Sunday	Monday	Tuesday	Wednesday	Thursday	Friday	Saturday
					1	2
3	4	5	6	7	8	9
10	11	12	13	14	15	16
17	18	19	20	21	22	23
24	25	26	27	28	29	30

Cambridge Review

ARCO
Teach Yourself
the GRE*
in 30 Days

MACMILLAN • USA

GRE is a registered trademark of Educational Testing Service, which does not endorse this book.

First Edition

Macmillan General Reference
A Pearson Education Macmillan Company
1633 Broadway
New York, NY 10019

Macmillan Publishing books may be purchased for business, education
or sales promotional use. For information please write: Special Markets
Department, Macmillan Publishing USA, 1633 Broadway, New York,
NY 10019.

ISBN: 0-02-862829-2 (book only)
ISBN: 0-02-862517-X (book with CD-ROM)

Library of Congress number: 99-63225 (book only)
                                   99-63237 (book with CD-ROM)

Manufactured in the United States of America

01–00   99   10–9–8–7–6–5–4–3–2–1

Overview

Contents

From the desk of David Waldherr
President, Cambridge Educational Services

Dear Teacher or School Administrator,

This Teach Yourself Book has been designed by Cambridge Educational Services as a self-study program. However, as an educator, I know that many students need the structure of a course schedule and the discipline of a classroom environment in order to succeed on the computer adaptive GRE. Many individuals and families make a large financial sacrifice to enroll their children in expensive test preparation courses, and indeed, studies have shown that such programs can be very effective.

Now your students don't have to choose between spending a fortune on test prep coaching and perhaps risking rejection at a first-choice school or missing out on a scholarship.

Today, hundreds of schools in every state use materials that Cambridge has created to provide top-quality, on-campus GRE preparation. These materials are designed especially for use by your teachers in your classrooms. Cambridge has more school partners than all the expensive test preparation companies combined!

Cambridge makes it easy for you to establish and expand your own high-quality, affordable test prep programs. Here's what you get:

- **The finest teaching materials:** Affordable student textbooks, official diagnostic and final exams and explanations, classroom-tested programs, practice tests, remedial review, quizzes, skill-builders, and adaptive computer software.

- **First-rate teacher assistance:** Teacher training, toll-free 24-hour teacher assistance hotline, class formats and schedules, teacher guides, concept outlines and summary sheets, test prep strategies, and local teacher training conferences.

- **Administrative convenience**: Administrators handbook including sample brochures, evaluations, schedules, parent and student letters, teacher selection criteria, and detailed course outlines for intensive, premium, overlapping and revolving courses.

Your school will schedule classes and set course fees (if any), select and compensate the teachers you choose, and register your own students. Schedules are available for after-school, weekend, or semester-long credit and non-credit courses.

For more information about offering Cambridge courses at your school, and to obtain a free sample of our GRE, PSAT, SAT, ACT, PLAN, EXPLORE, GMAT, TOEFL, LSAT, MCAT, GED, NTE, PPST, ITBS, Standardized Test Math, or College Prep materials please call us at 847-299-2930 or visit our website at **www.CambridgeEd.com.**

About This Book

The testmakers, otherwise known as ETS, would like you to believe that you can't beat the GRE. Well that's only half true. You can't study for the GRE, but you sure can prepare for it—and that's where this book comes in. We have examined the GRE question by question and answer choice by answer choice. We've literally taken each test apart, analyzed every component, and then put the pieces back together again. The result of all of our efforts is a proven plan. We call it the Cambridge Action Plan. It's the surefire method that works so well for students in our classes. And we're using many of these methods in this exciting new book.

By working your way through these pages, you'll get a structured course covering all the key points you need to know to raise your GRE score. In just 30 lessons, you'll review all of the topics and concepts that are tested on the GRE, and you will learn powerful strategies for answering every question type.

How to Use this GRE Book

This book has been designed as a 30-day teach-yourself training course complete with examples, workshops, quizzes, and full-length sample test sections. It is expected that you can complete each lesson in about two hours. However, you should work at your own rate. If you think you can complete a lesson in less than two hours, go for it! Also, if you think that you should spend more than two hours on a certain topic, spend as much time as you need.

Who Should Use This Book

- Students looking for a self-paced tutorial developed by Cambridge Publishing—the test-prep curriculum provider to over 500 educational institutions in the U.S.

- Students who are too busy to spend many hours in a classroom

- Students who cannot afford a private course costing thousands of dollars

- Students who want extended practice—you'll get extra drills at **www.CambridgeEd.com**

About the Authors

Who are we? We're Cambridge Educational Services, the fastest growing new powerhouse in on-campus test prep. On hundreds of high school and university campuses nationwide, we help students raise their test scores and get into the college or graduate school of their choice. We wrote this book to help you beat the GRE. We don't promise to raise your GPA or to get you on the honor roll. And we won't ask you to spend every night for the next six months chained to your desk, studying. What we do promise is that absolutely everything in this book has just one purpose: to help you earn the highest GRE score you can. And isn't that exactly what you want?

We're on your side, so count on us to make your graduate school dreams come true!

—The Curriculum Committee
at Cambridge Educational Services

Acknowledgments

Many, many thanks to all of the hardworking teachers, authors, and educators who have helped make Cambridge Educational Services the largest campus-based test-prep in the United States. Ever since Cambridge was started in 1990, our mission has been to provide schools all across America with first-rate test-prep at an affordable price. And now teachers all over America are teaching their own students test-prep strategies. Over three thousand teachers have put forth an extraordinary effort to make our mission come true.

My special thanks to Tom Martinson, Senior Cambridge author and Chair of the Cambridge Review Curriculum Committee; and to my wife, Kathy, for her extraordinary insight as a mathematics teacher. I also wish to thank my dedicated staff, especially Matthew and Sally.

And of course to the hundreds of high schools, colleges, and universities across America who chose Cambridge materials for their campus-based test preparation programs—your devotion and loyalty have truly launched a test-prep revolution.

Thanks for being a part of Cambridge Educational Services!

David P. Waldherr
President

Find out more about Cambridge!

Whether you are a student, parent, teacher or school administrator, you can get more information about our low-cost, top-quality TestPrep PLUS® courses and study materials just by filling out this form below. Mail the information to River Road Office Center, 2720 River Road, Des Plaines, IL 60018. Or e-mail us at: testprep@cambridgereview.com.

Cambridge TestPrep PLUS® Information Request Form

Attach or Staple Business Card or Label Here	Name: _____
	Job Title (position): _____
	School: _____
	School Address: _____
	City/State/Zip: _____
	Phone: _____ Fax: _____
	E-mail: _____

Total School Enrollment: _____

School Grade (circle all that apply):

K 1 2 3 4 5 6 7 8 9 10 11 12 College

Circle choices below to receive (fill in quantity) _____ complimentary sample(s) of Cambridge TestPrep® materials for you, your school, or your district:

ACT	MCAT	EXPLORE	SAT
TOEFL	PLAN	PSAT	PRAXIS I PPST
COLLEGE PREP	GRE	PRAXIS II NTE	ITBS (Iowa)
GMAT	GED	LSAT	Standardized Test Math

OTHER (please specify)

Do you currently offer any test preparation programs? ☐ Yes ☐ No

If yes what material(s) do you use? _____

_____

If not, have you ever considered implementing a test preparation program at your school? ☐ Yes ☐ No

Would you coordinate your test preparation course programs? ☐ Yes ☐ Someone Else? _____

I am primarily interested in receiving Cambridge's free sample(s) for (circle all that apply):

Teaching Our Own Course

Outside Party Teaches Course

Student Self-Study Course

Diagnostic Assessment

Software Preparation (take home)

Software Preparation (school lab)

Semester-Long Course

After-School Course

My School

My Community

Myself

Son/Daughter

Part I

GRE Basics

Day 1   Teach Yourself All About the GRE

Teach Yourself
All About the GRE

Today, you'll study the first of thirty lessons in this comprehensive self-study guide for the GRE.

Learn How to Use this Important Book

The fact that you're reading this book means that you already know that the GRE is an important test. It also says something important about you: You want to take charge of this important event.

Rather than wait for the test to happen to you, you're going to take control of the test and make sure that you get the best score possible. This book will help you do that; but to get the most out of it, you need to know how to use it.

As you can see at a glance, the book is divided into thirty, self-contained lessons. Each lesson takes about two hours to complete (depending on your prior familiarity with the subject matter and level of concentration that day).

The lessons are arranged according to an overall plan. For each subject, you begin with the basics; then you put the basics into a plan for that subject; then you assemble all of the subjects together in an area (like verbal); and at the end of the book, you'll have a complete plan for getting a top score on the GRE.

Along the way, the plan weaves together instruction and practice. You take a Verbal PreTest on Day 2 to diagnose your strengths and weaknesses. In the lessons that follow, you learn all about each of the different question types in that area. Day 3 tells you all about sentence completions, develop basic techniques, explains advanced strategies, and tells you what to do when you have to guess. As you progress through the various levels in

What You'll Do Today

- Learn How to Use this Important Book
- Get All the Inside Info on the GRE
- Workshop: MiniTest
- Master Important Strategies for the GRE
- Get Answers to Frequently Asked Questions

Day 3, you'll find workshops so that you can practice the material that you've just studied. Then in Day 4, you put together all of the elements of your plan for sentence completions, practice that question kind, and check your progress.

After you've mastered sentence completions, you move on to analogies, then to antonyms, then to reading comprehension until you take the Verbal Final on Day 11. You'll benefit from doing a full-length timed exercise, plus you'll be able to see how far you've progressed.

Then you'll follow the sequence for math and analytical ability.

NOTE   Each Day's lesson is *approximately* two hours. The time need can be shorter or longer depending on your individual strengths and weaknesses.

To get the maximum benefit from this book, you need to set up a workable study plan for yourself. In principle, that's easy: you've got to cover 30 two-hour lessons before the test, so you decide how many you can do each week and on what days, count backwards on a calendar and fill in the dates, get started, and then faithfully stay on schedule.

Easier said than done, so you'd better build in a time cushion. Start earlier than you think you need to and schedule some "make-up" days in case you don't get through a lesson or two in the time you've set aside.

TIP   Build some "wiggle room" into your study schedule, that is, start a little earlier and add in a couple of make-up days. That way you won't feel pressed or guilty if you fall a little behind.

You can't expect that you'll be perfect, but try to stay as close to your schedule as possible. The results will be worth it.

Get All the Inside Info on the GRE

The GRE is a grad school entrance exam. Your score on the test will be a part of your application along with your academic record, letters of recommendation, and personal history. Your GRE score can also affect decisions about financial aid.

The GRE is sponsored by the Graduate Record Examination Board, an association of schools. The GRE is written and administered by Educational Testing Service. You can get the forms you need to register to take the GRE from your advisor or guidance office. You can also find them on-line at:

http://www.gre.org

What's Tested?

The GRE uses four different kinds of verbal questions.

- **Sentence Completions:** Sentence Completions are "fill-in-the-blanks." Each question has a series of dashes to indicate where some word or words has been left out. Using your reading skills and vocabulary, you have to pick an appropriate completion for the sentence.

- **Analogies:** Analogies are "this-is-like-that" questions. You're given a pair of words like "CAP : HEAD" and asked to pick another pair, like "glove : hand," that expresses a similar relationship.

- **Antonyms:** Antonyms are "opposite of" questions. You're given a word in capital letters, say "TRANSITORY," and you're supposed to pick an opposite, like "permanent."

- **Reading Comprehension:** Reading Comprehension questions are based upon reading selections taken from an article, textbook, or other source that you're likely to be asked to read in graduate school. Questions ask things like "What's the main idea of the selection?" and "What's the author's attitude about the topic?"

The GRE uses three different kinds of math questions:

- **Problem Solving:** Problem Solving questions are your typical multiple-choice math questions. They may ask you to find a value for an unknown in an equation or to solve a word problem.

- **Quantitative Comparisons:** Quantitative Comparisons are math questions that were specially designed for the SAT. You're given two quantities (one called "Column A" and one called "Column B"). You determine which is larger.

- **Graphs:** Graphs questions are almost like regular multiple-choice math questions, but the data are presented in graphic format, e.g., pie charts or line graphs.

The GRE uses two kinds of analytical ability questions:

- **Analytical Reasoning:** Analytical Reasoning, also called logical puzzles, describe a situation such as people standing in a line or a group of students that must be divided into committees. The situation is controlled by various conditions such as "John is not standing behind Ralph" and "Peter can't be on the same committee as Alvin." The questions then ask about the logical possibilities.
- **Logical Reasoning:** Logical Reasoning, also called arguments, looks like reading comprehension—only shorter. The argument is developed in a short passage, and the questions asks you to weaken the argument, describe it, identify an assumption, or some similar task.

Your GRE may also include a Writing Assessment. The Writing Assessment is an essay test that uses two topics:

- **Issue Topic:** The issue topic is a statement on an issue of general interest. You have to take a position on the issue and write an essay supporting that position.
- **Argument Topic:** The argument topic is an argument in support of a conclusion. You have to analyze the argument and critique it.

 NOTE

> Your GRE may also include an equating section, but it won't count toward your scores.

How Is the GRE Scored?

The GRE is a computer adaptive test. The computer actually assembles your test during the testing session based upon your answers to previous questions.

At the risk of oversimplifying this, it works like this. The computer has access to a data base of questions that are classified according to concept tested and level of difficulty. The program starts you off with a couple of items of medium level difficulty. If you get those correct, it gives you an item of higher difficulty; if you miss the first ones, you get an easier item. Then, based on your response to each successive question, the computer moves you up or down the ladder of difficulty in smaller and smaller increments until it finally zeroes in on your score.

1

Of course, all of this goes on behind your back. You never see the pool of questions or how their classified. You just see the ones the computer selects for you.

At the end of the testing session, the computer will have to calculate three different scores for you:

Subject Area	Minimum Score	Maximum Score
Verbal Skills	200	800
Math Skills	200	800
Verbal Skills	200	800

Your essay responses on the Writing Assessment are not computer graded. Instead, they are given to teams of graders who assign them scores on a scale of 0 (the minimum) to 6 (the maximum). You'll learn more about the scoring of the essay in Day 28.

TIP

> As you go through your test, the adjustments become smaller and smaller. So, questions earlier in the section count for more than later ones. Take extra care with those in the first half of each part.

Workshop: MiniTest

The best way to get started is just to jump right in. So here's a MiniTest to familiarize you with the various types of questions used by the GRE. Each part has a 15 minute time limit. Indicate your answer choices in your book. Then check your answers against the explanations given below. (The MiniTest doesn't include a Writing Assessment; you'll get to that in Days 27 through 29.)

Verbal Part

15 Questions • Time—15 Minutes

DIRECTIONS: Choose the best answer to each of the questions below. Indicate your answer by circling the letter of your answer choice.

DIRECTIONS: Each of the sentences below has one or two blanks. Each blank indicates that a word or phrase has been omitted. Following each sentence is a series of five lettered words or phrases. Choose the word or phrase for each blank that *best* fits the meaning of the sentence in its entirety.

1. The two trails ran side-by-side for two miles until they ——, one rising high into the mountains and the other following an easier track along the river.

   (A) coincided
   (B) diverged
   (C) disappeared
   (D) terminated
   (E) extended

2. Her naturally —— outlook encouraged her to see possibilities where others saw insurmountable obstacles.

   (A) optimistic
   (B) gloomy
   (C) incomplete
   (D) humorous
   (E) fearful

3. The police failure to supervise carefully the blood sample and keep a record of everyone who handled the vial —— the integrity of the evidence and prompted the judge to rule that it was —— .

   (A) ensured . . conclusive
   (B) violated . . reliable
   (C) attained . . unprovable
   (D) underwrote . . unacceptable
   (E) compromised . . inadmissible

4. Although it is not ——, Virginia Parrot's book on the history of Washington County is often cited because of the —— of other sources.

   (A) published . . bias
   (B) comprehensive . . dearth
   (C) accurate . . reliability
   (D) outdated . . success
   (E) official . . authoritativeness

1

DIRECTIONS: In each of the following items, a related pair of capitalized words or phrases is followed by five lettered pairs of words or phrases. Choose the lettered pair that best expresses a relationship similar to that expressed by the capitalized pair.

5. THRIFTY : STINGY ::

— (A) generous : sympathetic
   (B) proud : arrogant
   (C) quiet : talkative
   (D) sincere : intense
   (E) calm : steadfast

6. NAVIGABLE : SAILING ::

— (A) arable : farming
   (B) fettered : movement
   (C) exposed : elements
   (D) healthy : treatment
   (E) persistent : commitment

7. WHIFF : AROMA ::

   (A) stench : odor
   (B) blast : sound
   (C) food : cuisine
   (D) fiery : taste
   (E) glimmer : light

8. DIVERSIONARY : DISTRACT ::

— (A) didactic : instruct
   (B) frenetic : occupy
   (C) disrespectful : esteem
   (D) conclusive : introduce
   (E) caustic : smooth

DIRECTIONS: Each item below consists of a word or phrase printed in capital letters, followed by five lettered words or phrases. Choose the lettered word or phrase that is most nearly *opposite* in meaning to the capitalized word or phrase.

9. CAPITULATE:

   (A) reinvent
   (B) persevere
   (C) flaunt
— (D) derive
   (E) harvest

10. TACIT:

   (A) express
— (B) crass
   (C) whole
   (D) strained
   (E) cloudy

Fractur is a uniquely American folk art rooted in the Pennsylvania Dutch (Pennsylvania German) culture. In German, *fraktur* refers to a particular typeface used (5) by printers. Derived from the Latin *fractura*, a "breaking apart," *fraktur* suggests that the letters are broken apart and reassembled into designs. *Fraktur* as a genre of folk art refers to a text (usually (10) religious) that is decorated with symbolic designs.

Fraktur was primarily a private art dealing with the role of the individual in Pennsylvania Dutch society and its various rites (15) of passage: birth and baptism; puberty and schooling; courtship and marriage; and death and funeral rites. Special *fraktur* documents were associated with each: the *Taufschein* or Birth-Baptismal Certificate, (20) the *Vorschrift* for the student, the *Trauschein* for marriage, and the *Denkmal* or Memorial. Of these, the *Taufschein* and the *Vorshrift* are the most numerous. Wedding and death certificates are rare because of (25) the availability of alternative forms of memorialization, the wedding plate with its humorous inscription and the engraved tombstone.

In Pennsylvania during the early settle- (30) ment era, *fraktur* art flowered, at least in part, to fill an artistic vacuum that existed in the everyday world of the Pennsylvania Dutch farmer. While *fraktur* were produced by folk artists, these were not studio artists (35) producing public art for a wealthy clientele, but individuals who, in addition to their major occupation, produced private art for individuals. The great majority were either ministers in the Lutheran or Reformed (40) Church or schoolmasters in parochial schools. Because of the close association with religious life, fraktur was permitted as an art form in a culture that frowned upon public display in general. As art, *fraktur* (45) both delights the eye and refreshes the spirit with its bright colors, ingenious combination of text and pictures, and symbols drawn from folk culture. For example, mermaids were often put on baptismal (50) certificates to represent water spirits that, in Germanic mythology, were believed to deliver newborns to midwives who then took them to their waiting mothers. Still, though art, *fraktur* was rarely displayed (55) even in the home. Instead, it was usually kept in Bibles or other large books, pasted onto the inside lids of blanket chests, or rolled up in bureau drawers.

Fraktur is uniquely Pennsylvania (60) Dutch, but manuscript art did develop in other American sectarian groups. The New England Puritans decorated family registers, the Shakers produced "spirit drawings," and the Russian-German (65) Mennonites created *Zierschriften* or ornamental writings.

11. The author is primarily interested in

(A) tracing German influences on American art

(B) describing *fraktur* art of the Pennsylvania Dutch

(C) cataloging the symbolism of German mythology

(D) surveying important trends in American folk art

(E) outlining the social structures of the Pennsylvania Dutch

12 In line 12, "private art" means art

(A) created by individual artists

(B) commemorating the lives of individuals

(C) exhibiting Germanic influences

(D) produced in manuscript form

(E) found in small communities

13 The wedding plate and the engraved tombstone correspond to the

(A) *Taufschein* and *Vorschrift*

(B) *Taufschein* and *Trauschein*

(C) *Vorschrift* and *Denkmal*

(D) *Trauschein* and *Denkmal*

(E) *Vorschrift* and *Trauschein*

14 "Flowered" (line 30) most nearly means

(A) exhibited bright colors

(B) served a useful function

(C) grew and spread vigorously

(D) challenged conventional wisdom

(E) lasted only a brief time

15 According to the author, *fractur* was NOT

(A) accented with bright colors

(B) produced using broken face text

(C) decorated with mythological symbols

(D) prominently displayed in the home

(E) valued for their commemorative significance

Math Part

15 Questions • Time—15 Minutes

DIRECTIONS: Choose the best answer to each of the questions below. Indicate your answer by writing down the letter of your answer choice next to each question.

DIRECTIONS: For each of the following questions, mark

    (A) if the quantity in Column A is greater;
    (B) if the quantity in Column B is greater;
    (C) if the two quantities are equal;
    (D) if the relationship cannot be determined from the information given.

	Column A	Column B
1.	0.51	0.501
2.	$-(-m)$	0

3.   Twice the sum of x and y is 12.

Column A	Column B
Three times the sum of x and y	18

4. x is a member of the set $\{1, 3, 5, 7\}$

     y is a member of the set $\{2, 4, 6, 8\}$

Column A	Column B
$x - y$	$y - x$

Column A   Column B

5.

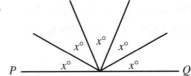

PQ is a line segment.

Column A	Column B
x	30

6.

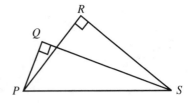

Column A	Column B
$PQ^2 + QS^2$	$PR^2 + RS^2$

Column A   Column B   **Column A   Column B**

7. A test tube contains 200 milliliters of water and is $\frac{4}{5}$ full.

The number of additional milliliters of water need to fill the test tube to capacity	50

8. $5 > x > y > 4$

20% of x	25% of y

9. $x > 1$

$(x^2)^5$	$(x^5)(x^2)$

10.   a and b are positive and $a \neq b$

$(a-b)(a+b)$	$a^2 + 2ab + b^2$

DIRECTIONS: Each of the *following questions* has five answer choices. For each question, choose the best answer given.

11. Which of the following numbers is the *least*?

(A) $1 + \frac{1}{2}$

(B) $1 - \frac{1}{2}$

(C) $1 \times \frac{1}{2}$

(D) $1 \div \frac{1}{2}$

(E) $\frac{1}{2} - 1$

12. If $2y + x = 10$ and $z - y = 5$, what is the value of $x + y + z$?

(A) 5
(B) 10
(C) 15
(D) 18
(E) 25

13 During a charity fund-raising event, an anonymous donor pledged d dollars in addition to the amount already pledged. If the total amount pledged after the donation was equal to t times the amount pledged before the donation, how many dollars had been pledged before the donation?

(A) $t - d$

(B) $\frac{t}{d}$

(C) $\frac{d}{t}$

(D) $\frac{d}{t-1}$

(E) $\frac{t}{d-1}$

Questions 14–15

BUDGET FOR SCHOOL X (TENS OF THOUSANDS OF DOLLARS)					
	1995	1996	1997	1998	1999
Faculty Salaries	130	145	150	160	175
Books and Equipment	65	75	90	100	125
Administration	100	110	115	120	125
Garage and Transportation	25	27	32	36	40
Physical Plant	20	27	23	20	35
Other	50	60	75	80	100
Total	390	444	485	516	600

14. For the five year period show, what was the average annual expenditure for books and equipment?

    (A) $910,000
    (B) $1,250,000
    (C) $1,900,000
    (D) $2,750,000
    (E) $3,550,000

15. For how many years, was the amount of money spent on Administration more than 25% of the total budget?

    (A) 1
    (B) 2
    (C) 3
    (D) 4
    (E) 5

Analytical Part

10 Questions • Time—15 Minutes

DIRECTIONS: Each question or group of questions is based on a passage or a set of conditions. You may find it useful to draw a rough diagram for some questions. For each question, select the best answer choice given.

Questions 1–4

Six people—Fred, Gina, Hiram, Ida, Jean, and Kaye—are standing in a single-file line waiting to buy tickets to a movie.

Fred is closer to the ticket window than Gina.

Jean is farther from the ticket window than Kaye.

Ida is standing somewhere between Fred and Gina.

Hiram is the last person in the line.

1. Which of the following CANNOT be true?

    (A) Gina is second in line.
    (B) Gina is third in line.
    (C) Jean is second in line.
    (D) Jean is third in line.
    (E) Jean is fourth in line.

2. If Jean is fourth in line, which of the following must be true?

    (A) Fred is third in line.
    (B) Fred is fifth in line.
    (C) Ida is second in line.
    (D) Ida is fourth in line.
    (E) Gina is fifth in line.

3. If Ida and Fred are separated by exactly two people, which of the following must be true?

    (A) Fred is first in line.
    (B) Kay is fifth in line.
    (C) Kaye is somewhere behind Ida.
    (D) Jean is somewhere between Gina and Ida.
    (E) Jean and Kay are separated by exactly one person.

4. If Fred is standing somewhere behind Jean, then how many different arrangements of the people are possible?

    (A) 1
    (B) 2
    (C) 3
    (D) 4
    (E) 5

5. Prices of prescription drugs are 30 to 100 percent higher in the United States than in many foreign countries. Through price controls, foreign governments force drug prices down to levels that almost equal manufacturing costs because they know that the regulated firms still have access to unregulated markets in the U.S. where above normal profits can offset the lost profits in those countries.

The argument above assumes that

(A) Foreign governments are less concerned about the health of their citizens than the U.S. government is about its citizens.

(B) Pharmaceutical firms don't want to make high profits on the drugs that they sell to citizens of foreign countries.

(C) Pharmaceutical firms would continue to supply prescription drugs to foreign markets even if prices dropped below manufacturing cost.

(D) Pharmaceutical firms raise the price of prescription drugs in domestic markets to levels higher than might prevail were prices allowed to rise in foreign markets.

(E) Consumers in the United States are less sophisticated about the pricing policies of pharmaceutical companies than their counterparts in other countries.

6. Everyone admitted to the practice of law after 1990 had to pass an ethics exam. Janice was admitted to the practice of law in 1980. Therefore, Janice did not pass an ethics exam.

The argument above is most similar in its logical structure to which of the following?

(A) No one who wears abbreviated attire will be admitted to the box seat area. Shorts are abbreviated attire. So anyone wearing shorts will not be admitted to the box seat area.

(B) Anyone who wins a major tournament during the year automatically qualifies for the Tournament of Champions. Sid did not win a major tournament during the year. Therefore, Sid did not qualify for the Tournament of Champions.

(C) The liquid in the beaker will turn blue if an acid is introduced and pink if a base is introduced. A chemical is introduced that caused no change in color. Therefore, the chemical was neither an acid nor a base.

(D) All students who score 90 or better on their final exam will receive As. Ursula scored 95 on the final exam. Therefore, Ursula will get an A.

(E) Anyone who established residency before 1990 is permitted to run for governor. Eileen did not establish residence until 1995. Therefore, Eileen is permitted to run for governor.

Questions 7–10

The coach of a basketball team must name five persons to the starting team. The players include three guards—J, K, L—and five forwards—M, N, O, P, Q. The starting team must include two guards and three fowards.

If Q is a starter, neither K nor N can start.

P and O cannot both be starters.

7. Which of the following is an acceptable starting team?

   (A) J, K, O, M, N
   (B) K, L, N, O, P
   (C) K, J, L, M, O
   (D) L, J, M, N, Q
   (E) L, K, N, P, Q

8. If K is named to the starting team, then which of the following must also be named to the starting team?

   (A) J
   (B) L
   (C) N
   (D) O
   (E) P

9. If L is not named to the starting team, then all of the following players must be named to the starting team EXCEPT:

   (A) J
   (B) K
   (C) M
   (D) N
   (E) P

10. If Q is named to the starting team, then how many different combinations of players can complete the starting team?

   (A) 1
   (B) 2
   (C) 3
   (D) 4
   (E) 5

1

Review

Verbal Part

1. **(B)** The "although" is an important verbal signal because it tells you to contrast the professor's warning with another idea.

2. **(B)** The "," is an important signal because it describes what happens to the trails: one goes into the mountains and the other along the river. The best description is "diverged."

3. **(A)** The one outlook contrasts with the other: one is ——, the other is defeatist.

4. **(E)** The first blank has to explain the outcome of the failure to supervise carefully: integrity was compromised. And then the second blank explains what happened after that: it was ruled inadmissible.

5. **(B)** The "although" signals a contrast: it isn't that good (comprehensive), but it is all that was available. (Dearth means scarcity.)

6. **(C)** A helmet protects the head, and goggles protect the eyes.

7. **(B)** Stingy is very thrifty, and arrogant is very proud.

8. **(A)** A waterway that is suitable for sailing is navigable, and a field that is arable is suitable for farming.

9. **(B)** Capitulate means to give in; persevere means to refuse to give up.

10. **(A)** Tacit means unstated; express means stated explicitly.

11. **(B)** This question asks about the main idea of the selection. The author talks mainly about *fraktur* art in the Pennsylvania Dutch region.

12. **(B)** In the second paragraph, the author explains that the purpose of *fraktur* was to commemorate important moments in an individual's life. This is to be seen in contrast to art intended primarily for public viewing.

13. **(D)** According to the second paragraph, the *Trauschein* was a *fraktur* to commemorate a marriage and the *Denkmal* a fraktur of remembrance.

14. **(C)** In this context, flowered means flourished or grew vigorously. A good clue is the juxtaposition of the word with "vacuum." In other words, there was little else in the way of art, but frakturs filled in the space.

15. **(D)** The author specifically says that *fraktur* was private art and that even in the home it was often stored away from sight.

1

Math Part

1. **(A)** 0.51 is larger than 0.501.

2. **(D)** You have no information about m. m could be positive, negative, or even 0.

3. **(C)** Since twice the sum of x and y is 12, $2(x + y) = 12$, and $x + y = 6$. And $3 \times 6 = 18$.

4. **(D)** $x - y$ could be as much as $7 - 2 = 5$ or as little as $1 - 8 = -7$; and $y - x$ could be as much as $8 - 1 = 7$ or as little as $2 - 7 = -5$.

5. **(C)** $x + x + x + x + x = 5x = 180$, so $x = 30$.

6. **(C)** By the Pythagorean Theorem, both columns are equal to PS^2.

7. **(C)** $\frac{4}{5}T = 200$, so $T = 250$; and $250 - 200 = 50$.

8. **(D)** $1.25 > x > 1$, and $1.25 > y > 1$; but you have no basis for comparing x and y within those ranges.

9. **(A)** Column A is x^{10}, and Column B is x^7.

10. **(B)** $(a - b)(a + b) = a^2 - 2ab + b^2$. So the only difference between the two columns is the $2ab$ term. And it's negative in Column A and positive in Column B.

11. **(E)** The expression in (E) has a negative value.

12. **(C)** Just add the two equations together.

13. **(D)** $x + d = t(x)$

$$d = t(x) - x$$

$$d = x(t - 1)$$

$$x = \frac{d}{t - 1}$$

14. **(A)** The average is:

$$\frac{65 + 75 + 90 + 100 + 125}{5} = \frac{455}{5} = 91 =$$

$910,000

15. **(A)** Twenty-five percent is $\frac{1}{4}$, so the only year in which Administration exceeded $\frac{1}{4}$ of the total was 1995.

Analytical Part

1. **(B)** Gina is behind both Ida and Fred.

2. **(E)** With Jean fourth, Fred, Ida, and Kaye must all be ahead of Jean. So Gina must be fifth.

3. **(A)** If Ida is two people behind Fred, then Fred is first, Ida is fourth, and Gina is fifth.

Jean and Kaye are second and third, though not necessarily respectively.

4. **(A)** If Fred is behind Jean, then Kaye too must be in front of Fred, and the order must be: Kaye, Jean, Fred, Ida, Gina, Hiram.

5. **(D)** The argument maintains that U.S. consumers subsidize consumers in other countries because foreign government depress prices just to the point where companies would prefer to sell than to get out of the market altogether. But that assumes that the companies will raise prices in the U.S. to levels above "normal" in order to offset those lost profits.

6. **(B)** The weakness in the argument is that Janice might have taken an ethics exam even though she was admitted before 1990. The premise states only that admission after 1990 guarantees that the person took an ethics exam. (B) makes a similar mistake. Winning a major tournament is one way to qualify, but perhaps not the only way to qualify, for the Tournament of Champions.

7. **(A)** (B) is not acceptable because O and P are on the team. (C) is not acceptable because it includes three guards. (D) and (E) are not acceptable because Q is included with either K or N.

8. **(C)** If K is named as a starter, then Q cannot be a starter, and that leaves M, N, O, and P for forwards. O and P cannot both be named to the team, so M and N must both be starters.

9. **(E)** If L is not named, then J and K must be the guards. If K is named as a starter, then Q cannot be. That leaves M, N, O, and P for the three forward positions. Both M and N must be named along with either P or O.

10. **(B)** If Q is named, then K cannot be, so J and L are the guards. Then, of M, O, and P, M must be chosen along with either O or P.

Get Answers to Frequently Asked Questions

1

Q: **Does the computer-based GRE test reward people who are computer geniuses?**

A: No. In fact, you don't really need to know anything at all about how a computer works. You just have to be able to use a mouse and a keyboard.

Q: **Doesn't a special program administer the GRE?**

A: Yes, so in addition to knowing about the mouse and the keyboard, you have to learn how to find your way about the testing, for example, how to move from one problem to the next. The first segment of the testing session is an untimed tutorial during which you'll have the opportunity to practice these techniques. However, it would be better to have prior experience with computer adaptive testing before you get to the test. If you purchased a copy of this book that included the Cambridge Review software on CD, make sure that you use it. If your edition did not include a CD, you can purchase a copy by contacting:

Cambridge Educational Services
2720 River Road, Suite 36
Des Plains, IL 60018
Telephone: 1 (847) 299-2930

Q: **I've heard a lot of hot tips about the GRE like "Pick the longest answer in reading because the test-writers are lazy and aren't going to write a long answer unless it's the correct one." Do these work?**

A: No, they don't, but we've heard a lot of them also, like, "In reading, don't pick a choice with an "always," "every," or "all." We've done studies of these so-called tips; and not only do they not work, they can actually hurt your score. You can't "beat" the GRE with a few cheap tricks like that, and that's good news for you. You'll have a distinct advantage because you're willing to invest the time and effort in the serious preparation offered by this book.

Today's Review

1. This book will help you get the high score you want on this all important exam. Make a workable study plan for yourself.

2. The GRE uses four kinds of verbal questions (sentence completions, analogies, antonyms, and critical reading), three types of math questions (quantitative comparisons, problem solving, and graphs), and two types of analytical questions (puzzles and arguments). There is also a Writing Assessment. Each type of question is covered in detail later in this book.

3. The test is computer-based. You don't need to be computer literate to take the test, but you do need to know how to perform certain basic operations such a using a mouse to point-and-click and to scroll text. You can learn how to do this by practicing with a computer before you get to the test. Also, the first part of the test is a tutorial that familiarizes you with the special features of the GRE. Even if you are very familiar with computers, pay careful attention to the tutorial.

4. The computer constructs your GRE test during the testing session based upon your answers to previous questions. You must enter an answer to a question before it will let you move to the next question. (Even if you have to guess.) You'll get your best score if you answer all of the questions in a part, so keep an eye on the passing time.

Part II

Verbal Skills

Test Your
Verbal Skills

Day
2

Today, you'll take the Verbal PreTest and use specially designed evaluation tools to make some judgments about where you stand. You'll also review explanations of the correct answers to the items used in the PreTest as a first step in your in-depth study of GRE verbal questions.

Preview the Verbal PreTest

The likelihood is that you'll be taking the GRE on computer. This diagnostic exercise, which is presented in pencil-and-paper format, has been carefully designed to yield results that are comparable to a computer-based version of the test. You'll get the most out of this PreTest if you keep the following important points in mind.

The GRE CAT uses the four different kinds of verbal questions you learned about in Day 1. You'll find these same four kinds in today's Verbal PreTest.

- **Sentence Completions.** Sentence Completions are "fill-in-the-blank" items. Each sentence includes one or two blanks indicating a missing word or words. Using structural and verbal clues provided by the sentence, pick the answer choice that best completes each sentence.

- **Analogies.** Analogies are "this-is-like-that" items. A capitalized pair of words expresses a verbal relationship. Pick the answer choice that best expresses a similar verbal relationship.

What You'll Do Today

- Preview the Verbal PreTest
- Take the Verbal PreTest
- Evaluate Your Performance
- Review the Correct Answers

- **Reading Comprehension.** Reading Comprehension questions are based upon a reading selection. The questions ask about the main idea of the selection, points the author specifically made, ideas that can be inferred from the text, and the structure and organization of the selection. Pick the answer choices that best answers each question.
- **Antonyms.** Antonyms are "pick-the-opposite" items. Pick the answer choice that best expresses an idea opposite to that expressed by the capitalized word.

The PreTest has been carefully crafted to give results that are comparable to those generated by a computer-based test. The mix of questions, the range of difficulty, and the 30-minute time limit are features that help to make this a true diagnostic exercise.

Circle your answers or write them on a separate piece of paper and, please, observe faithfully the 30-minute time limit.

Finally, since the computer-based GRE CAT does not give you the option of omitting a question, you should answer *all* items. You don't lose points for wrong answers.

Take the Verbal PreTest

Verbal PreTest

38 Questions • Time—30 Minutes

DIRECTIONS: Each of these sentences below has one or two blanks. Each blank indicates that a word or phrase has been omitted. Following each sentence is a series of five lettered words or phrases. Choose the word or phrase for each blank that *best* fits the meaning of the sentence in its entirety.

1. In the State of Nature, described by Thomas Hobbes in *Leviathan* as a state of war, one against all others, no individual has sufficient physical strength to be assured of personal security, so all rely on ——.

   (A) animosity
   (B) premeditation
   (C) principles
   (D) prowess
   (E) allies

2. Members of the Research and Development Council had been warned that the prototype was extremely ——, but were pleasantly surprised to see a model with many —— usually incorporated only much later in the design process.

   (A) crude . . . refinements
   (B) flexible . . . advances
   (C) rudimentary . . . deficiencies
   (D) unreliable . . . trappings
   (E) casual . . . advantages

3. Although the developmental sequence of the reproductive cycle in insects is similar for many species, the timing can —— greatly in regard to the beginning and duration of each stage.

   (A) endure
   (B) accelerate
   (C) vary
   (D) proceed
   (E) coincide

4. The "framers' original intent" theory of Constitutional interpretation, though now —— within academic circles, still has considerable practical effect because it is —— by many sitting judges.

   (A) propounded . . . accepted
   (B) disseminated . . . rejected
   (C) corroborated . . . critiqued
   (D) dismissed . . . espoused
   (E) encapsulated . . . emphasized

5. Proponents of a flat tax hope to substitute a single federal revenue-raising measure for the —— of convoluted and even self-contradictory provisions of the present tax code.

   (A) tapestry
   (B) concordance
   (C) cacophony
   (D) duplicity
   (E) welter

6. An examination of the psychological forces that shape the personality of the title character of *The Magus* naturally invites closer study of its form, as story content and form are carefully —— by Fowles in the novel.

   (A) delineated
   (B) anticipated
   (C) integrated
   (D) determined
   (E) reserved

7. The broadcast of the story has seriously compromised the credibility of the entire news department: the key piece of information, though not —— on the one particular point, is expected to support a vast —— of implications for which no other proof is offered.

   (A) fabricated . . . contradiction
   (B) unconvincing . . . superstructure
   (C) persuasive . . . convocation
   (D) inextricable . . . skein
   (E) conclusive . . . facsimile

2

DIRECTIONS: In each of the following items, a related pair of capitalized words or phrases is followed by five lettered pairs of words or phrases. Choose the lettered pair that best expresses a relationship similar to that expressed by the capitalized pair.

8. CAST : ACTOR ::

    (A) election : candidate
    (B) census : data
    (C) orchestra : conductor
    (D) meeting : speaker
    (E) chorus : singer

9. CROWD : DISPERSE ::

    (A) painting : restore
    (B) clog : dissolve
    (C) knot : tangle
    (D) population : reproduce
    (E) business : incorporate

10. MANDATE : COMPLIANCE ::

    (A) prohibit : abstention
    (B) vacate : occupancy
    (C) recall : retreat
    (D) vindicate : guilt
    (E) defame : reputation

11. TORPOR : MOTION ::

    (A) insipidness : taste
    (B) gangrene : infection
    (C) elegance : style
    (D) cowardice : discipline
    (E) winsomeness : appeal

12. INSINUATE : ACCUSE ::

    (A) beckon : refuse
    (B) alter : enhance
    (C) activate : sustain
    (D) vanquish : reconcile
    (E) discourage : forbid

13. HETEROGENEOUS : VARIETY ::

    (A) adulterous : commitment
    (B) capricious : change
    (C) imperious : backbone
    (D) benighted : desire
    (E) preemptory : plan

14. TAXONOMIST : CLASSIFICATION ::

    (A) scholar : study
    (B) acolyte : experience
    (C) podiatrist : infection
    (D) architect : design
    (E) vigilante : injustice

15. PLACEBO : EFFICACY ::

    (A) transparency : vision
    (B) concentrate : mixture
    (C) rigorousness : effectiveness
    (D) platitude : originality
    (E) comprehension : entirety

16. CALUMNY : FALSEHOOD ::

    (A) encomium : praise
    (B) plagarism : authorship
    (C) diversity : stereotype
    (D) turpitude : virtue
    (E) notoriety : anonymity

DIRECTIONS: Each selection below is followed by questions based on its content. After reading a selection, choose the best answer to each question, answering on the basis of what is *stated* or *implied* in the selection.

Silicon carbide is a highly promising material for many semiconductor applications, numbering among its other advantages excellent physical stability and
(5) hardness, great strength at high temperatures, high thermal conductivity, and a low friction coefficient, all of which make it particularly useful for integrated circuits operating under extreme conditions.

(10) Unfortunately, silicon carbide is not in wide use because it is extremely difficult to work with. Large-area crystals are not easily grown, and its inertness makes it difficult to etch. Dry etching techniques
(15) are both slow and problematic, as are chemical-vapor deposition techniques.

However, an elegant new technique for manufacturing silicon carbide microchips combines existing silicon technology with
(20) the unique way that C_{60} reacts with a heated silicon surface. The C_{60} molecule, the third member of the pure carbon family which also includes diamond and graphite as the two more commonly
(25) known family members, has a perfect soccer-ball-like structure. Standard lithographic techniques are first applied to deposit a controlled pattern of silicon dioxide to a thickness of about 1 micrometer
(30) on a silicon wafer. After the wafer is heated to 1100K (kelvin), it is exposed to a beam or flux of C_{60} vapor for about an hour. The carbon molecules stick to the bare silicon and essentially bounce off the oxide. To

(35) remove the unwanted silicon dioxide, the wafer is then dipped in concentrated hydrofluoric acid. The end result is a silicon wafer with a silicon carbide microstructure in place.

(40) Recently, successful attempts have grown films of silicon carbide to thicknesses greater than one micrometer. Because the adhesion of silicon carbide films thicker than one micrometer on a silicon
(45) wafer is relatively weak, it is possible to use the tip of an atomic force microscope to apply a force in the range of 10^{-8} N (newtons) so that a microcomponent can be maneuvered into position. Also, new
(50) procedures are used to coat the top of a silicon atomic-force microscope with a thin (approximately 0.5 micrometers) layer of silicon carbide. C_{60} has great surface mobility and is able to diffuse into
(55) areas that are not in the direct line of the sight of the beam of applied vapor. Thus, the tip of the atomic-force microscope is uniformly coated even though some of the surfaces are inclined at various angles with
(60) respect to the C_{60} source.

Silicon carbide microcomponents have considerable potential in a variety of applications; and although they will not replace silicon chips and may not be suit-
(65) able for some electrical uses, they do have the practical benefit of surviving extreme mechanical and thermal conditions. They could, for example, be used to detect

2

flameouts in aircraft engines by measuring
(70) pressure and temperature in the engine
quickly enough to stop and then restart
the engine. They may also have a use in
solving friction and wear problems encountered at crucial junctures in microelectro-
(75) mechanical systems such as tiny sensors,
actuators, resonators, and even motors,
devices the operation of which can be
limited by the relatively rapid wear
of contacting silicon surfaces and other
(80) mechanical properties. Recent test results
suggest that when use in microelectromechanical systems, films of silicon
carbide grown from C_{60} may lessen wear
and improve operation. The coefficient of
(85) friction for the silicon carbide film was
one-half to one-third that of the silicon
currently in use, and its hardness, based
on a compared elastic modulus of the
two materials, was almost 12 times greater.
(90) Silicon carbide films grown from C_{60} may,
therefore, present opportunities for application not previously considered.

17. Which of the following would be the most
appropriate title for the passage?

(A) The Use of Elemental Carbon as a
Component in the Manufacture of
Silicon Carbide Microchips
(B) Possible Electrical and Mechanical
Applications of Silicon Carbide
Microchip Technology
(C) New Techniques for Manufacturing
and Using Silicon Chips for Electri-
cal and Mechanical Applications
(D) Some Challenges to Producing
Silicon Carbide Microchips for Use
in Microelectromechanical Systems

(E) Semiconductor Applications for
Silicon Carbide Made Possible by
New Manufacturing Techniques

18. The passage mentions all of the following
as advantages of silicon carbide EXCEPT:

(A) strength at high temperatures
(B) high thermal conductivity
(C) excellent physical stability
(D) relative ease of manipulation
(E) low friction coefficient

19. According to the passage, it is possible to
maneuver microcomponents into position
on a film of silicon carbide thicker than
one micrometer because

(A) an atomic force microscope applies
force in the range of 10^{-8} N
(B) C_{60} does not react readily with
silicon dioxide
(C) such films have relatively weak
adhesive properties
(D) C_{60} has a perfect soccer-ball-like
structure
(E) C_{60} has great surface mobility and
diffuses into all areas

20. The author mentions dry etching and
chemical-vapor deposition techniques
(lines 14–16) primarily in order to

(A) illustrate some of the advantages of
silicon carbide technology over
conventional semiconductor
technology
(B) highlight the shortcomings of
silicon carbide microcomponents
when compared with silicon chips
(C) establish that certain common
manufacturing techniques cannot be
used with silicon carbide

(D) suggest some ways of overcoming the difficulty of working with silicon carbide

(E) define more precisely the physical processes at work in silicon carbide components

21. It can be inferred that silicon carbide microcomponents may be useful in microelectromechanical systems because

(A) silicon carbide film has a comparatively low coefficient of friction

(B) silicon carbide has high electrical conductivity

(C) microelectromechanical systems operate at extreme temperatures and pressures

(D) C$_{60}$ has considerable surface mobility and diffuses rapidly into obscured areas

(E) carbon molecules adhere easily to bare silicon but are deflected by silicon oxide

22. The use of concentrated hydrofluoric acid (lines 35–37) is most like which of the following?

(A) adding a new ingredient to a mixture to produce a new chemical

(B) breaking a mold to leave behind a product with a particular shape

(C) removing a naturally occurring impurity from raw ore during refining

(D) reconditioning a surface by scrubbing in order to remove contaminants

(E) applying a finish coat to protect the painted surfaces of a new product

23. The author's attitude toward the use of silicon carbide can best be described as

(A) qualified optimism

(B) fatalistic discouragement

(C) calculated indifference

(D) unrestrained enthusiasm

(E) sincere resignation

Early criminal law, which grew out of the blood feud, was almost totally lacking in the modern ethical notion of wrongdoing. Wherever a barbaric society was
(5) organized along the lines of blood kinship, revenge aimed not at atonement for the bodily harm inflicted as for the humiliation suffered by the family unit. So too, the primary goal of the early law was
(10) to provide an alternative to the feud by substituting a system of monetary compensation, and there emerged a definite tariff or *wer* with amounts reflecting the affront to clan dignity. Thus, the
(15) Welsh King Howell the Good decreed that a scar on the face was worth eighty pence, while the permanent loss of a thumb (an injury that would disable the hand) brought only seventy-six pence.
(20) In a parallel development, the institution of the *deodand* for cases involving a fatality required the surrender of the agent of death, whether that was a sword, a cart, a millwheel, or even an ox. It was not even
(25) required that the object have been under the direct control of the owner at the time, as in a case involving a sword hanging on a wall that fell killing a visitor. The fact that early law attributed responsibility to
(30) insensible objects is further indication that the notion of ethical wrongdoing was a much later innovation.

24. The primary purpose of the passage is to

    (A) compare and contrast the roles of the
        wer and the *deodand* in the early
        stages of the law's development
    (B) argue that early criminal law was
        lacking one of the important
        elements of modern criminal law
    (C) theorize about the origins of the
        kinship relations that gave rise to
        the practice of the blood feud
    (D) discuss some possible implications
        of early notions of criminal liability
        for modern legal systems
    (E) identify various economic and
        social factors that lead eventually to
        the decline of the *wer* and *deodand*

25. The author cites the decree of King Howell
    the Good in order to

    (A) clarify the distinction between the
        requirements of the *wer* and the
        deodand
    (B) prevent a possible misunderstanding
        about forfeiture in cases involving
        fatalities
    (C) demonstrate that violence and
        physical injury were common
        occurrence during the period of the
        blood feud
    (D) prove that the *wer* was a function of
        public injury to clan honor rather
        than physical injury to the victim
    (E) suggest that modern criminal law is
        more concerned with ethical notions
        than monetary compensation

26. The author's argument would be most
    strengthened by discovery of an early case
    that

    (A) established the *wer* for a visible
        bruise at double that for a similar
        bruise concealed by clothing.
    (B) relieved the owner of an object from
        the obligation of forfeiture if the
        owner was not at fault
    (C) refused to apply the requirement of
        the *deodand* because the instrument
        of death had been misused by the
        fatally injured person
    (D) required the payment of damages in
        equal amount for injuries to two
        persons of the same clan of unequal
        rank
    (E) stated that the amount of *wer* to be
        levied should be determined in large
        measure by the evil intention of the
        wrongdoer

27. It can be inferred from the passage
    that the establishment of the *wer* was
    intended to

    (A) deter malefactors from inflicting
        injury on innocent people
    (B) maintain public order by providing
        for alternative dispute resolution
    (C) punish wrongdoers for breaking the
        law against injuring another
    (D) prevent clan members from suing
        another clan for a wrongful injury
    (E) discourage careless practices by
        making owners liable for injuries

DIRECTIONS: Each item below consists of a word or phrase printed in capital letters, followed by five lettered words or phrases. Choose the lettered word or phrase that is most nearly *opposite* in meaning to the capitalized word or phrase.

28. ABASE:

    (A) recall
    (B) tangle
    (C) elevate
    (D) deter
    (E) quench

29. IMPERMEABLE:

    (A) explicable
    (B) mature
    (C) satiated
    (D) porous
    (E) reckless

30. DISSONANT:

    (A) unlikely
    (B) harmonious
    (C) flagrant
    (D) vibrant
    (E) tedious

31. PARSIMONY:

    (A) cleverness
    (B) valor
    (C) jaundice
    (D) inattention
    (E) generosity

32. MEDIATED:

    (A) inexpensive
    (B) horrific
    (C) vacuous
    (D) implausible
    (E) direct

33. REDOLENT:

    (A) foul spelling
    (B) needing repair
    (C) inviting disaster
    (D) becoming ill
    (E) incurring debt

34. INVETERATE:

    (A) reconstructed
    (B) serious-minded
    (C) exuberant
    (D) undecided
    (E) quiescent

35. ANOMALOUS:

    (A) frequent
    (B) abridged
    (C) anticipated
    (D) imperfect
    (E) tendentious

2

36. SANCTIMONIOUS:

    (A) practical
    (B) liquid
    (C) pious
    (D) delicate
    (E) infirm

37. STYMIE:

    (A) corroborate
    (B) facilitate
    (C) abdicate
    (D) truncate
    (E) vituperate

38. DECORUM:

    (A) penitence
    (B) salinity
    (C) impropriety
    (D) audaciousness
    (E) xenophobia

STOP:

IF YOU FINISH BEFORE
TIME EXPIRES, USE THE
ADDITIONAL TIME TO
CHECK YOUR WORK.

Evaluate Your Performance

Use the following answer key to score your Verbal Diagnostic Test. (Put a "✓" beside those items you answered correctly.)

Sentence Completion

1. (E)
2. (A)
3. (C)
4. (D)
5. (E)
6. (C)
7. (B)

Number of Sentence Completions Correct: _____

Analogies

8. (E)
9. (B)
10. (A)
11. (A)
12. (E)
13. (B)
14. (D)
15. (D)
16. (A)

Number of Analogies Correct: _____

Reading Comprehension

17. (E)
18. (D)
19. (C)
20. (C)
21. (A)
22. (B)
23. (A)
24. (B)
25. (D)
26. (A)
27. (B)

Number Reading Comprehension Correct: _____

Antonyms

28. (C)
29. (D)
30. (B)
31. (E)
32. (E)
33. (A)
34. (A)
35. (C)
36. (C)
37. (B)
38. (C)

Number of Antonyms Correct: _____

TOTAL CORRECT: _____

2

When you ask "How did I do?", you probably have in mind a couple of different questions. You want to know how you did overall and whether you did significantly worse (or better) on one part of the test or another. The following "bell curves" will help you answer those questions.

Sentence Completion

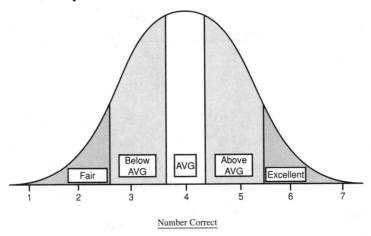

Number Correct

Analogies

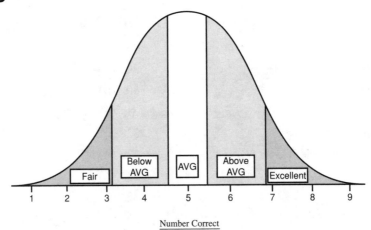

Number Correct

Reading Comprehension

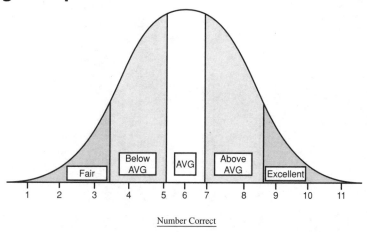

Antonyms

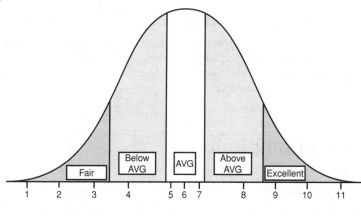

Verbal PreTest

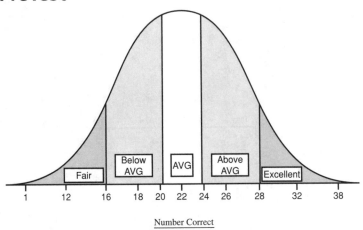

Number Correct

Review the Correct Answers

Now, you should review the explanations for the correct answers to the Verbal PreTest.

Before reviewing the explanations, go back over the PreTest and finish on your own any questions that you didn't have time for during the 30-minute time limit. Doing it on your own before reviewing an explanation is always good practice.

Sentence Completions

1. **(E)** According to Hobbes, no individual alone has sufficient strength to be assured of personal security. The solution to this problem is that there is safety in numbers, so individuals in the State of Nature seek allies.

2. **(A)** The "but" sets up a contrast between the expected result and the actual outcome: the Committee expected something crude but got something fairly refined.

3. **(C)** The "although" sets up a contrast between "similar" and the word that completes the sentence: the cycles are similar in some respects but —— in others. "Vary" provides the appropriate contrast.

4. **(D)** "Though" sets up a contrast between the status of the theory among academics and its status among sitting judges: it is *dismissed* by academics but *espoused* by sitting judges.

5. **(E)** The word that completes the sentence must suggest a "convoluted and self-contradictory" state of affairs. "Welter" means turmoil or confusion.

6. **(C)** The sentence suggests that two different viewpoints, form and content, that are often seen as independent perspectives, should be studied together for some reason. That must be because the two are somehow connected or "integrated" in *The Magus*.

7. **(B)** The sentence tells the reader that the story compromised the credibility of the news department, so you can infer that the story must have been untrue or unpersuasive. Then the "though" sets up a contrast between a description of that state of affairs and a description of the key piece of evidence, a contrast completed by "unconvincing": the story as a whole was not persuasive though a key piece of evidence was not unconvincing. Then, the other blank develops further the idea of the lack of persuasiveness: the rest of the story or the superstructure was unsupported.

MAKE CONNECTIONS You'll learn basic and advanced strategies for handling Sentence Completions on Day 3. And on Day 4 you can revisit the Sentence Completion items in this PreTest to see how those strategies would apply.

Analogies

8. **(E)** An actor is a member of a cast, and a singer is a member of a chorus.

9. **(B)** Dispersal is the method for breaking up a crowd, and dissolving is the method for breaking up a clog.

10. **(A)** A mandate is issued to result in compliance, and a prohibition is issued to result in abstention.

11. **(A)** Torpor is a state of inactivity or dormancy, and insipidness is a state of lacking flavor or taste.

12. **(E)** Insinuate is a milder form of accuse, and discourage is a milder form of forbid.

13. **(B)** Heterogenous means characterized by unlike elements, and capricious means characterized by change.

14. **(D)** A taxonomist is a person skilled in creating a classificatory scheme, and an architect is a person skilled in creating a design.

15. **(D)** The defining characteristic of a placebo is that it is totally lacking in efficacy, and the defining characteristic of a platitude is that it is totally lacking in originality.

16. **(A)** Calumny is by definition a false accusation, and encomium is by definition praise.

MAKE CONNECTIONS | You'll learn basic and advanced strategies for handling Analogies on Day 5. And on Day 6 you can revisit the Analogies in this PreTest to see how those strategies would apply.

Reading Comprehension

17. **(E)** The passage focuses upon possible uses of silicon carbide in semiconductors that have been made possible new manufacturing techniques.

18. **(D)** (A), (B), (C), and (E) are all mentioned in the first paragraph as advantages of silicon carbide. "Ease of manipulation" comes up in the second paragraph, but it is not the silicon carbide that is easily manipulated in the process described there, but the microcomponent to be embedded in the layer of silicon carbide.

19. **(C)** The answer to this question is found in the second paragraph where the author explains that the adhesion of a silicon carbide film thicker than one micrometer is "relatively weak."

20. **(C)** The answer to this question is not specifically stated in the passage, but you can infer the conclusion stated by (C). In the first paragraph, the author lists both advantages and disadvantages of working with silicon carbide. Mentioned as a disadvantage is the fact that it is difficult to work with—in part because large crystals are hard to make. But the author goes on to note that other techniques are also unavailable. The reason for mentioning these other techniques is to alert the reader that techniques that might ordinarily be employed in this situation are not effective.

21. **(A)** The use of silicon carbide in microelectromechanical systems is discussed in the last paragraph. There the author explains that silicon carbide components may last longer that those made of silicon because they generate less friction.

22. **(B)** The author explains that the process for making a silicon wafer with a silicon carbide microstructure requires several steps: use standard lithographic techniques to create a pattern of silicon dioxide, bombard the wafer with C_{60} for an hour or so, then wash off the silicon dioxide using acid. Left behind is the silicon carbide microstructure—just as though the mold had been removed leaving behind the formed product.

23. **(A)** Several clues in the passage let you know that the author is optimistic about the new developments: the new technique is "elegant,"the new microcomponents have "considerable potential in a variety of applications," and they have "practical benefit." This enthusiasm, however, is tempered because the new devices are not suitable for all purposes and probably will not replace entirely existing technology.

24. **(B)** The first sentence of the passage sets forth the main point: early criminal law lacks an important element found in modern criminal law. And the last point of the passage echoes this point.

25. **(D)** The author notes that the facial scar is worth more than the loss of a thumb, even though the loss of a thumb has considerably greater economic value (in terms of earning a living, say) than disfiguration. The point is that the *wer* was calculated to reflect the embarrassment suffered by the group and not the injury sustained by the individual.

26. **(A)** A key point in the argument is that the earliest forms of law were more concerned with the rights of the clan than of the individual. (A) provides further evidence of this contention: of two injuries that might cause the same pain to the individual, the one that is open to public view is more important when measured by the size of the *wer*.

27. **(B)** The passage is dealing with the earliest forms of criminal law, and the author notes that the overriding objective was to find a substitute for the blood feud. You can infer, therefore, that the goal of adopting the *wer* was to provide an alternative to the blood feud.

2

You'll learn basic and advanced strategies for handling Reading Comprehension questions on Day 9. And on Day 10 you can revisit the Reading Comprehension items in this PreTest to see how those strategies would apply.

Antonyms

28. **(C)** To abase means literally to lay low and by extension to humiliate, and to elevate means literally to raise up and by extension to raise to a higher intellectual or moral plane.

29. **(D)** Impermeable is the quality of not permitting passage, especially of liquids, and porous is the quality of permitting their passage.

30. **(B)** Dissonant means discordant, harsh, jarring, or out-of-tune.

31. **(A)** Parsimony means stinginess or miserliness.

32. **(E)** Mediated means to be dependent upon an intervening agency.

33. **(A)** Redolent means sweet-smelling or fragrant.

34. **(A)** Inveterate means deep-rooted or firmly established over a longer period of time, while reconstructed means made over again.

35. **(A)** Anomalous means abnormal or irregular.

36. **(B)** Stymie means to hinder or obstruct, while facilitate means to make easier.

37. **(B)** Decorum means that which is suitable or proper, and impropriety means that which is improper or unacceptable.

You'll learn basic and advanced strategies for handling Antonyms on Day 7. And on Day 8 you can revisit the Antonyms in this PreTest to see how those strategies would apply.

Day

3

Teach Yourself Sentence Completions

Today, you'll teach yourself how to answer GRE Sentence Completion items. Sentence Completions are the "fill-in-the-blanks" that appear on the verbal part of the GRE CAT; they test reading skills as well as vocabulary. You'll learn how to use your reading skills and vocabulary to maximize your performance on this question kind.

Get All the Inside Info on Sentence Completions

With any question type on the GRE, you'll want to feel comfortable with the format. The basic "fill-in-the-blank" format of Sentence Completions is fairly intuitive, but there are some subtleties that you need to be aware of.

The basic idea of a Sentence Completion is described in the directions.

DIRECTIONS: Each of the following sentences has one or two blanks. Each blank indicates that a word or phrase has been omitted. Following each sentence is a series of words or phrases. Choose the word or phrase for each blank that *best* fits the meaning of the sentence in its entirety.

TIP

Forget about the formal directions. When you see a sentence with one or two blanks, just choose the best "fill-in" using the strategies you learn today.

As the directions indicate, a Sentence Completion may have one blank or it may have two blanks. Here is an example of a one-blank question:

QUESTION To compensate for the funds that will no longer be available due to a decline in the value of the endowment's portfolio, the university will need to find an —— sum from another source.

(A) anticipated

(B) equivalent

(C) unofficial

(D) unstated

(E) inconsequential

ANALYSIS The answer to this question is **(B)**. Since funds will no longer be available from the present source, it will be necessary to replace those funds: to do so, the university will need to find an *equivalent* sum from another source.

And here is an example of a typical two-blank question:

QUESTION Although the mobster's efforts to appear mentally unstable and therefore unable to stand trial were —— and even ——, the defense lawyers, through clever strategies, were able to postpone the criminal proceedings for several years.

(A) unrelenting . . predictable

(B) contrived . . convincing

(C) unpersuasive . . ludicrous

(D) predictable . . amusing

(E) ill-advised . . heroic

ANALYSIS Here the answer is **(C)**. The "were —— and even ——" tells you that the second substitution word makes a more extreme statement than the first. And, the "Although" at the beginning of the sentence tells you that the substitutions describe an effort that seemed unlikely to work, but in fact resulted in partial success for the lawyers.

A typical GRE Verbal Part has 5 to 7 Sentence Completions, some of which may be experimental items that do not count toward your score. And you'll almost surely get a mix of one-blank and two-blank items.

 NOTE

> A two-blank item is not necessarily more difficult than a one-blank item. A two-blank item may sometimes even be easier because you have twice as many ways to eliminate wrong answers.

The basic idea of Sentence Completion is "fill-in-the-blank." How does it work? Studies have shown that people don't need to hear every word that is said in order to understand the point of what was said. And if you think about it, that makes sense. You could be talking to someone on a cellphone in an area of poor reception and hear:

On your way back to the house, please pick up a medium —— with mushrooms on it but no anchovies.

The most important word in the sentence is missing, but you understand that you're supposed to pick up a pizza. On the GRE, it would look like this:

QUESTION On your way back to the house, please pick up a medium —— with mushrooms on it but no anchovies.

  (A) hat

  (B) hammer

  (C) computer

  (D) aquarium

  (E) pizza

Actual GRE Sentence Completions aren't quite so easy as the "pizza" example. Although they're basically fill-in-the-blanks, several factors can make them more challenging. You need to know what those factors are so that you can learn strategies to neutralize them. The added difficulty factors are:

1. The Vocabulary Factor

2. The Complexity Factor

3. The Excess Baggage Factor

These factors are used by the GRE to make the ladder-of-difficulty behind the CAT for Sentence Completions. Let's take a look at each of the factors and how they work. Then, we can discuss ways that you can overcome them.

1. The Vocabulary Factor

One of the most important differences between a Sentence Completion at the bottom of the ladder of difficulty and one at the top of the ladder is the vocabulary used in the answer choices. Compare the following items:

Easy

 After working together for several years, members of the crew had developed specialized terms for the tools they used, —— only they could understand.

    (A) procedures

    (B) customs

    (C) jargon

    (D) appetite

    (E) rhythm

Hard

 After working together for several years, members of the crew had developed specialized terms for the tools they used, a(n) —— only they could understand.

    (A) procedures

    (B) customs

    (C) argot

    (D) appetite

    (E) rhythm

ANALYSIS The correct answer to both items is **(C)**. A specialized vocabulary is called jargon or, less commonly, argot. Although the sentence is the same in both cases, the level of difficulty is not. The second item stands higher on the ladder of difficulty because "argot" is a word that many people may not be familiar with. In general, the more obscure the vocabulary words in the answer choices, the more difficult the Sentence Completion item. Here is another illustration:

Easy

QUESTION Awed by the credentials of the reviewing committee, the doctoral candidate set forth the central thesis of the paper tentatively and answered questions with ——— .

(A) confidence

(B) delight

(C) uncertainty

(D) recklessness

(E) directness

Hard

QUESTION Awed by the credentials of the reviewing committee, the doctoral candidate set forth the central thesis of the paper tentatively and answered questions with ——— .

(A) aplomb

(B) relish

(C) diffidence

(D) abandon

(E) imperiousness

ANALYSIS The correct answer to both items is **(C)**. The sentence indicates that the candidate was awed and set forth the argument tentatively, that is, not confidently. This suggests that the candidate answered questions the same way, and uncertainty is a good word to complete the sentence. Diffidence, which means reserve, shyness, or modesty, is also a good completion.

Notice that the sentence is the same in both items. The answer choices, however, are different—all of them this time, and not just the correct answer. You should be able to see that an entire array of difficult vocabulary words moves an item up the ladder of difficulty by several rungs.

 NOTE

Very few Sentence Completions are "pure" vocabulary items. Most involve a significant element of reading comprehension as well.

3

2. The Complexity Factor

A second factor that makes a Sentence Completion item difficult is the structure of the sentence: the more complex the overall structure, the more difficult the item. Compare the following Sentence Completions:

Easy

 Every society has a concept of justice, but what counts as a just or an unjust act is —— .

(A) variable

(B) laudable

(C) foreseeable

(D) crucial

(E) implicit

Hard

 The concept of justice is universal, found in every society from the most primitive to the most advanced; but the actions to which these terms attach are —— .

(A) variable

(B) laudable

(C) foreseeable

(D) crucial

(E) implicit

ANALYSIS The correct answer is **(A)** in both cases, and the justification the same. The "but" sets up a contrast between an idea in the first part of the sentence and an idea in the second part of the sentence. The important idea in the first part is "universal," so the important idea in the second part must be something like unique or variable.

Now, compare the difficulty of these examples:

Easy

QUESTION Although the Best in Show was awarded to a dog owned by a relative of the judge, the decision was entirely —— .

(A) unwarranted

(B) conclusive

(C) unacceptable

(D) inappropriate

(E) justified

Hard

 Although the Best in Show was awarded to a dog owned by a relative of the judge, it cannot be argued that the decision was —— .

(A) warranted

(B) inconclusive

(C) acceptable

(D) appropriate

(E) unjustified

 The correct answer to both items is **(E)**. The "although" sets up a contrast between the first idea in the sentence and an idea that follows. The first part of the sentence explains that the prize was awarded to a relative of the judge, so a natural inference might be a suggestion of unfairness. But the "although" signals the opposite of this natural inference: no, the judging was fair. And both correct answers make this point, but the second does so in a more round about way:

The decision was entirely justified.

It cannot be argued that the decision was unjustified.

Added complexity can be injected into a sentence in many different ways: extra clauses, parenthetical notes, negative or other round-about phrasing, and so on. The best antidote to added complexity is to know what to expect; and later in this Day, you'll learn the most common techniques used to move a Sentence Completion up the ladder of difficulty and strategies for bringing it back down to a manageable level.

> **TIP**
>
> If a Sentence Completion seems overly complex, try breaking it down into simpler parts. For a two-blank item, focus first on one blank and then the other.

3. The Excess Baggage Factor

A third factor that makes Sentence Completions difficult is excess baggage. Excess baggage is detail such as the name of an historical person, a date, a place, or any other "real world" information that you don't really need to answer the question. Compare the following examples:

Easy

QUESTION For Thomas, the question was not —— but a —— issue of vital import.

(A) whimsy . . profound

(B) insightful . . complex

(C) comical . . superficial

(D) premeditated . . serious

(E) caprice . . fanciful

Hard

QUESTION For Thomas Aquinas, the Scholastic thinker and author of the *Summa Theologica*, the question of angels dancing on a pinhead was not —— but a —— issue of vital import to his project of reconciling Aristotelean metaphysics with medieval Church doctrine.

(A) whimsy . . profound

(B) insightful . . complex

(C) comical . . superficial

(D) premeditated . . serious

(E) caprice . . fanciful

ANALYSIS The correct answer to both items is **(A)**. The "not" signals a contrast between two ideas. The second element must support a notion described as "vital," and the first must stand in contrast. Whimsy and profound provide the needed contrast.

Now look at another pair, and try to identify for yourself the special features that make the second item more difficult than the first:

Easy

QUESTION They had expected the mission to be aborted; but the astronauts —— the problem, and the mission continued.

(A) recreated

(B) transmitted

(C) misjudged

(D) circumvented

(E) proscribed

Hard

QUESTION The rocket scientists had fully expected the thermothrockle to hydrolize under the intense ionizing radiation requiring the mission to be aborted; but the astronauts —— the problem by tekelating the suborbital flexion, and the mission continued.

(A) recreated

(B) transmitted

(C) misjudged

(D) circumvented

(E) proscribed

ANALYSIS The correct answer to both items is **(D)**. The sentence contrasts probable failure with actual success and attributes the outcome to the ability of the astronauts to solve the problem. A good match-up for "solve" is circumvent.

Each of these easy/hard items makes it clear that excess baggage kicks an item up the ladder of difficulty a couple of rungs by needlessly complicating the issue. But the underlying logic that is the key to the item remains the same.

In other words, you don't have to be a rocket scientist to solve Sentence Completions. In fact, all of the added detail in the second example is gibberish made up for this one example—not a technique ever used by the GRE, but you get the point: you can ignore excess baggage.

If excess baggage is irrelevant, you may wonder "Why not ignore it altogether?" That's a good strategy. It's developed for you later in greater detail.

 CAUTION Excess baggage is designed to stop you dead in your tracks because you start thinking about an obscure historical person or an exotic location or some other superfluous detail. So don't go there. Sentence Completion is about structure and vocabulary, not content.

Learn the Basic Technique for Sentence Completions

Whether or not they have added complexity factors, Sentence Completions are "fill-in-the-blanks," and that's the basic technique you should try first. Here it is broken down for you step-by-step:

ACTION PLAN **The Basic Tecnique**

Step 1: Read through the sentence for meaning. Read the sentence to yourself at normal speed—as though someone were speaking to you.

Step 2: Formulate a possible completion and choose an answer. Based on your reading and understanding of the intention of the sentence, formulate a possible completion by anticipating one or two words or phrases that might be used to complete the sentence. If you're lucky, your formulation will actually match up with an answer choice, and you'll have your correct answer. But you can't always count on luck. So be prepared to accept an answer choice that is similar in meaning to your formulation.

Now let's apply the Basic Technique to an example:

QUESTION After his novel was rejected by six publishers, John became embittered and ——, so much so that his friends feared for his sanity.

(A) gentle

(B) wary

(C) morose

(D) pacified

(E) prudent

ANALYSIS The correct answer is (**C**). Your reading tells you that John was affected negatively and became embittered as well as something else that is like embittered, that is, another negative emotion. Possible completions are words such as disappointed, angry, depressed, or sullen. The best match is found in (C): morose.

  TIP

As you read the sentence to yourself, say "bleep" (or some similar word) to indicate that something is missing. Articulating a place holder in this way will preserve the rhythm of the sentence and help you understand what the meaning is.

Now let's walk through some other examples together using the Action Plan for the Basic Technique:

QUESTION Given the rapidly changing nature of today's technological society, schools can no longer hope to teach eternal principles for by tomorrow today's knowledge is ——— .

(A) enriched

(B) reproduced

(C) adequate

(D) precarious

(E) obsolete

ANALYSIS The correct answer is (**E**). Your reading tells you that the sentence sets up a contrast between eternal principles and knowledge that is not eternal. So some possible completions are words such as temporary, outdated, or transient. The best match is given by (E): obsolete.

QUESTION Retiring by nature and ——— even in private, Eleanor hardly ever spoke in public.

(A) confident

(B) taciturn

(C) preoccupied

(D) untamed

(E) courageous

ANALYSIS The correct answer is (**B**). Your reading tells you that Eleanor was unwilling to speak. Some possible completions are quiet and silent. The best match is "reticent."

The Basic Approach is all you need for many Sentence Completions, especially those that are not complicated by added-difficulty factors. This should always be your first approach.

TIP

> Once you've found a possible match, then read the sentence a final time with your completion in place. If the result is a smooth-reading sentence that makes sense to you, then the problem yielded the correct answer. Enter your choice and move on to the next item.

Workshop A: The Basic Technique

This Workshop provides the opportunity to practice the Basic Technique. Do the Drill portion first, and then check your work against the explanations in the Review part.

Drill

Solve the following items using the Basic Technique. Read the sentence through for meaning. Then in the space provided, enter your anticipated completion. Match your anticipated completion to one of the choices.

1. Even those who vigorously disagreed with the goals of the plan —— admitted that it had been well designed.

   (A) erroneously
   (B) valiantly
   (C) successfully
   (D) defiantly
   — (E) grudgingly

2. The so-called "road rage" is just one more example of a more general —— that includes disrespect for rules, traditions, and institutions.

   — (A) incivility
   (B) caution
   (C) curiosity
   (D) passion
   (E) apprehension

3. Random noises have been shown to —— sleep cycles, causing fatigue and irritability in test subjects.

   (A) reinforce
   — (B) disrupt
   (C) solidify
   (D) undermine
   (E) fracture

4. Increasingly, state legislatures have enacted laws that use a standardized exam as the sole —— by which the success or failure a school system is to be judged.

   (A) prediction
   (B) guarantee
   (C) actuality
   — (D) criterion
   (E) aspiration

5. A fine public servant with an otherwise untarnished reputation has become the latest —— in a war being waged by unscrupulous journalists against those who espouse principles they reject.

   (A) happenstance
   (B) victory
   —(C) casualty
   (D) detriment
   (E) fiasco

6. The new bookstore, with its coffee bar and classical music, hopes that its literature selections will appeal to a ⸺ clientele.

— (A) sophisticated
   (B) conventional
   (C) provocative
   (D) restrictive
   (E) passive

7. The corporation's spokesperson ⸺ the report as junk science and accused the researchers of pursuing a political agenda.

   (A) highlighted
— (B) denounced
   (C) withdrew
   (D) fomented
   (E) inscribed

8. By the terms of the extremely ⸺ curriculum, all students at the Academy were required to take two years of Latin, two years of algebra, and two years of fine arts.

   (A) industrious
   (B) fractured
   (C) provocative
   (D) valiant
— (E) regimented

9. The polite veneer that John exhibits in public ⸺ a violent temper that frequently erupts in private, especially when his authority is challenged.

   (A) condemns
— (B) belies
   (C) validates
   (D) queries
   (E) presages

10. Long hours of ⸺ rehearsal ensured that the orchestra performed the difficult piece flawlessly.

— (A) arduous
   (B) spontaneous
   (C) influential
   (D) jubilant
   (E) temporary

3

Review

1. Anticipated completions: reluctantly, gradually

   Correct Answer: **(E)**

2. Anticipated completions: impoliteness, rebelliousness

   Correct Answer: **(A)**

3. Anticipated completions: interfere with, break up

   Correct Answer: **(B)**

4. Anticipated completions: standard, rule

   Correct Answer: **(D)**

5. Anticipated completions: victim, target

   Correct Answer: **(C)**

6. Anticipated completions: mature, intelligent

   Correct Answer: **(A)**

7. Anticipated completions: condemned, attacked

   Correct Answer: **(B)**

8. Anticipated completions: structured, rigorous

   Correct Answer: **(E)**

9. Anticipated completions: conceals, hides

   Correct Answer: **(B)**

10. Anticipated completions: careful, painstaking

    Correct Answer: **(A)**

Master Advanced Strategies for Difficult Items

If you can't dispose of an item using the Basic Technique, it's probably because of added-difficulty factors such as excess baggage or complicated sentence structures. Advanced strategies will help you neutralize those factors and bring the item down to a manageable level. Here's an Action Plan to help you implement the Advanced Strategies for difficult items.

ACTION PLAN   **Advanced Strategies**

Step 1: Dispose of any excess baggage. Mentally eliminate any superfluous detail, so that you can concentrate on the underlying logic of the sentence. Then try the Basic Approach again.

Step 2: Use the verbal signals. One of the most important added-difficulty factors is extra complexity that can be built into a sentence. When the pattern is complex, you have to pay careful attention to verbal signals to understand the underlying structure.

Here's how the Advanced Strategies work. First, you need to dispose of any excess baggage cluttering up the sentence and making your job more difficult. If you get a Sentence Completion that looks like this:

QUESTION Luciano Pavarotti may be the greatest tenor of all time; but even the greatest voice is not —— to the passage of time, and his voice shows the wear and tear of —— career.

(A) susceptible . . an illustrious

(B) immune . . a protracted

(C) transparent .. a lengthy

(D) ineluctable . . a contentious

(E) resistant . . an unenviable

ANALYSIS Then you can mentally cross out details so that you are left with this:

~~Luciano Pavarotti may be the greatest tenor of all time; but~~ even the greatest voice is not —— to the ravages of time, and his voice shows the wear and tear of —— career.

(A) susceptible . . an illustrious

(B) immune . . a protracted

(C) transparent .. a lengthy

(D) ineluctable . . a contentious

(E) resistant . . an unenviable

Now read the simplified sentence through and anticipate possible completions. The voice shows wear and tear and so is not invulnerable or immortal. And the passing of time indicates a long career. So the best completions are provided by (**B**): immune and protracted.

You can't literally cross out the words on the monitor screen, so you'll have to do it mentally. Just ignore the unnecessary details.

What qualifies as unnecessary detail? There is no hard-and-fast rule, but generally all of the following can be safely ignored:

Names: Georges Braque, Emily Dickinson, Marie Curie, W.H. Auden

Places: Lesotho, Mount Saint Helens, SoHo, Triton

Dates: The 1890s, 1776, the Renaissance, Post-Modern

Titles: *Omoo, Our Town,* "Death of a Salesman," "The Jupiter"

Theories: stellar evolution, continental drift, psychoanalysis, classical physics

Movements: French opera, Cubism, Russian Revolution, Saint-Simonian feminism

Since names, places, and so on are unnecessary details, the information needed to fill-in-the-blank is somewhere else in the sentence. So don't just ignore the unnecessary, look elsewhere in the sentence for the information that will help you fill in the blank.

 CAUTION | Don't memorize the list of "Unnecessary Details." The GRE can use almost anything to distract your attention. Instead, learn by practice to recognize what is useful and what is not.

A second advanced technique is to use the verbal signals provided. Verbal signals tell you how the various parts of a sentence fit together, e.g., whether one part of the sentence clarifies or adds detail to another, whether a later element contradicts an earlier element, whether one idea is qualified or overruled by another. Study the following examples:

QUESTION It is a rare individual who bothers to examine his or her fundamental ethical beliefs; indeed, the effort required —— most people from even starting.

(A) cautions

(B) discourages

(C) sustains

(D) recalls

(E) withdraws

ANALYSIS The correct answer is (**B**). "Indeed" is a verbal signal that indicates that the second part of the sentence supports the idea contained in the first part. More specifically, "indeed" suggests an added emphasis, so the second idea is stated even more strongly than the first.

QUESTION Although —— in her criticism of the minutest details, she often —— the larger picturer; so her input was incomplete.

(A) understated . . conspired

(B) sparing . . omitted

(C) exhaustive . . overlooked

(D) creative . . presented

(E) meticulous . . emphasized

ANALYSIS The correct answer is (**C**). The "although" is a verbal signal that indicates that the second part of the sentence contrasts with the first part of the sentence, so the two substitutions must result in a tension between two ideas: she was exhaustive, but she overlooked.

Here is a list of signals that are commonly used in Sentence Completions on the GRE and what you should look for:

Signal	Look For
therefore, thus, consequently, so, as a result	a further conclusion, the effect of a cause, an expected outcome
if, since, because	a premise of a logical argument, a cause leading to an effect, a condition(s) leading to an outcome
and, additionally, further, moreover, similarly, likewise	further extension of a thought, a parallel or similar idea, added emphasis
although, though, while, but, rather, however, despite, unlike, rather, yet, not	contrasting ideas, an exception, a reversal of thinking
indeed, in fact	an example, an idea for added emphasis
colon (:)	enumeration, clarification, further detail

The list of signals is by no means exhaustive, but it should give you an idea of what you should be looking for.

Workshop B: Advanced Strategies

This Workshop provides the opportunity to practice the Advanced Strategies. Do the Drill portion first, and then check your work against the explanations in the Review part.

Drill

Use the following ten items to practice the Advanced Strategies developed in this part. Begin by disposing of excess baggage. (In this case, you can use your pen if you care to.) Then, use the verbal signals to analyze the logical structure of the sentence in order to arrive at your choices.

1. When Ghana achieved independence from colonial domination in 1957, the first country in sub-Saharan Africa to do so, it —— economic and political advantages unrivaled elsewhere in tropical Africa.

   (A) demanded
   — (B) enjoyed
   (C) proclaimed
   (D) denounced
   (E) incited

2. Fraktur, a genre of folkart which has its roots in the Rhine Valley, is —— to the Pennsylvania Dutch region, though Russian-German Mennonites produced similar but —— ornamental drawings.

   (A) endemic . . characteristic
   (B) inherent . . distinct
   (C) native . . unusual
   (D) reduced . . inconsequential
   — (E) unique . . unrelated

3. The *Free Trade Zone* law was enacted in order to —— legal issues left open by the Supreme Court case of <u>California v. Bond</u>.

   — (A) resolve
   (B) undermine
   (C) redress
   (D) present
   (E) nullify

4. Scholars often speak of an early and a late Heidegger, but a more careful reading reveals only —— shift rather than a radical —— in his thought.

   (A) an evolutionary . . bent
   (B) a discernible . . consistency
   (C) an inevitable . . temper
   (D) an unpredictable . . change
   — (E) a gradual . . discontinuity

5. Van Gogh was virtually —— at the time of his death: his agent, brother Theo, had sold only one of his paintings.

   —(A) unknown
   (B) famous
   (C) wealthy
   (D) victorious
   (E) adored

6. Legalized gambling seems to offer unlimited governmental revenue without the need to raise taxes; however, experience shows that casino gambling is not the financial —— claimed by its proponents.

   —(A) panacea
   (B) calamity
   (C) incentive
   (D) predicament
   (E) validation

7. Low on supplies and badly in need of fresh troops, General Burgoyne's —— and even —— decision to push ahead resulted in disaster at Saratoga.

   (A) reflective . . conscientious
   (B) valorous . . cowardly
   — (C) rash . . foolhardy
   (D) ill-advised . . calculated
   (E) victorious . . generous

8. Although the Ford Edsel of the 1950s is commonly thought of as a "lemon," the car was actually ——; it was the victim of marketing not —— failures.

   (A) attractive . . sales
   — (B) well-made . . engineering
   (C) high-priced . . design
   (D) desirable . . advertising
   (E) well-known . . manufacturing

9. No reasonable trade-off between unemployment and inflation can be achieved by
either monetary or fiscal policy alone;
rather, both must be regarded as —— tools
for managing the economy.

(A) complementary
(B) intelligible
(C) unnecessary
(D) delicate
(E) unlimited

10. Professional schools assemble —— student
body not for the sake of enriching extra-
curricular life for the variety of personal
and academic backgrounds that enhance the
learning experience.

(A) a homogeneous
(B) a knowledgeable
(C) an elite
(D) an unexceptional
(E) a diverse

Review

1. **(B)** You can dispose of some excess
baggage:

~~When Ghana achieved independence from
colonial domination in 1957, the first
country in sub-Saharan Africa to do so,~~ it
—— economic and political advantages
unrivaled ~~elsewhere in tropical Africa.~~

This isolates the logic of the sentence: it
enjoyed advantages that were unrivaled.

2. **(E)** You can dispose of some excess baggage because the logic of the sentence is
not about Fraktur:

~~Fraktur, a genre of folkart which has its
roots in the Rhine Valley,~~ is —— to the
~~Pennsylvania Dutch~~ region, though
~~Russian-German Mennonites~~ produced
similar but —— ornamental drawings.

So the sentence says that the type of folkart
is unique to one region even though other
people produced similar but unrelated
drawings.

3. **(A)** Dispose of some excess baggage:

The ~~Free Trade Zone~~ law was enacted in
order to —— legal issues left open *by the*
~~Supreme Court case of California v. Bond~~.

And the phrase "in order to" tells you that
the blank must explain why something
occurred: since the issues were left open,
the law resolved them.

4. **(E)** You certainly don't need to know
anything about Heidegger to answer this
question:

Scholars often speak of an early and a late
~~Heidegger,~~ but a more careful reading
reveals only —— shift rather than a
radical —— in his thought.

And there are two clear verbal signals in
the sentence. "But" signals a contrast between the view that sees "early and late,"
so the second idea must downplay that
distinction. Then, the "rather" signals a
contrast between the first blank and the
second.

3

5. **(A)** You may know something about Van Gogh and his life, but you don't need that information for this item:

~~Van Gogh~~ was virtually —— at the time of his death: his agent, ~~brother Theo,~~ had sold only one ~~of his paintings~~.

So you see that even the fact that Van Gogh was a painter is not essential to the logic of the sentence. In this case, the signal is the colon. It tells you that the second half of the sentence is going to explain or illustrate the first half of the sentence.

6. **(A)** Start by eliminating the unnecessary detail:

~~Legalized gambling~~ seems to offer unlimited governmental revenue ~~without the need to raise taxes~~; however, ~~experience shows that casino~~ gambling is not the financial —— ~~claimed by its proponents~~.

"However" is an important verbal signal that tells you the second part of the sentence contrasts with the first part. But be careful. The "not" in the second part of the sentence adds another wrinkle. The blank has to be filled by a word that means just about the same thing as "unlimited": it seems to offer unlimited resources, but it is not a panacea.

7. **(C)** You don't need to know anything about the American Revolutionary War to answer this question:

~~Low on supplies and badly in need of fresh troops, General Burgoyne's~~ —— and even —— decision to push ahead resulted in disaster ~~at Saratoga~~.

The "and even" is a signal that tells you that two similar ideas are needed to complete the sentence and also that the second will probably be a stronger statement than the first: rash and even foolhardy.

8. **(B)** Since names and dates don't count:

Although the ~~Ford Edsel of the 1950s~~ is commonly thought of as a "lemon," the car was actually ——; it was the victim of marketing not —— failures.

And there are two strong verbal signals. The "although" tells you that the car was not the "lemon" most people believed it to be, so a good completion would be well-built. Then, the "not" later in the sentence tells you to set up a contrast between "marketing" and some other department.

9. **(A)** You don't have to be an economist to answer this question:

No reasonable trade-off ~~between unemployment and inflation~~ can be achieved by either ~~monetary or fiscal~~ policy alone; rather, both must be regarded as —— tools ~~for managing the economy~~.

The verbal signal "rather" tells you that the blank must be the opposite of things working alone, and complementary means working together.

10. **(E)** There isn't much excess baggage here in the way of names or places. The key signal is the "not . . . but." You are looking for a word that means just about the same as "providing different perspectives."

Develop a Fail-Safe Plan for Sentence Completion Emergencies

No matter how conscientiously you apply the Basic Approach and the Advanced Strategies, you're may still find times when you have to guess. But there is guessing, and then there is educated guessing.

ACTION PLAN   **The Fail-Safe Plan**

Step 1: Test answer choices.

Step 2: Choose the most obscure word.

This Action Plan is designed to give you something to do even when you can't think of anything to do.

First, some answer choices are wrong because, when substituted into the sentence, the result is simply not good English, that is, the word substituted just doesn't work in the context. Here is an example:

QUESTION   A new approach to psychotherapy encourages people to reconcile themselves to the complexities of life by —— rather than rejecting the conflicting elements of their lives.

(A) confronting

(B) embracing

(C) improving

(D) announcing

(E) diluting

opposite vb
rejecting

ANALYSIS   The correct answer is **(B)**. The key signal word in this sentence, "rather," sets up a contrast between the completion and the word "rejecting." And "embrace" and "reject" are opposites.

Assume that you overlooked the key signal in this sentence and so could not reach the conclusion given in the Analysis above. In order to improve your chances of guessing, eliminate any choice that, when substituted into the blank, fails to make an idiomatic phrase:

(A) confronting . . . the conflicting elements

(B) embracing . . . the conflicting elements

(C) improving . . . the conflicting elements

(D) announcing . . . the conflicting elements

(E) diluting . . . the conflicting elements

3

You can safely eliminate (C), (D), and (E) because they don't result in phrases that are idiomatic. So the correct answer must be either (A) or (B), and that gives you a 50-50 chance of getting the item right.

> **CAUTION**
>
> An exact opposite of the correct choice may make just as much sense as the right answer when you look only at a small part of the sentence. So use the technique of eliminating non-idiomatic choices to *disqualify* a choice as wrong not to *qualify* a choice as right.

Additionally, the technique of substitution is absolutely essential for a handful of Sentence Completions. These unusual items don't have a uniquely correct answer choice. Or rather, these items could be satisfactorily completed with different sets of substitutions—even ones that are contradictory. Consider the following pair of items:

QUESTION A professional violinist for most of her adult life, at age sixteen, Mary was —— musician and —— to lead the orchestra.

    (A) an accomplished . . able

    (B) an uneducated . . inclined

    (C) a dedicated . . unwilling

    (D) a presumptuous . . failing

    (E) an isolated . . expected

QUESTION A professional violinist for most of her adult life, at age sixteen, Mary was —— musician and —— to lead the orchestra.

    (A) an unaccomplished . . unable

    (B) an uneducated . . inclined

    (C) a dedicated . . unwilling

    (D) a presumptuous . . failing

    (E) an isolated . . expected

ANALYSIS The correct answer to each is (**A**). At sixteen, Mary might have been an accomplished musician who lead the orchestra and who later became a professional violinist; or she might equally well have been an unaccomplished musician who was unable to lead the orchestra and who nonetheless went on to become a professional violinist as an adult. Both make sense.

What makes both choices possible is that the sentence itself contains no clues that might let you know which would be the preferred reading. Consequently, the answer choices—and the answer choices alone—dictate the correct completion. And the only way of finding the correct choice is by substitution. (You would never be put in the impossible position of having to choose between (A) of the first example and (A) of the second.)

Here is another example:

QUESTION Adams was very much a —— who was —— to contribute to charity.

    (A) prodigal . . eager

    (B) scoundrel . . proposing

    (C) malingerer . . hoping

    (D) curmudgeon . . promising

    (E) philanthropist . . willing

ANALYSIS The correct answer is **(E)**. Neither the Basic Approach nor the Advanced Strategies is going to get the job done here because the sentence itself is pretty much devoid of signals. For all that you know, Adams might be a generous person who is always contributing to charity, but Adams might just as well be a tightwad who never contributes to charity. By substituting choices, however, you find that Adams was generous and did contribute to charity because (E) is the only pair of elements that creates a meaningful sentence.

The example could equally well have been:

QUESTION Adams was very much a —— who was —— to contribute to charity.

    (A) prodigal . . eager

    (B) scoundrel . . proposing

    (C) malingerer . . hoping

    (D) curmudgeon . . promising

    (E) miser . . unwilling

ANALYSIS Again, the correct answer is **(E)** even though the meaning is different. (E) is correct simply because (E) is the only completion given that makes sense.

Finally, you may encounter an item that simply defies analysis: the Basic Approach doesn't work and the Advanced Strategies don't work. What might cause this? One of the added-difficulty factors in this part is vocabulary; and, unfortunately, if you just don't know the meaning of one or more words, you're going to have to guess. As a last attempt, if you have an item the defies analysis, choose a vocabulary word that you don't know the meaning of. Here is an example:

QUESTION Kant focused on Descartes' proof of the existence of the ego in the *Meditations* to demonstrate the danger of a(n) —— or drawing a conclusion that is unwarranted by the premises.

    (A) inference

    (B) conclusion

    (C) paralogism

    (D) rationale

    (E) justification

ANALYSIS The correct answer is **(C)**. A paralogism is reasoning which is incorrect as a matter of form or logical structure.

In this case, four of the five choices are probably words that you know, even if you can't give a dictionary definition for them. "Paralogism," however, is a term with a highly specific definition that few people will recognize. So if you have to *guess,* then pick (C), the most obscure word in the list, on the theory that the item defies analysis because the correct answer is a tough vocabulary word.

 CAUTION

> Having to guess is never pleasant, so there is always the temptation to spend just a little more time on an item, hoping that you'll finally see the light. This is a score-killer. Go ahead and guess, and get on to the next item

 TIP

> When it comes time to guess, two-blank items are doubly easy because eliminating one or the other substitution element—for any reason whatever—eliminates that answer choice entirely.

Workshop C: The Fail-Safe Plan

This Workshop provides the opportunity to practice the Fail-Safe Plan. Do the Drill portion first, and then check your work against the explanations in the Review part.

Drill

Use the following five items to practice the Fail-Safe Plan. Even if you know that you can solve the problem using one of the other approaches, play around with the technique of substituting choices. And test your ability to spot the most obscure choice in the answer set just to practice that technique.

1. The Senator frequently —— other members of the chamber with unwarranted attacks on their personal lives.

— (A) provokes
  (B) analyzes
  (C) enhances
  (D) deprives
  (E) elevates

2. Clyde's —— occasionally astonished even his closest friends who knew full-well that his had been —— childhood.

  (A) sophistication . . an extended
— (B) naivete . . a sheltered
  (C) wit . . a precocious
  (D) knowledge . . a difficult
  (E) wisdom . . an uneducated

3. Research into sleep suggest that there are several —— states between sleeping and waking and that it is difficult to determine where one ends and another begins.

  (A) serious
  (B) permissive
  (C) predetermined
  (D) unalterable
— (E) intermediate

4. The playwright took a story so sublime that it has offered the ultimate challenge to composers, choreographers, and writers for centuries and, with a wanton heavy-handedness, gave the audience a hackneyed version that descended into —— .

  (A) confusion
— (B) bathos
  (C) inattention
  (D) significance
  (E) indecision

5. Sensing his position was all but lost, the speaker launched into ——, hoping to save the day by rhetoric rather than reason.

  (A) rationalization
  (B) recapitulation
  (C) dramatization
  (D) exactitude
— (E) peroration

3

Review

1. **(A)** The Basic Approach will work here because the clue "unwarranted attacks" indicates that you should use a word like "provokes." But substitution also produces the right choice:

   (A) provokes other members with attacks (Possible)
   (B) analyzes other members with attacks (Not possible)
   (C) enhances other members with attacks (Not possible)
   (D) deprives other members with attacks (Not possible)
   (E) elevates other members with attacks (Not possible)

2. **(B)** For this item you have to use substitution. It's one of those Sentence Completions that doesn't have a unique set of substitutions, that is, there are no signals that require a certain word or words: Clyde's unhappy childhood could have made him morose, his uneventful childhood could have made him boring, his tumultuous childhood could have made him volatile, and so. But of the five choices you are give, only one works:

   Clyde's naivete was the result of a sheltered childhood.

3. **(E)** Again, no particular solution is uniquely required by the verbal signals. So you should use the technique of substitution:

   (A) several serious states (Not idiomatic)
   (B) several permissive states (Not idiomatic)
   (C) several predetermined states (Not idiomatic)
   (D) several unalterable states (Idiomatic but not supported)
   (E) several intermediate states (Possible and therefore correct)

4. **(B)** "Bathos" refers to something once sublime or exalted that has been reduced to triteness. And what is the most obscure word in the list? Bathos would be a good choice for a guess.

5. **(E)** A "peroration" is a harangue. And what is the most obscure word in the list? Peroration would be a good choice for a guess.

Get Answers to Frequently Asked Questions

Q: How long should I spend on a Sentence Completion?

A: As a rule, no more than a minute. Some will take less time, some more.

Q: Should I be worried about using roots, prefixes, and so on?

A: No. You don't have time to do that on the test. More importantly, it's just not useful. Over the past 25 years, only one out of every thousand or so key words could be analyzed that way—maybe even fewer.

Q: What if I don't know some of the important words?

A: Then you're normal. No one is expected to know all the words, and you can do very, very well even when you don't know some.

Q: What should I do now?

A: If you have time, it would be a good idea to do the practice exercises in the lesson for Day 4. If not, then you should proceed directly to Day 5 and learn how to tackle GRE Analogies.

Today's Review

1. Sentence Completions appear in the verbal part of the GRE and test reading skills and vocabulary.

2. Sentence Completions are fill-in-the-blanks. You'll be able to answer many of them because you understand what is intended even though one or two parts of the sentence are missing.

3. Some Sentence Completions use two or even three of the added-difficulty factors (vocabulary, complexity, excess baggage) to place an item high on the ladder of difficulty. For those items that exhibit one or more of the added difficulty factors, you'll need additional strategies.

   Your Basic Approach should be to read the sentence for meaning, formulate a possible completion, look for an answer choice, and then check your choice by substitution.

   Your Advanced Strategies include disposing of excess baggage and analyzing verbal signals.

   When you must guess, guess intelligently: eliminate non-idiomatic substitutions and—when all else fails—guess the most difficult word in the list.

Day

4

Apply Your Action Plan to Sentence Completions

Today, you'll assemble all the pieces to the Action Plan that you developed in Day 3. After a quick review of some important points, you'll revisit the Sentence Completions from the PreTest to see how the Action Plan would have helped you perform better. Then you'll have the opportunity to do timed exercises for further practice and to see the Action Plan applied to those items.

Review Your Action Plan

In Day 3, you developed an Action Plan for Sentence Completions. You'll recall that the plan takes into account the defining characteristic of Sentence Completions as "fill-in-the-blank" items and further that it is designed to neutralize the added-difficulty factors (vocabulary, complexity, excess baggage) used by the GRE. The plan was developed at three levels: the Basic Technique, Advanced Strategies, and a Fail-Safe plan. The complete plan looks like this:

The Sentence Completion Action Plan

ACTION PLAN **The Basic Technique**

Step 1: Read Through the sentence for meaning.

Step 2: Formulate a possible completion and choose an answer.

What You'll Do Today

- Review Your Action Plan
- Apply Your Action Plan to the PreTest
- Workshop A
- Workshop B
- Get Answers to Frequently Asked Questions

ACTION PLAN   **Advanced Strategies**

              Step 1: Dispose of any excess baggage.

              Step 2: Use the verbal signals.

ACTION PLAN   **Fail-Safe Plan**

              Step 1: Test answer choices.

              Step 2: Choose the most obscure word.

              Now let's apply the integrated plan to the items from the PreTest.

Apply Your Action Plan to the PreTest

The following items appeared on the Verbal PreTest in Day 2. Here's how the Action Plan would have helped you.

QUESTION   1. In the State of Nature, described by Thomas Hobbes in *Leviathan* as a state of war, one against all others, no individual has sufficient physical strength to be assured of personal security, so all rely on ——.

(A) animosity

(B) premeditation

(C) principles

(D) prowess

(E) allies

Basic Technique

Possible Completions: assistance, cooperation, alliances
Best Completion: allies

Advanced Strategies

Dispose of Excess Baggage:

~~In the State of Nature, described by Thomas Hobbes in *Leviathan* as a state of war, one against all others,~~ no individual has sufficient physical strength to be assured of personal security, so all rely on ——.

Use the Verbal Signals: The key verbal signal is "so," a word that indicates a logical inference or causal consequence: no individual is secure, so everyone belongs to a group.

Fail-Safe

You can also eliminate two of the five choices by testing them:

(A) rely on <u>animosity</u> (Not possible)

(B) rely on <u>premeditation</u> (Not possible)

QUESTION   2. Members of the Research and Development Council had been warned that the prototype was extremely ——, but were pleasantly surprised to see a model with many —— usually incorporated only much later in the design process.

(A) crude . . . refinements

(B) flexible . . . advances

(C) rudimentary . . . deficiencies

(D) unreliable . . . trappings

(E) casual . . . advantages

Basic Technique

Possible Completions: vague, new, unfinished; extras, fancy doodads, elements,
Best Completion: crude; refinements

Advanced Strategies

Dispose of Excess Baggage:

Members ~~of the Research and Development Council~~ had been warned that the prototype was extremely ——, but were pleasantly surprised to see a model with many —— usually incorporated only much later in the design process.

Use the Verbal Signals: The "but" is an extremely important verbal signal. It sets up a contrast between "prototype" and the "model." Since prototype means the first example, you would expect it to be fairly primitive and the later versions to be more sophisticated.

Fail-Safe

Only one choice can be eliminated by testing:

(E) prototype was extremely <u>casual</u> (Not likely)

But even that would improve the odds if you had to guess.

QUESTION 3. Although the developmental sequence of the reproductive cycle in insects is similar for many species, the timing can —— greatly in regard to the beginning and duration of each stage.

(A) endure

(B) accelerate

(C) vary

(D) proceed

(E) coincide

Basic Technique

Possible Completions: differ, change, vary
Best Completion: vary

Advanced Strategies

Dispose of Excess Baggage:

There is so little detail in this item that it's not worth trying to simplify matters further.

Use the Verbal Signals: The "although" is an important verbal signal. It sets up a contrast between the idea that the sequence mentioned in the first part of the sentence is similar and the idea that the timing is something other than similar. So a good completion would be as close an opposite of dissimilar as you can find, and "vary" does the job.

Fail-Safe

You can eliminate choices (A), (D), and (E) by substitution:

(A) the timing can <u>endure</u> greatly (Not possible)

(D) the timing can <u>proceed</u> greatly (Not possible)

(E) the timing can <u>coincide</u> greatly (Not possible)

QUESTION 4. The "framers' original intent" theory of Constitutional interpretation, though now —— within academic circles, still has considerable practical effect because it is —— by many sitting judges.

(A) propounded . . . accepted

(B) disseminated . . . rejected

(C) corroborated . . . critiqued

(D) dismissed . . . espoused

(E) encapsulated . . . emphasized

Basic Technique

Possible Completions: in disfavor, not fashionable, pooh-poohed; accepted, used, endorsed

Best Completion: dismissed; espoused

Advanced Strategies

Dispose of Excess Baggage:

The ~~"framers' original intent"~~ theory ~~of Constitutional interpretation~~, though now —— within academic circles, still has considerable practical effect because it is —— by many sitting judges.

Use the Verbal Signals: The key verbal signal is "though." The word sets up a contrast between "academic circles" and the "practical" world. The sentence tells you that the theory has "considerable practical" effect, so the first blank has to be filled with a word indicating that the theory does not have much force in academe. Then, to complete the thought, the second blank needs to affirm that it does have influence insofar as judges are concerned.

Fail-Safe

You can at least eliminate choice (E):

the theory, though now <u>encapsulated</u> in academic circles. (Not possible)

QUESTION 5. Proponents of a flat tax hope to substitute a single federal revenue-raising measure for the —— of convoluted and even self-contradictory provisions of the present tax code.

(A) tapestry

(B) concordance

(C) cacophony

(D) duplicity

(E) welter

Basic Technique

Possible Completions: confusion, turmoil
Best Completion: welter

Advanced Strategies

Dispose of Excess Baggage:

~~Proponents of a flat tax hope to substitute a single federal revenue-raising measure for~~ the —— of convoluted and even self-contradictory provisions ~~of the present tax code.~~

Use the Verbal Signals: The sentence does not contain verbal signal to announce a shift but the structure of the sentence indicates that the blank must be filled by a word that means "convoluted" and "self-contradictory." Welter is the best choice. "Cacophony" is perhaps the second best answer, but the notion of noise is not supported by the sentence.

Fail-Safe

You could eliminate (A), (B), and (D) by substitution:

tapestry of convoluted and even self-contradictory provisions (Not possible)

concordance of convoluted and even self-contradictory provisions (Not possible)

duplicity of convoluted and even self-contradictory provisions (Not possible)

Finally, it would have been appropriate to guess "welter" on the ground that its meaning is less well-known than those of the other choices.

QUESTION 6. An examination of the psychological forces that shape the personality of the title character of *The Magus* naturally invites closer study of its form, as story content and form are carefully —— by Fowles in the novel.

(A) delineated

(B) anticipated

(C) integrated

(D) determined

(E) reserved

Basic Technique

Possible Completions: meshed, tied together, connected
Best Completion: integrated

Advanced Strategies

Dispose of Excess Baggage:

An examination ~~of the psychological forces that shape the personality~~ of the title character ~~of *The Magus*~~ ~~naturally~~ invites closer study of its form, as story content and form are carefully —— ~~by Fowles in the novel~~.

Use the Verbal Signals: The "as" signals a continuation of the idea developed earlier in the sentence: study the character and the form because the two are ——.

Fail-Safe

You could also have eliminated (E) by substitution:

content and form are carefully <u>reserved</u>. (Not possible)

QUESTION 7. The broadcast of the story has seriously compromised the credibility of the entire news department: the key piece of information, though not —— on the one particular point, is expected to support a vast —— of implications for which no other proof is offered.

(A) fabricated . . . contradiction

(B) unconvincing . . . superstructure

(C) persuasive . . . convocation

(D) inextricable . . . skein

(E) conclusive . . . facsimile

Basic Technique

Possible Completions: wrong, erroneous, unbelievable; framework, network
Best Completion: unconvincing; superstructure

Advanced Strategies

Dispose of Excess Baggage: There are really no specific, irrelevant details here. (Though you might choose to simplify the sentence for your own purposes in various ways.)

Use the Verbal Signals: The most important signal in this sentence is the colon. It announces that the rest of the sentence is going to explain how credibility was compromised.

4

So everything that follows the colon needs to suggest something that is unbelievable, and a vast network or superstructure of unproved inferences would not be readily believable. Then, the "though" signals the status of the parenthetical note. It contrasts with the overall weakness of the report, so you need to create a phrase that suggests believability: not unconvincing.

Now you have seen how the entire Action Plan is applied to Sentence Completion items. In the workshops that follow, you'll be given a chance to apply it under timed conditions.

Workshop A

This workshop consists of ten Sentence Completion items. The time limit for the Drill portion of the workshop is ten minutes. This reflects the general strategy of spending *on average* only about one minute per Sentence Completion—though some will require less time and others more. But you should then spend whatever time you need on the Review portion of the workshop. Before going on to the Review, however, you should finish any items you omitted or were unsure of on your own.

Drill

10 Questions • Time—10 Minutes

DIRECTIONS: Each of these sentences below has one or two blanks. Each blank indicates that a word or phrase has been omitted. Following each sentence is a series of five lettered words or phrases. Choose the word or phrase for each blank that *best* fits the meaning of the sentence in its entirety.

1. By and large, Wittgenstein's treatment of language in *The Philosophical Investigations* will be —— to the lay person, but the more —— points will be grasped only by specialists in the philosophy of language.

   (A) granted . . general
   X (B) accessible . . esoteric
   (C) concrete . . ingenious
   —— (D) alien . . technical *too severe*
   (E) attractive . . abstract

2. For many years, the cost of faculty salaries and benefits rose faster than tuition and contributions to endowments (so)that some —— were in danger of becoming ——.

   (A) colleges . . expensive
   — (B) universities . . insolvent
   (C) students . . dropouts
   (D) unions . . superfluous
   (E) teachers . . replaceable

   insolvent - bankrupt

signals
explanation this in
did order for that

3. In an effort to render as accurately as possible —— lighting conditions, French Impressionist Claude Monet worked on several paintings at once, frantically changing canvases as —— alterations in illumination created almost imperceptible new visual effects. _└ subtle_

   (A) essential . . unimportant
   ✗ (B) transitory . . subtle
   — (C) momentary . . evident
   (D) prototypical . . minute
   (E) classical . . improbable

4. During the 1980s, fortunes were made on a seemingly daily basis by —— traders who —— conventional wisdom on investing in the stock market.
   flouted
   ✗ (A) maverick . . flouted — _scorned_
   (B) rogue . . applied
   (C) impoverished . . acknowledged
   (D) devious . . promulgated
   — (E) renegade . . propounded _conventional vs_
   propounded - propose fortunes

5. A fire in the Peoples Republic of China destroyed the factory responsible for producing most of the world's RAM memory components; the ensuing shortage was so —— that computer users came to believe that the high prices were the result of —— by suppliers.

   (A) prolonged . . coddling
   (B) insignificant . . touting
   (C) ineffectual . . directing
   ➤ (D) severe . . gouging
   (E) unpredictable . . misleading

6. The idea that a single individual can alter the course of history is not mere speculation; in fact, well-documented instances are not even ——.

   ➤ (A) established
   (B) confirmable
   (C) conceivable
   (D) actualized
   ✗ (E) exceptional

7. Some proponents of an author's lending royalty plan argue that borrowing a book from a library is a form of —— since the reader enjoys the intellectual property without —— the author.

   (A) theft . . acknowledging
   (B) piracy . . protecting
   (C) contract . . paying
   (D) servitude . . releasing
   — (E) larceny . . compensating

8. Though it seemed that director Robert Altman had firmly established his artistic reputation with the nomination of _Nashville_ for Best Film of 1970, the 1979 film _Quintet_, perhaps the —— of his career, earned him only the —— of the critics.

   ➤ (A) nadir . . disapprobation
   (B) continuation . . notice
   (C) denouement . . acclaim
   (D) climax . . commentary
   (E) low point . . recommendation

4

1st part sets up opposing view of 2ND

NADIR - lowest point

9. Albert's advanced degree in urban planning made him the most qualified person on the committee, but his status as the junior member made his criticism of transportation policy seem —— even though his remarks were always —— .

   (A) unwarranted . . superficial
   (B) opportunistic . . spontaneous
   (C) presumptuous . . incisive ~ acute
   (D) vapid . . insincere
   (E) practical . . inappropriate

10. The professor's —— treatment of students in the classroom contrasted with her behavior in the office where those who sought advice found her to be genuinely —— to their problems.

    (A) supercilious . . sympathetic
    (B) arrogant . . indifferent
    (C) cavalier . . calloused
    (D) cautious . . attentive
    (E) inconsistent . . hardened

Review

Use the answer key to find how many you answered correctly, then compare your performance on the Drill to the graph below. Then you can review the discussion of the items that follows.

1. (B)   5. (D)   8. (A)
2. (B)   6. (E)   9. (C)
3. (B)   7. (E)   10. (A)
4. (A)

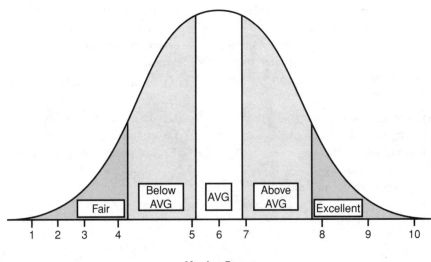

Number Correct

1. **(B)**

Basic Technique

Possible Completions: understandable, open, available; sophisticated, difficult, obscure
Best Completion: accessible; esoteric

Advanced Strategies

Dispose of Excess Baggage:

> ~~By and large, Wittgenstein's~~ treatment ~~of language in *The Philosophical Investigations*~~ will be —— to the lay person, but the more —— points will be grasped only by specialists in the philosophy of language.

Use the Verbal Signals: The "but" signals a contrast between the lay person and the specialist. You would expect that the lay person would understand the basics and that only the specialist would get the finer points.

Fail-Safe

Test Answer Choices:

(A) treatment will be granted to the lay person (Not possible)

2. **(B)**

Basic Technique

Possible Completions: schools, institutions, colleges; bankrupt, broke
Best Completion: universities; insolvent

Advanced Strategies

Dispose of Excess Baggage: There are no superficial details in this sentence of the sort that this strategy is designed for.

Use the Verbal Signals: The "so" signals a logical inference or causal outcome. Rising costs and stagnant revenues usually result in one expected outcome: insolvency.

Fail-Safe

You can test answer choices, but ultimately you'll have to rely on the verbal signal mentioned above for your answer.

4

3. **(B)**

Basic Technique

Possible Completions: changing, impermanent; quick, small, tiny
Best Completion: transitory; subtle

Advanced Strategies

Dispose of Excess Baggage:

In an effort to render as accurately as possible —— lighting conditions, ~~French Impressionist Claude Monet~~ worked on several paintings at once, frantically changing canvases as —— alterations in illumination created almost imperceptible new visual effects.

Use the Verbal Signals: "In an effort to" signals an explanation: he did this in order to do that. Since the "this" is frantically changing things around, the "that" must be something that has some sense of urgency. Transitory suggests urgency. Then the second blank must parallel the idea of "almost imperceptible," and "subtle" is the best choice.

Fail-Safe

Test the Answer Choices: You can eliminate both (A) and (E):

(A) essential lighting conditions (Not likely)

(E) improbable alterations (Not likely)

4. **(A)**

Basic Technique

Possible Completions: The structure of the sentence doesn't permit you to anticipate with any confidence. The traders might be unimaginative people who followed conventional wisdom or free-thinkers who ignored it. So you'll have to use another strategy.

Advanced Strategies

Dispose of Excess Baggage:

~~During the 1980s, fortunes were made on a seemingly daily basis by~~ — traders who —— conventional wisdom on investing in the stock market.

Use the Verbal Signals: The sentence sets up a parallel between the "—— traders" and people who "—— conventional wisdom." But the parallel could be completed in different ways. So you should move on to the third level.

Fail-Safe

Test the Answer Choices:

(A) maverick traders who flouted conventional wisdom (Yes)

(B) rogue traders who applied conventional wisdom (No) *Rogue suggests Non-conv*

(C) impoverished traders who acknowledged conventional wisdom (No)

(D) devious traders who promulgated conventional wisdom (No)

(E) renegade traders who propounded conventional wisdom (No)

5. **(D)**

Basic Technique

Possible Completions: bad, pronounced, great; rip-offs, manipulation
Best Completion: severe; gouging

Advanced Strategies

Dispose of Excess Baggage:

A fire ~~in the Peoples Republic of China~~ destroyed ~~the factory responsible for producing~~ most of the world's RAM memory components; the ensuing shortage was so —— that computer users came to believe that the high prices were the result of —— by suppliers.

Use the Verbal Signals: The semicolon signals the start of a new idea, in this case, one that explains what happens when the output of a major supplier is no longer available: a severe shortage. And a severe shortage would lead to much higher prices.

Fail-Safe

Test the Answer Choices:

(B) insignificant shortage (No, because it was a major supplier)

(C) ineffectual shortage (Not likely)

6. **(E)**

Basic Technique

Possible Completions: unusual, rare, uncommon
Best Completion: unexceptional

Advanced Strategies

Dispose of Excess Baggage: There are no superfluous details here.

Use the Verbal Signals: The "in fact" is an important verbal signal. It tells you that the second idea in the sentence is included for added emphasis. Since the first idea tells you that the phenomenon is not "mere speculation," the second should reinforce that by saying that "it's even very common."

Fail-Safe

Test the Answer Choices:

> (D) instances are not even actualized (Probably not)

7. **(E)**

Basic Technique

Possible Completions: theft, rip-off, stealing; paying, reimbursing
Best Completion: larceny; compensating

Advanced Strategies

Dispose of Excess Baggage:

> Some proponents ~~of an author's lending royalty plan~~ argue that borrowing a book from a library is a form of —— since the reader enjoys the intellectual property without —— the author.

Use the Verbal Signals: The "since" is an important verbal signal. The dependent clause that it introduces establishes a condition that is logically or temporally prior to the outcome described in the main clause: since the readers does this, it's really that. Or since the reader gets the benefit of the author's effort without paying for it, library lending is a form of theft or larceny.

Fail-Safe

Test the Answer Choices:

> (B) without protecting the author (Not likely)
>
> (D) without releasing the author (Not likely)

8. **(A)**

Basic Technique

Possible Completions: low point, trough, bottom; criticism, panning, bad remarks
Best Completion: nadir; disapprobation

Advanced Strategies

Dispose of Excess Baggage:

Though it seemed that director ~~Robert Altman~~ had firmly established his artistic reputation ~~with the nomination of *Nashville* for Best Film of 1970~~, the ~~1979~~ film *~~Quintet,~~* perhaps the —— of his career, earned him only the —— of the critics.

Use the Verbal Signals: "Though" is almost always an important verbal signal. In this sentence, it tells you that the first idea (the director established his reputation) contrasts with the second idea (the other film). So you're looking for a completion that indicates that the second film was a bad one.

Fail-Safe

Test the Answer Choices:

(C) earned him only the acclaim of the critics (Not likely)

(D) earned him only the commentary of the critics (Not likely)

Guess the most obscure word: For this item, if you were really, really left with nothing else to do, you should go ahead and choose an answer with a difficult vocabulary word. This would almost surely be either (A) or (C); and since (C) has been eliminated, you'd guess (A).

9. **(C)**

Basic Technique

Possible Completions: out of place, inappropriate; correct, accurate, on point
Best Completion: presumptuous; incisive

Advanced Strategies

Dispose of Excess Baggage:

~~Albert's advanced degree in urban planning made him~~ the most qualified person on the committee, but his status as the junior member made his criticism of transportation policy seem —— even though his remarks were always —— .

Use the Verbal Signals: The "but" signals a contrast between the idea of what a qualified person has to contribute and what the perception of the other members was. Additionally, the "even though" sets up another contrast within the second clause between the perception and the actuality.

Fail-Safe

Test the Answer Choices: The internal contrast within the second clause gives you a good opportunity for testing choices:

     (A) seemed unwarranted though they were superficial (Impossible)

     (B) seemed opportunistic though they were spontaneous (Impossible)

     (C) seemed presumptuous though they were incisive (Yes)

     (D) seemed vapid though they were insincere (Impossible)

     (E) seemed practical though they were inappropriate (Not likely)

  10. **(A)**

Basic Technique

Possible Completions: It doesn't seem possible to anticipate with any satisfaction. The teacher might be rude in public but polite in private or the opposite, polite in public and rude in private. So you should go on to the second level.

Advanced Strategies

Dispose of Excess Baggage: There is little superfluous detail here.

Use the Verbal Signals: The verbal signal "contrast" tells you that there are two opposing ideas; but, as noted above, the sentence structure doesn't tell what the content of the two will be.

Fail-Safe

Test the Answer Choices:

     (A) supercilious treatment contrasted with her genuinely sympathetic behavior (Yes)

     (B) arrogant treatment contrasted with her genuinely indifferent behavior (No)

     (C) cavalier treatment contrasted with her genuinely calloused behavior (No)

     (D) cautious treatment contrasted with her genuinely attentive behavior (No)

     (E) inconsistent treatment contrasted with her genuinely hardened behavior (No)

Workshop B

This workshop consists of ten Sentence Completion items. The time limit for the Drill portion of the workshop is ten minutes. This reflects the general strategy of spending *on average* only about one minute per Sentence Completion—though some will require less time and others more. But you should then spend whatever time you need on the Review portion of the workshop. Before going on to the Review, however, you should finish any items you omitted or were unsure of on your own.

Drill

10 Questions • Time—10 Minutes

DIRECTIONS: Each of these sentences below has one or two blanks. Each blank indicates that a word or phrase has been omitted. Following each sentence is a series of five lettered words or phrases. Choose the word or phrase for each blank that *best* fits the meaning of the sentence in its entirety.

1. Legal positivists deny that international law can properly be called law because international organizations can only —— prohibited conduct but do nothing to —— it.

    (A) investigate . . review
    (B) identify . . encourage
    (C) provoke . . rectify
    (D) outline . . satisfy
    — (E) define . . punish

2. Following the —— emotional pleas for passage of the bill by members known for rambling speeches, the —— argument for its rejection was a welcome relief for the House.

    ✗ (A) protracted . . trenchant
    — (B) lengthy . . specious
    (C) flowery . . ornate
    (D) undisguised . . deceiving
    (E) blatant . . unfocused

    [handwritten: clue- establishes difference btween arguments]

3. In his treatment of science, Ernst Cassirer rejects the traditional —— of fact and theory, approvingly quoting Goethe as saying "All fact is theory."

    (A) asymmetry
    — (B) dichotomy
    (C) frequency
    (D) conjunction
    (E) dysfunction

4. Although Jacques Derrida's writings held considerable theoretical promise, deconstructionism in America quickly deteriorated into a —— as academics of limited intellectual ability mimicked its style without —— its secrets.

    ✗ (A) farce . . plumbing
    — (B) battle . . understanding
    (C) burlesque . . concealing
    (D) comedy . . purporting
    (E) pretense . . sharing

[margin: 4]

5. Students had become so —— to the principal's capriciousness that they greeted the announcement of yet another dress code with complete indifference.

(A) receptive
(B) inured
(C) sensitive
(D) attuned
(E) evasive

6. Recent journalistic reports of respected researchers —— experimental results favorable to their own theories —— the popular conception of science as a pure search for the truth.

(A) manufacturing . . supports
(B) presenting . . belies
(C) finding . . reinforces
(D) fabricating . . contradicts
(E) concealing . . undermines

7. A recurring theme in science fiction is the contest between good and evil for control over technology that is, in itself, —— .

(A) productive
(B) ill-conceived   *something*
(C) independent   *Not good*
(D) amoral   *or*
(E) inconsequential   *evil*

8. In *The Ontology of Political Violence*, Professor Nogarola argues that so-called —— evidence often dismissed as unreliable would be admissible in a court of law as testimony and has value in the political arena as well.

(A) anecdotal
(B) practical
(C) sensational
(D) collaborative
(E) probative

9. Ironically, the modern Olympic games, which are held up as the ideal of amateur athletics, originated with games in honor of Athena in which winners were rewarded not with laurel wreaths of little —— worth but oil-filled amphorae with considerable —— value.

(A) practical . . sentimental
(B) financial . . honorific
(C) market . . aesthetic
(D) capital . . sacrificial
(E) intrinsic . . economic

10. Supply creates its own demand; and advertising, if sufficiently ——, can convince consumers to —— products for which they have little desire and even less need.

(A) strident . . approve
(B) pervasive . . purchase
(C) unscrupulous . . honor
(D) distasteful . . disregard
(E) vehement . . anticipate

Review

Use the answer key to find how many you answered correctly, then compare your performance on the Drill to the graph below. Then you can review the discussion of the items that follows.

1. (E)   5. (B)   8. (A)
2. (A)   6. (D)   9. (E)
3. (B)   7. (D) 2ND choice   10. (B)
4. (A)

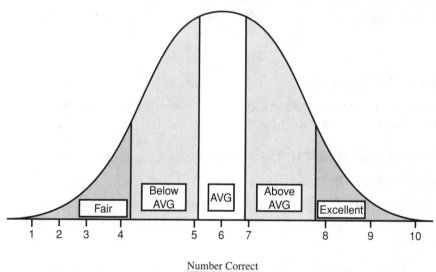

Number Correct

1. **(E)**

Basic Technique

Possible Completions: describe, define, list; enforce, punish, stop
Best Completion: define; punish

Advanced Strategies

Dispose of Excess Baggage:

~~Legal positivists~~ deny that international law can properly be called law because international organizations can only —— prohibited conduct but do nothing to — it.

Use the Verbal Signals: The "can only . . . but do nothing" sets up a contrast between two ideas: what the international organizations can do and what they cannot do.

Fail-Safe

Test the Answer Choices: You could make an argument that any of the suggested choices might, under some conceivable circumstances, be used to fill in the blank. So your strongest attack here is to use the verbal signals.

2. **(A)**

Basic Technique

Possible Completions: unfocused, long; logical, focused, well-constructed
Best Completion: protracted; trenchant

Advanced Strategies

Dispose of Excess Baggage:

Following the —— emotional pleas ~~for passage of the bill~~ by members known for rambling speeches, the —— argument for its rejection was a welcome ~~relief for the House~~.

Use the Verbal Signals: The structure of the sentence sets up a contrast between the idea of an emotional appeal and a different approach. So your choice for the second blank needs to be something that conveys the idea of logic or rationality. And the first blank needs to parallel the idea of rambling.

Fail-Safe

Test the Answer Choices:

(D) the deceiving argument (Not a likely English phrase, so eliminate)

3. **(B)**

Basic Technique

Possible Completions: distinction, division, separation
Best Completion: dichotomy

Advanced Strategies

Dispose of Excess Baggage:

~~In his treatment of science, Ernst Cassirer~~ rejects the traditional —— of fact and theory, approvingly quoting ~~Goethe as saying~~ "All fact is theory."

Use the Verbal Signals: The "approvingly" tells you that Cassirer endorsed the idea advanced by Goethe: fact and theory are not distinct. So the blank has to be filled by a word that will let the sentence say that Cassirer thought fact and theory were not distinct.

Fail-Safe

Test the Answer Choices:

(C) the traditional frequency of fact and theory (Not likely)

(E) the traditional dysfunction of fact and theory (Not likely)

4. **(A)**

Basic Technique

Possible Completions: mess, something ridiculous; learning, understanding
Best Completion: farce; plumbing

Advanced Strategies

Dispose of Excess Baggage:

Although ~~Jacques Derrida's~~ writings held considerable theoretical promise, ~~deconstructionism in America~~ quickly deteriorated into a —— as academics of limited intellectual ability mimicked its style without — its secrets.

Use the Verbal Signals: The "although" signals a contrast between "promise" and actual result. Therefore, the word that fills in the first blank must be a word with negative overtones and the opposite of "promise." Then, the "without" suggests a contrast between mimickery and real understanding, so the second blank should be something like "understanding."

4

Fail-Safe

Test the Answer Choices:

(D) without purporting its secrets (Not possible)

5. **(B)**

Basic Technique

Possible Completions: uncaring, used, nonchalant
Best Completion: inured

Advanced Strategies

Dispose of Excess Baggage: There is very little, if any, excess baggage in this item.

Use the Verbal Signals: The "so . . . that" signals that the blank must be completed by a word that explains the students' indifference to the new directive. "Inured" means accustomed or habituated.

Fail-Safe

Here's a good item for the "Pick the most obscure word" strategy. If you run out of other options, go ahead and pick "inured."

6. **(D)**

Basic Technique

Possible Completions: You probably won't be able to anticipate possible completions for this item. The structure of the sentence is neutral, that is, the sentence might say that the researchers published their results and this supports the conventional view. Or the sentence might equally well mean something almost the opposite—as the correct fill-ins do in this case.

Advanced Strategies

Dispose of Excess Baggage: There are no details in this item that might be considered "baggage," though you might want to simplify the sentence for yourself just to make it easier to work with.

Use the Verbal Signals: As noted above, possible completions are probably not possible. So you should go on to the third level of strategies.

Fail-Safe

Test the Answer Choices:

researchers manufacturing results supports the popular conception (No)

researchers presenting results belies the popular conception (No)

researchers finding results reinforces the popular conception (No)

researchers fabricating results contradicts the popular conception (Yes)

researchers concealing results undermines the popular conception (No, because it is unfavorable to their own theory.)

7. **(D)**

Basic Technique

Possible Completions: neither, neutral, not good or evil
Best Completion: amoral

Advanced Strategies

Dispose of Excess Baggage: There is no excess baggage to be eliminated here. In fact, the sentence itself is fairly short.

Use the Verbal Signals: The sentence sets up a contrast between good and evil on the one hand and a third alternative on the other. So you have to find a word that means neither good nor evil, and the best choice is "amoral."

Fail-Safe

Test the Answer Choices: You could also test all of the answer choices. In this case, that would be tantamount to determining which one provides the third alternative mentioned above. Testing takes a little longer, but you should use the strategy if it is needed to get the answer.

8. **(A)**

Basic Technique

Possible Completions: eye-witness, reported, narrative
Best Completion: anecdotal

Advanced Strategies

Dispose of Excess Baggage:

In ~~The Ontology of Political Violence,~~ ~~Professor Nogarola argues that~~ so-called —— evidence often dismissed as unreliable would be admissible in a court of law as testimony and has value in the political arena as well.

Use the Verbal Signals: The sentence structure tells you that the blank has to describe a kind of evidence that is like testimony. Since testimony is telling a story or relating events, a good description would be anecdotal evidence.

Fail-Safe

If you absolutely had to guess on this item, "anecdotal" ought to be your preferred choice.

9. **(E)**

Basic Technique

Possible Completions: monetary, real; financial, monetary, economic
Best Completion: intrinsic; economic

Advanced Strategies

Dispose of Excess Baggage:

Ironically, the modern Olympic games, which are held up as the ideal of amateur athletics, originated with games ~~in honor of Athena~~ in which winners were rewarded not with laurel wreaths of little —— worth but oil-filled amphorae with considerable —— value.

Use the Verbal Signals: The word "ironically" is an important verbal signal. It tells you that the modern games, which are touted as being for amateurs, contrast with the original games. So you would expect a completion that describes the original games as being for professionals and entailing compensation. Additionally, the "but" sets up another contrast, this one between the two completions. So the words that complete the sentence must be, in some sense, opposites.

Fail-Safe

Test the Answer Choices:

(D) with considerable sacrificial value (Not likely)

10. **(B)**

Basic Technique

Possible Completions: extensive, persuasive, widespread; buy, want, desire
Best Completion: pervasive; purchase

Advanced Strategies

Dispose of Excess Baggage: There is no excess baggage here. Most of the sentence is needed in order to understand the overall point.

Use the Verbal Signals: The second half of the sentence explains what it means to say "Supply creates its own demand." So the first blank has to describe a situation in which consumers are told about the supply of a good, and the second blank needs to say that, once aware of it, consumers will want it.

Fail-Safe

Test the Answer Choices:

(C) consumers to honor products (Not likely)

(E) consumers to anticipate products (Not likely)

4

Get Answers to Frequently Asked Questions

Q: Is it okay to deviate from the strict order of the Action Plan?

A: Sure. The Action Plan contains guidelines, not rules. The more comfortable you become with Sentence Completions, the less you'll need any step-by-step guidance. You've probably already noticed this. In fact, when you are truly proficient, you'll be using all of the strategies almost simultaneously without even realizing it.

Q: I'm still seeing words that I don't know. Is that a problem?

A: It's to be expected. There is no way that anyone could hope to master all of the possible vocabulary that the GRE might use. Expect that you'll keep on seeing words that are not a part of your core vocabulary. But remember that while the GRE is designed to test the limits of your abilities, it's not intended to overwhelm you.

Q: What should I do now?

A: Move on to the next topic. You're probably never going to be completely satisfied with your performance on any part of the GRE, but keep in mind that your score is not based on any one type of question. Your verbal score is also a function of your performance on Analogies. So you need to prepare for that topic as well.

Teach Yourself Analogies

Today, you'll teach yourself how to answer GRE Analogy items. Analogies are the "this-is-like-that" questions that appear on the verbal part of the GRE CAT. Analogies are a test of vocabulary and verbal reasoning power. You'll learn how to use your vocabulary and verbal reasoning skills to maximize your performance on this question kind.

Get the Inside Info on Analogies

You'll want to feel comfortable with the Analogies format. The basic "this-is-like-that" format of Analogies is fairly intuitive, but there are some subtleties that you need to be aware of.

The basic idea of an Analogy is described in the directions:

DIRECTIONS: In each of the following items, a related pair of capitalized words or phrases is followed by five pairs of words or phrases. Choose the pair that best expresses a relationship similar to that expressed by the capitalized pair.

A typical GRE Verbal Part has 6 to 8 Analogies, some of which may be embedded experimental items that do not count toward your score.

What You'll Do Today

- **Get All the Inside Info on Analogies**
- **Learn the Basic Technique for Analogies**
- **Workshop A: Practice the Basic Technique**
- **Master Advanced Strategies for Difficult Items**
- **Workshop B: Practice Advanced Strategies**
- **A Fail-Safe Plan for Emergencies**
- **Workshop C: Practice the Fail-Safe Plan**
- **Get Answers to Frequently Asked Questions**

TIP The directions are longer than an individual Analogy item, so don't waste any time with them. When you see the capitalized words followed by the five pairs, think "Which choice is most like the capitalized words?"

The basic idea of an Analogy is "this-is-like-that." How does it work? Every pair of capitalized words expresses a relationship that can be articulated in a sentence:

Related Words	Analogy Relationship
SHIP : FLEET	A ship is a part of a fleet.
ARROW : MISSILE	An arrow is a kind of missile.
COURTROOM : ATTORNEY	A courtroom is a place for an attorney.
PERFIDY : TRAITOR	Perfidy is characteristic of a traitor.
ROENTGEN : RADIATION	A roentgen is a measure of radiation.
ASTERISK : FOOTNOTE	An asterisk is a symbol for a footnote.

Since the verbal relationship can be summarized in a sentence using general terms, other pairs of words can express a similar relationship. Study the following word pairs by substituting them into the relationship given:

Relationship	Related Words
. . . is a part of . . .	SYLLABLE : WORD REGIMENT : ARMY KEYSTONE : ARCHWAY
. . . is a kind of . . .	JAZZ : MUSIC PEWTER : ALLOY TONSILECHTOMY : SURGERY
. . . is a place for . . .	STAGE : THESPIAN FORMICARY : ANT FOOT : SABOT
. . . is characteristic of . . .	INDOLENCE : GOLDBRICK TARDINESS : PROCRASTINATOR SECRECY : ESPIONAGE
. . . is a measure of . . .	DECIBEL : SOUND CALORIE : HEAT FATHOM : DEPTH
. . . a symbol for . . .	DOVE : PEACE CADUCEUS : MEDICINE CORNUCOPIA : PLENTY

The crucial element of the analogy is the verbal or conceptual relationship between the two words. The correct answer will match the capitalized pair:

- GAVEL : CHAIRPERSON :: WHISTLE : REFEREE

  A GAVEL is the tool used by a CHAIRPERSON to keep order, and a WHISTLE is the tool used by a REFEREE to keep order.

- MALNUTRITION : FOOD :: INSOMNIA : SLEEP

  MALNUTRITION is a lack of FOOD, and INSOMNIA is a lack of SLEEP.

- BANAL : ORIGINALITY :: INSIPID : TASTE

  Something that is BANAL lacks ORIGINALITY, and something that is INSIPID lacks TASTE.

 NOTE
In an analogy, the single colon ":" is read "is to" and the double colon "::" is read "as."

Every pair of capitalized words expresses a clear connection that can be articulated in a sentence, and the correct answer is correct because it fits the same pattern. This match is the basis for the Basic Approach that you will master later in this Day.

 CAUTION
Order counts. Since analogies are read from left to right, the order of the words is important. CHAPTER : BOOK is *not* equivalent to BOOK : CHAPTER.

GRE Analogies aren't all of the same difficulty. Although all of them are basically "this-is-like-that," you'll find that several factors can make some more challenging than others. You need to know what those factors are so that you can learn strategies to overcome them.

The Complexity Factor

You'll notice that for some Analogies it's harder to articulate the analogy relationship to yourself than it is for others. This is because some analogy relationships are fairly obvious, others are more subtle. Compare the following items:

Easy

QUESTION CHAPTER : BOOK ::

   (A) shoe : clothing

   (B) verse : poem

   (C) gallon : milk

   (D) road : distance

   (E) animal : lair

ANALYSIS The correct answer is **(B)**. A CHAPTER is a part of a BOOK, and a verse is a part of a poem.

Hard

QUESTION LUBRICANT : FRICTION ::

   (A) salve : pain

   (B) harmony : dissonance

   (C) plastic : flexibility

   (D) warning : danger

   (E) restriction : taboo

ANALYSIS The correct answer is **(A)**. LUBRICANT is applied to stop FRICTION, and a salve is applied to stop pain.

The second item is of a higher level of difficulty than the first. The relationship "is a part of" is fairly concrete and direct; the relationship "is applied to stop" is more abstract and less direct.

NOTE GRE Analogies do *not* use "This is the same as that" or "This is the opposite of that." (Antonyms are "opposites," but that is a different question type.) Simple synonyms and antonyms, as analogy relations, are just not refined enough for testing the sophisticated GRE population.

The Other-Meaning Factor

A second factor that makes some Analogies more difficult is the use of a word or words that have more than one meaning. Sometimes this occurs because the same word can serve as different parts of speech with different (though sometimes related) meanings. For example,

Word	Noun	Verb
LEAVE	permission	depart
BAFFLE	obstruction	bewilder
FLOWER	blossom	thrive
STEEL	rugged metal alloy	harden against
OBJECT	thing	voice opposition

This interplay of meanings can complicate things as you are working on analogies. Example:

QUESTION   NOOSE : TRAP ::

    (A) chain : lock

    (B) anvil : horse

    (C) axe : tree

    (D) club : weapon

    (E) saw : carpenter

ANALYSIS   The correct answer is **(D)**. A NOOSE is a kind of TRAP, and a club is a kind of weapon.

"Trap" can be either a noun or a verb, so at first you might think that the relation is "a noose is used to trap prey." But that relationship doesn't fit any of the answer choices. Instead, "trap" must be a noun, and the relationship is "a noose is a kind of trap."

Here is another example:

QUESTION   RESCIND : ORDER ::

    (A) retry : accused

    (B) requite : affection

    (C) repeal : enactment

    (D) refill : prescription

    (E) redraft : document

ANALYSIS   The correct answer is **(C)**. To RESCIND is to invalidate an ORDER, and to repeal is to invalidate an enactment.

The word "order" can be either a verb or a noun, but here it must be a noun because "prescription," "enactment," and "affection" are unequivocally nouns. So the analogy relationship is "to RESCIND an ORDER is to make it void and to repeal a law is to make it void."

5

In addition to the confusion generated by part-of-speech, different English words can have the same spelling. And an Analogy may be constructed with the less commonly used word. For example:

Word	More Common	Less Common
REPORT	written document	gun shot
STANDARD	rule or norm	flag or insignia
FOLD	crease	group of sheep
REFRAIN	hold back from	repeated song part
STRUT	proud walk	structural brace

Other-meanings of this type can also make your job more difficult. Example:

QUESTION   DEFILE : MOUNTAINS ::

    (A) keyhole : door

    (B) window : wall

    (C) bell : horn

    (D) picket : fence

    (E) gap : teeth

ANALYSIS   The correct answer is (**E**). A DEFILE is a narrow opening between mountains, and a gap is a narrow opening between teeth.

The word "defile" can be a verb meaning to pollute, but it is also a noun that refers to a narrow mountain pass. You can determine that it is intended here to be a noun by looking at the parallel entries in the answer choices: keyhole and window are nouns. Here is another example:

QUESTION   RENT : FABRIC ::

    (A) schism : society

    (B) divorce : spouse

    (C) crime : law

    (D) harvest : crop

    (E) objection : claim

ANALYSIS The correct answer is (**A**). RENT is a tear in a FABRIC, and schism is a breach of relations in an organized group.

In this item, "rent" is intended to be a noun (as is confirmed by the other parallel entries in the list which are also nouns, e.g., schism, crime, objection). The most common meaning of "rent" is the payment to a landlord for temporary possession of property, e.g., rent on an apartment. And that word comes into English via the French "rente" meaning rent or revenue. But there is another noun "rent" in English which derives from the Anglo-Saxon "rend" meaning to tear or rip apart. And it is the second word that is intended by this analogy.

The Vocabulary Factor

One of the most important differences between an Analogy at the bottom of the ladder of difficulty and one at the top of the ladder is the vocabulary used—both for the capitalized pair and for the answer choices. Compare the following items:

Easy

QUESTION PAINTER : STUDIO ::

(A) angler : aquarium

(B) artisan : workshop

(C) coach : team

(D) conductor : baton

(E) calligrapher : pen

Hard

QUESTION PAINTER : ATELIER ::

(A) angler:aquarium

(B) artisan:workshop

(C) coach:team

(D) conductor:baton

(E) calligrapher:pen

ANALYSIS The correct answer is (**B**) in both cases. A studio is a place where a painter works, and a workshop is a place where an artisan works. Similarly, an atelier is a place where a painter works.

The correct answer is the same in both cases, and the only difference between the two items is the use of "atelier" instead of "studio." "Atelier" makes the second analogy a bit

5

more difficult than the first. In the next pair, the more difficult item is loaded with vocabulary teasers:

Easy

QUESTION   IRRITABLE : COMPLAIN ::

    (A) fearless : brag

    (B) terse : speak

    (C) greedy : refrain

    (D) arrogant : defer

    (E) wasteful : spend

Hard

QUESTION   PETULANT : COMPLAIN ::

    (A) intrepid : brag

    (B) laconic : speak

    (C) avaricious : refrain

    (D) supercilious : defer

    (E) profligate : squander

ANALYSIS   The correct answer to both items is **(E)**, and the analogy relationship can be summarized as:

Someone who is IRRITABLE COMPLAINS a lot, and someone who is wasteful spends a lot.

Someone who is PETULANT COMPLAINS a lot, and someone who is PROFLIGATE SPENDS a lot.

Again, the relationship is the same in both items, but the vocabulary used to build the second item is considerably more difficult. You can see that an entire array of difficult vocabulary words moves an item up the ladder of difficulty, by several rungs.

CAUTION   Difficult vocabulary does not necessarily mean longest word. Even short, one syllable words can be difficult simply because they are not often used or because they have less commonly used meaning, e.g., gull (to cheat or trick), moot (arguable), pith (core or heart).

Analogies are "this-is-like-that" items. You'll be able to answer many of them because you understand the vocabulary and can articulate the relationship being used. Other Analogies cannot be solved so easily. Some are high on the ladder of difficulty because the verbal relationship is hard to articulate. And some use two or even three of the added-difficulty factors (vocabulary, part-of-speech, secondary meaning). For all of these reasons, you'll need strategies and a systematic approach to do your best on analogies. And that is the topic of the next section.

Learn the Basic Technique for Analogies

Regardless of added complexity factors, Analogies are "this-is-like-that" items, and that's the basic technique you should try first. Here it is broken down:

ACTION PLAN   **The Basic Technique**

> **Step 1: Summarize the relationship in a sentence. Make up a sentence that summarizes the relationship between the capitalized words. Then use that sentence to test choices.**
>
> **Step 2: Adjust the sentence if necessary. If your sentence doesn't work, make some minor adjustments: change the word order, play around with the parts of speech of the words, or look for another, less common meaning.**

You saw this procedure illustrated earlier in the discussion of various examples above. And it should come as no surprise to you that it works in the majority of cases, because it corresponds precisely to the basic concept of a GRE Analogy. And a lot of the time, the Basic Approach works almost automatically:

QUESTION   PARODY : RIDICULE ::

  (A) memorial : erase

  (B) fantasy : condemn

  (C) testimonial : recommend

  (D) eulogy : amuse

  (E) burlesque : respect

ANALYSIS   The correct answer is (**C**).

5

QUESTION PARODY : RIDICULE ::

Sentence: The purpose of a PARODY is to RIDICULE.

(A) memorial : erase The purpose of a memorial is to erase. (Wrong)

(B) fantasy : condemn The purpose of a fantasy is to condemn. (Wrong)

(C) testimonial : recommend The purpose of a testimonial is to recommend. (Right)

(D) eulogy : amuse The purpose of a eulogy is to amuse. (Wrong)

(E) burlesque : respect The purpose of a burlesque is to respect. (Wrong)

ANALYSIS You can see that **(C)** is correct because it is the only choice that is captured by the sentence that we created.

TIP

> Once you've found a possible choice, then read your sentence a final time. If the result is a smooth-reading sentence that makes sense to you, then the Basic Approach has probably yielded the correct answer. Enter your choice and move on to the next item.

But what do you do if the order of the words threatens to ruin your sentence?

QUESTION RIDICULE : PARODY ::

(A) erase : memorial

(B) condemn : fantasy

(C) recommend : testimonial

(D) amuse : eulogy

(E) respect : burlesque

Just put the words into a the more convenient order. This example is exactly the same as the previous one—except for the order of the words. The underlying conceptual relationship between the words hasn't changed, so you can still use the sentence "The purpose of . . . is to . . . ." You'll just need to change the order of the words in your mind.

CAUTION

> If you reverse the *order* of the elements of the capitalized words to make it easier to create your sentence, be sure that you also change the order of the elements of the answer choices when you make your substitutions or you won't get the correct result. "A chapter is a part of a book" is not equivalent to "A book is a part of chapter."

Similarly, if an inconvenient choice for part of speech, say an adjective where you might want a noun, makes it difficult to create a sentence, then just rewrite the problem:

QUESTION PARODY : RIDICULOUS ::

(A) memorial : erased

(B) fantasy : condemnatory

(C) testimonial : recommended

(D) eulogy : amusing

(E) burlesque : respectful

In this version, the second word is an adjective. (How do you know? Because "condemnatory" and "amusing" are unequivocally adjectives.) And now the sentence doesn't read correctly:

The purpose of PARODY is RIDICULOUS, and the purpose of testimonial is recommended.

But there is absolutely no reason to throw away a perfectly good sentence simply because it's a bit awkward. Just change all of the adjectives to verbs

QUESTION PARODY : RIDICULE ::

(A) memorial:erase

(B) fantasy:condemn

(C) testimonial:recommend

(D) eulogy:amuse

(E) burlesque:respect

ANALYSIS The purpose of a PARODY is to RIDICULE.

(A) The purpose of a memorial is *to erase*.

(B) The purpose of a fantasy is *to condemn*.

(C) The purpose of a testimonial is *to recommend*.

(D) The purpose of a eulogy is *to amuse*.

(E) The purpose of a burlesque is *to respect*.

Or even to nouns, if that's more convenient:

(A) The purpose of a memorial is *erasing*.

(B) The purpose of a fantasy is *condemnation*.

(C) The purpose of a testimonial is *recommendation*.

(D) The purpose of a eulogy is *amusement*.

(E) The purpose of a burlesque is *respect*.

You don't get "style points" for an elegant sentence. So just do whatever it takes to get the answer.

 CAUTION | If you change the part of speech of a capitalized word to make your sentence read more evenly, make sure that you change the part of speech of the corresponding answer choices before testing them in the sentence.

Workshop A: Practice the Basic Technique

This Workshop provides you the opportunity to practice the Basic Technique for Analogies. Do the Drill portion first, and then check your work against the explanations in the Review part.

Drill

In the space provided, jot down a sentence that summarizes the relationship between the capitalized words. Then use that sentence to find the correct answer.

1. SWITCH : ELECTRICITY ::

   Your Sentence: _Turn on a switch to provide electricity_

   (A) tree : sap
   — (B) valve : liquid
   (C) trap : game
   (D) gasket : seal
   (E) knot : rope

2. MAINSPRING : WATCH ::

   Your Sentence: _A Mainspring powers a watch_

   (A) runway : airplane
   (B) staircase : elevator
   — (C) engine : automobile
   (D) wheel : bicycle
   (E) coolant : radiator

3. CAST : PLAY ::

   A CAST PLAYS The Play
   Your Sentence: _A cast is one element of a play_

   — (A) chorus : song
   (B) class : teacher
   (C) electorate : candidate
   (D) audience : drama
   (E) platoon : unit

4. DECLAIM : POMPOUS ::

   TO D
   Your Sentence: _TO DECLAIM IS TO speak in a pompous manner_

   (A) plagiarize : original
   (B) condemn : blameworthy
   (C) ponitifcate : dogmatic
   (D) allocate : victorious
   (E) relegate : important

5. ACRID : ODOR ::

Your Sentence: _ACRid is AN unpleasant odor_

(A) painful : nerve
(B) obscure : view
(C) aglow : bulb
— (D) harsh : sound
(E) weepy : tear

6. FUNDS : DISBURSEMENT ::

Your Sentence: _DISBURSEMENT is METHOD for distributing funds_

✶ (A) knowledge : dissemination
(B) emission : pollution
— (C) benefits : compensation
(D) conclusion : inferrence
(E) agenda : itemization

7. HOMESICKNESS : SEPARATION ::

Your Sentence: _homesicKNess can be caused by separation_

(A) nostalgia : sadness
— (B) melancholy : loss
(C) despondency : cure
(D) indifference : anticipation
(E) grief : expectation

8. ALIAS : IDENTITY ::

Your Sentence: _ALIAS hides an identity_

(A) mask : face
(B) hat : head
(C) collar : shirt
(D) shoe : sock
(E) glove : hand

9. EMACIATION : BODY ::

Your Sentence: _emaciation is a weakened body_

(A) instantiation : clue
(B) desparation : motive
(C) extraction : dentist
(D) inaction : sanction
—(E) devaluation : currency

10. CHAOTIC : ORDER ::

Your Sentence: _chaotic means without order_

✶ (A) ponderous : animation
(B) trustworthy : temptation
(C) ill-fated : predilection
(D) dominant : haphazard
(E) unfettered : liberation

Ponderous means without ANimation

5

Review

1. **(B)** A SWITCH controls the flow of ELECTRICITY, and valve controls the flow of liquid.

2. **(C)** A MAINSPRING powers a WATCH, and an engine powers an automobile.

3. **(A)** A CAST plays the PLAY, and a chorus sings the song.

4. **(C)** To DECLAIM is to speak in a POMPOUS manner, and to pontificate is to speak in a dogmatic manner.

5. **(D)** An ACRID ODOR is a disagreeable odor, and a raucous sound is a disagreeable sound.

6. **(A)** DISBURSEMENT is the method for distributing FUNDS, and dissemination is the method for distributing knowledge.

7. **(B)** HOMESICKNESS is caused by SEPARATION, and melancholy is caused by loss.

8. **(A)** An ALIAS is a device to obscure an IDENTITY, and a mask is a device to obscure a face.

9. **(E)** EMACIATION is a loss of mass in the BODY, and devaluation is a loss of value in currency.

10. **(A)** Something that is CHAOTIC lacks ORDER, and something that is ponderous lacks animation.

Master Advanced Strategies for Difficult Items

Sometimes the Basic Technique will seem to fail you. How could that occur given that "this-is-like-that" is the very essence of the Analogy? Simply stated, you may overlook the intended conceptual relationship; and when that happens, you're not going to find the correct answer on the first try. So you'll need a couple of other strategies to help you advance the issue. Here is your Advanced Strategies Action Plan.

ACTION PLAN   **Advanced Strategies for Analogies**

Use a prepared template. If your Basic Technique sentence doesn't work, then scrap it, and use a template, that is, a "canned" sentence that represents one of the common analogy relationships tested by the GRE.

1. Place for: . . . is a place for . . .

2. Device for: . . . is a device for . . .

3. Kind of: . . . is a kind of . . .

4. Part of: . . . is a part of . . .

5. Sequence: . . . precedes (follows) . . .

6. Degree: . . . is more (less) than . . .

7. Key element: . . . is a key element of the definition of . . .

8. Absence of: absence of . . . is a key element of the definition of . . .

For all of the variety in vocabulary, GRE Analogies display a remarkable constancy in the relationships used. In fact, the vast majority of the Analogies on GREs fall into one of eight categories:

1. **place for:** . . . is a place for . . .

   CAVE : SPELUNKER   A CAVE is a place for a SPELUNKER.

   SEMINARY : THEOLOGIAN   A SEMINARY is a place for a THEOLOGIAN.

   COLUMN : CAPITAL   A COLUMN is a place for a CAPITAL.

2. **device for:** . . . is a device for . . .

   CLEAVER : BUTCHER   A CLEAVER is a device for a BUTCHER.

   AUGER : DRILLING   AN AUGER is a device for DRILLING.

   SEMAPHORE : COMMUNICATION   A SEMAPHORE is a device for COMMUNICATION.

5

3. **kind of:** . . . is a kind of . . .

   CROISSANT : BREAD   A CROISSANT is a kind of BREAD.

   MISDEMEANOR : CRIME   A MISDEMEANOR is a kind of CRIME.

   BARITONE : VOICE   A BARITONE is a kind of VOICE.

4. **part of:** . . . is a part of . . .

   SLEEVE : SHIRT   A SLEEVE is a part of a SHIRT.

   MOVEMENT : SYMPHONY   A MOVEMENT is a part of a SYMPHONY.

   CELL : MATRIX   A CELL is a part of a MATRIX.

5. **sequence:** . . . precedes (follows) . . .

   ENGAGEMENT : MARRIAGE   An ENGAGEMENT precedes a MARRIAGE.

   RELAPSE : RECOVERY   A RELAPSE follows a RECOVERY.

   PLEA : INDICTMENT   A PLEA follows an INDICTMENT.

6. **degree:** . . . is a large (small) . . .

   CONFLAGRATION : FIRE   A CONFLAGRATION is a large FIRE.

   TEMPEST : SQUALL   A TEMPEST is a large SQUALL.

   RILL : STREAM   A RILL is a small STREAM.

7. **key element:** . . . is a key element of . . .

   FOOD : MEAL   FOOD is a key element of the definition of MEAL.

   CONFIDENCE : PANACHE   CONFIDENCE is a key element of the definition of PANACHE.

   STARS : SIDEREAL   STARS is a key element of the definition of SIDEREAL.

8. **absence of:** absence of . . . is a key element of the definition of . . .

   WATER : DROUGHT   Absence of WATER is a key element of the definition DROUGHT.

   SPEECH: : LACONIC   Absence of SPEECH is a key element of the definition of LACONIC.

   COMMITMENT : VASCILLATION   Absence of COMMITMENT is a key element of the definition of VACILLATION.

These eight template sentence should capture the analogy relationship of as many as 80% of the Analogies you get on your GRE.

You should memorize these eight templates and use them as a checklist. If your Basic Technique sentence doesn't work, then go down the list until you find one that does work. Be sure to use the same techniques to adjust a template sentence that you use to adjust a Basic Technique sentence: invert word order or change a part of speech in order to make the sentence read easily. And once you've identified what you think is the correct answer, substitute the words into your template sentence to make sure that you get a sentence that makes sense.

An analogy may sometimes fit into more than one category. For example, HAMMER : DRIVE might be read as a "device" analogy (a HAMMER is a device for DRIVING) or as a "key element" analogy (a key element of the definition of hammering is driving). Both are equally effective, so use whichever occurs first to you.

GRE analogies do *not* fit the pattern "same as" or "opposite of." In other words, you should not be looking for synonyms or antonyms. Although templates 7 and 8 sound a little like synonyms and antonyms, they are not the same thing.

5

Workshop B: Practice Advanced Strategies

This Workshop provides you the opportunity to practice the Advanced Strategies for Analogies. Do the Drill portion first, and then check your work against the explanations in the Review part.

Drill

Use the eight template sentences you learned above as a checklist to answer to the following Analogies. Enter a sentence (or the number of the template, if you prefer), and circle the correct answer.

1. ORGAN : LUNG ::

   Sentence: _A lung is a kind of organ_

   (A) stomach : intestine
   (B) mouth : tooth
   (C) foot : hand
   (D) ear : hearing
   — (E) joint : elbow

2. PAIN : AGONY ::

   Sentence: _pain is a key element in defenition of agony_

   — (A) joy : ecstacy
   (B) care : indifference
   (C) hope : fulfillment
   (D) cause : outcome
   (E) battle : victory

3. COOLANT : HEAT ::

   Sentence: _A coolant is used to lessen heat_

   (A) extender : impurity
   (B) insulation : temperature
   (C) conductor : electricity
   (D) computor : information
   — (E) lubricant : friction

4. CLAIRVOYANT : FUTURE ::

   Sentence: _clairvoyance is device for predicting future_

   (A) telescope : tripod
   — (B) oracle : knowledge
   (C) administrator : participant
   (D) doorkeeper : entry
   (E) clergy : religion

5. BERTH : SHIP ::

   Sentence: _A berth is where a ship rests_

   (A) highway : automobile
   (B) racecourse : horse
   — (C) hangar : airplane
   (D) anchor : chain
   (E) pedal : bicycle

6. VEGETARIAN : MEAT ::

   Sentence: _Absence of meat key element of veg._

   — (A) omnivore : vegetation
   ✱(B) teetotaller : alcohol
   (C) theist : belief
   (D) gourmand : food
   (E) dispatcher : route

7. CARAVANASARY : TRAVELLER ::

Sentence: *a traveller is element in caravanasary*

(A) government : academic
(B) musician : instrument
(C) district : voter
(D) domicile : resident
(E) laboratory : technician

8. WORD : LEXICON ::

Sentence: *words are part of a lexicon*

(A) retrieval : data bank
(B) item : catalogue
(C) performer : repertoire
(D) wanderer : destination
(E) orator : speech

9. THRESH : GRAIN ::

Sentence: *thresh is key element of defining grain*

(A) harvest : seed
(B) refine : slag
(C) glean : harvest
(D) employ : idler
(E) tan : hide

10. INTERMISSION : PERFORMANCE ::

Sentence: *intermission follows a performance*

(A) recess : hearing
(B) suspension : student
(C) conclusion : climax
(D) halftime : score
(E) seal : proceedings

Review

1. (E) Template 3.
2. (A) Template 6.
3. (E) Template 2.
4. (B) Template 7.
5. (C) Template 1.

6. (B) Template 8.
7. (D) Template 7.
8. (B) Template 4.
9. (E) Template 7.
10. (A) Template 5.

5

A Fail-Safe Plan for Emergencies

Although GRE Analogies are fairly predictable, you're likely to encounter some that you just can't seem to solve. You don't want to waste a lot of time here, particularly since these items are very short. So you need a couple of techniques for eliminating as many wrong answers as possible, so that you can make a guess and get along to the next item on your test. Here is an Action Plan to help you.

ACTION PLAN **Fail-Safe Plan**

> **Step 1: Eliminate non-starters. Non-starters are word pairs that do not exhibit any clear, necessary connection. You can eliminate all such pairs.**
>
> **Step 2: Use templates 7 and 8. If you don't know the meaning of one or both of the capitalized words, assume that the connection is either "key element" or "absence of key element," and use those sentences to find a guess.**

Here's how to apply the action plan.

First, you eliminate non-starters—those are pairs that don't show any analogy connection at all. Because the very notion of an analogy is dependent upon a connection between two words, a pair of words that doesn't show a connection *cannot possibly* be part of an analogy. They're non-starters because they can't qualify for *any* analogy sentence. Eliminate them immediately.

Here are some examples of non-starters:

- calf : mare
- vine : apple
- microphone : sight
- ambulatory : captive
- furtive : success
- outrage : melancholy
- misanthrope : courage
- dentist : organs
- philanthropist : pragmatic
- impervious : fanaticism

These word pairs just don't show a clear connection. If you doubt that, then try to create a sentence to express such a relationship. You'll find that you cannot.

Another way of proving to yourself that these are non-starters is to ask yourself whether changing one or the other word would give you a possible analogy connection. For example, if "calf:mare" were "foal:mare," then you could use the sentence "A foal is the newborn offspring of a mare." The fact that the change creates a relationship where there wasn't one before is not absolute proof that the pair is a non-starter, but it is as close as you can come.

Here are some suggestions for converting the non-starters above into possible analogy choices:

- calf : cow   A calf is the offspring of a cow.
- vine : grape   A grape grows on a vine.
- microphone : speaking   A microphone enhances speaking.
- ambulatory : walk   A key element of the definition of ambulatory is walking.
- furtive : secrecy   A key element of the definition of furtive is secrecy.
- outrage : disapproval   Outrage is very strong disapproval.
- misanthrope : hatred   A key element of the definition of misanthrope is hatred.
- dentist : teeth   A dentist works on teeth.
- philanthropist : generous   A key element of the definition of philanthropy is generosity.
- impervious : penetrability   Lack of penetrability is a key element of the definition of impervious.

You won't have to write your own GRE answers as we just did; the exercise was just to show you that if it is possible to create a connection where none existed, then the pair was a non-starter to begin with.

The non-starter guessing technique is easy to use—once you know what to look for. Here's how to use it:

QUESTION   CURTAIN : LIGHT ::

    (A) dam : water

    (B) signal : sound

    (C) heat : cook

    (D) frock : modesty

    (E) victim : wound

5

ANALYSIS The correct answer is (**A**). A curtain is a device for stopping the passage of light, and a dam is a device for stopping the passage of water.

This is a fairly easy analogy, but it will let you see how non-starters can be eliminated. You can eliminate (B) because there is no clear connection between a sound and a signal. To be sure, a sound, such as a gunshot or a shout, *might* be used as a signal; but then so could a flare, an odor, a painted mark, or many other things. The "might" is important. If your sentence includes "might," "could," "sometimes," "perhaps," or some similar word, then you probably are looking at a non-starter. In this case, (D) and (E) are also non-starters. A frock might be used to preserve modesty, but it might not; a victim might receive a wound, or might not. In other words, there is no clear connection between those word pairs, so they cannot possibly be the basis for an analogy connection. On the other hand, by definition, cooking requires heat, so there is a necessary connection between those words—just not the same one as between the capitalized words.

Here's another example:

QUESTION DEYHDRATION : WATER ::

   (A) insomnia : daydream

   (B) recalcitrance : will

   (C) fearlessness : complain

   (D) culpability : blame

   (E) malnutrition : food

ANALYSIS The correct answer is (**E**). Lack of water is a key element of the definition of dehydration, and lack of food is a key element of the definition of malnutrition.

You can eliminate (A) as a non-starter. Someone with insomnia might or might not daydream. And the same treatment can be given to (C). Someone who is fearless might or might not complain. (B) and (D) both exhibit clear connections: Someone who is recalcitrant has a lot of will, and someone who is culpable is blameworthy. But those are not the same connections as that given by the capitalized pair of words.

The mix of wrong answers in a set is likely to include some that show a clear connection (but the wrong one) as well as some that are non-starters because they do not show a clear connection. You probably won't be able to eliminate all four wrong choices using this guessing technique, but by eliminating one or even two, you will have greatly improved your chances of guessing the right answer.

TIP	If you think you've found a non-starter but aren't sure, try changing one or the other word to get a better connection. If you can get a better connection, then the pair as originally written is probably a non-starter.

The second Fail-Safe strategy is for use when you don't know one or both of the capitalized words. In that case, you won't be able to use the Basic Approach (because you can't formulate a sentence using words you don't know the meaning of), and you won't be able to use the Advanced Strategy (for a similar reason). However, you can still apply a sentence to the answer choices (assuming you know the words). But which sentence would be best?

The two most important GRE analogy relationships are the definitional relationships: "this is a key element of the definition of that" and "absence of this is a key element of the definition of that." So if you can't capture the relationship between the capitalized words, *assume* that it is one of these two because they are so common. Then find an answer choice that fits the template, and enter that choice as your guess.

Here's how to apply the strategy:

QUESTION   XXXXXXXXXX : SLEEP ::

(A) inhabit : kitchen

(B) vacation : relaxation

(C) remonstrate : blame

(D) mollify : exclusion

(E) depart : preparation

ANALYSIS   One of the capitalized words has been x'd out, so there is no way for you to make a sentence. This is very much the position you'll find yourself in when you don't know the meaning of one of the words. So assume that the capitalized words should be joined by one of the definitional templates, say number seven: . . . is a key element of the definition of . . . . And apply that template to the answer choices:

(A) A key element of the definition of inhabit is kitchen. (Impossible)

(B) A key element of the definition of vacation is relax. (Possible)

(C) A key element of the definition of remonstrance is blame. (Possible)

(D) A key element of the definition of mollification is exclude. (Impossible)

(E) A key element of the definition of departure is prepare. (Impossible)

So you would eliminate (A), (D), and (E), and choose (guess) between (B) and (C). Here is the full analogy:

QUESTION   LATIBULIZE : SLEEP ::

    (A) inhabit : kitchen

    (B) vacation : relaxation

    (C) remonstrate : blame

    (D) mollify : exclusion

    (E) depart : preparation

ANALYSIS   The correct answer is (**B**). A key element of latibulizing is to find a place to sleep or hibernate, and a key element of vacation is to find a place to relax.

Don't be disappointed if this strategy fails in particular cases. Remember that you're guessing at this point, so you have to play the odds. Even though the strategy won't work in every single case, it will, on balance, work in enough cases to produce a significant positive result.

CAUTION
> Don't pick an answer choice just because it is directly related to one of the capitalized words. For example, the correct answer to CALLIGRAPHY : PEN would not be handwriting:letters—even though calligraphy and handwriting are directly related. (Embroidery:needle would be a good choice since it's a "device" analogy.)

Workshop C: Practice the Fail-Safe Plan

The following Drill contains analogies rank high on the ladder of difficulty. If you can't solve them using the Basic Technique or the Advanced Strategy, then apply the rules for guessing.

Drill

demur - express misgivings

1. DEMUR : MISGIVINGS ::

    — (A) endorse : support

    (B) enhance : coddle

    (C) entrust : captivate

    (D) encompass : limit

    (E) enrapture : liberate

A PUN solves a conundrum

2. PUN : CONUNDRUM ::

    — (A) key : code

    (B) gem : opal

    (C) cap : hand

    (D) web : spider

    (E) edge : cup

3. CATAPHRACT : PENETRATION ::

    (A) elevator : highrise
    (B) ticket :admission
    (C) rampway : progress
 — (D) barricade : passage
    (E) funnel : filter

4. QUISLING : COUNTRY ::

    (A) patriot : war
 — (B) apostate : religion
    (C) coward : flight
    (D) mediator : quotation
    (E) abductor : ransom

5. RATITE : FLIGHT ::

    (A) beard : face   *place for*
 — (B) mute : speech   *lacks ✻ template 8*
    (C) hair : comb   *device for*
    (D) eye : lid   *device for*
    (E) sandal : shoe   *type of*

Review

1. **(A)** To DEMUR is to express MIS-GIVINGS, and to endorse is to express support. You can eliminate (B), (C), and (E) as non-starters because they do not express a possible analogy relationship.

2. **(A)** A PUN is the solution to a CONUN-DRUM, and a key is the solution to a code. You can eliminate (C) and (E) as non-starters. ("lip:cup" would be different.) (B) and (D) show an analogy type connection, but neither is parallel to that of PUN:CONUNDRUM.

3. **(D)** There is absolutely no reason that you should know the word CATAPHRACT unless you're some sort of military history buff or a student of ancient Greek. For the rest of us, we should eliminate (C) and (E) as non-starters, and then try Template 7. (A) fails the Template 7 test (it's a "place where" connection). So you would guess either (B) or (D).

4. **(B)** A QUISLING is a traitor who abandons a COUNTRY, and an apostate is a disciple who abandons a religion. You could eliminate (A) and (D) as non-starters. Then apply Template 7 to get either (B), (C), or (E). Only a 1 out of 3 chance, but better than nothing at all.

5. **(B)** A RATITE is a bird that lacks the power of FLIGHT, and a mute is a person who lacks the power of speech. There are no non-starters in this list; each one exhibits a possible analogy connection:

    (A) beard : face (place for)

    (B) mute : speech (lack of)

    (C) hair : comb (device for)

    (D) eye : lid (device for)

    (E) sandal : shoe (type of)

And none of them fits Template 7, so you should try Template 8. Then you get (B), and (B) alone. (Not bad work, we'd say, for folks like us who didn't know about ratites until we went looking in *Webster's* for an obscure word for an analogy.)

5

Get Answers to Frequently Asked Questions

Q: How long should I spend on an Analogy?

A: Certainly less than a minute. On some, only 30 to 45 seconds. There's really not that much to do, and either you know the vocabulary or you don't.

Q: Should I be worried about learning roots, prefixes, and so on?

A: No. For the same reasons that this is not useful for other verbal types. You don't have time to do that on the test. More importantly, it's just not useful. Over the past 25 years, only one out of every thousand or so key words could be analyzed that way—maybe even fewer.

Q: What if I don't know some of the important words?

A: Then you're normal. No one is expected to know all the words, and you can do very, very well even when you don't know some. Also, remember that you have a powerful guessing tool to use in that case.

Q: What should I do now?

A: If you have time, it would be a good idea to do the practice in the lesson for Day 6. If not, then you should proceed directly to Day 7 and learn how to tackle GRE Antonyms.

Today's Review

1. Analogies appear in the verbal part of the GRE and test vocabulary and word power.

2. Analogies are "this-is-like-that" items. The relationship between the key words can always be summarized by an appropriate sentence, but this task is made more difficult by abstract relationships, other meanings, and vocabulary.

3. Your Basic Technique is to formulate a sentence based on the capitalized words and to use that sentence to locate the right answer. You may need to adjust the sentence by playing around with order and parts of speech.

4. Your Advanced Strategy is a checklist of eight template sentences already prepared for you. Use them to find the intended analogy relationship.

5. Your Fail-Safe Plan is designed to maximize your chances of answering correctly when all else fails. You should eliminate non-starters (choices that do not exhibit a clear and necessary relationship) and prefer a choice for a guess that exhibits a definitional connection.

Apply Your Action Plan to Analogies

Today, you'll assemble all the pieces to the Action Plan that you developed in Day 5. After a quick review of some important points, you'll revisit the Analogies from the PreTest to see how the Action Plan would have helped you perform better. Then you'll have the opportunity to do timed exercises for further practice and to see the Action Plan applied to those items.

Review Your Action Plan

In Day 5, you developed an Action Plan for Analogies. You'll recall that the plan takes into account the defining characteristic of Analogies as "this-is-like-that" and further that it is designed to neutralize the added-difficulty factors (complexity, other meaning, vocabulary) used by the GRE. The plan was developed at three levels: the Basic Technique, the Advanced Strategy, and a Fail-Safe Plan. The complete plan looks like this:

The Analogies Action Plan

ACTION PLAN **The Basic Technique**

> **Step 1: Summarize the relationship in a sentence.**
>
> **Step 2: Adjust the sentence if necessary.**

ACTION PLAN **Advanced Strategy**

> **Use a prepared template.**
>
> **place for: . . . is a place for . . .**
>
> **device for: . . . is a device for . . .**
>
> **kind of: . . . is a kind of . . .**

What You'll Do Today

- **Review Your Action Plan**
- **Apply Your Action Plan to the PreTest**
- **Workshop A**
- **Workshop B**
- **Get Answers to Frequently Asked Questions**

> **part of:** . . . is a part of . . .
>
> **sequence:** . . . precedes (follows) . . .
>
> **degree:** . . . is more (less) than . . .
>
> **key element:** . . . is a key element of . . .
>
> **absence of:** absence of . . . is a key element of . . .

ACTION PLAN **Fail-Safe Plan**

> **Step 1: Eliminate non-starters.**
>
> **Step 2: Use templates 7 and 8.**

Now let's apply the integrated plan to the items from the PreTest.

Apply Your Action Plan to the PreTest

The following items appeared on the Verbal PreTest in Day 2. Here's how the Action Plan would have helped you.

QUESTION   8. CAST : ACTOR ::   *An actor is part of cast*
                                          actor is member of cast

   (A) election : candidate

   (B) census : data

   (C) orchestra : conductor

   (D) meeting : speaker

— **(E) chorus : singer**

Basic Technique

An actor is a member of a cast, and a singer is a member of a chorus.

Remember that it's okay to change the order of words. Just remember to change the order of the words in the answer choices as well.

Advanced Strategy

Template #4.

Fail-Safe

Nonstarters: (D)

QUESTION   9.   CROWD : DISPERSE ::

(A) painting : restore

(B) clog : dissolve

(C) knot : tangle

(D) population : reproduce

(E) business : incorporate

Basic Technique

Dispersing is the method for breaking up a crowd, and dissolving is the method for breaking up a clog.

Remember that it's okay to play around with the parts of speech used. Just remember to conform the answer choices to the capitalized words.

Advanced Strategy

Template #5 or #7.

Fail-Safe

Nonstarters: (A), (E)

QUESTION   10. MANDATE : COMPLIANCE ::

(A) prohibit : abstention

(B) vacate : occupancy

(C) recall : retreat

(D) vindicate : guilt

(E) defame : reputation

issue mandate to have compliance

issue prohibition

6

Basic Technique

A mandate is issued to ensure compliance, and a prohibition is issued to ensure abstention.

Advanced Strategy

Template #7.

Fail-Safe

Nonstarters: (C)

QUESTION   11. TORPOR : MOTION ::

Absence of torpor is motion
Torpor

—   **(A) insipidness : taste**

(B) gangrene : infection

(C) elegance : style

(D) cowardice : discipline

(E) winsomeness : appeal

Basic Technique

Torpor is a total lack of motion, and insipidness is a total lack of taste.

Advanced Strategy

Template #7.

Fail-Safe

Nonstarters: (D)

QUESTION   12. INSINUATE : ACCUSE ::

degree
accusation is
strong
insinuation

(A) beckon : refuse

(B) alter : enhance

(C) activate : sustain

(D) vanquish : reconcile

(E) discourage : forbid

Basic Technique

An accusation is a strong insinuation, and a forbidding is strong discouragement.

Advanced Strategy

Template #6.

Fail-Safe

Nonstarters: (A), (B)

QUESTION 13. HETEROGENEOUS : VARIETY ::

(A) adulterous : commitment
(B) capricious : change
(C) imperious : backbone
(D) benighted : desire
(E) preemptory : plan

heterogeneous characterized by variety

Basic Technique

Heterogenous means characterized by unlike elements, and capricious means characterized by change.

Advanced Strategy

Template #7.

Fail-Safe

Nonstarters: (A), (C), (D)

QUESTION 14. TAXONOMIST : CLASSIFICATION ::

(A) scholar : study
(B) acolyte : experience
(C) podiatrist : infection
— (D) architect : design
(E) vigilante : injustice

classification is device for a taxonomist
taxonomist produces classification

Basic Technique

A taxonomist produces a classification, and an architect produces a design.

Advanced Strategy

Template #7.

6

Fail-Safe

Nonstarters: (C)

QUESTION 15. PLACEBO : EFFICACY ::

    (A) transparency : vision
    (B) concentrate : mixture
    (C) rigorousness : effectiveness
    (D) platitude : originality
    (E) comprehension : entirety

the absence of efficacy
key element of placebo

Basic Technique

A placebo is totally lacking in efficacy, and a platitude is totally lacking in originality.

Advanced Strategy

Template #8.

Fail-Safe

Nonstarters: (C), (E)

QUESTION 16. CALUMNY : FALSEHOOD ::

    (A) encomium : praise
    (B) plagarism : authorship
    (C) diversity : stereotype
    (D) turpitude : virtue
    (E) notoriety : anonymity

key element of calumny is falsehood

Basic Technique

Calumny is a statement of falsehood, and encomium is a statement of praise.

Advanced Strategy

Template #7.

Fail-Safe

Nonstarters: None

Now you have seen how the entire Action Plan is applied to Analogies items. In the workshops that follow, you'll be given a chance to apply it under timed conditions.

Workshop A

This workshop consists of 15 Analogy items. The time limit for the Drill portion of the workshop is ten minutes. This reflects the general strategy of spending *on average* less than one minute per Analogy—though some will require less time and others more. But you should then spend whatever time you need on the Review portion of the workshop. Before going on to the Review, however, you should finish any items you omitted or were unsure of on your own.

Drill

15 Questions • Time—10 Minutes

DIRECTIONS: In each of the following items, a related pair of capitalized words or phrases is followed by five lettered pairs of words or phrases. Choose the lettered pair that best expresses a relationship similar to that expressed by the capitalized pair.

1. MELLIFLUOUS : SOUND ::
   - (A) searing : heat
   - (B) acrid : displeasure
   - (C) cacophonous : hearing
   - (D) honeyed : taste
   - (E) flaccid : digestion

2. NOMENCLATURE : TERM ::
   - (A) lexicon : word
   - (B) orthography : spelling
   - (C) dictionary : meaning
   - (D) glossary : pronunciation
   - (E) vocabulary : speech

3. DAREDEVIL : CAUTION ::
   - (A) theocrat : religion
   - (B) adversary : foe
   - (C) demagogue : government
   - (D) prodigal : thrift
   - (E) sychophant : purpose

4. PROTEAN : VARIATION ::
   - (A) sublime : imperfection
   - (B) unseemly : actuality
   - (C) malcontented : dissatisfaction
   - (D) contentious : agreement
   - (E) erroneous : penalty

5. SOLITUDE : COMPANIONSHIP ::
   - (A) boredom : stimulation
   - (B) destitution : need
   - (C) valor : reward
   - (D) sanctity : health
   - (E) kinship : blood

6. REDACT : PUBLISH ::
   - (A) solidify : enhance
   - (B) frame : exhibit
   - (C) denude : prune
   - (D) fracture : assemble
   - (E) delete : craft

6

7. GUAGE : MEASURE ::

    (A) vagabond : travel
    (B) watch : sychnonize
    (C) vacuum : refill
    (D) spice : ingredient
    — (E) pump : circulate

8. CONSERVE : MISERLINESS ::

    — (A) spend : profligacy
    (B) exhaust : emptiness
    (C) instruct : graduation
    (D) abstain : contrariness
    (E) separate : codependency

    miserliness is strongly conservative

9. NEGOTIATIONS : IMPASSE ::

    (A) communications : cypher
    (B) nuptials : betrothal
    — (C) production : shipment
    (D) blueprint : structure
    ✗ (E) commerce : boycott

    impasse can stop negotiations

10. CONTIGUOUS : PLACE ::

    ✗ (A) sequential : time
    (B) inferential : logic
    (C) imperious : ruler
    — (D) material : spirit
    (E) colonial : rebellion

    contigous- next to in place

11. AUGER : BORE ::

    (A) balloon : inflate
    (B) hammer : drive
    (C) propeller : spin
    — (D) kiln : glaze
    (E) wrench : expel

12. LABORATORY : EXPERIMENT ::

    (A) auditorium : audience
    (B) studio : musician
    (C) capitol : debate
    (D) stable : training
    — (E) gymnasium : workout

    experiment is performed in a lab

13. HYPOCRITE : PIETY ::

    (A) medal : bravery
    (B) judge : sincerity
    — (C) gaud : value
    (D) fragrance : nose
    (E) cashew : nut

    opposites hypocrite pretends to have piety

14. ROSEMARY : HERB ::

    — (A) balsam : tree
    (B) aloe : pain
    (C) signal : response
    (D) log : fire
    (E) curtain : window

    rosemary is kind of herb

15. WIRE : CABLE ::

    (A) gorge : bridge
    (B) link : chain
    — (C) fiber : rope
    (D) plow : field
    (E) stamp : envelope

    wire is part of a cable

    wire forms a cable

Review

Use the answer key to find how many you answered correctly, then compare your performance on the Drill to the graph below.

1. (D)	6. (B)	11. (B)
2. (A)	7. (E)	12. (E)
3. (D)	8. (A)	13. (C)
4. (C)	9. (E)	14. (A)
5. (A)	10. (A)	15. (C)

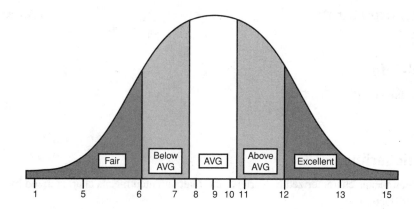

1. **(D)**

Basic Technique

A mellifluous sound is a sweet sound, and a honeyed taste is a sweet taste.

Advanced Strategy

Template #7.

Fail-Safe

Nonstarters: (E)

2. **(A)**

Basic Technique

A term is a part of a nomenclature, and a word is a part of lexicon.

Advanced Strategy

Template #4.

Fail-Safe

Nonstarters: (D)

3. **(D)**

Basic Technique

A daredevil is completely lacking in caution, and a prodigal is completing lacking in thrift.

Advanced Strategy

Template #8.

Fail-Safe

Nonstarters: (C), (E)

4. **(C)**

Basic Technique

Protean means characterized by variety, and malcontented means characterized by dissatisfaction.

Advanced Strategy

Template #7.

Fail-Safe

Nonstarters: (B), (E)

5. **(A)**

Basic Technique

Solitude means lacking companionship, and boredom means lacking stimulation.

Advanced Strategy

Template #8.

Fail-Safe

Nonstarters: (C),(D)

6. **(B)**

Basic Technique

To redact means to put in order prior to publishing, and to frame means to get ready to exhibit.

Advanced Strategy

Template #5.

Fail-Safe

Nonstarters: (A), (E)

7. **(E)**

Basic Technique

A gauge is a tool for measuring, and a pump is a tool for circulating.

Advanced Strategy

Template #2.

Fail-Safe

Nonstarters: None

8. **(A)**

Basic Technique

Miserliness is to conserve to an extreme degree, and profligacy is to spend to an extreme degree.

Advanced Strategy

Template #6.

Fail-Safe

Nonstarters: (D), (E)

6

9. **(E)**

Basic Technique

An impasse stops the negotiations, and a boycott stops commerce.

Advanced Strategy

Template #5.

Fail-Safe

Nonstarters: (C)

10. **(A)**

Basic Technique

Contiguous means next to in place, and sequential means next to in time.

Advanced Strategy

Template #7.

Fail-Safe

Nonstarters: (E)

11. **(B)**

Basic Technique

An auger is a tool used for boring, and a hammer is a tool used for driving.

Advanced Strategy

Template #2.

Fail-Safe

Nonstarters: (E)

12. **(E)**

Basic Technique

A laboratory is a place to do an experiment, and a gymnasium is a place to do exercise.

Advanced Strategy

Template #1.

Fail-Safe

Nonstarters: (C), (D)

   13. **(C)**

Basic Technique

A hypocrite pretends to have but really lacks piety, and a gaud seems to have but really lacks value.

Advanced Strategy

Template #8.

Fail-Safe

Nonstarters: (A), (B)

   14. **(A)**

Basic Technique

Rosemary is a kind of herb, and balsam is a kind of tree.

Advanced Strategy

Template #3.

Fail-Safe

Nonstarters: (C)

   15. **(C)**

Basic Technique

A wire is a part of a cable, and a fiber is a part of a rope.

Advanced Strategy

Template #4.

Fail-Safe

Nonstarters: none

Workshop B

This workshop consists of 15 Analogy items. The time limit for the Drill portion of the workshop is ten minutes. This reflects the general strategy of spending *on average* less than one minute per Analogy—though some will require less time and others more. But you should then spend whatever time you need on the Review portion of the workshop. Before going on to the Review, however, you should finish any items you omitted or were unsure of on your own.

Drill

15 Questions • Time—10 Minutes

DIRECTIONS: In each of the following items, a related pair of capitalized words or phrases is followed by five lettered pairs of words or phrases. Choose the lettered pair that best expresses a relationship similar to that expressed by the capitalized pair.

1. WARM : TORRID ::
   (A) timid : brave
   (B) calm : removed
   (C) tepid : caring
   (D) casual : costly
   — (E) cool : gelid

2. STEVEDORE : PIER ::
   — (A) welder : factory
   (B) epicure : restaurant
   (C) general : army
   X (D) roustabout : circus
   (E) plumber : kitchen

3. STOICISM : RESIGNATION ::
   (A) asceticism : indulgence
   — (B) hedonism : moderation
   — (C) epicureanism : luxury
   (D) modernism : temporality
   (E) celibacy : sexuality

   stoic is someone who is resigned

   epicurean is someone who is luxurious

4. STANCH : BLOOD ::
   (A) operate : organ
   (B) winnow : grain
   (C) carve : course
   — (D) dam : water
   (E) cull : herd

5. ALTO : CHOIR ::
   — (A) viola : orchestra
   (B) brush : painter
   (C) wave : ocean
   (D) layer : cake
   (E) spice : ingredient

6. KEYNOTE : CONVENTION ::
   (A) epilogue : documentary
   (B) intermission : play
   — (C) crescendo : symphony
   (D) encore : concert
   X (E) salutation : letter

   keynote speaker opens a convention

   salutation opens a letter

7. SPLINT : FRACTURE :

    (A) microbe : infection

— (B) suture : laceration

    (C) lavage : digestion

    (D) allergen : reaction

    (E) scalpel : operation

8. PLEBISCITE : SOVEREIGNTY ::

—(A) referendum : law

    (B) audit : accounting

    (C) declaration : war

    (D) impeachment : crime

    (E) recall : ambassador

9. APPETIZER : MEAL ::

    (A) sketch : portrait

    (B) superstructure : ship

    (C) postscript : letter

    (D) interment : funeral

— (E) portico : building

10. TACITURNITY : SILENCE ::

— (A) cupidity : acquisitiveness

    (B) felicity : mournfulness

    (C) toxicity : antidote

    (D) complicity : innocence

    (E) validity : rationality

11. FEN : WATER ::

X (A) lea : grass

    (B) bog : brush

    (C) plain : trees

    (D) hillock : crops

— (E) field : rows

fen - piece of land covered by water

lea - piece of land covered by grass

12. AMBIGUOUS : CLARITY ::

    (A) raucous : noise

— (B) enigmatic : solution

    (C) iridescent : color

    (D) anarchic : disorder

    (E) glorious : praise

Ambiguous Absence of clarity

enigmatic - lack of solution

13. PATENT : INVENTOR ::

    (A) manuscript : editor

    (B) royalty : producer

— (C) product : manufacturer

X (D) copyright : author

    (E) draught : writer

Duh!

inventor protects by patent

author protects by copyright

14. BIRD : BEVY ::

    (A) shepherd : flock

    (B) kennel : lodging

    (C) hunter : prey

    (D) chicken : poultry

— (E) cow : herd

bird is part of bevy

15. BASTION : DEFENSE ::

— (A) pedagogy : education

    (B) extrovert : psychology

    (C) terror : capitulation

    (D) perimeter : fencing

    (E) fashion : expense

6

Review

Use the answer key to find how many you answered correctly, then compare your performance on the Drill to the graph below.

1. (E)	6. (E)	11. (A)
2. (D)	7. (B)	12. (B)
3. (C)	8. (A)	13. (D)
4. (D)	9. (E)	14. (E)
5. (A)	10. (A)	15. (A)

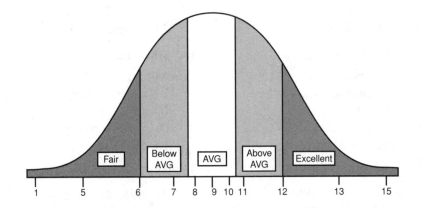

1. **(E)**

Basic Technique

Torrid means very, very warm, and gelid means very, very cold.

Advanced Strategy

Template #6.

Fail-Safe

Nonstarters: (B), (C), (D)

2. **(D)**

Basic Technique

A stevedore is a special name for a worker who works on the pier, and a roustabout is a special name for a worker who works in a circus.

Advanced Strategy

Template #1 or #7.

Fail-Safe

Nonstarters: (A), (E)

3. **(C)**

Basic Technique

By definition, a stoic is someone who is resigned; and by definition, an epicure is someone who loves luxury.

Advanced Strategy

Template #7.

Fail-Safe

Nonstarters: (D)

4. **(D)**

Basic Technique

Stanch means to stop the flow of blood, and dam means to stop the flow of water.

Advanced Strategy

Template #7.

Fail-Safe

Nonstarters: (A), (C)

5. **(A)**

Basic Technique

An alto is a voice in the choir, and a viola is an instrument in the orchestra.

Advanced Strategy

Template #4.

Fail-Safe

Nonstarters: None

   6. **(E)**

Basic Technique

The keynote is the speech that opens a convention, and a salutation is the part that opens the letter.

Advanced Strategy

Template #4.

Fail-Safe

Nonstarters: (A)

   7. **(B)**

Basic Technique

A splint is a device that is used to treat a fracture, and a suture is a device that is used to treat a laceration.

Advanced Strategy

Template #2.

Fail-Safe

Nonstarters: (C)

   8. **(A)**

Basic Technique

A plebiscite is a vote that determines sovereignty, and a referendum is a vote that determines law.

Advanced Strategy

Template #2 or #7.

Fail-Safe

Nonstarters: (C)

9. **(E)**

Basic Technique

An appetizer is the opening part of a meal, and a portico is the opening to a building.

Advanced Strategy

Template #4.

Fail-Safe

Nonstarters: None

10. **(A)**

Basic Technique

By definition, someone who is taciturn is silent; and by definition, someone who has cupidity is acquisitive.

Advanced Strategy

Template #7.

Fail-Safe

Nonstarters: None

11. **(A)**

Basic Technique

A fen is a piece of land covered with water, and a lea is a piece of land covered with grass.

Advanced Strategy

Template #7.

Fail-Safe

Nonstarters: (D), (E)

6

12. **(B)**

Basic Technique

Something that is ambiguous lacks clarity, and something that is enigmatic lacks a solution.

Advanced Strategy

Template #8.

Fail-Safe

Nonstarters: None

13. (D)

Basic Technique

A patent protects the intellectual property of an inventor, and a copyright protects the intellectual property of an author.

Advanced Strategy

Template #2 or #7.

Fail-Safe

Nonstarters: (B), (C)

14. (E)

Basic Technique

A bird is a member of a bevy, and a cow is a member of a herd.

Advanced Strategy

Template #4 or #7.

Fail-Safe

Nonstarters: None

15. (A)

Basic Technique

By definition, a bastion is designed for defense; and by definition, pedagogy is designed for education.

Advanced Strategy

Template #7.

Fail-Safe

Nonstarters: (B), (C), (E)

Get Answers to Frequently Asked Questions

Q: Is it okay to deviate from the strict order of the Action Plan?

A: Sure. The Action Plan contains guidelines, not rules. The more comfortable you become with Analogies, the less you'll need any step-by-step guidance. You've probably already noticed this. In fact, when you are truly proficient, you'll be using all of the strategies almost simultaneously without even realizing it.

Q: I'm still seeing words that I don't know. Is that a problem?

A: It's to be expected. There is no way that anyone could hope to master all of the possible vocabulary that the GRE might use. Expect that you'll keep on seeing words that are not a part of your core vocabulary. But remember that while the GRE is designed to test the limits of your abilities, it's not intended to overwhelm you.

Q: What should I do now?

A: Move on to the next topic. You're probably never going to be completely satisfied with your performance on any part of the GRE, but keep in mind that your score is not based on any one type of question. Your verbal score is also a function of your performance on Antonyms. So you need to prepare for that topic as well.

6

Teach Yourself Antonyms

Today you'll teach yourself how to answer GRE Antonym items. Antonyms are the "opposite of" questions that appear on the verbal part of the GRE CAT. Antonyms are primarily a test of vocabulary and, to a lesser extent, of verbal reasoning power. You'll learn how to use your vocabulary and verbal reasoning skills to maximize your performance on this question kind.

Get the Inside Info on Antonyms

The basic "opposite of" format of Antonyms is fairly intuitive, but there are some subtleties that you need to be aware of. These subtleties become important as you work every angle to maximize your performance on these items.

The basic idea of an Antonym is described in the directions:

DIRECTIONS: In each of the following items, a word is printed in capital letters and is followed by five words or phrases. Choose the word or phrase that is most nearly *opposite* to the word in capital letters.

TIP

Antonyms are the briefest of all verbal items, typically only six words long. (The capitalized word and the five choices.) Don't even think about reading the directions again. When you see the capitalized word followed by the five choices, think "Which choice is most nearly opposite to the capitalized word?"

What You'll Do Today

- **Get All the Inside Info on Antonyms**
- **Learn the Basic Technique for Antonyms**
- **Workshop A: Practice the Basic Technique**
- **Master Advanced Strategies for Difficult Items**
- **Workshop B: Practice Advanced Strategies**
- **Develop a Fail-Safe Plan for Emergencies**
- **Workshop C: Practice the Fail-Safe Plan**
- **Get Answers to Frequently Asked Questions**

As the directions indicate, most of the Antonyms that you'll see will consist of exactly six words, a capitalized word and five one-word answer choices:

QUESTION ARROGANT

    (A) predictable

    (B) knowledgeable

    (C) confused

    (D) humble

    (E) composed

ANALYSIS The correct answer is **(D)**: "humble" is an exact opposite of "arrogant." Another Antonym form you might see uses phrases for the answer choices:

QUESTION AJAR:

    (A) tightly shut

    (B) very late

    (C) even tempered

    (D) pleasant scented

    (E) carefully planned

ANALYSIS The correct answer is **(A)**: "ajar" means open slightly, so "tightly shut" is an exact opposite. You might even have an Antonym that mixes one word choices and phrases:

QUESTION ALIENATE:

    (A) welcome

    (B) expose

    (C) inspect

    (D) listen carefully

    (E) answer sharply

ANALYSIS The correct answer is **(A)**: "alienate" means to estrange or to make averse, and "welcome" means to receive cheerfully.

A typical GRE Verbal Part has 7 to 9 Antonyms, some of which may be embedded experimental items that do not count toward your score.

NOTE Although Antonyms exhibit some slight variations in format (one word choices versus phrases), you don't need to worry about the differences. The strategies you learn today will apply to all formats.

GRE Antonyms aren't all of the same difficulty. You'll find that three added-difficulty factors can place an Antonym higher up on the ladder of difficulty. If you know what the added-difficulty factors are, then you can use various strategies to neutralize them and make the items more manageable.

1. The Vocabulary Factor

As you would expect, some Antonyms are more difficult than others because they use difficult vocabulary. Compare the following three items:

Easy

QUESTION TALKATIVE:

    (A) modest

    (B) hardened

    (C) fearless

    (D) polite

    (E) quiet

More Difficult

QUESTION GARRULOUS:

    (A) modest

    (B) hardened

    (C) fearless

    (D) polite

    (E) quiet

Even More Difficult

QUESTION GARRULOUS:

    (A) diffident

    (B) inured

    (C) intrepid

    (D) deferential

    (E) taciturn

7

ANALYSIS The correct answer to each item is (**E**), and all of the parallel words (including the answer choices) are similar in meaning. "Garrulous" just means "talkative," but the use of "garrulous" makes the second item more difficult than the first because "garrulous" is a less commonly used word. And the third example is even more difficult. "Taciturn" means "quiet," "diffident" means "modest," "inured" means "hardened," "intrepid" means "fearless," and "deferential" means "polite." So the third item is conceptually the same as the second (and the first) but with much more difficult vocabulary.

The vocabulary added-difficulty factor can be particularly vexing because it leaves you with a sense of frustration: there's not much you can do with an item if you just don't have any idea about the meaning of the key word. Fortunately, this will not happen to you with any frequency. The CAT algorithm is designed to present you with challenging but not impossible items.

| **CAUTION** | Difficult vocabulary in Antonyms does not necessarily mean longest word. Even short, one syllable words can be difficult simply because they are not often used or because they have less commonly used meaning, e.g., loll (lounge about), fledge (grow feathers), flag (weaken). |

2. The Uncommon Word Form Factor

A second added-difficulty factor you'll encounter is the Uncommon Word Form Factor. This factor shows in several related ways. First, more or less commonly used words can have secondary or rarely intended meanings. For example:

Word	Primary Meaning	Secondary Meaning
DIFFUSE	not concentrated	to disperse
FREQUENT	often	to visit regularly
PROFANE	unholy	to debase
SALVE	ointment	to soothe

Although vocabulary is idiosyncratic (you don't know all the same words as your neighbor), in general an Antonym constructed using the secondary meaning above is going to be more difficult—at least for the average person. The following pairs of examples illustrate the point:

More Common Form	Less Common Form
DIFFUSE:	DIFFUSE:
(A) reliable	(A) placate
(B) unfinished	(B) inundate
(C) haphazard	(C) elevate
(D) casual	(D) invert
(E) concentrated	(E) focus

The correct answer to both Antonyms is (E). In the first Antonym, "diffuse" means spread out or not concentrated, so a good opposite is simply "concentrated." In the second Antonym, "diffuse" means to scatter about in every direction, so a good opposite is "focus."

In the example above, the extra difficulty is created by using a different part of speech, a verb instead of a noun. And you learned in Day 5, with regard to Analogies, that the way to resolve any question about the part of speech intended is to look at the parallel entries in the answer choices.

Sometimes the added difficulty is accomplished by using a different word altogether but with the same spelling. Example:

More Common Usage	Less Common Usage
SOUND:	SOUND:
(A) deflate	(A) irresponsible
(B) silence	(B) unhealthy
(C) cultivate	(C) excited
(D) opine	(D) bereft
(E) encircle	(E) ravenous

The correct answer to both Antonyms is (B). In the first Antonym, "sound" has the more common usage related to noise, as in to sound the alarm. So a good opposite is "silence." The second Antonym uses an unrelated word. In the second example, "sound" means "whole" or "unimpaired." A good opposite is given by (B): sound health as opposed to unhealthy.

The use of less common meanings can make finding the opposite difficult because the less common usage simply does not come as readily to mind. So later in this Day, you'll learn strategies that will help to ensure that you won't overlook an intended meaning.

7

You first encountered the "uncommon form" wrinkle in Analogies on Day 5; but it's even more important in Antonyms since Antonyms are almost entirely a function of vocabulary. (Note: If you want to see some other examples, you can go back to Day 5.)

Yet another way of changing the word form to make an item more difficult is the deliberate use of a cumbersome part of speech. For example, you're accustomed to making a noun out of a verb by adding -tion so that "notify" becomes "notification" or by adding an -iness so that adjective "clumsy" becomes the noun "clumsiness." But sometimes the GRE seems to take this to extreme, as shown here:

Word	Normal Transformation	GRE Transformation
responsible	responsibility	responsibleness
beautiful	beauty	beauteousness
ferment	fermentation	fermentability
approbate	approbation	approbativeness
rudiment	rudimentary	redimentariness

There is nothing wrong with any of these words *per se*, it's just that those in the third column are not ones most people are likely to use. As a result, you get antonyms that are more difficult than they might otherwise be. Here are some examples:

 SIMILITUDE:

(A) difference

(B) inaction

(C) cleanliness

(D) importance

(E) wilfulness

ANALYSIS The correct answer is **(A)**. Similitude is just a variation on similar and is equivalent to similarity. And a good opposite for similarity is difference.

QUESTION ANARCHISM:

(A) stealth

(B) preference

(C) pessimism

(D) defiance

(E) order

ANALYSIS The correct answer is (**E**). "Anarchism" is just a less frequently used form of "anarchy," and it simply means "anarchy." So a good opposite is "order."

QUESTION EFFICACIOUSNESS:

(A) disregard

(B) sociability

(C) impotence

(D) generosity

(E) amicability

ANALYSIS The correct answer is (**C**). "Efficaciousness" is just a longer way of saying "efficacy" or "effectivenss," so a good opposite is impotence.

As the examples above demonstrate, an Antonym may seem more difficult than it actually is. So don't let a "big word" intimidate you. Below you will find a strategy that will help you meet this challenge on its own terms.

TIP

> If the part of speech of the capitalized word is ambiguous, check the answer choices. The capitalized word will have the same part of speech.

3. The Strength of Opposition Factor

The third added difficulty factor in this part is strength of opposition. For example, what is the opposite of "twilight?" Is it "total darkness," "noonday," or "dawn?" All of those choices are arguably "opposite" to "twilight," so only one would appear in any given version of the item. In other words, you don't have to worry about *degrees* of oppositeness within an item, but you do need to be open to the possibility that the correct answer will not be exactly the one that you anticipated. Compare the following:

IMPEDE:	*IMPEDE:*
(A) assist	(A) stand aside
(B) inform	(B) inform
(C) rename	(C) rename
(D) delight	(D) delight
(E) incur	(E) incur

7

The correct answer to each problem is (**A**), and "to assist" is the opposite of "to impede" just as "to stand aside" is the opposite of "to impede." "Assist," however, seems to be a somewhat "stronger" opposite, that is, it is "more opposite" than "stand aside." But since both are opposites, either could be the correct choice. (Again, you wouldn't find them both in the same list of choices.)

> Although the directions for Antonyms tell you to look for the choice that is "most nearly *opposite*," within an item there are no degrees of opposition. The correct choice is the *only one* that stands in opposition to the capitalized word.

Antonyms are "opposite of" items. You'll be able to answer many of them because you know the vocabulary word. Other Antonyms cannot be solved so easily. Some are high on the ladder of difficulty because they use two or even three of the added-difficulty factors (vocabulary, uncommon form, strength of opposition). For all of these reasons, you'll need strategies and a systematic approach to do your best on antonyms. And that is the topic of the next section.

Learn the Basic Technique for Antonyms

Regardless of added complexity factors, Antonyms are "opposite of" items. You're looking for the best opposite, and that's the basic technique you should try first. Here it is broken down for you:

 Basic Technique for Antonyms

Step 1: Read the capitalized word, check the part of speech, and try to formulate possible opposites. Read the capitalized word, think about its meaning, and try to come up with at least one and preferably two or even three possible opposites.

Step 2: Match your formulated responses to an answer choice. Read the answers, and select the one that most closely matches one or more of your formulated opposites.

You should begin by reading the capitalized word; and if you recognize it and know its meaning, try to formulate one to three opposites. Your possible opposites can be phrases even if the answer choices are each one word, and it won't matter if your formulation isn't elegant. You're not writing an Antonym item; you're just using this technique to get ready to pick an opposite of the capitalized word. Here's how you should proceed:

QUESTION EMBELLISH:

    (A) aribtrate

    (B) counteract

    (C) reassure

    (D) simplify

    (E) tamper

ANALYSIS You don't have to provide a formal dictionary definition of "embellish." The word means "decorate" or "adorn," so possible opposites would include "strip down" or "make plainer." With your formulated opposites in mind, you would then read the choices:

    (A) aribtrate is to "strip down" or "make plainer?" No.

    (B) counteract is to "strip down" or "make plainer?" No.

    (C) reassure is to "strip down" or "make plainer?" No.

    (D) simplify is to "strip down" or "make plainer?" Yes.

    (E) tamper is to "strip down" or "make plainer?" No.

And so the correct answer is **(D)**.

Here's another example:

QUESTION SERENE:

    (A) frigid

    (B) jaded

    (C) mealy

    (D) agitated

    (E) spacious

ANALYSIS "Serene" means "calm" or "quiet," so you're looking for an opposite that means "disturbed" or "upset."

    (A) frigid means disturbed or upset? No.

    (B) jaded means disturbed or upset? No.

    (C) mealy means disturbed or upset? No.

    (D) agitated means disturbed or upset? Yes.

    (E) spacious means disturbed or upset? No.

7

Therefore, the correct answer is (**D**).

QUESTION   And here is an example with a twist:

PROMPT:

(A) discourage

(B) fortify

(C) dazzle

(D) align

(E) persist

ANALYSIS   You might reason "prompt" means "punctual" or "on time," so I'm looking for a word like "late" or "tardy." But it seems that there is no correct answer. What happened? In this case, "prompt" is not an adjective; it's a verb. You know this because "discourage," "fortify," and the other choices are unequivocally verbs. "Prompt" means to "suggest" or to "encourage," so you're looking for a word like "discourage." And you find an exact match in choice (**A**), which is the correct answer.

> **TIP**   Read *all* the choices before making your selection, so that you'll be sure of finding the one that is most clearly the opposite of the capitalized word.

This last example demonstrates why it is important to read all of the choices before making your selection. Don't settle for "Well, this could be an opposite under some circumstances." The correct answer will be the only choice that is truly opposite to the capitalized word.

> **CAUTION**   Don't pick a synonym of the capitalized word. The GRE is not out to trick you; but if you're not careful, you might inadvertently pick a wrong choice because "it's kind of like" the capitalized word.

Workshop A: Practice the Basic Technique

This Workshop will give you the chance to practice the Basic Technique for solving Antonyms.

Drill

In the space provided, jot down at least one or as many as three words that are opposite to the capitalized word. Then use those opposites to find the correct choice.

1. AFFIRM:

   Possible Opposites: _to Not agree with_

   (A) activate
   (B) renounce
   (C) deliver
   (D) withhold
   (E) pretend

2. RECLUSIVE:

   Possible Opposites: _sociable_

   (A) inept
   (B) moody
   (C) sociable
   (D) protracted
   (E) animated

3. SQUANDER:

   Possible Opposites: _save_

   (A) account for
   (B) focus on
   (C) reserve
   (D) quarrel
   (E) improvise

4. VERBOSE:

   Possible Opposites: _simple_

   (A) subdued
   (B) terse
   (C) constant
   (D) doubtful
   (E) ornery

5. MONOTONY:

   Possible Opposites: _not the same_

   (A) insularity
   (B) casuality
   (C) felicity
   (D) enmity
   (E) variety

6. SAP:

   Possible Opposites: _enliven_

   (A) energize
   (B) betray
   (C) supplant
   (D) verify
   (E) idolize

7

7. CONCILIATORY:

Possible Opposites: _____

_____

    (A) observant
    (B) indefinable
    (C) succulent
— (D) recalcitrant
    (E) qualified

8. EXTRINSIC:

Possible Opposites: _____

_____

— (A) inherent
    (B) defensible
    (C) appealing
    (D) divisive
    (E) sanctified

9. CHARISMATIC:

Possible Opposites: *dull*

_____

    (A) melodramatic
    (B) inconsequential
    (C) indecisive
    (D) outspoken
— (E) uninspiring

10. DECORUM:

Possible Opposites: _____

_____

— (A) impropriety
    (B) propensity
    (C) puncuality
    (D) insincerity
    (E) instability

Review

1. **(B)** *Possible opposites:* deny, disavow, or say no.

2. **(C)** *Possible opposites:* friendly, outgoing, affable.

3. **(C)** *Possible opposites:* save, hold back, retain.

4. **(B)** *Possible opposites:* using few words, succinct, brief.

5. **(E)** *Possible opposites:* variation, heterogeneity, selection.

6. **(A)** *Possible opposites:* enliven, strengthen, bolster.

7. **(D)** *Possible opposites:* stubborn, obstinate, bullheaded.

8. **(A)** *Possible opposites:* belong to, a part of, defining element.

9. **(E)** *Possible opposites:* dull, lifeless, boring.

10. **(A)** *Possible opposites:* improper behavior, taboo, misstep.

Master Advanced Strategies for Difficult Items

Sometimes the Basic Technique will seem to fail you even when you think that you know the meaning of the capitalized word. How could that occur when the word is familiar to you? Probably because one of the added-difficulty factors is creating trouble for you. Here's how to deal with that.

 Advanced Strategies for Antonyms

Step 1: Correct for part of speech. Some of your Antonyms will probably include capitalized words that you recognize as being a familiar word presented in odd form. Just correct for part of speech to turn it into something more familiar.

Step 2: Work backwards from the answer choices. Turn the Antonym on its head. Let each answer choice be the capitalized word and the capitalized word the choice.

Above you learned that an Antonym can seem more difficult because it is written using an unusual form of the word: beauteousness rather than beauty. The solution to this problem is just to change the word into its more familiar form:

If you get:	Treat it as:
VENERATIVE	VENERATE
CALAMITOUS	CALAMITY
SUBVERSION	SUBVERT
TENUOUSNESS	TENUOUS
SUPERFICIALITY	SUPERFICIAL

You change the part of speech to make the solution easier. If it doesn't help, then don't do it for that item. But for the words in this list, it would probably make things easier:

	If you get:	Treat it as:
	VENERATIVE	VENERATE
Possible Opposites	abohorable	disrespectfulness
	abhor	disrespect
	CALAMITOUS	CALAMITY
Possible Opposites	good luck	good fortune
	good luck	good fortune

continues

7

continued

	If you get:	*Treat it as:*
	SUBVERSION	SUBVERT
Possible Opposites	preservation	support
	preserve	support
	TENUOUSNESS	TENUOUS
Possible Opposites	solidity	substantialiness
	solid	substantial
	SUPERFICIALITY	SUPERFICIAL
Possible Opposites	fundamentality	incisiveness
	fundamental	incisive

If you change the part of speech of the capitalized word, then you'll also need to make an adjugment to the choices:

Turn these:	*Into these:*
VENERATIVE:	VENERATE:
(A) condemnatory	(A) condemn
(B) invasive	(B) invade
(C) illustrative	(C) illustrate
(D) merited	(D) merit
(E) deferential	(E) defer
SUPERFICIALITY:	SUPERFICIAL:
(A) redundancy	(A) redundant
(B) zealousness	(B) zealous
(C) flamboyance	(C) flamboyant
(D) depth	(D) deep
(E) plausibility	(E) plausible

The correct answer to the first item is (**A**), and the correct answer to the second is (**D**). Changing the part of speech of the capitalized word plus the answer choices should make it easier to spot the correct answer.

CAUTION If you change the part of speech of a capitalized word to make your sentence read more evenly, make sure that you change the part of speech of the corresponding answer choices before testing them in the sentence.

A second Advanced Strategy is to invert the item: let each answer choice stand for a capitalized word and the capitalized word be an answer choice. Here's how it works:

 QUESTION POSTURE:

    (A) act naturally

    (B) close securely

    (C) limit severely

    (D) place carefully

    (E) breathe heavily

ANALYSIS Let's assume that the Basic Technique, for one reason or another, did not produce an answer to this item. You could then try:

ACT NATURALLY:

(-) posture

And the opposite of "act naturally" is "put on airs" or "posture," so **(A)** is the correct answer. What the second way of looking at the item shows is that you might have overlooked the fact that "posture" in this case is a verb rather than a noun. By inverting the item, you are forced to think of the capitalized word as a verb. This should make it easier to identify (A) as the correct response.

Here's another example:

QUESTION PLUCK:

    (A) craftiness

    (B) cowardice

    (C) complicity

    (D) coolness

    (E) caprice

7

ANALYSIS Again, let's assume that the Basic Technique did not generate an answer. So you could try:

CRAFTINESS: COWARDICE:

(-) pluck   (-) pluck

The first doesn't exhibit a relationship of oppositeness, but the second does. "Pluck" means "courage" or "spirit," so a good opposite would be "cowardice." And the correct answer is (**B**).

The Advanced Strategies for Antonyms are somewhat like aspirin. They're a good treatment for a variety of minor symptoms. Just changing the problem by correcting the part of speech or by turning it upside-down may be all that's needed to shake out the correct answer.

 NOTE

> The strategies presented in the Action Plans are not rules but guidelines. Use them wisely; don't follow them slavishly.

Workshop B: Practice Advanced Strategies

Use the ten items in this exercise to practice the Action Plan for Advanced Strategies.

Drill

For each of the following items, choose the best opposite of the capitalized word.

1. DULL:

— (A) burnish
   (B) qualify
   (C) waste
   (D) harvest
   (E) detach

2. VOLUBILITY:

   (A) enhancement
   (B) clarification
   (C) endearment
   (D) disgruntlement
— (E) reticence

3. DORMANCY:

   (A) incompleteness
   (B) rancidity
   (C) domination
— (D) manifestness
   (E) inanity

4. INEBRIATION:

— (A) generosity
— (B) sobriety
   (C) apprehensiveness
   (D) tenacity
   (E) cleverness

5. GROUP:

— (A) disband
   (B) gratify
   (C) determine
   (D) arise
   (E) frazzle

6. EXTOLLMENT:

   (A) fabrication
   (B) delusion
— (C) criticism
   (D) maximum
   (E) classification

7. DELIGHT:

— (A) misery
   (B) calumny
   (C) profanity
   (D) salinity
   (E) unanimity

8. PRESUMPTUOUSNESS:

   (A) callousness
   (B) divinity
   (C) imbalance
— (D) humility
   (E) congeniality

9. COLOSSUS:

   (A) mirth
— (B) miniature
   (C) original
   (D) climax
   (E) fragment

10. FACETIOUSNESS:

— (A) solemnity
   (B) rapidity
   (C) engagement
   (D) singularity
   (E) squalor

Review

1. **(A)** Here dull is a verb. Turning the problem upside-down will reveal that to you. Also, it would help you to see that burnish is the correct answer since burnish means to make shiney.

2. **(E)** You can start here by changing volubility to voluble, meaning very talkative. So a good opposite is reticent.

3. **(D)** Change dormancy to the more convenient dormant and the other choices to adjectives as well. Manifest is the best opposite.

4. **(B)** Change inebriation to the adjective inebriated, and you'll see immediately that a good opposite is sober.

5. **(A)** Here's a problem that you might want to turn upside-down. Group is used here as a verb meaning to bring items together. So disband is a good opposite.

6. **(C)** Change extollment to extol and criticism to criticize. Criticize is a good opposite of extol.

7

7. **(A)** Delight is often a verb, but here it has to be a noun. A delight is something very pleasurable, so a good opposite is misery.

8. **(D)** Change presumptuousness to presumptuous and humility to humble. Humble is a good opposite of presumptuous.

9. **(B)** This is a fairly difficult item, but you can make some headway by inverting it. Miniature (a noun) means something small, and collosus means something large.

10. **(A)** Change facetiousness to facetious, which means in jest. So a good opposite is solemn.

Develop a Fail-Safe Plan for Emergencies

You're likely to encounter some Antonyms that you just can't seem to solve. You don't want to waste a lot of time here, particularly since these items are very short. So you need a strategy that will get you an answer quickly and move you along to the next item. Here is an Action Plan to do that.

ACTION PLAN **Fail-Safe Plan**

Step 1: Associate the capitalized word with a context. A context is the situation or circumstance in which the word might be applied. The context may guide you in making a guess.

Step 2: Guess. If you have absolutely no idea of the meaning of the capitalized word, then guess.

The Fail-Safe Action Plan is your plan of last resort. It's there for you when all else fails. Here's how to apply it.

First, try to establish a context for the capitalized word. Establishing a context is not an attempt at definition. Rather, a context is a set of circumstances with which you associate the word: a film, a conversation, a book, an article, or somewhere else where you've heard or read the word. Suppose, for example, that you encountered the following Antonym:

QUESTION UNCTUOUS:

(A) impolite
(B) accursed
(C) flighty
(D) mature
(E) sincere

ANALYSIS If you know that "unctuous" means "too suave or oily" as in an attempt to curry favor, then you know, as a matter of definition, that the best opposite is **(E)**, "sincere." But imagine that you don't know the meaning of "unctuous," even if you, in fact, do. Perhaps you've heard the term used in reference to someone who is not particularly well-liked, say, "an unctuous slimeball who sucks up to the teacher"— not a very nice thing to say but pretty vivid imagery. The context makes it clear that "unctuous" carries a powerful negative charge, so it's opposite must have positive overtones. This alone should allow you to eliminate choices (A), (B), and (C), giving you a 50/50 chance of guessing correctly. And since "slimeball" sounds for all the world like "greasy or oily," you might even settle on (E).

Here's another example—with a story as to how finding a context might lead you to the correct answer:

QUESTION RUMINATION:

    (A) honest effort

    (B) qualified endorsement

    (C) unwarranted cynicism

    (D) snap judgment

    (E) urgent message

ANALYSIS Assume that you don't have a clue as to the formal definition of "rumination," but let's imagine that you know that a cow is a ruminant. So you have this mental image of a cow chewing its cud—and chewing, and chewing. So, for an opposite, you would pick either (D), "snap," or (E), "urgent"—words suggesting quick action. And (D) is correct because "ruminate" means "chew and chew again" and by extension "to think and think again, to ponder."

 CAUTION Don't waste time trying to dissect an unknown word into a root with suffix or prefix. If you recognize the meaning of the word from its structure, that's fine; but trying to puzzle out the meaning with Latin or Greek roots is a score killer.

Second, when you have absolutely no idea of the meaning of the word—no formal definition, no contextual association, no inkling—then guess. That means, pick an answer, select it, confirm it, and move to the next item.

7

Now let's put the business of guessing and Antonyms into perspective. It is an inherent feature of standardized exams such as the GRE that, other things remaining equal, the more complex the question structure, the more susceptible the item type is to a variety of alternative strategies, including guessing. The simpler the question structure, the less susceptible the item type is to short-term preparation. It's hard to imagine a question structure simpler than the Antonyms.

Our best advice about guessing is this: don't think overly long on it; instead, just do it; and get on with your test.

 NOTE

A guess is an answer too. With Antonyms, it is sometimes better to answer with a guess than to study too hard on an item. Remember that the computer won't let you move on to the next item until you have answered the one that you are working on.

Workshop C: Practice the Fail-Safe Plan

Use the "in context" guessing strategy to solve the following five Antonyms. Even if you can solve them using the Basic Approach or an Advanced Strategy, try to think how you'll use the guessing strategies when you need to.

Drill

1. SUMPTUOUS:

   (A) inexpensive
   (B) fearless
   (C) insincere
   (D) expansive
   (E) guaranteed

2. EXTENUATING:

   (A) ingrained
   (B) spiritual
   (C) enclosed
   (D) practical
   (E) aggravating

3. FULMINATE:

   (A) walk quickly
   (B) look carefully
   (C) speak softly
   (D) listen attentively
   (E) wait patiently

4. SIGMOIDAL:

   (A) humorous
   (B) straight
   (C) flawed
   (D) outlandish
   (E) partial

5. PANACHE:

(A) simplicity
(B) correctness
(C) valor
(D) lubricant
(E) concept

Review

1. **(A)** Sumptuous means lavish or costly, so a good opposite is inexpensive. You might have heard the word in the phrase "a sumptuous meal." That must mean a meal that is unusual, very good, or elaborate. And that could lead you to (A).

2. **(E)** To extenuate means to lessen the severity of something such as a crime, so a good opposite is (E). And you've probably heard the phrase "extenuating circumstances" applied to the commission of a crime.

3. **(C)** To fulminate means to thunder and by extension to speak in such a manner. And perhaps you have heard something like "His fulminations could be heard all the way into the next county."

4. **(B)** Sigmoidal means curved like an "s." It's a reach, but you might think of a fraternity with the Greek letter "sigma" in its name.

5. **(A)** Panache refers literally to decorative feathers in a helmet and so by extension means with flair or style. You might have heard the word used to describe someone who is very stylish, who does things "with panache."

Get Answers to Frequently Asked Questions

Q: How long should I spend on an Antonym?

A: That depends on whether you have a good idea of the meaning of the word, some idea of the meaning of the word, or no idea of the meaning of the word. If you have a good idea of the meaning of the word, you might want to spend as much as 30 or 45 seconds on the item because you can be confident of banking a correct answer. If you have some idea of the meaning of the word, you might also spend 30 or 45 seconds trying the various strategies you learned. If you have literally no idea of the meaning, spend only as much time as is required to select at random an answer, confirm it, and signal the computer to present the next item.

7

Q: Should I be worried about learning roots, prefixes, and so on?

A: No. For the same reasons that this is not useful for Analogies. You don't have time to do that on the test. This doesn't mean that you shouldn't try to reason out the meaning of a word by changing it from a noun to a verb or from an adjective to a noun. But this technique is really simplifying the word.

Q: What if I don't know some of the capitalized words?

A: Remember that the computer is programmed to give you items that are challenging but within your capabilities. So this should not happen often. When it does, you need to guess, keeping in mind that guessing itself is a strategy: when you guess and move on, you are using the test structure to your advantage because your verbal score is based on your performance overall in the section—not just on the Antonyms.

Q: What should I do now?

A: If you have time, it would be a good idea to do the practice in the lesson for Day 8. If not, then in your next study session, you should go to Day 9 and learn the best way to handle Reading Comprehension.

Today's Review

1. Antonyms appear in the verbal part of the GRE. They test vocabulary and, to a lesser extent, word power.

2. Antonyms are "opposite of" items. The three added-difficulty factors are vocabulary, other-meanings, and variety of opposition.

3. Your Basic Technique is to formulate possible opposites to the capitalized word and to use those to locate the right answer. You need to be alert for less common meanings to commonly used words.

4. You have two Advanced Strategies. One, correct the part of speech of the capitalized word to make it easier to formulate an opposite. Two, work backward from the answer choices.

5. Your Fail-Safe Plan is designed to maximize your chances of answering correctly when all else fails. You can try to "contextualize" the word by thinking of the circumstances in which you've seen it before. Otherwise, you should "declare victory" by making a guess and quickly move on.

Apply Your Action Plan to Antonyms

Today, you'll assemble all the pieces to the Action Plan that you developed in Day 7. After a quick review of some important points, you'll revisit the Antonyms from the PreTest to see how the Action Plan would have helped you perform better. Then you'll have the opportunity to do timed exercises for further practice and to see the Action Plan applied to those items.

Review Your Action Plan

In Day 7, you developed an Action Plan for Antonyms. You'll recall that the plan takes into account the defining characteristic of Antonyms as "opposite ofs" and further that it is designed to neutralize the added-difficulty factors (vocabulary, other meanings, variety of opposition) used by the GRE. The plan was developed at three levels: the Basic Technique, Advanced Strategies, and a Fail-Safe plan. The complete plan looks like this:

The Antonyms Action Plan

ACTION PLAN **The Basic Technique**

> **Step 1: Read the capitalized word, check the part of speech, and try to formulate possible opposites.**
>
> **Step 2: Match your formulated responses to an answer choice.**

ACTION PLAN **Advanced Strategies**

> **Step 1: Correct for part of speech.**
>
> **Step 2: Work backwards from the answer choices.**

What You'll Do Today

- **Review Your Action Plan**
- **Apply Your Action Plan to the PreTest**
- **Workshop A**
- **Workshop B**
- **Get Answers to Frequently Asked Questions**

Fail-Safe Plan

>   **Step 1: Associate the capitalized word with a context.**

>   **Step 2: Guess.**

Now let's apply the integrated plan to the items from the PreTest.

Apply Your Action Plan to the PreTest

The following items appeared on the Verbal PreTest in Day 2. Here's how the Action Plan would have helped you.

QUESTION   28. ABASE:

>   (A) recall

>   (B) tangle

>   **(C) elevate**

>   (D) deter

>   (E) quench

The Basic Technique

Possible Opposites: raise, make higher, lift up
Match: elevate

Advanced Strategies

There is no confusion regarding the part of speech for this word or possible meanings. Thus, the Advanced Strategies are not relevant.

Fail-Safe

You might think of a context here: he abased himself before the high authority.

QUESTION   29. IMPERMEABLE:

>   (A) explicable

>   (B) mature

>   (C) satiated

>   **(D) porous**

>   (E) reckless

8

The Basic Technique

Possible Opposites: permeable, possible to infiltrate, sponge-like
Match: porous

Advanced Strategies

There is no confusion regarding the part of speech for this word or possible meanings. Thus, the Advanced Strategies are not relevant.

Fail-Safe

A good context guess might go like this: a raincoat is impermeable to water.

QUESTION 30. DISSONANT:

 (A) unlikely

 (B) harmonious

 (C) flagrant

 (D) vibrant

 (E) tedious

The Basic Technique

Possible Opposites: consonant, meshing, in agreement
Match: harmonious

Advanced Strategies

You could change the capitalized word to "dissonance," in which case (B) would be "harmony."

Fail-Safe

Perhaps you've heard the phrase "cognitive dissonance," meaning a clash of beliefs. If so, that could help you with the meaning of dissonant.

QUESTION 31. PARSIMONY:

 (A) cleverness

 (B) valor

 (C) jaundice

 (D) inattention

 (E) generosity

Basic Technique

Possible Opposites: openness, charitable, giving
Match: generosity

Advanced Strategies

You might want to change the capitalized word to "parsimonious," in which case (E) becomes "generous."

Fail-Safe

Perhaps you have a special context for this word. If not, and you just don't know the meaning of "parsimony," then you should guess and move on to the next item.

QUESTION 32. MEDIATED:

   (A) inexpensive

   (B) horrific

   (C) vacuous

   (D) implausible

   (E) direct

Basic Technique

Possible Opposites: unmediated, without a middle link, direct
Match: direct

Advanced Strategies

At first, you might think "mediated" is a verb, but a quick look at choice (A) shows that it is an adjective

Fail-Safe

You might think of "mediation," in which a third person acts as a go between during a discussion. So an opposite would be direct.

QUESTION 33. REDOLENT:

   (A) foul smelling

   (B) needing repair

   (C) inviting disaster

   (D) becoming ill

   (E) incurring debt

Basic Technique

Possible Opposites: stinky, rotten smelling
Match: foul smelling

Advanced Strategies

This item is pretty much a straight-forward test of vocabulary. Without some knowledge of the meaning of the word, you'd have to try the third set of strategies.

Fail-Safe

Here you might think of a context of redolent: the redolence of flowers on a warm summer evening—or something else like that you might have read or heard somewhere. Anyway, the idea is that redolent means sweet or good smelling, so (A) must be the opposite.

QUESTION 34. INVETERATE:

(A) reconstructed

(B) serious-minded

(C) exuberant

(D) undecided

(E) quiescent

Basic Technique

Possible Opposites: cured, recovered, changed
Match: reconstructed

Advanced Strategies

This is pretty much a test of the meaning of "inveterate," so Advanced Strategies won't be useful.

Fail-Safe

You can probably think of a good context for "inveterate:" an inveterate liar. So "inveterate" must mean habitual, and a good opposite would be reconstructed.

QUESTION 35. ANOMALOUS:

(A) frequent

(B) abridged

(C) anticipated

(D) imperfect

(E) tendentious

Basic Technique

Possible Opposites: expected, according to a rule
Match: anticipated

Advanced Strategies

Again, you have an item that is pretty much just a test of vocabulary.

Fail-Safe

Perhaps you have heard a phrase such as "anomalous results," meaning unexpected results or outcome.

QUESTION 36. SANCTIMONIOUS:

    (A) practical

    (B) liquid

    (C) pious

    (D) delicate

    (E) infirm

Basic Technique

Possible Opposites: holy, pious
Match: pious

Advanced Strategies

"Sanctimonious" presents no possible confusion—other than its proper meaning.

Fail-Safe

Perhaps you have heard the word in the phrase "sanctimonious so-and-so." If so, then you might surmise that the word has negative overtones, so the correct answer would have to have positive overtones. This would give a pretty good chance of picking (C).

QUESTION 37. STYMIE:

    (A) corroborate

    (B) facilitate

    (C) abdicate

    (D) truncate

    (E) vituperate

Basic Technique

Possible Opposites: assist, abet, help, aid
Match: facilitate

Advanced Strategy

This item is just a test of vocabulary. Remember that difficult vocabulary doesn't always mean a long word.

Fail-Safe

Perhaps you've heard the phrase "I'm stymied," meaning the person doesn't know what to do. That suggests that "stymied" means stumped by or beaten by, so you would look for an opposite like helped by.

QUESTION 38. DECORUM:

(A) penitence

(B) salinity

(C) impropriety

(D) audaciousness

(E) xenophobia

Basic Technique

Possible Opposites: misbehavior, bad actions
Match: impropriety

Advanced Techniques

This is just a test of the meaning of "decorum."

Fail-Safe

You might have a context for "decorum:" he acted with decorum. And you would recall that the word has positive overtones and so look for an opposite with negative overtones. That would produce (C) as the correct answer.

Now you have seen how the entire Action Plan is applied to Antonyms items. In the workshops that follow, you'll be given a chance to apply it under timed conditions.

Workshop A

This workshop consists of 20 Antonyms. The time limit for the Drill portion of the workshop is ten minutes. This reflects the general strategy of spending *on average* 30 seconds or so per Antonym. But you should then spend whatever time you need on the Review portion of the workshop. Before going on to the Review, however, you should finish any items you omitted or were unsure of on your own.

Drill

20 Questions • Time—10 Minutes

DIRECTIONS: Each item below consists of a word or phrase printed in capital letters, followed by five lettered words or phrases. Choose the lettered word or phrase that is most nearly *opposite* in meaning to the capitalized word or phrase.

1. INCOMPATIBILITY:
   (A) finitude
   (B) sensitivity
   (C) receptiveness
   (D) spaciousness
   (E) captainship

2. LIQUIFICATION:
   (A) coagulation
   (B) intransigence
   (C) eccentricity
   (D) prevarication
   (E) inconvenience

3. PLASTICITY:
   (A) rigidity
   (B) calculation
   (C) solvency
   (D) cultivation
   (E) incongruity

4. INSOUCIANCE:
   (A) tardiness
   (B) concern
   (C) guarantee
   (D) humor
   (E) defiance

5. CRAVEN:
   (A) zealous
   (B) careful
   (C) direct
   (D) humid
   (E) brave

6. CAMOUFLAGE:
   (A) retract
   (B) highlight
   (C) predate
   (D) vanquish
   (E) interpret

8

7. PERENNIAL:

— (A) short-lived
    (B) ill-fated
    (C) over burdened
    (D) fast paced
    (E) little known

8. SWAY:

X   (A) align
    (B) remind
— (C) defend   *Duh*
    (D) value
    (E) untied

9. DAMP:

    (A) meander
    (B) evict
    (C) bruise
—   (D) amplify
    (E) desist

10. CONFIDENCE:

    (A) pressure
    (B) serenity
    (C) perseverance
—   (D) trepidation
    (E) casualness

11. GUTTER:

    (A) bring toward
— (B) let overflow
    (C) remain calm
    (D) renew vows
    (E) stop progress

12. INCULCATE:

    (A) delight
X (B) erase
⇒ (C) subdue
    (D) berate
    (E) embody

13. HACKNEY:

    (A) settle
    (B) praise
    (C) opine
    (D) delete
— (E) refresh

14. INTEMPERANCE:

    (A) improvisation
⇗ (B) moderation
    (C) sacrilege
    (D) medication
    (E) literacy

15. ACRIMONY:

X (A) good will
    (B) careful planning
    (C) slow response
—   (D) unlimited space
    (E) apt characterization

16. GLIB:

X (A) halting
    (B) agile
—   (C) withdrawn
    (D) special
    (E) transparent

17. RIDER:

    (A) stanza
    (B) review
    (C) conflict
    (D) conviction
— (E) preamble

18. WANTONNESS:

    (A) crudeness
    (B) resistence
—   (C) restraint
    (D) dalliance
    (E) blasphemy

19. CONVICTION: X 20. TRAIN:
    (A) gaiety   (A) point away
    (B) doubt   (B) empty out
    (C) insight   (C) make smooth
    (D) devotion   (D) cut evenly
    (E) onus   (E) take up

Review

Use the answer key to find how many you answered correctly, then compare your performance on the Drill to the graph below.

1. (C)   8. (A)   15. (A)
2. (A)   9. (D)   16. (A)
3. (A)   10. (D)   17. (E)
4. (B)   11. (B)   18. (C)
5. (E)   12. (B)   19. (B)
6. (B)   13. (E)   X 20. (A)
7. (A)   14. (B)

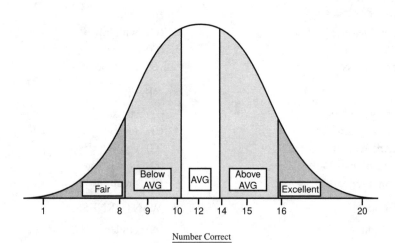

Number Correct

8

1. **(C)**

Basic Technique

Possible Opposites: acceptivity, getting along, working together
Match: receptiveness

Advanced Strategies

You might want to change "incompatibility" to "incompatible," in which case "receptiveness" becomes "receptive."

Fail-Safe

You should be able to handle this item using one of the first two levels of attack. Otherwise, you would probably need to guess.

2. **(A)**

Basic Technique

Possible Opposites: setting, hardening, solidifying
Match: coagulation

Advanced Strategies

You might want to change "liquification" to "liquify," in which case "coagulation" becomes "coagulate."

Fail-Safe

If you weren't able to dispose of this item on the first two levels, then you should have guessed before spending too much time on it.

3. **(A)**

Basic Technique

Possible Opposites: hardness, straightness, unbendability
Match: rigidity

Remember that your possible opposites don't have to be real words. They can be words such as "unbendability" that you use just to set up a possible match with a real word that is the correct answer.

Advanced Strategies

This is an excellent case for changing the part of speech. You are almost surely more familiar with the words "plastic" and "rigid."

Fail-Safe

Again, the first two levels should have let you dispose of this item. Otherwise, you would need to guess.

4. **(B)**

Basic Technique

Possible Opposites: worry, fretfulness
Match: concern

Advanced Strategies

You might have wanted to change "insouciance" to "insouciant," in which case "concern" would have become "concerned."

Fail-Safe

Changing "insouciance" to "insouciant" might set up a context guess for you.

5. **(E)**

Basic Technique

Possible Opposites: bold, brave, courageous
Match: brave

Advanced Strategies

This item is pretty much a test of whether you know the word "craven." If you do, then the Basic Technique will dispose of it; if you don't, then you should guess without further ado.

Fail-Safe

At this point, you would need to guess.

6. **(B)**

Basic Technique

Possible Opposites: reveal, pinpoint, make obvious
Match: highlight

Advanced Strategies

It might not be clear to you at first that "camouflage" is a verb rather than a noun. But a quick look at choice (A), which is a verb, shows you that all of the words in this item are verbs. Also, if you turn each of the choices into a possible capitalized word, you might be better able to see the relationship of oppositeness:

HIGHLIGHT: camouflage

Fail-Safe

A context might also help you to uncover the ambiguous part of speech problem, e.g., he camouflaged himself for the night maneuvers.

7. **(A)**

Basic Technique

Possible Opposites: quickly dying, temporary
Match: short-lived

Advanced Strategies

This item is pretty-much a test of the meaning of a single word.

Fail-Safe

Here you might think of a context such as: "Jones, the perennial candidate for Town Supervisor." That would suggest to you that perennial means recurring or long-lived and prompt you to look for an opposite such as (A).

8. **(A)**

Basic Technique

Possible Opposites: stay in one place, remain still
Match: align

Advanced Strategies

This item is made difficult because of an other-meaning factor. Ordinarily, we use sway to mean to rock to and fro, and so you might be looking for an opposite like "sit still." But you don't find one. So you should turn the question upside-down:

ALIGN: sway

This shows that (A) is an opposite of sway.

Fail-Safe

If you missed the other meaning here, you'd be forced to guess.

9. **(D)**

Basic Technique

Possible Opposites: increase, escalate
Match: amplify

Advanced Strategies

Here you have to pay careful attention to part of speech. "Damp" is ordinarily an adjective meaning filled with moisture. Here, however, "damp" is a verb, as you'll notice when you look at the choices. Even so, you might still keep looking for an opposite such as "dry out," but you won't find one. So turn the question upside-down:

AMPLIFY: damp

This could help you to see that "damp," as it appears here, is intended to mean silence or stop from vibrating, as to damp a string on an instrument.

Fail-Safe

If the insight above escaped you, you would almost surely be forced to guess. And this item should remind you that guessing itself is a strategy. Unless you uncover the other-meaning of damp, there is little chance that spending 10 or even 15 minutes with an item will get you a correct answer. So, it's better to make a guess and move along.

10. **(D)**

Basic Technique

Possible Opposites: fear, afraid-ness
Match: trepidation

8

Advanced Strategies

The possible matches, above, set up a solution, but you have to know the meaning of trepidation.

Fail-Safe

This is pretty much a test of your knowledge of the word "trepidation." If you know that it means fear, dread, or alarm, then you see immediately that it is a good opposite of "confidence." If not, then you'd be forced to guess. Here you can use the Fail-Safe strategy of guessing the most obscure word. You probably know "pressure," "serenity," "perseverance," and "casualness." So the fly in the ointment, so to speak, is likely to be "trepidation." It's all that stands between you and the correct solution. So guess (D).

11. (B)

Basic Technique

Possible Opposites: spread out
Match: let overflow

Advanced Strategies

The key to this item is to recognize that "gutter" is a verb—not the usual noun. You can then use your understanding of the function of a gutter to deduce that as a verb, the word means to channel the flow of liquid. And so a good opposite would be to let spread out or to let overflow.

Fail-Safe

Unless you pick up on the fact that "gutter" is a verb here, you'll just have to guess.

12. (B)

Basic Technique

Possible Opposites: remove from memory
Match: erase

Advanced Strategies

This item is just a test of the meaning of the capitalized word.

Fail-Safe

If you weren't sure of the meaning of "inculcate," you might contextualize the word and remember having heard it associated with the learning process: inculcate values. Therefore, it must mean something like instruct or teach, and you could come up with "erase" as a possible opposite.

13. (E)

Basic Technique

Possible Opposites: invent, originate
Match: refresh

Advanced Strategies

"Hackney" is used here as a verb, but you might be more comfortable with "hackneyed," meaning trite.

Fail-Safe

The solution to this item is facilitated by changing "hackney" to "hackneyed," but, beyond that, there is little to be done with it.

14. (B)

Basic Technique

Possible Opposites: temperance, caution
Match: moderation

Advanced Strategies

You might want to change the nouns "intemperance" and "moderation" to adjective forms: intemperate and moderate.

Fail-Safe

A good contextualized phrasing might be: an intemperate remark by the Senator. This would clue you into the fact that the word means rash or poorly thought out, and so a possible opposite would be moderate, or in this case, moderation.

15. **(A)**

Basic Technique

Possible Opposites: warmth, congeniality, friendliness
Match: good will

Advanced Strategies

You might want to change the word to an adjective "acrimonious," in which case you could use "characterized by good will" for choice (A).

Fail-Safe

A good contextualized phrasing with this word might be: an acrimonious debate between the two candidates who dislike each other. This would remind you that the word has negative overtones and probably means something like bitter or harsh.

16. **(A)**

Basic Technique

Possible Opposites: not smooth, tentative, halting
Match: halting

Advanced Strategies

This item serves as a reminder that a difficult vocabulary word doesn't have to be a long word. Glib means fluent or facile. So a good opposite is halting. It's not really possible to change the part of speech or to invert the question. If you know the meaning of glib, then you see that the correct choice is (A), or you try the third level.

Fail-Safe

A good context for glib could be: he was a glib speaker. This indicates someone who speaks easily and confidently, so "halting" would be a good opposite.

17. **(E)**

Basic Technique

Possible Opposites: core, body, center
Match: preamble

Advanced Strategies

Here added difficulty is introduced by the other-meaning factor. "Rider" is a noun that could have many different usages, one of the most common meaning a passenger in a vehicle. Here, however, it is used to mean an attachment or an add-on. This is a good time to turn the question upside-down:

PREAMBLE: rider

Juxtaposing the two words in this way could very well prompt you to recognize that a preamble comes ahead of the body of a text and a rider is an add-on.

Fail-Safe

If you overlook the other-meaning of rider, then you should guess.

18. (C)

Basic Technique

Possible Opposites: discipline, circumspection, restraint
Match: restraint

Advanced Strategies

You probably should change the form of the capitalized word to "wanton," in which case the correct answer becomes "restrained."

Fail-Safe

Here you probably have a ready-to-hand context: his lewd and wanton behavior. The opposite of such behavior would be disciplined behavior, circumspect behavior, or restrained behavior.

19. (B)

Basic Technique

Possible Opposites: wavering, self-doubt, second thoughts
Match: doubt

Advanced Strategies

The key to this item is the other-meaning factor. Often, we use "conviction" to mean a guilty finding at a trial, but here the word means confidence or certainty. Turning the question upside-down could help you see this:

8

DOUBT: conviction

The opposite of "doubt" is "conviction."

Fail-Safe

Here you don't really need a context to help you guess about the meaning of a word you do know. However, contextualizing might still be helpful: have the courage of one's convictions. This phrase uses the word "conviction" in the sense intended and could lead you to choice (B).

20. **(A)**

Basic Technique

Possible Opposites: look away, point away
Match: point away

Advanced Strategies

For this item, turning the question upside-down will have some very noticeable benefits:

POINT AWAY: train

At first, you might overlook the fact that "train" means to "aim," as "to train a gun on someone." Turning the question upside-down, however, forces this other-meaning into your mind because "point away" is likely to suggest aiming.

Fail-Safe

When all else fails, go ahead and guess. You could probably drive yourself crazy with this item since "train" is a very common word. You might keep thinking "put cars together," "go to the gym," or "make the dog obey." And all of these are meanings of the word. But until you find the one having to do with pointing a gun, you're no closer to a solution. So after you've tried the Basic Technique and the Advanced Strategy of turning the item upside-down, you should implement the final strategy: guess.

Workshop B

This workshop consists of 20 Antonyms. The time limit for the Drill portion of the workshop is ten minutes. This reflects the general strategy of spending *on average* 30 seconds or so per Antonym. But you should then spend whatever time you need on the Review portion of the workshop. Before going on to the Review, however, you should finish any items you omitted or were unsure of on your own.

Drill

20 Questions • Time—10 Minutes

DIRECTIONS: Each item below consists of a word or phrase printed in capital letters, followed by five lettered words or phrases. Choose the lettered word or phrase that is most nearly *opposite* in meaning to the capitalized word or phrase.

1. LEVEL:

    (A) turn about
    (B) heat up
    (C) send home
    (D) forget about
    (E) make uneven

2. SLACKEN:

    (A) intensify
    (B) gratify
    (C) intimidate
    (D) equalize
    (E) conform

3. PRAISEWORTHY:

    (A) incomplete
    (B) execrable
    (C) valid
    (D) temporary
    (E) instantaneous

4. EMBELLISHMENT:

    (A) confrontation
    (B) randomness
    (C) perpetuity
    (D) deletion
    (E) cleverness

5. IMPORT:

    (A) insignificance
    (B) premeditation
    (C) validation
    (D) vanity
    (E) attraction

6. MEANDERING:

    (A) direct route
    (B) thoughtlessness
    (C) wishful thinking
    (D) embarrassment
    (E) incompetence

7. PLENTY:

    (A) improvement
    (B) comfort
    (C) dearth
    (D) decision
    (E) omission

8. PALLIATIVE:

    (A) conclusive
    (B) aggravating
    (C) dissimilar
    (D) innocent
    (E) titular

8

9. EROSION:

  (A) excuse
  (B) recall
  (C) limitation
  (D) show off
— (E) build up

10. CALIBRATED:

  (A) replete
  (B) grievous
— (C) approximate
  (D) definitive
  (E) exquisite

11. PURIFIED:

  (A) intended
— (B) debauched
  (C) codified
  (D) welcomed
  (E) sensitized

12. HARBOR:

  (A) keep quiet
  (B) withstand
— (C) turn out
  (D) invoke
  (E) capture

13. LIONHEARTED:

  (A) jovial   ?
X (B) pusillanimous
  (C) excessive
  (D) romantic
— (E) tendentious

14. OCCULT:

  (A) harmful
  (B) elusive
  (C) bereft
— (D) public
  (E) arid

15. VILIFICATION:

  (A) counsel
  (B) elitism
  (C) usurpation
  (D) arbitration
⌐ (E) reverence

16. PERTURBATION: perturbed

  (A) distance
  (B) viability
— (C) composure   composed
  (D) opulence
  (E) disability

17. EPHEMERAL:

  (A) generous
  (B) vicious
  (C) untoward
— (D) permanent
  (E) oblique

18. BLANDISHMENT: blandish

  (A) retrenchment   retrench
— (B) containment   contain
  (C) indebtedness   indebt
X (D) discouragement
  (E) ratification

19. PUNCTUATED:

X (A) uninterrupted
— (B) equalized
  (C) predatory   Duh
  (D) singular
  (E) hazardous

20. HYPERBOLE:

— (A) generalization
  (B) legitimacy
  (C) materialism
  (D) conservancy
X (E) understatement

Review

Use the answer key to find how many you answered correctly, then compare your performance on the Drill to the graph below.

1. (E)   8. (B)   15. (E)
2. (A)   9. (E)   16. (C)
3. (B)   10. (C)   17. (D)
4. (D)   11. (B)   18. (D)
5. (A)   12. (C)   19. (A)
6. (A)   13. (B)   20. (E)
7. (C)   14. (D)

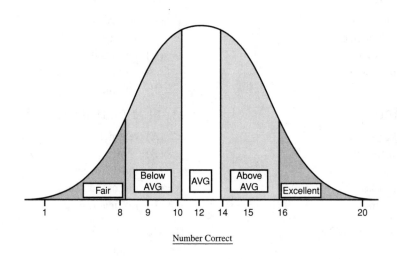

Number Correct

1. **(E)**

Basic Technique

Possible Opposites: unbalance, throw out of kilter
Match: make uneven

Advanced Strategies

The difficult thing about this item is the other-meaning factor. Ordinarily, we use "level" as an adjective, but here it is a verb. You might need to turn the item upside-down to see this:

MAKE UNEVEN: level

8

Fail-Safe

The first two levels of attack should take care of this item for you. If not, then you should go ahead and guess.

2. **(A)**

Basic Technique

Possible Opposites: tighten, aggravate, elevate
Match: intensify

Advanced Strategies

The difficulty here is created by the form of the word because you are probably accustomed to using "slack off" rather than just "slacken." The two, however, mean the same. So it would be okay to try "slack off," and then you can see that intensify is an appropriate choice.

Fail-Safe

If neither the Basic Technique nor the Advanced Strategies worked here, then you should go ahead and guess. "Slacken" is not a word that is unknown to you. And if you can't seem to find an opposite fairly quickly, this indicates that you are overlooking something. You can't afford to spend a whole lot of time looking for the missing key, so be prepared to guess and move along.

3. **(B)**

Basic Technique

Possible Opposites: damnable, condemnable, loathsome
Match: execrable

Advanced Strategies:

This is pretty much a straight-forward test of the meaning of "execrable," but you might have some luck by changing the parts of speech from "praiseworthy" to "praise" and from "execrable" to "execrate." If not, then be prepared to guess.

Fail-Safe

"Execrable" is a fairly difficult word, so you might have to guess. On this item, it would be appropriate to use the "most obscure word" guessing strategy. "Execrable" is probably the only word not familiar to you, so assume that it is the cause of your worries and make it your guess.

4. **(D)**

Basic Technique

Possible Opposites: simplification, de-ornamentation, elimination
Match: deletion

Advanced Strategies

Here is a good candidate for changing parts of speech: "embellishment" to "embellish" and "deletion" to "delete." The change may help you see the relationship of opposition.

Fail-Safe

The difficulty factor here is the invocation of the other-meaning factor. To embellish means to add something to beautify. So a key element in the antonym relationship is the "add." If your "vocabulary ear" doesn't hear this, then you're probably not going to pick (D) as the right answer. Since you're not dealing with very obscure vocabulary here, you'd be better advised to guess when you realize that you're not making any headway.

5. **(A)**

Basic Technique

Possible Opposites: lack of importance, meaninglessness
Match: insignificance

Advanced Strategies

The difficulty here is seeing that "import" is a noun meaning "significance" and not a verb or a noun pertaining to trade across national borders. You know that you need to check the choices to clarify any ambiguity regarding part of speech, and you might also find it helpful to turn the problem upside-down:

INSIGNIFICANCE: import

Fail-Safe

You can probably come up with a good context for this word: the decision to declare war was a matter of great import. Something like that should be enough to lead you toward choice (A).

6. **(A)**

Basic Technique

Possible Opposites: straight route
Match: direct route

Advanced Strategies

At first, you might read the capitalized word as a verb meaning wandering or as an adjective of the same meaning. But a quick glance at the choices tells you that it is a noun. You can't really change the part of speech, but try to think of the idea of circuitous or round about as a noun, and you'll have choice (A).

Fail-Safe

A good context guess could be: in her meanderings. That suggests wandering without direction.

7. **(C)**

Basic Technique

Possible Opposites: lack, scarcity, need
Match: dearth

Advanced Strategies

Plenty is a noun here and has the meaning of abundance. If you were uncomfortable with that, you could use "plentiful" instead. But you'd still have the problem of recognizing that dearth means lack or scarcity.

Fail-Safe

If you have to guess, here's a good time to guess the most obscure word in the list: dearth.

8. **(B)**

Basic Technique

Possible Opposites: easing, soothing, minimizing
Match: aggravating

Advanced Strategies

"Palliative" might be a noun or an adjective, but the answer choices tell you that it is here an adjective. There isn't any good reason to try changing the part of speech, so you just have to know the meaning of the word.

Fail-Safe

This is a straight-forward vocabulary item. Either you know or have some idea of the meaning of "palliative," or you guess.

9. **(E)**

Basic Technique

Possible Opposites: restoration, replacing
Match: build up

Advanced Strategies

You might want to change "erosion" to "erode," in which case the choices become:

    (A) excuse

    (B) recall

    (C) limit

    (D) show off

    (E) build up

Only one of them changes spelling, but you can now think of them as verbs, and "build up" something as the opposite of "eroding" or "eating away" at it.

Fail-Safe

The key to this item is the part of speech confusion. Once you've cleared that up, you shouldn't need to guess.

10. **(C)**

Basic Technique

Possible Opposites: inexact, rough, unmeasured
Match: approximate

Advanced Strategies

You might want to change the problem from an adjective to a verb form: calibrate and approximate. (The spelling of "approximate" doesn't change, though the part of speech does.) To calibrate means to measure precisely, so a good opposite would be approximate.

Fail-Safe

This is pretty much a test of the core meaning of "calibrate," so if the word is not known to you, you'd have to guess.

11. **(B)**

Basic Technique

Possible Opposites: contaminated, made impure, sullied
Match: debauched

Advanced Strategies

Everything turns on the meaning of "debauched." Changing the part of speech or inverting the item is not likely to help.

Fail-Safe

Here is another case for the "guess the obscure word" strategy. The meanings of "intended," "codified," "welcomed," and "sensitized" shouldn't be a mystery, and you know that they don't work. So, when it comes time to guess, guess the other word—the strange word: debauched.

12. **(C)**

Basic Technique

Possible Opposites: evict, turn away, refuse sanctuary
Match: turn out

Advanced Strategies

"Harbor" might be a noun or a verb," but here it must be a verb. It might help to see that if you turn the item upside-down:

TURN OUT: harbor

This should help you see that the intended meaning of "harbor" is "give sanctuary to" and that "turn out" is the best available opposite.

Fail-Safe

You don't need any fancy guessing strategy here. If you don't see the other-meaning in "harbor," just guess and move along.

13. **(B)**

Basic Technique

Possible Opposites: cowardly
Match: pusillanimous

Advanced Strategies

This item is pretty much a test of whether you know the meaning of a fairly difficult vocabulary word "pusillanimous." If you do, you'll recognize it immediately as the opposite of "lionhearted." If you don't, you'll probably have to guess.

Fail-Safe

If you have to guess on this item, you should go ahead and guess what seems to be the most obscure word in the list. This would surely be either "tendentious" or "pusillanimous." The strategy is not perfect. Just remember, it's intended to give you something to do when everything else seems to have failed.

14. **(D)**

Basic Technique

Possible Opposites: natural, normal, usual, well-known
Match: public

Advanced Strategies

This is a test of the key meaning of occult, and the best opposite is "public." No amount of changing the item is going to avoid the necessity for knowing the meaning of the word here.

Fail-Safe

Even if you don't know the dictionary definition of "occult," you might still be able to contextual it: magic and other occult sciences. This suggests that "occult" means dark and mysterious, and the best opposite seems to be "public."

15. (E)

Basic Technique

Possible Opposites: speaking well of, praise, positive regard
Match: reverence

Advanced Strategies

You might fare better if you change the part of speech: vilification to vilify and reverence to revere.

Fail-Safe

And if you have to guess, then perhaps you have a context in which you can place the word. Otherwise, pick a choice, enter it, and move on.

16. (C)

Basic Technique

Possible Opposites: sedateness, calmness
Match: composure

Advanced Strategies

Here is a good item for changing parts of speech: perturbation to perturb and composure to compose or to perturbed and composed. Remember that the purpose of this maneuver is just to make it easier for you to identify the correct choice.

Fail-Safe

The item depends entirely on either knowing the meaning of perturbation or recentering it changing the part of speech so that you have a word that you are comfortable with.

17. **(D)**

Basic Technique

Possible Opposites: permanent, long-lasting, eternal
Match: permanent

Advanced Strategies

This is about as pure a vocabulary item as you can imagine. If you know the meaning of "ephemeral," then the answer is easy to find; otherwise, you'll probably have to guess.

Fail-Safe

If you have to guess, then do so and move along.

18. **(D)**

Basic Technique

Possible Opposites: impediment, hurdle, advice not to
Match: discouragement

Advanced Strategies

Changing the part of speech could be very helpful here: blandish instead of blandishment and discourage instead of discouragement.

Fail-Safe

Perhaps you have a context for this word: in spite of her banishments, he went ahead on his own. This suggests that the word means something like advice not to do something.

19. **(A)**

Basic Technique

Possible Opposites: unpunctuated, continuous
Match: uninterrupted

Advanced Strategies

First, you'll probably be more comfortable with "punctuate." Still, this item is difficult because it tests an uncommon meaning: interrupt or break into segments. Turning the problem upside could help you find this key:

UNINTERRUPTED: punctuated

Fail-Safe

There is no reason to prefer one choice over another here. If you have to guess, then guess.

20. **(E)**

Basic Technique

Possible Opposites: down playing
Match: understatement

Advanced Strategies

This is really a vocabulary item. If you know that hyperbole means exaggeration, then you have choice (E).

Fail-Safe

And if you have to guess, pick a choice and move on.

Get Answers to Frequently Asked Questions

Q: Is it okay to deviate from the strict order of the Action Plan?

A: Sure. The Action Plan contains guidelines, not rules. The more comfortable you become with Antonym, the less you'll need any step-by-step guidance. You've probably already noticed this. In fact, when you are truly proficient, you'll be using all of the strategies almost simultaneously without even realizing it. Plus, they're so short that it's difficult to keep applying the Action Plan in a step-by-step fashion.

Q: I'm still seeing words that I don't know. Is that a problem?

A: It's to be expected. There is no way that anyone could hope to master all of the possible vocabulary that the GRE might use. Expect that you'll keep on seeing words that are not a part of your core vocabulary. But remember that while the GRE is designed to test the limits of your abilities, it's not intended to overwhelm you.

Q: Antonyms seem to be pretty a much a test of vocabulary. Is there anything else I need to do?

A: That's correct. Most of the Antonyms are straight-forward tests of vocabulary. Either you know the word or you don't, and there are only a few things you can try if you don't. The simple structure of the item type doesn't leave much room for maneuvering, but then remember that everyone else against whom you are competing is in the same boat.

Q: What should I do now?

A: Move on to the next topic. You're probably never going to be completely satisfied with your performance on any part of the GRE, but keep in mind that your score is not based on any one type of question. Your verbal score is also a function of your performance on Reading Comprehension. So you need to prepare for that topic as well.

Day

9

Teach Yourself Reading Comprehension

Today, you'll teach yourself how to answer GRE Reading Comprehension items. Reading Comprehension, as the name suggests, is a reading selection (passage) followed by two to four questions based on the content of the selection. You'll learn how to use your reading ability to maximize your performance on this question kind.

Get All the Inside Info on Reading Comprehension

The idea of GRE Reading Comprehension *seems* fairly intuitive, and the description given in the directions makes it sound so very simple:

DIRECTIONS: The reading selection is followed by questions based on its content. After reading the selection, choose the best answer to each question, answering on the basis of what is *stated* or *implied* in the selection.

That seems straight-forward enough: read a selection and then answer some questions. But, in fact, GRE Reading Comprehension is not quite so simple.

The GRE uses added-difficulty factors to make the exam sufficiently challenging for the testing population as well as to adjust the positioning of questions on the ladder of difficulty. Once again, you will learn about these added-difficulty factors and master strategies to neutralize their effects.

What You'll Do Today

- **Get All the Inside Info on Reading Comprehension**
- **Learn Methods of Reading for Comprehension**
- **Workshop A**
- **Master Techniques for Identifying Question Stems**
- **Workshop B**
- **Develop Strategies for Choosing Right Answers**
- **Workshop C**
- **Get Answers to Frequently Asked Questions**

The typical GRE reading selection is two or three paragraphs long for a total of about 250 to 400 words and supports two to four questions. A GRE verbal part usually has three such selections during the 30-minute time limit.

| CAUTION | The name "Reading Comprehension" is an oversimplification. Reading Comprehension is more than "reading a selection and answering a couple of questions." You need all the inside information about this question type to do your best. |

Inside the Selection

The selection, which is also called the passage, is the reading material upon which the questions are based. A selection may discuss a recent archaeological find, a scientific theory, a work of literature, a political or historical event, or almost anything else. The GRE uses three added-difficulty factors to make the selections challenging:

1. Unpredictable Mix
2. Surprise Beginnings
3. Compaction

Let's take a look at each of the factors and how they work. Knowing what the rules of the game are will give you an important edge.

1. Unpredictable Mix

The GRE uses a bewildering variety of topics for its reading selections. Consider just a few that have appeared in recent memory:

Willard Quine's neo-empiricist philosophy

Specialized feeding adaptations in zooplankton

Pulsating giant star IRC _ 10216

Sinistral and dextral shells in *Lymnaea peregra*

The classical formula for a piano rag

Fortunately, you're not expected to know anything about these topics—other than what you read on the GRE itself. Still, the fact that there are literally endless possibilities for the GRE to choose from automatically makes Reading Comprehension more difficult than it might seem at first. The best advice on this count is "Don't Panic." Yes, the topic may be obscure, but you *know* that everything you need to answer the questions is there for you.

 Don't let the selections intimidate you. No one is expected to be familiar with the topics, and everything you need to know for the questions is in the selection.

9

2. Surprise Beginnings

The psychological burden of confronting an unknown topic is compounded by the abruptness of the opening sentence of the selection. It would not be an exaggeration to call this the "surprise beginning."

You can get some idea of what to expect on your GRE from the following opening sentences that have appeared on previous tests:

Two relatively recent independent developments stand behind the current major research effort on nitrogen fixation, the process by which bacteria symbi-

(5) otically render leguminous plants independent of nitrogen fertilizer.[1]

Whether the languages of ancient American peoples were used for expressing abstract universal concepts can be

(10) clearly answered in the case of Nahuatl.[2]

Initially, the Vinaver theory that Malory's eight romances, once thought to be fundamentally unified, were in fact eight independent works produced both a

(15) sense of relief and an unpleasant shock.[3]

It is a popular misconception that nuclear fusion power is free of radioactivity; in fact, the deuterium-tritium reaction that nuclear scientists are currently

(20) exploring with such zeal produces both alpha particles and neutrons.[4]

EDUCATIONAL TESTING SERVICE, *GRE: PRACTICING TO TAKE THE GENERAL TEST*, 1995, P. 595.

[2]IBID, P. 614.

[3]IBID, P. 659.

[4]IBID, P. 712.

The selections went on to explain each of the notions in terms that we can all understand, even those of us who don't have any special background in these areas. But the initial jolt of the surprise beginning can be somewhat unpleasant. Again, don't let it panic you. Just keep reading in the assurance that everything you need to know to answer the questions will be right there for you.

TIP

> To mitigate surprise beginning shock, preview the first and last sentences of the selection before you begin your reading. They will tell you what the selection is about.

3. Compaction

The third added-difficulty factor used in the selections is compaction. The selections are not very long, but they are filled with information. For example, the selection introduced by the last "surprise beginning" sentence above (the one on nuclear fusion) is only seven sentences long. Yet, it supports *four* questions whose total word count is *greater* than the selection itself.

How is that possible? How can the questions be longer than the passage? The answer is compaction. The selection is carefully edited so that as much information as possible can be packed into a very few words.

Since the selections are so compact, you'll need to adapt your reading style to the GRE. Later today, you'll learn strategies for reading the selections that will help you overcome all three of the added-difficulty factors associated with the selections.

NOTE

> Because the selections are so compact, speed reading techniques are not useful and would even be counterproductive. The GRE stresses *comprehension* not *speed*.

Inside the Question Stems

The GRE uses exactly *six* different Reading Comprehension question stems. This may seem somewhat curious given the variety of topics mentioned above, but it's true. Regardless of topic, the same six questions are used over and over again. (Though not all six will necessarily be used on any given selection since there may be only three or four total.) The six types ask about different aspects of the selection:

1. Thesis or main idea

2. Facts or points specifically stated

3. Development or logical structure of the argument

4. Further implications or ideas that are logically deducible

5. Possible applications of the reading material

6. The author's judgment about the topic

9

It's important to learn what each of the six types of questions is asking for and what a correct answer will probably look like. Later, you'll learn more about each question type and how they are worded.

NOTE

The six question types reflect the GRE's theory that reading involves three skills: general understanding (thesis and development questions), specific understanding (fact questions), and drawing further conclusions (implication, application, and judgment questions).

Inside the Choices

The most striking difference between the exams you're used to taking and the GRE reading comprehension is the answer choices. An ordinary multiple-choice exam has short answers; the answer choices to a set of GRE reading comprehension questions may use *more* words than the selection itself. This, in and of itself, is an added-difficulty factor. Plus, the GRE can manipulate the length and wording of answer choices to move an item up or down the ladder of difficulty. For example, a Thesis question with short, uncomplicated choices might be situated on the lowest rung of the reading comprehension ladder, but a Thesis question worded in exactly the same way with long, convoluted choices could belong on the highest rung of the ladder.

Regardless of where on the ladder the question is situated, it is important for you to learn about the patterns that characterize right and wrong answers to each of the six question types. And later today, this will become a central feature in one of the Reading Comprehension Action Plans.

NOTE

The answer choices is where you'll do your "heavy lifting" in Reading Comprehension. The correct choice is surrounded by four "distractors" that are meant to draw your attention away from the right answer.

Each of the three parts of a Reading Comprehension exercise (the selection, the question stems, the answer choices) presents you with different challenges. You have to learn how to cope with each of the three aspects. And they are the subjects of the next three sections.

Learn Methods of Reading for Comprehension

You now know what to expect when you encounter a new selection: a strange topic, a surprise beginning, compact reading. You have to read the selection, but you can't read like you usually do. Instead, you have to read for the things that the GRE has put there for you to find. Here is the approach broken down for you step-by-step:

 Reading for Comprehension

Step 1: Read the first and last sentences. Begin your reading with the first and last sentences of the selection.

Step 2: Track the development. As you read through the selection, take note of the way the argument unfolds.

Step 3: Read "through" details. Don't try to memorize details. Try to understand what point is being made, but more importantly, make sure that you understand the position the detail occupies in the structure of the selection.

Step 4: Summarize the Development. After you've finished your reading and before you go to the first question, pause to summarize in your mind the development of the selection and the author's main point.

Step 1 of the Action Plan does two things. One, the first and last sentences taken together will help to neutralize the "surprise beginning" factor by giving you a general idea of what the passage is about—somewhat like having a headline over a newspaper article. Two, one of the sentences will usually include a statement of the main theme of selection. This is likely to be the answer to a Thesis question.

 The thesis or main idea of the selection is your key to understanding the selection. If you can articulate the main idea, then you'll understand the significance of the details and the other parts of the argument.

Step 2 of the Action Plan also does two things. First, you are tracking the development of the selection, and some questions ask about development of the selection directly. Plus, a clear understanding of the argument structure is essential to assessing the significance of details.

TIP

Transitions words are important. Some transition words signal a continuation of a line of thought: additionally, moreover, not only but, another, furthermore, moreover, and for example. Other transition words signal a reversal in a line of thought: however, on the other hand, but, and yet. And still others signal a conclusion: therefore, thus, in sum, and in short.

9

Step 3 of the Action Plan makes sure that you don't waste a lot of time on details. Your main objective is to understand what role the details play in the development of the selection. GRE Reading Comprehension is an "open book" test. You can always go back to the selection if you need to look up something.

CAUTION

Passages are sprinkled with undefined terms such as "oxidative metabolic sources," "extrasocial symbols," and "the Berkeley-Klaus model." You are not expected to know these terms in advance of your reading; and even though they appear in the selection, they may not turn up in a question.

Step 4 of the Action Plan helps you to digest what you've just read. Having a clear idea of the overall development of the selection is essential both to answering a Thesis question and to understanding how the various parts of the argument fit together.

TIP

Most selections contrast two points of view, e.g., the conventional theory and a recent finding, the dominant belief and a challenge, an outmoded view and the contemporary perspective.

Now let's apply the Action Plan for reading to a selection:

Government bailouts of failing banks and other institutions are harmful because moral-hazard incentives magnify truly exogenous shocks that confront financial
(5) systems. Indeed, moral hazard is the villain in the recent, unprecedented wave of financial system collapses. Banks willingly and knowingly take on more risks—especially default risks and
(10) exchange risks—than they would if they were not protected by government safety nets. Banking collapses lead to the fiscal insolvency of governments that bail out banks and to exchange rate collapse.
(15) In the absence of safety net distortions, macroeconomic shocks would encourage the opposite behavior—a reduction in bank risk exposure to reassure bank debt holders. But overly generous protection
(20) of banks insulates them from market discipline and makes them willing to increase their asset risk in the wake of adverse shocks. Banks are not the only entities protected by government safety
(25) nets: large, politically influential firms often receive implicit protection from the government on their debts, which encourages a similar tendency to bear risk.

The mechanism by which the bailout is
(30) usually funded, the general revenue fund, also results in economic dislocation because it entails large increases in taxation of average citizens to transfer resources to wealthy risk-takers. Tax
(35) increases are always distortionary and serve to accentuate the unequal wealth distribution. In addition, there is a longer term cost from the way bailouts affect the political process. Bailouts encourage
(40) crony capitalism in emerging market economies and thus stunt the growth of democracy and reform. Bailouts also undermine democracy and economic competition in industrialized countries
(45) because they are often a means for the executive to provide subsidies to international lenders and foreign governments without legislative approval under the guise of liquidity assistance.

(50) It is possible to provide banks with liquidity protection without bailouts through a responsible lender of last resort provided that the plan ensures market discipline. This presupposes, however, an
(55) *economic* and not a *political* definition of liquidity assistance. Politicians and bureaucrats often define "liquidity" crises and "liquidity" assistance broadly and vaguely to disguise transfers of wealth
(60) that have nothing to do with true liquidity assistance. Thus, the moral-hazard incentive re-emerges at the political level, and special interests will surely fight to preserve the mechanism that affords
(65) them the luxury of moral-hazard risk assumption. The challenge of political economy, then, is to design an alternative to bailouts that will survive the attack of special interests.

The first thing you'll notice is that this passage is characterized by the three added-difficulty factors mentioned above. First, the topic is not one that most people will be familiar with. (Even though the term "bailout" is occasionally in the news.) Second, the selection begins abruptly with its references to "bailouts" and "moral-hazard incentives." Finally, the prose is quite dense because the original publication from which this selection is excerpted was carefully edited to delete as many excess words as possible.

Step 1: The first sentence informs you that the selection is about bailouts, and the last sentence sets forth the conclusion of the argument: there is an alternative to bailouts.

Step 2: Read the passage, paying careful attention to the logical development.

9

In the first paragraph, the author states that moral- hazard incentives are the cause of financial system collapses and goes on to explain that moral-hazard incentives aggravate the effects of economic shocks by encouraging banks to take even greater risks. Collapses have other harmful effects, and other institutions are affected as well.

The second paragraph describes other harmful effects of bailouts. The "also" in the first sentence of the paragraph signals that the author is continuing with the list of harmful effects of bailouts. The "in addition" in the middle of the paragraph lets you know that the flow of the argument is continuing in the same direction. And the "also" in the last sentence of the paragraph signals yet another harmful affect of bailouts.

The third paragraph introduces a different or competing point of view: there is an alternative to bailouts. The author describes what the alternative might look like. Finally, the "then" in the last sentence lets you know that you are looking at a conclusion.

Step 3: The long list of harmful effects of bailouts is obviously important, but you don't have to memorize anything. The first paragraph discusses moral-hazard risk, which is defined implicitly. The second paragraph talks about tax implications and political consequences. And the final paragraph addresses the practical difficulties of introducing a plan with market discipline.

Step 4: The author says that bailouts are harmful in a lot of different ways. There is an alternative to bailouts, but whether or not such a plan would ever be accepted is problematic.

Now you've read the selection and understand the author's argument. You could write a summary of it in your own words, but that is not the way the GRE works. Instead, you'll be given three or four multiple-choice question that require you to map your understanding onto answer choices prepared by the GRE. In order to demonstrate that you really do understand the selection, you have to make sure you fit your understanding of what you've read into the questions that are asked. Learning how to do that is the next phase of your Action Plan. First, however, you should practice what you've learned about reading by doing Workshop A.

Workshop A

This workshop consists of a reading selection. Analyze it using the Action Plan for Reading in the way we did the passage above.

Drill

Disregarding the obvious differences in phrasing, scholars have tended to assimilate the "I am, I exist" of Descartes' *Meditations* to the "I think, therefore I am"
(5) which appears in Descartes' *Discourse on Method* published three years earlier. Hintikka, for example, treats both formulations as performative utterances when in fact only the former qualifies.

(10) The "cogito," in its familiar form of "I think therefore I am," appears in the *Discourse*; but in this rendering, Descartes is describing not an intuition of the thinking subject's existence but a deduc-
(15) tion from thought to existence. The particle "therefore" is a very clear signal and is absent in the formulation of the *Meditations*. Additionally, the first person point of view adopted in the *Meditations*
(20) is no mere accident of literary preference. The meditative posture is dictated by the philosophical and forensic exigencies of the case: there is no single, universal thinking subject who can assume the burden of
(25) demonstrating for all persons in all times the certainty of the "*I* am, *I* exist" that each individual ego must establish for itself.

This distinction is also supported by the development of Descartes' thought from
(30) the *Rules* to the *Discourse* and thence to the *Meditations*. In all three works, Descartes' skepticism about knowledge drives the argument. In the *Rules*, the doubt is not at all extraordinary; it is simply a
(35) resolve not to accept anything as true but can be "clearly and perspicuously" known and is directed primarily against the testimony of the senses which can be misleading. The skepticism of the *Rules* is the
(40) prudent mistrust of a scientist wishing to avoid rash conclusions. The theme of doubt is taken up again in the *Discourse* with renewed vigor. The skeptical attitude is no longer mere caution but a firm policy
(45) of refusing credence to anything that might be infected with falsity. It is in the *Meditations*, that Descartes' skepticism reaches its full power. The penultimate moment occurs with the addition of the hypothesis
(50) of the *malin genie* which, Descartes fears, might have deceived him regarding even those things that are taken for granted such as body, figure, extension, movement, and place. Skepticism cannot be maintained at
(55) this level, and doubt turns back on and destroys itself giving way to the certainty of the "I am, I exist."

The "I am, I exist" that results from the intensified skepticism of the *Meditations*
(60) is not merely a reformulation of the "I think, therefore I am" of the *Discourse*; it is an ontological rather than a logical claim. Respect for this crucial distinction would facilitate scholarly research into the
(65) significance of Descartes philosophical thought.

Review

Step 1: In the first sentence, the author states that scholars have tended to misinterpret Descartes' writings; and in the last, the author states that the distinction drawn in the selection would help researchers understand Descartes.

Step 2: The first paragraph sets forth the thesis of the selection. Then the second paragraph develops a reason supporting the thesis: the different wordings. The third paragraph provides another reason (the "also" in the first sentence is important): Descartes' philosophical skepticism grew stronger and stronger. And the final paragraph sets forth the conclusion of the argument.

Step 3: There are a lot of details in the passage that you may or may not need to understand. In the first paragraph, the author refers to Hintikka, apparently a philosopher who is one of those who, according to the author, misconstrued Descartes' writings. In the second paragraph, the author discusses the literary style of the various works in some detail. And in the third, the author contrasts them in terms of their philosophical content. All of this detail ultimately helps determine whether the argument is persuasive or not, but you don't have to worry about that issue. All you need to know is where the detail appears so that you can find it if you need it.

Step 4: The author argues that some scholars have overlooked an important distinction in Descartes' writings, discusses that distinction, and then concludes that scholars would benefit from paying attention to the differences outlined.

Master Techniques for Understanding Question Stems

Every GRE question stem falls into one of six categories, and the right and wrong answers are carefully written to fit the type of question. So the next step is for you to learn to recognize each of the six types.

ACTION PLAN **Identify each question as you come to it by its characteristic wording:**

1. Thesis. Thesis questions typically use a phrase like "main idea," "main purpose," or "primary concern."

2. Fact. Fact questions typically use a phrase like "according to the passage," "according to the author," or "the author mentions which of the following."

3. Development. A Development question may include a phrase such as "in order to," or it may directly ask "why" the author introduces an idea.

4. Implication. Implication questions uses phrases such as "inferred" or "suggests."

5. Application. Application questions are often characterized by the phrases "most likely" and "most probably."

6. Judgment. Judgment questions typically include phrases such as "author's attitude" or "tone."

Each of the six different question kinds asks about a different aspect of reading. If you can recognize each question type by its characteristic wording, then you'll be in a better position to know what kind of answer the GRE is looking for.

Thesis questions always ask you about the main point or the central theme of the passage. They are usually phrased like this:

The author is primarily concerned to . . .

The passage is chiefly concerned with . . .

Which of the following best expresses the main idea of the passage?

Which of the following titles best summarizes the content of the passage?

The author is primarily concerned with . . .

Every selection is edited so that it has a central thesis; and since "main idea" is a generic concept, the wording of Thesis questions doesn't vary from selection to selection. (The answer choices are very different, but that's a matter discussed below.) The correct answer to a Thesis question is always a summary of the central thesis of the selection.

TIP

> The phrases "main idea" and "primarily concerned" always signal a Thesis question.

Fact questions always ask you about an idea that is explicitly stated somewhere in the selection. Since the facts that are mentioned are different for each selection, the wording of Fact questions is context dependent and varies from selection to selection. Here are some examples:

According to the passage, the Missalifu Ice Floe is unusual because . . .

According to the author, early inhabitants of the Lesser Antilles had what type of kinship relationships?

The author mentions which of the following as a toxic byproduct of the Prekovian Reductive Cycle?

For each question like this, the correct answer is an idea explicitly mentioned somewhere in the selection.

> The phrases "according to the passage" and "according to the author" always signal a Fact question.

9

Development questions ask you about the structure of the selection, either about the overall development of the argument or about why the author made some particular point. Again, the correct answer to a Development depends on the logical structure of that particular selection, so the questions vary in their wording. Here are some examples:

The author mentions Carl Hempel (line 21) in order to . . .

Which of the following best explains why the author introduces the Freedom of Information Act in the second paragraph?

Why does the author cite Benedetto Croce in the first paragraph?

Which of the following best describes the overall structure of the selection?

The correct answer to a Development question always explains *why* the author did something in the selection.

> The phrases "in order to" and "why does" always signal a Development question.

Implication questions ask you about inferences that you can draw from the text of the selection. The following examples illustrate the typical wording of an Implications question:

Which of the following conclusions can be inferred from the discussion of the solar mass of a supernova in paragraph three?

The author suggests which of the following about the extinction of species in the atoll?

Words such as "inferred" and "suggests" signal Implication questions.

> **TIP** The phrases "implies," "suggests," and "inferred" always signal an Implication question.

Application questions are the most abstract of the six question types—even more abstract than Implications. Whereas Implications ask you for an inference based upon a particular reference, say a sentence or two, Applications often require you to distill the underlying thinking from a large part of the passage. Here are some examples:

With which of the following statements would the author most likely agree?

The author analysis of the ethical treatment of laboratory test animals could most easily be applied to which of the following situations?

Which of the following topics would be the most logical for the author to take up in the next paragraph of a continuation of the passage?

Since the correct answer to an Application question is correct not as a matter of explicit statement or logical inference, it is often the correct choice by default, that is, it is correct because the other choices are unsatisfactory. It is for this reason that this kind of question usually uses a phrase such as "most likely" or "most probably."

> **TIP** The phrases "most likely" and "least likely" usually signal an Application question.

The final type of question asks you about the author's Judgment on a topic. Here are some examples:

The author's attitude toward the proposed treaty can best be described as . . .

Which of the following best characterizes the tone of the selection?

This type of question requires you to determine how the author feels about a topic. You'll need to look for value judgments in words and phrases like "unfortunately," "happily," "justified," and "as expected."

> **TIP** The words "attitude" and "tone" always signal a Judgment question.

NOTE GRE questions are completely predictable. You don't even need to read the passage to know which of the categories a question belongs to.

Here are the question stems for the "bailout" passage, grouped according to category. Study them so that you know why each fits into the category that it does.

Thesis Questions

Each of the following questions asks about the central thesis of the selection:

1. Which of the following is the main point of the selection?
2. The author is primarily concerned with
3. Which of the following would be the most appropriate title for the selection?

Fact Questions

Each of the following questions asks about a fact specifically stated in the selection:

4. According to the passage, tax increases used to fund bailouts
5. According to the author, a reduction in assets risk in response to exogenous shocks would
6. The passage mentions all of the following as a harmful effect of bailouts EXCEPT:

Development Questions

Each of the following questions about the logical development of the selection:

7. Which of the following best describes the logical development of the selection?
8. Which of the following best describes why the author mentions politically influential firms at the end of paragraph one?
9. Which of the following best describes the logical function of the final paragraph?

Implication Questions

Each of the following questions asks about a further implication that can be drawn from the selection:

10. It can be inferred that the economic definition of liquidity assistance mentioned in line 39

11. The author implies that in an industrialized country the decision to provide subsidies to a foreign government should be

12. It can be inferred that in the absence of a government guaranteed safety-net, non-financial firms would respond to an exogenous shock by

Application Questions

Each of the following questions asks about a further application of the material given in the selection:

13. With which of the following statements would the author most likely agree?

14. The author is most likely addressing a meeting of

15. With which of the following statements would the author LEAST likely agree?

Judgment Questions

Each of the following questions asks about the author's attitude or tone:

16. The tone of the passage can best be described as

17. The author's attitude toward moral-hazard incentives is one of

18. The author regards an alternative to bailout assistance as

Workshop B

This Workshop will help you learn how to identify question stems by their unique wording.

Drill

The following question stems are based on the passage on Descartes that you read above. The purpose of this exercise is for you to practice identifying questions by their characteristic wordings. So identify the questions stems below using the following abbreviations:

T = Thesis question

F = Fact question

D = Development question

I = Implication question

A = Application question

J = Judgment question

There are six questions, more than you would have on an actual GRE passage. And there is one of each type of question.

1. The author is primarily concerned to   *T*

2. The author implies that the hypothesis of the *malin genie* (line 38) is   *I*

3. The author's attitude toward the scholars mentioned in paragraph one can best be described as   *J*

4. According to the author, Descartes used the first person point of view in the *Meditations* because it was   *F*

5. Which of the following best describes the logical development of the selection?   *D*

6. Which of the following topics would the author most likely take up in the next paragraph after the last to continue the discussion?   *A*

Review

1. This is a Thesis question. The "primarily concerned to" phrasing is typical of this question type.

2. This is an Implication question. The word "implies" definitely signals that this question is looking for a further inference that might be drawn from the selection.

3. This is a Judgment question. The "author's attitude toward something" format is a commonly used structure for a question that asks you to show that you know what judgment the author has made about a point.

4. This is a Fact question. The "According to . . . " wording is a dead give-away for this question, and it is asking about a detail that is specifically given somewhere in the selection.

5. This is a Development question. The phrase "logical development" explicitly says that you are supposed to describe the structure of the argument.

6. This is an Application question. The "most likely" is typical of this type of question. The question will ask that you apply your understanding of the selection to the answer choices to determine which is the "most likely" candidate for a fit.

Develop Strategies for Choosing Right Answers

Now you know how to read the selection to learn what you need to know for the specific purpose of answering GRE-type questions based on the particular text. And you've learned how to identify questions according to type so that you'll know what kind of correct answer choice to be looking for. In this section, you'll be concentrating on the choices in order to learn how the wrong answers differ from the correct response. The pattern is different for each of the six types.

ACTION PLAN **After you have identified the question type, identify the right answer.**

Thesis Questions

Right Answer: Describe the main theme of the selection

Wrong Answers: Describes only a subpart of the selection or refers to material beyond the passage altogether

Fact Questions

Wrong Answers: Nowhere mentioned in the text, a distorted rendering of a fact mentioned in the text, or a fact mentioned that is not responsive to the question asked

Development Questions

Right Answer: Explains *why* the author introduces a specific point or *how* the entire selection is organized

Wrong Answers: Fail to explain *why* the author makes a certain point or fail to explain *how* the selection is organized

Implication Questions

Right Answer: A statement logically inferrable from the text of the selection

Wrong Answers: Statements that do not follow from the text either because they are not supported or because they go too far

Application Questions

Right Answer: A statement that is *plausibly* a conclusion the author would accept

Wrong Answers: Statements that are *unlikely* to be conclusions the author would accept

Judgment Questions

Right Answer: A description that reflects the author's attitude or tone

Wrong Answers: Descriptions that are too positive, too negative, or simply not descriptive of the author's tone or attitude

Now let's apply the Action Plan for answers to the questions for the "bailout" passage that you read above.

Thesis Questions

QUESTION   1. Which of the following is the main point of the selection?

(A) The use of general tax revenues to fund bailouts of failing banks and other financial institutions is inequitable.

(B) Bank bailouts weaken democratic institutions and slow economic reform in both emerging and industrialized nations.

(C) Government bailouts of financial institutions cause harms that could be avoided by a system that imposes market discipline.

(D) Governmental manipulation of financial markets encourages financial institutions to assume risks greater than are warranted by economic considerations.

(E) Government spending relies on taxation and therefore manifests itself in harmful economic distortions.

ANALYSIS   The correct answer is **(C)**, as noted above in our discussion of the Action Plan for reading the selection. (A) and (B) refer to subparts of the discussion: (A) to the discussion in the second paragraph on taxation, and (B) to the discussion in the third paragraph. So neither can be a correct answer to a Thesis question. (D) and (E) go beyond the scope of the selection. Notice, for example, that neither of the choices mentions bailouts. They, too, must be wrong.

QUESTION   2. The author is primarily concerned with

(A) proving that government funded bailouts of banks and other financial institutions are inequitable

(B) highlighting the threat to democratic institutions and economic reform posed by bailouts

    (C) arguing that a plan imposing market discipline can avoid the harms caused by bailouts

    (D) demonstrating that moral-hazard incentives have been the cause of the recent rash of financial failures

    (E) protesting the practice of government intervention into financial markets

ANALYSIS The correct answer is **(C)**, for the reasons noted in the discussion of the preceding question. (A), (B), and (D) are all topics the author discusses, but they are subparts of the discussion. Because they refer to subparts and not the main thesis, none of the three could be the correct choice. (E) goes beyond the scope of the passage. Notice that (E) refers generally to "government intervention" and does not focus particularly on bailouts.

QUESTION 3. Which of the following would be the most appropriate title for the selection?

    (A) Inequitable Taxing Policies and Government Funded Bank Bailouts

    (B) Bank Bailouts as a Threat to Democratic Institutions and Economic Reform

    (C) Market Discipline as an Alternative to Harmful Bailouts of Financial Institutions

    (D) Moral-Hazard Incentives: The Dangers of Government Bailouts of Failing Financial Institutions

    (E) Government Spending: Inequities and other Market Distortions

ANALYSIS The correct answer is **(C)**, for the reasons given above. The only difference between this question and 1 and 2 is its format: what is the best title. You should apply the Action Plan for Thesis questions to this type of question just as you would to the others. (A) and (B) are wrong because, like (A) and (B) of the two questions above, they refer to subparts of the passage. (Tax and reform) (D) too refers to only a part of the selection. To be sure, the moral-hazard incentives offered by bailouts are an important topic of the selection, but (D) makes no mention of that other important element: how to fix the problem. (E) goes beyond the scope of the selection. It refers generally to "government spending" and is not focused on bailouts.

TIP | Look for the correct answer to a Thesis question in the first or last sentence of the selection.

Fact Questions

QUESTION 4. According to the passage, tax increases used to fund bailouts

(A) lead directly to the collapse of exchange rates

(B) shift power from the executive to the legislature

(C) encourage crony capitalism in emerging market economies

(D) prompt financial institutions to increase risk

(E) aggravate existing inequities in wealth distribution

ANALYSIS The correct answer is **(E)**. You'll find the reference that you need in the second sentence of the second paragraph. (E) doesn't exactly quote from the selection, but it is a pretty close restatement of the point that the author makes. The other choices refer to aspects of the passage, but even though they mention facts that appear in the selection, they are not answers to the question asked: what are the tax consequences of bailouts.

QUESTION 5. According to the author, a reduction in assets risk in response to exogenous shocks would

(A) insulate banks from market discipline

(B) alleviate concerns of a bank's debt holders

(C) transfer economic resources to wealthy risk-takers

(D) encourage influential firms to increase risks

(E) guarantee liquidity without tax increases

ANALYSIS The correct answer is **(B)**, and the reference that you need is in sentence four of the first paragraph: banks would try to appease debt holders by minimizing risk. The other choices use language that you can find at various places in the development, but none of the phrases is an appropriate response to the question "What would be the effect of reducing risk?"

QUESTION 6. The passage mentions all of the following as a harmful effect of bailouts EXCEPT:

(A) making moral-hazard risk more attractive to financial institutions

(B) arbitrarily redistributing wealth from one economic class to another

(C) weakening democratic institutions in emerging and industrialized nations

(D) encouraging crony capitalism in emerging markets

(E) increasing the number of banking institutions

The correct answer is **(E)**. Notice that this question uses what is called a "thought reverser:" EXCEPT. This is a fairly common feature of this type of question. The "EXCEPT" means that four of the five ideas are facts mentioned in the selection. The one that is not mentioned is the correct answer. You'll find the ideas mentioned by (A), (B), (C), and (D) in the selection, but the idea of an increase in the number of banking institutions does not appear.

CAUTION

> The correct answer to a Fact question must meet two criteria: explicitly stated in the text *and* responsive to the question asked. Some wrong answers meet the first but not the second.

Development

 7. Which of the following best describes the logical development of the selection?

(A) The author describes a problem and then proposes a possible solution.

(B) The author refutes a conventional explanation and then advances a new theory.

(C) The author defines a key concept and then discusses examples of the concept.

(D) The author lists several possible causes of a phenomenon and then analyzes one.

(E) The author criticizes a government policy and then assigns blame for its effects.

ANALYSIS The correct answer is **(A)**. This Development question is similar to a Thesis question, except that it asks about the *form* of the development rather than the *content*. (A) is correct for the reasons given in the discussion of the Thesis questions, above. (B) is wrong because, while the author criticizes a practice, the author does not refute a theory. (C) is wrong because the author does not define a key concept, e.g., the author uses "bailout" without offering a formal definition. (D) is incorrect because the author does not analyze just one cause or effect. And (E) is wrong because the main purpose of the selection is not to assign blame but to propose a solution to a problem.

QUESTION 8. Which of the following best describes why the author mentions politically influential firms at the end of paragraph one?

(A) To contrast the behavior of banks with that of non-financial institutions

(B) To draw a distinction between bailouts with acceptable and unacceptable consequences

(C) To demonstrate that the problem of moral-hazard risk is not restricted to banks

(D) To reconcile the need for liquidity assistance with dangers of abuse

(E) To prove that moral-hazard incentives are not unique to bailouts

ANALYSIS The correct answer is **(C)**. The author explains that bailouts create moral-risk incentives for banks and then adds that this affects other firms as well. (A) must be wrong since the author wants to suggest that the behavior of the non-banking firms is like that of banks—at least when it comes to bailout incentives. (B) must be wrong for the same reason, since the author regards the consequences as unacceptable in both cases. (D) would be an interesting answer had the question asked about the author's proposal: the author recognizes that a trade-off will be necessary. But the question did not ask for that answer. As for (E), while the phrase "not unique" is interesting, the rest of the wording of the choice makes it wrong because the author seems to think that the incentives are particularly strong in the case of bailouts.

QUESTION 9.   Which of the following best describes the logical function of the final paragraph?

(A) The author quantifies the extent of the problem discussed earlier.

(B) The author clarifies a key term that was used earlier in an ambiguous manner.

(C) The author begins a discussion of a new problem more serious than the one described earlier.

(D) The author outlines a possible alternative to the policies criticized earlier.

(E) The author invites the reader to formulate a solution to the problem described earlier.

ANALYSIS The correct answer is **(D)**. This type of question occupies a kind of middle ground between questions that ask about the overall logical development of the selection (see #7) and those that ask about the logical significance of a particular point (see #8). But there should be no mystery in how to approach it. (D) correctly states that the last paragraph contains the author's alternative solution. (A) is wrong because the author never offers quantification of the problem. (B) is wrong because the author does not clarify terminology, and you shouldn't confuse the point about the "economic" and "political" definitions in the final paragraph. The author there is not really defining terms but rather prescribing what ought to qualify as a definition: liquidity should be defined as an economic phenomenon and not be used as a term to justify government policy on an *ad hoc* basis. (C) is wrong because the alternative solution is not a new problem. And (E) is wrong because the author specifically proposes a solution and does not invite the reader to speculate.

> **TIP**
>
> Treat a Development question that asks about the overall structure of the passage just as you would a Thesis question. The correct answer will summarize the development without being too narrow or too broad.

Implications

QUESTION 10. It can be inferred that the economic definition of liquidity assistance mentioned in line 39

    (A) is narrower than the political definition

    (B) is used primarily by government officials

    (C) covers more cases than the political definition

    (D) obscures the need for liquidity assistance

    (E) increases reliance on government bailouts

ANALYSIS The correct answer is **(A)**. In the final paragraph, the author calls for an economist's use of the term liquidity and disparages the use of the term to justify government bailouts that are merely politically expedient. You can infer that the economist would apply to the term to fewer cases than the politician would. (B) is "in the right pew but the wrong church." (B) correctly implies that government officials use the term in a special way, but the danger is not that they use it "primarily" but that they use it in a bad fashion. (C) must be wrong for the reasons that (A) is correct. (D) is wrong for the same reason that (B) is correct: the term is used not to obscure need but to find need where there is none. And finally, (E) is wrong because a "tighter" definition of the sort called for by the author would mean fewer bailouts.

QUESTION 11. The author implies that in an industrialized country the decision to provide subsidies to a foreign government should be

    (A) the prerogative of the legislature and not the executive

    (B) a function entirely of the need for assistance and the ability to pay

    (C) determined by the executive on a case-by-case basis

    (D) contingent upon a commitment by the recipient to reduce moral-hazard risk

    (E) calculated according to an economic rather than a political formula

ANALYSIS   The correct answer is **(A)**. In the third paragraph, the author says that bailouts are often a subterfuge for the executive branch to funnel monies to a foreign government or firm without the approval of the legislative; and this practice, according to the author, is anti-democratic. So you can infer that the author believes this type of policy should be subject to legislative approval. (B) is incorrect since the author questions whether or not there really is a need for assistance. (C) is an interesting observation, but it is not responsive to the question asked. (D) is wrong because no such string is presently attached, and that is a problem, according to the author. Finally, (E) is wrong because politicians too often use a political rather than an economic formula to determine "need."

QUESTION   12. It can be inferred that in the absence of a government guaranteed safety-net, non-financial firms would respond to an exogenous shock by

(A) increasing risk to reassure debt holders

(B) reducing exposure to asset risk

(C) shifting economic resources to foreign markets

(D) transferring funds from one shareholder group to another

(E) abandoning crony capitalism in favor of democracy and reform

ANALYSIS   The correct answer is **(B)**, and the reference you need is in the comparison of non-financial firms to banks in the first paragraph. Since the author suggests that there is a parallel to be drawn between the two, you can infer that non-financial firms react to moral-hazard incentives in the same way that banks do: they'll take the guarantee and increase risk. (A) is wrong because increasing risk does not reassure debt holders. (C) and (D) simply go beyond anything suggested by the selection, e.g., where does the passage mention foreign markets or different shareholder groups. (E) overstates the author's cases. To be sure, you would expect that reform would tend to alleviate the harms identified by the author, but it goes beyond what you have available to you for the basis of a conclusion to suggest that crony capitalism would be *abandoned*.

MAKE CONNECTIONS | Drawing further conclusions is a topic covered in more detail in Day 25: "Teach Yourself Analytical Ability Questions." Pay particularly close attention to the material on reading choices carefully.

Application

QUESTION 13. With which of the following statements would the author most likely agree?

(A) A plan for a lender of last resort that includes a measure of market discipline would reduce moral-hazard incentives.

(B) Emerging market economies would be better advised to allow banks to fail during a liquidity crisis than offer any kind of government assistance.

(C) Non-financial institutions are more likely than banks to increase moral-hazard risk when a government safety net is assured.

(D) Bailouts could be financed out of the general revenue fund without side-effects if market discipline were a condition of assistance.

(E) Leaders of banks and other financial institutions would be less likely to increase risk if they were aware that they were responding to moral-hazard incentives.

ANALYSIS The correct answer is **(A)**. The key to an Application question is the "most likely" or similar wording. The correct answer to an Application question will not fit the text as neatly as the correct answer to an Implication question. The correct answer to an Application question will be correct because it is generally supported by the text and not because it is logically deducible. Here the author would likely agree with (A): lack of market discipline is the problem with moral-hazard incentives. (B) is wrong because the author does not say that banks should be allowed to fail. In fact, the last paragraph suggests that the author would strongly disagree with this statement since the author is proposing a plan for liquidity assistance—but one that avoids moral-hazard incentives by introducing market discipline. You should apply the same kind of thinking to choice (C) because the author would probably disagree with (C). In the first paragraph, the author lumps non-financial firms with banks insofar as their behavior in the presence of moral-hazard incentives is concerned. So the author would expect their behavior to be like that of banks, not different. (D) is just a confused reading of the passage. The economic distortion mentioned in paragraph two is a direct result of taxation not bailouts. And (E) is wrong because the author seems to think that leaders respond in a rational way to moral-hazard incentives: hey, the money's there so let's take advantage of it for our firm.

QUESTION 14. The author is most likely addressing a meeting of

(A) government policy makers

(B) leaders of emerging market countries

(C) heads of politically influential firms

(D) directors of banks and other financial institutions

(E) experts on the economic effects of taxation

ANALYSIS The correct answer is (A). You don't have any way of knowing where this article appeared. In fact, it is excerpted from the testimony given by an economist before a Congressional committee in a hearing on bailouts. While you could never reach that precise conclusion (except as a wild guess), you can figure out that it is probably addressed to policy makers who have the authority to entertain argument on the alternative plan suggested in the last paragraph. It would not be addressed to foreign leaders, nor to private firms, nor to tax experts. Those readers might have an interest in the topic, but the structure of the argument (identify the problem and propose a solution) indicates that none of those are the primary audience.

9

QUESTION 15. With which of the following statements would the author LEAST likely agree?

(A) A plan for government intervention in times of illiquidity is not necessary.

(B) Moral-hazard incentives have both financial and psychological appeal.

(C) Emerging market economies should be encouraged to adopt democracy and reform.

(D) Tax policies should be designed to minimize economic distortions.

(E) Bailouts are defended in political terms even when unnecessary in economic terms.

ANALYSIS The correct answer is (A), and the "LEAST" is a thought-reverser. Whereas in question 13 you were looking for the statement the author would endorse, here you are looking for the statement the author would *not* endorse. The author would not accept (A) for the very reason that the author has proposed an alternative to bailouts for addressing liquidity crises. The author would, however, probably accept (B), because the first paragraph indicates that firms are not acting irrationally when they "follow the money." (C) and (D) are ideas the author appears to endorse in paragraph two. And (E) is a direct consequence of a point made by the author in the final paragraph.

NOTE Application questions are the most abstract of the six types and therefore the most difficult. If you are getting a lot of Application questions, then you are probably working at the `very top of the ladder of difficulty for the Verbal Part.

Judgment

QUESTION 15. The tone of the passage can best be described as

(A) critical but professional

(B) laudatory but cautious

(C) neutral and indifferent

(D) derogatory and insensitive

(E) hypercritical and demeaning

ANALYSIS The correct answer is **(A)**. The author is critical of bailouts, but the critical evaluation is also professional

QUESTION 16. The author's attitude toward moral-hazard incentives is one of

(A) tolerance

(B) condemnation

(C) unconcern

(D) endorsement

(E) uncertainty

ANALYSIS The correct answer is **(B)**. The author is critical of moral-hazard incentives. Indeed, the very choice of phrasing to describe the phenomenon, *moral*-hazard, suggests that the author has very strong negative feelings about the phenomenon.

QUESTION 17. The author regards an alternative to bailout assistance as

(A) economically feasible but politically unacceptable

(B) politically desirable but theoretically impossible

(C) economically unnecessary but politically attractive

(D) politically contrived but economically sound

(E) theoretically possible but practically difficult

ANALYSIS The correct answer is **(B)**. The author proposes a plan in the last paragraph but acknowledges the political realities that make it difficult to implement.

TIP Often the answer choices to a Judgment question can be arranged on a scale from 1 to 5 where 1 is the most negative emotion and 5 the most positive. Then you can easily decide whether the author's judgment is positive or negative (eliminating two or three choices) and from there how strong the judgment is (leaving you with the correct choice).

Workshop C

This workshop will give you the opportunity to apply what you have just learned about right and wrong answers to the questions on the "Descartes" passage that you read earlier. If you need to, first refer to your classification of the items so that you'll know what kind of correct answer you're looking for.

Drill

9

1. The author is primarily concerned to

   (A) explore the history of skepticism in philosophical writings

   (B) demonstrate that Descartes' "cogito" has two different forms

   (C) refute the notion that "I think, I am" is a performative utterance

   (D) criticize Descartes for not being consistent in his treatment of the "cogito"

   (E) explain why Descartes used the first person point of view in the *Meditations*

2. The author implies that the hypothesis of the *malin genie* (line 50) is

   (A) used by Descartes in all of his important philosophical works

   (B) incidental to the skepticism expressed in the *Meditations*

   (C) uniquely a feature of the skepticism of the *Meditations*

   (D) a central element of Descartes' rules of scientific inquiry

   (E) a literary device that has little real significance in Descartes' writings

3. The author's attitude toward the scholars mentioned in paragraph one can best be described as

   (A) critical

   (B) enthusiastic

   (C) supportive

   (D) neutral

   (E) rancorous

4. According to the author, Descartes used the first person point of view in the *Meditations* because it was

   (A) less likely to be misunderstood by subsequent scholars than another point of view

   (B) the only point of view appropriate to an argument that did not rely on skepticism

   (C) uniquely suited to demonstrate the certainty of the conclusion "I am, I exist"

   (D) best calculated to ensure that the reader would not be mislead by the senses

   (E) more suitable to a work on philosophy than to a work on scientific theory

5. Which of the following best describes the logical development of the selection?

   (A) The author outlines a commonly accepted theory and then provides new evidence for it.

   (B) The author claims conventional wisdom is mistaken and offers proof for that claim.

   (C) The author cites an authority on a topic and then demonstrates the authority is wrong.

   (D) The author reviews the history of a philosophical debate and offers a new interpretation.

   (E) The author presents conflicting interpretations of a point and then reconciles them.

6. Which of the following topics would the author most likely take up in the next paragraph after the last to continue the discussion?

   (A) A discussion of the concept of performative utterance and how it might apply to Descartes' writings

   (B) A listing of other writers who have used skepticism as an important element in their philosophical writings

   (C) A detailed examination of Descartes' conclusions about scientific observation in the *Rules*

   (D) A comparison of the philosophy of Descartes with the philosophy of Hintikka

   (E) A history of the development of philosophy since Descartes wrote the Meditations

Review

1. The correct answer is **(B)**; and, as suggested, you can find the answer in the first sentence. (A) is too broad: the author does not offer a general *history*. (C) is too narrow: the only reference to performative utterance is in the first paragraph. (D) is wrong because the author does not criticize Descartes himself. And (E) is wrong because this idea is but a part of the selection.

2. The correct answer is **(C)**. The author comments that the thesis of the *malin genie* is the penultimate step in the development of the *Meditations*. You can infer, therefore, that it appears only there. Additional support is provided by the discussion about the special role of skepticism in the argument of the *Meditations*. Since the other choices are statements that contradict this idea, they must be wrong.

3. The correct answer is **(A)**. The author says that scholars such as Hintikka have fallen into error because they do not realize that there are two formulations for the "cogito." You can arrange the choices, from negative to positive, in the following way: E . . A . . D . . C . . B. The author's judgment is negative, so you can eliminate (B), (C), and (D). But the judgment isn't highly negative, so (A) is the best answer.

4. The correct answer is **(C)**. In the third paragraph the author explains that the skepticism of the *Meditations* is of a different order of magnitude than that that appears in earlier works and that it culminates in the second formulation of the "cogito." (A) is simply not mentioned in the selection, and (B) is contradicted by the correct answer. (D) and (E) represent confused readings of facts mentioned in the passage.

5. The correct answer is **(B)**. You can treat this Development question as you would a Thesis question. (B) is correct for the reasons given in the discussion of #1 above.

6. The correct answer is **(A)**. With an Application question, you are often looking for the "best of the worst." Since there is no strictly logical basis for preferring one choice to another, you are looking for any "peg to hang your hat on." Here a good peg is provided by the first paragraph. The author refers to Hintikka noting that failure to observe the distinction between the formulations led him into error. An appropriate continuation would be to apply the distinction on behalf of the mistaken scholars. (B) is an interesting idea, but there is no "peg" to hang this choice on. (C) is also interesting but the mention of the *Rules* is primarily to set up the discussion for the *Meditations*, so there is no reason for the author to return to this topic. (D) has some merit, but it is really an overstatement of (A). Finally, (E) is just too broad: an entire history?

9

Get Answers to Frequently Asked Questions

Q: **How long should I spend on Reading Comprehension?**

A: About two minutes to read the passage and then one minute per question. This works out to five minutes per Reading Comprehension exercise (assuming three questions); and since you'll probably have three exercises, you'll spend a total of 15 minutes on Reading Comprehension. If you check the recommended time allocations for the other question types for this part, you'll see that this puts you on schedule to finish within the 30 minutes time limit.

Q: **Does this assume that I know speed reading?**

A: No. First of all, remember that this is a test of *comprehension* not *speed*. Second, the Action Plan for reading the selection was designed to keep you from wasting time in order to make sure that you'd be able to finish the reading itself in about two minutes.

Q: **What if I really don't know anything about the topics I see?**

A: Then you're normal. You're not expected to know anything at all—except how to read. Everything you need to answer the question is right there in the selection.

Q: **What should I do now?**

A: If you have time, it would be a good idea to do the practice in the lesson for Day 10. If not, then you should proceed directly to Day 11 and take the Verbal PostTest. It'll allow you to practice everything that you've learned in Days 3 through 9.

Today's Review

1. Reading Comprehension appears in the verbal part of the GRE and tests reading *comprehension* and not *speed* or *prior knowledge* or anything else.

2. GRE Reading Comprehension is not just reading and answering questions. There are added-difficulty factors for the selection, for the question stems, and for the answer choices.

3. You have an Action Plan for reading the selection that is designed to give you everything you need to know to answer questions without getting sidetracked.

4. You have an Action Plan for identifying question stems because each of the six types calls for a different kind of right answer.

5. You have an Action Plan for pinpointing the right choice and avoiding the wrong choices for each of the six question kinds.

Day

10

Apply Your Action Plan to Reading Comprehension

Today, you'll assemble all the pieces to the Action Plan that you developed in Day 9. After a quick review of some important points, you'll revisit the Reading Comprehension from the PreTest to see how the Action Plan would have helped you perform better. Then you'll have the opportunity to do timed exercises for further practice and to see the Action Plan applied to those items.

Review Your Action Plan

In Day 9, you developed an Action Plan for Reading Comprehension. You'll recall that the plan treats Reading Comprehension not as a routine "read this and answer that" exercise but as a highly specialized question type created especially for the GRE. The plan was developed in three parts: Reading for Comprehension, Identifying Question Stems, and Selecting the Right Choice. The complete plan looks like this:

ACTION PLAN

The Reading Comprehension Action Plan

Read for Comprehension

Step 1: Read the first and last sentences.

Step 2: Track the development.

Step 3: Read "through" details.

Step 4: Summarize the development.

Identify Question Stems and Choose the Right Answer

What You'll Do Today

- Review Your Action Plan
- Apply Your Action Plan to the PreTest
- Workshop A
- Workshop B
- Get Answers to Frequently Asked Questions

Thesis Questions

Right Answer: Describes the main theme of the selection

Wrong Answers: Describes only a subpart of the selection or refers to material beyond the passage altogether

Fact Questions

Right Answer: Specifically mentioned in the text (though perhaps not in the same words)

Wrong Answers: Nowhere mentioned in the text, a distorted rendering of a fact mentioned in the text, or a fact mentioned that is not responsive to the question asked

Development Questions

Right Answer: Explains *why* the author introduces a specific point or *how* the entire selection is organized

Wrong Answers: Fail to explain *why* the author makes a certain point or fail to explain *how* the selection is organized

Implication Questions

Right Answer: A statement logically inferrable from the text of the selection

Wrong Answers: Statements that do not follow from the text either because they are not supported or because they go too far

Application Questions

Right Answer: A statement that is *plausibly* a conclusion the author would accept

Wrong Answers: Statements that it is *unlikely* the author would accept

Judgment Questions

Right Answer: A description that reflects the author's attitude or tone

Wrong Answers: Descriptions that are too positive, too negative, or simply not descriptive of the author's tone or attitude

Now let's apply the integrated plan to the items from the PreTest.

Apply Your Action Plan to the PreTest

Here's how the Action Plan would have helped you. The following items appeared on the Verbal PreTest in Day 2. (You'll probably need to refer to the reading passages on pages 29 and 31 to refresh your memory.)

The first passage is longer than those you'll encounter when you take the GRE on computer. The extra length was good practice, and now you can use the passage to explore the Action Plan in greater detail. First, read the passage:

Step 1: Read the first and last sentences.

Here are the first and last sentences:

> Silicon carbide is a highly promising material for many semiconductor applications, numbering among its other advantages excellent physical stability and hardness, great strength at high temperatures, high thermal conductivity, and a low friction of coefficient, all of which make it particularly useful for integrated circuits operating under extreme conditions.

> Silicon carbide films grown from C_{60} may, therefore, present opportunities for application not previously considered.

These two sentences alone tell you quite a lot about the passage. The topic is silicon carbide and, more particularly, some engineering uses of silicon carbide. According to the first sentence, the material has some nice advantages; and according to the last sentence, it presents new opportunities. You can imagine that the passage will be filled with details about these advantages and new opportunities. And you can expect that the correct answer to a thesis question will be something like "silicon carbide film from C_{60} is an important new engineering material."

Step 2: Track the development.

The second sentence of the first paragraph notes that large-area crystals are hard to grow, but then the first sentence of the second paragraph (note the "however") announces a shift in the author's thinking: a new technique exists. The second paragraph then goes on to describe the new technique.

The third paragraph provides further information about the new technique. Then the fourth paragraph describes some potential uses of the new microcomponents, e.g., aircraft components and microelectromechanicalsystems, and explains why they are useful.

Step 3: Read "through" details.

The passage is filled with detail. For example, in the second paragraph the author mentions other members of the carbon family. The second paragraph also explains how components are made using the new technique. The third paragraph talks about newtons and micrometers and so on. This is all heavy going, so don't try to become an expert in silicon technology. Just make a note of where to find the details if you need them. The fourth paragraph talks about applications of the new technology. Again, don't try to learn what they are, just make a note that the fourth paragraph is the place to look in case a question asks about them.

Step 4: Summarize the Development.

The passage talks about silicon carbide. The material has advantages. A new technique gives it even more potential. There is a lot of discussion of the technical details for making the stuff. It's good in airplanes and other applications for several reasons. And, all in all, it has great potential.

That gives you a pretty good look at a very long and difficult passage. Now turn to the questions. For each question, you'll want to identify the category to which the stem belongs and then identify the correct answer using the patterns you've learned.

Identify Question Stems and Choose the Right Answer

QUESTION   17. Which of the following would be the most appropriate title for the passage?

(A) The Use of Elemental Carbon as a Component in the Manufacture of Silicon Carbide Microchips

(B) Possible Electrical and Mechanical Applications of Silicon Carbide Microchip Technology

(C) New Techniques for Manufacturing and Using Silicon Chips for Electrical and Mechanical Applications

(D) Some Challenges to Producing Silicon Carbide Microchips for Use in Microelectromechanical Systems

(E) Semiconductor Applications for Silicon Carbide Made Possible by New Manufacturing Techniques

ANALYSIS   This is a thesis question, and the correct answer is (**E**). Notice especially that (E) uses the phrase "new manufacturing techniques," a topic of importance in the selection. By contrast, (A) is too narrow in scope. It seems to refer only to paragraph two where the author mentions elemental carbon during the discussion of the manufacturing process. (B) also is too narrow in scope. It seems to refer only to the final paragraph where the author discusses possible applications. (C) is perhaps the second best choice; but it mentions silicon chips, and the passage is about silicon carbide. (D) is too narrow in two respects: the manufacturing difficulties (as opposed to the new techniques) are a subpart of the selection found in paragraph one, and the microelectromechical use is only one of the applications discussed in paragraph four.

QUESTION   18. The passage mentions all of the following as advantages of silicon carbide EXCEPT:

(A) strength at high temperatures

(B) high thermal conductivity

(C) excellent physical stability

(D) relative ease of manipulation

(E) low friction of coefficient

ANALYSIS   This is a fact question, and the correct answer is **(D)**. Often fact questions include a thought-reverser, as this one does here. So four of the five choices are explicitly mentioned in the selection. You're looking for the one that is not mentioned. The advantages of silicon carbide are mentioned in the first sentence and include stability, high temperature strength, high temperature conductivity, and low friction of coefficient. (D), however, is not mentioned there.

QUESTION   19. According to the passage, it is possible to maneuver microcomponents into position on a film of silicon carbide thicker than one micrometer because

(A) an atomic force microscope applies force in the range of 10^{-8} N

(B) C_{60} does not react readily with silicon dioxide   *Not responsive*

(C) such films have relatively weak adhesive properties

(D) C_{60} has a perfect soccer-ball-like structure   *Not resp*

(E) C_{60} has great surface mobility and diffuses into all areas   *Not resp*

ANALYSIS   This is a fact question, and the correct answer is **(C)**. In the second sentence of the third paragraph, the author specifically says that the adhesion of films thicker than one micrometer is relatively weak and this allows microcomponents to be manipulated on their surface. Notice that choice (C) doesn't quote from the selection, but it does express substantially that idea even if in somewhat different terms. (A) is a fact mentioned in the paragraph, but remember that in order to be a correct answer to a fact question the choice has to satisfy two criteria: stated in the text and responsive to the question. (A) is a fact stated in the passage, but it is not responsive to the question. What the microscope can do is not the same as what the film is susceptible to. (B), (D), and (E) are also a facts mentioned in the passage, but they are mentioned in the second paragraph in the discussion of the manufacturing process.

10

QUESTION 20. The author mentions dry etching and chemical-vapor deposition techniques (lines 14–16) primarily in order to

(A) illustrate some of the advantages of silicon carbide technology over conventional semiconductor technology

(B) highlight the shortcomings of silicon carbide microcomponents when compared with silicon chips *Not comparing w/ silicon chips*

(C) establish that certain common manufacturing techniques cannot be used with silicon carbide

(D) suggest some ways of overcoming the difficulty of working with silicon carbide

(E) define more precisely the physical processes at work in silicon carbide components

ANALYSIS This is a development question, and the correct answer is **(C)**. In the first paragraph, the author explains that silicon carbide is difficult to work with and adds that two techniques, dry etching and chemical-vapor, are not particularly useful. So the question is why the author mentions those two techniques by name, and the answer is in order to preempt any objection that they might overcome the difficulties of working with the material. (A) is incorrect because this is not an idea connected with the reference you are given. The author has mentioned advantages of silicon carbide, but the question refers you to where the author is talking about production problems. As for (B), the comparison of silicon carbide and silicon chips comes in the last paragraph. (D) is wrong because the previously available technologies did not work with silicon carbide. And (E) is wrong because this discussion doesn't come until the next paragraph.

QUESTION 21. It can be inferred that silicon carbide microcomponents may be useful in microelectromechanical systems because

(A) silicon carbide film has a comparatively low coefficient of friction

(B) silicon carbide has high electrical conductivity

(C) microelectromechanical systems operate at extreme temperatures and pressures

(D) C_{60} has considerable surface mobility and diffuses rapidly into obscured areas

(E) carbon molecules adhere easily to bare silicon but are deflected by silicon oxide

ANALYSIS This is an implication question, and the correct answer is **(A)**. The answer to this type of question will not be explicitly given in the selection, but it will be clearly inferrable from the information given. The material you need is in the last paragraph where the author is discussing uses for silicon carbide microcomponents. There the author explains that these components have the advantage of improved wear in microelectromechanical systems and mentions their lower coefficient of friction. From this, you can infer that it is the lower coefficient of friction that provides the advantage. (B) seems to be a misreading of paragraph one where it is stated that silicon carbide has high *thermal* conductivity; and, in any case, the fourth paragraph states that silicon carbide may not be suitable for all electrical uses. The idea of extreme temperature and pressure can be found in paragraph four but in connection with systems such as airplane engines, not microelectromechanical systems. (D) and (E) are features of the manufacturing process, not aspects of the applications.

QUESTION 22. The use of concentrated hydrofluoric acid (lines 35–37) is most like which of the following?

(A) adding a new ingredient to a mixture to produce a new chemical

(B) breaking a mold to leave behind a product with a particular shape

(C) removing a naturally occurring impurity from raw ore during refining

(D) reconditioning a surface by scrubbing in order to remove contaminants

(E) applying a finish coat to protect the painted surfaces of a new product

ANALYSIS This is an application question, and the correct answer is (**B**). The author describes the manufacturing process in the second paragraph. It begins with creating a pattern of silicon dioxide on a silicon wafer. Then, the wafer is "doused" with carbon which sticks to the wafer but not to the silicon dioxide that defines the pattern. Later, the silicon dioxide is washed off with acid leaving behind the silicon carbide film that formed during the process. It's kind of like making a mold and filling it up and then breaking away the mold to leave the finished product. It's not a perfect analogy, but you have to remember that the correct answer to an application question is the one that is "most likely" or some similar wording. The explanations given by the other choices are interesting but they aren't analogous to the process described in the selection.

QUESTION 23. The author's attitude toward the use of silicon carbide can best be described as

(A) qualified optimism

(B) fatalistic discouragement

(C) calculated indifference

(D) unrestrained enthusiasm

(E) sincere resignation

ANALYSIS This is a judgment question, and the correct answer is (**A**). The phrase "highly promising" in the first sentence tells you immediately that the author has a positive attitude about this new technology, so you can eliminate (B), (C), and (E) using the "negative to positive" technique. The only question that remains is whether the author's attitude is wildly enthusiastic or just fairly positive, and the fact that the author discusses limitations as well as advantages lets you know that the author's enthusiasm is not unbridled.

10

Now let's look at the second passage that appeared on the PreTest:

Step 1: Read the first and last sentences.

The first and last sentences of the selection are:

> Early criminal law, which grew out of the blood feud, was almost totally lacking in the modern ethical notion of wrongdoing.

> The fact that early law attributed responsibility to insensible objects is further indication that the notion of ethical wrongdoing was a much later innovation.

The two sentences tell you that the topic is the early criminal law and that the selection tries to prove that the idea of ethical wrongdoing was absent during the earliest stages of the law's development.

Step 2: Track the development.

The first paragraph goes on to explain the idea of the blood feud. and how monetary compensation arose as an alternative. The second paragraph sites a "parallel development" in the institution of the *deodand* which called for the surrender of the instrumentality of death in a case involving a fatality. These two themes are subarguments that support the main claim that the ethical notion of wrongdoing came into the law only at some later stage.

Step 3: Read "through" details.

Remember that you don't have to memorize details. In the first paragraph, for example, the last sentence gives an illustration. Don't worry about the details of the illustration (what the injury was, how much it cost, who set up the law, etc.), just remember that at the end of the paragraph there is an illustration. Similarly, in paragraph two, the author mentions several objects that might be subject to forfeiture. You don't need to know this list, just that there is a list in that paragraph if a question asks about such objects.

Step 4: Summarize the Development.

The thesis of the argument is that, contrary to what one might believe, certain ethical considerations were not a part of the early law. The author offers two main arguments for this thesis.

Now let's turn to the questions.

Identify Question Stems and Choose the Right Answer

QUESTION   24. The primary purpose of the passage is to

(A) compare and contrast the roles of the wer and the deodand in the early stages of the law's development

(B) argue that early criminal law was lacking one of the important elements of modern criminal law

(C) theorize about the origins of the kinship relations that gave rise to the practice of the blood feud

(D) discuss some possible implications of early notions of criminal liability for modern legal systems

(E) identify various economic and social factors that lead eventually to the decline of the wer and deodand

10

ANALYSIS   This is a thesis question, and the correct answer is **(B)**. The first and last sentences as well as the summary of the development given above show that (B) must be the correct choice. (A) is wrong because, though the author refers to both ideas and calls them "parallel," the passage doesn't compare and contrast them. They are treated as independent pieces of evidence for the main theme. (C) goes beyond the scope of the passage: the kinship relations are taken as a given for purposes of the argument. (D) is perhaps the second best answer because one implication of the argument is that our notions of right and wrong came into the law later, but a further implication of the text is not its main idea. And finally, (E) goes beyond the scope of the passage because it refers to later history that the author does not discuss.

QUESTION   25. The author cites the decree of King Howell the Good in order to

(A) clarify the distinction between the requirements of the wer and the deodand

(B) prevent a possible misunderstanding about forfeiture in cases involving fatalities

(C) demonstrate that violence and physical injury were common occurrences during the period of the blood feud

(D) prove that the wer was a function of public injury to clan honor rather than physical injury to the victim

(E) suggest that modern criminal law is more concerned with ethical notions that monetary compensation

ANALYSIS This is a development question, and the correct answer is **(D)**. In the first paragraph where the author mentions King Howell the Good, the author is discussing the system of monetary compensation that arose to replace the vengeance of the blood feud. So the mention must be an illustration of that point. And, in fact, the details of the illustration show that a thumb, which has earning potential, was valued less than a highly visible scar to the face, which did not impede the ability of the injured person to earn a living but which was highly embarrassing to the clan. (A) and (B) have to be wrong since they refer to ideas that are not developed until the second paragraph. (C) is an interesting idea and is suggested by the word "barbaric," but an implication is not an answer to a development question. Finally, (E) does not answer the question: *why* does the author mention Howell?

QUESTION 26. The author's argument would be most strengthened by discovery of an early case that

    (A) established the wer for a visible bruise at double that for a similar bruise concealed by clothing.

    (B) relieved the owner of an object from the obligation of forfeiture if the owner was not at fault

    (C) refused to apply the requirement of the deodand because the instrument of death had been misused by the fatally injured person

    (D) required the payment of damages in equal amount for injuries to two persons of the same clan of unequal rank

    (E) stated that the amount of wer to be levied should be determined in large measure by the evil intention of the wrongdoer

ANALYSIS This is an application question, and the correct answer is **(A)**. Remember that with an application question, you have to abstract from the information given and reach a further conclusion. The essence of the *wer* was compensation in lieu of vengeance, and an important element of the argument is that humiliation counted for more than physical pain and suffering. The finding suggested by (A) supports this idea. (B) and (C) would actually weaken the author's argument about the *deodand*. (D) would weaken the argument about the *wer* because it implies that all clan members were equal, whereas the *wer*, as described by the author, assumed that some were more important than others. And (E) is wrong because the whole point of the argument is that ethical notions such as evil intent weren't a part of the early law.

QUESTION 27. It can be inferred from the passage that the establishment of the *wer* was intended to

(A) deter malefactors from inflicting injury on innocent people

(B) maintain public order by providing for alternative dispute resolution

(C) punish wrongdoers for breaking the law against injuring another

(D) prevent clan members from suing another clan for a wrongful injury

(E) discourage careless practices by making owners liable for injuries

ANALYSIS This is an implication question, and the correct answer **(B)**. The author refers to the *wer* as a tariff that represented an alternative to the feud. (A), (B), and (E) are wrong because satisfaction of the blood lust was the key factor in the early law—not deterrence or punishment. As for (D), the author is talking about a time before there were even courts of law.

Now you have seen how the entire Action Plan is applied to Reading items. In the workshops that follow, you'll be given a chance to apply it under timed conditions.

10

Workshop A

This workshop consists of drill, evaluation, and review. The drill has a time limit, but you should spend as much time as you need on the evaluation and review portions of the workshop.

Drill

This drill consists of two Reading Comprehension selections each with three questions. The time limit is ten minutes. This reflects the general strategy of spending *on average* two minutes reading the passage and one minute per question.

6 Questions • Time—10 Minutes

DIRECTIONS: Each selection below is followed by questions based on its content. After reading a selection, choose the best answer to each question, answering on the basis of what is *stated* or *implied* in the selection.

Except that their output is alternating current rather than direct current, electro-mechanical batteries, or EMBs, would power an electric car in the same way as a bank of electrochemical batteries.
(5) The modular device contains a flywheel stabilized by nearly frictionless magnetic bearings integrated with a special ironless generator motor and housed in a sealed vacuum enclosure. The EMB is "charged"
(10) by spinning its rotor to maximum speed with an integral generator/motor in its "motor mode." It is "discharged" by slowing the rotor of the same generator/motor to draw out the kinetically stored
(15) energy in its "generator mode." Initial research focused on the possibility of using one or two relatively large EMBs, but subsequent findings point in a different direction.
(20) Compared to stationary EMB applications such as with wind turbines, vehicular applications pose two special problems. Gyroscopic forces come into play whenever a vehicle departs from a straight-line course,
(25) as in turning. The effects can be minimized by vertically orienting the axis of rotation, and the designer can mount the module in limited-excursion gimbals to resist torque. By operating the EMB modules in pairs—
(30) one spinning clockwise and the other counterclockwise—the net gyroscopic effect on the car would be nearly zero.

The other problem associated with
(35) EMBs for vehicles is failure containment.
Any spinning rotor has an upper speed limit
determined by the tensile strength of the
material from which it is made. On the other
hand, at a given rotation speed, the amount
(40) of kinetic energy stored is determined by
the mass of the flywheel. It was originally
thought that high-density materials such as
metals were optimal for flywheel rotors,
and a metal flywheel does store more
(45) energy than an equivalent-size flywheel
made of low-density material and rotating
at the same speed. However, a low-density
wheel can be spun up to a higher speed until
it reaches the same internal tensile stresses
(50) as the metal one, where it stores the same
amount of kinetic energy at a much lower
weight. Lightweight graphite fiber, for
example, is more than ten times more
effective per unit mass for kinetic energy
(55) storage than steel. Plus, tests show that a
well-designed rotor made of graphite fibers
that fails turns into an amorphous mass
of broken fibers. This failure is far more
benign than that of metal flywheels, which
(60) typically break into shrapnel-like pieces
that are difficult to contain.

Not only is the uncontrolled energy that
can be released by each unit reduced, but
the danger posed by a failed rotor is
(65) very small compared to that of rotors just
two or three times larger. Thus, an array
of small EMB modules offers major
advantages over one or two large units.

1. The author is primarily concerned to

   (A) describe technological advances
       that make possible containment of
       uncontrolled kinetic energy discharge
       due to cataclysmic rotor failure

   (B) report on new technologies that will
       make electric cars competitive with
       vehicles employing conventional
       internal combustion engines

   (C) argue that an array of small EMB
       modules mounted in an electric car
       is more energy efficient than a
       single large EMB

   (D) construct field tests that will prove
       whether or not mobile EMBs can
       be arranged so as to minimize
       unwanted torque

   (E) demonstrate how a group of small
       EMB modules for use in an electric
       car can avoid technological problems
       associated with a single large EMB

2. It can be inferred that a non-metallic, low-
   density flywheel that has stored kinetic
   energy equivalent to that of a metallic,
   high-density flywheel is

   (A) operating in its "motor mode" and
       discharging energy as it spins

   (B) oriented vertically to the axis of
       rotation of the metallic flywheel

   (C) spinning in the opposite direction
       of the metallic flywheel

   (D) rotating at a higher speed than the
       metallic fly-wheel

   (E) made of graphite fibers that disinte-
       grate into harmless fragments upon
       failure

10

3. With which of the following statements would the author of the passage LEAST likely agree?

(A) Gyroscopic forces in applications such as wind turbines are not relevant factors because wind turbines remain in one place.

(B) Lightweight non-metallic flywheels made of materials such as graphite fiber are less likely to fail at maximum stress than non-metallic flywheels.

(C) An array of small EMB modules can provide the same amount of energy to the system of an electric car as one or two relatively large EMBs.

(D) The amount of kinetic energy that can be stored by a flywheel is a function of the weight of its constituent materials and its maximum rotational speed.

(E) Technological innovations such as frictionless bearings can help to make electromechanical batteries sufficiently efficient for use in electric cars.

The tendency of formalistic labor market historians to focus on status has made it difficult for these scholars to understand the fundamental forces that
(5) have shaped the structure of labor markets. On their view, at the beginning of the nineteenth century, workers were differentiated by skill, income, and relative opportunities for advancement. The unskilled fared poorly.
(10) Laborers, weavers, and mill workers, who constituted perhaps forty percent of the urban working class, received about a dollar per day. Skilled workers—variously known as craftsman, artisans,
(15) or mechanics—received nearly double that. Working with others as journeymen in small shops directed by master craftsmen who supervised the production of goods for a custom market, they could
(20) realistically anticipate becoming masters someday.

A hundred years later, little had changed in terms of the formal structure. In the typical shop the master was still the chief,
(25) and the craftsmen he presided over still owned their tools. But masters had begun to demand greater productivity from skilled workers and to resort to cheaper labor—prisoners, women, children, and the
(30) unskilled. The conclusion of formalistic scholars was that the master, motivated by greed, had found ways to exploit workers for greater profit.

While it cannot be denied that the lot
(35) of workers was by and large an unhappy one, this analysis fails to address a fairly obvious question: why, suddenly, had masters become greedy? In fact, they had not. Improvements in turnpikes or toll
(40) roads, the introduction of steamboats on canals, and the construction of railroads sharply reduced transportation costs and enabled sellers to compete successfully in distant markets, opening up great
(45) profit-making opportunities to efficient large-scale manufacturers.

Merchants possessed substantial capital and easy access to credit that enabled them to contract for massive orders all *(50)* over the country. The size of their operations allowed them to cut prices below those fixed by masters and journeymen. The masters became small contractors employed by the merchant capitalist and, in turn, *(55)* employed one to a dozen journeymen. Since the profits of masters came solely out of wages and work, they sought to lessen dependence on skill and to increase productivity. Limited custom order and *(60)* local trade gave way to a massive national market, inevitably affecting the conditions of the workers who produced for this market. By this time, the master, the traditional locus of authority in the pri- *(65)* vate shop, had ceased to exist except in name only.

4. Which of the following best describes the logical structure of the question in line 37?

(A) A challenge to the formalistic theory the answer to which undermines the assumption that masters were greedy.

(B) A rhetorical device that has no correct or incorrect answer but serves to focus the reader's attention on the role of the master.

(C) A suggestion that further research is needed before it can be determined whether masters were the villains or the victims of changing labor market conditions.

(D) An inquiry into the fundamental conditions of labor markets in the 19th Century that can only be answered in light of further research.

(E) A question with a hidden assumption that contradicts what the formalistic historians believed about the masters' motivations.

5. Which of the following is NOT mentioned by the author as a factor contributing to the changed status of the master?

(A) The use of women and children and other cheap sources of labor

(B) Lower transportation costs associated with the advent of railroads

(C) Economies of scale available to large manufacturers

(D) Merchant access to credit to finance contracts for large orders

(E) A decline of the demand for custom-made products

6. The tone of the selection can best be described as

(A) polemical and biased

(B) aloof and condescending

(C) argumentative and one-sided

(D) deferential and solicitous

(E) critical but restrained

Review

Use the following answer key to find how many you answered correctly, then compare your performance on the Drill to the graph below.

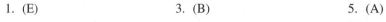

1. (E)   3. (B)   5. (A)
2. (D)   4. (A)   6. (E)

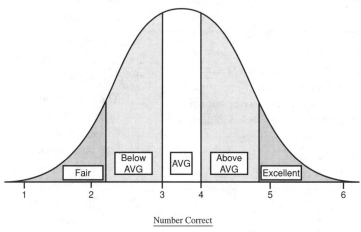

Number Correct

Now let's analyze the drill using the Action Plan for reading comprehension. Start with the first selection:

Step 1: Read the first and last sentences.

The first sentence tells you that the topic of the selection is electromechanical batteries or EMBs that can be used in cars. And the last sentence provides the conclusion of the argument: small EMBs are better than big ones.

Step 2: Track the development.

The first paragraph is intended primarily to introduce the reader to the concept of EMBs. Then the first sentence of the second paragraph announces the direction for the rest of the selection: vehicular applications pose special problems. One of these problems is the gyroscopic forces, though, the author says, these can be minimized. The other problem, announced in the first sentence of the third paragraph, is the danger posed by a rapidly spinning heavy metal flywheel. That paragraph goes on to discuss the physics of flywheels and some implications for safety. The last paragraph is a summary of the argument: small units are better than big.

Step 3: Read "through" details.

There is some pretty tough detail in the first paragraph: generator/motor, motor mode, discharge, and so on. Don't slow down to master the theory of EMBs, just note to yourself that their operation is discussed in the first paragraph. The second paragraph also contains a couple of details: what is a limited-excursion gimbal, how does it resist torque, why do opposite spins neutralize gyroscopic forces? Those are interesting questions that may or may not appear, so don't try to answer them in advance. If you see one or more of them, you know where to find the answers. The same reasoning applies to paragraph three where the selection gives you a lot of detail about flywheels.

Step 4: Summarize the development.

EMBs can be used in electric cars but (1) there's a problem with gyroscopic forces and (2) a danger that the spinning flywheel will come apart with some fairly serious consequences. Small units minimize these problems.

Now let's apply the Action Plan to the questions.

Identify Question Stems and Choose the Right Answer

1. This is a thesis question, and the correct answer is **(E)**. The first and last sentences of the selection effectively provide the answer you're looking for. (A) is too narrowly drafted because the author discusses not just the containment issue (the second issue). (B) goes beyond the explicit scope of the selection because "competitiveness" is not mentioned. (C) likewise is wide of the mark. The author focuses on physical forces not energy efficiency. And finally, (D) is incorrect because the author doesn't suggest any new experiments.

2. This is an implication question, and the correct answer is **(D)**. In paragraph three, the author explains that the energy stored by a flywheel is a function of its weight and speed and that a lighter weight flywheel would have to spin faster to store the same energy as a heavier one. So you can infer that if the weights are different but the stored energy is the same, the lighter wheel is spinning faster—and that's choice (D). (A) is just a confused reading of the first paragraph, and that information doesn't help answer the question asked. Similarly, (B) and (C) come out of paragraph two and aren't relevant here. Finally, (E) bears on the issue of safety, not on the physics by which energy is stored.

3. This is an application question, and the correct answer is **(B)**. The author says that lighter weight flywheels cause less damages when they fail, but the author does not say that they are less likely to fail. In fact, in paragraph three the author talks of spinning a light-weight wheel until it "reaches the same internal tensile stresses"

as the heavier one. At this point it is just as likely to break; it is just that the consequences are not so horrendous. The author would probably agree with (A) since windmills are stationary. And the author would probably agree with (C) since the opening sentence says that EMBs would power an electric car. (D) is based upon the third paragraph. And (E), finds adequate support in the first paragraph.

Now let's analyze the second reading passage.

Step 1: Read the first and last sentences.

The first sentence introduces you to the formalistic historians and lets you know that the author thinks that this approach is wanting. The last sentence states some kind of change has occurred to the status of a master. You don't want to spend too much time here, but you could probably figure out that the last sentence must be an example of the criticism set forth in the first sentence.

Step 2: Track the development.

The author uses paragraph one to describe a certain set of labor markets in the nineteenth century. Paragraph two then notes that some changes occurred during the ensuing hundred years. The third paragraph is critical to the development. The author issues a challenge to the formalist thinkers: why had the masters changed? The author then says categorically that they had not. The rest of the paragraph is the author's explanation of what really happened.

Step 3: Read "through" details.

Most people will probably find the detail here less intimidating than the physics in the previous passage, but that doesn't mean that you should spend any more time on it. Detail is just that—detail. It may or may not be the basis for a question. In the first paragraph, the comparison of the working conditions for skilled and unskilled workers is a detail that you should bracket. In the third paragraph and fourth, just note that several changes reshaped market conditions. If you need to analyze them further, you can find them later.

Step 4: Summarize the development.

The author announces that the formalists are myopic. They have a certain explanation for the change in the structure of the labor market for skilled craftsman. But, according to the author, they are wrong. The real explanation of the change is underlying economic forces.

Now let's apply the Action Plan to the questions.

Identify Question Stems and Choose the Right Answer

4. This is a development question, and the correct answer is (**A**). (The phrase "logical structure" is sometimes used for this purpose.) As we noted above, the third paragraph is a pivotal point in the argument, for it's there that the author begins the constructive portion of the argument: here's what really happened. The question in line 37 is used to dramatize the author's challenge to the formalists. (B) is wrong because the author believes that the question has an answer, one that the author develops in the rest of the passage. (C) and (D) are wrong because, among other things, the author believes that all the necessary research to answer the question has already been done. And (E) is incorrect because the hidden assumption (that masters had become greedy) doesn't contradict the formalist's theory. In fact, it is the conclusion of the formalist's theory.

5. This is a fact question, and the correct answer is (**A**). Remember that with a question stem that uses a thought-reverser, in this case "NOT," four of the five choices will be mentioned as facts in the selection. Because they are mentioned, they are not the answer to the question. (A) is not mentioned as a *cause* of the change but as an *effect*.

6. This is a judgment question, and the correct answer is (**E**). You can see that (A), (B), and (C) are highly charged; (D) is neutral; and (E) is somewhat negative. The passage doesn't include any extreme statements, so the first three choices can be eliminated. Then the issue is whether the author is "deferential" or "critical." The author is openly critical of the formalist (even though restrained in the criticism), so the best choice is (E).

10

Workshop B

This workshop consists of drill, evaluation, and review. The drill has a time limit, but you should spend as much time as you need on the evaluation and review portions of the workshop.

Drill

This drill consists of two Reading Comprehension selections each with questions. The time limit is ten minutes. This reflects the general strategy of spending *on average* two minutes reading the passage and one minute per question.

6 Questions • Time—10 Minutes

> **DIRECTIONS:** Each selection below is followed by questions based on its content. After reading a selection, choose the best answer to each question, answering on the basis of what is *stated* or *implied* in the selection.

Dogmatic sensationalism provides an inadequate and distorted view of language and knowledge because it wrongly imagines that sensibility is an impression of (5) the immediately given. The theory of language of dogmatic sensationalism has as its centerpiece learning by ostensive definition. A fluent speaker of the language points to an object and names it: rabbit. But, (10) as Quine has observed, what does "rabbit" signify to the one learning the language? The entire animal denoted by the English "rabbit" or "undetached rabbit part?" Its peculiar ears? Its queer tail?

(15) The answer of dogmatic sensationalism is found in its epistemology. The sensory impression that corresponds to "rabbit" is simply the idea of the "rabbit" created by the sense impression of a "rabbit." So, too, (20) the idea of a circle is just the impression created by a series of round objects or rather, the dogmatic sensationalist would say, "roundish" objects—"roundish" because no perfectly round figure is ever (25) found in nature. So the idea of a perfectly round circle is an extrapolation from a series of more or less round objects. But this move is unsatisfactory: if the idea of "round" does not come from immediate (30) sensory experience but only from a series of mediated steps, then where did the notion of "round" to which the "roundish" objects are compared first arise? The very notion of "roundish" already presupposes (35) the concept of "round."

If the concept of round is not found in the objects themselves, then it can only have originated in the knowing subject. "Round" is an innate idea with which
(40) humans are naturally equipped and by virtue of which they recognize imperfectly round objects as "roundish." So too "rabbit" corresponds to that animal which is denoted by the appropriate word. Innate
(45) concepts are the template of the mind into which the objects of experience are accommodated. *authors conclusion*

1. The author is primarily concerned to

    (A) sketch the outlines of a philosophical system that can be the basis for a theory of language and knowledge
    (B) reconcile dogmatic sensationalism with the theory that concepts are innate and correspond to objects in the world
    (C) prove that dogmatic sensationalism cannot account for the formation of concepts nor explain how it is that language is taught
    (D) demonstrate that the theory of innate ideas provides a more satisfactory account of language and knowledge than dogmatic sensationalism
    (E) rescue the theory of innate ideas from the attacks mounted by proponents of the philosophical view that concepts are the product of immediate experience

2. Which of the following best describes the logical structure of the author's argument?

    (A) All observed examples of x have also been y, therefore, all x observed in the future will be y.
    (B) Either p or q is the correct explanation; p is not acceptable; therefore, the correct explanation is q.
    (C) If m is true, then n is true; m may or may not be true; therefore, n may or may not be true.
    (D) If a is an acceptable theory, then b is an acceptable theory; b is not an acceptable theory; therefore, a is not an acceptable theory.
    (E) All s are m; all m are p; therefore, all s are p.

3. The author would most likely agree with which of the following statements?

    (A) No two observers will apply the term "roundish" to the same set of objects.
    (B) It is impossible to find an exact word-for-word equivalent in another language for a concept described in English.
    (C) The concept of round-ness must eventually be based upon the sensory experience some perfectly round object.
    (D) Our knowledge of mathematical objects such as geometry figures is less dependable than our knowledge of other objects.
    (E) Mathematical concepts such as the number two depend upon an innate idea of "two-ness."

10

Speaking unscientifically, we say that lightning strikes an object on the ground; but from a scientific point of view, this language is inaccurate. Cloud-to-ground (5) lightning begins when complex meteorological processes cause a tremendous electrostatic charge to build up within a cloud. Typically, the bottom of the cloud is negatively charged. When the charge (10) reaches 50 to 100 million volts, air is no longer an effective insulator, and lightning occurs within the cloud itself. Ten to 30 minutes after the onset of intracloud lightning, negative charges called stepped (15) leaders emerge from the bottom of the cloud, moving toward the earth in 50-meter intervals at speeds of 100 to 200 kilometers per second and creating an ionized channel. As the leaders near the (20) Earth, their strong electric field causes streamers of positively charged ions to develop at the tips of pointed objects connected directly or indirectly to the ground. These positively charged streamers (25) flow upward.

When the distance, known as the striking distance, between a stepped leader and one of the streamers reaches 30 to 100 meters, the intervening air breaks down (30) completely and the leader is joined to the Earth via the streamer. Now a pulse of current known as a return stroke ranging from thousands to hundreds of thousands of amperes moves at one tenth to one third (35) the speed of light from the Earth through the object from which the streamer emanated and up the ionized channel to the charge center within the cloud. An ionized channel remains in the air and

(40) additional negative charges called dart leaders will quickly move down this path resulting in further return strokes. It is this multiplicity that causes the flash to flicker. The entire event typically lasts (45) about one second. The return stroke's extremely high temperature creates the visible lightning and produces thunder by instantly turning moisture into steam.

4. According to the passage, which of the following is NOT true of stepped leaders?

(A) They develop 10 to 30 minutes after intracloud lightning.

(B) As they traverse the distance from cloud to ground, they create an ionized channel.

(C) Their powerful positive charge causes streamers to develop in grounded objects.

(D) They emerge from the bottom of the cloud and move downward in intervals of 50 meters.

(E) Their rate of progress is 100 to 200 kilometers per second.

5. The passage answers which of the following questions?

(A) How does lightning produce the associated thunder?

(B) How far about the ground is bottom of the typical lightning producing cloud?

(C) How frequently will lightning strike a given object?

(D) How long does it take a cloud to build up an electrostatic charge?

(E) How does intracloud lightning cross from one area of a cloud to another?

6. The author is primarily concerned to

(A) warn about the dangers posed by lightning strikes

— (B) describe the sequence of events that make up a lightning strike

(C) discuss fundamental scientific laws pertaining to electricity

(D) support the commonly held view that lightning strikes the ground

(E) prove that lightning occurs because of a charge imbalance between a cloud and the ground

10

Review

Use the following answer key to find how many you answered correctly, then compare your performance on the Drill to the graph below.

1. (D)   3. (E)   5. (A)

2. (B)   4. (C)   6. (B)

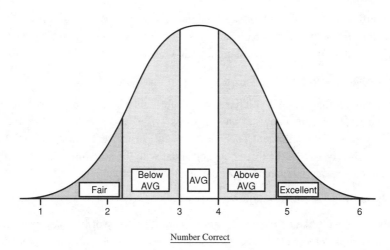

Number Correct

Now let's analyze the second drill using the Action Plan for reading comprehension. Start with the first selection:

Step 1: Read the first and last sentences.

The first says that something called dogmatic sensationalism is a bad idea, and the last sentence says that innate concepts are the template of the mind. This tells you that the topic is something philosophical (language and knowledge), and you can probably guess that the author prefers the innate idea explanation over dogmatic sensationalism.

Step 2: Track the development.

After announcing the topic and pronouncing judgment on "dogmatic sensationalism," the author presents an argument against the theory of language as learned by ostensive definition:

> Here's a rabbit.
>
> A what?
>
> A rabbit!
>
> The ears? The tail? What's a rabbit?

In the next paragraph, the author examines the epistemology of dogmatic sensationalism: a rabbit is just a rabbit—the thing you see right in front of you. The author attacks this view with the "round" example.

In the third paragraph, the author says that the view that concepts are formed by receiving impressions from objects is unsatisfactory, so the concept must be an element of knowledge. This solves the problems of language and epistemology of dogmatic sensationalism.

Step 3: Read "through" details.

Unlike many of the passages you have seen so far, this passage is not particularly rich in detail, that is, there are no laws of physics or lists of items. Even so, you need to keep the formal features of the argument, such as the overall structure, separate from the details. As you'll see shortly, two of the three questions deal with the structure. Only the third question requires an understanding of the details of the argument.

Step 4: Summarize the development.

The author doesn't like dogmatic sensationalism. It's theory of language is weak; and it's epistemology is defective. The theory of innate ideas provides a better explanation.

Now let's apply the Action Plan to the questions.

Identify Question Stems and Choose the Right Answer

1. This is a thesis question, and the correct answer is **(D)**, as shown by the analysis above. (A) is too broad: an entire philosophical system? (B) is based on a misunderstanding of the development of the selection. The author wants to refute one theory and advance another. The passage does not attempt to *reconcile* the two. (C) is wrong because it is too narrow. Yes, the author attacks dogmatic sensationalism, but that is only half of the argument. The constructive portion of the argument presents innate ideas as an alternative theory. (E) reverses the point of the passage. The author doesn't try to "rescue" the innate ideas theory.

2. This is a development question, and the correct answer is **(B)**. Since this question asks about the overall structure of the passage, you can treat it much the same way that you would a thesis question. And the analysis above shows that the overall development is best described by (B).

3. This is an application question ("likely agree"), and the correct answer is **(E)**. The author argues in favor of the theory of innate ideas, so the author would accept the assertion that a mathematical concept such as "two-ness," like "round-ness," comes from an innate idea. (A) would be rejected by the author since this is a weakness of the dogmatic sensationalism theory that the author attacks. (B) is incorrect for the same reason, since the theory of innate ideas is supposed to answer the objection that sense impression could not guarantee that people have the experience of the same object. (C) is an idea the author would reject, since the author tacitly agrees that nowhere in nature is there a perfectly round object. And the author would also reject (D) since mathematical concepts are guaranteed by the innateness of ideas.

And now let's do the second selection.

Step 1: Read the first and last sentences.

The first sentence announces that the passage will discuss lightning and that it will give a scientific explanation that is inconsistent with the naive view of lightning. The last says that it is the return or upward stroke that is the lightning that we see and that causes thunder.

Step 2: Track the development.

The development of the passage is a "story" about formation of a lightning strike: charge build-up, intracloud lightning, leaders move down, streamers move upward, the return stroke moves through the ionized channel causing visible lightning and thunder, secondary dart leaders and return strokes cause the appearance of flickering.

Step 3: Read "through" details.

Whereas the first passage in this drill had relatively few details, this one is filled with minutiae: how long does it take, how far apart are these things, how fast do they move, what happens when they meet, and so on. And two of the three questions ask about details. But on your first reading, you shouldn't be worried about the details. Instead, you should be reading for the overall development, that is, the general sequence of events described above.

Step 4: Summarize the development.

Lightning starts with a charge buildup. Then it goes through stages: intracloud lightning, leaders moving down, streamers moving up, a return stroke, and secondary strokes.

Now let's apply the Action Plan to the questions.

Identify Question Stems and Choose the Right Answer

4. The "according to" indicates that this is a fact question, and the correct answer is **(C)**. Note the thought-reverser. (C) is the only idea in the choices NOT mentioned in the passage.

5. This is a fact question, and the correct answer is **(A)**. Although this is not the most common wording for a fact question, you know that it has to fit the pattern because the questions in the choice could only be answered by facts. The passage supplies facts to answer (A): moisture turns to steam. (See the last sentence.) You just won't find the facts you need to answer the other questions explicitly stated in the text, though a not-so-careful reading might mislead you. For example, the time frame of 10 to 30 minutes is the interval between the onset of intracloud lightning and the emergence of streamers, but this does not answer question (D).

6. This is a thesis question, and the correct answer is **(B)** for the reasons discussed above. (A) goes beyond the scope of the selection because the author does not discuss the dangers of lightning. (C) is also too broad. Though the author refers indirectly to concepts from physics (amperes and so on), the main idea is not to discuss scientific laws. (D) is wrong because the author discusses the more accurate, scientific explanation. And finally, (E) is too narrow since this is but one event leading to a lightning strike.

Get Answers to Frequently Asked Questions

Q: **Should I expand my preview of the selection to include more than the first and last sentences?**

A: No. The strategy is designed to move you ahead of the learning curve that each new selection requires. It's value is its ability to save you time. If one or the other preview sentence isn't helpful, that's disappointing; but resist the temptation to go looking for the "magic formula" elsewhere in the selection. You could be a wild goose chase; and, in any event, you'll find the key sentence or sentences during your reading of the selection.

Q: **Will I always get the same number of each question stem type?**

A: Probably not for two reasons. First, thesis questions and fact questions tend to appear with greater frequency because they test core reading skills (the main idea and the details). Second, not all types are of the same level of difficulty. Judgment questions tend to be easy while application questions tend to be hard. So your mix of questions will also depend a lot on the progress that your making at any given time during the test. We try to show you approximately equal numbers of each in this *30 Days* guide so that you'll be prepared for all of them.

Q: **Once I've found what I think is the correct answer, should I bother reading the rest of the choices?**

A: Yes, you should read all of the choices before making and confirming your selection. As you've seen, some wrong answer choices can be very attractive. You might not notice a weakness until you've seen something better. Only if you know that you're about to run out of time and haven't yet finished should you take a short cut.

10

Take the Verbal Final

Today, you'll take the Verbal Final.

The Verbal Final has a format similar to that you will encounter on your computer-based GRE: 30 questions with a 30 minute time limit. The Final uses all four verbal types presented in an order similar to that of the actual exam. Do the Final under strict timing conditions. After the Final proper, evaluate your performance and review your work.

Take the Verbal Final

This is the Verbal Final. It consists of 30 questions with a time limit of 30 minutes. Mark your answers by filling in the oval next to the answer choice that you select.

1 Ⓐ Ⓑ Ⓒ Ⓓ Ⓔ   9 Ⓐ Ⓑ Ⓒ Ⓓ Ⓔ   17 Ⓐ Ⓑ Ⓒ Ⓓ Ⓔ   25 Ⓐ Ⓑ Ⓒ Ⓓ Ⓔ
2 Ⓐ Ⓑ Ⓒ Ⓓ Ⓔ   10 Ⓐ Ⓑ Ⓒ Ⓓ Ⓔ   18 Ⓐ Ⓑ Ⓒ Ⓓ Ⓔ   26 Ⓐ Ⓑ Ⓒ Ⓓ Ⓔ
3 Ⓐ Ⓑ Ⓒ Ⓓ Ⓔ   11 Ⓐ Ⓑ Ⓒ Ⓓ Ⓔ   19 Ⓐ Ⓑ Ⓒ Ⓓ Ⓔ   27 Ⓐ Ⓑ Ⓒ Ⓓ Ⓔ
4 Ⓐ Ⓑ Ⓒ Ⓓ Ⓔ   12 Ⓐ Ⓑ Ⓒ Ⓓ Ⓔ   20 Ⓐ Ⓑ Ⓒ Ⓓ Ⓔ   28 Ⓐ Ⓑ Ⓒ Ⓓ Ⓔ
5 Ⓐ Ⓑ Ⓒ Ⓓ Ⓔ   13 Ⓐ Ⓑ Ⓒ Ⓓ Ⓔ   21 Ⓐ Ⓑ Ⓒ Ⓓ Ⓔ   29 Ⓐ Ⓑ Ⓒ Ⓓ Ⓔ
6 Ⓐ Ⓑ Ⓒ Ⓓ Ⓔ   14 Ⓐ Ⓑ Ⓒ Ⓓ Ⓔ   22 Ⓐ Ⓑ Ⓒ Ⓓ Ⓔ   30 Ⓐ Ⓑ Ⓒ Ⓓ Ⓔ
7 Ⓐ Ⓑ Ⓒ Ⓓ Ⓔ   15 Ⓐ Ⓑ Ⓒ Ⓓ Ⓔ   23 Ⓐ Ⓑ Ⓒ Ⓓ Ⓔ
8 Ⓐ Ⓑ Ⓒ Ⓓ Ⓔ   16 Ⓐ Ⓑ Ⓒ Ⓓ Ⓔ   24 Ⓐ Ⓑ Ⓒ Ⓓ Ⓔ

Day 11

What You'll Do Today

- Take the Verbal Final
- Evaluate Your Performance
- Review Your Work
- Get Answers to Frequently Asked Questions

GRE Verbal Final

30 Questions • Time—30 minutes

DIRECTIONS: Each item below consists of a word or phrase printed in capital letters, followed by five words or phrases. Choose the word or phrase that is most nearly *opposite* in meaning to the capitalized word or phrase.

1. AUGMENT:
   (A) reduce
   (B) excuse
   (C) avow
   (D) impel
   (E) emit

2. SUPERFLUOUS:
   (A) caustic
   (B) precise
   (C) deceitful
   (D) essential
   (E) becoming

DIRECTIONS: Each of the sentences below has one or two blanks. Each blank indicates that a word or phrase has been omitted. Following each sentence is a series of five words or sets of words. Choose the word or sets of words for each blank that *best* fits the meaning of the sentence in its entirety.

3. The directors who favored the plan to diversify overseas operations, though in —— following their failed experiment on the domestic side, constituted a sufficiently —— political force on the Board to gain a favorable vote.

   (A) retreat . . cohesive
   (B) disarray . . ineffective
   (C) control . . powerful
   (D) abeyance . . contentious
   (E) disfavor . . fragmented

4. Our relegation of the fairy tale to the status of bedtime reading for children has resulted in the —— of the goriest details from the *Grimm Tales*.

   (A) ratification
   (B) reinsertion
   (C) accentuation
   (D) expurgation
   (E) codification

DIRECTIONS: In each of the following items, a related pair of capitalized words or phrases is followed by five pairs of words or phrases. Choose the pair that best expresses a relationship similar to that expressed by the capitalized pair.

5. TREE : ARBORETUM ::

(A) soloist : conductor
(B) flower : stamen
(C) seedling : mulch
(D) document : archivist
(E) bee : apiary

6. ETCH : GLASS ::

(A) chisel : sculpture
(B) embroider : cloth
(C) paint : mural
(D) tune : instrument
(E) stage : drama

etch a piece of glass

embroider a piece of cloth

DIRECTIONS: The selection below is followed by questions based on its content. After reading the selection, choose the best answer to each question, answering on the basis of what is *stated* or *implied* in the selection.

The historian distinguishes between the outside of an event and its inside. The outside of the event is everything that can be described in terms of physical
(5) bodies, their movements, and their interactions: Caesar crossed the Rubicon on a particular date, soldiers came with Caesar, on a later date Caesar's blood covered the floor of the Roman Senate.
(10) The inside of the event is intention: Caesar *defied* the Constitutional authority of Rome by crossing the Rubicon with the soldiers and was later killed by assassins who *believed* they were defending the
(15) Constitution. The historian is concerned with the surrounding objective conditions and will read letters, examine documents, interview witnesses, and visit sites; but the physical objects and surroundings are
(20) important only insofar as they provide access to the inner of the event.

The task of the historian is distinguished from that of the natural scientist in two ways. On the one hand, the historian
(25) employs investigative tools neither needed by nor available to the natural scientist because the historian inquires after the "why" of the event. On the other hand, the task of the historian is somewhat simpler
(30) than that of the natural scientist because once that question has been answered, there is no further question to be raised. There is no reason to look behind the thought to find a supervening law. There are no laws
(35) of historical development; and this is a consequence of the view that the inside of the event is what distinguishes an historical event from a natural one. A natural or purely physical event can only
(40) be regarded as a particular classified under a universal or general law, but the inside of the event is a thought, unique, and as such,

11

not subject to law-like explanation. The historian is not concerned with one order
(45) of events to the exclusion of the other, but as between the two, the second enjoys a certain logico-historical priority.

7. The author is primarily concerned to

(A) explain why Caesar crossed the Rubicon in defiance of the Roman Constitution

(B) contrast the methodology of history as a discipline with that of the natural sciences

(C) defend history as a science equal in status to the natural sciences

(D) demonstrate that history lacks the rigor of the natural sciences

(E) distinguish the inside of an historical event from its outside

8. The author would most likely agree with which of the following statements?

(A) An exchange of letters between two world leaders regarding the events leading to an armed conflict would be the best evidence available to an historian as to why the conflict had occurred.

(B) A natural scientist who asks "why" a certain chemical reaction took place is asking a different sort of question from that asked by the historian who wants to know "why" a war broke out.

(C) Physical evidence such as a document speaks for itself, so, in the absence of ambiguity, two historians reading the same document should arrive at substantially identical conclusions.

(D) Historical laws are more difficult to uncover and articulate than natural laws because it is impossible to create experimental conditions to verify or disconfirm historical hypotheses.

(E) The value of the study of history, like the study of the natural sciences, is the formulation general rules of human behavior that will allow the prediction of future events.

9. The author mentions all of the following as aspects of the objective conditions in which an event takes place that the historian might consider EXCEPT:

(A) correspondence about the event
(B) documents pertaining to the event
(C) eyewitness accounts of the event
(D) physical setting of the event
(E) intentions of key participants in the event

word olve

DIRECTIONS: Each item below consists of a word or phrase printed in capital letters, followed by five words or phrases. Choose the word or phrase that is most nearly *opposite* in meaning to the capitalized word or phrase.

10. TOUT:

   (A) remember
   (B) uncover
   (C) weather
   (D) prolong
   (E) downplay

11. CANONICAL:

   (A) pretentious
   (B) heretical
   (C) supportable
   (D) gargantuan
   (E) vehement

12. INDIGENOUS:

   (A) pensive
   (B) infected
   (C) undeserved
   (D) foreign
   (E) expressive

13. SOPHISTICAL:

   (A) inherent
   (B) bellicose
   (C) contrived
   (D) valid
   (E) random

11

DIRECTIONS: Each of the sentences below has one or two blanks. Each blank indicates that a word or phrase has been omitted. Following each sentence is a series of five words or sets of words. Choose the word or sets of words for each blank that *best* fits the meaning of the sentence in its entirety.

14. For all of his outlandish costumes and immoderate behavior on-stage, rock musician Arlen Quigby was, in his private life, —— person who was described by associates as a simple businessman.

   (A) an enigmatic
   (B) a subdued
   (C) a conventional
   (D) an unstable
   (E) a conservative

15. As vaccines have become increasingly ——, cases of Haemophilius influenzae among children under the age of five dropped nearly 99% in the last ten years, and the disease has been nearly ——.

   (A) routine .. eradicated
   (B) virile .. annihilated
   (C) innocuous .. obliterated
   (D) problematic .. rampant
   (E) inefficacious .. contained

INNOCUOUS doesn't work

16. The script writers for the stage version of Kipling's *Just So Stories* wisely decided to make only —— use of the author's original diction; the occasional flashes of alliteration are charming but overdone, and their arcane sound would quickly have become —— to the modern ear.

    (A) judicious . . familiar
    (B) intermittent . . inaudible
    (C) sporadic . . cloying
    (D) exacting . . familiar
    (E) limited . . dissonant

DIRECTIONS: The selection below is followed by questions based on its content. After reading the selection, choose the best answer to each question, answering on the basis of what is *stated* or *implied* in the selection.

Geothermal energy offers enormous potential for direct, low-temperature applications. Unlike indirect applications, this new technology relies on the Earth's

(5) natural thermal energy to heat or cool a house or multi-family dwelling directly without the need to convert steam or other high-temperature fluids into electricity using expensive equipment.

(10) A geothermal system consists of a heat pump and exchanger plus a series of pipes, called a loop, installed below the surface of the ground or submerged in a pond or lake. Fluid circulating in the loop is

(15) warmed and carries heat to the home. The heat pump and exchanger use an electrically powered vapor compression cycle—the same principle employed in a refrigerator—to concentrate the energy

(20) and to transfer it. The concentrated geothermal energy is released inside the home at a higher temperature, and fans then distribute the heat to various rooms through a system of air ducts. In summer,

(25) the process is reversed: excess heat is drawn from the home, expelled to the loop, and absorbed by the Earth.

Geothermal systems are more effective than conventional heat pumps that use the

(30) outdoor air as their heat source (on cold days) or heat sink (on warm days) because geothermal systems draw heat from a source whose temperature is more constant than that of air. The temperature

(35) of the ground or groundwater a few feet beneath the Earth's surface remains relatively stable—between 45°F and 70°F. In winter, it is much easier to capture heat from the soil at a moderate 50°F than from

(40) the atmosphere when the air temperature

is below zero. Conversely, in summer, the relatively cool ground absorbs a home's waste heat more readily than the warm outdoor air.

(45)   The use of geothermal energy through heat pump technology has almost no adverse environmental consequences and offers several advantages over conventional energy sources. Direct
(50)   geothermal applications are usually no more disruptive of the surrounding environment than a normal water well. Additionally, while such systems require electricity to concentrate and distribute
(55)   the energy collected, they actually reduce total energy consumption by one-fourth to two-thirds, depending on the technology used. For each 1,000 homes with geothermal heat pumps, an electric
(60)   utility can avoid the installation of 2 to 5 megawatts of generating capacity. Unfortunately, only a modest part of the potential of this use for geothermal energy has been developed because the
(65)   service industry is small and the price of competing energy sources is low.

17. The author regards the new technology as

(A) promising but underutilized
(B) dependable but costly
(C) inexpensive but unreliable
(D) unproven but efficient
(E) successful but dangerous

18. The passage implies that a rise in cost of conventional energy would result in

(A) an expanded reliance on direct geothermal technology for climate control of smaller structures
(B) a decrease in the cost for installing geothermal heating and cooling equipment
(C) an economic incentive in favor of the use of conventional energy sources
(D) a decrease in the number of new homes constructed using geothermal heating
(E) a reduction in expenditures on research and development for indirect geothermal technology

19. Which of the following would be the most logical continuation of the passage?

(A) A listing of geological features of the Earth such as geysers and volcanoes that might be potential geothermal energy sources
(B) A review of the history of the use of geothermal energy and associated technologies
(C) A description of experimental techniques for converting geo-thermal energy into electricity
(D) An overview of the environmental hazards to be faced in the next 20 years due to pressures for increased energy consumption
(E) A discussion of some ways of expanding reliance on geothermal energy for direct, low-temperature applications

11

DIRECTIONS: In each of the following items, a related pair of capitalized words or phrases is followed by five pairs of words or phrases. Choose the pair that best expresses a relationship similar to that expressed by the capitalized pair.

20. EAT : GOBBLE ::

    (A) plan : premeditate
    (B) listen : discriminate
    (C) chew : ingest
    (D) drink : quaff
    (E) consume : direct

21. SPECIOUS : AUTHENTICITY ::

    (A) radical : impulsiveness
    (B) incongruous : specificity
    (C) imaginary : actuality
    (D) secretive : accountability
    (E) perilous : direction

DIRECTIONS: The selection below is followed by questions based on its content. After reading the selection, choose the best answer to each question, answering on the basis of what is *stated* or *implied* in the selection.

Although patterns vary, it is possible to classify drinkers as social drinkers, alcohol abusers, and alcoholic-dependent persons. While alcohol consumption is
(5) never entirely a risk-free activity, these categories represent a range from relatively benign to extremely problematic. An evaluation of treatment for any alcohol-related disorder must be situated
(10) historically. For nearly two hundred years, the explanation of alcoholism as a disease competed with explanations in which character or moral defects were believed to lead to drinking behavior. It wasn't
(15) until the 1930s that serious consideration was given to the concept of alcoholism as a disease with psychological, biochemical, endocrinological, and neurological implications. Even as late as the 1960s, some
(20) researchers still defined alcoholism broadly to include any drinking having harmful consequences.

Evidence accumulated, however, suggesting that alcohol abuse and alcohol
(25) dependence are distinguishable. "Alcohol abuse" refers either to transitory or long-term problems in accomplishing basic living activities in which alcohol is implicated, and "alcohol dependence" describes
(30) a severe disability in which dependence brings about a reduction in the individual's ability to control the drinking behavior. This delineation was endorsed in 1987 by the Institute of Medicine which defined
(35) alcohol abuse as "repetitive patterns of heavy drinking associated with impairment of functioning and/or health" and discussed alcoholism (dependency) as a separate phenomenon. Alcohol
(40) dependence is associated with additional

symptoms such as craving, tolerance, and physical dependence that bring about changes in the importance of drinking in the individual's life and impaired ability *(45)* to exercise behavioral restraint.

The distinction has important clinical implications. For some nondependent alcohol abusers, drinking patterns may be modified by exhortations or by societal *(50)* sanctions. For alcohol-dependent persons, exhortations and sanctions are insufficient, and the goal of modified drinking inappropriate. The goal for these persons is abstinence, and a range of treatment *(55)* options is available, including pharmacologic interventions, psychotherapy, and counseling. Knowledge of the differences among persons who drink is important because treatment methods are differen- *(60)* tially effective according to patient characteristics.

22. Which of the following best describes the development of the selection?

(A) The author draws a distinction, provides evidence for that distinction, and points out some policy implications of the distinction.

(B) The author outlines the history of a social problem, describes attempts to solve the problem, and concludes that efforts thus far have been futile.

(C) The author defines a key term, shows that the term is frequently misused by scholars and researchers, and offers a better definition of the term.

(D) The author presents an accepted theory, reviews some recent challenges to the theory, and concludes that the theory is still viable.

(E) The author clarifies a possible ambiguity in a widely accepted theory, shows that the ambiguity produces harmful results, and presents a plan for avoiding similar problems in the future.

23. The authors regard the conclusions of the researchers mentioned in lines 10–24 as

(A) unfounded rejections of a traditional model

(B) conclusively proven and valid for current models

(C) scientific advances but only partially correct

(D) irrelevant to the subject of the discussion

(E) essentially accurate but of limited utility

24. The author mentions all of the following as characteristic of alcohol dependence but not alcohol abuse EXCEPT:

(A) severely compromised ability to exercise behavioral restraint

(B) magnified importance of drinking as a function in the routine life

(C) increased tolerance for and physical addiction to alcohol

(D) repetitive patterns of substantial consumption with impairment of health

(E) marked resistance to hortatory measures as a means of behavior modification

11

DIRECTIONS: Each item below consists of a word or phrase printed in capital letters, followed by five words or phrases. Choose the word or phrase that is most nearly *opposite* in meaning to the capitalized word or phrase.

25. PRECARIOUS:

   (A) not contingent
   (B) closely observed
   (C) open ended
   (D) hastily assembled
   (E) without sanction

26. DECREPITUDE:

   (A) vitality
   (B) belatedness
   (C) insecurity
   (D) harshness
   (E) redundancy

DIRECTIONS: In each of the following items, a related pair of capitalized words or phrases is followed by five pairs of words or phrases. Choose the pair that best expresses a relationship similar to that expressed by the capitalized pair.

27. FAVONIAN : GENTLENESS ::

   (A) blasphemous : libel
   (B) reckless : danger
   (C) therapeutic : illness
   (D) corrosive : integrity
   (E) mecurial : volatility

28. ANACHRONOUS : TIME ::

   (A) impetuous : consideration
   (B) immortal : death
   (C) sequential : stage
   (D) cacophonous : tune
   (E) moralistic : taboo

29. FOOTNOTE : TEXT ::

   (A) overture : symphony
   (B) heat : race
   (C) aside : dialogue
   (D) artist : painting
   (E) irony : drama

30. OBLIGATORY : CONTRAINT ::

   (A) repugnant : acceptance
   (B) impartial : bias
   (C) impeccable : taint
   (D) ludicrous : amusement
   (E) awesome : nonchalance

Evaluate Your Performance

Use the following answer key to find out how many questions you answered correctly, then compare your performance on the Verbal Final with the graph below.

1. (A)	11. (B)	21. (C)
2. (D)	12. (D)	22. (A)
3. (A)	13. (D)	23. (C)
4. (D)	14. (C)	24. (D)
5. (E)	15. (A)	25. (A)
6. (B)	16. (C)	26. (A)
7. (B)	17. (A)	27. (E)
8. (B)	18. (A)	28. (D)
9. (E)	19. (E)	29. (C)
10. (E)	20. (D)	30. (D)

Overall Verbal

11

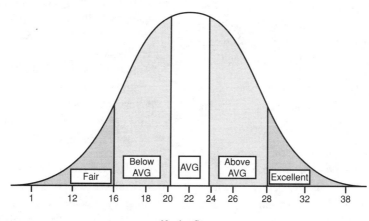

Number Correct

Review Your Work

1. **(A)** Augment means to increase or to enlarge, so reduce is an exact opposite.

2. **(D)** Superfluous means excessive or unnecessary, so essential is an exact opposite.

3. **(A)** "Though" signals a contrast between the efforts of the directors in the failed experiment and their efforts regarding overseas operations; and the two elements of the correct choice must create that contrast: they were in retreat, but they still were sufficiently cohesive to attain their goal.

4. **(D)** The "result in" signals an effect or an outcome. What kind of book would be the result of treating a fairy tale as bedtime reading for children? It would have to be fairly innocuous, so the gory details would have to be eliminated, or expurgated.

5. **(E)** An arboretum is a place where trees are raised, and an apiary is a place where bees are raised.

6. **(B)** You can think of this as a "place where" analogy: glass is where an etching is done, and cloth is where embroidery is done. Or you can also think of it as a "device" analogy: glass is a device used in making an etching, and cloth is a device used in making embroidery.

7. **(B)** This is a thesis question. The first sentence of the selection distinguishes between the inside and the outside of historical events, and the last sentence says that the historian is more concerned with the former than the latter. In the discussion, the author spends a good bit of the passage explaining why history (as thus described) is not like the natural sciences. This development is best summarized by (B). (A) refers only to a small part of the selection. (C) is incorrect because the author doesn't offer a "defense." Indeed, there is no mention of any "attack" on history in the first place. The same analysis disposes of (D). And (E) is a correct description of part of the passage but not of the overall development.

8. **(B)** This is an application question. The author says that the historian and the natural scientist are engaged in different enterprises. When the historian asks "why" something occurred, the historian wants to know about the states of mind of the actors involved. The natural scientist is looking for an explanation couched in terms of a natural law.

9. **(E)** This is a fact question. The author specifically says that (A), (B), (C), and (D) are physical aspects of an historical event. The intentions of the participants, however, belong to the "inside" of the event.

10. **(E)** Tout means to praise or to recommend highly, so a good opposite is downplay.

11. **(B)** Canonical means accepted or authoritative, so a good opposite is heretical.

12. **(D)** Indigenous means native to a certain region or country, so a good opposite is foreign.

13. **(D)** Sophistical means pertaining to sophistry or reasoning that seems to have merit but is actually fallacious. So valid is a good opposite.

14. **(C)** Although it may not be obvious at first, the "for all" introduces a contrast between the outlandish costumes and stage behavior and the private life of the performer. So you need a word to complete the sentence that conveys the idea of staid or normal, and conventional does the job.

15. **(A)** The "as" introduces as causal connection or explanation, so the word that completes the first blank has to explain why the incidence of the disease has declined: routine vaccinations would account for that. Additionally, the second blank must explain the outcome of the drop in the incidence of the disease: the disease has been wiped out. And "eradicated" is a good completion.

16. **(C)** The "but" in the second part of the sentence signals a contrast: occasional is charming but overdone would be something. So you need a word with negative overtones, and "cloying" is a good choice. You might also note that the first blank must be completed with a word that suggests only limited reliance on the original diction, and "sporadic" is a good choice.

17. **(A)** This is a judgment question. The author says in the first sentence that geothermal energy offers "enormous potential" but in the last sentence adds that only a "modest part" has been realized.

18. **(A)** This is an implication question. In the last sentence, the author notes that the potential for geothermal energy remains largely untapped because the cost of competing energy sources is low. You can infer, therefore, that were the cost of competing sources to rise, geothermal energy would become increasingly attractive.

19. **(E)** As just noted, the author says that the potential for geothermal applications is great but largely untapped. A logical next step, given the author's enthusiasm for the technology, would be to go on and discuss some ways of exploiting the new technology.

20. **(D)** This is a degree analogy: To gobble is to eat large quantities of food, and to quaff is to drink large quantities of liquid.

21. **(C)** This is an absence of analogy: the absence of authenticity is a key element of speciousness, and the absence of actuality is a key element of anything imaginary.

11

22. **(A)** This is a development question that functions like a thesis question. The author begins by distinguishing social drinkers, alcohol abusers, and alcohol-dependent persons. Most of the paragraph is devoted to further refining the distinction between the second two terms. And in the last paragraph, the author notes some of the implications for treatment of the distinction.

23. **(C)** This is a judgment question. In the first paragraph, the author notes the outmoded view of alcoholism as a moral or character weakness and explains that this conception gradually gave way to the view of alcoholism as a disease. But, the author explains, the initial steps in that direction did not clearly distinguish between alcohol abuse and alcohol dependency. Even as late as the 1960s, this distinction was not entirely clear. So the author views this stage as a first-step but not the final word on alcoholism.

24. **(D)** This is a fact question. The author mentions (A), (B), and (C) in paragraph two as being elements of the view that alcohol dependency is different from abuse. And in the last paragraph, the author explains that dependent behavior is not likely to change in response to moral suasion. (D), however, is mentioned in the third paragraph as an element of abuse as opposed to dependency.

25. **(A)** Precarious means dependent upon the will of someone else or on some circumstance outside of one's control. So not contingent is a good opposite.

26. **(A)** You might find it easier to deal with the word "decrepit" which means old and worn out from use.

27. **(E)** This is a key element of analogy. Favonian means pertaining to the west wind and conveys the idea of calmness or gentleness. And mercurial derives from the god Mercury and connotes volatility or changeability.

28. **(D)** You could analyze this either as an absence of or as a sequence analogy, though it doesn't fit easily into either category. Anachronous means occurring out of the correct time, and cacophonous means out of sequence with the harmony or melody.

29. **(C)** You can analyze this as a place for analogy: the text is a place for a footnote, and the dialogue is a place for an aside. If you need to refine your sentence further, you might note that a footnote occurs in the middle of the text and is intended to amplify the text, and the same can be said of an aside.

30. **(D)** This is a key element analogy: Anything that is obligatory is intended to convey constraint, and anything that is ludicrous is intended to convey amusement.

Get Answers to Frequently Asked Questions

Q: Do I need to do more work on the verbal part?

A: Probably not. You have learned all about the four types of verbal questions and have mastered strategies for each one. Plus, you have done the equivalent of *six full-length practice exams* for this area.

Q: Should I be worried if I still miss some questions?

A: No. You have to remember that the GRE is a challenging exam. It's not like the tests you're used to taking. Only a handful of people every year answer all of the questions correctly. Even the people who are scoring in the 700s are missing questions.

Q: What if I want to practice the GRE on the computer?

A: That would be a good idea. You've mastered the content of the test, but you could still probably benefit from some hands-on experience with a computer-based delivery system. Even if you are computer literate, you would still need to get used to the idiosyncracies of the GRE program.

11

Part III

Math Skills

Test Your Math Skills

Today, you'll take the Math PreTest and use specially designed evaluation tools to make some judgments about where you stand. You'll also review explanations of the correct answers to the items used in the PreTest as a first step in your in-depth study of GRE Math questions.

The PreTest has two major purposes. First, it will give you some idea of where you stand on the Math part right now—before you begin learning techniques and strategies that will boost your confidence and help you to improve your performance. Second, it will help you to diagnose any math weaknesses you may have. You should pay extra attention to those items that you miss. The explanations will guide you to Day 14, 15, 16 or 21. The lessons for those Days are a review of important math concepts tested by the GRE.

Preview the Math PreTest

The likelihood is that you'll be taking the GRE on computer. This PreTest exercise, which is presented in pencil-and-paper format, has been carefully designed to yield results that are comparable to a computer-based version of the test. In Day 1, you learned about the format for the GRE math sections. Here's a brief re-cap of that information.

The GRE CAT uses three different kinds of math questions. You'll find these same three kinds in the PreTest.

1. **Problem-Solving.** Problem-Solving is your basic, multiple-choice math question type. It's the kind of problem that you've been doing since you first started standardized testing in grade school. It tests your understanding of arithmetic, algebra, and geometry and your ability to apply those concepts in different ways.

A problem-solving item may ask you to do a simple calculation:

What is the value of 0.02×0.03?

Or you may be asked to solve an equation:

If $2x + 4 = 12$, then what is the value of x?

Or analyze a geometry figure:

If a right triangle has legs of 3 and 4, what is the length of the hypotenuse?

Or solve a word problem involving a real life situation:

Maria opened a savings account with a $1,000 deposit. The money earned 5% simple interest compounded semi-annually. If all interest payments were reinvested in the account and no other contributions or withdrawals were made, how much money was in the account 24 months after it was opened?

Problem Solving presents a variety of challenges, but basically all of the items are standard multiple-choice questions.

2. **Graphs.** The graphs element of the math part of the GRE is very much like Problem Solving *except* that the data needed to answer are presented in graphic form rather than in text form. Additionally, a single graphic presentation usually supports two or three questions.

    The GRE tends to favor common sorts of graphs such as lines, bars, and pies. You may find a graphic presentation that combines two or more graphic elements.

    The graphs items ask question such as:

    In what year, did the population of Country X first exceed 10 million people?

    How much greater was the Gross Domestic Product in 1995 than in 1985?

    What percent of the National Budget was spent on Defense?

3. **Quantitative Comparisons.** Quantitative Comparison are special GRE math questions that use an unusual set of instructions:

    Choose:

    A if the quantity in Column A is greater;

    B if the quantity in Column B is greater;

    C if the two quantities are equal;

    D if the relationship cannot be determined from the information given.

The PreTest has been carefully crafted to give results that are comparable to those generated by a computer-based test. The mix of questions, the range of difficulty, and the 30-minute time limit are features that help to make this a true Pre-Test.

In order to obtain the most accurate results possible, you must follow the directions. Circle the letter of your answer choice or write your answers on a separate piece of paper, and observe faithfully the 30-minutes time limit.

Finally, since the computer-based GMAT CAT does not give you the option of omitting a question, you should answer *all* items. You don't lose points for wrong answers.

12

Take the Math PreTest

Math PreTest

30 Questions • Time—30 Minutes

Numbers: All numbers are real numbers.

Figures: Figures that accompany items are included to provide information for answering the questions. However, unless a note specifically states that a figure is drawn to scale, you should solve problems NOT by visual estimation or measurement but by using your knowledge of mathematical principles.

Lines shown as straight can be assumed to be straight.

Angle measures are positive.

Positions of points, angles, regions, etc. can be assumed to be in the order depicted.

All figures lie in a plane unless otherwise indicated.

DIRECTIONS: Each of the *Items 1–15* consists of two quantities, one in Column A and one in Column B. Compare the quantities and choose:

(A) if the quantity in Column A is greater;

(B) if the quantity in Column B is greater;

(C) if the two quantities are equal;

(D) if the relationship cannot be determined from the information given.

Centered information applies to both columns, and a symbol appearing in both columns has the same meaning in both quantities.

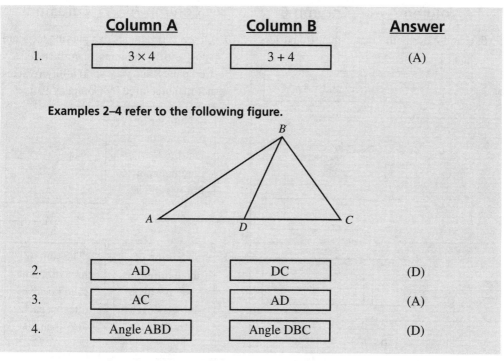

	Column A	Column B	Answer
1.	3×4	$3 + 4$	(A)

Examples 2–4 refer to the following figure.

	Column A	Column B	Answer
2.	AD	DC	(D)
3.	AC	AD	(A)
4.	Angle ABD	Angle DBC	(D)

Column A	Column B

1.
3^5	5^3

2. The total rainfall in August for Region R was 4 centimeters.

Amount of rain that fell during the first 10 days of August.	Amount of rain that fell during the first 20 days of August.

3. A triangle has angles with measures $x°$, 100°, and $y°$.

x	80

Column A   Column B

4. On a landscaping plan, 1 centimeter represents 5 meters.

The actual distance in meters between two trees that are shown on the plan as 19 centimeters apart.	100

5.
$$5 + x < 12$$
$$5 + y < 12$$

x	y

12

Column A	**Column B**

6. j and k are both greater than 0 and less than 1.

7.

$x + y$	z

8.

$\dfrac{6^{10}}{3^5}$	$2^{10} \times 3^5$

9. $0 < k < 1$

$$\frac{\dfrac{1}{x}}{\dfrac{1}{y}} = k$$

$\dfrac{x}{y}$	$\dfrac{y}{x}$

Column A	**Column B**

10. Of the 100 vehicles in a parking lot, x are sport utility vehicles manufactured by Company P and y are sport utility vehicles not manufactured by Company P.

Number of vehicles in the parking lot that are not sport utility vehicles.	$100 - x - y$

11.

The sum of three different odd positive integers each less than 10	The sum of three different even positive integers each less than 10

12.

$0.89(x - y)$	$0.89x - y$

13.

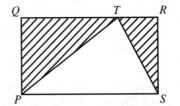

PQRS is a rectangle.

Area of *PTS*	Shaded Area

Column A	**Column B**

14. $x^2 - 2x - 3 = 0$

The sum of the possible values for x.	-1

Column A	**Column B**

15.   Average (arithmetic) mean of Test Scores of job applicants

Average score for female applicants: 89

Average score for male applicants: 80

Average score for all applicants: 85

Number of scores of male applicants	Number of scores of female applicants

---

DIRECTIONS: Each of the *Questions 16–20* has five answer choices. For each question, choose the best answer given.

16. $\dfrac{(13)(23) - (23)(7)}{13 - 7} =$

(A) 0
(B) 7
(C) 13
(D) 20
(E) 23

17. A certain book sells for $15.00 in the bookstore, but the book can be purchased on-line for $12.00. An on-line purchaser saves what percent of the bookstore price of the book?

(A) 0.20%
(B) 0.25%
(C) 3%
(D) 20%
(E) 25%

18.

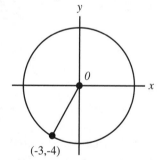

(-3,-4)

If O is the center of the circle above, what is the circumference of the circle?

(A) 5π
(B) 7π
(C) 10π
(D) 25π
(E) 49π

12

19. If 12 identical stamping machines require 20 hours to fill an order, how much less time, in hours, will be required to fill the order if 4 additional stamping machines are used?

   (A) 5
   (B) $9\frac{4}{5}$
   (C) 10
   (D) 15
   (E) 18

20. The length of a rectangular room R is 1 meter longer than the side of square room S, and the width of room R is 1 meter shorter than the side of room S. If x^2 is the floor area of room S, what is the floor area, in square meters, of room R?

   (A) $x^2 - 2$
   (B) $x^2 - 1$
   (C) x^2
   (D) $x^2 + 1$
   (E) $x^2 + 2$

Questions 21–25 refer to the following graph.

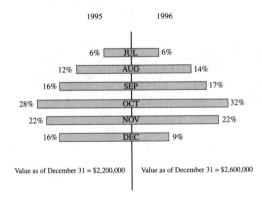

Warehouse Inventory for Company X
By Month of Acquisition

21. For 1995, what percent of the dollar value of inventory held on December 31 was acquired in September?

   (A) 1%
   (B) 15%
   (C) 16%
   (D) 28%
   (E) 34%

22. During which of the following months was the dollar value of inventory acquired the greatest?

   (A) August, 1996
   (B) September, 1995
   (C) September, 1996
   (D) November, 1995
   (E) December, 1996

23. If Company X acquired $500,000 of inventory in September, 1996, what was the dollar value of the inventory acquired that month that was no longer in the warehouse on December 31, 1996?

 (A) $58,000
 (B) $110,000
 (C) $165,00
 (D) $390,000
 (E) It cannot be determined from the information given.

24. What was the dollar value of the inventory held by Company X on August 31, 1996?

 (A) $520,000
 (B) $450,000
 (C) $360,000
 (D) $275,000
 (E) It cannot be determined from the information given.

25. Which of the following statements can be inferred from the graph?

 I. Company X had fewer units in the warehouse on December 31, 1995 than on December 31, 1996.

 II. The total cost of inventory acquired by Company X for the period August, 1996 through November, 1996 was $2,210,000.

 III. Company X acquired $880,000 more in inventory during November, 1996 than November, 1995.

 (A) none
 (B) I only
 (C) III only
 (D) II and III only
 (E) I, II, and III

26. At a certain company, 60 percent of the employees are women. If 20 percent of the women and 15 percent of the men hold MBAs, what percent of the total number of employees hold MBAs?

 (A) 6
 (B) 9
 (C) 12
 (D) 15
 (E) 18

27. If a triangle in the coordinate plan has vertices of (-2,2), (4,4), and (0,0), what is the perimeter of the triangle?

 (A) $2 + 6\sqrt{2}$
 (B) $2 + 6\sqrt{10}$
 (C) $4 + 2\sqrt{10}$
 (D) $4\sqrt{2} + 6\sqrt{10}$
 (E) $6\sqrt{2} + 2\sqrt{10}$

28. If a solid right circular cylinder of diameter 4 and height of 5 inches is placed into a rectangular box that is 3 inches by 3 inches by 5 inches, the volume of the box that is not occupied by the cylinder is how many cubic inches?

 (A) $45 - 20\pi$
 (B) $45 - 16\pi$
 (C) $15 - 5\pi$
 (D) $20\pi - 30$
 (E) $16\pi - 45$

12

29. If x and y are different positive integers, then the ratio of $\frac{x}{y}$ to its reciprocal is

   (A) $\dfrac{y^2}{x^2}$

   (B) $\dfrac{x^2}{y^2}$

   (C) $\dfrac{x}{y}$

   (D) $\dfrac{y}{x}$

   (E) 1

30. Which of the following is the graph of all x values such that $x \geq 1$ and $-x \leq -2$?

   (A)

   (B)

   (C)

   (D)

   (E)

STOP:

IF YOU FINISH BEFORE TIME
EXPIRES, USE THE ADDITIONAL
TIME TO CHECK YOUR WORK.

Evaluate Your Performance

Use the following answer key to score your Math PreTest. Put a "✓ "beside those items you answered correctly.

Quantitative Comparisons

1. (A)
2. (D)
3. (B)
4. (B)
5. (D)
6. (B)
7. (A)
8. (C)

9. (A)
10. (C)
11. (D)
12. (D)
13. (C)
14. (A)
15. (B)

Number of Quantitative Comparisons Correct: _____

Problem Solving

16. (E)
17. (D)
18. (C)

19. (A)
20. (B)

(Enter total below.)

Graphs

21. (C)
22. (D)
23. (A)

24. (E)
25. (A)

Number of Graphs Correct: _____

Problem Solving

26. (E)
27. (E)
28. (A)

29. (B)
30. (C)

Number of Problem Solving Questions Correct: _____
(16–20 plus 26–30)

TOTAL CORRECT: _____

12

You'll find explanations for the Math PreTest below. Right now, however, you're probably more interested in learning how you did. So use the graphs below to find out how you did. Then review the Explanations before you go on to another lesson.

Quantitative Comparisons

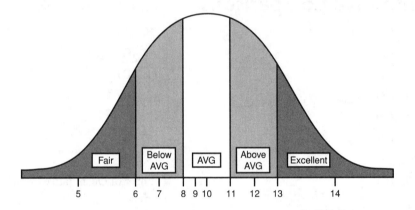

Number Correct

Problem Solving

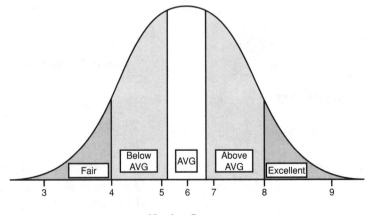

Number Correct

Graphs

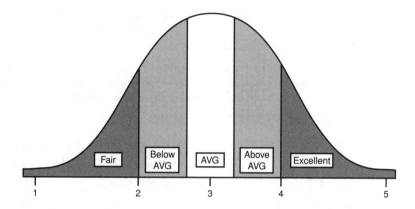

Number Correct

Overall Math

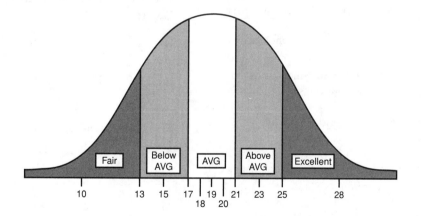

Number Correct

12

Review the Correct Answers

You should now review the explanations for the correct answers to the Math PreTest.

TIP — Before reviewing the explanations, go back over the PreTest and finish on your own any questions that you didn't have time for during the 30-minute time limit. Doing it on your own before reviewing an explanation is always good practice.

1. **(A)**

   $3^5 = 3 \times 3 \times 3 \times 3 \times 3 = 243$

   $5^3 = 5 \times 5 \times 5 \times = 125$

   For more information on powers, see Day 14.

2. **(D)** The Centered Information gives the total rainfall for the region for the entire month. But it provides no information about how much rain fell on any given day.

3. **(B)** Since the sum of the measures of the interior angles of a triangle is $180°$, $x + y = 180 - 100 = 80$. Since y must have some measure, x must be less than 80.

   For more information on triangles, see Day 16.

4. **(B)** Since $1\text{cm} = 5$ m, the actual distance is $19 \times 5\text{m} = 95\text{m}$.

5. **(D)** The Centered Information establishes only that both x and y are less than 7. But that is not sufficient to permit you to make a comparison of x and y.

   For more information on inequalities, see Day 14.

6. **(B)** Since j and k are both positive fractions, $j^2 < j$ and $k^2 < k$, and therefore $j^2 + k^2 < j + k$.

   For more information on inequalities, see Day 14.

7. **(A)** For any given triangle, the sum of the lengths of two of the legs must be greater than the length of the third leg.

   For more information on triangles, see Day 16.

8. **(C)**

   $$\frac{6^{10}}{3^5} = \frac{2^{10} \times 3^{10}}{3^5} = 2^{10} \times 3^5$$

   For more information on exponents, see Day 14.

9. **(A)**

   $$\frac{\frac{1}{x}}{\frac{1}{y}} = \frac{y}{x} = k$$

   Since k is a positive fraction $y < x$ and therefore $\left|\frac{x}{y}\right| > \left|\frac{y}{x}\right|$.

For more information about multiplying algebraic terms, see Day 15.

10. **(C)** The total number of vehicles in the parking lot less the total number of sports utilities in the parking lot is equal to the number of vehicles in the parking lot that are not sport utilities.

11. **(D)** The three odd integers might be $1 + 3 + 5 = 9$ or they might be $3 + 5 + 7 = 15$ or even $5 + 7 + 9 = 21$. The three even integers might be $2 + 4 + 6 = 12$ or $4 + 6 + 8 = 18$. So the relationship is indeterminate.

For more information on odd and even numbers, see Day 13.

12. **(D)** $0.89(x-y) = 0.89x - 0.89y$. $0.89x = 0.89x$, but you have no information about y, which could be negative, positive, or 0.

For more information about multiplying algebraic terms, see Day 15.

13. **(C)** *PTS* is a triangle with altitude equal to *PQ* and base of *PS*. So the area of *PTS* is $\frac{1}{2} \times PQ \times PS$. But that is equal one-half the area of the rectangle *PQRS*. So the area of the triangle is one-half of the area of the rectangle and so is the shaded area.

For more information on triangles and rectangles, see Day 16.

14. **(A)**

$x^2 - 2x - 3 = 0$

$(x - 3)(x + 1) = 0$

$x - 3 = 0 \text{ or } x + 1 = 0$

$x = 3 \text{ or } x = -1$

For more information on solving quadratic equations, see Day 15.

15. **(B)** Let x be the number of women and y be the number of men:

$x(89) + y(80) = (x + y)85$

$89x + 80y = 85x + 85y$

$4x = 5y$

$\dfrac{x}{y} = \dfrac{5}{4}$

So $x > y$.

For more information on averages, see Day 14.

16. **(E)**

$$\frac{(13)(23) - (23)(7)}{13 - 7} =$$

$$\frac{(23)(13 - 7)}{13 - 7} = 23$$

For more information on factoring, see Day 15.

17. **(D)**

$$\frac{\$15.00 - \$12.00}{\$15.00} = \frac{\$3.00}{\$15.00} = \frac{1}{5} = 20\%$$

For more information on percent, see Day 14.

12

18. **(C)** You can use the Distance Formula or the Pythagorean Theorem to find the radius of the circle:

$$r^2 = 3^2 + 4^2$$

$$r = 5$$

And:

$$C = 2\pi r = 2\pi(5) = 10\pi$$

For more information on coordinate geometry, see Day 16.

19. **(A)** Use an indirect proportion:

$$\frac{12}{16} = \frac{x}{20}$$

Where x is the time required to do the job with 16 machines. Cross-multiply:

$$x = \frac{12 \times 20}{16} = 15$$

And:

$$20 - 15 = 5$$

For more information on proportions, see Day 14.

20. **(B)** Since x^2 is the area of the square room, the side of S is equal to x. Therefore, the dimensions of the rectangular room are:

$$L = x + 1$$

$$W = x - 1$$

And the area of the rectangular room is:

$$L \times W = (x + 1)(x - 1) = x^2 - 1$$

For more information about squares and rectangles, see Day 16.

21. **(C)** You can read the number directly off the graph.

For more information about graphs, see Day 21.

22. **(D)** The dollar figures are:

(A) 14% of $2,600,000 = $364,000

(B) 16% of $2,200,000 = $352,000

(C) 17% of $2,600,000 = $442,000

(D) 22% of $2,200,000 = $484,000

(E) 9% of $2,600,000 = $234,000

For more information about graphs, see Day 21.

23. **(A)** The dollar value of inventory acquired in September, 1996 that was still on hand on December 31, 1996 was:

17% of $2,600,000 = $442,000

And:

$500,000 - $442,000 = $58,000

For more information about graphs, see Day 21.

24. **(E)** The graph tells you only about inventory that was on-hand on December 31. It gives you no information about what was in stock in any other month.

For more information about graphs, see Day 21.

25. **(A)** Statement I is not inerrable since the graph give you information about dollar value and not about number of units. Statement II is not inferrable because the graphs gives you information only about the dollar value of inventory acquired during a certain month that will still be on hand on December 31. It tells you nothing about the total acquired during a month. And statement III is not inerrable for the same reason.

For more information about graphs, see Day 21.

26. **(E)** The percent of women with MBAs is:

20% of 60% = 12%

And the percent of men with MBAs is:

15% of 40% = 6%

The two figures combined are:

12% + 6% = 18%

For more information on percent, see Day 14.

27. **(E)** You can use the Distance Formula or the Pythagorean Theorem. The distance from (-2,2) to (0,0) is $2\sqrt{2}$, the distance from (0,0) to (4,4) is $4\sqrt{2}$, and the distance from (-2,2) to (4,4) is $2\sqrt{10}$. So the perimeter of the triangle is $6\sqrt{2} + 2\sqrt{10}$.

For more information about coordinate geometry, see Day 16.

28. **(A)** The cylinder goes inside the box. The volume of the cylinder is:

$$V_{cyldinder} = \pi r^2 \times h = \pi(2)^2 \times 5 = 20\pi$$

And the volume of the cube is:

$$V_{cube} = 3 \times 3 \times 5 = 45$$

The volume that is not occupied by the cylinder is the difference between the two:

$$45 - 20\pi$$

For more information on solid geometry, see Day 16.

29. **(B)** The reciprocal of $\frac{x}{y}$ is $\frac{y}{x}$ and the ratio is:

$$\frac{\frac{x}{y}}{\frac{y}{x}} = \frac{x^2}{y^2}$$

For more information on manipulating algebraic terms, see Day 15.

30. **(C)** The second inequality is equivalent to $x \geq 2$, so $x \geq 1$.

For more information on inequalities, see Day 15.

12

Teach Yourself
GRE Arithmetic (I)

Today's lesson focuses on some basic math concepts such as proprties of the numbers system and using negative numbers. These concepts are so fundamental that, in addition to sometimes being the focus of a test problem, they permeate the math part with one or more showing up in almost every problem. So a solid working knowledge of them is essential to a good score.

Review Properties of the Number System

Whole numbers are the numbers we use for counting, plus the number zero: 0, 1, 2, 3, 4, . . .

The counting system is based on groups of ten, so it is called the base ten system. When we write a number, the positions of the digits indicate their value. The first digit (at the far right) always indicates the number of units; the second digit indicates the number of groups of ten; the third digit always indicates the number of ten groups of ten, or hundreds; the fourth digit indicates the number of ten groups of ten groups of ten, or thousands; and so on.

So 1,234,567 is equivalent to one group of one million plus two groups of one hundred thousand plus three groups of ten thousand plus four groups of a thousand plus five groups of one hundred plus six groups of ten plus seven additional units.

Operations with Whole Numbers

Begin by making sure that you know the meaning of some key terms that might be used on the test.

sum or total: The result of adding numbers together. For example, the sum (or total) of 2 and 3 is 5: $2 + 3 = 5$.

difference: The result of subtracting one number from another. For example, the difference between 5 and 2 is 3: $5 - 2 = 3$.

product: The result of multiplying numbers together. For example, the product of 2 and 3 is 6: $2 \times 3 = 6$.

quotient: The result of dividing one number by another. For example, the quotient when 6 is divided by 2 is 3: $6 \div 2 = 3$.

remainder: In division, if the quotient is not itself a whole number, the result can be written as a whole number quotient plus a whole number remainder. For example, $7 \div 3 = 2$ plus a remainder of 1.

Next, you need to make sure that you remember the basic rules governing operations. In math, the basic punctuation mark is the parenthesis. Sets of parentheses will tell you in what order operations are to be performed, and operations in parentheses are always done first. Here is an example:

$(2 + 3) \times 4 = 20$, BUT $2 + (3 \times 4) = 14$

Here is a more complex example:

$$\frac{(2 \times 3) \times (2 + 1)}{3 \times (5 - 4)} = \frac{(6) \times (3)}{3 - (1)} = \frac{18}{3} = 6$$

A particularly complex statement might use brackets as well. Here is an example that uses additional punctuation:

$[(2 \times 3) - 5] + [2 \times (4 - 1)]$

With such a problem, work from the inside out. Start with the operations within parentheses:

$[(2 \times 3) - 5] + [2 \times (4 - 1)] = [6 - 5] + [2 \times 3]$

Then do the operations within brackets:

$[6 - 5] + [2 \times 3] = 1 + 6$

And finish the problem off:

$1 + 6 = 7$

Punctuation eliminates ambiguity, but it does not always dictate the order in which operations must be done. That's what the following example demonstrates:

$2 + 3 + 4 = 4 + 3 + 2$

$2 \times 3 \times 4 = 4 \times 3 \times 2$

Even when multiplication and addition are combined, you have a choice about order of operations. For example:

$5(2 + 3 + 4) =$

Most people would probably do the addition first and then the multiplication:

$5(2 + 3 + 4) = 5(9) = 45$

It is also permissible, however, to do the multiplication first:

$5(2 + 3 + 4) = 2(5) + 3(5) + 4(5) = 10 + 15 + 20 = 45$

And here is another illustration:

$(1 + 4)(2 + 3) =$

Again, most people would probably do the addition first:

$(1 + 4)(2 + 3) = (5)(5) = 25$

But it is possible to do the multiplication first:

$(1 + 4)(2 + 3) = (1)(2) + (1)(3) + (4)(2) + (4)(3) = 2 + 3 + 8 + 12 = 25$

It just so happens that the first method (addition before multiplication) is easier, so it's the one we naturally use.

We have just seen that $10 + 15 + 20$ is equal to $2(5) + 3(5) + 4(5)$, which in turn equals $5(2 + 3 + 4)$. We might call this process, which is the reverse of multiplication, "de-multiplication." "De-multiplying" can be a tremendous labor-saving device, as demonstrated by the next example:

$(723)(34) - (723)(33) =$

You could do this calculation by first multiplying and then subtracting:

$(723)(34) - (723)(33) = 24,582 - 23,859 = 723$

13

A better way of handling the calculation is to "de-multiply":

$$(723)(34) - (723)(33) = 723(34 - 33) = 723(1) = 723$$

"De-multiplication" can be combined with division for even greater simplifying power. Here's how:

$$\frac{24 + 36}{12} = \frac{12(2 + 3)}{12} = (1)(2 + 3) = 2 + 3 = 5$$

In this case, 12 can be extracted from both 24 and 36. Then it is possible to divide 12 by 12, which is 1. This last step is also known as cancelling.

 TIP

This of "factoring" "de-multiplying." "De-multiplying" is an invaluable labor-saving device.

Factors, Multiples, and Primes

Factor, multiple, and prime are properties of numbers that are often the basis for a test question. So we'll go over each concept. First, numbers that evenly divide another number are called the factors of that number. (What we called "de-multiplication" above is usually called factoring. The process is called factoring because it breaks a number into its factors.)

If a number is evenly divisible by another number, it is considered to be a multiple of that number. 2, 3, 4, and 6 are all factors of 12. And conversely, 12 is a multiple of 2, a multiple of 3, and so on.

Some numbers are not evenly divisible except by 1 and themselves. For example, 13 is evenly divisible by 1 but not by 2 through 12. And, of course, it can be divided by itself. A number such as this (which can be divided evenly only by 1 and itself) is called a prime number. Examples of prime numbers are 2, 3, 5, 7, 11, 13, 17, 19, and 23. (Note: 1 is not considered a prime number even though it is not evenly divisible by any other number.)

 CAUTION

1 is not considered a prime number even though it is not even divisible by another counting number. 2 is the first prime number.

A second important concept is that of even and odd. An even number is a number that is divisible by 2; an odd number is one that is not divisible by 2. Any number the last digit of which is 0, 2, 4, 6, or 8 is divisible by 2 and therefore even. Any number the last digit of which is 1, 3, 5, 7, or 9 is not divisible by 2 and therefore odd.

Here are some important principles that govern the behavior of odd and even numbers:

EVEN + EVEN = EVEN   For example, $2 + 4 = 6$

EVEN + ODD = ODD   For example, $4 + 3 = 7$

ODD + EVEN = ODD   For example, $3 + 4 = 7$

ODD + ODD = EVEN   For example, $3 + 5 = 8$

EVEN $\times$ EVEN = EVEN   For example, $2 \times 4 = 8$

EVEN $\times$ ODD = EVEN   For example, $2 \times 3 = 6$

ODD $\times$ EVEN = EVEN   For example, $3 \times 2 = 6$

ODD $\times$ ODD = ODD   For example, $3 \times 5 = 15$

> **CAUTION** The even/odd rules on multiplication do NOT apply to division. For example, if you divide the even number 4 by the even number 8, the result is $\frac{1}{2}$. Odd and even are characteristics of whole numbers (plus negative integers), but not fractions. A fraction is neither odd nor even.

The third important concept in this series is *consecutive* numbers. Consecutive numbers are ones that follow each other immediately. For example, 3, 4, 5, and 6 are consecutive numbers, but 3, 7, 21, and 45 are not. In a string of consecutive numbers, the next number is always one more than the preceding number. Thus, if n is the first number in a string of consecutive numbers, the second number is $n + 1$, the third number is $n + 2$, the fourth number is $n + 3$, and so on.

13

1st	2nd	3rd	4th
3	4	5	6
n	$n + 1$	$n + 2$	$n + 3$

We can also speak of consecutive even numbers and consecutive odd numbers. 2, 4, 6, and 8 are consecutive even numbers; 3, 5, 7, and 9 are consecutive odd numbers. In a string of consecutive even (or odd) numbers, the next number is always two more than the preceding number. Thus, if n is the first number in a string of consecutive even (or odd) numbers, the second number is $n + 2$, the third number is $n + 4$, the fourth number is $n + 6$, and so on.

1st	2nd	3rd	4th
4	6	8	10
n	$n + 2$	$n + 4$	$n + 6$
3	5	7	9
n	$n + 2$	$n + 4$	$n + 6$

NOTE Even though 2, 4, etc., are even numbers, $n + 2$, $n + 4$, etc. will be odd numbers when n, the starting point, is odd.

Workshop A: Properties

Use the 20 problems in this drill to practice working with whole numbers. There is no time limit for the drill. You'll find the answers in the Review section immediately following the Drill section.

Drill

1. Subtracting 1 from which digit in the number 12,345 will decrease the value of the number by 1,000?

    (A) 1
    (B) 2
    (C) 3
    (D) 4
    (E) 5

2. $(1 \times 10{,}000) + (2 \times 1{,}000) + (3 \times 100) + (4 \times 10) + (5 \times 1) =$

    10,000 + 2,000 + 300 + 400 + 5

    (A) 5,000
    (B) 15,000
    (C) 12,345
    (D) 54,321
    (E) 543,210

[handwritten: 20,000.^{00} 8,000.^{00} + 40]

3. $(2 \times 10,000) + (8 \times 1,000) + (4 \times 10) =$

(A) 284
(B) 482
(C) 2,084
(D) 2,840
(E) 28,040 *[circled]*

4. What is the remainder when 18 is divided by 2?

(A) 0 *[circled]*
(B) 1
(C) 3
(D) 6
(E) 9

5. When both 8 and 13 are divided by a certain number, the remainder is 3. What is that number?

(A) 4
(B) 5 *[circled]*
(C) 6
(D) 7
(E) 8

6. When both 33 and 37 are divided by a certain number, the remainder is 1. What is that number?

(A) 4 *[circled]*
(B) 9
(C) 10
(D) 16
(E) 18

7. $[(36 \div 12) \times (24 \div 3)] \div [(1 \times 3) - (18 \div 9)] =$

(A) 3
(B) 8
(C) 16
(D) 20
(E) 24 *[circled]*

[handwritten: [3 × 8] ÷ [3-2]   24 ÷ 1]

8. $[(12 \times 3) - (3 \times 12)] + [(8 \div 2) \div 4] =$

(A) 0
(B) 1 *[circled]*
(C) 4
(D) 8
(E) 16

[handwritten: [36 - 36] + [(4 ÷ 4)]   0 + 1]

9. Which of the following statements is (are) true?

I. $(4 + 3) - 6 = 4 + (6 - 2)$ *[handwritten: 7-6 = 4-4]*

II. $3(4 + 5) = (3 \times 4) + (3 \times 5)$ *[handwritten: (9) 27 = 12 + 15]*

III. $(3 + 5) \times 4 = 4 \times (5 + 3)$ *[handwritten: 32 = 32]*

(A) I only
(B) II only
(C) III only
(D) II and III only *[circled]*
(E) I, II, and III

10. $\dfrac{99(121) - 99(120)}{33} =$

[handwritten: $\dfrac{99(121-120)}{33} = 33$]

(A) 1
(B) 3
(C) 33 *[circled]*
(D) 99
(E) 120

11. $1,234(96) - 1,234(48) =$

(A) $1,234 \times 48$ *[circled]*
(B) $1,234 \times 96$
(C) $1,234(48 + 96)$
(D) $(1,234 \times 1,234) \times 48$
(E) 59,232

[handwritten: 96 - 48 = 48]

[handwritten: 1,234 (96-48)   1234 × 48   9872   49360   59232]

12. How many prime numbers are greater than 20 but less than 30?

    (A) 0   23

    (B) 1

    (C) 2   29

    (D) 3

    (E) 4

13. How many prime numbers are greater that 50 but less than 60?

    (A) 0   51

    (B) 1   53

    (C) 2   57

    (D) 3   59

    (E) 4

14. Which of the following numbers are prime numbers?

    I. 11

    II. 111

    III. 1,111

    (A) I only

    (B) II only

    (C) I and II only

    (D) I and III only

    (E) I, II, and III

15. What is the smallest multiple of both 12 and 18?

    (A) 36

    (B) 48

    (C) 72

    (D) 128

    (E) 216

16. Which of the following is (are) even?

    I. $333,332 \times 333,333$

    II. $999,999 + 101,101$

    III. $22,221 \times 44,441$

    (A) I only

    (B) II only

    (C) I and II only

    (D) I and III only

    (E) I, II, and III

17. If n is an even number, all of the following must also be even EXCEPT

    (A) $(n \times n) + n$

    (B) $n \times n - n$

    (C) $n + 2$

    (D) $3(n + 2)$

    (E) $\dfrac{n}{2}$

18. For any whole number n, which of the following must be odd?

    I. $3(n + 1)$

    II. $3n + 2n$

    III. $2n - 1$

    (A) I only

    (B) II only

    (C) III only

    (D) I and II only

    (E) I, II, and III

19. If 8 is the third number in a series of three consecutive whole numbers, what is the first number in the series?

    (A) 0
    (B) 1
    (C) 6
    (D) 7
    (E) 11

20. If *m*, *n*, and *o* are consecutive whole numbers that total 15, what is the largest of the three numbers?

    (A) 4
    (B) 5
    (C) 6
    (D) 14
    (E) 17

13

Review

Review Procedures for Manipulating Fractions

When one whole number is divided by another whole and the result is not a third whole number, the result is a fraction. Thus, when 2 is divided by 3, the result is not a whole number. The result is the fraction $2 \div 3$, which is written $\frac{2}{3}$.

The number above the line in the fraction is called the numerator; the number below the line is called the denominator.

In a proper fraction, the numerator is less than the denominator, so the fraction has a value of less than 1, e.g., $\frac{1}{2}$ and $\frac{3}{4}$, which are both less than 1.

In an improper fraction, the numerator is greater than the denominator, so the fraction has a value greater than 1, e.g., $\frac{3}{2}$ and $\frac{4}{3}$ are both greater than 1.

A mixed number consists of both a whole number and a fraction written together, for example, $2\frac{1}{2}$ which is equivalent to $2 + \frac{1}{2}$ and $3\frac{4}{5}$ which is equivalent to $3 + \frac{4}{5}$.

Before you add, subtract, multiply, or divide, you should change mixed numbers to improper fractions. To convert a mixed number to an improper fraction:

1. Use the denominator of the old fractional part of the mixed number as the new denominator.

2. Multiply the whole number part of the mixed number by its denominator and add to that product the numerator of the old fractional part. This is the new numerator.

This is more difficult to describe than it is to do. Take the mixed number $2\frac{3}{7}$. First, the denominator of your new fraction will be 7. Next, multiply 7 by 2, which is 14. Then add 3 to that: $14 + 3 = 17$. 17 is the new numerator, and 7 is the denominator. So the result is $\frac{17}{7}$.

To convert an improper fraction to a mixed number, you reverse the process:

1. Divide the denominator into the numerator. The quotient becomes the whole number part of the mixed number.
2. Using the same denominator, create a fraction the numerator of which is the remainder of the division process in step one.

For example, to convert $\frac{30}{7}$ into a mixed number, first divide 7 into 30. The result is 4 with a remainder of 2. The 4 is now the whole number part of the mixed number. Next, the numerator of the fraction is the remainder 2, and the denominator is 7. So the result is $4\frac{2}{7}$.

For reasons of convenience, it is customary to reduce all fractions to their lowest terms. When you reduce a fraction to lowest terms, you really are doing nothing but rewriting it in an equivalent form. This is accomplished by eliminating redundant factors in both the numerator and the denominator of the fraction. Here is an example:

$$\frac{8}{16} = \frac{1(8)}{2(8)} = \frac{1}{2}$$

There are various ways of describing what goes on when you reduce a fraction. You might think of taking out a common factor, such as 8 in the example above, and dividing 8 into 8 (or cancelling the 8s). It's also possible to think of the process as dividing both numerator and denominator by the same number:

$$\frac{8}{16} = \frac{8 \div 8}{16 \div 8} = \frac{1}{2}$$

It doesn't really matter which way you would describe the process, so long as you know how to reduce a fraction to its lowest terms.

A fraction is expressed in lowest terms when there is no number (other than 1) that can be evenly divided into both numerator and denominator. For example, $\frac{8}{15}$ is in lowest terms, since there is no number (other than 1) that evenly goes into 8 that also evenly goes into 15. On the other hand, $\frac{8}{12}$ is not in lowest terms, since both 8 and 12 can be evenly divided by 4. If you reduce $\frac{8}{12}$ by a factor of 4, you get $\frac{2}{3}$, which is in lowest terms since no number (other than 1) evenly divides both 2 and 3.

13

If a fraction is particularly large, you may need to reduce it in steps. The process is largely a matter of trial and error, but there are a couple of rules that can guide you. Remember that if both numerator and denominator are even numbers, you can reduce the fraction by a factor of 2. Here's an example:

$$\frac{32}{64} = \frac{16(2)}{32(2)} = \frac{8(2)}{16(2)} = \frac{4(2)}{8(2)} = \frac{2(2)}{4(2)} = \frac{1}{2}$$

If both the numerator and the denominator end in either 0 or 5, they are both divisible by 5. Here's an example:

$$\frac{55}{100} = \frac{11(5)}{20(5)} = \frac{11}{20}$$

NOTE

On the test, fractions in the answer choices are often presented in lowest terms.

A common denominator is a number that is a multiple of the denominators of two or more fractions. For example, 12 is a multiple of both 3 and 4 (both 3 and 4 divide evenly into 12), so it is a suitable common denominator for $\frac{1}{3}$ and $\frac{3}{4}$. Converting a fraction to another denominator is the reverse of reducing it to lowest terms. Here's how it goes:

$$\frac{1}{4} = \frac{1 \times 3}{4 \times 3} = \frac{1}{12}$$

When you multiply both the numerator and the denominator by the same number, you are really just multiplying the fraction by 1 ($\frac{3}{3} = 1$), so you don't change its value.

In the example above, how do we know to use 3? We want to convert a fraction with a denominator of 4, so we ask the question, "What number, when multiplied by 4, yields the product 12?" The answer is found by dividing 12 by 4. Since $12 \div 4 = 3$, we know we must multiply 4 by 3 to get 12.

To take another example, by what number must you multiply the numerator and denominator of the fraction to get a fraction with a denominator of 30? Since $30 \div 6 = 5$, you must use 5:

$$\frac{5}{6} = \frac{5 \times 5}{6 \times 5} = \frac{25}{30}$$

In grade school you were taught to find the lowest common denominator for fractions. But in truth, any old common denominator will work. The easiest way to find a common denominator is to multiply the two denominators you are working with. Thus, a common denominator for 2 and 3 is 2×3, or 6; a common denominator for 3 and 4 is 3×4, or 12; a common denominator for 2 and 5 is 2×5, or 10.

What, then, was the big deal about lowest common denominators? It's the same as reducing fractions to lowest terms: it's easier to work with. Thus, a common denominator for 2 and 8 is 16, but 8 is also a possibility. And it's easier to deal with a fraction of denominator 8 than 16.

In the final analysis, however, you can use any common denominator, because you can always reduce a fraction to its lowest terms.

The procedure for adding fractions varies depending on whether or not the fractions already share the same denominator. To add fractions with the same denominator, create a new fraction using that denominator. The new numerator is the sum of the old numerators. For example:

$$\frac{3}{7} + \frac{2}{7} = \frac{5}{7}$$

$$\frac{21 + 14}{49} = \frac{35}{49} = \frac{5}{7} = \frac{5}{7}$$

If you are adding a fraction and a mixed number, remember to change the mixed number to an improper fraction and then add:

$$2\frac{1}{3} + \frac{1}{3} = \frac{7}{3} + \frac{1}{3} = \frac{8}{3} = 2\frac{2}{3}$$

To add fractions with different denominators, you must first find a common denominator and convert the fractions in the manner described above. For example, $\frac{1}{3}$ and $\frac{1}{5}$. Since these fractions have unlike denominators, you must find a common denominator such as 15. Next, you convert each fraction to a fraction with denominator of 15. Here's an example:

$$\frac{1}{3} + \frac{1}{5} = \frac{1(1)}{3(5)} + \frac{1(3)}{5(3)} = \frac{5}{15} + \frac{3}{15} = \frac{8}{15}$$

$$\frac{1}{3} + \frac{1}{5} = \left(\frac{1}{3}\right)\left(\frac{5}{5}\right) + \left(\frac{1}{5}\right)\left(\frac{3}{3}\right)$$
$$= \frac{5}{16} + \frac{3}{15} = \frac{8}{15}$$

13

If you are adding a fraction and a whole number, you can treat the whole number as a fraction with a denominator of 1. For example:

$$2 + \frac{1}{5} + \frac{1}{2} = \frac{2}{1} + \frac{1}{5} + \frac{1}{2} = \frac{20}{10} + \frac{2}{10} + \frac{5}{10} = \frac{27}{10}$$

$$\left(\frac{10}{10}\right)\frac{2}{1} + \frac{1}{5}\left(\frac{2}{2}\right) + \frac{1}{2}\left(\frac{5}{5}\right) = \frac{20}{10} + \frac{2}{10} + \frac{5}{10} = \frac{27}{10}$$

You follow the same procedure for subtraction except that you subtract rather than add. When the fractions have the same denominators, you simply subtract one numerator from another. When you have fractions with different denominators, it's first necessary to find a common denominator.

You really don't need to worry about finding a lowest common denominator as long as you remember to reduce the result of an operation to lowest terms. The procedure can be described generally as:

1. Multiply the denominators to get a new denominator.

2. Multiply the numerator of the first fraction by the denominator of the second.

3. Multiply the numerator of the second fraction by the denominator of the first.

4. The new numerator is the sum (or difference) of the results of steps 2 and 3.

It's more difficult to describe the process than it is to do it. Perhaps the easiest way to learn it is to see it done. Let $\frac{a}{b}$ and $\frac{c}{d}$ be any two fractions). Add them:

$$\frac{a}{b} + \frac{c}{d} = \frac{ad + bc}{bd}$$

And the same method can be used for subracting fractions:

$$\frac{a}{b} - \frac{c}{d} = \frac{ad - bc}{bd}$$

Of course, this may not give you the lowest terms of the fractions, so it may be necessary to reduce.

TIP

To add or subtract fractions in a hurry, multiply denominators to get your new denominator. Then cross-multiply the numerator/denominator combinations and add or subrtact. Remember to reduce to lowest terms.

Multiplication of fractions does not require a common denominator. Or perhaps we should say that multiplication produces a common denominator automatically. To multiply fractions, just multiply numerators to create a new numerator, and multiply denominators to create a new denominator. Here's an example:

$$\frac{3}{4} \times \frac{1}{5} = \frac{3 \times 1}{4 \times 5} = \frac{3}{20}$$

Division is the opposite of multiplication. To divide by a fraction, you invert the divisor (the fraction by which you are dividing) and then multiply:

$$2 \div \frac{1}{4} = 2 \times \frac{4}{1} = 8$$

Workshop B: Fractions

Use the 20 problems in this drill to practice working with fractions. There is no time limit for the drill. You'll find the answers in the Review section immediately following the Drill section.

Drill

1. $5\frac{3}{8} =$

   (A) 1

   (B) $\frac{15}{8}$

   (C) $\frac{23}{8}$

   (D) $\frac{35}{8}$

   (E) $\frac{43}{8}$

2. $\frac{23}{13} =$

   (A) 10

   (B) $7\frac{7}{13}$

   (C) $1\frac{10}{13}$

   (D) $\frac{13}{23}$

   (E) $\frac{7}{13}$

3. $\frac{125}{625} =$

   (A) $\frac{1}{5}$

   (B) $\frac{2}{5}$

   (C) $\frac{7}{10}$

   (D) $\frac{4}{5}$

   (E) $\frac{14}{15}$

4. $\frac{3}{8}$ is equal to all of the following EXCEPT

   (A) $\frac{6}{16}$

   (B) $\frac{15}{40}$

   (C) $\frac{31}{81}$

   (D) $\frac{33}{88}$

   (E) $\frac{120}{320}$

13

5. $\frac{3}{8} + \frac{5}{6} =$ $\frac{18 + 40}{48} = \frac{58}{48}$

(A) 848

(B) $\frac{8}{14}$

(C) $\frac{29}{24}$

(D) $\frac{3}{2}$

(E) $\frac{14}{8}$

(handwritten) $\frac{29}{2\overline{)58}}$ $2\overline{)\frac{24}{48}}$ $= \frac{29}{24}$

6. $\frac{4}{9} + \frac{5}{8} =$ $\frac{32 + 45}{72} = \frac{77}{72}$

(A) $\frac{8}{9}$

(B) $\frac{25}{24}$

(C) $\frac{84}{80}$

(D) $\frac{77}{72}$

(E) $\frac{27}{24}$

7. $\frac{1}{7} + \frac{1}{8} =$ $\frac{8 + 7}{56} = \frac{15}{56}$

(A) $\frac{1}{15}$

(B) $\frac{1}{27}$

(C) $\frac{1}{5}$

(D) $\frac{3}{5}$

(E) $\frac{15}{56}$

8. $\frac{1}{12} + \frac{1}{7} =$ $\frac{7 + 12}{84} = \frac{19}{84}$

(handwritten top) $\frac{12}{\frac{7}{84}}$

(A) $\frac{19}{84}$

(B) $\frac{19}{42}$

(C) $\frac{10}{19}$

(D) $\frac{20}{19}$

(E) $\frac{5}{4}$

(handwritten) $\frac{1}{12}\left(\frac{7}{7}\right) + \frac{1}{7}\left(\frac{12}{12}\right)$

9. $\frac{1}{2} + \frac{1}{3} + \frac{1}{6} =$

(A) $\frac{1}{36}$

(B) $\frac{1}{12}$

(C) 1

(D) $\frac{7}{6}$

(E) $\frac{7}{3}$

(handwritten) $\frac{1}{2}\left(\frac{3}{3}\right) + \frac{1}{3}\left(\frac{2}{2}\right) + \frac{1}{6}\left(\frac{1}{1}\right)$

$\frac{3}{6} + \frac{2}{6} + \frac{1}{6}$

10. $\frac{9}{10} - \frac{1}{5} =$

(A) $\frac{7}{1}$

(B) $\frac{7}{5}$

(C) $\frac{10}{7}$

(D) $\frac{7}{5}$

(E) $\frac{20}{7}$

(handwritten) $\frac{9}{10} - \frac{1}{5}\left(\frac{2}{2}\right) = \frac{7}{1}$

1

11. $2\frac{1}{3} - 1\frac{1}{6} =$

   (A) $1\frac{1}{16}$

   (B) $1\frac{1}{3}$

   (C) $1\frac{1}{2}$

   (D) $1\frac{2}{3}$

   (E) 2

12. $\frac{2}{7} \times \frac{1}{4} =$

   (A) $\frac{1}{63}$

   (B) $\frac{1}{14}$

   (C) $\frac{1}{4}$

   (D) $\frac{3}{8}$

   (E) $\frac{5}{9}$

13. $\frac{1}{4} \times \frac{1}{8} \times 3 =$

   (A) $\frac{3}{32}$

   (B) $\frac{1}{8}$

   (C) $\frac{1}{4}$

   (D) $\frac{1}{2}$

   (E) $\frac{3}{4}$

14. $\frac{7}{8} \div \frac{3}{4} =$

   (A) $\frac{7}{6}$

   (B) 1

   (C) $\frac{3}{4}$

   (D) $\frac{1}{3}$

   (E) $\frac{1}{8}$

15. $\frac{8}{9} \div \frac{7}{8} =$

   (A) $\frac{64}{63}$

   (B) $\frac{9}{7}$

   (C) $\frac{7}{9}$

   (D) $\frac{1}{2}$

   (E) $\frac{1}{3}$

16. $\left(\frac{1}{4} \div \frac{1}{8}\right) \times \left(\frac{1}{2} + \frac{3}{4}\right) =$

   (A) $\frac{3}{4}$

   (B) 1

   (C) $1\frac{3}{4}$

   (D) 2

   (E) $2\frac{1}{2}$

13

17. $\left(\dfrac{1}{4}+\dfrac{2}{3}\right)\times\left(\dfrac{3}{2}+\dfrac{1}{4}\right) =$

(A) $\dfrac{21}{47}$

(B) $\dfrac{33}{49}$

(C) $\dfrac{51}{48}$

(D) $\dfrac{77}{48}$

(E) $\dfrac{105}{51}$

18. $\left(\dfrac{2}{3}\times\dfrac{1}{6}\right)\div\left(\dfrac{1}{2}\times\dfrac{1}{4}\right) =$

(A) $\dfrac{1}{18}$

(B) $\dfrac{2}{9}$

(C) $\dfrac{8}{9}$

(D) $\dfrac{11}{8}$

(E) $\dfrac{15}{75}$

19. $\left(\dfrac{1}{3}+\dfrac{1}{2}\right)\times\left(\dfrac{2}{3}-\dfrac{1}{3}\right)18 =$

(A) 5

(B) $\dfrac{7}{8}$

(C) $\dfrac{5}{6}$

(D) $\dfrac{4}{5}$

(E) $\dfrac{2}{3}$

20. $\left(\dfrac{1}{3}\div\dfrac{1}{6}\right)\times\left(\dfrac{2}{3}\div\dfrac{1}{3}\right)\times\left(\dfrac{1}{2}+\dfrac{3}{4}\right) =$

(A) 5
(B) 4
(C) 3
(D) 2
(E) 1

Review

1. (E)	8. (B)	15. (A)
2. (C)	9. (C)	16. (E)
3. (E)	10. (A)	17. (D)
4. (C)	11. (C)	18. (C)
5. (C)	12. (B)	19. (A)
6. (D)	13. (A)	20. (A)
7. (E)	14. (A)	

Review Rules for Working with Decimal Numbers

A decimal fraction is nothing more than a special way of writing fractions using a denominator of ten, or one hundred, or one thousand and so on. For example, the ordinary fraction $\frac{3}{10}$ written as a decimal is 0.3, and the ordinary fraction $\frac{72}{100}$ written as a decimal is 0.72.

Decimal fractions are written with a period, called a decimal point, placed to the left of the left-most digit in order to distinguish them from whole numbers. The positions to the right of the decimal point are called decimal places. Decimal places are analogous to the positions of the digits in whole numbers (units column, tens column, etc.). The number of decimal places indicates the denominator of the decimal fraction. One decimal place indicates a denominator of 10; two places indicate a denominator of 100; three indicate a denominator of 1,000; and so on.

 NOTE

In some formats, a zero is placed to the left of the decimal point. This has no mathematical significance; it's there just to make the decimal fractions more readable.

If the ordinary fraction already has a denominator that is ten, a hundred, a thousand, etc., the conversion is very easy. The numerator of the fraction becomes the decimal fraction. The placement of the decimal point is governed by the number of zeros in the denominator. Starting just to the right of the last digit of the numerator, you count over one digit to the left for each zero in the denominator. For example, to express in decimal form, take the numerator, 127, as the decimal fraction. Then, starting just to the right of the 7, count over three places to the left (one for each zero in 1,000). The decimal equivalent is 0.127. Here are some more examples:

$\frac{3}{10} = 0.3$ (One zero in the denominator means one decimal place.)

$\frac{13}{100} = 0.13$ (Two zeros in the denominator means two decimal places.)

$\frac{522}{1000} = 0.522$ (Three zeros in the denominator means three decimal places.)

13

If there are fewer numbers in the numerator than there must be decimal places, add zeros to the left of the number until you have enough decimal places. Take as an example. The denominator contains three zeros, but 53 is only a two-digit number. So we must add one zero to the left of the 5: $\frac{53}{1000} = 0.053$. (Remember, the zero to the left of the decimal point has no mathematical significance. It's there as a matter of style.) Here are some more illustrations:

$$\frac{3}{100} = 0.03 \text{ (Two zeros means two decimal places, but 3 is a single-digit number.)}$$

$$\frac{71}{10,000} = 0.0071 \text{ (Four zeros means four decimal places, but 71 is a two-digit number.)}$$

$$\frac{9}{100,000} = 0.00009 \text{ (Five zeros means five decimal places, but 9 is a single-digit number.)}$$

To convert a proper fraction with a denominator other than 10, 100, etc., you first convert the fraction to an equivalent form using a decimal denominator such as ten, one hundred, etc. For example, to convert the ordinary fraction to a decimal, you first change it into a fraction with a denominator of 100: $\frac{3}{4} = \frac{3 \times 25}{4 \times 25} = \frac{75}{100}$. Then you change $\frac{75}{100}$ to 0.75, as described above. Here some other exmaples:

$$\frac{2}{5} = \frac{4}{10} = 0.4$$

$$\frac{3}{8} = \frac{375}{1000} = 0.375$$

$$\frac{1}{50} = \frac{2}{100} = 0.02$$

To determine which decimal denominator you should use, divide the denominator of the ordinary fraction into 10, then into 100, then into 1,000, until you find the first decimal denominator that is evenly divisible by the denominator of the ordinary fraction. For example, $\frac{3}{8}$ doesn't have an equivalent form with a denominator of 10, but it does have an equivalent form with a denominator of 100. This is the same process you use to change a mixed number into a decimal number, convert the fractional part of the mixed number to a decimal fraction as just discussed, and then place the whole number part of the mixed number to the left of the decimal point. For example, in the mixed number $2\frac{3}{4}$, $\frac{3}{4}$ is the fractional part. You would convert $\frac{3}{4}$ to a decimal number as just shown ($\frac{3}{4}$ = 0.75), and then you would place the whole-number part to the left of the decimal point (2.75). (Notice that the superfluous zero is dropped. There is no reason to write 02.75.)

To convert an improper fraction to a decimal, just treat the improper fraction as a mixed number and follow the procedure just outlined. For example:

$$\frac{9}{4} = 2\frac{1}{4} = 2.25$$

$$\frac{8}{5} = 1\frac{1}{5} = 1.6$$

(Note: It's also possible, and even easier, to convert such fractions to decimals by dividing the numerator by the denominator. Again, we will postpone this part of the discussion until we have studied division of decimals.)

To convert a decimal fraction back to an ordinary fraction, it is necessary only to create a fraction using the digits of the decimal number as a numerator and a denominator of 1 plus a number of zeros equal to the number of decimal places. Thus, to convert 0.125 back to an ordinary fraction, use 125 as the numerator and 1 plus 3 zeros as the denominator: $\frac{125}{1000}$. Then reduce to lowest terms: $\frac{1}{8}$.

Finally, if the decimal number consists of both a whole part and a decimal fraction, the conversion will result in a mixed number. The whole part of the mixed number will be the whole part of the decimal number. Then you convert the fractional part of the decimal as just shown. For example, to convert 2.05 to a mixed number convert 0.05 to a fraction as just shown: 0.05 = $\frac{5}{100}$ = $\frac{1}{20}$. Then create a mixed number, the whole-number part of which is 2 and the fractional part of which is $\frac{1}{20}$. So 2.05 = $2\frac{1}{20}$.

Decimals can be manipulated in very much the same way that whole numbers can. You can add and subtract decimals:

$$0.2 + 0.3 + 0.1 = 0.6$$
$$0.7 - 0.2 = 0.5$$

13

Remember, however, that decimals are fractions, and that before you can add, you must have a common denominator. For example, the addition problem 0.25 + 0.1 + 0.825 is equivalent to the addition problem $\frac{25}{100} + \frac{1}{10} + \frac{825}{1000}$. So it is necessary to find a common denominator.

Fortunately, it's easy to find a common denominator for decimal numbers. Adding zeros to the right of the number doesn't change the value of the number, so you find a common denominator by lining up the decimal points in the numbers to be added or subtracted. If they don't all have the same number of decimal places, add zeros to the right of those that don't until every number has the same number of decimal places, which is to say the same denominator. So:

$$0.25 + 0.1 + 0.825 = 1.175$$

You can also multiply decimals. As with ordinary fractions, there is no need to find a common denominator: the multiplication process generates its own. To multiply decimal fractions, you simply multiply as you would whole numbers and then adjust the decimal point. To find the correct position for the decimal point, you count the total number of decimal places in the numbers being multiplied, count that many places to the left from the right of the final number in the product, and put the decimal point there. Here's an example:

$$0.25 \times 0.2 =$$

First, multiply as though the numbers were not decimals: $25 \times 2 = 50$. Next, adjust the decimal point. 0.25 consists of two decimal places, and 0.2 has one decimal place, for a total of three decimal places. Therefore, we count three places to the left, starting at the right of 50, so the final product is 0.050, or just 0.05.

You can also divide decimal numbers. And, like multiplication, division generates a common denominator by a suitable adjustment of zeros. But there are two slightly different situations in division that make things a little tricky. Let's take them one at a time.

First, when the number doing the dividing is a whole number, place the decimal point in the quotient (result of division) immediately above the decimal point in the number being divided. Then, keep dividing until there is no remainder, adding zeros as needed to the right of the number being divided. (This is how you change the denominator.) For example:

$$2.5 \div 2 = 1.25$$

The second situation occurs when the number doing the dividing is a decimal. In these cases, you must "clear" the fractional part of the decimal number by moving the decimal point to the right. For example, if you are dividing by 0.1 you must change 0.1 to a whole number, or 1. Or if you are dividing by 2.11, you must convert that to 211 by moving the decimal point two places to the right. But when you do this, you must also move the decimal point of the number being divided by the same number of places to ensure that you don't change their relative values. For example:

$$5 \div 2.5 = 2$$

There are two final things to say about dividing decimals. First, as was promised above, you can use division of decimals to convert ordinary fractions to decimals. Thus, if you need to convert to a decimal number, you just divide 9 by 2, as we did above.

Second, some fractions don't have exact decimal equivalents. Try converting to a decimal fraction using the division route. You'll be at it forever, because you keep getting an endless succession of 3s. Or try converting to a decimal using the division method. Again, you wind up with an endless succession, this time, repeating 1s. By convention, repeating decimals are shown using ellipses: 0.333 . . . .

TIP

You can save yourself some time if you know the fraction equivalents of certain common fractions. So memorize these:

$$\frac{1}{2} = 0.50 \qquad\qquad \frac{1}{6} \approx 0.166$$

$$\frac{1}{3} = 0.33 \ldots \qquad\qquad \frac{1}{7} \approx 0.143$$

$$\frac{1}{4} = 0.25 \qquad\qquad \frac{1}{8} = 0.125$$

$$\frac{1}{5} = 0.20 \qquad\qquad \frac{1}{9} \approx 0.11$$

Workshop C: Decimals

Use the 20 problems in this drill to practice working with decimal numbers. There is no time limit for the drill. You'll find the answers in the Review section immediately following the Drill section.

Drill

13

1. What is $\frac{257}{100}$ expressed as a decimal?

   (A) 25.7
   (B) 2.57
   (C) 0.257
   (D) 0.0257
   (E) 0.00257

2. What is $\frac{57}{10}$ expressed as a decimal?

   (A) 57
   (B) 5.7
   (C) 0.57
   (D) 0.057
   (E) 0.0057

3. What is $\frac{5}{8}$ expressed as a decimal?

   (A) 0.125
   (B) 0.625
   (C) 0.850
   (D) 1.25
   (E) 5.80

4. What is $\frac{4}{5}$ expressed as a decimal?

   (A) 0.4
   (B) 0.6
   (C) 0.8
   (D) 1.2
   (E) 2.4

5. What is $\frac{1}{20}$ expressed as a decimal?

   (A) 0.05
   (B) 0.005
   (C) 0.0005
   (D) 0.00005
   (E) 0.000005

6. What is $\frac{1}{50}$ expressed as a decimal?

   (A) 0.2
   (B) 0.02
   (C) 0.002
   (D) 0.0002
   (E) 0.00002

7. $0.1 + 0.1 =$

   (A) 0.002
   (B) 0.02
   (C) 0.2
   (D) 2
   (E) 20

8. $0.27 + 0.13 + 0.55 =$

   (A) 0.21
   (B) 0.36
   (C) 0.47
   (D) 0.85
   (E) 0.95

9. $57.1 + 23.3 + 35.012 =$

   (A) 412.115
   (B) 115.412
   (C) 115.0412
   (D) 11.5412
   (E) 1.15412

10. $0.01 + 0.001 + 0.0001 + 0.00001 =$

   (A) 1
   (B) 0.10
   (C) 0.1111
   (D) 0.01111
   (E) 0.001111

11. $0.7 - 0.3 =$

   (A) 0.004
   (B) 0.021
   (C) 0.04
   (D) 0.21
   (E) 0.4

12. $0.75 - 0.25 =$

   (A) 5
   (B) 1
   (C) 0.5
   (D) 0.25
   (E) 0.005

13. $25.125 - 5.357 =$

    (A) 19.768
    (B) 15.432
    (C) 12.115
    (D) 4.108
    (E) 2.288

14. $1 - 0.00001 =$

    (A) 0.9
    (B) 0.99
    (C) 0.999
    (D) 0.9999
    (E) 0.99999

15. $0.2 \times 0.1 =$

    (A) 0.3
    (B) 0.2
    (C) 0.1
    (D) 0.02
    (E) 0.006

16. $0.1 \times 0.1 \times 0.1 =$

    (A) 0.3
    (B) 0.1
    (C) 0.01
    (D) 0.001
    (E) 0.0001

17. $6 \div 0.2 =$

    (A) 0.03
    (B) 0.3
    (C) 3
    (D) 30
    (E) 300

18. $0.2 \div 5 =$

    (A) 0.4
    (B) 0.04
    (C) 0.004
    (D) 0.0004
    (E) 0.00004

19. $25.1 \div 2.51 =$

    (A) 100
    (B) 10
    (C) 0.1
    (D) 0.01
    (E) 0.001

20. $0.12345 \div 0.012345$

    (A) 100
    (B) 10
    (C) 1
    (D) 0.1
    (E) 0.01

Review

1. (B)	8. (A)	15. (D)
2. (B)	9. (B)	16. (D)
3. (B)	10. (D)	17. (D)
4. (C)	11. (E)	18. (B)
5. (A)	12. (C)	19. (B)
6. (B)	13. (A)	20. (A)
7. (C)	14. (E)	

13

Review Conventions Governing Negative Numbers

On first hearing, the notion of a negative number seems a strange idea. After all, the positive numbers we have been studying are used to count real things like marbles, and rocks, and people. So what could a negative number do? Count negative things, like negative rocks and negative people? This sounds a little too much like Star Trek: "Aye, Captain, the anti-matter bubble burst!"

But numbers are just positions in a system. Each number is one greater than the preceding one and one less than the succeeding one. And there is no logical objection to continuing this in a "negative" direction.

So the negative numbers don't refer to negative objects. The minus sign indicates the direction in which the number system is moving with reference to zero. If you move to the right, you are going in the positive direction; to the left, in the negative direction.

In fact, there are everyday situations, such as games and banking, in which it is quite natural to use negative numbers. in some games, you might score "minus ten"; or if your checking account is overdrawn, you have a minus balance.

Negative numbers can be manipulated by the basic operations of addition, subtraction, multiplication, and division. To help explain these operations, we need to introduce the concept of absolute value.

Absolute value just means the size of a number without regard to its sign. Absolute value is like distance without regard to direction. Five miles in an easterly direction and five miles in a westerly direction are both five miles, but they move in different directions. So, too, –5 and +5 are five units large, but one signifies a change toward the negative, the other a change toward the positive. This idea of value, without regard to direction, should help you understand the operations with negative numbers. (Note: The symbol for absolute value is $|(x)|$, e.g., $|-10| = 10$.)

To add a negative number to some other number, just subtract the absolute value of the negative number. Here's an example:

$$10 + (-4) = 10 - 4 = 6$$

The absolute value of –4 is 4, so just subtract 4 from 10.

You follow this procedure even if you wind up with a negative result:

$$10 + (-12) = 10 - 12 = -2$$

And the procedure works when you need to add a negative number to another negative number:

$$-3 + -2 = -3 - 2 = -5$$

Subtraction of negative numbers is a little different. When you subtract something you are taking it away, so when you subtract a negative number, you are really adding. This is like a double negative. "It is not the case that John is not a student" means that John is a student.

To subtract a negative number from another quantity, add the absolute value of the negative number to the other quantity. Here's an example:

$$10 - (-5) = 10 + 5 = 15$$

Follow this procedure if you are subtracting a negative number from zero or from another negative number:

$$-5 - (-10) = -5 + 10 = 5$$

You can also understand the rules for multiplying negative numbers through the concept of absolute value. To multiply a positive number by a negative number, you multiply the absolute values of the two numbers (just as if they were positive), but the product is a negative number. Here are two examples:

$$3 \times -6 = -18$$
$$-2 \times 4 = -8$$

In both examples, the final result is the product of the absolute values of the two numbers, $3 \times 6 = 18$ and $2 \times 4 = 8$. But both results are negative. A way of remembering this is to think that the minus sign has "tainted" the problem, so the final result must be negative.

To multiply a negative number by a negative number, you multiply the absolute values of the numbers, but the final result is positive. For example:

$$-3 \times -6 = 18$$
$$-1 \times -4 = 4$$

In both examples, the result is the product of the absolute values of the two numbers, $3 \times 6 = 18$ and $1 \times 4 = 4$. But both results are positive. This is somewhat like saying two wrongs do make a right—a negative times a negative produces a positive.

13

And if you multiply more than two numbers, the result toggles back and forth between positive and negative, like an on/off switch. In multiplication, three negatives produce a negative number, four a positive number, five a negative number, six a positive number, and so on. For example:

$$-1 \times -1 = 1$$
$$-1 \times -1 \times -1 = -1$$
$$-1 \times -1 \times -1 \times -1 = 1$$
$$-1 \times -1 \times -1 \times -1 \times -1 = -1$$
$$-1 \times -1 \times -1 \times -1 \times -1 \times -1 = 1$$

Division is the reverse of multiplication, so the same rules apply. To divide a positive number by a negative number or to divide a negative number by a positive number, you divide using absolute values, and the result of the final sign is negative. Here's are two examples:

$$6 \div -3 = -2$$
$$-8 \div 2 = -4$$

In both examples, we divided using absolute values: $6 \div 3 = 2$ and $8 \div 2 = 4$; and in both cases, the sign of the final result is negative.

To divide a negative number by another negative number, you divide using absolute values, but the final sign is positive. For example:

$$-8 \div -4 = 2$$

Dividing by using the absolute values of -8 and -2, you get $8 \div 4$, which is 2, and in this case the "double negative" gives a positive sign to the final result.

These are the rules that govern all operations with signed numbers. But you must be careful how you apply them to more complicated problems. Just remember to take things one step at a time.

TIP

An important feature of multiplying by negative numbers is the sign of the product:

POSITIVE × NEGATIVE = NEGATIVE

NEGATIVE × NEGATIVE = POSITIVE

And division gives similar results.

Workshop D: Negative Numbers

Use the 20 problems in this drill to practice working with negative numbers. There is no time limit for the drill. You'll find the answers in the Review section immediately following the Drill section.

Drill

1. $16 \div -1 =$
   - (A) −16
   - (B) −1
   - (C) 1
   - (D) 8
   - (E) 16

2. $-12 \div 4 =$
   - (A) −4
   - (B) −3
   - (C) −2
   - (D) 3
   - (E) 4

3. $-12 \div -12 =$
   - (A) −144
   - (B) −1
   - (C) 1
   - (D) 24
   - (E) 144

4. $(7 - -6) + 3(2 - 4) =$
   - (A) −2
   - (B) 0
   - (C) 7
   - (D) 12
   - (E) 23

5. $(2 \times -3)(1 \times -4)(2 \times -1) =$
   - (A) −48
   - (B) −16
   - (C) 2
   - (D) 28
   - (E) 56

6. $(6 \times -2) \div (3 \times -4) =$
   - (A) −12
   - (B) −1
   - (C) 1
   - (D) 3
   - (E) 24

7. $(4 - -3 + 7 - -1)(-3 - -2) =$
   - (A) −25
   - (B) −15
   - (C) −7
   - (D) −1
   - (E) 8

8. $[(2 \times -1) + (4 \div -2)] \times [(-6 + 6) - (2 - 3)] =$
   - (A) 5
   - (B) 2
   - (C) −2
   - (D) −4
   - (E) −23

13

9. $(2-3)(3-2)(4-3)(3-4)(5-4)(4-5) =$
    (A) −625
    (B) −1
    (C) 1
    (D) 50
    (E) 625

10. $[2 \times (3-4)] + [(125 \div -25) \times (1 \times -2)] =$
    (A) −12
    (B) −8
    (C) 2
    (D) 8
    (E) 125

11. $-\frac{1}{2} \times 2 \times -\frac{1}{2} \times -\frac{1}{2} \times 2 =$
    (A) −16
    (B) −8
    (C) −1
    (D) 1
    (E) 2

12. $[(2 \times 3) \div (-6 \times 1)] \times [(21 \div 7) \times \frac{1}{3}] =$
    (A) −5
    (B) −1
    (C) 1
    (D) 12
    (E) 36

13. $(-5 \times -2) - (-2 \times -5) =$
    (A) 0
    (B) 2
    (C) 10
    (D) 12
    (E) 18

14. $\frac{6}{-3} =$
    (A) −18
    (B) −2
    (C) 2
    (D) 3
    (E) 18

15. $(-3 - -3) - (-2 - -2) - (-1 - -1) =$
    (A) −12
    (B) −6
    (C) 0
    (D) 6
    (E) 12

16. If n is any negative number, which of the following must also be negative?

    I. $n + n$

    II. $n \times n$

    III. $n - n$

    (A) I only
    (B) II only
    (C) I and III only
    (D) II and III only
    (E) I, II, and III

17. If n is any negative number, which of the following must also be negative?

    I. $n \times -n$

    II. $-n \times -n$

    III. $-n + n$

    (A) I only
    (B) II only
    (C) III only
    (D) II and III only
    (E) I, II, and III

18. If n is any positive number, which of the following must be negative?

    I. $n \times -n$

    II. $-n \div -n$

    III. $n - (-n)$

(A) I only
(B) II only
(C) I and II only
(D) I and III only
(E) I, II, and III

19. If n is any positive number, which of the following must be positive?

    I. $-n - (-n)$

    II. $-n \times -n$

    III. $n \div (-n \times -n)$

(A) I only
(B) II only
(C) III only
(D) I and III only
(E) II and III only

20. Given any number such that $n \neq 0$, which of the following must be equal to 0?

    I. $-n \times -n \times -n \times -n \times -n \times -n$

    II. $[(n - n) - n] - [(n - n) - n]$

    III. $n \div [(n \div n) \div n]$

(A) I only
(B) II only
(C) I and II only
(D) I and III only
(E) I, II, and III

Review

1. (A)	8. (D)	15. (C)
2. (B)	9. (B)	16. (A)
3. (C)	10. (D)	17. (A)
4. (C)	11. (C)	18. (C)
5. (A)	12. (B)	19. (E)
6. (C)	13. (A)	20. (B)
7. (B)	14. (B)	

13

Get Answers to Frequently Asked Questions

Q: **Does the exam cover long division, addition of columns of numbers, and so on?**

A: No. That's donkey math, and the exam does not test donkey math. The test-writers can find out whether you understand those concepts without the need to make you work out lengthy calculations.

Q: **What's the best way to determine whether a number is a prime, a multiple of another number, or perhaps a factor of a number?**

A: Play around with the number itself. Try dividing it by smaller numbers to determine whether it is a multiple or a prime. Divide it into a number to determine whether it's a factor. If it divides evenly, then it is a factor.

Q: **Is there an easy way of determining whether a variable has to be even or odd, positive or negative?**

A: Aside from analyzing the unknown using the principles you've learned today, you can usually make a pretty good guess based upon testing some representative numbers.

Today's Review

1. The test presupposes that you are comfortable with the mechanics of basic math, e.g., working with fractions, manipulating decimals, playing around with negative numbers. But some of the peculiar features of each of these topics also are the core concepts tested by some problems.

2. Factors, multiples, primes, odds and evens, and consecutive numbers can be the focus of a math question.

3. A problem may ask for you to demonstate that you know how to work with fractions. Also, be sure to reduce fractions in your final result to lowest terms.

4. Decimals are just fancy fractions. You may get a problem that asks you to add, subtract, multiply, or divide decimals.

5. Negative numbers are an important component of math in general, but they are also featured by certain problems, especially the behavior of negative numbers when they are multiplied or divided.

Teach Yourself
GRE Arithmetic (II)

Today, you'll review the important arithmetic concepts that you need to do well on the test. And you will get several chances to practice what you've reviewed.

Today's review is broken down in several subject areas:

Percents

Averages

Ratios and Proportions

Powers and Roots

Review the Methods for Solving Percent Problems

A percent is nothing but another special fraction form, one which always uses the denominator 100. The percent sign, "%," is shorthand for "$\frac{}{100}$;" for example, $67\% = \frac{67}{100}$.

What You'll Do Today

- Review the Methods for Solving Percent Problems
- Workshop A: Percents
- Review the Concept of Average
- Workshop B: Averages
- Review the Use of Ratios and Proportions
- Workshop C: Ratios and Proportions
- Review the Conventions Governing Powers and Roots
- Workshop D: Powers and Roots
- Get Answers to Frequently Asked Questions

Converting to and from Percent

Since a percent is just a special fraction form, you can convert both ordinary and decimal fractions to percents, and vice versa. The easiest conversion is the one changing a decimal to a percent. Here's how its done:

$0.27 = 27\%$

$0.50 = 50\%$

$0.275 = 27.5\%$

TIP

> To change any decimal to a percent, just move the decimal point two places to the right and add the percent sign. To change a percent back to a decimal number, just move the decimal point two places to the left and drop the percent sign.

All that this does is substitute the "%" for two decimal places—just a matter of changing things from one form into an equivalent form. And the process can be reversed. Here's how:

$27\% = 0.27$

$50\% = 0.50$

$27.5\% = 0.275$

And to convert an ordinary fraction to a percent, just convert the fraction to a decimal number and follow the rule just given. Like this:

$$\frac{3}{4} = 0.75 = 75\%$$

$$\frac{5}{8} = 0.625 = 62.5\%$$

$$\frac{1}{10} = 0.10 = 10\%$$

And to reverse the process, follow the rule given above for turning percentages back into decimals and then use the procedure outlined in the previous section for converting decimals to ordinary fractions. This is the way:

$$75\% = 0.75 = \frac{75}{100} = \frac{3}{4}$$

$$62.5\% = 0.625 = \frac{625}{1000} = \frac{5}{8}$$

$$10\% = 0.1 = \frac{1}{10}$$

There are two types of percents that are a little tricky: those greater than 100% and those less than 1%. First, it is possible to have a percent that is larger than one hundred. This would be the result of converting a mixed number, such as $2\frac{3}{4}$, to a percent: $2\frac{3}{4} = \frac{11}{4} = 2.75 = 275\%$.

Percents can also be less than 1, in which case they are written with decimals; for example, 0.5%. But these strange numbers follow the general rules outlined above. We can convert 0.5% to a fraction: $0.5\% = 0.005 = \frac{5}{1000} = \frac{1}{200}$. And, conversely, fractions smaller than will yield a percent less than 1: $\frac{1}{2500} = 0.0004 = 0.04\%$.

 CAUTION | Percents can be greater than 100 and less than 1. The numbers look a little strange, but they're governed by the same rules that govern all percents.

Manipulating Percents

Because percents are fractions, they can be manipulated just like other fractions. Addition and subtraction of percents are easy, because you already have a common denominator. (Remember, all percentages use 100 as their denominator.)

You can add percents: 25% + 15% + 10% = 50%. When would you need to add percents?

Paul originally owned 25 percent of the stock of a certain company. He purchased another 15 percent of the stock privately, and he received a gift of another 10 percent of the stock. What percent of the stock of the company does Paul now own?

$$25\% + 15\% + 10\% = 50\%$$

14

And you can subtract percents: $50\% - 20\% = 30\%$. When would you need to subtract percents?

In a certain election, Peter and Mary received 50 percent of all the votes that were cast. If Peter received 20 percent of the votes cast in the election, what percent of the votes did Mary receive?

$50\% - 20\% = 30\%$

You can also multiply percents. First, convert the percents to decimal numbers, and then multiply the decimal numbers, according to the procedure described in the preceding section: $60\% \times 80\% = 0.60 \times 0.80 = 0.48$. When would you multiply percents?

In a certain group, 80 percent of the people are wearing hats. If 60 percent of those wearing hats are also wearing gloves, what percent of the entire group is wearing both a hat and gloves?

60% of $80\% = 60\% \times 80\% = 0.60 \times 0.80 = 0.48 = 48\%$

Finally, you can also divide percents, by converting them to decimal numbers: $100\% \div 12.5\% = 1 \div 0.125 = 8$. When would you divide percents?

Peter is purchasing an item on a lay-away plan. If he pays weekly installments of 12.5 percent of the purchase price, how many weeks will he need to pay the entire purchase price?

$100\% \div 12.5\% = 8$

Common Problems Using Percents

There are three common uses of percents that form the basis of questions in the exam:

1. What is x percent of something?
2. This is what percent of that?
3. What is the percent change from this quantity to that quantity?

We will review each of the three types.

1. What is *x* percent of something?

One common problem involving percents has the form "What is *x* percent of some quantity?" Since a percent is also a fraction, the *of* indicates multiplication. Here are a couple of problems to illustrate the concept:

QUESTION A certain class is made up of 125 students. If 60 percent of the students are men, how many men are in the class?

60% of 125 = 60% × 125 = 0.60 × 125 = 75

QUESTION If Sam originally had $25 and gave 25 percent of that amount to his friend Samantha, how much money did Sam give to Samantha?

25% of $25 = 25% × 25 = 0.25 × 25 = $6.25

QUESTION If Paula had 50 marbles and gave 20 percent of them to her friend Paul, how many marbles did Paula give to Paul?

20% of 50 = 20% × 50= 0.20 × 50 = 10

2. What percent is this of that?

A second common problem involving percents has the form "What percent of this is that?" Here are how these problems are worded:

QUESTION What percent is 3 of 12?

$$\frac{3}{12} = 0.25 = 25\%$$

ANALYSIS The question asks that you express the fraction as a percent. To do that, first convert to a decimal (by dividing 3 by 12) and then change that decimal number to a percent.

There are other ways of phrasing the same question:

3 is what percent of 12?

Of 12, what percent is 3?

These questions are equivalent and have the general forms:

What percent is this of that?

This is what percent of that?

Of that, what percent is this?

(Although the order of words is different, they ask the same thing: Express a fraction as a percent.)

14

TIP

In any question having the form "This is what percent of that?" set up your fraction, making sure that the "of that" is the denominator and that the "this" is the numerator.

Here are examples of the "this of that" kind of percent question:

5 is what percent of 25?

Of 25, what percent is 5?

What percent is 5 of 25?

Notice that these questions are equivalent. Using the Tip:

$$\frac{\text{this}}{\text{of that}} = \frac{5}{\text{of 25}} = \frac{5}{25} = 0.2 = 20\%$$

As long as you remember that the *of that* goes on the bottom of the fraction and the other number goes on the top, you can't make a mistake.

QUESTION What percent is 20 of 50?

$$\frac{20}{50} = 0.40 = 40\%$$

QUESTION Of 125, what percent is 25?

$$\frac{25}{125} = 0.20 = 20\%$$

QUESTION 12 is what percent of 6?

$$\frac{12}{6} = 2 = 200\%$$

There is a variation on this theme that can also be attacked using the "of that" Tip. For example, what number is 20% of 25?

This is very much like the examples just analyzed, except here the percent is given but one of the two numbers is missing. Still, the "of that" Tip works. (Here "this" represents "what number"—a slight variation in wording.)

QUESTION What number is 20% of 25?

$$\frac{\text{this}}{\text{of that}} = \text{percent}$$

$$\frac{\text{this}}{\text{of 25}} = 20\%$$

$$\text{this} = 0.20 \times 25 = 5$$

QUESTION 5 is 20% of what number?

$$\frac{\text{this}}{\text{of that}} = \text{percent}$$

$$\frac{5}{\text{of that}} = 20\%$$

$$\frac{5}{20\%} = \text{that}$$

$$\text{that} = \frac{5}{0.20} = 25$$

No matter how wordy or otherwise difficult such questions get, they are all answerable by following the "of that" tip:

QUESTION John received a dividend check in the amount of $200. Of that amount, he paid Ed $25. Of the original dividend check, John gave Ed what percent?

ANALYSIS What's the "of that"? The $200. So the other number is $25. And the solution is:

$$\frac{25}{100} = \frac{1}{8} = 0.125 = 12.5\%$$

3. What is the percent change?

A third type of percent problem involves the change in a quantity over time. Here is an example:

QUESTION The price of an item increased from $20 to $25. What was the percent increase in the price?

ANALYSIS This type of question asks you to express the relationship between the change and the original amount in percent terms. To answer, you create a fraction that is then expressed as a percent:

$$\frac{\text{change}}{\text{original amount}} = \frac{5}{20} = \frac{1}{4} = 0.25 = 25\%$$

Think of this as the "change-over" tip, because the fraction places the change over the original amount. Here's how it works:

QUESTION Mary was earning $16 per hour when she received a raise of $4 per hour. Her hourly wage increased by what percent?

$$\frac{\text{change}}{\text{original amount}} = \frac{4}{16} = 0.25 = 25\%$$

14

When a question asks about percent change, put the "change" over the "original amount" and convert to a fraction.

The "change-over" tip works for decreases as well. Here's how:

QUESTION The value of a certain stock declined from $50 per share to $45 per share. What was the percent decline in the value of a share?

$$\frac{\text{change}}{\text{original amount}} = \frac{5}{50} = 0.10 = 10\%$$

And here's another example:

QUESTION Student enrollment at College X dropped from 5,000 students in 1970 to 4,000 students in 1980. What was the percent drop in the number of students enrolled at College X?

$$\frac{\text{change}}{\text{original amount}} = \frac{1,000}{5,000} = 0.20 = 20\%$$

Workshop A: Percents

This workshop includes a Drill part and a Review part. The drill consists of 25 items. There is no time limit for the drill.

Drill

Practice working with percents using the following problems. Circle your answer choice in your book. Then compare you work to the answer key given in the Review part

1. What is 0.79 expressed as a percent?

   (A) 0.0079%
   (B) 0.079%
   (C) 0.79%
   (D) 7.9%
   (E) 79%

2. What is 0.5555 expressed as a percent?

   (A) 5555%
   (B) 555.5%
   (C) 55.55%
   (D) 5.555%
   (E) 0.555%

3. What is 2.45 expressed as a percent?

   (A) 2,450%

   (B) 245%

   (C) 24.5%

   (D) 2.45%

   (E) 0.245%

4. What is 1.25 expressed as a percent?

   (A) 125%

   (B) 12.5%

   (C) 1.25%

   (D) 0.125%

   (E) 0.0125%

5. What is 25 percent expressed as a decimal?

   (A) 25.0

   (B) 2.5

   (C) 0.25

   (D) 0.025

   (E) 0.0025

6. What is 100% expressed as a decimal?

   (A) 100.0

   (B) 10.0

   (C) 1.0

   (D) 0.1

   (E) 0.001

7. If from 9:00 a.m. to noon Mary mowed 35 percent of a lawn, and from noon to 3:00 she mowed another 50 percent of the lawn, what percent of the lawn did she mow between 9:00 a.m. and 3:00 p.m.?

   (A) 17.5%

   (B) 60%

   (C) 74.3%

   (D) 85%

   (E) 98%

Questions 8–10

SCHEDULE FOR COMPLETING PROJECT X				
Day by which a portion of work is to be completed				
Monday	Tuesday	Wednesday	Thursday	Friday
Percent to be completed 8%	17%	25%	33%	17%

8. By the end of which day is one-half of the work scheduled to have been completed?

   (A) Monday

   (B) Tuesday

   (C) Wednesday

   (D) Thursday

   (E) Friday

9. By the end of Tuesday, what percent of the work is scheduled to have been completed?

   (A) 8%

   (B) 17%

   (C) 25%

   (D) 50%

   (E) 88%

14

10. If production is on schedule, during which day will of the project have been completed?

    (A) Monday
    (B) Tuesday
    (C) Wednesday
    (D) Thursday
    (E) Friday

11. A bucket is filled to 33 percent of its capacity. If an amount of water equal to of the bucket's capacity is added, the bucket is filled to what percent of its capacity?

    (A) 8%
    (B) 25%
    (C) 33%
    (D) 58%
    (E) 75%

12. If Edward spends 15 percent of his allowance on a book and another 25 percent on food, what percent of his allowance remains?

    (A) 10%
    (B) 40%
    (C) 45%
    (D) 60%
    (E) 80%

13. 50% of 50% =

    (A) 1%
    (B) 2.5%
    (C) 25%
    (D) 100%
    (E) 250%

14. If 75 percent of the 240 cars in a certain parking lot are sedans, how many of the cars in the parking lot are sedans?

    (A) 18
    (B) 24
    (C) 60
    (D) 180
    (E) 210

15. If 0.1 percent of the 189,000 names on a certain mailing list have the initials B.D., how many names on the list have initials B.D.?

    (A) 1.89
    (B) 18.9
    (C) 189
    (D) 18,900
    (E) 189,000

16. What number is 250 percent of 12?

    (A) 3
    (B) 15
    (C) 24
    (D) 30
    (E) 36

17. If 25 of the employees at a bank are women and 15 are men, then what percent of the bank's employees are women?

    (A) 37.5%
    (B) 40%
    (C) 60%
    (D) 62.5%
    (E) 90%

18. If the price of an item increases from $5.00 to $8.00, the new price is what percent of the old price?

   (A) 20%
   (B) 60%
   (C) 62.5%
   (D) 92.5%
   (E) 160%

19. If the price of a share of stock drops from $200 to $160, what was the percent decline in the price?

   (A) 20%
   (B) 25%
   (C) 50%
   (D) 80%
   (E) 125%

20. If a merchant raised the selling price of an item by 10% and he reduces the new selling price by 10% the net result on the selling price is

   (A) an increase of 11%
   (B) an increase of 1%
   (C) no change
   (D) a decrease of 1%
   (E) a decrease of 11%

Questions 21–25

ENROLLMENTS FOR A ONE-WEEK SEMINAR	
Week Number	*Number of Enrollees*
1	10
2	25
3	20
4	15
5	30

21. The number of people who enrolled for the seminar in Week 1 was what percent of the number of people who enrolled in Week 2?

   (A) 5%
   (B) 40%
   (C) 50%
   (D) 80%
   (E) 250%

22. The number of people who enrolled for the seminar in Week 4 was what percent of the number of people who enrolled in Week 5?

   (A) 15%
   (B) 25%
   (C) 50%
   (D) 100%
   (E) 200%

14

23. The number of people who enrolled for the seminar in Week 5 was what percent of the number of people who enrolled in Week 4?

    (A) 15%
    (B) 25%
    (C) 50%
    (D) 100%
    (E) 200%

24. What was the percent increase in the number of people enrolled for the seminar from Week 1 to Week 2?

    (A) 40%
    (B) 80%
    (C) 100%
    (D) 150%
    (E) 250%

25. What was the percent decrease in the number of people enrolled for the seminar from Week 3 to Week 4?

    (A) 25%
    (B) 33%
    (C) 75%
    (D) 125%
    (E) 133%

Review

1. (E)	10. (D)	18. (E)
2. (C)	11. (D)	19. (A)
3. (B)	12. (D)	20. (D)
4. (A)	13. (C)	21. (B)
5. (C)	14. (D)	22. (C)
6. (C)	15. (C)	23. (E)
7. (D)	16. (D)	24. (D)
8. (C)	17. (D)	25. (A)
9. (C)		

Review the Concept of Average

Averages are a staple of the test. You won't necessarily have a lot of problems involving average, but the concept almost always appears on the test; and sometimes, it is the centerpiece of an item. There are three important things you need to know about averages.

1. Simple Averages

To calculate an average, just add the quantities to be averaged and then divide that sum by the number of quantities involved. For example, the average of 3, 7, and 8 is 6: $3 + 7 + 8 = 18$, and $18 \div 3 = 6$. Here's a sample problem:

QUESTION A student's final grade is the average (arithmetic mean) of her scores on five exams. If she receives scores of 78, 83, 82, 88, and 94, what is her final grade?

ANALYSIS To find the average, add the five grades and divide that sum by 5.

$$\frac{78 + 83 + 82 + 88 + 94}{5} = \frac{425}{5} = 85$$

 NOTE
> An average is also called an arithmetic mean, and exam questions that ask for averages may include the phrase arithmetic mean in parentheses following the word average.

Since there won't be any misunderstanding now, we will omit the phrase arithmetic mean, and on the exam you can just ignore the extra terminology.

It's possible that an easy question might ask that you find the average of a few numbers, as above; but questions about averages can take several other forms.

2. Missing Elements of an Average

Some questions provide the average of a group of numbers and some—but not all—of the quantities involved. You are then asked to find the missing quantity or quantities. For example, if the average of 3, 8, and a third number is 6, what is the value of the third number? Since the average of the three numbers is 6, the sum or total of the three numbers is $3 \times 6 = 18$. The two numbers we know total $3 + 8 = 11$. So the third number must be 7. You can check this solution by averaging 3, 8, and 7: $3 + 8 + 7 = 18 \div 3 = 6$. Here's an example:

QUESTION For a certain five-day period, the average high temperature (in degrees Fahrenheit) for City X was 30°. If the high temperatures recorded for the first four of those days were 26°, 32°, 24°, and 35°, what was the high temperature recorded on the fifth day?

14

ANALYSIS The sum of the five numbers is 5 ¥ 30 = 150. The sum for the four days we know about is only 26 + 32 + 24 + 35 = 117. So the fifth day must have had a high temperature of 150 – 117 = 33.

QUESTION The average of Jose's scores on four tests is 90. If three of those scores are 89, 92, and 94, what is the fourth score?

ANALYSIS The sum of all four scores must be 4 × 90 = 360. The three scores that are known total 89 + 92 + 94 = 275. So the remaining score must be 360 – 275 = 85.

A variation on this type of question might ask about more than one missing element. Here's an example:

QUESTION In a group of children, three of the children are ages 7, 8 and 10, and the other two are the same age. If the average of the ages of all five children is 7, what is the age of the other two children?

ANALYSIS We know that the total of the five ages must be 5 ¥ 7 = 35. The known ages total only 7 + 8 + 10 = 25. So the ages of the two other children must total 10. Since there are two of them, each one must be 5 years old. And here's another:

QUESTION The average of a group of eight numbers is 9. If one of these numbers is removed from the group, the average of the remaining numbers is 7. What is the value of the number removed?

ANALYSIS The sum of the original numbers is 8 × 9 = 72. The sum of the remaining numbers is 7 × 7 = 49. So the value of the number that was removed must be 72 – 49 = 23.

> **TIP**
>
> For a question that asks about a missing number in an average, compare the sum of all numbers in the average to the sum of the numbers without the missing number. The difference between the two sums is the missing number.

3. Weighted Averages

In the average problems discussed thus far, each element in the average has been given equal weight. Sometimes, averages are created that give greater weight to one element than to another. Here's what this looks like:

QUESTION Paula bought four books that cost $6.00 each and two books that cost $3.00 each. What is the average cost of the six books?

ANALYSIS The average cost of the six books is not just the average of $6.00 and $3.00, which is $4.50. She bought more of the higher priced books, so our average must take into account that fact. One way of doing the arithmetic is to treat each book as a separate expense:

$$\frac{6+6+6+6+3+3}{6} = \frac{30}{6} = 5$$

Another way of arriving at the same result is to *weight* the two different costs:

$$4(6) + 2(3) = 30$$

TIP

> To calculate a weighted average, multiply each value in the group by the number of times it appears, total all values, and divide by the number of elements in the average.

Workshop B: Averages

This workshop includes a Drill part and a Review part. The drill consists of 25 items. There is no time limit for the drill.

Drill

1. What is the average of 8, 6, and 16?

    (A) 10
    (B) 12
    (C) 13
    (D) 15
    (E) 18

2. What is the average of 0 and 50?

    (A) 0
    (B) 5
    (C) 10
    (D) 25
    (E) 50

3. What is the average of 5, 11, 12 and 8?

    (A) 6
    (B) 8
    (C) 9
    (D) 10
    (E) 12

4. What is the average of 25, 28, 21, 30, and 36?

    (A) 25
    (B) 28
    (C) 29
    (D) 34
    (E) 44

14

5. What is the average $\frac{1}{4}$, $\frac{3}{4}$, $\frac{5}{8}$, $\frac{1}{2}$, and $\frac{3}{8}$?

   (A) $\frac{3}{32}$

   (B) $\frac{5}{16}$

   (C) $\frac{1}{2}$

   (D) $\frac{5}{8}$

   (E) $\frac{27}{32}$

6. What is the average of $0.78, $0.45, $0.36, $0.98, $0.55, and $0.54?

   (A) $0.49
   (B) $0.54
   (C) $0.56
   (D) $0.60
   (E) $0.61

7. What is the average of 0.03, 0.11, 0.08, and 0.5?

   (A) 0.18
   (B) 0.25
   (C) 0.28
   (D) 0.50
   (E) 1.0

8. What is the average of 1,001, 1,002, 1,003, 1,004, and 1,005?

   (A) 250
   (B) 1,000
   (C) 1,003
   (D) 2,500
   (E) 5,000

9. What is the average of –8, –6, and –13?

   (A) –18
   (B) –15
   (C) –13
   (D) –12
   (E) –9

10. A student receives test scores of 79, 85, 90, 76, and 80. What is the average of these test scores?

    (A) 82
    (B) 83
    (C) 84
    (D) 85
    (E) 86

11. A shopper bought five different items costing $4.51, $6.25, $3.32, $4.48, and $2.19. What is the average cost of the five items?

    (A) $3.40
    (B) $3.80
    (C) $3.90
    (D) $4.00
    (E) $4.15

12. A gymnast received scores of 8.5, 9.3, 8.2, and 9.0 in four different events. What is the average of her scores?

    (A) 8.5
    (B) 8.75
    (C) 8.9
    (D) 9
    (E) 9.1

13. Five people have ages of 44, 33, 45, 44, and 29 years. What is the average of their ages in years?

    (A) 36
    (B) 39
    (C) 40
    (D) 41
    (E) 43

14. In a certain government office, if 360 staff hours are needed to process 120 building permit applications, on the average how long (expressed in hours) does it take to process one application?

    (A) 3
    (B) 6
    (C) 12
    (D) 24
    (E) 36

15. In a chemical test for Substance X, a sample is divided into five equal parts. If the purity of the five parts is 84 percent, 89 percent, 87 percent, 90 percent, and 80 percent, then what is the overall purity of the sample (expressed as a percent of substance X)?

    (A) 83
    (B) 84
    (C) 86
    (D) 87
    (E) 88

16. The average of three numbers is 24. If two of the numbers are 21 and 23, what is the third number?

    (A) 20
    (B) 24
    (C) 26
    (D) 28
    (E) 30

17. The average of three numbers is 5. If two of the numbers are zero, what is the third number?

    (A) 1
    (B) 3
    (C) 5
    (D) 10
    (E) 15

18. The average of the weight of four people is 166 pounds. If three of the people weigh 150 pounds, 200 pounds, and 180 pounds, what is the weight of the fourth person?

    (A) 134
    (B) 140
    (C) 155
    (D) 161
    (E) 165

19. For a certain student, the average of five test scores is 83. If four of the scores are 81, 79, 85, and 90, what is the fifth test score?

    (A) 83
    (B) 82
    (C) 81
    (D) 80
    (E) 79

20. Sue bought ten items at an average price of $3.60. The cost of eight of the items totaled $30. If the other two items were the same price, what was the price she paid for each?

    (A) $15.00
    (B) $7.50
    (C) $6.00
    (D) $3.00
    (E) $1.50

14

21. In a certain shipment, weights of 12 books average 2.75 pounds. If one of the books is removed, the weights of the remaining books average 2.70 pounds. What was the weight, in pounds, of the book that was removed?

    (A) 1.7
    (B) 2.3
    (C) 3.0
    (D) 3.3
    (E) 4.5

22. The average of a group of seven test scores is 80. If the lowest and the highest scores are thrown out, the average of the remaining scores is 78. What is the average of the lowest and highest scores?

    (A) 100
    (B) 95
    (C) 90
    (D) 88
    (E) 85

23. In a certain group, 12 of the children are age 10, and eight are age 15. What is the average of the ages of all the children in the group?

    (A) 9.5
    (B) 10.5
    (C) 11
    (D) 11.5
    (E) 12

24. Robert made the following deposits in a savings account:

Amount	Frequency
$15	4 times
$20	2 times
$25	4 times

What was the average of all the deposits Robert made?

    (A) $18.50
    (B) $20.00
    (C) $21.50
    (D) $22.00
    (E) $22.50

25. The average of the weights of six people sitting in a boat is 145 pounds. After a seventh person gets into the boat, the average of the weights of all seven people in the boat is 147 pounds. What is the weight (in pounds) of the seventh person?

    (A) 160
    (B) 159
    (C) 155
    (D) 149
    (E) 147

Review

1. (A)	10. (A)	18. (A)
2. (D)	11. (E)	19. (D)
3. (C)	12. (B)	20. (D)
4. (B)	13. (B)	21. (D)
5. (C)	14. (A)	22. (E)
6. (E)	15. (C)	23. (E)
7. (A)	16. (D)	24. (B)
8. (C)	17. (E)	25. (B)
9. (E)		

Review the Use of Ratios and Proportions

Ratios and proportions show up on the exam both as featured concepts, e.g., in problems that simply ask "What is the ratio?", and as problem-solving aids, "Use a proportion to find how much five items would cost instead of three."

Simple Ratios

A ratio is a statement about the relationship between any two quantities, or we might say a ratio is a statement that compares any two quantities. Suppose that in a certain classroom there are five girls and eight boys. We can compare those quantities by saying that the ratio of girls to boys is 5 to 8. Conversely, the ratio of boys to girls is 8 to 5.

Notice that in stating a ratio, order is very important. The order of the numbers in the ratio must reflect the order of the categories you are comparing. Thus, it would be incorrect to say of the above example that the ratio of girls to boys is 8 to 5.

A phrase such as "5 to 8" is one way of stating a ratio, but there are several other ways. A ratio can also be described using a colon: "The ratio of girls:boys is 5:8"; "The ratio of boys:girls is 8:5." Or, we can write the ratio in fraction form:

The ratio $\dfrac{\text{girls}}{\text{boys}}$ is $\dfrac{5}{8}$. The ratio $\dfrac{\text{boys}}{\text{girls}}$ is $\dfrac{8}{5}$.

CAUTION   In a ratio, order is critical: $\dfrac{3}{5}$ is *not* $\dfrac{5}{3}$. One of the typical wrong answers you'll find in a test problem dealing with a ratio is the *reverse* of the correct answer.

14

You can also speak of ratios as though they refer to pure numbers instead of a number of objects. Thus, you can speak abstractly of the ratio 5:8, which is the ratio of any set of five things to any set of eight things, e.g., "The ratio of five girls to eight boys is 5:8"; "The ratio of five donuts to eight donuts is 5:8"; and "The ratio of five teachers to eight students is 5:8."

Since ratios can be treated just as numbers having the form a:b or $\frac{a}{b}$, a ratio can be manipulated in the same way a fraction is manipulated. You can convert a ratio to an equivalent form by multiplying both terms of the ratio by the same number:

$$\frac{5}{8} = \frac{5 \times 2}{8 \times 2} = \frac{10}{16}$$

$$\frac{8}{5} = \frac{8 \times 5}{3 \times 3} = \frac{24}{15}$$

(Just as you would rewrite a fraction to get a form with a different denominator.)

And it is customary to reduce a ratio to its lowest terms (just as you reduce fractions to lowest terms). For example, in a certain classroom there are ten girls and 16 boys; the ratio of girls to boys is $\frac{10}{16}$, which is $\frac{5}{8}$.

Although you may not be aware of it, you probably also use ratios in an informal way in ordinary conversation. A common phrase that signifies a ratio is "for every (number) . . . there are (number) . . . ." For example, in the classroom just described, for every ten girls there are 16 boys, or in lowest terms, for every five girls there are eight boys. And for every eight boys there are five girls.

Finally, a ratio can also be stated as a rate using the word per. If a car travels 200 miles and uses 10 gallons of fuel, the car gets 200 miles per 10 gallons, or 20 miles per gallon. Cost, too, is often described as a ratio. If it is possible to purchase a dozen greeting cards for $2.40, the cost of the cards is $2.40 per dozen, or 20 cents per card.

Three-Part Ratios

When a comparison is to be made of three quantities, it can be stated using ordinary ratios. For example, if a bowl of fruit contains two apples, three pears, and five oranges, the ratio of apples to pears is 2:3; the ratio of apples to oranges is 2:5; and the ratio of pears to oranges is 3:5. This same information can be conveyed in a single statement. The ratio of apples to pears to oranges is 2:3:5.

A three-part ratio depends on the middle term to join the two outside terms. Above, the ratio of apples to pears is 2:3, and the ratio of pears to oranges is 3:5. Since 3 is common to both ratios, it can be the middle term. Sometimes it will be necessary to find a common middle term. Here's an example:

QUESTION On a certain day, a bank has the following rates of exchange:

$$\frac{\text{dollar}}{\text{mark}} = \frac{1}{3}$$

$$\frac{\text{mark}}{\text{pound}} = \frac{6}{1}$$

What is the ratio of dollars to pounds?

ANALYSIS To find the ratio dollars:pounds, we will use marks as the middle term. But the ratio of dollars to marks is 1:3, and the ratio of marks to pounds is 6:1. We must change the first ratio so that it is expressed in terms of six marks rather than three marks. This is like finding a common denominator before adding fractions:

$$\frac{1}{3} = \frac{1 \times 2}{2 \times 3}\left(\frac{2}{6}\right)$$

So the ratio of dollars to marks is 2:6, and the ratio of dollars to marks to pounds is 2:6:1. Thus the ratio of dollars to pounds is 2:1.

TIP | To build a three-part ratio, create a middle term that has the same value in both the normal ratios.

Dividing a Quantity by a Ratio

A problem may require that you divide a quantity according to a certain ratio. Here's an example:

QUESTION A $100 prize is to be divided between two contestants according to the ratio 2:3. How much should each contestant receive?

ANALYSIS To solve the problem, add the terms of the ratio to determine how many parts the prize is to be divided into. Divide the prize by that many parts, and multiply the result by the number of parts to be given to each contestant. 2 + 3 = 5, so the prize is to be divided into five parts. Each part is $100 ÷ 5 = $20. One contestant gets 2 × $20 = $40, and the other contestant receives 3 × $20 = $60. And here's another example:

14

QUESTION   Bronze is 16 parts tin and nine parts copper. If a bronze ingot weighs 100 pounds, what is the weight (in pounds) of the tin?

ANALYSIS   First, the number of parts in the ratio is $16 + 9 = 25$. Second, $100 \div 25 = 4$. So each part is worth four pounds. And since there are 16 parts of tin, the tin must weigh $16 \times 4 = 64$ pounds.

TIP

> To divide a quantity according to a ratio, divide the total by the number of ratio parts, then multiply the result by each of the number parts in each component of the ratio.

Proportions

A proportion is the mathematical equivalent of a verbal analogy. For example, 2:3::8:12 is read, "Two is to three as eight is to twelve." The main difference between a verbal analogy and a mathematical proportion is precision. Whereas a verbal analogy depends upon words that don't have single unique and precise meanings, mathematical proportions are made up of numbers which are very exact.

In a mathematical proportion, the first and last terms are called the extremes of the proportion (because they are on the extreme outside), and the two middle terms are called the means (mean can mean "middle"). In a mathematical proportion, the product of the extremes is always equal to the product of the means:

$$2 : 3 :: 8 : 12$$
$$2 \times 12 = 3 \times 8$$

Since any ratio can be written as a fraction, a proportion, which states that two ratios are equivalent, can also be written in fraction form:

$$\frac{2}{3} = \frac{8}{12}$$
$$2 \times 12 = 3 \times 8$$

This is the foundation for the process that is sometimes called cross–multiplication, a process useful in solving for an unknown element in a proportion. Here's how it works:

$$\frac{6}{9} = \frac{12}{x}$$
$$6x - 108 =$$
$$x = 18$$

(It's called cross-multiplication because you "cross" from upper left to lower right and from lower right to upper left.) After cross-multiplying, you divide both sides of the equality by the number next to the unknown.

> **TIP** You can check your solution to a proportion problem by substituting your solution for the unknown and cross-multiplying. If the two sides of the equation are equal, then your solution is correct.

Problem-Solving with Proportions

A proportion can be a very powerful problem—solving tool. Here's how you can use it:

QUESTION If the cost of a dozen donuts is $3.60, what is the cost of four donuts? (Assume there is no discount for buying in quantity.)

ANALYSIS Most people would probably solve this problem by calculating the cost of one donut ($3.60 ÷ 12 = $0.30) and then multiplying that cost by four ($0.30 × 4 = $1.20). This procedure is mathematically correct, but the same result can be reached in a way that is conceptually simpler.

The more donuts you buy, the greater the total cost, and vice versa. Since the cost of one donut is the same as the cost of any other donut, we say that the total cost increases in direct proportion to the number of donuts purchased. This can be described by a mathematical proportion:

$$\frac{\text{Total Cost } X}{\text{Total Cost } Y} = \frac{\text{Number } X}{\text{Number } Y}$$

(The X and Y just indicate the two different situations.)

$$\frac{\$3.60}{x} = \frac{12}{4}$$

Cross-multiply:

$3.60(4) = 12x$

Divide by 12:

$14.40 = 12x$

$x = \$1.20$

In this question we set up the proportion by grouping like terms; that is, "cost" is on one side of the proportion and "number" is on the other side. It would be equally correct to set up this proportion:

$$\frac{\text{Total Cost } X}{\text{Number } X} = \frac{\text{Total Cost } Y}{\text{Number } Y}$$

Nor does it make any difference whether "number" goes on the top or bottom. The following is also correct:

$$\frac{\text{Number } X}{\text{Total Cost } X} = \frac{\text{Number } Y}{\text{Total Cost } Y}$$

Although this other form is mathematically correct, it's a good idea to group like terms to avoid confusion. Also, you can simplify the calculation at any stage you choose to. Thus, in the example just discussed, you could reduce the right-hand side before cross-multiplying:

$$\frac{\$3.60}{x} = \frac{\cancel{12}^3}{\cancel{4}^1}$$

$3.60 = 3x$

$x = \$1.20$

But since different people will use different techniques for simplifying, we can't indicate every instance where simplification might be used. Instead, we will explain the problems without simplifying.

TIP

When working with a proportion, before you start your calculation, reduce fractions to their lowest terms in order to save time.

Here are some other types of problems that can be solved using proportions:

The Longer the Traveling Time, the Greater the Distance Traveled (Assuming a Constant Speed).

Here's an example:

QUESTION If a plane moving at constant speed flies 300 miles in six hours, how far will the plane fly in eight hours?

ANALYSIS First, set up a proportion grouping like terms:

$$\frac{\text{Time } X}{\text{Time } Y} = \frac{\text{Distance } X}{\text{Distance } Y}$$

$$\frac{6}{8} = \frac{300}{x}$$

Cross-Multiply:

$$6x = 300(8)$$

Divide by 6:

$$x = \frac{300(8)}{6}$$

$$x = 400$$

The Longer the Time of Operation, the Greater the Output.

Here's an example:

QUESTION If a stamping machine operating at a constant rate without interruption can post-mark 320 envelopes in five minutes, how long will it take the machine to postmark 480 envelopes?

ANALYSIS First, set up a proportion grouping like terms:

$$\frac{\text{Time } X}{\text{Time } Y} = \frac{\text{Output } X}{\text{Output } Y}$$

$$\frac{5}{x} = \frac{320}{480}$$

14

Cross-multiply:

$$320x = 5(480)$$

$$x = \frac{5(480)}{320} = 7.5 \text{ minutes}$$

The Greater the Number of Items, The Greater the Weight.

Here's how the proportion would work in this case:

QUESTION If 20 jars of preserves weigh 25 pounds, how much do 15 jars of preserves weigh?

ANALYSIS Group like terms:

$$\frac{\text{Weight } X}{\text{Weight } Y} = \frac{\text{Jars } X}{\text{Jars } Y}$$

$$\frac{25}{x} = \frac{20}{15}$$

Cross-multiply:

$$15(25) = 20x$$

$$x = \frac{15(25)}{20} = 18.75$$

Indirect Proportions

In the situations just discussed, quantities were related in direct proportion. The more of one, the more of the other—and vice versa. In some situations, quantities are related indirectly; that is, an increase in one results in a decrease in the other. For example, the more workers or machines doing a job, the less time it takes to finish. In this case, quantities are related indirectly or inversely to each other.

To solve problems involving indirect relationships, you must use an indirect or inverse proportion. The procedure is:

1. Set up an ordinary proportion, making sure that you group like quantities.
2. Invert the right side of the proportion.
3. Cross-multiply and solve for the unknown.

Here's how you use the indirect proportion:

QUESTION   Traveling at constant rate of 150 miles per hour, a plane makes the trip from City P to City Q in four hours. How long will the trip take if the plane flies at a constant rate of 200 miles per hour?

ANALYSIS   First, set up a proportion grouping like terms:

$$\frac{\text{Speed } X}{\text{Speed } Y} = \frac{\text{Time } X}{\text{Time } Y}$$

$$\frac{150}{200} = \frac{4}{x}$$

Now invert the right side:

$$\frac{150}{200} = \frac{x}{4}$$

Cross-multiply:

$$150(4) = 200x$$

Solve for the unknown:

$$x = \frac{150(4)}{200} = 3 \text{ hours}$$

Earlier, you learned that it is possible to set up a direct proportion without grouping like terms—though we advised against it. With an indirect proportion, it is absolutely essential that you group like terms. And this is one reason we recommend always grouping like terms: so you won't make a mistake if the problem involves an indirect proportion.

 CAUTION

> When quantities vary indirectly (faster speed, shorter time, etc.), you must use an indirect proportion. Be sure that you group like terms, so that you will invert the right side properly.

14

Workshop C: Ratios and Proportions

This workshop includes a Drill part and a Review part. The drill consists of 25 items. There is no time limit for the drill.

Drill

1. If a jar contains three blue marbles and eight red marbles, what is the ratio blue marbles:red marbles?

   (A) 3:11
   (B) 3:8
   (C) 8:3
   (D) 11:3
   (E) 4:1

2. If a school has 24 teachers and 480 students, what is the ratio of teachers to students?

   (A) $\frac{1}{20}$

   (B) $\frac{1}{24}$

   (C) $\frac{1}{48}$

   (D) $\frac{1}{56}$

   (E) $\frac{1}{200}$

3. If a library contains 12,000 works of fiction and 3,000 works of nonfiction, what is the ratio of works of fiction to works of nonfiction?

   (A) $\frac{1}{9}$

   (B) $\frac{1}{5}$

   (C) $\frac{1}{4}$

   (D) $\frac{4}{1}$

   (E) $\frac{5}{1}$

4. Which of the following is equivalent to $\frac{1}{3}$?

   I. $\frac{40}{120}$

   II. $\frac{75}{100}$

   III. $\frac{120}{360}$

   (A) I only
   (B) III only
   (C) I and III only
   (D) II and III only
   (E) I, II, and III

Questions 5 and 6

STUDENTS AT TYLER JUNIOR HIGH SCHOOL		
	Girls	*Boys*
7th Grade	90	85
8th Grade	80	75

5. What is the ratio of seventh-grade girls to the total number of girls at Tyler Junior High School?

   (A) $\dfrac{9}{17}$

   (B) $\dfrac{8}{9}$

   (C) $\dfrac{18}{17}$

   (D) $\dfrac{9}{8}$

   (E) $\dfrac{17}{9}$

6. What is the ratio of eighth-grade girls to the total number of students at Tyler Junior High School?

   (A) $\dfrac{8}{33}$

   (B) $\dfrac{9}{33}$

   (C) $\dfrac{8}{15}$

   (D) $\dfrac{8}{17}$

   (E) $\dfrac{17}{33}$

7. If an airplane flies 275 miles on 25 gallons of fuel, then what is the average fuel consumption for the entire trip expressed in miles per gallon?

   (A) 25
   (B) 18
   (C) 15
   (D) 11
   (E) 7

8. If an assortment of candy contains 12 chocolates, six caramels, and nine mints, what is the ratio of chocolates:caramels:mints?

   (A) 4:3:2
   (B) 4:2:3
   (C) 3:4:2
   (D) 3:2:4
   (E) 2:4:3

9. If Maria has twice as much money as Tim, who has three times as much money as William, then what is the ratio of the amount of money William has to the amount of money Maria has?

   (A) $\dfrac{1}{8}$

   (B) $\dfrac{1}{6}$

   (C) $\dfrac{1}{4}$

   (D) $\dfrac{1}{2}$

   (E) $\dfrac{2}{1}$

14

10. If three farkels buy two kirns, and three kirns buy five pucks, then nine farkels buy how many pucks?

    (A) 2
    (B) 5
    (C) 8
    (D) 10
    (E) 17

11. If machine x operates at twice the rate of machine y, and machine y operates at $\frac{2}{3}$ the rate of machine z, then what is the ratio of the rate of operation of machine x to the rate of operation of machine z?

    (A) $\frac{4}{1}$

    (B) $\frac{3}{1}$

    (C) $\frac{4}{3}$

    (D) $\frac{3}{4}$

    (E) $\frac{1}{3}$

12. If 48 marbles are to be divided between Bill and Carl in the ratio of 3:5, how many marbles should Bill get?

    (A) 6
    (B) 8
    (C) 18
    (D) 24
    (E) 30

13. If the sum of $10 is to be divided between Molly and Fred so that Fred receives only of what Molly receives, then how much should Molly receive?

    (A) $10.00
    (B) $8.00
    (C) $7.50
    (D) $6.00
    (E) $2.00

14. If a $1,000 reward is to be divided among three people in the ratio of 2:3:5, what is the largest amount that will be given to any one of the three recipients?

    (A) $200
    (B) $300
    (C) $500
    (D) $750
    (E) $900

15. If $\frac{6}{8} = \frac{x}{4}$, then $x =$

    (A) 12
    (B) 6
    (C) 4
    (D) 3
    (E) 2

16. If $\frac{14}{x} = \frac{2}{7}$, then $x =$

    (A) 7
    (B) 14
    (C) 28
    (D) 49
    (E) 343

17. If $\dfrac{3}{4} = \dfrac{4}{x}$, then $x =$

   (A) $\dfrac{3}{16}$

   (B) $\dfrac{3}{4}$

   (C) $\dfrac{4}{3}$

   (D) $\dfrac{7}{3}$

   (E) $\dfrac{16}{3}$

18. If 240 widgets cost $36, what is the cost of 180 widgets?

   (A) $8
   (B) $16
   (C) $24
   (D) $27
   (E) $32

19. If a kilogram of a certain cheese costs $9.60, what is the cost of 450 grams of the cheese? (1 kilogram = 1,000 grams)

   (A) $2.78
   (B) $3.14
   (C) $3.88
   (D) $4.32
   (E) $5.12

20. If 50 feet of electrical wire cost $4.80, then $10.80 will buy how many feet of the wire?

   (A) 60
   (B) 62.5
   (C) 67.25
   (D) 75
   (E) 112.5

21. In a certain group of people, 100 people have red hair. If only 25 percent of the people have red hair, then how many people do not have red hair?

   (A) 75
   (B) 125
   (C) 300
   (D) 400
   (E) 500

22. If a certain fundraising project has raised $12,000, which is 20 percent of its goal, how much money will have been raised when 50 percent of the goal has been reached?

   (A) $60,000
   (B) $30,000
   (C) $18,000
   (D) $15,000
   (E) $4,800

23. If 48 liters of a certain liquid weigh 50 kilograms, then how much (in kilograms) do 72 liters of the liquid weigh?

   (A) 25
   (B) 60
   (C) 75
   (D) 90
   (E) 120

24. If the trip from point x to point y takes two hours walking at the constant rate of four miles per hour, how long (expressed in hours) will the same trip take walking at a constant rate of five miles per hour?

   (A) 2.5
   (B) 1.75
   (C) 1.6
   (D) 1.5
   (E) 1.25

14

25. A swimming pool is filled by either of two pipes. Pipe A supplies water at the rate of 200 gallons per hour and takes eight hours to fill the pool. If Pipe B can fill the pool in five hours, what is the rate (in gallons per hour) at which Pipe B supplies water?

(A) 125
(B) 320
(C) 360
(D) 480
(E) 575

Review

1. (B)	10. (D)	18. (D)
2. (A)	11. (C)	19. (D)
3. (D)	12. (C)	20. (E)
4. (C)	13. (B)	21. (C)
5. (A)	14. (C)	22. (B)
6. (A)	15. (D)	23. (C)
7. (D)	16. (D)	24. (C)
8. (B)	17. (E)	25. (B)
9. (B)		

Review the Conventions Governing Powers and Roots

Powers and roots often appear on the exam as featured concepts, that is, they're the whole story. If you know the math, you get the right answer.

The Power of a Number

A power of a number is the product obtained by multiplying the number by itself a specified number of times. If we multiply 3 by itself five times, the result is $3 \times 3 \times 3 \times 3 \times 3 = 243$. So 243 is the fifth power of 3:

The second power of 2 is $2 \times 2 = 4$.

The third power of 2 is $2 \times 2 \times 2 = 8$.

The fourth power of 2 is $2 \times 2 \times 2 \times 2 = 16$.

The second power of 3 is $3 \times 3 = 9$.

The third power of 3 is $3 \times 3 \times 3 = 27$.

The second power of a number is also called the square of the number: $3 \times 3 = 9$

And the third power of a number is also called the cube of the number: $2 \times 2 \times 2 = 8$

Beyond the square and the cube, powers are referred to by the number of times the number is multiplied, e.g., fourth, fifth, sixth, and so on.

Exponents

There is a notational system for powers. To indicate the power of a number, we use a superscript (a small number placed in the upper right-hand corner). For example:

2 to the third power is written 2^3.

3 to the fifth power is written 3^5.

4 to the second power is written 4^2.

14

The superscript is called an exponent, and the number that is being multiplied is called the base. The exponent is an instruction to multiply the base by itself the number of times specified by the exponent:

$$2^3 = 2 \times 2 \times 2$$
$$3^2 = 3 \times 3$$

A number that is not to be multiplied by itself is, of course, just itself, and it is called the first power of the number. But by convention, the 1 is left out:

$$2^1 = 2$$
$$3^1 = 3$$
$$1,000^1 = 1,000$$

Rules for Working with Powers

Because powers are written using the special device of an exponent, the ordinary rules for manipulating numbers don't apply. So you must learn the special rules that apply to exponents. Here are the five rules. Don't try to memorize them all at once, and don't be put off by our use of letters instead of numbers. Everything will be explained shortly.

Rules for Working with Exponents

1. $x^m \cdot x^n = x^{m+n}$
2. $x^m \div x^n = x^{m-n}$
3. $(x^m)^n = x^{mn}$
4. $(xy)^m = (x^m)(y^m)$
5. $\left(\dfrac{x}{y}\right)^m = \dfrac{x^m}{y^m}$

The first rule covers those situations where you have multiplication of powers of the same base. In such cases, you add exponents:

$$2^2 \times 2^3 = 2^{2+3} = 2^5$$

The rule may seem a bit more plausible if we actually do the multiplication:

$$2^2 \times 2^3 = (2 \times 2) \times (2 \times 2 \times 2) = 2^5$$

The multiplication done without the rule shows that the rule does reach the correct result.

$$3^2 \times 3^5 = 3^{2+5} = 3^7$$
$$5^2 \times 5^3 \times 5^5 = 5^{2+3+5} = 5^{10}$$
$$2^{10} \times 2^{10} = 2^{10+10} = 2^{20}$$

Notice that in each of the examples there is only one base. In the first example, the base is 3; in the second, it is 5; and in the third, it is 2. This is absolutely essential. This rule for manipulating exponents doesn't apply when you have different bases in a single expression:

$$2^4 \times 3^4 =$$

You cannot use the rule here since 2 and 3 are not the same base. To carry out this manipulation, you would have to multiply out the numbers:

$$2^4 \times 3^4 = (2 \times 2 \times 2 \times 2)(3 \times 3 \times 3 \times 3) = 16 \times 81 = 1{,}296$$

Nor does the first rule apply to terms that are added, even if they use the same base. For example, $2^2 + 2^3$ is not equal to 2^5, as you can show by multiplying out the numbers.

$$2^2 + 2^3 = (2 \times 2) + (2 \times 2 \times 2) = 4 + 8 = 12$$
But 2^5 is $2 \times 2 \times 2 \times 2 \times 2 = 32$.

CAUTION The rule for multiplying terms by adding exponents does not apply when the bases are different.

The second rule governs those situations where you have a power divided by a power of the same base. You subtract exponents:

$$2^5 \div 2^3 = 2^{5-3} = 2^2$$

Again, the rule may seem more plausible if you actually do the manipulation.

$$2^5 \div 2^3 = (2 \times 2 \times 2 \times 2 \times 2) \div (2 \times 2 \times 2) = 32 \div 8 = 4$$

And 4 is 2^2, so our manipulation confirms the correctness of the rule.

$$5^4 \div 5^2 = 5^{4-2} = 5^2$$
$$10^8 \div 10^6 = 10^{8-6} = 10^2$$
$$2^3 \div 2^2 = 2^{3-2} = 2^1 = 2$$

14

Again, you will notice that in each example the bases are the same, and also that the operation is division (not addition or subtraction).

Since division of powers is accomplished by subtracting exponents, it is possible that you could end up with a zero exponent! How would that happen? Like this:

$$3^2 \div 3^2 = 3^{2-2} = 3^0$$

But what does the zero exponent signify? The zero exponent was the result of dividing a quantity into itself (3^2 and 3^2 are the same number), and you know that the result of such division is always 1. (A number goes into itself exactly one time.) For this reason, we define any number with a zero exponent to be 1:

$$5^3 \div 5^3 = 5^{3-3} = 5^0 = 1$$
$$3^{12} \div 3^{12} = 3^{12-12} = 3^0 = 1$$

In both cases, we are dividing a number into itself, so the result must be simply 1.

It is even possible to end up with a negative exponent! What does that mean?

$$2^2 \div 2^3 = 2^{2-3} = 2^{-1}$$

The meaning of a negative exponent becomes clearer if we do the problem by first multiplying:

$$2^2 \div 2^3 = (2 \times 2) \div (2 \times 2 \times 2) = 4 \div 8 = \frac{1}{2}$$

The negative exponent, therefore, does not signify a negative number. Instead, it signifies a fraction. Or, more precisely, the negative exponent indicates the reciprocal of the number written:

$$3^{-2} = \left(\frac{1}{3}\right)^2 = \frac{1}{9}$$

$$2^{-3} = \left(\frac{1}{2}\right)^3 = \frac{1}{8}$$

 CAUTION A negative exponent does not signifiy a negative number. It signifies the *reciprocal* of a number.

The third rule covers those situations where a power is raised to another power. For example:

$(2^2)^3 =$

In such situations, according to the third rule, we must multiply the exponents:

$(2^2)^3 = 2^{2 \times 3} = 2^6$

Again, the rule gains plausibility if we actually do the multiplication:

$(2^2)^3 = (2 \times 2)^3 = 4^3 = 4 \times 4 \times 4 = 64 = 2^6$

Since $(2^2)^3$ is equal to 2^6, this suggests that the rule is correct.

$(5^2)^3 = 5^{2 \times 3} = 5^6$

$(3^2)^4 = 3^{2 \times 4} = 3^8$

$(2^3)^4 = 2^{3 \times 4} = 2^{12}$

The fourth and fifth rules are really just rules for rewriting expressions using powers, and both say essentially the same thing. An exponent outside parentheses governs all the terms inside the parentheses. The fourth rule applies to situations where powers of different bases are multiplied, and the fifth rule to those where powers of different bases are divided. Here's how the fourth and fifth rules are applied:

$(2 \times 3)^2 = 2^2 \times 3^2$

$\dfrac{2}{3} = \dfrac{2^2}{3^2}$

Again, you can verify the correctness of the rules by doing the multiplication or the division.

$(2 \times 3)^2 = 2^2 \times 3^2 = 4 \times 9 = 36$ and $(2 \times 3)^2 = 6^2 = 36$

$\left(\dfrac{2}{3}\right)^2 = \dfrac{2^2}{3^2} = \dfrac{4}{9}$ and $\dfrac{2}{3} \times \dfrac{2}{3} = \dfrac{4}{9}$

As you might anticipate, more complex expressions may require the application of two or even more of the rules. And you would be correct. But no matter how complex a problem gets, it can be solved by a series of simple steps following the basic rules. Here are some examples of problems that combine operations:

$(2^3 \times 3^2)^2 = 2^{3 \times 2} \times 3^{2 \times 2} = 2^6 \times 3^4$

$\left(\dfrac{3^3 \times 5^5}{3^2 \times 5^2}\right)^2 = (3^{3-2} \times 5^{5-2})^2 = (3^1 \times 5^3)^2 = 3^2 \times 5^6$

14

Roots

When you perform the multiplication indicated by an exponent, you are in effect answering the question "What do I get when I multiply this number by itself so many times?" Now ask the opposite question: "What number, when multiplied by itself so many times, will give me a certain value?" For example, when you raise 2 to the third power, you find out that $2^3 = 8$. Now ask the question in the other direction. What number, when raised to the third power, is equal to 8?

This reverse process is called "finding the root of a number." For example, since $2^6 = 64$, the sixth root of 64 is 2.

We rarely deal with sixth roots. Mostly, we deal with numbers that have two roots: $2 \times 2 = 4$, so the second or square root of 4 is 2; and occasionally with numbers having three roots: $2 \times 2 \times 2 = 8$, so the third or cube root of 8 is 2.

The operation of taking a square root of a number is signaled by the radical sign,. (Radical comes from the Latin word rad, which means "root.") Here's what they look like:

$\sqrt{1} = 1$ $\qquad\qquad\qquad$ $\sqrt{49} = 7$

$\sqrt{4} = 2$ $\qquad\qquad\qquad$ $\sqrt{64} = 8$

$\sqrt{9} = 3$ $\qquad\qquad\qquad$ $\sqrt{81} = 9$

$\sqrt{16} = 4$ $\qquad\qquad\qquad$ $\sqrt{100} = 10$

$\sqrt{25} = 5$ $\qquad\qquad\qquad$ $\sqrt{121} = 11$

$\sqrt{36} = 6$ $\qquad\qquad\qquad$ $\sqrt{144} = 12$

 NOTE | The $\sqrt{}$ symbol always denotes a positive number.

If the radical sign is adorned with a little number, it indicates a different root:

$\sqrt[3]{8} = 2$ (The cube root of 8 is 2.)

$\sqrt[3]{27} = 3$ (The cube root of 27 is 3.)

$\sqrt[3]{125} = 5$ (The cube root of 125 is 5.)

Theoretically, even greater roots are possible, but you probably won't run across any on the exam.

Extracting Square Roots

If a number is a perfect square (e.g., 4, 9, 16, etc.), then extracting its square root is easy. You just use the values given in the table above.

Not every number, however, has an exact square root. In such cases, you can do one of two things. First, you may be able to find in the number a factor that does have an exact square root and extract that (pull it out) from under the radical sign. Here are some examples:

$$\sqrt{125} = \sqrt{25 \times 5} = 5\sqrt{5}$$

In this case, 125 does not have an exact square root, but 25, which does, is a factor of 125. So we factor 125 into 25 and 5. Then we take the square root of 25, which is 5. The final expression is 5, which means 5 multiplied by the square root of 5.

$$\sqrt{27} = \sqrt{9 \times 3} = 3\sqrt{3}$$
$$\sqrt{32} = \sqrt{16 \times 2} = 4\sqrt{2}$$
$$\sqrt{52} = \sqrt{4 \times 13} = 23\sqrt{13}$$

Your second option is to approximate a value for the square root. For the exam, it is useful to know that $\sqrt{2}$ is approximately 1.4 and that $\sqrt{3}$ is approximately 1.7. You can approximate other values by using ranges. For example, must be between 2 and 3 ($\sqrt{4} < \sqrt{7} < \sqrt{9}$). And since 7 is closer to 9 than to 4, a good approximation of $\sqrt{7}$ is 2.6 to 2.7. For the test, you would not need greater accuracy.

TIP   Memorize the two most important non-exact radical values: $\sqrt{2} \approx 1.4$ and $\sqrt{3} \approx 1.7$.

Manipulating Radicals

Radicals are really just a form of exponents. In fact, radicals can be written using fractional exponents:

$$\sqrt{4} = 4^{\frac{1}{2}} = 2$$
$$\sqrt[3]{8} = 8^{\frac{1}{3}} = 2$$

14

The exam doesn't often make use of fractional exponents; but fractional exponents do make it easier to explain how to manipulate radicals, since all of the rules for manipulating exponents apply to fractional exponents and therefore to radicals as well.

You know, for example, that when you multiply a square root by itself, the result is the number beneath the radical:

$$\sqrt{2} \times \sqrt{2} = 2$$

This result is consistent with common sense. But it is also explained by the first rule of exponents. Since $\sqrt{2} = 2^{\frac{1}{2}}$, $\sqrt{2} \times \sqrt{2} = 2^{\frac{1}{2}+\frac{1}{2}} = 2^1 = 2$.

The fourth and fifth rules of exponents are the ones you are most likely to use in working with radicals. Those are the rules for rewriting. Here is how the fourth rule applies to radicals:

$$\sqrt{125} = 125^{\frac{1}{2}} = (25 \times 5)^{\frac{1}{2}} = 25^{\frac{1}{2}} \times 5^{\frac{1}{2}} = \sqrt{25} \times \sqrt{5} = 5\sqrt{5}$$

Notice that this is just the process of extracting a square root by finding a factor, but what makes that process work is the fourth rule of exponents. The fifth rule is used in the following example:

$$\sqrt{\frac{4}{9}} = \left(\frac{4}{9}\right)^{\frac{1}{2}} = 25^{\frac{1}{2}} \times 5^{\frac{1}{2}} = \sqrt{25} \times \sqrt{5} = 5\sqrt{5}$$

Importantly, since radicals are just a form of exponents, you cannot just add radicals. $\sqrt{4} + \sqrt{9}$ is not equal to $\sqrt{13}$, and you can prove this by taking the square root of 4, which is 2, and the square root of 9, which is 3. And $2 + 3$ is 5, which is not $\sqrt{13}$.

 NOTE | Radicals can be expressed as fractional exponents.

Workshop D: Powers and Roots

This workshop includes a Drill part and a Review part. The drill consists of 35 items. There is no time limit for the drill.

Drill

1. What is the third power of 3?

   (A) 1
   (B) 3
   (C) 9
   (D) 15
   (E) 27

2. What is the fourth power of 2?

   (A) 2
   (B) 4
   (C) 8
   (D) 16
   (E) 32

3. What is the first power of 1,000,000?

   (A) 0
   (B) $\dfrac{1}{1,000,000}$
   (C) 1
   (D) 10
   (E) 1,000,000

4. $100^0 =$

   (A) 0
   (B) 1
   (C) 10
   (D) 100
   (E) 100,000

5. $2^3 \times 2^2 =$

   (A) 6
   (B) 8
   (C) 2^5
   (D) 2^6
   (E) 4^6

6. $3^{10} \times 10^3 =$

   I. 30^{30}

   II. $300 \times 1,000$

   III. $30 + 30$

   (A) I, but not II or III
   (B) II, but not I or III
   (C) I and III, but not II
   (D) II and III, but not I
   (E) Neither I, II, nor III

7. $5^4 \times 5^9 =$

   (A) 25^{36}
   (B) 5^{36}
   (C) 5^{13}
   (D) 5^5
   (E) 5

8. $2^3 \times 2^4 \times 2^5 =$

   (A) 2^{12}
   (B) 2^{60}
   (C) 8^{12}
   (D) 4^{60}
   (E) 8^{60}

14

9. $(2 + 3)^{20} =$
   (A) 5^{20}
   (B) $2^{20} + 3^{20}$
   (C) 6^{20}
   (D) 20^5
   (E) 20^6

10. $\dfrac{2^5}{2^3} =$
    (A) 2^2
    (B) 4^4
    (C) 2^8
    (D) 4^8
    (E) 2^{15}

11. $\dfrac{3^{10}}{3^8} =$
    (A) 3
    (B) 3^2
    (C) 9^2
    (D) 3^{18}
    (E) 3^{80}

12. $\dfrac{5^2}{5^2} =$
    I. 0

    II. 1

    III. 5^0
    (A) I and II only
    (B) I and III only
    (C) II and III only
    (D) III only
    (E) Neither I, II, nor III

13. $\dfrac{5^2}{5^3} =$
    I. 3^{-1}

    II. $\dfrac{1}{3}$

    III. -1
    (A) I only
    (B) II only
    (C) I and II only
    (D) I and III only
    (E) I, II, and III

14. $(2^2)^3 =$
    (A) 2^5
    (B) 2^6
    (C) 4^5
    (D) 4^6
    (E) 6^5

15. $(5^2)^6 =$
    (A) 5^8
    (B) 5^{12}
    (C) 10^4
    (D) 10^8
    (E) 10^{12}

16. $(7^7)^7 =$
    (A) 21
    (B) 7^{14}
    (C) 7^{49}
    (D) 21^7
    (E) 49^{49}

17. $(3 \times 2)^2 =$

    I. 36

    II. $3 \times 3 \times 2 \times 2$

    III. $3^2 \times 2^2$

    (A) I only
    (B) II only
    (C) III only
    (D) I and III only
    (E) I, II, and III

18. $(5 \times 3)^2 =$

    I. 15^2

    II. $5^2 \times 3^2$

    III. 8^2

    (A) I only
    (B) II only
    (C) III only
    (D) I and II only
    (E) I, II, and III

19. $\left(\dfrac{8}{3}\right)^2 =$

    I. $\dfrac{64}{9}$

    II. $\dfrac{8^2}{3^2}$

    III. 11^2

    (A) I only
    (B) II only
    (C) I and II only
    (D) I and III only
    (E) I, II, and III

20. $\left(\dfrac{4}{9}\right)^2 =$

    (A) $\dfrac{2}{3}$

    (B) $\dfrac{4}{9}$

    (C) $\dfrac{16}{81}$

    (D) $\dfrac{4^2}{9}$

    (E) $\dfrac{4}{9^2}$

21. $(2 \times 2^2 \times 2^3)^2 =$

    (A) 2^8
    (B) 2^{10}
    (C) 2^{12}
    (D) 2^{16}
    (E) 2^{18}

22. $\dfrac{2^4 \times 5^4}{2^2 \times 5^2} =$

    (A) $2^4 \times 5^4$
    (B) $2^6 \times 2^6$
    (C) 4^6
    (D) 4^8
    (E) 24

23. $\dfrac{3^6 \times 5^3 \times 7^9}{3^4 \times 5^3 \times 7^8} =$

    (A) $3^2 \times 5 \times 7$
    (B) $3^2 \times 5 \times 7^2$
    (C) $3 \times 5 \times 7$
    (D) $3^2 \times 5$
    (E) $3^2 \times 7$

14

24. $\left(\dfrac{5^{12} \times 7^6}{5^{11} \times 7^5}\right)^2 =$

    (A) 25
    (B) 49
    (C) 5^7
    (D) 5^{11}
    (E) 7^5

25. $\left(\dfrac{12^{12} \times 11^{11} \times 10^{10}}{12^{12} \times 11^{11} \times 10^{10}}\right)^2 =$

    (A) 0
    (B) 1
    (C) 10
    (D) 100
    (E) 1,000

26. $\sqrt{36} =$

    I. 6

    II. -6

    III. $3\sqrt{3}$

    (A) I only
    (B) I and II only
    (C) I and III only
    (D) II and III only
    (E) I, II, and III

27. $\sqrt{81} + \sqrt{4} =$

    I. $\sqrt{85}$

    II. $\sqrt{9} + \sqrt{2}$

    III. 11

    (A) I only
    (B) II only
    (C) III only
    (D) I and II only
    (E) II and III only

28. $\sqrt{27} =$

    (A) 3
    (B) $3\sqrt{3}$
    (C) $3\sqrt{9}$
    (D) 27
    (E) 81

29. $\sqrt{52} =$

    (A) $\sqrt{5} + \sqrt{2}$
    (B) 7
    (C) $2\sqrt{13}$
    (D) $13\sqrt{4}$
    (E) 13^2

30. $\sqrt{\dfrac{9}{4}} =$

  (A) $\dfrac{\sqrt{3}}{2}$

  (B) $\dfrac{3}{\sqrt{2}}$

  (C) $\dfrac{3}{2}$

  (D) 5

  (E) $\sqrt{5}$

31. $\dfrac{\sqrt{81}}{\sqrt{27}} =$

  (A) $\sqrt{3}$
  (B) 3
  (C) $3\sqrt{3}$
  (D) 9
  (E) $9\sqrt{3}$

32. $2 \times \sqrt{2}$ is most nearly equal to
  (A) 2.8
  (B) 3.4
  (C) 4
  (D) 7
  (E) 12

33. $\sqrt{27}$ is most nearly equal to
  (A) 3
  (B) 4
  (C) 4.5
  (D) 5.1
  (E) 9

34. $\sqrt{12}$ is most nearly equal to
  (A) 2
  (B) 3.4
  (C) 4
  (D) 6
  (E) 8

35. $\sqrt{23}$ is most nearly equal to
  (A) 4
  (B) 4.8
  (C) 6
  (D) 7
  (E) 8

14

Review

1. (E)	13. (C)	25. (D)
2. (D)	14. (B)	26. (A)
3. (E)	15. (B)	27. (C)
4. (B)	16. (C)	28. (B)
5. (C)	17. (E)	29. (C)
6. (E)	18. (D)	30. (C)
7. (C)	19. (C)	31. (A)
8. (A)	20. (C)	32. (A)
9. (A)	21. (C)	33. (D)
10. (A)	22. (A)	34. (B)
11. (B)	23. (E)	35. (B)
12. (C)	24. (A)	

Get Answers to Frequently Asked Questions

Q: Are percents very important?

A: Yes, percents can appear in many different forms. Sometimes the test asks you to do a calculation and express a fraction as a percent. You might also have a pie chart which uses percents. And there are many different kinds of word problems that ask for answers in percent terms. So you not only need to know how to do things like multiply with a percent, you also need to know how to use percents in practical situations.

Q: How do averages come up on the test?

A: Usually in a word problem, e.g., "Ten students took a test, and the average for the class was, etc."

Q: How often are ratios and proportions tested?

A: Pretty often. You may get a problem that asks you to find a ratio or solve a proportion. But more important, proportions are very powerful problem solvers. Remember that you can use them on word problems, too.

Q: When am I most likely to have to use power, squares, cubes, and so on?

A: A few questions may just you to show that you know how to manipuate the symbols, but you also need a working knowledge of those concepts to solve some algebra problems (those involving certain questions, for example) and some geometry problems (those involving area where quantities are squared or volume where quantities are cubed).

Today's Review

1. Today, you studied the more advanced arithmetic concepts that appear on the test: percent, average, ratio and proportions, and powers and roots.

2. The two kinds of percent problems that you're most likely to encounter have the general forms "What percent is this of that?" and "What was the percent change?"

3. The two kinds of average problems that you're most likely to encounter will ask about a missing element of an average or about a weighted average.

4. The test uses ratios and proportions as the basis for math problems, but you'll also find that proportions are useful tools for solving word problems.

5. A few problems are likely to be a straight-forward test of your ability to manipulation roots and powers.

14

Teach Yourself GRE Algebra

Today, you'll review the essential algebra concepts that you need to do well on the test. And you will get several chances to practice what you've reviewed.

Basic Grammar of Algebra

Algebra is that branch of mathematics that uses letter symbols to represent numbers. The letter symbols are in essence place holders. They function somewhat like English words such as *someone* or *somewhere*. For example, in the English sentence "Someone took the book and put it somewhere," neither the identity of the person in question nor the new location of the book is known. Using letters in the way algebra does, we might say "x put the book in y place." The identity of x is unknown, and the new location of the book is unknown. It is for this reason that letter symbols in algebra are often referred to as "unknowns."

Algebra, like English, is a language, and for making certain statements, algebra is much better than English. For example, the English statement "There is a number such that, when you add 3 to it, the result is 8" can be rendered more easily in algebraic notation: $x + 3 = 8$. In fact, learning the rules of algebra is really very much like learning the grammar of any language.

With this analogy between algebra as a language and English in mind, let's begin by studying the components of the language of algebra. Just as English is built up from words, phrases, and sentences, the language of algebra is built up from terms (words), expressions (phrases), and equations (sentences).

What You'll Do Today

- Review Methods for Working with Expressions
- Workshop A: Expressions
- Review Procedures for Solving Equations
- Workshop B: Equations
- Get Answers to Frequently Asked Questions

The basic unit of the English language is the word. The basic unit of the language of algebra is the *term*. In English, a word consists of one or more letters. In algebra, a term consists of one or more letters (or numbers). For example, x, $2z$, xy, N, 2, , and π can all be algebraic terms.

In English, a word may have a root, a prefix, a suffix, an ending, and so on. In algebra, a term may have a coefficient, an exponent, and a sign.

 NOTE

In math in general, and on the test in particular, when the sign is positive, the "+" is not written but understood, e.g., $3x$ is $+3x$. Also, when the coefficient is 1, it is understood, not written out, e.g., x and not $1x$.)

The elements in an algebraic term are all joined by the operation of multiplication. The coefficient (and its sign) is multiplied by the variable. Thus, $-3x$ means -3 times x; $5a$ means $(+)5$ times a; and N means times N.

The exponent, as you have already learned, also indicates multiplication. Thus, x^2 means x times x; a^3 means a times a times a; and N^5 means N times N times N times N times N. When you are working with algebraic terms, be careful not to confuse the coefficient with the exponent. $3x$ means 3 times x, while x^3 means x times x times x.

 CAUTION

When working with algebraic terms, don't confuse coefficients and exponents. For example, $(x + x + x)$ is $3x$—not x^3. But one of the the wrong answers on the test would probably be x^3.

Many terms have both a coefficient and an exponent. Thus, $3x^2$ means "3 times (x times x)," and $-5a^3$ means "-5 times (a times a times a)."

In English, words are organized into phrases. In algebra, terms are grouped together in *expressions*. An expression is a collection of algebraic terms that are joined by addition, subtraction, or both. Here are some examples of algebraic expressions:

$x + y$

$-2x + 3x + z$

$3x^2 - 2y^2$

$x^2 + y^2$

A *monomial* is an expression with a single term.

A *polynomial* is any expression with more than one term.

A *binomial* is a polynomial with exactly two terms.

In algebra, a complete sentence is called an *equation*. An equation asserts that two algebraic expressions are equal. Compare the algebraic translation of an English expression:

$2x + 4 = 3x - 2$

2 times a certain unknown plus 4 is equal to 3 times that unknown minus 2.

Inequalities are also complete algebra statements. Again, here is both the English and the algebra:

3 plus twice some number is more than 5.

$3 + 2x > 5$

The rules for working with inequalities, however, are different from the rules for working with equations. You'll learn more about the distinction later in this day.

Some test problems don't have to be solved. They just ask you to "translate" English into algebra, that is, create an expression for a concept or set up an equation that can be solved. Other problems require you to solve for an unknown

Review Methods for Working with Expressions

Like numbers in arithmetic, algebraic terms can be added and subtracted, multiplied and divided.

Addition and subtraction are indicated in algebra, as they are in arithmetic, with the signs "+" and "–." In arithmetic, these operations result in the combining of numbers into a third number. For example, the addition of 2 and 3 results in the combining of 2 and 3 to form the number $5:2 + 3 = 5$. In algebra, however, this process of combining can take place only with *like* terms. Two terms are considered like terms if, and only if, they (1) have exactly the same variable and (2) are raised to exactly the same power. The coefficient does not determine whether terms are like terms. Study these examples:

$3x^2$, $40x^2$, and $-2x^2$ are like terms.

$3x$ and $3x^2$ are not like terms.

xy, $5xy$, $-23xy$, and πxy are like terms.

xy and x^2y are not like terms.

$10xyz$, $-xyz$, and xyz are like terms.

xy, yz, and xz are not like terms.

To add or subtract algebraic terms, group like terms and then add or subtract the coefficients:

QUESTION   What is $x^2 + 2x^2 + 3x^2$?

ANALYSIS   All three terms are like terms: x raised to the second power. To add, simply add the coefficients: $1 + 2 + 3 = 6$. (Remember, a term with no explicit coefficient is understood to have a coefficient of 1 .) So the result is $6x^2$. Here's another example:

QUESTION   What is $y + 2x +3y -x$?

ANALYSIS   Here we have two different types of terms, x and y terms. First, group like terms together:

$(2x - x) + (y + 3y)$

Next, add the coefficients for each type of term. For the x terms, the coefficients are $2 - 1 = 1$, and for the y terms, $1 + 3 = 4$. So the final result is $1x + 4y$, which is written as $x + 4y$. And here is another example:

QUESTION   What is $x - 3x + 5x - 2x$?

ANALYSIS   Here, all of the terms are like terms, x. Simply add the coefficients: $1 - 3 + 5 -2 = 1$, so the result is $1x$, or simply x.

QUESTION   What is $2x - y - 3x + 4y + 5x$?

ANALYSIS   Here, we have both x and y terms. First group like terms:

$(2x - 3x + 5x) + (4y - y)$

Now add coefficients for each. For the x terms, $2 - 3 + 5 = 4$, and for the y terms, $4 - 1 = 3$. So the result is $4x + 3y$.

QUESTION What is $5x^2 + 3x^3 - 2x^2 + 4x^3$?

ANALYSIS Here, we have two different terms, x^2 and $x3$. Group like terms:

$(5x^2 - 2x^2) + (3x^3 + 4x^3)$

Now add the coefficients for each term. For the x^2 terms, the result is $5 - 2 = 3$, or $3x2$. For the x^3 terms, the result is $3 + 4 = 7$, or $7x3$. So the final result is $3x^2 + 7x3$.

> **CAUTION**
>
> When you have combined all like terms, it is not possible to carry the addition or subtraction further. For example, $x + y$ is just that, $x + y$. But a wrong answer choice could be xy.

The laws of exponents apply to algebraic terms just as they apply to numbers in arithmetic:

1. To multiply the same variable raised to powers, add the exponents:

   $(x^2)(x^3) = x^{2+3} = x^5$

2. To divide the same variable raised to powers, subtract the exponents:

   $x^3 - x^2 = x^{3-2} = x^1 = x$

3. To raise an algebraic term to a power, multiply the exponents:

   $(x^2)^3 = x^{(2)(3)} = x^6$

4. An exponent outside parentheses governs all terms within the parentheses:

   $(x^2y^3)^2 = x^{(2)(2)}y^{(3)(2)} = x^4y^6$

   $$\left(\frac{x^2}{y^3}\right)^2 = \left[\frac{x^{(2)(2)}}{y^{(3)(2)}}\right] = \left[\frac{x^4}{y^6}\right]$$

> **MAKE CONNECTIONS**
>
> The rules for working with exponents in algebra are the same as those for working with numbers.

Multiplication in algebra can be indicated in four ways:

$a \times b$

$(a)(b)$

$a \cdot b$

ab

To multiply two or more monomial (single) terms, just multiply their coefficients and use the laws of exponents. Here's a simple example:

QUESTION What is $(4x)(2x)$?

ANALYSIS First, multiply the coefficients: $(4)(2) = 8$. Second, use the law of exponents: $(x)(x) = x^2$. So the final result is $8x^2$. Here's a little more complicated example:

QUESTION What is $(3x^2)(xy)$?

ANALYSIS First, multiply the coefficients: $(3)(1) = 3$. Second, use the laws of exponents: $(x^2)(xy) = x^{2+1}y = x^3y$. So the final result is $3x^3y$. And now an even more complicated example:

QUESTION What is $(2xyz)(3xy)(4yz)$?

ANALYSIS First, multiply the coefficients: $(2)(3)(4) = 24$. Next, use the laws of exponents: $(xyz)(xy)(yz) = x^{1+1}y^{1+1+1}z^{1+1} = x^2y^3z\mathbf{2}$. So the result is $24x^2y^3z\mathbf{2}$.

To divide one monomial by another, divide coefficients and use the laws of exponents. Here's a simple example:

QUESTION What is $4x^3y^4 + 2xy^3$?

ANALYSIS First, divide the coefficients: $4 \div 2 = 2$. Next, use the second law of exponents: $x^3y^4 \div xy^3 = x^{3-1}y^{4-3} = x^2y$. So the result is $2x^2y$. And a little more complicated example:

QUESTION What is $2x^4y^3 \div x^2z$?

ANALYSIS First, divide exponents: $2 \div 1 = 2$. Next, use the second law of exponents:

$$x^4y^3 \div x^2z = \frac{x^{4-2}y^3}{z} = \frac{x^2y^3}{z}. \text{ So the result is } \frac{2x^2y^3}{z}.$$

Addition and subtraction of algebraic fractions, like the addition and subtraction of ordinary fractions, require the use of common denominators.

When you already have like denominators, simply add the numerators of the fractions, using the already existing denominator. Here are examples of this procedure:

$$\frac{5}{x} + \frac{3}{x} = \frac{5+3}{x} = \frac{8}{x}$$

$$\frac{2x}{y} - \frac{x}{y} = \frac{2x - x}{y} = \frac{x}{y}$$

$$\frac{a}{cd} + \frac{x}{cd} = \frac{a+x}{cd}$$

To add or subtract algebraic fractions with unlike denominators, you must first find a common denominator. Here's how:

$$\frac{2}{x} + \frac{3}{y} + \frac{4}{z} = \frac{2yx + 3xy + 4yz}{xyz}$$

 CAUTION   You can add algebraic fractions just as you do numerical fractions. Create a new denominator by multiplying the old denominators. "Cross-multiply" the numberator of each fraction by the denominators of the others. Add. But be sure to reduce to lowest terms.

To multiply fractions, follow the rules for multiplying arithmetic fractions. Multiply terms in the numerators to create a new numerator, and multiply terms in the denominator to create a new denominator. Here are some examples:

$$\frac{2}{x} \times \frac{3}{y} = \frac{6}{xy}$$

$$\frac{a}{b} \times \frac{b}{c} = \frac{ab}{cd}$$

$$\frac{x^2 y^3}{z} \times \frac{x^3 y^2}{wz} = \frac{x^5 y^5}{xz^2}$$

To divide algebraic fractions, follow the rule for dividing arithmetic fractions. Invert the divisor and multiply. For example:

$$\frac{2}{y} \div \frac{3}{x} = \frac{2}{y} \times \frac{x}{3} = \frac{2x}{3y}$$

$$\frac{2x^2}{y} \div \frac{y}{x} = \frac{2x^2}{y} \times \frac{x}{y} = \frac{2x^3}{y^2}$$

Multiplying Polynomials

A polynomial is an algebraic expression with more than one term, e.g., $x + y$. A multiplication problem such as $(x + y)(x + y)$ requires a special procedure.

The fundamental rule for multiplying is that every term of one expression must be multiplied by every term of the other expression. This principle can be illustrated using numbers.

First, take the case in which a polynomial is to be multiplied by a single term; for example, $2(3 + 4 + 5)$. One way of solving the problem is to do the addition first and then multiply:

$2(3 + 4 + 5) = 2(12) = 24$

It is also possible, however, to multiply each term in the parentheses by 2 and then add. Just multiply every term inside the parentheses by the term outside the parentheses:

$2(3 + 4 + 5) = (2)(3) + (2)(4) + (2)(5) = 6 + 8 + 10 = 24$

Notice that the result is the same no matter which method we use.

Now take the case in which it is necessary to multiply two polynomials; for example, $(2 + 3)(1 + 4)$. Again, this can be accomplished by first adding and then multiplying:

$(2 + 3)(1 + 4) = (5)(5) = 25$

But it can also be done by first multiplying and then adding:

$(2 + 3)(1 + 4) = (2)(1) + (2)(4) + (3)(1) + (3)(4) = 2 + 8 + 3 + 12 = 25$

We get the same result with either method!

With algebraic expressions such as $(x + y)$, you must use the second method (multiply and then add), because you cannot add (beyond just saying "$x + y$"). So now we will apply the technique to algebraic expressions. Here's how it works:

$x(y + z) = xy + xz$

$a(b + c + d) = ab + ac + ad$

The multiplication of two binomials (two two-term expressions) presents a special case that arises often enough that you should learn a special technique for handling it. The following diagram illustrates how to multiply two binomials:

$(x + y)(x + y) = x^2 + xy + xy + y^2 = x^2 + 2xy + y^2$

The method described in the diagram is often referred to as the FOIL method. FOIL is an acronym for First, Outer, Inner, and Last. Stated more fully, when multiplying two binomials, e.g., $(x + y)(x + y)$, you first multiply the *first* terms together, then the *outer* terms together, then the *inner* terms together, and then the *last* terms together. Finally, combine like terms.

$(x + y)(x + y) =$

First: $(x)(x) = x^2$

Outer: $(x)(y) = xy$

Inner: $(y)(x) = xy$

Last: $(y)(y) = y^2$

Add: $x^2 + xy + xy + y^2 = x^2 + 2xy + y^2$

$(x - y)(x - y) =$

First: $(x)(x) = x^2$

Outer: $(x)(-y) = -xy$

Inner: $(-y)(x) = -xy$

Last: $(-y)(-y) = y^2$

Add: $x^2 - xy - xy + y^2 = x^2 - 2xy + y^2$

TIP

Memorize the following common multiplications so you don't have to do them each time you see one:

$(x + y)^2 = (x + y)(x + y) = x^2 + 2xy + y^2$

$(x - y)^2 = (x - y)(x - y) = x^2 - 2xy + y^2$

$(x + y)(x - y) = x^2 - y2$

It is also possible that you would be asked to multiply something more complex than two binomials; for example, $(x + y)^3$. The process is tedious and time–consuming, but ultimately it is executed the same way. First, multiply $(x + y)(x + y)$, as shown above. The result is $x^2 + 2xy + y^2$. Then, complete the multiplication by multiplying every term in that result by both x and y, as follows:

$$(x + y)(x^2 + 2xy + y^2) =$$
$$x(x^2) + x(2xy) + x(y^2) + y(x^2) + y(2xy) + y(y^2) =$$
$$x^3 + 2x^2y + xy^2 + x^2y + 2xy^2 + y^3 =$$
$$x^3 + 3x^2y + 3xy^2 + y^3$$

Factoring

Although mention of the term *factoring* strikes fear into the hearts of many students, factoring is really nothing more than the reverse of multiplication. For example, if $(x + y)(x + y) = x^2 + 2xy + y^2$, then $x^2 + 2xy + y^2$ can be factored into $(x + y)(x + y)$. Fortunately, for purposes of taking the test, any factoring you might need to do will fall into one of three categories.

1. Finding a Common Factor
2. Reversing a Known Multiplication Process
3. Reversing an Unknown Multiplication Process

Let's look at each.

1. Finding a Common Factor

If all the terms of an algebraic expression contain a common factor, then that term can be factored out of the expression. Here are some examples:

$$ab + ac + ad = a(b + c + d)$$
$$abx + aby + abz = ab(x + y + z)$$
$$x^2 + x^3 + x^4 = x^2(1 + x + x^2)$$
$$3a + 6a^2 + 9a^3 = 3a(1 + 2a + 3a^2)$$

2. Reversing a Known Multiplication Problem

Some patterns recur with such frequency on the exam that you must simply *memorize* them.

$$x^2 + 2xy + y^2 = (x + y)(x + y)$$
$$x^2 - 2xy + y^2 = (x - y)(x - y)$$
$$x^2 - y^2 = (x + y)(x - y)$$

15

You will observe that these are the same three patterns you were asked to memorize above while we were studying the FOIL method.

3. Reversing an Unknown Multiplication Process

Occasionally, and only occasionally, you may find it necessary to factor an expression that does not fall into one of the two categories above. The expression will almost surely have the form $ax^2 + bx + c$; for example, $x^2 + 2x + 1$. To factor such expressions, set up a blank diagram: ( )( ). The diagram is then filled in by answering a series of questions:

1. What factors will produce the first, the x^2, term?
2. What possible factors will produce the last, the c, term?
3. Which of the possible factors from step 2, when added together, will produce the middle, the bx, term?

Here's how the method works:

 Factor $x^2 + 3x + 2$.

 1. What factors will produce the first, the x^2 term? x times x yields x^2, so the factors, in part, are $(x\ )(x\ )$.

2. What possible factors will produce the last term? The possibilities are $(2,1)$ and $(-2, -1)$.
3. Which of the two sets of factors just mentioned, when added together, will produce a final result of $3x$? The answer is $(2,1)$: $2 + 1 = 3$. You can confirm this by performing the multiplication using the FOIL method:

$$(x + 2)(x + 1) = x^2 + x + 2x + 2 = x^2 + 3x + 2$$

Try this yourself:

 Factor $x^2 + 4x - 12$.

 1. What factors will generate x^2? $(x\ )(x\ )$

2. What factors will generate -12? $(1,-12),(12,-1),(2,-6)(6,-2),(3,-4)(4,-3)$
3. Which factors, when added together, will produce the middle term of $+ 4x$? The answer is $(6,-2)$: $6 + (-2) = 4$.

So the factors are $(x + 6)$ and $(x - 2)$, a fact that you can confirm by using the FOIL method to multiply together these two binomials:

$$(x + 6)(x - 2) = x^2 - 2x + 6x - 12 = x^2 + 4x - 12$$

Workshop A: Expressions

This workshop will let you practice the procedures that you've just reviewed. There is no time limit for the workshop; but after you have finished, check your work against the Review part.

Drill

1. Which of the following pairs of terms are like terms?

    I. $34x$ and $-18x$

    II. $2x$ and $2xy$

    III. x^3 and $3x$

    (A) I only
    (B) II only
    (C) I and III only
    (D) II and III only
    (E) I, II, and III

2. Which of the following pairs of terms are like terms?

    I. $\sqrt{3x}$ and $\sqrt{3x}$

    II. π and 10

    III. x^2 and $2x^2$

    (A) I only
    (B) II only
    (C) I and II only
    (D) I and III only
    (E) I, II, and III

3. $x + 2x + 3x =$

    (A) $6x^6$
    (B) x^6
    (C) $6x$
    (D) $x + 6$
    (E) $x - 6$

4. $2x + 3x - x + 4x =$

    (A) $8x^8$
    (B) x^8
    (C) $8x$
    (D) $x + 8$
    (E) $x - 8$

5. $a^3 + a^2 + a =$

    (A) $3a^3$
    (B) a^3
    (C) $2a^2$
    (D) a^2
    (E) $a^3 + a^2 + a$

6. $z^2 + 2z^2 - 5z^2 =$

    (A) $-9z^2$
    (B) $-2z^2$
    (C) 0
    (D) $2z^2$
    (E) $5z^2$

7. $a^3 - 12a^3 + 15a^3 + 2a^3 =$

   (A) $6a^3$
   (B) $2a^2$
   (C) $6a$
   (D) $3a$
   (E) a

8. $3c + 2a - 1 + 4c - 2a + 1 =$

   (A) $2a + 4c + 1$
   (B) $4a + 3c - 2$
   (C) $a + c - 1$
   (D) $2a + 1$
   (E) $7c$

9. $-7nx + 2nx + 2n + 7x =$

   (A) 0
   (B) $-5nx + 2n + 7x$
   (C) $18nx$
   (D) $9nx + 9xn$
   (E) $4nx$

10. $c^2 + 2c^2d^2 - c^2 =$

   (A) $4c^2d^2$
   (B) $2c^2d^2$
   (C) c^2d^2
   (D) $2cd$
   (E) cd

11. $2x^2 + 2x^2 + 2x^2 =$

   (A) $6x^6$
   (B) $2x^6$
   (C) $6x^2$
   (D) $6x$
   (E) 6

12. $3xy + 3x^2y - 2xy + y =$

   (A) $6xy - y$
   (B) $x + xy + y$
   (C) $3x^2y + xy + y$
   (D) $x^2y^2 + xy$
   (E) $3xy + x$

13. $x^2 + 2xy - 3x + 4xy - 6y + 2y^2 + 3x - 2xy + 6y =$

   (A) $x^2 - 2xy + y^2$
   (B) $x^2 + y^2 + 3x + 2y$
   (C) $x^2 + 2y^2 + 4xy + 6x + 6y$
   (D) $x^2 + 2y^2 + 4xy + 6x$
   (E) $x^2 + 2y^2 + 4xy$

14. $8p + 2p^2 + pq - 4p^2 - 14p - pq =$

   (A) $-2p^2 - 6p$
   (B) $-p^2 + 6p$
   (C) $2p^2 + 6p$
   (D) $p^2 + 3p$
   (E) $3p^2 - pq$

15. $pqr + qrs + rst + stu =$

   (A) $pqrst$
   (B) $pq + qr + rs + st + tu$
   (C) $pqr + rst$
   (D) $4pqrst$
   (E) $pqr + qrs + rst + stu$

16. $(x^2)(x^3) =$

   (A) $\dfrac{x^2}{x^3}$

   (B) $\dfrac{x^5}{x^6}$

   (C) x^2
   (D) x^5
   (E) x^6

17. $(a)(a)(a)(a) =$

   (A) $10a$
   (B) $24a$
   (C) a^5
   (D) a^{10}
   (E) a^{24}

15

18. $y^5 \div y^2 =$

   (A) $3y$
   (B) $7y$
   (C) y
   (D) y^3
   (E) y^7

19. $(x^2y)(xy^2) =$

   (A) $4xy$
   (B) x^3y^3
   (C) xy^4
   (D) x^4y^4
   (E) x^{16}

20. $(abc)(a^2bc^2) =$

   (A) $4abc$
   (B) a^2bc^2
   (C) $a^3b^2c^3$
   (D) $a^3b^3c^3$
   (E) abc^6

21. $(xy^2)(x^2z)(y^2z) =$

   (A) $8xyz$
   (B) x^2y^4z
   (C) $x^3y^4z^2$
   (D) $x^3y^3z^2$
   (E) $x^3y^3z^3$

22. $\dfrac{x^2y^4}{xy} =$

   (A) y^3
   (B) xy^3
   (C) x^2y^3
   (D) x^3y^5
   (E) xy^8

23. $\dfrac{a^3b^4c^5}{abc}$

   (A) $a^2b^3c^4$
   (B) $a^3b^4c^5$
   (C) $(abc)^3$
   (D) $(abc)^{12}$
   (E) $(abc)^{60}$

24. $(x^2y^3)^4 =$

   (A) $(xy)^9$
   (B) x^6y^7
   (C) x^8y^{12}
   (D) xy^{20}
   (E) xy^{24}

25. $\left(\dfrac{a^2}{b^3}\right)^3 =$

   (A) $\left(\dfrac{a^5}{b}\right)$
   (B) $\left(\dfrac{a^6}{b^9}\right)$
   (C) a^5b
   (D) a^6b
   (E) a^6b^9

26. $\dfrac{x^3y^4z^5}{x^4y^2z} =$

   (A) y^2z^4
   (B) xy^2z^4
   (C) $\dfrac{y^2z^4}{z}$
   (D) $\dfrac{y^2z^5}{x}$
   (E) $\dfrac{y^6z^6}{x}$

15

27. $\left(\dfrac{c^4 d^2}{c^2 d}\right)^3$

    (A) $c^5 d^3$
    (B) $c^5 d^5$
    (C) $c^6 d^3$
    (D) $c^6 d^4$
    (E) $c^6 d^6$

28. $\left(\dfrac{x^2 y^3}{xy}\right) \times \left(\dfrac{x^3 y^4}{xy}\right) =$

    (A) $x^2 y^3$
    (B) $x^3 y^4$
    (C) $x^3 y^5$
    (D) $x^5 y^6$
    (E) $x^6 y^7$

29. $\left(\dfrac{abc^2}{abc^3}\right) \times \left(\dfrac{a^2 b^2 c}{ab}\right) =$

    (A) $\dfrac{ab}{c}$

    (B) $\dfrac{bc}{a}$

    (C) ab
    (D) c
    (E) 1

30. $\left(\dfrac{x^5 y^3 z^2}{x^4 y^2 z}\right) \times \left(\dfrac{x^2 y^3 z^5}{xy^2 z^4}\right) =$

    (A) xyz
    (B) $x^2 y^2 z^2$
    (C) $x^5 y^5 z^5$
    (D) $x^6 y^6 z^6$
    (E) xyz^{12}

31. $\dfrac{a}{c} + \dfrac{b}{c} =$

    (A) $\dfrac{ab}{c}$

    (B) $\dfrac{a+b}{c}$

    (C) $\dfrac{a+b}{2c}$

    (D) $\dfrac{a+b}{c^2}$

    (E) $\dfrac{a+b}{abc}$

32. $\dfrac{x}{2} + \dfrac{y}{2} + \dfrac{z}{2} =$

    (A) $\dfrac{x+y+z}{2}$

    (B) $\dfrac{x+y+z}{6}$

    (C) $\dfrac{x+y+z}{8}$

    (D) $\dfrac{xyz}{2}$

    (E) $\dfrac{xyz}{8}$

33. $\dfrac{ab}{x} + \dfrac{bc}{x} + \dfrac{cd}{x} =$

    (A) $\dfrac{abcd}{x}$

    (B) $\dfrac{a+b+c+d}{3x}$

    (C) $\dfrac{ab+bc+cd}{x}$

    (D) $\dfrac{ab+bc+cd}{3x}$

    (E) $\dfrac{ab+bc+cd}{x^3}$

34. $\dfrac{x^2}{k} + \dfrac{x^3}{k} + \dfrac{x^4}{k} =$

    (A) $\dfrac{x^9}{k}$

    (B) $\dfrac{x^9}{3k}$

    (C) $\dfrac{x^2 4}{k}$

    (D) $\dfrac{x^2 + x^3 + x^4}{k}$

    (E) $\dfrac{x^2 + x^3 + x^4}{3k}$

35. $\dfrac{2x}{z} - \dfrac{y}{z} =$

    (A) $\dfrac{2x - y}{z}$

    (B) $\dfrac{2x - y}{2x}$

    (C) $\dfrac{2x - y}{x^2}$

    (D) $\dfrac{2xy}{z}$

    (E) $\dfrac{2xy}{2z}$

36. $\dfrac{x}{y} + \dfrac{y}{x} =$

    (A) $\dfrac{xy}{x} + y$

    (B) $\dfrac{x + y}{y + x}$

    (C) $\dfrac{x + y}{xy}$

    (D) $\dfrac{xy + yx}{xy}$

    (E) $\dfrac{x^2 + y^2}{xy}$

37. $\dfrac{a}{b} - \dfrac{b}{a} =$

    (A) $\dfrac{ab}{a - b}$

    (B) $\dfrac{a - b}{b - a}$

    (C) $\dfrac{a - b}{ab}$

    (D) $\dfrac{ab - ba}{ab}$

    (E) $\dfrac{a^2 - b^2}{ab}$

38. $\dfrac{x^2}{y} + \dfrac{x^3}{z} =$

    (A) $\dfrac{x^2 + x^3 + y}{yz}$

    (B) $\dfrac{x^5}{yz}$

    (C) $\dfrac{x^6}{yz}$

    (D) $\dfrac{x^2 + x^3}{yz}$

    (E) $\dfrac{x^2 z + x^3 y}{yz}$

39. $\dfrac{x}{a} + \dfrac{y}{b} + \dfrac{z}{c} =$

    (A) $\dfrac{xyz}{abc}$

    (B) $\dfrac{x + y + z}{z + b + c}$

    (C) $\dfrac{xbc + yac + zab}{abc}$

    (D) $\dfrac{xbc + yac + zab}{z + b + c}$

    (E) $\dfrac{xa + yb + zc}{abc}$

40. $\dfrac{x^2}{y^2} - \dfrac{y^3}{x^3} =$

    (A) $\dfrac{x^2 - x^3}{y^5}$

    (B) $\dfrac{x^3 - x^2}{y^6}$

    (C) $\dfrac{x^2 - y^3}{x^2 - y^2}$

    (D) $\dfrac{x^5 - y^5}{x^3 y^2}$

    (E) $\dfrac{x^6 - y^6}{x^3 y^2}$

41. $2(x + y) =$

    (A) $2xy$
    (B) $2x + 2y$
    (C) $2 + x + y$
    (D) $4xy$
    (E) $2x^2 + 2y^2$

42. $a(b + c) =$

    (A) $ab + bc$
    (B) $ab + ac$
    (C) $2abc$
    (D) $ab^2 + b^2 c$
    (E) $ab + ac + bc$

43. $3(a + b + c + d) =$

    (A) $3abcd$
    (B) $3a + b + c + d$
    (C) $3a + 3b + 3c + 3d$
    (D) $3ab + 3bc + 3cd$
    (E) $12a + 12b + 12c + 12d$

44. $2x(3x + 4x^2) =$

    (A) x^{10}
    (B) $6x + 8x^2$
    (C) $5x^2 + 6x^3$
    (D) $6x^2 + 8x^3$
    (E) $6(x^2 + x^3)$

45. $3a^2(ab + ac + bc) =$

    (A) $3a^3 b^2 c$
    (B) $3a^3 + 3b^2 + 3c$
    (C) $3a^2 b + 3a^2 c + 3a^2 bc$
    (D) $3a^3 b + 3a^3 c + 3a^2 bc$
    (E) $3a^5 b + 3a^5 c$

46. $(x + y)(x + y) =$

    (A) $x^2 + y^2$
    (B) $x^2 - y^2$
    (C) $x^2 + 2xy - y^2$
    (D) $x^2 - 2xy + y^2$
    (E) $x^2 + 2xy + y^2$

47. $(a + b)^2 =$

    (A) $a^2 + b^2$
    (B) $a^2 - b^2$
    (C) $a^2 + 2ab - b^2$
    (D) $a^2 - 2ab + b^2$
    (E) $a^2 + 2ab + b^2$

48. $(x - y)^2 =$

    (A) $x^2 + 2xy - y^2$
    (B) $x^2 + 2xy + y^2$
    (C) $x^2 - 2xy + y^2$
    (D) $x^2 - 2xy - y^2$
    (E) $x^2 + y2$

49. $(a + b)(a - b) =$

    (A) $a^2 - b^2$
    (B) $a^2 + b^2$
    (C) $a^2 + 2ab + b^2$
    (D) $a^2 - 2ab + b^2$
    (E) $a^2 + 2ab - b^2$

50. $(x - 2)^2 =$

    (A) $2x$

    (B) $4x$

    (C) $x^2 - 4$

    (D) $x^2 - 4x + 4$

    (E) $x^2 - 4x - 4$

51. $(2 - x)^2 =$

    (A) $4 - x^2$

    (B) $x^2 + 4$

    (C) $x^2 + 4x + 4$

    (D) $x^2 - 4x + 4$

    (E) $x^2 - 4x - 4$

52. $(ab + bc)(a + b) =$

    (A) $a^2b + ab^2 + b^2c + abc$

    (B) $a^2b + ab^2 + abc$

    (C) $a^2b + ab^2 + a^2bc$

    (D) $a^2b + ab + bc + abc$

    (E) $a^2 + b^2 + c^2 + abc$

53. $(x - y)(x + 2) =$

    (A) $x^2 + 2xy + 2y$

    (B) $x^2 + 2xy + x + y$

    (C) $x^2 + 2xy + x - 2y$

    (D) $x^2 - xy + 2x - 2y$

    (E) $x^2 + 2x + 2y - 2$

54. $(a + b)(c + d) =$

    (A) $ab + bc + cd$

    (B) $ab + bc + cd + ad$

    (C) $ac + bd$

    (D) $ac + ad + bc + bd$

    (E) $ab + ac + ad$

55. $(w + x)(y - z) =$

    (A) $wxy - z$

    (B) $wy + xy - yz$

    (C) $wy - wz + xy + xz$

    (D) $wy + wz + xy - xz$

    (E) $wy - wz + xy - xz$

56. $(x + y)(w + x + y) =$

    (A) $x^2 + wx + wy + xy$

    (B) $x^2 + y^2 + wx + wy + 2xy$

    (C) $x^2 + y^2 + wxy$

    (D) $x^2 + y^2 + wx^2y^2$

    (E) $x^2y^2 + wxy$

57. $(2 + x)(3 + x + y) =$

    (A) $x^2 + 6xy + 6$

    (B) $x^2 + 6xy + 3x + 2y + 6$

    (C) $x^2 + 2xy + 6x + 6y + 6$

    (D) $x^2 + xy + 5x + 2y + 6$

    (E) $x^2 + 3xy + 2x + y + 6$

58. $(x + y)^3 =$

    (A) $x^3 + 5x^2y + y^2z + xyz$

    (B) $x^3 + 3x^3y + 3xy^3 + y^3$

    (C) $x^3 + 3x^2y + 3xy^2 + y^3$

    (D) $x^3 + 6x^2y^2 + y^3$

    (E) $x^3 + 12x^2y^2 + y^3$

59. $(x - y)^3 =$

    (A) $x^3 - 3x^2y + 3xy^2 - y^3$

    (B) $x^3 + 3x^2y + 3xy^2 + y^3$

    (C) $x^3 + 3x^2y - 3xy^2 - y^3$

    (D) $x^3 + 6x^2y^2 + y^3$

    (E) $x^3 + 6x^2y^2 - y^3$

60. $(a + b)(a - b)(a + b)(a - b) =$

    (A) 1

    (B) $a^2 - b^2$

    (C) $a^2 + b^2$

    (D) $a^4 - 2a^2b^2 + b^4$

    (E) $a^4 + 2a^2b^2 + b^4$

61. $2a + 2b + 2c =$

    (A) $2(a + b + c)$

    (B) $2(abc)$

    (C) $2(ab + bc + ca)$

    (D) $6(a + b + c)$

    (E) $8(a + b + c)$

15

62. $x + x^2 + x^3 =$

   (A) $x(x + 2x + 3x)$
   (B) $x(1 + 2x + 3x)$
   (C) $x(1 + 2 + 3)$
   (D) $x(1 + x + x^2)$
   (E) $x(1 + 3x)$

63. $2x^2 + 4x^3 + 8x^4 =$

   (A) $2x^2(1 + 2x + 4x^2)$
   (B) $2x^2(1 + 2x + 4x^3)$
   (C) $2x^2(x + 2x + 4x^2)$
   (D) $2x^2(x + 2x^2 + 4x^3)$
   (E) $2x^2(x^2 + 2x^3 + 4x^4)$

64. $abc + bcd + cde =$

   (A) $ab(c + d + e)$
   (B) $ac(b + e)$
   (C) $b(a + c + de)$
   (D) $c(ab + bd + de)$
   (E) $d(a + b + c + e)$

65. $x^2y^2 + x^2y + xy^2 =$

   (A) $(x + y)^2$
   (B) $x^2 + y^2$
   (C) $x^2y^2(x + y)$
   (D) $xy(xy + x + y)$
   (E) $xy(x + y + 1)$

66. $p^2 + 2pq + q^2 =$

   (A) $(p + q)(p - q)$
   (B) $(p + q)(p + q)$
   (C) $p^2 - q^2$
   (D) $p^2 + q^2$
   (E) $(p - q)^2$

67. $144^2 - 121^2 =$

   (A) 23
   (B) $(144 + 121)(144 - 121)$
   (C) $(144 + 121)(144 + 121)$
   (D) $(23)^2$
   (E) $(144 + 121)^2$

68. $x^2 - y^2 =$

   (A) $(x + y)(x - y)$
   (B) $(x + y)(x + y)$
   (C) $(x - y)(x - y)$
   (D) $x^2 + y^2$
   (E) $2xy$

69. $x^2 + 2x + 1 =$

   (A) $(x + 1)(x - 1)$
   (B) $(x + 1)(x + 1)$
   (C) $(x - 1)(x - 1)$
   (D) $x^2 - 1$
   (E) $x^2 + 1$

70. $x^2 - 1 =$

   (A) $(x + 1)(x + 1)$
   (B) $(x - 1)(x - 1)$
   (C) $(x + 1)(x - 1)$
   (D) $(x - 1)^2$
   (E) $(x + 1)^2$

71. $x^2 + 3x + 2 =$

   (A) $(x + 1)(x - 2)$
   (B) $(x + 2)(x + 1)$
   (C) $(x + 2)(x - 1)$
   (D) $(x - 2)(x - 1)$
   (E) $(x + 3)(x - 1)$

72. $a^2 - a - 2 =$

   (A) $(a + 2)(a - 1)$
   (B) $(a - 2)(a + 1)$
   (C) $(a + 1)(a + 2)$
   (D) $(a + 2)(a - 2)$
   (E) $(a + 1)(a - 1)$

73. $p^2 + 4p + 3 =$

   (A) $(p + 3)(p + 1)$
   (B) $(p + 3)(p - 1)$
   (C) $(p - 3)(p - 1)$
   (D) $(p + 3)(p + 4)$
   (E) $(p + 3)(p - 4)$

74. $c^2 + 6c + 8 =$

    (A) $(c + 2)(c + 4)$
    (B) $(c + 2)(c - 4)$
    (C) $(c + 4)(c - 2)$
    (D) $(c + 3)(c + 5)$
    (E) $(c + 8)(c - 1)$

75. $x^2 + x - 20 =$

    (A) $(x + 5)(x - 4)$
    (B) $(x + 4)(x - 5)$
    (C) $(x + 2)(x - 10)$
    (D) $(x + 10)(x - 2)$
    (E) $(x + 20)(x - 1)$

76. $p^2 + 5p + 6 =$

    (A) $(p + 1)(p + 6)$
    (B) $(p + 6)(p - 1)$
    (C) $(p + 2)(p + 3)$
    (D) $(p - 3)(p - 2)$
    (E) $(p + 5)(p + 1)$

77. $x^2 + 8x + 16 =$

    (A) $(x + 2)(x + 8)$
    (B) $(x + 2)(x - 8)$
    (C) $(x - 4)(x - 4)$
    (D) $(x + 4)(x - 4)$
    (E) $(x + 4)(x + 4)$

78. $x^2 - 5x - 6 =$

    (A) $(x + 1)(x + 6)$
    (B) $(x + 6)(x - 1)$
    (C) $(x + 2)(x + 3)$
    (D) $(x - 6)(x + 1)$
    (E) $(x - 2)(x - 3)$

79. $a^2 - 3a + 2 =$

    (A) $(a - 2)(a - 1)$
    (B) $(a - 2)(a + 1)$
    (C) $(a + 1)(a - 2)$
    (D) $(a - 3)(a + 1)$
    (E) $(a + 3)(a + 1)$

80. $x^2 + x - 12 =$

    (A) $(x + 6)(x + 2)$
    (B) $(x + 6)(x - 2)$
    (C) $(x + 4)(x - 3)$
    (D) $(x - 4)(x - 3)$
    (E) $(x + 12)(x + 1)$

Review

1. (A)	28. (C)	55. (E)
2. (E)	29. (C)	56. (B)
3. (C)	30. (C)	57. (D)
4. (C)	31. (B)	58. (C)
5. (E)	32. (A)	59. (A)
6. (B)	33. (C)	60. (D)
7. (A)	34. (D)	61. (A)
8. (E)	35. (A)	62. (D)
9. (B)	36. (E)	63. (A)
10. (B)	37. (E)	64. (D)
11. (C)	38. (E)	65. (D)
12. (C)	39. (C)	66. (B)
13. (E)	40. (D)	67. (B)
14. (A)	41. (B)	68. (A)
15. (E)	42. (B)	69. (B)
16. (D)	43. (C)	70. (C)
17. (D)	44. (D)	71. (B)
18. (D)	45. (D)	72. (B)
19. (B)	46. (E)	73. (A)
20. (C)	47. (E)	74. (A)
21. (C)	48. (C)	75. (A)
22. (B)	49. (A)	76. (C)
23. (A)	50. (D)	77. (E)
24. (C)	51. (D)	78. (D)
25. (B)	52. (A)	79. (A)
26. (C)	53. (D)	80. (C)
27. (C)	54. (D)	

Review Procedures for Solving Equations

Pursuing the analogy between English and algebra as a language, the algebraic analogue of a complete sentence in English (with subject and verb) is an equation. An equation is an algebraic statement that two expressions are equivalent. Here are some examples:

English	*Algebra*
Ed is three years older than Paul.	$E = P + 3$
Paul is twice as old as Mary.	$P = 2M$
Ned has $2 more than Ed.	$N = E + \$2$
Bill has three times as much money as Ted.	$B = 3T$

NOTE Some test questions require you to translate English into algebra, and then solve for an unknown.

Solving Linear Equations

An equation containing variables of just the first power is called a first degree or linear equation. Although a linear equation can in principle contain any number of variables, in practice, equations on the exam usually contain only one variable. (Those containing two variables will be discussed in Simultaneous Equations.)

The fundamental rule for working with equations is that you can add, subtract, multiply, and divide both sides of the equation by any value without changing the statement of equality. (The one exception is that you cannot multiply or divide by zero.) Follow the logic of this illustration:

$5 = 5$

This is obviously a true statement. And you can add any value to both sides of the equation, say 10, and the statement will remain true:

Add 10: $5 + 10 = 5 + 10$

$15 = 15$

You can also subtract the same value from both sides, say, 7:

$15 - 7 = 15 - 7$

$8 = 8$

And you can multiply both sides by the same value (except zero), say, –2:

$$8 \times -2 = 8 \times -2$$
$$-16 = -16$$

And finally, you can divide both sides by the same value (except zero), for example, –4:

$$-16 \div -4 = -16 \div -4$$
$$4 = 4$$

This principle holds true for variables as well:

$$5 = 5$$
Add x: $5 + x = 5 + x$

Whatever x is, since it appears on both sides of the equation, both sides of the equation must still be equal. Now subtract a value, say, y:

$$5 + x - y = 5 + x - y$$

Again, since y appears on both sides of the equation, the statement that the two expressions are equal remains true. And you can surely see by now that you can multiply and divide (so long as you don't do it by zero) without changing the truth of the equality.

This fundamental rule for working with equations is the key to solving linear equations containing just one variable. Here's an example:

QUESTION   If $2x + 3 = x + 1$, what is x?

ANALYSIS   To find what x is equal to, we will manipulate both sides of the equation, according to the rule set forth above, until we have a single x equal to a value. First, subtract an x from both sides of the equation:

$$2x + 3 - x = x + 1 - x$$
$$x + 3 = 1$$

Next, subtract 3 from both sides of the equation:

$$x + 3 - 3 = 1 - 3$$
$$x = -2$$

Now we have the value of x.

QUESTION   If $4x + 2 = 2x + 10$, what is x?

ANALYSIS   First, subtract $2x$ from both sides of the equation:

$$4x + 2 - 2x = 2x + 10 - 2x$$
$$4x - 2x + 2 = 2x - 2x + 10$$
$$2x + 2 = 10$$

Now subtract 2 from both sides of the equation:

$$2x + 2 - 2 = 10 - 2$$
$$2x = 8$$

Now, to isolate a single x on the left side of the equation, divide both sides of the equation by 2:

$$2x \div 2 = 8 \div 2$$
$$x = 4$$

TIP | To solve for an unknown, isolate the unknown on one side of the equation.

So far, we have been very formal in following the fundamental rule for solving equations. Now it is time to introduce a shortcut called "transposition." Transposing is the process of moving a term or a factor from one side of the equation to the other by changing it into its mirror image.

To transpose a term that is added or subtracted, move it to the other side of the equation and change its sign. Thus, a term with a positive sign on one side is moved to the other side and becomes negative, and vice versa. Here's how it works:

$$x + 5 = 10$$

Rather than thinking "subtract 5 from both sides," just transpose the 5, that is, move it from the left side to the right side and change the sign from "+" to "−":

$$x = 10 - 5$$
$$x = 5$$
$$x - 5 = 10$$

15

Transpose the –5 by moving it to the right side of the equation and changing the sign from "+" to "–":

$x = 10 + 5$

$x = 15$

$3x = 5 + 2x$

Transpose the $+ 2x$ by moving it from the right side of the equation to the left side and changing the sign from "–" to "+":

$3x - 2x = 5$

$x = 5$

To transpose a *factor*, move the factor to the other side of the equation and invert it (to make its reciprocal):

$$\frac{2x + 6}{2} = 9$$

In this equation, you may not transpose the 6 without first taking care of the 2, because the 6 is really 6 divided by 2. So you first tranpose the 2. Instead of thinking "multiply both sides of the equation by 2," simply move the 2, which is really to the right side and invert it. The equation now looks like this:

$2x + 6 = 9(2)$

$2x + 6 = 18$

Now transpose the 6:

$2x = 18 - 6$

$2x = 12$

Finally, solve for x by transposing the 2:

$x = 12 = 6$

TIP

> To save time, think of "transposing" terms from one side of the equation to other using their mirror images: addition turns into subtraction; multiplication turns into division.

Systems of Equations

Ordinarily, if an equation has more than one variable, it is not possible to find specific solutions for those variables. For example, the equation $x + y = 10$ does not have one, unique solution set for x and y. x and y could be 1 and 9, 5 and 5, –2 and 12, and so on.

There is a situation, however, in which it is possible to find specific values for x and y: when two equations are taken together. Here's an example of the special case:

$$x + y = 10$$
$$x - y = 6$$

If we treat both of the equations as making true statements at the same time, then there is only one solution set for x and y, for there is only one pair of numbers that will satisfy both equations, $x = 8$ and $y = 2$. This technique is called "solving simultaneous equations," because both equations are taken to be true at the same time or simultaneously.

How do you find that one solution set? There are two methods. One way of finding the solution for simultaneous equations is to solve by substitution:

1. In one of the two equations, define one variable in terms of the other.
2. Substitute that value for the defined variable in the other equation and solve.
3. Substitute your solution back into either equation to solve for the remaining variable.

Here's how to use this approach:

$$2x + y = 13$$
$$x - y = 2$$

1. Choose either equation. Let's take the first. Redefine either variable in terms of the other. Since we already have a single y variable (as opposed to a $2x$ variable), let's define y in terms of x:

    $$y = 13 - 2x$$

2. Substitute $13 - 2x$ for y in the second equation:

    $$x - (13 - 2x) = 2$$

    Now you have an equation with a single variable. Solve for x:

    $$x - (13 - 2x) = 2$$

15

Combine like terms: $x - 13 + 2x = 2$

$x + 2x - 13 = 2$
$3x - 13 = 2$

Transpose 13: $3x = 2 + 13$
$3x = 15$

Transpose 3: $x = 15 = 5$

3. Solve for y by substituting 5 for x in either equation:

$2x + y = 13$
$2(5) + y = 13$
$10 + y = 13$
$y = 13 - 10$
$y = 3$

And here's another example:

$3x + 2y = 16$
$2x - y = 6$

1. Choose either equation, and define either variable in terms of the other. In this case, since you have a simple y term in the second equation, it will be easier to use the second equation. (You won't have to deal with a fraction.) Define y in terms of x:

$2x - y = 6$
$-y = 6 - 2x$
$y = -6 + 2x$
$y = 2x - 6$

2. Substitute this value for y in the first equation:

$3x + 2(2x - 6) = 16$

Solve for x:

$3x + 4x - 12 = 16$
$7x - 12 = 16$
$7x = 28$
$x = 4$

3. Substitute 4 for x into either equation:

$$2x - y = 6$$
$$2(4) - y = 6$$
$$8 - y = 6$$
$$-y = 6 - 8$$
$$-y = -2$$
$$y = 2$$

There is a second method for attacking simultaneous equations. Eliminate one of the two variables by adding or subtracting. Here's how to use the second approach:

$$2x + y = 8$$
$$x - y = 1$$

In this system of equations, you have a $+ y$ term in one equation and a $-y$ term in the other. Since $+y$ and $-y$ added together yield zero, you can eliminate the y term by adding the two equations together. (Actually, you will be adding the left side of the second equation to the left side of the first equation and the right side of the second to the right side of the first, but it is easier to speak of the process as "adding equations.")

$$2x + y = 8$$
$$\underline{+(x - y = 1)}$$
$$3x = 9$$
$$x = 3$$

Now you can find the value of y by substituting 3 for x in either equation.

Here's another example to be solved using the second approach:

$$4x + 3y = 17$$
$$2x + 3y = 13$$

In this pair, each equation has a $+3y$ term, which you can eliminate by subtracting the second equation from the first:

$$4x + 3y = 17$$
$$\underline{-(2x + 3y = 13)}$$
$$2x = 4$$
$$x = 2$$

Finally, you can solve for y simply by substituting 2 for x in either equation.

$4x + 3y = 17$

$4(2) + 3y = 17$

$8 + 3y = 17$

$3y = 9$

$y = 3$

TIP

With two unknowns in one equation, you can't find values for the unknowns. But with two unknowns in two equations, you can find values either by redefining one unknown and substituting that value into the other equation or by adding or subtracting to eliminate an unknown from one of the equations.

Quadratic Equations

Equations that involve variables of the second power (e.g., x^2) are called quadratic equations. Unlike a linear equation with a single variable, which has a single solution, a quadratic may have two solutions. By convention, quadratic equations are written so that the left side of the equation is equal to zero. The general form is:

$ax^2 + bx + c = 0$

Notice how the following examples fit the format of the general form for the quadratic equation:

$x^2 + x - 2 = 0$

$x^2 - 3x - 4 = 0$

To solve a quadratic equation, factor the expression on the left side:

$x^2 + x - 2 = 0$

$(x + 2)(x - 1) = 0$

Since $(x + 2)$ times $(x - 1)$ is equal to zero, either $(x + 2)$ or $(x - 1)$ must be equal to zero. If $x + 2$ is equal to zero, then x is equal to -2 ($-2 + 2 = 0$), and if $x - 1$ is equal to zero, then $x = 1$ ($1 - 1 = 0$). We conclude, therefore, that *either* x is equal to -2 or x is equal to $+ 1$.

There are two possible values for x, so this quadratic equation has two solutions. Here's another example:

$$x^2 - 3x - 4 = 0$$

Factor the left side of the equation:

$$(x + 1)(x - 4) = 0$$

Either $x + 1 = 0$, in which case $x = -1$, or $x - 4 = 0$, in which case $x = 4$. So the two solutions to this quadratic equation are -1 and $+4$.

Not every quadratic equation has two different solutions. Here's an example of a quadratic equation with only one solution:

$$x^2 + 2x + 1 = 0$$

Factor the left side of the equation:

$$(x + 1)(x + 1) = 0$$

Since the two factors are the same, the equation has but a single solution, -1.

If you encounter a quadratic equation that is not written in standard form, you must first rearrange its elements using the rules already studied to put it in standard form. Here's an illustration of the procedure:

$$2x^2 + 12 - 3x = x^2 + 2x + 18$$

To find the solution of this quadratic equation, you must first rewrite the equation, putting it in standard form:

$$2x^2 + 12 - 3x = x^2 + 2x + 18$$
$$(2x^2 - x^2) + (-3x - 2x) + (12 - 18) = 0$$
$$x^2 - 5x - 6 = 0$$

Now factor the left side:

$$(x - 6)(x + 1) = 0$$

So either $x - 6 = 0$, in which case $x = 6$, or $x + 1 = 0$, in which case $x = -1$. So the two solutions are 6 and -1.

NOTE   When a problem on the test uses a quadratic equation, the task is almost
always to find the possible solutions. You won't be asked to create a quadratic equation to solve a word problem.

15

Inequalities

An inequality is very much like an equation except, as the name implies, it is a statement
that two quantities are not equal. Four different symbols are used to make statements of
inequality:

>	**greater than**	$y < x$	y is less than x.
<	**less than**	$x \geq 0$	x is greater than or equal to
$\geq$	**greater than or equal to**		zero. (x could be zero or any
$\leq$	**less than or equal to**		number larger than zero.)

$5 > 1$ 5 is greater than 1.

$2 > -2$ 2 is greater than –2.

$x > 0$ x is greater than zero.

$x > y$ x is greater than y.

$8 < 9$ 8 is less than 9.

$-4 < -1$ –4 is less than –1.

$x < 0$ x is less than zero.

$x \geq y$ x is greater than or equal to y. (Either x is greater than y, or x and y are equal.)

$x \leq 0$ x is less than or equal to zero. (x could be zero or any number less than zero.)

$x \leq y$ x is less than or equal to y. (Either x is less than y, or x and y are equal.)

The fundamental rule for working with inequalities is similar to that for working with
equalities. You can add or subtract the same value to each side of an inequality without
changing the inequality, and you can multiply or divide each side of an inequality *by any
positive value* without changing the inequality.

To illustrate the rule, let's start with a statement of inequality that we know to be true:

$5 > 2$

You can add any value to both sides without changing this statement:

$5 + 25 > 2 + 25$

$30 > 27$

You can subtract any value from both sides without changing this statement:

$$30 - 6 > 27 - 6$$
$$24 > 21$$

You can multiply both sides of the inequality by the same *positive* number:

$$24(2) > 21(2)$$
$$48 > 42$$

And you can divide both sides of the inequality by the same *positive* number:

$$48 \div 6 > 42 \div 6$$
$$8 > 7$$

If you should multiply or divide by a *negative* number, however, you will change the direction of the inequality:

$$4 > 3$$
$$4(-2) > 3(-2) \text{ (FALSE!)}$$
$$-8 > -6 \text{ (FALSE!)}$$

You can multiply or divide by a negative number, so long as you remember to change the direction of the inequality:

$$4 > 3$$
$$4(-2) < 3(-2)$$
$$-8 < -6$$

 CAUTION | Don't multiply or divide across an inequality unless you are certain the value of the number or the unknown is positive.

Workshop B: Equations

This workshop will let you practice the procedures that you've just reviewed. There is no time limit for the workshop; but after you have finished, check your work against the Review part.

Drill

1. If $3x = 12$, then $x =$
    (A) 2
    (B) 3
    (C) 4
    (D) 6
    (E) 10

2. If $2x + x = 9$, then $x =$
    (A) 0
    (B) 1
    (C) 3
    (D) 6
    (E) 9

3. If $7x - 5x = 12 - 8$, then $x =$
    (A) 0
    (B) 1
    (C) 2
    (D) 3
    (E) 4

4. If $3x + 2x = 15$, then $x =$
    (A) 2
    (B) 3
    (C) 5
    (D) 6
    (E) 9

5. If $a - 8 = 10 - 2a$, then $a =$
    (A) –2
    (B) 0
    (C) 2
    (D) 4
    (E) 6

6. If $p - 11 - 2p = 13 - 5p$, then $p =$
    (A) –4
    (B) –1

    (C) 1
    (D) 2
    (E) 6

7. If $12x + 3 - 4x - 3 = 8$, then $x =$
    (A) –5
    (B) –1
    (C) 0
    (D) 1
    (E) 5

8. If $5x - 2 + 3x - 4 = 2x - 8 + x + 2$, then $x =$
    (A) –5
    (B) 0
    (C) 1
    (D) 3
    (E) 6

9. If $a + 2b - 3 + 3a = 2a + b + 3 + b$, then $a=$
    (A) –1
    (B) 0
    (C) 2
    (D) 3
    (E) 6

10. If $4y + 10 = 5 + 7y + 5$, then $y =$
    (A) –2
    (B) –1
    (C) 0
    (D) 4
    (E) 8

11. If $-4 - x = 12 + x$, then $x =$
    (A) –8
    (B) –2
    (C) 1
    (D) 2
    (E) 4

15

12. If $\frac{1}{2}x + \frac{1}{4}x = 3$, then $x =$

    (A) $\frac{1}{2}$

    (B) $\frac{2}{3}$

    (C) 1

    (D) 2

    (E) 3

13. If $\frac{2}{3}x + \frac{1}{4}x + 4 = \frac{1}{6}x + 10$, then $x =$

    (A) $\frac{11}{12}$

    (B) $\frac{3}{2}$

    (C) 5

    (D) 8

    (E) 20

14. If $\frac{a}{2} - \frac{a}{4} = 1$, then $a =$

    (A) $\frac{1}{2}$

    (B) $\frac{2}{3}$

    (C) 1

    (D) 2

    (E) 4

15. If $\frac{1}{p} + \frac{2}{p} + \frac{3}{p} = 1$, then $p =$

    (A) $\frac{2}{3}$

    (B) $\frac{3}{4}$

    (C) 1

    (D) 2

    (E) 6

16. If $\frac{2x-6}{3} = 8$, then $x =$

    (A) 1

    (B) 3

    (C) 6

    (D) 15

    (E) 18

17. If $\frac{5-x}{5} = 1$, then $x =$

    (A) −5

    (B) −1

    (C) 0

    (D) 1

    (E) 5

18. If $\frac{2-x}{10} = 1$, then $x =$

    (A) −8

    (B) −1

    (C) 8

    (D) 1

    (E) 5

19. If $\frac{5}{x+1} + 2 = 5$, then $x =$

    (A) $-\frac{2}{7}$

    (B) $\frac{2}{3}$

    (C) $\frac{7}{2}$

    (D) 7

    (E) 10

20. If $\dfrac{x}{2} + \dfrac{x}{3} = \dfrac{1}{2} + \dfrac{1}{3}$, then $x =$

   (A) $\dfrac{1}{3}$

   (B) $\dfrac{2}{3}$

   (C) 1

   (D) 2

   (E) 3

21. If $3x + y = 10$ and $x + y = 6$, then $x =$

   (A) 1

   (B) 2

   (C) 3

   (D) 4

   (E) 5

22. If $2x + y = 10$ and $x + y = 7$, then $y =$

   (A) 3

   (B) 4

   (C) 5

   (D) 6

   (E) 9

23. If $x + 3y = 5$ and $2x - y = 3$, then $x =$

   (A) 2

   (B) 4

   (C) 5

   (D) 6

   (E) 9

24. If $x + y = 2$ and $x - y = 2$, then $y =$

   (A) -2

   (B) -1

   (C) 0

   (D) 1

   (E) 2

25. If $a + b = 5$ and $2a + 3b = 12$, then $b =$

   (A) 1

   (B) 2

   (C) 3

   (D) 4

   (E) 6

26. If $5x + 3y = 13$ and $2x = 4$, then $y =$

   (A) 1

   (B) 2

   (C) 3

   (D) 4

   (E) 5

27. If $K - n = 5$, and $2K + n = 16$, then $K =$

   (A) -3

   (B) 0

   (C) 1

   (D) 5

   (E) 7

28. If $T = K - 5$ and $K + T = 11$, then $K =$

   (A) 2

   (B) 3

   (C) 8

   (D) 11

   (E) 14

29. If $a + 5b = 9$ and $a - b = 3$, then $a =$

   (A) 1

   (B) 4

   (C) 5

   (D) 7

   (E) 11

30. If $8 + x = y$ and $2y + x = 28$, then $x =$

   (A) 2

   (B) 4

   (C) 6

   (D) 12

   (E) 18

15

31. If $\dfrac{x+y}{2} = 4$ and $x - y = 4$, then $x =$

    (A) 1
    (B) 2
    (C) 4
    (D) 6
    (E) 8

32. If $\dfrac{x+y}{2} = 7$ and $\dfrac{x-y}{3} = 2$, then $x =$

    (A) 2
    (B) 4
    (C) 8
    (D) 10
    (E) 14

33. If $x + y + z = 10$ and $x - y - z = 4$, then $x =$

    (A) 2
    (B) 3
    (C) 6
    (D) 7
    (E) 12

34. If $x + 2y - z = 4$ and $2x - 2y + z = 8$, then $x =$

    (A) -2 –
    (B) 0
    (C) 4
    (D) 6
    (E) 8

35. If $x + y + z = 6$, $x + y - z = 4$, and $x - y = 3$, then $x =$

    (A) -2
    (B) 0
    (C) 4
    (D) 6
    (E) 8

36. If $x^2 - 3x + 2 = 0$, then $x =$

    (A) -2 or 1
    (B) 2 or 1

    (C) -1 or 2
    (D) -1 or 4
    (E) 2 or 4

37. If $x^2 - 3x - 4 = 0$, then $x =$

    (A) -4 or 1
    (B) -2 or 2
    (C) -1 or 2
    (D) 4 or -1
    (E) 6 or -1

38. If $x^2 + 5x + 6 = 0$, then $x =$

    (A) -3 or -2
    (B) -3 or 2
    (C) -1 or 6
    (D) 1 or -6
    (E) 6 or -2

39. If $x^2 + 3x + 2 = 0$, then $x =$

    (A) -2 or -1
    (B) -1 or 2
    (C) 1 or 2
    (D) 2 or 3
    (E) 3 or 5

40. If $x^2 + 3x + 2 = 0$, then which of the following are possible values of x?

    I.   1
    II. -1
    III. -2

    (A) I only
    (B) II only
    (C) III only
    (D) I and II only
    (E) II and III only

41. If $x^2 + 5x = -4$, then $x =$

    (A) -1 or -4
    (B) -1 or -2
    (C) 1 or 2
    (D) 1 or 4
    (E) 2 or 6

42. If $x^2 - 8 = 7x$, then $x =$

    (A) −8 and −1

    (B) −4 and 1

    (C) −1 and 8

    (D) 1 and 4

    (E) 1 and 8

43. If $k^2 - 10 = -3k$, then $k =$

    (A) −10 and −1

    (B) −10 and 1

    (C) −5 and 3

    (D) −3 and 5

    (E) 2 and −5

44. If $x^2 = 12 - x$, then $x =$

    (A) −4 and −3

    (B) −4 and 3

    (C) −3 and 4

    (D) −2 and 6

    (E) 1 and 6

45. If $x^2 = 6x - 8$, then $x =$

    (A) −8 and −2

    (B) −4 and −2

    (C) −2 and 2

    (D) 2 and 4

    (E) 2 and 8

46. If x is an integer and $6 < x < 8$, then what is the value of x?

    (A) 4

    (B) 5

    (C) 7

    (D) 9

    (E) 10

47. If x is an integer and $5 \le x \le 7$, which of the following are possible values of x?

    I.   5

    II. 6

    III. 7

    (A) II only

    (B) I and II only

    (C) I and III only

    (D) II and III only

    (E) I, II, and III

48. If x and y are integers such that $2 < x < 4$ and $8 > y > 6$, then what is the value of xy?

    (A) 12

    (B) 16

    (C) 21

    (D) 24

    (E) 32

49. If x and y are integers such that $5 > x \ge 2$ and $6 < y \le 9$, then what is the *minimum* value of xy?

    (A) 14

    (B) 18

    (C) 20

    (D) 45

    (E) 54

50. If $1 \le x \le 3$, then which of the following are possible values of x?

    I. $\dfrac{5}{2}$

    II. $\dfrac{7}{2}$

    III. $\dfrac{3}{2}$

    (A) I only

    (B) II only

    (C) I and II only

    (D) I and III only

    (E) I, II, and III

15

Review

1. (C)	18. (A)	35. (C)
2. (C)	19. (B)	36. (B)
3. (C)	20. (C)	37. (D)
4. (B)	21. (B)	38. (A)
5. (E)	22. (B)	39. (A)
6. (E)	23. (A)	40. (E)
7. (D)	24. (C)	41. (A)
8. (B)	25. (B)	42. (C)
9. (D)	26. (A)	43. (E)
10. (C)	27. (E)	44. (B)
11. (A)	28. (C)	45. (D)
12. (D)	29. (B)	46. (C)
13. (D)	30. (B)	47. (E)
14. (E)	31. (D)	48. (C)
15. (E)	32. (D)	49. (A)
16. (D)	33. (D)	50. (D)
17. (C)	34. (C)	

Get Answers to Frequently Asked Questions

15

Q: **Will I have to do a lot of factoring?**

A: No, and almost all of the time the factoring will fit one of the three common patterns you were asked to memorize.

Q: **With exponents, should I try to multiply out everything or just use the procedures?**

A: Use the procedures such as adding exponents when variables of like bases are multiplied. In the lesson, the multiplication was done just to show you why the rules actually work. Now, you should just rely on the rules.

Q: **Are quadratic equations an important test topic?**

A: Not really. If you want a top (and that means *top score*), you'll have to be good at doing quadratics. But there really are only a handful, maybe only two or three, such problems on a typical test.

Today's Review

1. Today, you studied the algebra concepts that are tested by the exam including basics such as adding, subtracting, multiplying, and dividing algebraic terms, intermediate concepts such as solving for one unknown in an equation, and advanced concepts like factoring quadratics.

2. Algebra is a lot like English, but you have to know the special "rules of grammar" that govern.

3. Many of the math problems on the exam just ask you to show that you know the rules, for example, solve this equation or factor this expression. Some of the more difficult items require that you actually create the equation and then solve it.

Teach Yourself
GRE Geometry

Today, you'll review the essential geometry principles that you need to do well on the test. At the end of the lesson, you'll have a chance to practice what you've learned.

If you have ever taken a basic course in geometry, you probably remember having to memorize theorems and do formal proofs. Fortunately, you won't be asked to do any formal proofs on the exam, and the formulas you need to know are fairly few in number and relatively simple.

Most often, test questions involve things like finding the measure of an angle, the length of a line, or the area of a figure. Here is an example:

What You'll Do
Today

- **Review Lines and Angles**
- **Review Triangles**
- **Review Rectangles and Squares**
- **Review Circles**
- **Workshop: Geometry Principles**
- **Get Answers to Frequently Asked Questions**

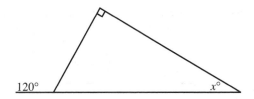

120° $x°$

QUESTION   In the figure above, $x =$

(A) 15

(B) 30

(C) 45

(D) 60

(E) 90

ANALYSIS The correct answer is **(B)**. The unmarked angle plus the 120° angle form a straight line, so their sum must be 180 ÷ :

120 + unmarked angle = 180

unmarked angle = 180 – 120

unmarked angle = 60

Then, since the unmarked angle is contained in a triangle:

$90 + 60 + x = 180$

$150 + x = 180$

$x = 180 - 150$

$x = 30$

This is a fairly easy test question, but it does illustrate the kind of principles you need to know.

The lesson plan for today was designed to make it easy for you to remember the principles you review. It begins with lines, then moves to triangles and rectangles, and finishes up with circles.

Review Lines and Angles

For purposes of our discussion (and for test–taking purposes), the word line means a straight line:

The line above is designated line L. The portion of line L from point *P* to point *Q* is called line segment *PQ*.

When two lines intersect, they form an angle, and their point of intersection is called the vertex of that angle.

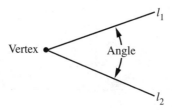

The size of an angle is measured in degrees. Degrees are defined by reference to a circle. By convention, a circle is divided into 360 equal parts, or degrees.

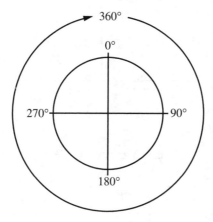

A 90° angle is also called a right angle. A right angle is often indicated in the following way:

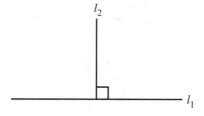

Two right angles form a straight line:

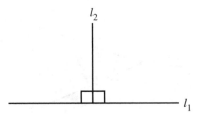

Since two right angles form a straight line, the measure of the angle of a straight line is 180°:

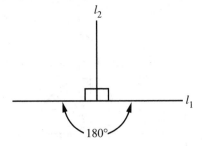

An angle that is less than 90° is called an acute angle:

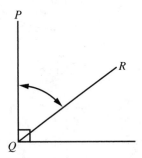

In the figure above, angle *PQR* is an acute angle.

An angle that is greater than 90° but less than 180° is called an obtuse angle.

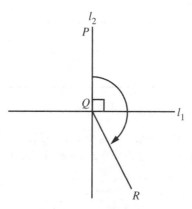

16

In the figure above, angle *PQR* is an obtuse angle.

When two lines intersect, the opposite (or vertical) angles created by their intersection are equal:

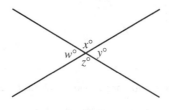

$$w = y$$
$$x = z$$

Two lines that do not intersect regardless of how far they are extended are parallel to each other:

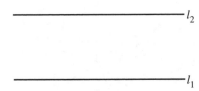

In the figure above, the symbol ∥ indicates that L₁ and L₂ are parallel. When parallel lines are intersected by a third line, the following angle relationships are created:

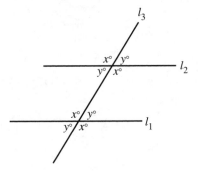

TIP

Here's everything you need to know about parallel lines:

All the big angles are equal to each other.
All the little angles are equal to each other.
Any big angle and any little angle total 180°.

Two lines that are perpendicular to the same line are parallel to each other:

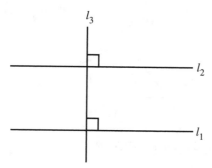

16

Since L_1 and L_2 are both perpendicular to L_3, we can conclude that L_1 and L_2 are parallel to each other.

Review Triangles

A polygon is a closed figure created by three or more lines.

A triangle is any polygon with exactly three sides.

A quadrilateral is any polygon with exactly four sides.

A pentagon is any polygon with exactly five sides.

A hexagon is any polygon with exactly six sides.

A polygon with more than six sides is usually referred to just as a polygon with a certain number of sides; for example, a polygon with ten sides is called a ten-sided polygon.

Every polygon has both a perimeter (the sum of the lengths of all of its sides) and an area.

A triangle is a three-sided figure. Within a given triangle, the larger the angle, the longer the opposite side; and, conversely, the longer the side, the larger the opposite angle.

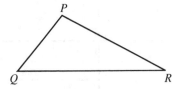

Since angle *P* > angle *Q* > angle *R*, *QR* > *PR* > *PQ*.

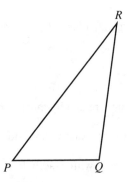

Since *PR* > *QR* > *PQ*, angle *Q* > angle *P* > angle *R*.

 CAUTION

Relationships between angles and lines exist only *within* particular triangles—not *between* two different triangles. Be careful with any test item that tells you about an angle in one triangle, an angle in a different triangle, and asks you to reach a conclusion comparing some aspect of the two triangles.

Within a given triangle, if two sides are equal their opposite angles are equal, and vice versa:

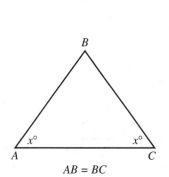
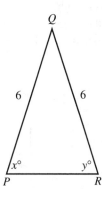

$AB = BC$

16

A triangle with exactly two equal sides is called an isosceles triangle.

A triangle with exactly three equal sides is called an equilateral triangle.

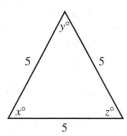

Since the equilateral triangle has three equal sides, all angles are also equal: $x = y = z$. Since all angles are equal in an equilateral triangle, each angle is 60°.

TIP

Think of the definitions of isoceles and equilater double-edged swords. A triangle that has equal angles also has equal sides. (Those opposite the equal angles.) And a triangle that has equal sides also has equal angles. (Those opposite the equal sides.) This can be used to cut through many test problems.

A triangle with a right angle is called a right triangle. The longest side of the right triangle, which is opposite the 90° angle, is called the hypotenuse.

The sides of every right triangle fit a special relationship called the Pythagorean Theorem: The square of the hypotenuse is equal to the sum of the squares of the other two sides. This is easier to understand when it is summarized in a formula:

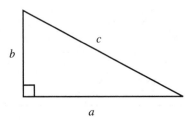

In the right triangle above, $c^2 = a^2 + b2$.

| TIP | The Pythagorean Theorem is a double-edged sword. On the one hand, if you are given the lengths of any two sides of a right triangle, you can find the length of the third. On the other hand, if you are told that a triangle has sides such that $c^2 = a^2 + b^2$, then the triangle must be a right triangle and the side opposite the largest angle the hypotenuse. |

The perimeter of a triangle is the sum of the lengths of the three sides:

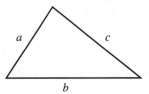

Perimeter $= a + b + c$

The altitude of a triangle is a line drawn from a vertex perpendicular to the opposite side.

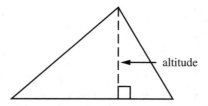

16

The formula for finding the area of a triangle is $\frac{1}{2}$ times the altitude times the base:
$Area = \frac{1}{2}$ (a)(b).

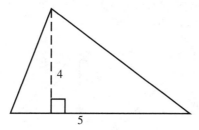

The area of the triangle above is $\frac{1}{2}(4)(5) = 10$.

 TIP

> If know the lengths of the altitude and base of a triangle, then you can calculate the area. Also, if you know the base (altitude) and the area, then you can find the length of the altitude (base).

Two right triangles deserve special mention. First, in a triangle with angles of $45 \div - 45° - 90°$, the length of the hypotenuse is equal to the length of either side multiplied by the square root of two:

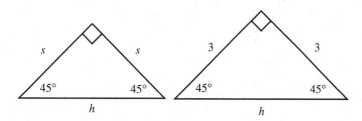

$h = s \times \sqrt{2} \quad h = 3\sqrt{2}$

Conversely, in a $45° - 45° - 90°$ triangle, the length of each of the two sides is equal to one-half the lengh of the hypotenuse multiplied by the square root of two.

$$s = \frac{1}{2} \times h \sqrt{2} \quad s = 2\sqrt{2}$$

TIP

Since two of the sides of the isoceles right triangle are equal you only need to know the length of one of them to find the length of the hypotenuse.

In a $30° - 60° - 90°$ triangle, the length of the side opposite the $30°$ angle is equal to one-half the length of the hypotenuse and the length of the side opposite the $60°$ angle is equal to one-half the length of the hypotenuse multiplied by $\sqrt{3}$.

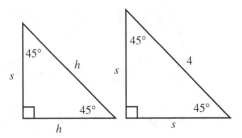

$$PR = \frac{1}{3}QR$$

$$PQ = \frac{\sqrt{3}}{2}QR$$

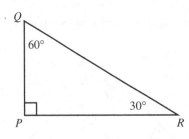
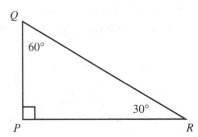

$$PR = 3$$

$$PQ = 3\sqrt{3}$$

The principle of the 30–60–90 triangle is a powerful problem-solving tool, but don't assume that any triangle that has a side of $\sqrt{3}$ fits this pattern. Many triangles could have a side of $\sqrt{3}$, but only those with sides in the ratio of $1 : \frac{1}{2} : \frac{\sqrt{3}}{2}$ fall within this principle.

Review Rectangles and Squares

16

A rectangle is any four-sided figure that has four right angles. Since the opposite sides of a rectangle are equal, it is customary to speak of the two dimensions of a rectangle, width and length:

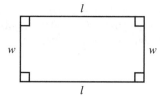

A square is a rectangle with four equal sides:

To find the perimeter of either a rectangle or a square, simply add the lengths of the four sides:

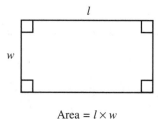

Area = $l \times w$

To find the area of a rectangle, multiply the width times the length:

In a square, the sides are all equal, so there is no difference between length and width. So to find the area of a square, just multiply: side × side.

Area: = side × side

 The diagonal of a square creates two 45–45–90 triangles, so you can use both the formulas governing the square and those governing the isoceles right triangle to reach further conclusion about such a figure.

Review Circles

The distance from the center of the circle to any point on the circle is called the radius:

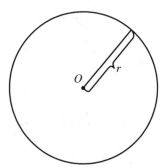

A line segment with end points on the circle which passes through the center of the circle is called the diameter:

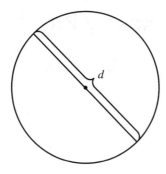

The diameter of a circle is twice the radius.

The "perimeter" of a circle is called the circumference. The formula for calculating the circumference of a circle is 2 times π times the radius: $2\pi r$.

The formula for calculating the area of a circle is π times the radius squared: $Area = \pi r^2$.

NOTE

Figures on the test, unless otherwise indiated, lie in a plane. Occasionally, a problem will ask about a cube or other rectangular solid, but you don't need a list of formulas for those.

16

Workshop: Geometry Principles

Use the problems in this workshop to practice with the principles of geometry that you review in this day. There is no time limit for the Drill. You can check your work using the answer key in the Review part.

Drill

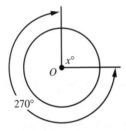

O is the center of the circle.

1. In the figure above, $x =$

    (A) 30
    (B) 60
    (C) 90
    (D) 120
    (E) 270

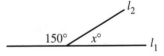

2. In the figure above, $x =$

    (A) 45
    (B) 60
    (C) 90
    (D) 120
    (E) 150

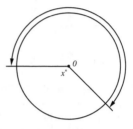

O is the center of the circle.

3. In the figure above, $x =$

    (A) 60
    (B) 90
    (C) 120
    (D) 150
    (E) 180

4. In the figure above, $x =$

    (A) 15
    (B) 30
    (C) 45
    (D) 90
    (E) 120

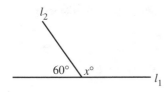

5. In the figure above, $x =$

(A) 15
(B) 30
(C) 45
(D) 90
(E) 120

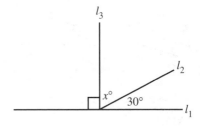

8. In the figure above, $x =$

(A) 15
(B) 30
(C) 45
(D) 60
(E) 90

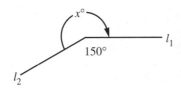

6. In the figure above, $x =$

(A) 210
(B) 180
(C) 150
(D) 135
(E) 120

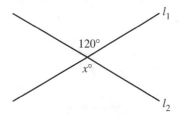

9. In the figure above, $x =$

(A) 45
(B) 60
(C) 75
(D) 90
(E) 120

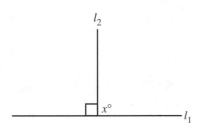

7. In the figure above, $x =$

(A) 15
(B) 30
(C) 45
(D) 60
(E) 90

16

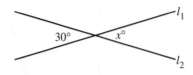

10. In the figure above, $x =$
    (A) 30
    (B) 45
    (C) 55
    (D) 65
    (E) 80

Questions 11 through 15 are based on the following figure.

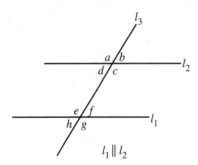

11. Which of the following is necessarily true?

    I. $a = b$

    II. $a = c$

    III. $g = h$

    (A) I only
    (B) II only
    (C) I and II only
    (D) II and III only
    (E) I, II, and III

12. Which of the following is necessarily true?

    I. $b = d$

    II. $d = e$

    III. $g = c$

    (A) I only
    (B) III only
    (C) I and III only
    (D) II and III only
    (E) I, II, and III

13. Which of the following is necessarily true?

    I. $c + d = 180$

    II. $e + a = 180$

    III. $b + g = 180$

    (A) I only
    (B) III only
    (C) I and III only
    (D) II and III only
    (E) I, II, and III

14. If $e = 120$, then g =
    (A) 60
    (B) 90
    (C) 120
    (D) 150
    (E) 180

15. If $d = 60$, then h =
    (A) 60
    (B) 90
    (C) 120
    (D) 150
    (E) 180

(A) I only
(B) II only
(C) III only
(D) I and II only
(E) I, II, and III

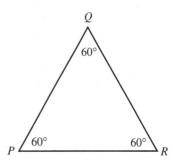

16. Which of the following is true of the figure above?

   I. $AB = BC$

   II. $BC = AC$

   III. $AC = AB$

   (A) I only
   (B) II only
   (C) I and II only
   (D) I and III only
   (E) I, II, and III

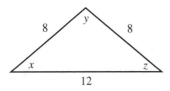

18. Which of the following is true of the figure above?

   I. $PQ = QR$

   II. $QR = PR$

   III. $PR = PQ$

   (A) I only
   (B) III only
   (C) I and II only
   (D) II and III only
   (E) I, II, and III

17. Which of the following is true of the figure above?

   I. $x = y$

   II. $y = z$

   III. $x = z$

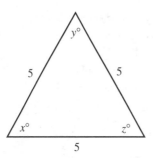

19. Which of the following is true of the figure above?

    I. $x = y$

    II. $y = z$

    III. $z = x$

(A) I only
(B) I and II only
(C) I and III only
(D) II and III only
(E) I, II, and III

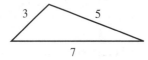

20. What is the perimeter of the triangle above?

(A) 3
(B) 5
(C) 15
(D) 20
(E) 30

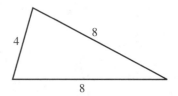

21. What is the perimeter of the triangle above?

(A) 20
(B) 18
(C) 12
(D) 10
(E) 8

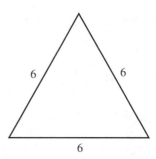

22. What is the perimeter of the triangle above?

(A) 6
(B) 12
(C) 18
(D) 21
(E) 24

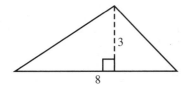

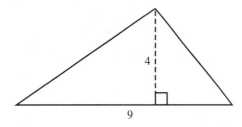

23. What is the area of the triangle above?

    (A) 3
    (B) 6
    (C) 12
    (D) 18
    (E) 24

16

25. What is the area of the triangle above?

    (A) 6
    (B) 12
    (C) 15
    (D) 18
    (E) 24

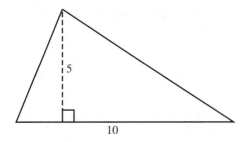

24. What is the area of the triangle above?

    (A) 5
    (B) 10
    (C) 12
    (D) 15
    (E) 25

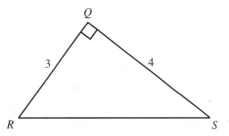

26. In the figure above, what is the length of *RS*?

    (A) 3
    (B) 5
    (C) 8
    (D) 12
    (E) 16

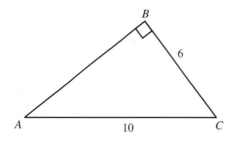

27. In the figure above, what is the length of *AB*?

(A) 4
(B) 8
(C) 12
(D) 16
(E) 24

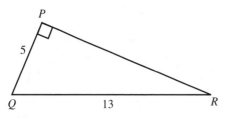

28. In the figure above, what is the length of *PR*?

(A) 12
(B) 23
(C) 27
(D) 36
(E) 48

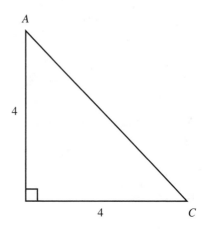

29. In the figure above, what is the length of *AC*?

(A) 2
(B) $2\sqrt{2}$
(C) 4
(D) $4\sqrt{2}$
(E) 8

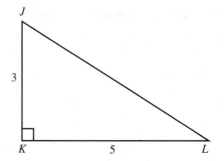

30. In the figure above, what is the length of *JL*?

(A) $\sqrt{2}$
(B) $2\sqrt{2}$
(C) $\sqrt{15}$
(D) $2\sqrt{2}$
(E) 8

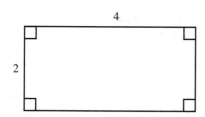

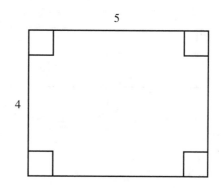

31. What is the perimeter of the figure above?

    (A) 6
    (B) 8
    (C) 10
    (D) 12
    (E) 16

16

33. What is the area of the figure above?

    (A) 10
    (B) 15
    (C) 16
    (D) 18
    (E) 20

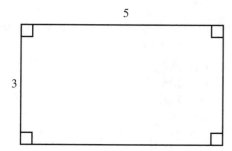

32. What is the perimeter of the figure above?

    (A) 8
    (B) 12
    (C) 14
    (D) 15
    (E) 16

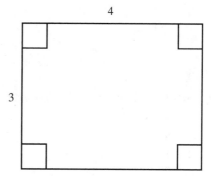

34. What is the area of the figure above?

    (A) 6
    (B) 8
    (C) 12
    (D) 16
    (E) 24

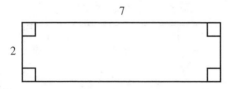

35. What is the area of the figure above?

    (A) 5
    (B) 9
    (C) 14
    (D) 25
    (E) 81

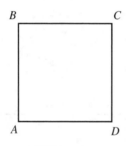

ABCD is a square

36. In the figure above, if AB = 5, what is the
    area of ABCD?

    (A) 5
    (B) 10
    (C) 20
    (D) 25
    (E) 40

37. If the radius of a circle is 2, then the
    diameter is

    (A) 1
    (B) 2
    (C) 3
    (D) 4
    (E) 8

38. If the diameter of a circle is 10, what is
    the radius?

    (A) 2
    (B) 5
    (C) 8
    (D) 15
    (E) 20

39. If the radius of a circle is 3, what is the
    circumference?

    (A) 2π
    (B) 3π
    (C) 6π
    (D) 9π
    (E) 12π

40. If the radius of a circle is 5, what is the
    circumference?

    (A) 5π
    (B) 10π
    (C) 15π
    (D) 20π
    (E) 24π

41. If the diameter of a circle is 8, what is the
    circumference?

    (A) 8π
    (B) 6π
    (C) 4π
    (D) 2π
    (E) π

42. If the radius of a circle is 3, what is the
    area?

    (A) π
    (B) 3π
    (C) 6π
    (D) 9π
    (E) 12π

43. If the radius of a circle is 5, what is the area?

    (A) 25π

    (B) 21π

    (C) 18π

    (D) 2π

    (E) π

44. If the diameter of a circle is 8, what is the area?

    (A) 16π

    (B) 12π

    (C) 10π

    (D) 8π

    (E) 4π

45. If the diameter of a circle is 12, what is the area?

    (A) 18π

    (B) 24π

    (C) 30π

    (D) 32π

    (E) 36π

16

Review

1. (C)	16. (A)	31. (D)
2. (D)	17. (C)	32. (E)
3. (C)	18. (E)	33. (E)
4. (B)	19. (E)	34. (C)
5. (E)	20. (C)	35. (C)
6. (A)	21. (A)	36. (D)
7. (E)	22. (C)	37. (D)
8. (D)	23. (C)	38. (B)
9. (E)	24. (E)	39. (C)
10. (A)	25. (D)	40. (B)
11. (B)	26. (B)	41. (A)
12. (C)	27. (B)	42. (D)
13. (C)	28. (A)	43. (A)
14. (C)	29. (D)	44. (A)
15. (A)	30. (E)	45. (E)

Get Answers to Frequently Asked Questions

Q: **Do I need to know technical terms like tangent and chord?**

A: No. When those terms are used (and that's very rarely), they're included to clarify the problem. For example, a note might say "*PQ* is tangent to Circle *O* at point *T*." You're not really being tested on the definition of a tangent; the note's included to make sure that you understand that, as the figure will show, the line *PQ* touches the circle at only one point.

16

Q: **Do I need to know formulas for things like cylinders and spheres?**

A: Not really. When those concepts come up, the question stem almost always includes the information you need. For example, if the question uses a water tank in the shape of a cylinder and asks about the volume given a certain water level, there will likely be a note: Volume of a cylinder = $\frac{4}{3}\pi r^3$.

Today's Review

1. Today you reviewed the most important geometry principles tested by your exam.

2. Intersecting lines and parallel lines create angle relationships that are often tested by the exam.

3. The perimeter of any triangle is the sum of the lengths of the sides and the area is: $\frac{1}{2} \times$ altitude $\times$ base. Isoceles triangles (two equal sides and angles), equilateral triangles (three equal sides and angles), and right triangles (the Pythagroean relationship) have special features that come up often.

4. A square is a particular type of rectangle. The perimeter of a rectangle or a square is sum of the lengths of all four sides and the area is found by multiplying width times length.

5. The formula for finding the circumference of a circle is: $(2\pi r)$. The formula for finding the area of a circle is πr^2.

Teach Yourself Quantitative Comparisons

Today you'll teach yourself how to answer GRE Quantitative Comparison (QC) items. QCs are math questions, but they have a special set of instructions. You'll be using your math skills, but you'll have to learn how to use those skills in the context of this unusual type of question.

Get the Inside Info on Quantitative Comparisons

QCs are math questions, so you'll be using your knowledge of arithmetic, algebra, and geometry to handle QC items, but QCs are governed by a special set of directions. The best place to begin your detailed study of QCs is with the directions. (You saw the directions earlier in Day 1 and again in Day 12, but now you need to dig a little deeper.) Here are the QC directions:

> **DIRECTIONS:** Each of the items below consists of two quantities, one in Column A and one in Column B. Compare the quantities and choose:
>
> (A) if the quantity in Column A is greater;
>
> (B) if the quantity in Column B is greater;
>
> (C) if the two quantities are equal;
>
> (D) if the relationship cannot be determined from the information given.
>
> Centered information applies to both columns, and a symbol appearing in both columns has the same meaning in both quantities.

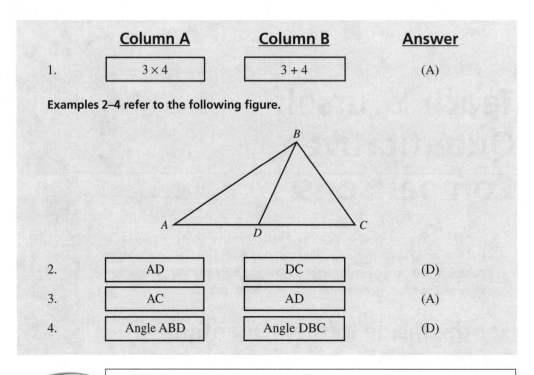

	Column A	Column B	Answer
1.	3×4	$3 + 4$	(A)

Examples 2–4 refer to the following figure.

	Column A	Column B	Answer
2.	AD	DC	(D)
3.	AC	AD	(A)
4.	Angle ABD	Angle DBC	(D)

NOTE

When QCs appear on your computer monitor during the GRE, your choices will look like this:

(A)   The quantity in Column A is greater.

(B)   The quantity in Column B is greater.

(C)   The two quantities are equal.

(D)   The relationship cannot be determined.

You will see ovals in place of the letters, but the order of the choices corresponds to A, B,C, and D.

At the core of every QC item is a math concept such as adding fractions, taking roots, manipulating algebraic expressions, finding the value of a variable, or calculating the area of a figure. If this were all there were to QC, then QC would be a straight-forward test of what you know about math. But it's not. Rather, QC is a test of your "quantitative ability." And what is "quantitative ability" as opposed to "math?" "Quantitative ability" is math with an attitude.

The GRE uses three added-difficulty factors to bring the extra dimension to QC. You have to know what these other factors are, so that you'll be able to recognize them and use strategies to neutralize their impact. We'll look at each one in turn.

1. The Strange Directions Factor

The QC directions themselves are strange and impart an element of confusion to problems of this type. The directions are long, longer than the directions for any other question type. And QCs are unlike multiple-choice math problems that you usually encounter. There are two aspects of the directions in particular that you simply have to know in order to make sure that you are answering according to the rules.

First, the four-answer schema has a very exact meaning. Here are problems to illustrate each answer choice:

Column A	**Column B**
3^2	2^3

QUESTION

ANALYSIS Column A is greater. Column A is $3 \times 3 = 9$, and Column B is $2 \times 2 \times 2 = 8$; and since $9 > 8$, you would select the first oval in the list.

17

Column A	**Column B**
$\frac{1}{2}(10)$	$\frac{10}{\frac{1}{2}}$

QUESTION

ANALYSIS Column B is greater. Column A is 5, and Column B is 20. Since $20 > 5$, you would select the second oval in the list.

Column A	**Column B**
Area of a circle with radius 2.	Area of a circle with diameter 4.

QUESTION

ANALYSIS Column A and Column B are equal. The area of both circles is 4π. So you would select the third oval in the list.

Column A	**Column B**
The total cost of 4 pounds of apples.	The total cost of 5 pounds of pears.

QUESTION

ANALYSIS You cannot determine which column is greater because you don't have any information about the cost per pound of either fruit. So you would select the fourth oval in the list.

NOTE

Any information centered above the two columns applies to both columns, and a symbol that appears in both columns means the same thing in Column A as it does in Column B.

TIP

When you take the GRE on computer, beside each oval you'll see a brief explanation of the answer choice. But you should be so familiar with the directions that you never read the explanations. Just think:

(A)   First oval means A's bigger.

(B)   Second oval means B's bigger.

(C)   Third oval means they're equal.

(D)   Fourth oval means "Can't be determined."

The second important thing you need to keep in mind about the QC directions is that the figures are not necessarily drawn to scale. You can assume that *relative positions* of points, angles, lines, and regions are accurate, but you cannot assume anything about the *magnitude* of angles, lines, or regions. Here is an example to illustrate the point:

Column A   Column B

Q

$(x+0.05)°$

P $x°$ $x°$ R

QUESTION PQ PR

ANALYSIS   Column B is greater than Column A, so you would use the mouse pointer to select the second oval in the list. Why is Column B greater when the figure makes it look like

PQ is equal to *PR*? Because angle *PQR* is greater than angle *QPR*—0.05° larger according to the information provided within the figure—and that means that *PR* is longer than *PQ*.

Because the figures in QC are not necessarily drawn to scale, estimating or measuring may get you a wrong answer. Try to solve the problem using your knowledge of geometry.

Now that you know what each of the four ovals in the list signifies and that you have to use your knowledge of geometry rather than estimation to solve problems that use figures you can be confident that you'll be playing QC by the rules.

2. The Excess Baggage Factor

17

A second added-difficulty factor that you'll encounter in QC is Excess Baggage. Excess Baggage is a technique used to make it more difficult to find the key to a QC problem. The technique is used to position a QC item on the ladder of difficulty.

The following pair of QC items illustrates the concept of Excess Baggage:

Column A	**Column B**
QUESTION $\dfrac{5^{23} - 5^{22}}{5^{22}}$	4
QUESTION $\dfrac{5^{3} - 5^{2}}{5^{2}}$	4

ANALYSIS In each case, the two columns are equal; but this conclusion is less obvious in the first case than in the second. In the second item, you can just do the arithmetic that is indicated:

$$\frac{5^{3} - 5^{2}}{5^{2}} = \frac{125 - 25}{25} = \frac{100}{25} = 4$$

You can't do the same thing with the first item because the numbers are too large, so the first item would be higher on the level of difficulty than the second.

Other Excess Baggage techniques include complicating algebraic expressions with extra terms and adding superfluous features to geometry drawings. Since Excess Baggage makes the item more difficult, you may wonder "Why don't I ignore it altogether?" That's a pretty good idea. You can't just *ignore* the excess baggage, but later today you'll learn strategies for disposing of it so that you won't be carrying around the extra burden.

NOTE

> In QC, the *appearance* of difficulty created by excess baggage *really* makes the problem difficult because you can't solve it directly using a technique such as calculation. Instead, you have to use one of the advanced strategies to unload the excess baggage.

3. The Unwelcome Surprise Factor

A third added difficulty factor is the unwelcome surprise. Many QC items take advantage of peculiarities of the number system, algebra, or geometry, and these peculiarities can produce some surprising results. Here is an example:

Column A	Column B

QUESTION

$$4x = 3y$$

| x | y |

ANALYSIS In this item, the relationship between the two columns cannot be determined, so you would select the fourth oval in the list. At first glance, however, it looks like Column B might be greater because:

$$4x = 3y$$

$$\frac{x}{y} = \frac{3}{4}$$

So the ratio of x to y is 3 to 4. For example, x and y might be 3 and 4, respectively, or 6 and 8, respectively. But no restriction has been placed on x and y, so x and y might also be negative, in which case they could have the values -3 and -4, respectively, or -6 and -8, respectively. And if x and y have negative values, then x is greater than y. And that's the unwelcome surprise: x and y might be negative.

Here is another item that holds an unwelcome surprise:

Column A	Column B

QUESTION

$$x > 0$$

| x | x^2 |

ANALYSIS At first glance, you might think that Column B has to be greater because x is squared in Column B. But what happens if x is a fraction between 0 and 1? In that case, Column A is greater. Or what happens if $x = 1$? In that case the two columns are equal. Once again, an unwelcome surprise awaits you: the correct answer is not Column B but "cannot be determined."

The best way to avoid unwelcome surprises is to learn where they might be hidden. And later today, you'll review items used by the GRE to generate surprises. If you're ready for them, then the surprises will not be unwelcome any longer.

QCs are math questions, so they would be challenging under the best of circumstances. The three added-difficulty factors—the strange directions, the excess baggage factor, and unwelcome surprises—just raise the bar a few notches. But with the strategies that you'll learn today, you'll lower the bar back down.

NOTE

QCs with unwelcome surprises are difficult because most test-takers overlook the unexpected possibility and so select a wrong answer. *By definition,* a QC that most test-takers get wrong is a difficult item. If you expect the unexpected, then the difficult QC becomes easier because the added difficulty factor of the unwelcome surprise is neutralized.

17

MAKE CONNECTIONS

Regardless of added-difficulty factors, at the core of every QC is a math concept. If you are unclear about the math, consult the appropriate review lesson in Day 14, 15, 16, or 21.

The core of every QC item is a math concept: add some fractions, solve for a variable, find the magnitude of some feature of a figure, and so on. Sometimes the core concept is disguised by added-difficulty factors; at other times, the core concept is presented directly. Provided that you know the math, the key to doing well in QC is summarized by your QC Action Plan.

Step 1: The Basic Technique: For simple QCs, do the arithmetic, the algebra, or the geometry.

Step 2: Advanced Strategy: For difficult QCs, simplify the math.

Step 3: Fail-Safe Plan: For very difficult QCs, use one of the guessing guidelines.

The basic idea behind the Action Plan is "first things first." If the problem has an easy solution, then do it that way; if the problem is too difficult, try to make it more manageable; and if the problem cannot be tamed, then maxmize your chances by making an intelligent guess.

Learn the Basic Technique for QCs

Simple QC problems tend to fall into one of three categories: manipulation problems, word problems, and properties problems. You won't need to sort problems into the three categories; we're using them primarily for purposes of discussion. The main point is that, regardless of what's being tested, these problems all have direct solutions.

Manipulation Problems

When you encounter a problem that calls for a simple arithmetic manipulation, a basic algebraic operation, or an uncomplicated application of a geometry principle, then attack the problem directly by doing the math suggested by the problem itself. Here are examples of each.

	Column A	**Column B**
QUESTION	$\dfrac{1}{6} - \dfrac{1}{7}$	$\dfrac{1}{42}$

ANALYSIS The math is simple; so just do it:

$$\frac{1}{6} - \frac{1}{7} = \frac{7-6}{42} = \frac{1}{42}$$

The two quantities are equal, and you would select the third oval in the list. Here is another manipulation problem:

	Column A	**Column B**
QUESTION	$(131)^2 - (37)^2$	$(131 - 37)^2$

ANALYSIS The manipulation here is a bit more complex than that required by the preceding problem. But you can do the arithmetic operations fairly quickly:

$(131)^2 - (37)^2 = (131)(131) - (37)(37) = 17,161 - 1,369 = 15,792$

$(131 - 37)^2 = (94)2 = 8,836$

Column A is greater, and you would select the first oval in the list.

Actually doing the multiplication is *not* the way that the GRE test-writers think that you should answer this question. They think that you should notice that the expression in Column A can be factored as follows:

$(131)^2 - (37)^2 = (131 + 37)(131 - 37) = (168)(94)$

And since Column B is (94)(94) and (168)(94) > (94)(94) Column A must greater.

There is a certain mathematical elegance about factoring Column A to get the solution. Fortunately, the GRE doesn't reward elegance. You get the same credit for the problem whether you grind out the multiplication and determine that Column A is greater or use the more elegant route—and in just about the same amount of time.

The beauty of this part of the Action Plan is that it is a real time saver. Just as soon as you see that you can get the solution fairly quickly using a crude approach such as multiplying, go ahead and implement it. Don't waste time wondering whether there might not be some more elegant alternative. The only thing that you have to watch out for is that you don't try to do a calculation that is totally impossible given the time limit. Here is an example of a problem that you should not try to solve by doing the manipulations:

Column A	**Column B**
QUESTION $\dfrac{3^{57} - 3^{56}}{3^{56}}$	2

ANALYSIS It would be a big, big mistake to start raising 3 to the 57th power. This is not a *simple* problem, so the Action Plan for simple problems doesn't apply. We'll return to this item later to discuss a solution when we talk about the Action Plan for difficult problems.

 CAUTION If the calculations would take more than 45 seconds, then the item is not a simple one. Don't do the calculation. Instead, try an advanced strategy.

Manipulation problems can also use alegebraic expressions and equations, but, again, the best approach is just to attack them directly. Here is an example:

Column A	**Column B**
QUESTION $(x + 1)^2$	$x^2 + 2x + 1$

ANALYSIS The expression in Column A can be multiplied:

$$(x + 1)^2 = (x + 1)(x + 1)\ x^2 + 2x + 1$$

This shows that the two columns are equal.

You should use the same strategy with problems that present equations:

17

Column A   Column B

QUESTION

$$2x + 1 = 3x - 2$$

| x | | 1 |

ANALYSIS The algebra is simple, so just solve for x:

$$2x + 1 = 3x - 2$$

$$x = 3$$

So Column A is greater.

TIP

> If the centered information contains an equation with one variable, solve for the unknown.

Some geometry-based QCs require nothing more than a quick calculation. Here's an example:

Column A   Column B

QUESTION

| The circumference of a circle with radius 3. | | The circumference of a circle with diameter 6. |

ANALYSIS The two columns are equal, as can be shown quickly by using formulas for calculating the circumference of a circle:

$$\text{Circumference} = 2\pi r = 2\pi(3) = 6\pi$$

$$\text{Circumference} = \pi d = \pi(6) = 6\pi$$

Here is another example of a QC that should be solved just by doing a quick calculation with a geometry formula:

Column A   Column B

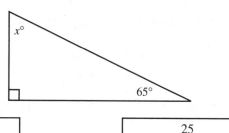

Column A	Column B
x	25

ANALYSIS Just calculate the value of x:

$$x + 65 + 90 = 180$$
$$x = 25$$

So the two columns are equal.

17

NOTE Geometry-based QCs that ask for the measure of an angle, length of a line, or area of a figure are just calculation problems. Use the appropriate formula to get the answer.

For this aspect of the Action Plan, it really doesn't matter whether the calculation involves arithmetic, algebra, or geometry. Once you see that you can get the right answer just by doing a manageable manipulation, go ahead and do the operations. You may not be using the most elegant technique; but it is effective, and you'll have one more right answer in the bank.

Word Problems

This aspect of the Action Plan is analogous to the one we just discussed, except that it applies to word problems. Again, if you see that by solving a word problem, you'll be able to make a comparison of the columns, then go ahead and do the math. Here's an example:

Column A   Column B

QUESTION

Column A	Column B
The number of miles a car travels in 2 hours at an average speed of 50 miles per hour	The number of miles a car travels in 4 hours at an average speed of 25 miles per hour

ANALYSIS Like a simple manipulation problem, a simple word problem can be solved with a fairly easy manipulation. In this case, the solution can be found by answering the question "How far does each car travel?" And you can get the answers directly:

50 miles per hour × 2 hours = 100 miles

25 miles per hour × 4 hours = 100 miles

The two quantities are equal, and you would select the third oval in the list. Here is another simple word problem:

Column A   ## Column B

QUESTION

A certain punch mixture calls for $7\frac{1}{2}$ liters of fruit juice. Alan used 30 percent more fruit juice than the mixture calls for.

| The number of liters of fruit juice Alan used | 10 |

ANALYSIS You can get the answer to this item by answering the question "How much fruit juice did Alan use?" And the direct solution is to multiply $7\frac{1}{2}$ by $\frac{3}{10}$ and add the product to $7\frac{1}{2}$:

$$7\frac{1}{2} \times \frac{3}{10} = 2\frac{1}{4}$$

$$2\frac{1}{4} + 7\frac{1}{2} = 9\frac{3}{4}$$

So Column B is greater, and you would select the second oval in the list. Is there a more elegant solution? Yes. Thirty percent is a little less than $\frac{1}{3}$. Had Alan used $\frac{1}{3}$ more juice, he would have used $2\frac{1}{2}$ liters more, for a total of 10 liters. In that case, the two columns would be equal. But since 30% is less than $\frac{1}{3}$, Alan must have used less than 10 liters. That's elegant, but simply doing the math is a purely mechnical and therefore effective approach as well.

Here is one final example of a simple word problem:

LAWN	x	y
Dimensions of Rectangular Lawn	40 meters by 60 meters	50 meters by 40 meters
Cost (per square meter) of Fertilizer	$0.05	$0.06

Column A   **Column B**

 | The cost of fertilizer for lawn X | The cost of fertilizer for lawn Y |

 The arithmetic required to calculate the cost of fertilizer for each lawn is not overly burdensome, so you should just do it:

Lawn X: $40 \times 60 \times \$0.05 = \$120$

Lawn Y: $50 \times 40 \times \$0.06 = \$120$

The two columns are equal, so you would select the third oval in the list. Is there a more elegant approach to this problem? Yes. Since both yards have a 40-meter dimension, you don't really need to include the number "40" in your calculation. Since $60 \times \$0.05 = 50 \times \$0.06$, the two columns must be equal. But you shouldn't waste time looking for the elegant solution once you have concluded that you can get the right answer fairly quickly just by doing a couple of calculations. (Of course, if you do see that the "40" is irrelevant, then, by all means simplify the calculation. In fact, that's a strategy you'll take up in the Action Plan for more difficult items, later.)

 TIP

> If a QC looks like a word problem that asks a question such as "How much?", "How long?", "How many?" or a similar question, then treat it as a word problem. First answer the question; then make the comparison.

Properties Problems

The third type of simple problem that you may encounter covers items that use a property of the number system, algebra, or geometry as the core concept for the item. This might be something about even and odd integers, about fractions, about factors, or areas and perimeters. The trick is usually to investigate the possibilities to see what conclusion you can reach. Here are some examples:

Column A   **Column B**

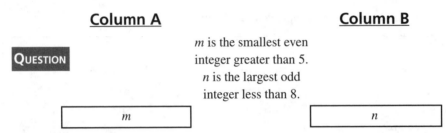

QUESTION

m is the smallest even
integer greater than 5.
n is the largest odd
integer less than 8.

m	n

ANALYSIS The smallest even integer greater than 5 is 6, and the largest odd integer less than 8 is 7. So Column B is greater than Column A.

Here is an example that uses signed numbers:

Column A   **Column B**

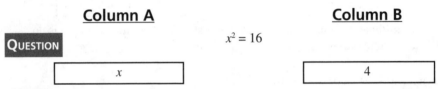

QUESTION

$$x^2 = 16$$

x	4

ANALYSIS This item tests whether or not you recognize that x could have a negative as well as a positive value, +4 or –4. So the relationship between the two quantities cannot be determined, and you would choose the fourth oval in your list on the monitor screen.

Here is a properties question that uses a geometry figure:

Column A   **Column B**

QUESTION

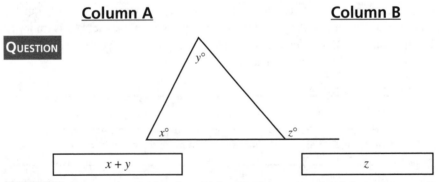

$x + y$	z

ANALYSIS You may remember from high school geometry that it is a property of a triangle that the measure of an exterior angle (like z) is equal to the sum of the measures of the two non-adjacent interior angles (in this case, x and y). If so, then you know without thinking further that the two columns are equal. If that insight has receded into the misty haze of time, don't worry. You can still arrive at the same conclusion by investigating the properties of the figure. Let w be the measure of the third, unlabelled interior angle of the figure. Then, you know:

$$w + z = 180$$
$$w = 180 - z$$

You now have w described in terms of z, and you know further:

$$x + y + w = 180$$

Substituting $(180 - z)$ for w:

$$x + y + (180 - z) = 180$$
$$x + y - z = 0$$
$$x + y = z$$

So the two columns are equal, and you would select the third oval in the list using your mouse pointer.

When you're defining a property of some numbers, watch out for unpleasant surprises. Remember to ask yourself whether negative values, 0, fractions, and 1 are permissible values.

There is one final point to keep in mind about simple problems: even though you can't find an exact value for a variable, a specific range may be sufficient to make a comparison. For example:

Column A	Column B

$$-1 < x < 1$$

QUESTION

x^2		1

ANALYSIS In this problem, Column B is greater. The centered information tells you that x ranges between -1 and 1, not inclusive. So the question becomes "What is the possible range of x^2? x^2 must be positive, and x^2 must also be less than 1, since x is a fraction: $0 < x^2 < 1$. Although this does not fix an exact value for x, defining the range of x in this way is sufficient to make the comparison.

Time is of the essence. When you see a solution, execute. So long as it is effective and does not consume an inordinate amount of time, it is a *good* approach. Don't worry about finding the *perfect* approach.

Simple problems have simple solutions—whether manipulations, word problems, or geometry problems. Once you have determined that there is a manageable solution, use it.

Workshop A: Practice the Basic Technique

This workshop consists of 15 QCs that fall into the category "simple." The first idea that comes to mind is probably the right way to solve it. Practice this technique by working each item, darkening the appropriate oval. Then check your work against the explanations given in the "Review" portion of the workshop, below.

Drill

	Column A	Column B
1.	$\dfrac{0.06}{0.005}$	30

2. $x = 3$

	Column A	Column B
	x^3	9

	Column A	Column B
3.	33(248)	249(32)

4. $4x + 3y = 5x + 2y$

	Column A	Column B
	x	y

	Column A	Column B
5.	The area of a circular region with a circumference of 4π	The circumference of a circular region with an area of 4π

6. For all integers m and n, let $m \blacksquare n$ be defined as folows:
$$m \blacksquare n = -|m + n|$$

	Column A	Column B
	$5 \blacksquare 4$	$-5 \blacksquare 4$

7. x and y are both greater than 0 and less than 1.

	Column A	Column B
	$x + y$	$x^2 + y^2$

8. n is an even integer and a multiple of 3

	Column A	Column B
	The remainder when n is divided by 6	0

9.

	Column A	Column B
	The area of a triangle with a base of 6 and an altitude of 4	The area of a triangle with a base of 4 and an altitude of 6

	Column A	Column B
10.	$\sqrt{x^2 + 2x + 1}$	$x + 1$

	Column A	Column B
11.	9^5	100,000

Column A	Column B		Column A	Column B

12.   Chris financed the purchase of a computer. The cash price of the computer was $1,000. Chris made an initial payment of $250 and 24 payments of $50 each.

The amount Chris paid for the computer in excess of the cash price	$250

15.

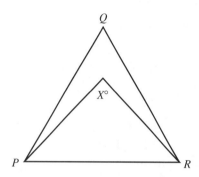

PQR is an equilateral triangle.

x	60

13.

The average (arithmetic mean) of 93, 87, and 89	The average (arithmetic mean) of 92, 89, and 88

17

14.
$$2x - y = 2$$
$$3x + y = 13$$

x	3

Review

1. **(B)** $\frac{0.06}{0.005} = 12$. So Column B is greater

2. **(A)** If $x = 3$, then $x^3 = 3^3 = 3 \times 3 \times 3 = 27$. And Column A is greater.

3. **(A)** 33(248) = 8,184 and 249(32) = 7,968. So Column A is greater.

4. **(C)** Manipulate the centered equation:
$$4x + 3y = 5x + 2y$$
$$x = y$$

5. **(C)** First, find the radius of the circle described in Column A:
$$C = 2\pi r$$
$$4\pi = 2\pi r$$
$$r = 2$$
And find the area of the cricular region:
$$A = \pi r^2$$
$$A = \pi(2)^2$$
$$A = 4\pi$$

Then find the radius of the circle described in Column B:

$$A = \pi r^2$$
$$4\pi = \pi r^2$$
$$r^2 = 4$$
$$r = 2$$

And find the cicumference:

$$C = 2\pi r$$
$$C = 2\pi(2)$$
$$C = 4\pi$$

6. **(B)** Find the value of each expression:

$$5 \blacksquare 4 = -|\,5+4\,| = -9$$
$$-5 \blacksquare 4 = -|\,-5+4\,| = -|\,-1\,| = -1$$

7. **(A)** This item asks about the properties of fractions. Since x and y are both fractions between 0 and 1, $x^2 < x$ and $y^2 < y$. Therefore, $x^2 + y^2 < x + y$.

8. **(C)** Since n is an even integer and a multiple of 3, n must be a number like 6, 12, 18, etc., all of which are divisible by 6 with no remainder.

9. **(C)** The formula for the area of a triangle is:

$$A = \frac{1}{2}ab$$

And:

$$A = \frac{1}{2}(4)(6) = 12$$

$$A = \frac{1}{2}(6)(4) = 1$$

10. **(C)** Do the indicated operation:

$$\sqrt{x^2 + 2x + 1} = \sqrt{(x+1)(x+1)}$$
$$= (x+1)$$

So the two columns are equal.

11. **(B)** The arithmetic required by Column A is not that difficult, so just do it:

$$9^5 = 9 \times 9 \times 9 \times 9 \times 9 = 59{,}049$$

12. **(A)** Figure out how much Chris paid for the computer:

Price = \$250 + 24(\$50) = \$250 + \$1,200 = \$1,450

So Chris paid \$1,450 − \$1,000 = \$450 more than the cash price.

13. **(C)** Calculate the average for each set of values:

$$\frac{93+87+89}{3} = \frac{269}{3} = 89\frac{2}{3}$$

$$\frac{92+89+88}{3} = \frac{269}{3} = 89\frac{2}{3}$$

14. **(C)** Solve for x:

$$\underline{2x - y = 2}$$
$$+\ 3x + y = 13$$
$$5x = 15$$
$$x = 3$$

15. **(A)** You can't figure an exact value for x, but you can determine a range. Since *PQR* is equilateral, angle *PQR* = 60°. So 60 is the lower limit of the magnitude of x, and Column A is greater.

Master Advanced Strategies for Difficult QCs

Simple QCs are simple because the solution is fairly obvious. Difficult QCs are difficult not so much because the math is very advanced (there is no trig or calculus on the GRE) but because the solution isn't obvious. Your advanced strategies for difficult QCs are designed to overcome the excess baggage problem that tends to obscure the solution.

There are several different techniques that you can use. Each technique is independent of the others; one does not depend upon your having tried another. In fact, more than one technique may be useful for a particular problem.

Simplify the Problem

First, try simplifying the problem. Here is an example:

17

Column A   Column B

QUESTION

$$x + 1 \neq 0$$

$$\frac{x^2 - 1}{x + 1}$$ $$x - 1$$

ANALYSIS Simplify the quantity in Column A by factoring and reducing:

$$\frac{x^2 - 1}{x + 1} = \frac{(x + 1)(x - 1)}{x + 1} = x - 1$$

So the two columns are equal.

Here is another example:

Column A   Column B

QUESTION

$$x > 0$$

$$1$$ $$\frac{1}{1} + \frac{1}{x}$$

ANALYSIS Begin by performing the operation indicated in Column B:

$$\frac{1}{1} + \frac{1}{x} = \frac{1}{x + \frac{1}{x}} = \frac{x}{x} + 1$$

And since x is positive, you can multiply both sides by $x + 1$. You're left with $x + 1$ in Column A and x in Column B, so Column A is greater.

TIP

> If at any point during the solution process you determine that one column is larger, then stop working immediately. You don't have to figure out how much larger.

Eliminate Redundant Elements

Excess baggage may show up in the form of redundant elements, that is, terms that are common to both sides. Because they appear in both columns, they don't usually make a difference to the comparison. You can eliminate them from both columns without changing the relationship and thereby simplify matters for yourself. Here is an example:

Column A	Column B
QUESTION $(0.041)^2(0.041)^3$	$(0.041)^6$

ANALYSIS This item is just over the line into the hard category. You might be able to pull off the calculation in a minute, but it would be hard. Instead, the fact that both sides of the comparison are made up of "0.041"s strongly suggests that you should eliminate as many as possible. In fact, the problem could be rewritten to look like this:

Column A	Column B
$(0.041) \times (0.041) \times$ $(0.041) \times (0.041) \times$ (0.041)	$(0.041) \times (0.041) \times$ $(0.041) \times (0.041) \times$ $(0.041) \times (0.041)$

Just get rid of five of the terms from Column A and five of the terms from Column B. You're left with:

Column A	Column B
1	(0.041)

So Column A must be greater.

 NOTE

> When you eliminate redundant information, you may change the *magnitude* of the difference between the two columns; but the *magnitude* of difference is not important. You are concerned with the question "Which is larger?" not "How much larger?"

We just used the phrase "get rid of" to describe the process of eliminating redundant elements. Actually, what we did was make use of one of the rules for manipulating inequalities. We divided each side of the comparison by the same number.

The rules for manipulating inequalities define what it's permissible for you to do with a comparison and what is not permissible. You can:

Add the same value to both sides.

Subtract the same value from both sides.

Multiply or divide both sides by the same positive value.

Square or take the square root of both sides, provided they are positive.

CAUTION
If you are eliminating redundant elements, do not multiply or divide by a value unless you know the value is positive. If you use a negative value, you'll reverse the direction of the relationship and get the wrong answer.

17

And the following item demonstrates why you must not multiply or divide unless you know that you are using a positive value:

Column A	Column B
x^3	$(x-1)(x)(x+1)$

ANALYSIS The problem places no restriction on the value of x, so x might be positive, negative, or even 0. But let's assume that you overlooked this fact and divided both sides by x. You'd be left with:

Column A	Column B
x^2	$(x-1)(x+1)$

And then you could multiply the expression in Column B:

$$(x-1)(x+1) = x^2 - 1$$

Then you could legitimately subtract x^2 from both sides. And you'd be left with:

Column A	Column B
0	-1

This would lead you to conclude erroneously that Column A is greater. In fact, the correct answer is "cannot be determined." (If $x = 0$, the columns are equal, so Column A is not utmost always greater.) How did the technique fail? Because we divided by x with first being sure that x has to be positive.

Here is another illustration of the proper use of the technique of eliminating redundant elements:

Column A

Column B

QUESTION

$$\frac{7^{11}}{7^7}$$

$$\frac{7^{13}}{7^9}$$

ANALYSIS You can multiply both sides by 7^7 and by 7^9:

Column A

Column B

$$\frac{7^{11}}{7^7}\left(7^7\right)\left(7^9\right) =$$

$$7^{11}\left(7^9\right) = 7^{20}$$

$$\frac{7^{13}}{7^9}\left(7^9\right)\left(7^7\right) =$$

$$7^{13}\left(7^7\right) = 7^{20}$$

So the two columns are equal. (You could also have simplified directly by subtracting exponents, but no extra points are given for using one method instead of the other.)

 NOTE

> There is usually more than one way to skin a QC cat, e.g., simplifying, eliminating redundant elements, a combination of both. All are equally acceptable.

And here is another example:

Column A

Column B

QUESTION

$$x > 1$$

$$\frac{x^2}{5}$$

$$\frac{x^3}{7}$$

ANALYSIS Multiply both sides by 5 and by 7:

Column A

Column B

$$\frac{x^2}{5}(5)(7) = 7x^2$$

$$\frac{x^3}{7}(7)(5) = 5x^3$$

At this point, you could probably conclude that the relationship is indeterminate; but if you were still not certain, you could do further consolidation:

Column A	**Column B**
$7x^2 \div x^2 = 7$	$5x^3 \div x^2 = 5x$

Since the only information about x is that $x > 1$, the relationship cannot be determined. If need be, you could even divide both sides by 5 and compare $\frac{7}{5}$ to x.

TIP

> Don't think of using one technique to the exclusion of another. Instead, think of using any tool at your disposal to move a problem from the difficult category into the easy category.

Redefine Elements of a Figure

17

Often a QC figure will actually be made up of two or even three figures. Here is an example:

QUESTION

Column A	**Column B**

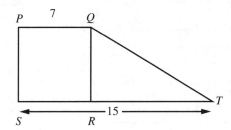

PQRS is a square.

One-half area of *PQRS*	Area of *QRT*

ANALYSIS   The key to this QC is recognizing that *QR* does two things in the figure. It is not only the side of square *PQRS*; it is also the altitude of *QRT*. So the area of *QRT* is one-half times 7 times 8 or 28, which is more than half the area of the square.

MAKE CONNECTIONS

> Composite figures are also important in Problem Solving. You'll return to this idea in Day 19.

Workshop B: Practice Advanced Strategies

This workshop consists of 15 QCs that fall into the category "difficult." You probably won't be able to solve them by a direct approach such as multiplying or dividing. Instead, use the strategies developed in the Action Plan for Difficult Problems. Darken the appropriate oval. Then check your work against the explanations given in the "Review" portion of the workshop, below.

Drill

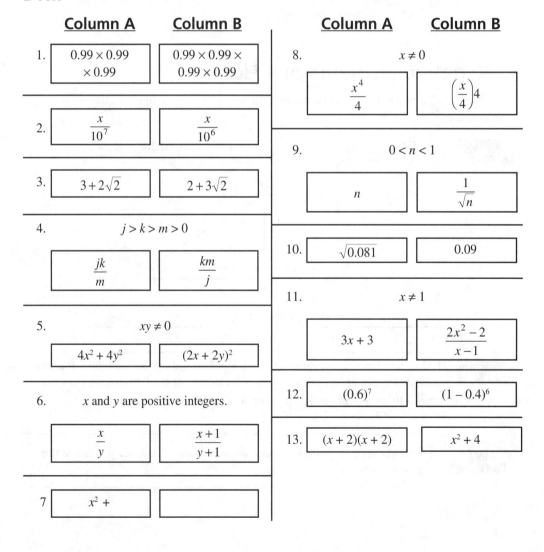

	Column A	Column B
1.	$0.99 \times 0.99 \times 0.99$	$0.99 \times 0.99 \times 0.99 \times 0.99$
2.	$\dfrac{x}{10^7}$	$\dfrac{x}{10^6}$
3.	$3 + 2\sqrt{2}$	$2 + 3\sqrt{2}$
4.	$j > k > m > 0$	
	$\dfrac{jk}{m}$	$\dfrac{km}{j}$
5.	$xy \neq 0$	
	$4x^2 + 4y^2$	$(2x + 2y)^2$
6.	x and y are positive integers.	
	$\dfrac{x}{y}$	$\dfrac{x+1}{y+1}$
7	$x^2 +$	

	Column A	Column B
8.	$x \neq 0$	
	$\dfrac{x^4}{4}$	$\left(\dfrac{x}{4}\right)4$
9.	$0 < n < 1$	
	n	$\dfrac{1}{\sqrt{n}}$
10.	$\sqrt{0.081}$	0.09
11.	$x \neq 1$	
	$3x + 3$	$\dfrac{2x^2 - 2}{x - 1}$
12.	$(0.6)^7$	$(1 - 0.4)^6$
13.	$(x + 2)(x + 2)$	$x^2 + 4$

Column A	Column B	Column A	Column B

14.

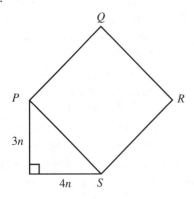

PQRS is a square.

Area of PQRS	$25n^2$

15.

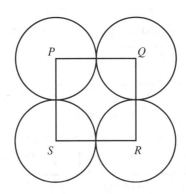

Square PQRS is formed by joining centers
P, Q, R, and S of the circles.
Each circle has at most one point
in common with another circle.

The perimeter of PQRS	The circumference of circle with with center P

17

Review

1. **(A)** It would be a mistake to do the arithmetic as shown. Instead, you can simplify matters by dividing both sides of the comparison by $0.99 \times 0.99 \times 0.99$. The result is:

Column A	Column B
1	0.99

2. **(D)** If you notice that there is no information about x, so the relationship is indeterminate, then indicate your choice and move on. But if you missed that, you could multiply each side of the comparison by 10^7:

Column A	Column B
$\dfrac{x}{10^7}\left(10^7\right) = x$	$\dfrac{x}{10^6}\left(10^7\right) = 10x$

But you don't have any basis for comparing x with $10x$.

3. **(B)** Subtract 2 and $2\sqrt{2}$ from both sides:

Column A	Column B
$3 + 2\sqrt{2} - \left(2 - \sqrt{2}\right) = 1$	$2 + 3\sqrt{2} - \left(2 - \sqrt{2}\right) = \sqrt{2}$

And since $\sqrt{2} > 1$, Column B is greater

4. **(A)** Since all variables are positive, you can divide both sides of the comparison by k:

Column A	Column B
$\dfrac{jk}{m} \div k = \dfrac{j}{m}$	$\dfrac{km}{j} \div k = \dfrac{m}{j}$

And you can multiply both sides by both j and m:

Column A	Column B
$\dfrac{j}{m} \times jm = j^2$	$\dfrac{m}{j} \times jm = m^2$

And you can even take the square root of both sides, so that you are left with just:

Column A	Column B
j	m

5. **(D)** You can begin by performing the indicated operations for Column B:

$$(2x + 2y)^2 = 4x^2 + 4xy + 4y^2$$

And you can subtract $4x^2 + 4y^2$ from both sides, so that you are left with:

Column A	Column B
0	$4xy$

Since you know only that xy is not equal to 0, the relationship cannot be determined.

6. **(D)** Since x and y are positive numbers, you can multiple both sides of the comparison by $(y + 1)$ and by y:

Column A	Column B
$\dfrac{x}{y} \times (y+1)(y) =$ $xy + x$	$\dfrac{x+1}{y+1} \times (y+1)(y)$ $= xy + y$

And if you then subtract xy from both sides, you are left with x for Column A and y for Column B. Without any additional information, the relationship cannot be determined.

7. **(C)** No matter what value x has, the expressions in the two columns cannot be negative, so you can square both sides of the comparison. The result is:

Column A	Column B
$x^4 + 4x^2 + 4$	$x^4 + 4x^2 + 4$

So the two columns are equal.

8. **(A)** Since $x \neq 0$, the variables raised to even powers in the problem must have positive values. Therefore, you are free to manipulate the comparison. Start by taking the square root of both sides. You're left with:

Column A	Column B
$\dfrac{x^2}{2}$	$\left(\dfrac{x}{4}\right)^2$

And Column B is $\dfrac{x^2}{16}$. You can divide both sides by x^2, and the final comparison will be between $\dfrac{1}{2}$ in Column A and $\dfrac{1}{16}$ in Column B. So Column A is greater.

9. **(B)** Since n is a positive number, you can square both sides of the comparison. The new comparison is:

Column A	Column B
n^2	$\dfrac{1}{n}$

And you can multiply both sides by n, so that you get:

Column A	Column B
n^3	1

Since n is a positive fraction, Column B is greater.

10. **(C)** The quantities are positive, so you can square both sides of the comparison. Column A becomes 0.081, and Column B becomes $0.09 \times 0.09 = 0.081$.

11. **(D)** You can begin by factoring the numerator of Column B:

$$2x^2 - 2 = 2(x^2 - 1)\ 2(x + 1)(x - 1)$$

So that Column B becomes $2(x + 1)$ or $2x + 2$. You can then subtract $2x$ and 2 from both sides so that Column A becomes $x + 1$ and Column B becomes 0. But you have no information that would let you make a comparison between these two quantities.

12. **(B)** You can begin by peforming the subtraction indicated in Column B. Column B becomes: $(0.6)^6$. And you can divide both sides of the comparison by $(0.6)^6$, so that you are left with 0.6 in Column A and 1 in Column B.

13. **(D)** Start by doing the multiplication indicated in Column A: $(x + 2)(x + 2) = x^2 + 4x + 4$. Then you can subtract $x^2 + 4$ from both sides. You must then compare $4x$ in Column A with 0 in Column B. But since you have no information about x, the relationship cannot be determined.

14. **(C)** The hypotenuse of the right triangle, which has a length of $5n$, is also the side of the square. So the square has an area of $25n^2$.

15. **(B)** Each side of the square consists of two radii. So if you let the radius of the circles be r, the perimeter of the square is $8r$. And the circumference of any one of the circles is $2\pi r$:

Column A	Column B
$8r$	$2\pi r$

And to make things really easy on yourself, you can divide both sides of the comparison by 2 and by r (since distances are always positive):

Column A	Column B
4	π

And since π is about 3.14, Column A is greater.

17

Develop a Fail-Safe Plan for QC Emergencies

If you don't see an easy solution at first, and if one does not emerge from simplifying the problem, then you have a QC emergency. You just can't afford to spend a lot of time on one of these items. Use one of the following guessing strategies.

Use a Proxy Problem

Let's return to an earlier problem:

Column A	**Column B**
QUESTION $\dfrac{3^{57} - 3^{56}}{3^{56}}$	2

ANALYSIS Above, we used this problem to emphasize that you should not try to do unmanageable calculations. And numbers like 3^{57} and 3^{56} are just too big. But you could write a similar problem, one that would allow you to do the arithmetic:

Column A	**Column B**
$\dfrac{3^{3} - 3^{2}}{3^{2}}$	2

Now the math is manageable:

$$\frac{3^{3} - 3^{2}}{3^{2}} = \frac{27 - 9}{9} = 2$$

If the two quantities are equal in your proxy problem, then the two quantities should be equal in the original. Here is another example:

Column A	**Column B**
QUESTION $(-1)^{500}(-2)^{3}$	-8

ANALYSIS The 500th power of -1 makes this problem more difficult than it should be. Since 500 is an even power, you could as easily use the second power:

Column A	**Column B**
$(-1)^{2}(-2)^{3}$	-8

Now the arithmetic is manageable:

$$(-1)^{2}(-2)^{3} = 1(-8) = -8$$

And the two columns are equal.

Test Numbers

One of the most annoying things about variables is that, unless otherwise restricted, they can represent any value. But you can also make this work for you. Pick some numbers to test. Here is an example:

Column A   Column B

$$xy \neq 0$$

| QUESTION | $x^2 + y^2$ | | $(x + y)^2$ |

ANALYSIS Your first line of attack on this QC should be to manipulate the expressions to try to simplify the problem, but let's assume for the purpose of the discussion that you didn't have any luck with that line. So you would need to guess. The only restriction on x and y is that $xy \neq 0$, so you can assume some values for x and y and test them. In fact, x and y don't even have to be different numbers. Let $x = 1$ and $y = 1$:

$$x^2 + y^2 = (1)^2 + (1)^2 = 2$$
$$(1 + 1)^2 = (2)^2 = 4$$

You have one substitution instance in which Column B is greater. You now know that Column A is not always greater, and you know also that the columns are not always equal. So try another set of values. Let $x = 1$ and $y = -1$:

$$(1)^2 + (-1)^2 = 1 + 1 = 2$$
$$(1 + -1)^2 = (0)^2 = 0$$

So it is possible also for Column A to be larger. This proves that the relationship cannot be determined.

TIP

A single substitution eliminates two of the four QC answer choices. If Column A is greater, you should eliminate the second and third ovals; if Column B is greater, you should eliminate the first and third ovals; and if the two columns are equal, you should eliminate the first and second ovals.

NOTE

Substituting numbers is not a *proof* of an answer choice because it is an inductive procedure. But it is a highly effective inductive technique given the structure of the QC exercise.

Distort Figures

Another vexing element of the QC problem type is the fact that figures are not necessarily drawn to scale. Consequently, you can't rely on the figure for conclusions. But you can also make this work for you:

Column A   ### Column B

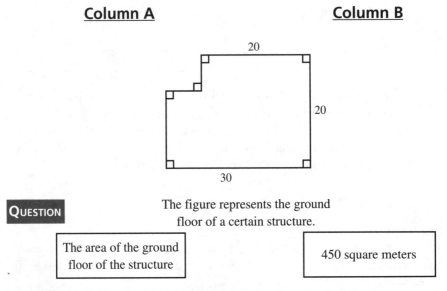

QUESTION The figure represents the ground floor of a certain structure.

| The area of the ground floor of the structure | 450 square meters |

ANALYSIS The figure makes it look as though the floor area is 600 square meters less a 10m × 10m cutout for a total of 500 square meters. But remember that the drawing is not necessarily accurate. You can redraw the lines:

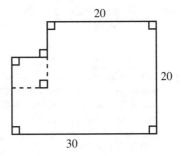

This demonstrates that the relationship between the columns cannot be determined.

Here is another example:

Column A	**Column B**

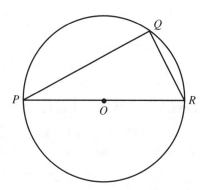

QUESTION

The radius of the circle is 1.

Area of *PQR*	1

ANALYSIS Point Q is on the circumference of the circle between P and R, but where is not known. Triangle PQR, however, will have its maximum area when the altitude formed by Q and the center of the circle is its greatest:

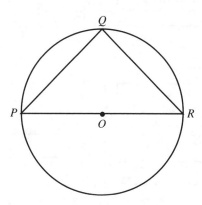

In this scenario, the area of *PQR* is:

$$A = \frac{1}{2}ab = \frac{1}{2}(1)(2) = 1$$

And the two columns would be equal. But the altitude can also be shorter, as illustrated by the figure that accompanies the problem. Therefore, the relationship cannot be determined.

TIP

> If a comparison does not include a variable or a figure, then the answer choice cannot possibly be "cannot be determined." So don't select the fourth oval in the list.

Guessing strategies are just that. Don't expect that they can substitute for a solid working knowledge of math. But, in a pinch, they're better than nothing.

Workshop C: Practice the Fail-Safe Plan

Use the 5 QCs below to practice the Fail-Safe methods outlined above. Darken the appropriate oval. Then check your work against the explanations given in the "Review" portion of the workshop, below.

Drill

	Column A	Column B
1.	Average (arithmetic mean) of 1,007, 1,010, and 1,005	Average (arithmetic mean) of 1,010, 1,008, and 1,004

2. m and n are positive numbers and $\sqrt{m}+1=\sqrt{m+n}$

Column A	Column B
$2\sqrt{m}+1$	n

3. $x>y>0$

Column A	Column B
$(x+1)y$	$(y+1)x$

4.

Column A	Column B

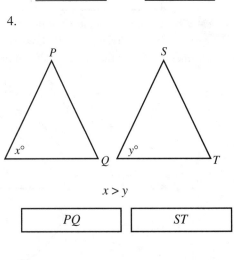

$x>y$

Column A	Column B
PQ	ST

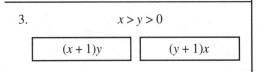

Column A   **Column B**

5.

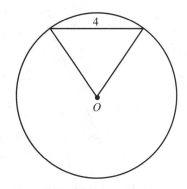

O is the center of the circle.

| Area of the circular region | 16π |

Review

1. **(C)** Use a proxy problem:

Column A	Column B
Average of 7, 10, and 5	Average of 10, 8, and 4

2. **(C)** Substitute some numbers. Let $m = 4$. Given the centered information, $n = 5$. And substituteing 4 for m and 5 for n into the columns:

Column A	Column B
$2\sqrt{4} + 1 = 5$	5

3. **(B)** Pick a couple of numbers, say $x = 3$ and $y = 2$, and substitute those into the expressions in the columns:

Column A	Column B
$(3 + 1)(2) = 8$	$(2 + 1)(3) = 9$

And that's a good basis for guessing that Column B is greater.

4. **(D)** Just distort the figures:

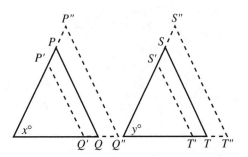

5. **(D)** Distort the figure:

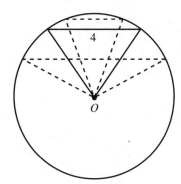

Get Answers to Frequently Asked Questions

Q: How long should I spend on an individual QC item?

A: A minute or so. Not much more; and on those that ask for nothing more than a simple manipulation, considerably less. By following this guideline, you'll spend about 15 minutes *total* on QCs in the math part—and you'll have plenty of time for the other two question types.

Q: Why doesn't the GRE just use regular old math questions of the kind we learned in school?

A: The math part of the GRE is not just intended to test your knowledge of math. It is also supposed to measure your ability to *reason* with math concepts. That's why the QC directions are so long and involved. They let the test-writer set up situations using things like positive and negative numbers or unusual geometry figures that test your reasoning power as well as your knowledge of math.

Q: Are QCs that use algebra always harder than QCs that use arithmetic?

A: No. You can have some very easy algebra-based QCs and some very hard arithmetic-based items. The reason that this is possible is because the special QC directions permit the extra dimension of "reasoning power" to be incorporated into an item.

Q: Are geometry figures *always* inaccurate?

A: No. Many of them are accurately drawn even in the QC part of the math. The problem is that you have no way of knowing which are and which aren't. So it's better to operate on the assumption that the figure is not accurately drawn.

Today's Review

1. Quantitative Comparisons involve a special set of directions. In addition to the meanings of each choice, the two most important things to remember about the directions are that the figures may not be drawn to scale and the fourth oval stands for "the relationship cannot be determined."

2. Simple problems have simple solutions. If you can see your way to an answer by a manageable calculation or manipulation, then execute that strategy immediately.

3. Difficult problems are difficult not because the math itself is extraordinary but because the solution has been obscured by excess baggage. You can use a variety of techniques to eliminate the excess baggage.

4. At some point you are probably going to have to guess. Use one of the guessing strategies developed in this lesson, but don't waste too much time trying to figure out a problem. Remember that time is of the essence.

17

Apply Your Action Plan to Quantitative Comparisons

What You'll Do Today

- **Review Your Action Plan**
- **Apply Your Action Plan to the PreTest**
- **Workshop A**
- **Workshop B**
- **Get Answers to Frequently Asked Questions**

Today, you'll be using the Action Plan that you developed in Day 17. After a quick review of some important points, you'll revisit the Quantitative Comparison part of the Math PreTest to see how the Action Plan would have helped you perform better. Then you'll have the opportunity to do timed exercises for further practice and to see the Action Plan applied to those items.

Review Your Action Plan

In Day 17, you developed an Action Plan for Quantitative Comparisons. You'll recall that the plan starts with the fact that QCs are not ordinary math questions in three important respects: one, they use a highly specific set of instructions; two, QCs often carry excess baggage; three, QCs often contain unwanted surprises. Your Action Plan is designed to neutralize the effects of these added-difficulty factors. The overall plan looks like this:

ACTION PLAN **Step 1: The Basic Technique: For simple QCs, do the arithmetic, the algebra, or the geometry.**

Step 2: Advanced Strategy: For difficult QCs, simplify the math.

Step 3: Fail-Safe Plan: For very difficult QCs, use one of the guessing guidelines.

Now let's apply the integrated plan to the items from the PreTest.

Apply Your Action Plan to the PreTest

Here's how the Action Plan would have helped you. The following items appeared on the Math PreTest in Day 12.

Column A	**Column B**

1.

3^5	5^3

ANALYSIS **(A)** This is a simple problem. You can solve it just by doing the arithmetic:

Column A	**Column B**

$3 \times 3 \times 3 \times 3$ $\times 3 = 243$	$5 \times 5 \times 5 = 125$

As the Action Plan suggests, when you see a direct line of attack, use it. Don't worry that there may be a more elegant approach.

Column A	**Column B**

2.

The total rainfall in August for
Region R was 4 centimeters.

Amount of rain that fell during the first 10 days of August.	Amount of rain that fell during the first 20 days of August.

ANALYSIS **(D)** This problem holds an unwanted surprise for the unwary. You're asked to compare the amount of rain during the first 10 days with the amount of rain during the last 20 days, but the centered information gives you information about rainfall for the *entire* month. With QCs, it is important to be alert for such surprises.

Column A	Column B

3.
A triangle has angles with measures $x°$, $100°$, and $y°$.

x	80

ANALYSIS **(B)** This items tests properties of triangles. The sum of the measures of the interior angles of a triangle is 180. Therefore:

$x + y + 100 = 180$

$x + y = 80$

Since both x and y must have some magnitude, x must be less than 80.

Column A	Column B

4.
On a landscaping plan, 1 centimeter represents 5 meters.

The actual distance in meters between two trees that are shown on the plan as 19 centimeters apart.	100

18

ANALYSIS **(B)** This is a simple problem that can be solved with a calculation:

$19 \times 5 = 95$

So Column B is greater. Remember also not to do anymore work than you have to. Once you see that you have to multiply 19 by 5, and if it occurs to you that 20×5 is equal to 100 (Column B), then you don't have to do any more work. You don't need to know *how much greater* Column B is than Column A—only that Column B *is greater*.

Column A	Column B

5.

$$5 + x < 12$$
$$5 + y < 12$$

x	y

ANALYSIS (D) You can simplify the centered information by subtracting 5 from both sides of each inequality. You're left with:

$5 + x < 12$

$x < 12$

$5 + y < 12$

$y < 12$

And so the relationship between x and y is indeterminate.

Column A	Column B

6. j and k are both greater than 0 and
                        less than 1.

$j^2 + k^2$	$j + k$

ANALYSIS (B) This QC has the potential of an unwanted surprise for those who think that a squared variable automatically has to be larger than the variable itself. The centered information tells you that j and k are positive fractions, and the result of squaring a fraction is less than the fraction itself. This is also a good time to test some numbers if you need to. You might try $\frac{1}{2}$ for both j and k. (j and k do not have to be different fractions.) When you test $\frac{1}{2}$, you learn that Column B is greater. You might also try $\frac{1}{4}$, and Column B is also greater. This doesn't constitute a proof that Column B is greater, but it is a pretty good basis for a guess.

Column A	Column B

7.

$x + y$	z

ANALYSIS **(A)** This item tests a property of triangles: the sum of the lengths of any two sides must be greater than the length of the third side. (Otherwise, you wouldn't have a triangle.) Since figures are not drawn to scale, you could use your pencil and some of the scratch paper provided to draw a couple of different triangles, and this technique should lead you to the conclusion that $x + y$ must always be greater than z.

Column A	Column B

8.

$\dfrac{6^{10}}{3^5}$	$2^{10} \times 3^5$

ANALYSIS **(C)** This is not a simple problem as written (the arithmetic is completely unmanageable), so the Action Plan tells you to try to simplify matters. Remember that there may be different ways of doing that. One way here is to reason that $6^{10} = (2 \times 3)^{10} = 2^{10} \times 3^{10}$. Then you might divide the numerator of Column A by its denominator and get $2^{10} \times 3^5$. Or you could multiply both side of the comparison by 3^5 leaving you with $2^{10} \times 3^{10}$ in both columns. Either way, you learn that the two quantities are equal.

18

Column A	Column B

9.

$$0 < k < 1$$

$$\frac{\frac{1}{x}}{\frac{1}{y}} = k$$

$\dfrac{x}{y}$	$\dfrac{y}{x}$

ANALYSIS (A) The significance of the centered information is probably not clear to you the way it is written, so perform the indicated operations just to see what you can learn:

$$\frac{\frac{1}{x}}{\frac{1}{y}} = k$$

$$\frac{1}{x} \times y = k$$

$$\frac{y}{x} = k$$

Since k is a positive fraction, $|x| > |y|$, and x and y have the same sign. (Both are positive or both are negative.) So $\frac{x}{y} > \frac{y}{x}$, and Column A is greater than Column B. If you were to lose your way in all of those twists and turns, you could use the third step of the Action Plan and test some numbers, say $x = 3$ and $y = 2$. That would make Column A equal to $\frac{3}{2}$ and Column B equal to $\frac{2}{3}$. So a good guess would be (A).

<table>
<tr><th>Column A</th><th>Column B</th></tr>
</table>

10.   Of the 100 vehicles in a parking lot,
                       x are sport utility vehicles manufactured
                       by Company P and y are sport utility vehicles
                       not manufactured by Company P.

Number of vehicles in the parking lot that are not sport utility vehicles.	$100 - x - y$

ANALYSIS (C) Since the total number of vehicles is 100, the number that are not sport utilities is 100 less the total number of sport utilities: $10 - x - y$. You could also reach the same conclusion by testing some numbers. For example, you might assume that there are 20 sport utilities made by Company P and 20 not made by company P. On that assumption, the number of vehicles that are not sport utilities is 60. And if you substitute 20 for x and 20 for y, Column B is 60, suggesting that the correct answer may be (C).

Column A	Column B

11.

The sum of three different odd positive integers each less than 10	The sum of three different even positive integers each less than 10

ANALYSIS   **(D)** A QC that tests properties of the number system is likely to contain an unwanted surprise, so you need to be careful. The three numbers for Column A could be 1, 3, and 5, in which case Column A would have the value 9, or they could be 5, 7, and 9, in which case Column A would have the value 21. The three numbers for Column B might be 2, 4, and 6, for a sum of 12. At this point you can stop working, because you have demonstrated that the relationship is indeterminate.

Column A	Column B

12.

$0.89(x - y)$	$0.89x - y$

ANALYSIS   **(D)** Since this is not a simple problem, try to simplify it as much as possible. First, do the operations indicated in Column A: $0.89(x - y) = 0.89x - 0.89y$. Then you can subtract $0.89x$ from both columns. You're left with:

Column A	Column B

$-0.89y$	y

At this point, you should be able to see that the relationship is indeterminate, but you could go further and even add $0.89y$ to both columns. You would be left with:

Column A	Column B

0	$1.89y$

But you have no information that will allow you to compare $1.89y$ with 0, so the answer is (D).

18

Column A   **Column B**

13.

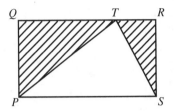

PQRS is a rectangle.

| Area of *PTS* | Shaded Area |

ANALYSIS **(C)** This figure consists of a rectangle and a triangle, and the shaded area is the difference between the area of the rectangle and the area of the triangle. With such figures, one aspect of the figure usually serves multiple roles; in this case, *QP* (or *RS*) is not just the side of the rectangle, it is also the altitude of the triangle. So the area of the rectangle is $QP \times PS$, and the area of the triangle is $\frac{1}{2} \times QP \times PS$. This means that the shaded area is also $\frac{1}{2} \times QP \times PS$, so the columns are equal.

Column A   **Column B**

14. $x^2 - 2x - 3 = 0$

| The sum of the possible values for *x*. | −1 |

ANALYSIS **(A)** There really isn't any alternative to factoring here:

$$x^2 - 2x - 3 = 0$$
$$(x - 3)(x + 1) = 0$$

So $x = 3$ or $x = -1$, and the sum of the possible solutions (or roots) of the equation is 2.

Column A	Column B

15.

AVERAGE (ARITHMETIC MEAN) OF TEST SCORES OF JOB APPLICANTS	
Average score for female applicants	89
Average score for male applicants	80
Average score for all applicants	85

Number of scores of male applicants	Number of scores of female applicants

ANALYSIS (B) You could solve this by using algebra:

Let x be the number of women and y be the number of men:

$$x(89) + y(80) = (x + y)85$$

$$89x + 80y = 85x + 85y$$

$$4x = 5y$$

$$\frac{x}{y} = \frac{5}{4}$$

This tells you that the ratio of the number of women to the number of men is 5 to 4. And that answers the QC question, but it also contains more information than you need. All you need to know is which is greater. You could reason like this: since the average for women is 89, and the average for men is 80, if there were equal numbers of each, the average of all scores would be 84.5. But the average is 85. Since $85 > 84.5$, there must have been more women in order to "pull the average up."

Now you have seen how the entire Action Plan is applied to QC items. In the workshops that follow, you'll be given a chance to apply it under timed conditions.

18

Workshop A

This workshop consists of drill and review. The drill has a time limit, but you should spend as much time as you need on the evaluation and review portions of the workshop.

Drill

This drill consists of 15 QCs. The time limit is 15 minutes. This reflects the general strategy of spending *on average* no more than a minute per QC. Indicate your response by darkening the appropriate oval.

15 Questions • Time—15 Minutes

Numbers: All numbers are real numbers.

Figures: Figures that accompany items are included to provide information for answering the questions. However, unless a note specifically states that a figure is drawn to scale, you should solve problems NOT by visual estimation or measurement but by using your knowledge of mathematical principles.

Lines shown as straight can be assumed to be straight.

Angle measures are positive.

Positions of points, angles, regions, etc. can be assumed to be in the order depicted.

All figures lie in a plan unless otherwise indicated.

DIRECTIONS: Each of the *Items 1–15* consists of two quantities, one in Column A and one in Column B. Compare the quantities and choose:

(A) if the quantity in Column A is greater;

(B) if the quantity in Column B is greater;

(C) if the two quantities are equal;

(D) if the relationship cannot be determined from the information given.

Centered information applies to both columns, and a symbol appearing in both columns has the same meaning in both quantities.

Column A	Column B	Answer
Column A	**Column B**	**Answer**

1. 3×4 $3 + 4$ (A)

Examples 2–4 refer to the following figure.

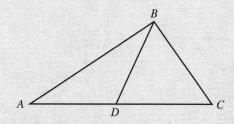

2. AD   DC   (D)

3. AC   AD   (A)

4. Angle ABD   Angle DBC   (D)

18

Column A	**Column B**

1. $m = \dfrac{2}{3}n,\ n = \dfrac{3}{4}p,\ p = 24$

     m 7

2. 20 percent of \$280   40 percent of \$140

Column A	**Column B**

3. $x \neq 0$

     $5x^2$ $(5x)^2$

4. The cost of lunch at a restaurant is $(5x + y)$, and the cost of a dinner is $(5y + x)$. The total cost of lunch and dinner is \$63.

     x y

Column A	**Column B**

5.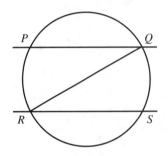

PQ is parallel to *RS*.

Length of minor arc *PR*	Length of minor arc *QS*

6. $\left(\sqrt{0.3}\right)^3$ | 0.3

7.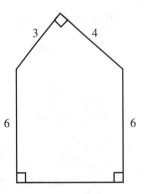

Area of figure	36

Column A	**Column B**

8. $(x + 2)(x - 5) = 0$

x	2

9. $\dfrac{2}{3}$ | 0.666

10. $\dfrac{1}{3} + \left(\dfrac{1}{4} + \dfrac{1}{5}\right)$ | $\dfrac{1}{5} + \left(\dfrac{1}{4} + \dfrac{1}{3}\right)$

11. $x^2 > 1$

x	1

12. The average (arithmetic mean) of *N* numbers if 39, and $N \geq 10$.

The sum of the *N* numbers	385

13. $xy = 15$

$x^2 = 25$

x	y

Column A	Column B		Column A	Column B

14.

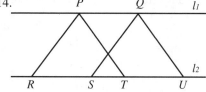

Line l_1 is parallel to line l_2, and the area of triangle *RPT* is greater than the area of triangle *SQU*.

RS	*TU*

15.   The width of a rectangular area is increased by x percent and the length is decreased by x percent.

The resulting area if $x = 20$	The resulting area if $x = 10$

18

Review

Use the following answer key to find how many you answered correctly, then compare your performance on the drill to the graph below.

1. (A)	6. (B)	11. (D)
2. (C)	7. (C)	12. (A)
3. (B)	8. (D)	13. (D)
4. (D)	9. (A)	14. (A)
5. (C)	10. (A)	15. (B)

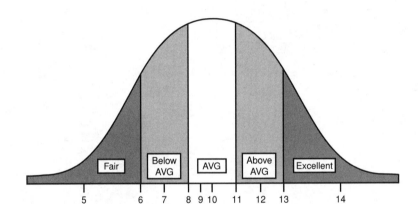

Number Correct

1. **(A)** This is a simple problem, so do the indicated operations. Since $p = 24$:

$$n = \left(\frac{3}{4}\right)24 = 18$$

And since $n = 18$:

$$m = \left(\frac{2}{3}\right)18 = 12$$

So Column A is greater than Column B.

2. **(C)** This is a simple problem because you can simply do the indicated manipulations:

20% of \$280 = \$56

40% of \$140 = \$56

Or you might avoid doing arithmetic altogether if you notice that 40% is twice 20% and \$140 half of \$280. Remember that the objective is only to make the comparison— not to determine how much greater or less one column is than the other.

3. **(B)** Begin by performing the manipulation as dictated in Column B. You get:

Column A

$$5x^2$$

Column B

$$25x^2$$

Since x is not equal to 0, x^2 is positive, and you can divide each side of the comparison by x^2. The result

Column A

$$5$$

Column B

$$25$$

So Column B is greater.

4. **(D)** You can perform the algebraic operations indicated in the centered information:

$(5x + y) + (5y + x) = \$6.30$

$6x + 6y = 6.3$

$6(x + y) = 6.3$

$x + y = 1.05$

But that is not enough information for a comparison of x and y.

5. **(C)** Since PQ is parallel to RS, the angles that intercept minor arcs PR and QS have equal measures. (A transverse cutting parallel lines creates equal angles and sets of supplemental angles.) So the two arcs are equal.

18

6. **(B)** Perform the operation indicated in Column A:

$$\left(\sqrt{0.3}\right)^3 = 0.3\sqrt{0.3}$$

Divide both columns by 0.3. The result is:

Column A	**Column B**
$\sqrt{0.3}$	1

Since $\sqrt{0.3}$ is less than 1, Column B is greater.

7. **(C)** Add a line to the figure:

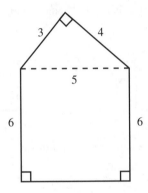

The new line creates a right triangle, so you can use the Pythagorean Theorem to find its length. Or better yet, you need only remember that a right triangle with sides of 3 and 4 must have a hypotenuse of 5. The area of the triangular region is:

Area of Triangular Region $= \dfrac{1}{2}(3)(4) = 6$

Area of Rectangular Region $= (6)(5) = 30$

So the area of the figure is $6 + 30 = 36$.

8. **(D)** Given the centered information, x must be equal either to -2 or to $+5$.

9. **(A)** Here is a good illustration of the principle of unpleasant surprises. The fraction $\dfrac{2}{3}$ is equal to the repeating decimal 0.6666... , while Column B is 0.6660. So Column A must be greater than Column B.

10. **(A)** This problem illustrates the difference between a simple and a difficult item. You <u>can</u> do the arithmetic as indicated. Column A turns out to be $\frac{5}{36}$ and Column B $\frac{3}{28}$. At that point, you should see that both are slightly less than $\frac{1}{7}$ but that $\frac{5}{36}$ is closer to $\frac{1}{7}$ than $\frac{3}{28}$, so Column A is greater. That's not an elegant solution, but it is effective; and you might be able to pull it off within a minute. A better approach would be to treat it with the Advanced Strategy of simplification. Multiply both side of the comparison by the numerator of each fraction. (In essence, cross-multiply.) You get:

Column A	**Column B**
$5 + \left(\dfrac{1}{4} + \dfrac{1}{3}\right)$	$3 + \left(\dfrac{1}{4} + \dfrac{1}{5}\right)$

And you can subtract 3 from both sides to get:

Column A	**Column B**
$2 + \left(\dfrac{1}{4} + \dfrac{1}{3}\right)$	$\left(\dfrac{1}{4} + \dfrac{1}{5}\right)$

At this point, you can see that Column A is "2 plus a fraction" while Column B is "a fraction," so Column A is greater. And it's worth a reminder at this juncture, that that's "good enough:" Column A is greater, and you don't have to know how much greater.

11. **(D)** Remember that squared variables may bring unwanted surprises. In this case, though x^2 is greater than 1, x itself may be less than 1 or greater than 1.

12. **(A)** This is a properties of numbers question, so you need to investigate to see what you've been given. If N were equal to 10, then you would have 10 numbers, the average of which is 39. The sum of the ten numbers would be $10 \times 39 = 390$. And Column A would be greater. Can Column A be less? No, because N is equal to *or greater* than 10. So the sum of the N numbers must be equal to or greater than 390.

13. **(D)** Again, you have to remember to watch out for unpleasant surprises. Since $x^2 = 25$, x could be +5 or −5. If $x = 5$, then $y = 3$, and $x > y$. But if $x = -5$, then $y = -3$, and $y > x$.

14. **(A)** The formula for calculating the area of a triangle is "$\frac{1}{2} \times$ altitude $\times$ base." In this case, the altitudes of the two triangles are equal, so if the area of one is greater than the area of the other, the base of the first must be greater than the base of the second. Since ST is common to the base of both triangles, $RS > TU$. And this item reminds you of the importance of solving problems by using your knowledge of geometry rather than (except in the case of a dire emergency) relying on the figure.

18

15. **(B)** You can solve this item algebraically. Let w be the width of the rectangle and l its length. For Column A, the new area is $(1.2w)(.8l) = .96wl$; and for Column B, the new area is $(1.1w)(.9l) = .99wl$. So Column B is greater. This would also be a good time to use one of the guessing strategies and substitute numbers. You could let $w = 10$ and $l = 10$. (A square is, after all, a rectangle.) The new rectangle described by Column A would have an area of $(12)(8) = 96$, and the one described by Column B would have an area of $(11)(9) = 99$.

Workshop B

This workshop consists of drill and review. The drill has a time limit, but you should spend as much time as you need on the evaluation and review portions of the workshop.

Drill

This drill consists of 15 QCs. The time limit is 15 minutes. This reflects the general strategy of spending *on average* no more than a minute per QC.

15 Questions • Time—15 Minutes

Numbers: All numbers are real numbers.

Figures: Figures that accompany items are included to provide information for answering the questions. However, unless a note specifically states that a figure is drawn to scale, you should solve problems NOT by visual estimation or measurement but by using your knowledge of mathematical principles.

Lines shown as straight can be assumed to be straight.

Angle measures are positive.

Positions of points, angles, regions, etc. can be assumed to be in the order depicted.

All figures lie in a plane unless otherwise indicated.

DIRECTIONS: Each of the *Items 1–15* consists of two quantities, one in Column A and one in Column. Compare the quantities and choose:

(A) if the quantity in Column A is greater;

(B) if the quantity in Column B is greater;

(C) if the two quantities are equal;

(D) if the relationship cannot be determined from the information given.

Centered information applies to both columns, and a symbol appearing in both columns has the same meaning in both quantities.

Column A	**Column B**	**Answer**
1. 3×4	$3 + 4$	(A)

Examples 2–4 refer to the following figure.

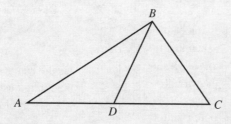

	Column A	**Column B**	**Answer**
2.	AD	DC	(D)
3.	AC	AD	(A)
4.	Angle ABD	Angle DBC	(D)

18

Column A	**Column B**
1.	$x > 0$

$$1 - \frac{1}{x+1} \qquad\qquad 1 + \frac{1}{x+1}$$

2. It costs \$13.56 to ship 3 pounds by Carrier X and \$18.52 to ship 4 pounds by Carrier Y.

The cost per pound of shipping via Carrier X	The cost per pound of shipping via Carrier Y

Column A	**Column B**
3.	N is an integer greater than 1.

$7N + 3$	$4N + 7$

4. $xy = 0$

$yz = 3$

x	0

Column A	Column B

5. $(0.03)^3$ | $(0.03)^5$

6. A driver can purchase a car for $15,000 or lease it for x months at $299 per month.

48	The greatest possible value of x such that the cost of leasing the car is less than the cost of purchasing it

7. $x < y < 0$

$x^2 + y^2$ | xy

8.

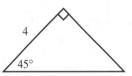

The area of the triangular region	8

9. 23 percent of 67 | 67 percent of 23

Column A	Column B

10.

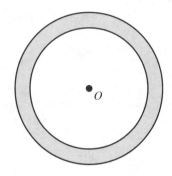

O is the center of two concentric circles, and the radius of the larger circle twice that of the smaller circle.

Shaded area	Area of smaller circle

11. On a course reading list with 72 entries, $\frac{1}{6}$ of the entries were published more than three years ago. Of the entries published within the last three years, there are 10 more required readings than optional readings.

The number of required readings on the list	40

12. A cube has a surface area of x square meters and a volume of x cubic meters.

The length of an edge of the cube	6

	Column A	**Column B**

13. n is a positive integer.

The remainder when $n^2 + n$ is divided by 2	0

14.

$\dfrac{x}{10^{10}}$	$\dfrac{x}{10^{9}}$

15.

$5(\sqrt{27} + 3)$	$3(\sqrt{75} + 5)$

18

Review

Use the following answer key to find how many you answered correctly, then compare your performance on the drill to the graph below.

1. (B)	6. (B)	11. (D)
2. (B)	7. (D)	12. (C)
3. (A)	8. (C)	13. (C)
4. (C)	9. (C)	14. (D)
5. (A)	10. (A)	15. (C)

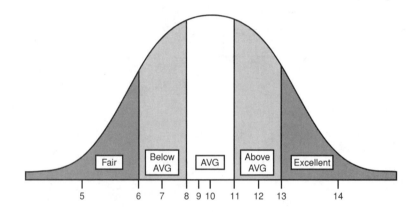

Number Correct

1. **(B)** You can simplify things by subtracting 1 from both sides of the comparison. You're left with:

Column A	**Column B**
$-\left(\dfrac{1}{x+1}\right)$	$\left(\dfrac{1}{x+1}\right)$

Since x is positive, you can multiply both sides by $x + 1$. You're left with:

Column A	**Column B**
-1	1

2. **(B)** The arithmetic is manageable, so just do it:

$$\frac{\$13.56}{3 \text{ pounds}} = \$4.52 \text{ per pound}$$

$$\frac{\$18.52}{4 \text{ pounds}} = \$4.63 \text{ per pound}$$

3. **(A)** This problems asks about properties of the number system (integers), but you can begin by simplifying matters. Subtracting $4N$ and 3 from both sides, you're left with:

Column A	**Column B**
$3N$	3

And you can even divide both sides by 3:

Column A	**Column B**
N	1

The centered information tells you that N is an integer greater than 1, so Column A is greater.

4. **(C)** This items asks about properties of numbers. Since the product of x and y is 0, either x or y or both x and y are 0. But the product of y and z is a non-zero number, so y cannot be 0. Therefore, $x = 0$.

5. **(A)** The arithmetic here appears to be unmanageable, so you should use one of the advanced strategies to simplify things. Start by dividing both sides of the comparison by $(0.03)^3$. You're left with:

Column A	**Column B**
1	$(0.03)^2$

Column B is less than 1, so Column A must be greater.

6. **(B)** You could attack this item by dividing $15,000 by $299: $15,000 ÷ $299 = 50 plus remainder 50. But you could also use a proxy problem. $15,000 ÷ $300 = 50. And since $299 < $300, $299 must go into $15,000 at least 50 times with a remainder left over.

18

7. **(D)** This item test properties of numbers, so you might want to reason about the behavior of the variables when they have various values. Or, better yet, why not substitute some numbers. If $x = -\frac{1}{2}$ and $y = -\frac{1}{4}$, then Column A is $\frac{5}{16}$ and Column B is $\frac{1}{8}$, so Column A would be greater on that assumption. But if $x = -2$ and $y = -1$, then Column A is 5 and Column B is 2, so Column A would be greater. Two substitutions shows that the correct answer is that the relationship is indeterminate.

8. **(C)** You can drop an altitude from the vertex of the triangle to the opposite base, bisecting the base. The length of the altitude, which is opposite a 45°, must be 4, and the area of the triangle is $\frac{1}{2}(4)(4) = 8$. Or you could use the Pythagorean Theorem to find the length of the other two sides of the triangle and find the area using them as altitude and base.

9. **(C)** You could just do the arithmetic here, but better would be to divide both sides of the comparison by 23 and by 67 to show that the two columns are equal.

10. **(A)** Let r be the radius of the smaller circle so that the larger circle has a radius of $2r$. Then the area of the smaller circle is πr^2. The area of the larger circle is $\pi(2r)^2 = 4\pi$, and the shaded area is the difference between the two: $4\pi - \pi = 3\pi$.

11. **(D)** Remember to watch out for unpleasant surprises. In this case, you can deduce that $72 - \frac{1}{6}72 = 60$ of the readings were published in the past three years, of which 35 are required and 25 are not. But there are still 12 other readings on the list (those published more than three years ago), and they may or may not be required readings.

12. **(C)** Since the volume in cubic meters of the cube is equal to its surface in square meters:

$$\text{edge}^3 = 6 \times \text{edge}^2$$
$$\text{edge} = 6$$

13. **(C)** You can reason about properties of numbers in this case. $n^2 + n = n(n + 1)$, and since n is a positive integer, n and $(n + 1)$ are consecutive integers, one of which is odd and the other even. Therefore, $n^2 + n$ is an even number and when divided by 2 generates a remainder of 0. This would also be a good problem to use the technique of substituting of numbers. It won't prove that the two columns are equal, but a couple of substitutions will strongly suggest that conclusion.

14. **(D)** A good start here would be to simplify matters by multiplying both sides of the comparison by 10^{10}. You're left with x in Column A and $10x$ in Column B. But you have no further information about x.

15. **(C)** Perform the indicated operations:

$$5(\sqrt{27} + 3) = 5(3\sqrt{3} + 3) = 15\sqrt{3} + 15$$
$$3(\sqrt{75} + 5) = 3(5\sqrt{3} + 5) = 15\sqrt{3} + 15$$

Get Answers to Frequently Asked Questions

Q: **I find it difficult to stay within the guideline of one minute or less per QC. What should I do?**

A: Don't be afraid to take your best shot and move on. If you're spending more than 60 seconds on an item, you're probably looking for certainty or for psychological reassurance that you'll never find. You have to accept that part of the test design is that your quantitative score is based not on this or that QC but your *overall* performance on the math part. The test is designed so that you'll score higher if you finish all questions.

Q: **If I get a question that can be solved by calculating, does that mean that I dropped down on the ladder of difficulty?**

A: No. In the first place, remember that we have defined "simple QCs" as those that can be attacked directly, but even some "difficult QCs" can also be handled in this way—even though it may not be the most elegant approach. So you may actually be using a "simple" technique to solve a "difficult" QC. Remember also that you'll probably have some embedded experimental questions that won't affect your score, and they could be of any level of difficulty.

Q: **Will I get equal numbers of arithmetic, algebra, and geometry QCs?**

A: Probably not, for two reasons. First, as the GRE algorithm constructs your individualized test, the most important factor will be positioning items on the ladder of difficulty. So how you're doing at any point during the test can have a lot to do with the kind of questions you're seeing. Second, the algorithm will also be choosing from the item pool according to a predetermined list of concepts that have to be covered.

Q: **I've noticed that in spite of the warning about figures, it seems possible to solve some QCs by estimating. Is that a viable option?**

A: Yes, but only in case of a dire emergency. In general, you shouldn't trust the figures; but if estimation is your only alternative to guessing at random, then go ahead and estimate. In fact, some figures *have* to be drawn to scale. For example, a circle inscribed in a square has to be drawn accurately because there is no way to inscribe a circle in a square except by having each side of the square tangent to exactly one point of the circle.

Day

19

Teach Yourself Problem Solving

Today, you'll teach yourself how to answer GRE Problem Solving items. Problem Solving items are multiple-choice math questions similar to—though not exactly like—those you used to do in school.

Get All the Inside Info on Problem Solving

Problem Solving items are math questions, so you'll be using your knowledge of arithmetic, algebra, and geometry to answer them. In fact, as curious as it may seem, you probably learned all of the math that you need for the GRE in high school. (Though you may have forgotten some of it.)

How can a test for admission to grad school be constructed of math for high school students? Because there's more to Problem Solving than just "math." Although the math concepts that drive this type of question are taught in high school, the applications that you'll be expected to make of them are intellectually more sophisticated than the tasks usually required of high schoolers.

The GRE uses three added-difficulty factors to control the level of difficulty of Problem Solving items. We'll look at each one in turn.

1. The Multiple Concepts Factor

Of the three types of math questions used by the GRE, Problem Solving comes to the closest to being "pure" math. Some items are easy because the math concept needed to answer is relatively basic; others are more difficult because more than one math concept is involved. And this is true of each of the three basic categories of math—arithmetic, algebra, and geometry.

The following pair of items illustrates how one GRE arithmetic problem is more difficult than another. First, here's an easier problem:

QUESTION $\sqrt{3}\left(\sqrt{12}\right) =$

    (A) 6

    (B) $3 + \sqrt{3}$

    (C) $3 + \sqrt{2}$

    (D) $2 + \sqrt{3}$

    (E) $\sqrt{3} + \sqrt{2}$

ANALYSIS The correct answer is **(A)**, and you get the answer simply by multiplying:

$$\sqrt{3}\left(\sqrt{12}\right) = \sqrt{3 \times 12} = \sqrt{36} = 6$$

And now here's a more difficult problem:

QUESTION $\dfrac{2+\sqrt{3}}{2-\sqrt{3}} =$

    (A) $1 - \sqrt{3}$

    (B) 1

    (C) $7 + 4\sqrt{3}$

    (D) $7 - 4\sqrt{3}$

    (E) $7\sqrt{2} + 7\sqrt{3}$

ANALYSIS The correct answer is **(C)**. To solve this problem, you have to multiply, but you also need to remember the technique for removing radicals from the denominator of a fraction:

$$\frac{2+\sqrt{3}}{2-\sqrt{3}} \times \frac{2+\sqrt{3}}{2+\sqrt{3}} = \frac{4+4\sqrt{3}+3}{4-3} = \frac{7+4\sqrt{3}}{1} = 7+4\sqrt{3}$$

Both of these problems use concepts drawn only from arithmetic (manipulating radicals), but the second problem is considerably more difficult than the first.

The same point is true of algebra. Here is a relatively easy algebra problem:

QUESTION If $2x + 3 = 9$, then $x =$

    (A) 3

    (B) 2

    (C) $\dfrac{3}{2}$

    (D) 1

    (E) $\dfrac{1}{3}$

ANALYSIS You just have to solve for x:

$$2x + 3 = 9$$
$$2x = 6$$
$$x = 3$$

So the correct answer is **(A)**.

Now, here's a more difficult problem that uses algebra:

QUESTION If $2x + y = 12$ and $x + y = 7$, then $x =$

    (A) 3

    (B) 4

    (C) 5

    (D) 6

    (E) 8

ANALYSIS The correct answer is **(C)**. For this problem, you not only have to solve for an unknown, you also need to remember how to work with a system of equations. First, redefine y in terms of x:

$$x + y = 7$$
$$y = 7 - x$$

Then, use that value for y in the other equation:

$$2x + (7 - x) = 12$$
$$x = 5$$

19

And the same point can be made with respect to geometry. First, here's a relatively easy item:

QUESTION What is the circumference of a circle with a radius of 4?

(A) 2π

(B) 4π

(C) 8π

(D) 16π

(E) $4\pi^2$

ANALYSIS The correct answer is **(C)**. This is a fairly easy problem that just requires you to use the formula for finding the circumference of a circle:

$Circumference = 2\pi r$

$C = 2\pi4 = 8\pi$

Other geometry problems are more difficult. Here's an example:

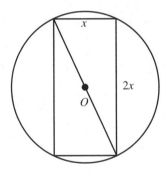

QUESTION In the figure above, if the area of the inscribed rectangular region is 16, then the circumference of the circle is

(A) 2π

(B) $\pi\sqrt{5}$

(C) $2\pi\sqrt{5}$

(D) $\pi\sqrt{10}$

(E) $2\pi\sqrt{10}$

ANALYSIS The correct answer is **(E)**. Like the first, easier item in this pair, you have to know the formula for finding the circumference of a circle. But for this more difficult item, you also need to know the formula for the area of a rectangle *plus* the Pythagorean Theorem:

$(x)(2x) = 16$

$2x^2 = 16$

$x^2 = 8$

$x = 2\sqrt{2}$

$hypotenuse^2 = (x^2)^2 + (2x^2)^2$

$h^2 = (2\sqrt{2})^2 + (2(2\sqrt{2}))^2$

$h^2 = (4 \times 2) + (4 \times 4 \times 2)$

$h^2 = (8) + (32)$

$h^2 = 40$

$h = 2\sqrt{10}$

And finally, since the hypotenuse of the right triangle is also the diameter of the circle:

$Circumference = \pi d = 2\pi \sqrt{10}$

Since Problem Solving is a lot like a traditional math exam, you have to expect that the level of difficulty of the items will be determined by the difficulty of the math.

NOTE

Since the algorithm selects problems according to whether you've been successful on earlier items, you shouldn't see a Problem Solving item that is way beyond your math ability. So the task is to use your math skills to maximum advantage by getting right all those you know how to answer and to use the advanced strategies outlined in the Action Plan below to push your score beyond the limits of your math knowledge.

19

2. The Additional Baggage Factor

A second added-difficulty factor that you'll encounter in some Problem Solving items is additional baggage. Additional baggage is data needed to answer the question asked that make answering more difficult than if the question were presented as a simple manipulation problem. Compare the following items:

QUESTION If $h\pi(8)^2 = 10\pi(16)^2$, then $h =$

    (A) 5

    (B) 16

    (C) 32

    (D) 40

    (E) 52

ANALYSIS The correct answer is **(D)**, and you only need to solve for h:

$$h\pi(8)^2 = 10\pi(16)^2$$
$$h(8)^2 = 10(16)^2$$
$$h = 40$$

Now compare this pure manipulation with the following word problem:

QUESTION A certain volume of molten metal when poured into molds will make 10 circular medallions that are each 16 centimeters in diameter. How many medallions of the same thickness but 8 centimeters in diameter can be made from the same volume of molten metal?

    (A) 5

    (B) 16

    (C) 32

    (D) 40

    (E) 52

ANALYSIS Again the correct answer is **(D)**, and the math required to answer is the same. But this second item is more difficult because of the additional baggage. You can think of each "stack" of medallions as being a cylinder, and the volumes of the two cylinders are equal:

$$Volume_1 = Volume_2$$
$$10 \times h\pi(16)^2 = m \times h\pi 8^2$$

Where h is the thickness of the medallions and m the number of medallions in the second "stack":

$$10 \times h\pi(16)^2 = m \times h\pi(8)^2$$
$$10(16)^2 = m(8)^2$$
$$m = 40$$

In QCs, you learned about additional information called "excess baggage." Problem Solving has "additional baggage." For QCs, you didn't need the extra information because you only needed to determine which column was larger—not how much larger. In Problem Solving, however, you'll need an exact answer, so the baggage is "additional" but not "excess."

3. The Unexpected Question Stem Factor

A third added-difficulty factor is created by the question stems themselves. Sometimes they ask a question other than the one that you're expecting. Here is an example:

 On a certain rack, there are twice as many medium sized shirts as shirts of all other sizes combined. Which of the following CANNOT be the number of shirts on the rack?

    (A) 84

    (B) 76

    (C) 69

    (D) 54

    (E) 36

ANALYSIS The correct answer is **(B)**, and the "CANNOT" is a potential problem for the unwary. Ordinarily, you would expect to be asked "What is?" But here you are asked "What cannot be?"

Don't overestimate the importance of this last point. The test-writers are not out to trick through misdirection. (In fact, the key word "CANNOT" is capitalized to call your attention to the fact that the question is subject to misinterpretation.) But you do need to avoid making a silly mistake.

19

 Make sure that you're answering the question asked. The wording of the question stem can sometimes be tricky, so read it carefully.

Learn the Basic Techniques for Problem Solving

Since Problem Solving is largely driven by traditional math concepts, the Basic Technique is to meet the math problems on their own terms. You need to become familiar with the most commonly used types of questions and make sure that you know the math needed to answer them.

Basic Techniques

Use familiar math techniques to solve the most common types of problems:

1. Problems about Operations

2. Problems about Approximations

3. Problems about Properties

4. Problems about Unknowns

5. Problems about Situations

6. Problems about Figures

The GRE is a carefully controlled situation; it has to be in order to produce scores that are comparable day in and day out. This need for order manifests itself in Problem Solving in the form of common question types that are used over and over again. You probably won't see exactly the same problems that you've studied, but you will see similar ones. And the list of math techniques that you need to master in order to handle the vast majority of these problems is fairly short. The Action Plan gives you the list of the common problem types, and now we'll discuss how to handle each.

Problems About Operations

Some Problem Solving items don't ask for anything more than a simple manipulation. Here is an example:

QUESTION What is the ratio of $3\frac{1}{2}$ to $2\frac{1}{3}$?

(A) $\dfrac{35}{4}$

(B) $\dfrac{9}{5}$

(C) $\dfrac{3}{2}$

(D) $\dfrac{12}{11}$

(E) $\dfrac{7}{8}$

ANALYSIS The correct answer is (C). Just create a ratio:

$$\frac{3\frac{1}{2}}{2\frac{1}{3}} = \frac{\frac{7}{2}}{\frac{7}{3}} = \frac{7}{2} \times \frac{3}{7} = \frac{3}{2}$$

Not all manipulation problems are this easy. If a problem indicates operations that are too complex to be solved in a minute or so, then look for a way to simplify the calculation. Here is an example:

QUESTION $\dfrac{3^8 - 3^5}{3^5} =$

(A) 1

(B) 3

(C) 9

(D) 24

(E) 26

ANALYSIS The correct answer is (E). Given the time limit for the math, you're not expected to multiply three by itself eight times, then multiply three by itself five times, and so on. Instead, you can simplify the problem by reducing:

$$\frac{3^8 - 3^5}{3^5} = 3^{(8-5)} - 3^{(5-5)} = 27 - 1 = 26$$

The category of manipulation problems also includes basic algebra problems. Here is an example:

QUESTION $2[2x + (3x + 4x)] - (5x + 2x) =$

(A) $7x$

(B) $11x$

(C) $13x$

(D) $15x$

(E) $22x$

ANALYSIS The correct answer is (B). Just do the indicated operations:

$2[2x + (3x + 4x)] - (5x + 2x) =$

$2(9x) - (7x) = 11x$

19

The distinction between manageable and unmanageable operations also applies to algebra-based items. If you see a complex algebraic expression, it can probably be simplified. Here is an example:

QUESTION If $x + y \neq 0$, then $\dfrac{\left(x^2 + 2xy + y^2\right)}{x+y} =$

(A) $x + y$

(B) $x - y$

(C) $2x + 2y$

(D) $2x - 2y$

(E) $2xy$

ANALYSIS The correct answer is **(A)**:

$$\frac{\left(x^2 + 2xy + y^2\right)}{x+y} = \frac{(x+y)(x+y)}{x+y} = x + y$$

TIP

> When a problem indicates manageable arithmetic or algebraic operations, do them. If the operation would take too long, first simplify the problem, then do the operations.

Problems About Approximations

Some Problem Solving items specifically ask for approximation. Approximation problems are used because they test whether you have a "feel" for what the numbers really mean, so the best technique is to approximate. Here is an example:

QUESTION If the circumference of Circle Q is 18.734 and the circumference of Circle R is 12.516, then the radius of Circle Q minus the Radius of Circle R is approximately

(A) 1

(B) 2

(C) 4

(D) 6

(E) 12

ANALYSIS The correct answer is **(A)**. The range of answer choices tells you that you don't have to be very precise. Since the circumference of Circle Q is 18.734, the diameter of Circle Q is "18 and change divided by π, which is 3 and change" or about 6, and the radius approximately 3. And since the circumference of Circle R is 12.516, the diameter of Circle R is approximately 4 and the radius approximately 2. So the difference is approximately 3 − 2 = 1.

Here is another example:

QUESTION Of the following, which is LEAST?

(A) $\dfrac{1}{2}$

(B) $\dfrac{8}{15}$

(C) $\dfrac{51}{100}$

(D) $\dfrac{374}{750}$

(E) $\dfrac{499}{1000}$

ANALYSIS The correct answer is **(D)**. You won't have time to do the arithmetic needed to convert each fraction to a decimal number for ready comparison. Instead, you can use the answer choices as a guide. (A), $\frac{1}{2}$, sets the mark. (B), $\frac{8}{15}$, is more than $\frac{8}{16}$ and therefore more than $\frac{1}{2}$, so (A) is less than (B). The same conclusion is true of (C): $\frac{51}{100} > \frac{50}{100} > \frac{1}{2}$. $\frac{374}{750}$, however, is less than $\frac{1}{2}$, so it becomes the new mark. (E), $\frac{499}{1000}$, is also less than $\frac{1}{2}$, but $\frac{1}{1000}$ is less than $\frac{1}{750}$ so (E) is closer to $\frac{1}{2}$ than (D). So (D) is the smallest answer choice.

And here's one final example of a problem asking for an approximation:

QUESTION A farmer receives $15.00 per hundredweight for fluid milk. If a hundredweight is on average equal to 12.55 fluid gallons, approximately how much will the farmer receive for 150 gallons of milk?

(A) $225
(B) $180
(C) $150
(D) $125
(E) $90

19

ANALYSIS The correct answer is **(B)**. Notice that the question stem specifically calls for an approximation, and notice also that the range of answer choices is such that even a rough approximation is going to be precise enough. 150 gallons of milk would be approximately 12 hundredweight, so the price would be approximately $15 \times 12 = \$180$.

CAUTION

When a problem asks for an approximation, don't look for an answer choice more precise than the answer choices. If you try for greater precision than the choices require, you're wasting valuable time.

Problems About Properties

Problems that ask about the properties of numbers focus on common features of the number system such as odd and even, positive and negative, and multiples or primes. Here is an example:

 If *n* is a positive integer, then which of the following must be even?

(A) $n - 1$

(B) $n + 1$

(C) $2n + 1$

(D) $2n - 1$

(E) $2n + 2$

ANALYSIS The correct answer is **(E)**. If *n* is a positive integer, then $2n$ must be even and $2n + 2$ must also be even.

And here is another example of a question that asks about the properties of numbers:

QUESTION Which of the following is the product of two positive integers whose sum is 5?

I. 4

II. 5

III. 6

(A) I only

(B) II only

(C) III only

(D) I and III only

(E) I, II, and III

ANALYSIS The correct answer is (**D**). There are two pairs of positive integers that total 5: 1 + 4 = 5 and 2 + 3 = 5. The product of 1 and 4 is 4, and the product of 2 and 3 is 6.

TIP With answer choices in a Roman numeral format, you can use partial information to eliminate choices. When you've decided that a statement is wrong or right, eliminate all of the choices that do or do not include it.

Problems About Unknowns

One of the most common categories of Problem Solving is algebra questions with unknowns, but what you should do with the unknowns depends on the structure of the problem. The simplest sort is one where you are asked to evaluate an expression by plugging in a number that you are given:

QUESTION If $x = 3$, $-x + 2x + 5 =$

    (A) 11

    (B) 8

    (C) 5

    (D) 3

    (E) 0

ANALYSIS The correct answer is (**B**). Just plug in 3 for x:

$$-3 + 2(3) + 5 = 8$$

A second common problem type built with algebra uses a single unknown in a single equation. The correct technique is almost always to find a value for the unknown. Here is an example:

QUESTION If $3x - 2 = 13$, then $x =$

    (A) 5

    (B) 3

    (C) 0

    (D) −1

    (E) −3

19

ANALYSIS The correct answer is **(A)**. Just solve for x:

$$3x - 2 = 13$$
$$3x = 15$$
$$x = 5$$

A variation on this theme uses two unknowns and two equations. For this type of problem, you treat both equations as a system of equations and solve for one or the other unknown. Here is an example:

QUESTION If $2x + y = 10$ and $x - y = 2$, then $x + y =$

    (A) -2

    (B) 0

    (C) 2

    (D) 5

    (E) 6

ANALYSIS The correct answer is **(E)**. First, redefine one unknown in terms of the other:

$$x - y = 2$$
$$x = 2 + y$$

And substitute that result into the other equation:

$$2(y + 2) + y = 10$$
$$2y + 4 + y = 10$$
$$3y = 6$$
$$y = 2$$

And using that value for y, you can find the value of x:

$$x - 2 = 2$$
$$x = 4$$
$$\text{So } x + y = 6.$$

Sometimes you won't be able to determine a value for an unknown. Instead, this kind of problem is solved by manipulating the algebraic expression you're given to produce some other expression specified by the question. Here's an example:

QUESTION If $2x + 3 = k$, then $2k - 6 =$

    (A) 3

    (B) 5

    (C) x

    (D) $2x$

    (E) $4x$

ANALYSIS The correct answer is **(E)**. You can't find a numerical value for x, but you don't have to. And the question stem itself points you toward a solution: you need $2k$. And the easiest way to get $2k$ is to multiply by 2:

$$2 \times (2x + 3) = 2 \times k$$
$$4x + 6 = 2k$$
$$2k - 6 = 4x$$

TIP

Questions about algebraic expressions often contain clues that guide you to a solution. Use the stem and the answer choices to determine what your final solution should look like and then work toward it from what you're given.

Problems About Situations

Problems about situations, also called word problems, can be very difficult. They tend to have a lot of additional baggage and require some thought about the math. Here is an example:

19

QUESTION At 7:00 a.m., train L left station S on the local track, and exactly three hours later train X left the same station on the express track. If train L averaged 40 kilometers per hour and train X averaged 55 kilomters per hour until X passed L, at what time did X pass L?

    (A) 12:00 noon

    (B) 2:00 p.m.

    (C) 4:00 p.m.

    (D) 6:00 p.m.

    (E) 8:00 p.m.

ANALYSIS The correct answer is **(D)**. At the moment that train X overtakes train L, the distance traveled by the two trains since leaving the station will be equal:

$$d_L = d_X$$

And since *distance = rate × time*:

$$rate_L \times time_L = rate_X \times time_X$$

But the time travelled by L is 3 hours more than the time travelled by X, so if t is the time travelled by L, $t - 3$ is the time travelled by X:

$$rt = r(t - 3)$$
$$40t = 55(t - 3)$$
$$40t = 55t - 165$$
$$15t = 165$$
$$t = 11$$

L leaves at 7:00 a.m. and is passed by X 11 hours later—at 6:00 p.m.

Not all situation problems are this difficult. Here is an example of an easier problem:

QUESTION If 24 square yards of carpeting cost a total of $432, then, at the same cost per square yard, what is the cost of 16 square yards of the carpeting?

(A) $142

(B) $164

(C) $202

(D) $288

(E) $299

ANALYSIS The correct answer is **(D)**. You can find the answer by using a direct proportion:

$$\frac{\text{Number of Yards}_x}{\text{Total Cost}_x} = \frac{\text{Number of Yards}_y}{\text{Total Cost}_y}$$

$$\frac{24}{\$432} = \frac{16}{x}$$

Cross-multiply:

$$x = 16\frac{432}{24} = 2 \times \frac{144}{3} = \$288$$

> **TIP**
>
> Approach a word problem by making a note on your scratch paper of the ultimate question to be answered. You'll probably be able to save yourself sometime by simplifying before doing the calculation.

Problems About Figures

Some geometry problems ask for nothing more than the application of some formula. Here is an example:

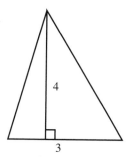

QUESTION   What is the area of the triangular region above?

   (A) 1

   (B) 3

   (C) 6

   (D) 9

   (E) It cannot be determined.

ANALYSIS   The correct answer is **(C)**. You just have to apply the formula for calculating the area of triangle:

$$Area = \frac{1}{2} \times altitude \times base$$

$$A = \frac{1}{2} \times 4 \times 3 = 6$$

Most Problem Solving items that use geometry, however, are not this easy. Many of the more difficult problems use figures constructed of more than one simple component. These are composite figures. Here's an example:

19

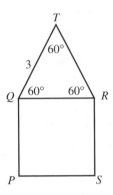

What is the perimeter of *PQTRS*, shown above?

(A) 9

(B) 12

(C) 15

(D) 18

(E) 21

The correct answer is (**C**). The key to the problem is that one side of the equilateral triangle *QTR* is also a side of square *PQRS*. So each of the line segments has length of 3.

And here is another kind of composite figure problem:

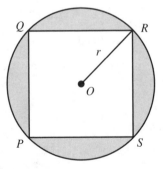

In the figure above, *PQRS* is a square inscribed in a circle with radius *r*. In terms of *r*, what is the area of the shaded portion of the figure?

(A) $r^2(\pi - 2)$

(B) $2r([2 - \pi)$

(C) $\pi - 2r$

(D) $\pi(r - 2)$

(E) $\pi(r^2 - 2)$

ANALYSIS The correct answer is **(A)**. This is a composite figure made up of a square inside of a circle, and the diagonal of the square is also the diameter of the circle. The diagonal of the square can be used to find the length of the side of the square and then to find its area. And the radius can be used to find the area of the circle. The shaded area is then:

Shaded Area = Area of Circle – Area of Square

Begin with the square. The diagonal of the square is $2r$. Using the Pythagorean Theorem, you can find the length of the side of the square:

$side^2 + side^2 = (2r)^2$

$2s^2 = 4r^2$

$s = r\sqrt{2}$

And now you can find the area of the square:

$Area\ of\ Square = s \times s$

$A_s = r\sqrt{2} \times r\sqrt{2}$

$A_s = 2r^2$

And the area of the circle is:

Area of Circle $= \pi r^2$

So the shaded area is:

$SA = \pi r^2 - 2r^2 = r^2(\pi - 2)$

TIP

For a composite figure problem, look for the key element that is a common feature of both simple figures.

19

Familiar math techniques will dispose of the vast majority of items in the GRE's Problem Solving data base, but you need to make sure that you're up to speed on your math. The following Workshop will help you.

Workshop A: Practice the Basic Techniques

This workshop consists of 15 Problem Solving items drawn from the six common types. There is no time limit. The problems can be solved using standard math techniques. Determine what technique is needed and work the problem, darkening the appropriate oval. Then check your work against the explanations given in the Review portion of the workshop, below.

Drill

1. What is the ratio of $2\frac{1}{3}$ to $3\frac{1}{2}$?

   (A) $\frac{2}{7}$

   (B) $\frac{1}{3}$

   (C) $\frac{3}{7}$

   (D) $\frac{2}{3}$

   (E) $\frac{7}{3}$

2. $\dfrac{\frac{1}{1}+\frac{2}{2}+\frac{3}{3}}{\frac{1}{3}\quad\frac{2}{5}\quad\frac{3}{7}} =$

   (A) $\frac{3}{5}$

   (B) 1

   (C) $\frac{5}{3}$

   (D) 9

   (E) 15

3. $\dfrac{7^{23}-7^{22}}{7^{22}} =$

   (A) 2
   (B) 6
   (C) 7
   (D) 42
   (E) 49

4. Which of the following is most nearly equal to $\frac{1}{3}$?

   (A) $\frac{1}{4}$

   (B) $\frac{1}{6}$

   (C) $\frac{2}{9}$

   (D) $\frac{4}{15}$

   (E) $\frac{6}{25}$

5. Of the following, which is the closest approximation to $\sqrt{\dfrac{(0.2498)(98.796)}{(0.49)^2}}$?

   (A) 100
   (B) 50
   (C) 20
   (D) 10
   (E) 1

6. If the product of six integers is an odd integer, exactly how many of the six *must* be odd?

   (A) Two
   (B) Three
   (C) Four
   (D) Five
   (E) Six

7. How many positive integers less than 25 are equal to the sum of a positive multiple of 3 and a positive multiple of 4?

   (A) Three
   (B) Eight
   (C) Eleven
   (D) Thirteen
   (E) Fourteen

8. If $3 \times 16 = x \times 4 \times 12$, then $x =$

   (A) 6
   (B) 3
   (C) 2
   (D) 1
   (E) $\dfrac{1}{3}$

9. If the sum of 10, 18, and x is 40, then the product of 3 and $(x + 2)$ is

   (A) 24
   (B) 42
   (C) 54
   (D) 78
   (E) 93

10. If $m = \dfrac{1}{4}(m + n)$, then what is m in terms of n?

   (A) $\dfrac{1}{4}n$
   (B) $\dfrac{1}{3}n$
   (C) $n + 3$
   (D) $3n$
   (E) $4n$

11. If 45 percent of the customers who bought tickets to a certain performance of a drama were students, what was the ratio of the number of students who purchased tickets to the number of non-students who purchased tickets?

   (A) $\dfrac{5}{9}$
   (B) $\dfrac{9}{11}$
   (C) $\dfrac{9}{10}$
   (D) $\dfrac{11}{9}$
   (E) $\dfrac{9}{5}$

12. The rate for a limousine service ride from a hotel to the airport in a car that can accommodate 4 passengers is $42 for one passenger plus x dollars for each additional passenger. If 3 people take the limousine service to the airport and each pays $26, what is the value of x?

   (A) 3
   (B) 4
   (C) 9
   (D) 12
   (E) 18

19

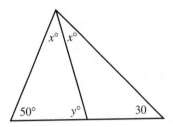

13. What is the value of *y* in the figure above?

    (A) 50
    (B) 65
    (C) 80
    (D) 105
    (E) 120

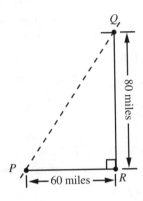

15. According to the map above, how many miles of travel are saved by flying directly from *P* to *Q* rather than flying from *P* to *R* and then from *R* to *Q*?

    (A) 40
    (B) 60
    (C) 80
    (D) 100
    (E) 120

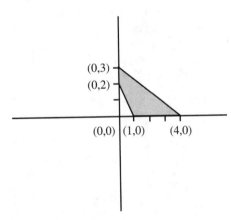

14. In the figure above, what is the area of the shaded region?

    (A) 3
    (B) $3\frac{1}{2}$
    (C) 4
    (D) $4\frac{1}{2}$
    (E) 5

Review

You may have noticed that the problems fall into the common categories in the following way:

Problems about Operations: 1, 2, 3

Problems about Approximations: 4, 5

Problems about Properties: 6, 7

Problems about Unknowns: 8, 9, 10

Problems about Situations: 11, 12

Problems about Figures: 13, 14, 15

1. **(D)** The operations required for this problem are not very complicated, so just do them:

$$\frac{2\frac{1}{3}}{3\frac{1}{2}} = \frac{\frac{7}{3}}{\frac{7}{2}} = \frac{7}{3} \times \frac{2}{7} = \frac{2}{3}$$

2. **(E)** Again, you have a problem that can easily be disposed of just by doing some arithmetic:

$$\frac{1}{\frac{1}{3}} + \frac{2}{\frac{2}{5}} + \frac{3}{\frac{3}{7}} = 3 + 5 + 7 = 15$$

3. **(B)** The operations here would be too time-consuming, so first you should simplify the problem:

$$\frac{7^{23} - 7^{22}}{7^{22}} + \frac{7^{23}}{7^{22}} - \frac{7^{22}}{7^{22}} = 7 - 1 = 6$$

4. **(D)** The "most nearly equal" in the question stem tells you that you should use approximation. Compare the fractions using the benchmark method. The first choice, $\frac{1}{4}$, is the mark. $\frac{1}{6}$ is less

than $\frac{1}{4}$, so (A) is closer to $\frac{1}{3}$ than (B), and (A) remains the mark. The third choice, $\frac{2}{9}$, is farther from $\frac{1}{3}$ than $\frac{1}{4}$, so (A) remains the mark. The fourth choice, $\frac{4}{15}$, is close to $\frac{5}{15}$, which is equal to $\frac{1}{3}$, so (D) replaces (A) as the mark. Finally, $\frac{6}{25}$ is closer to $\frac{1}{4}$ than to $\frac{1}{3}$, so the correct answer is (D).

5. **(D)** Here is another item that specifically calls for an approximation. Using the answer choices as a guide, you can see that you won't be needing three places of decimal point precision. Instead, you can use:

$$\sqrt{\frac{(0.25)(100)}{(0.5)^2}}$$

And that is:

$$\sqrt{\frac{25}{.25}} = \sqrt{100} = 10$$

19

6. **(E)** This item asks about even and odd properties of integers. You know that any integer, whether odd or even, when multiplied by an even integer, yields a product that is even, e.g., $3 \times 2 = 6$. So, for the product of two or more integers to be *odd*, none of the integers can be even; all must be odd.

7. **(B)** This items asks about a peculiar property of the number system. You don't need any advanced mathematical theory to answer, just patience and attention to detail. The multiples of 3 that are less than 25 are 6, 9, 12, 15, 18, 21, and 24; the multiples of 4 that are less than 25 are 8, 12, 16, 20, and 24.

   $6 + 8 = 14$

   $6 + 12 = 18$

   $6 + 16 = 22$

   $9 + 8 = 17$

   $9 + 12 = 21$

   $12 + 8 = 20$

   $12 + 12 = 24$

   $8 + 15 = 23$

8. **(D)** Here you have a simple equation with one unknown, so solve for x:

   $3 \times 16 = x \times 4 \times 12$

   $48 = 48x$

   $x = 1$

9. **(B)** Here is another equation with a single unknown, so you should solve for x. Then you'll have one more step in order to get the answer:

   $10 + 18 + x = 40$

   $x = 40 - (10 + 18) = 12$

   Then:

   $3 \times (12 + 2) = 3 \times 14 = 42$

10. **(A)** This is one of those algebra-based questions that cannot be answered with a value. Instead, you're asked to redefine one term by another:

    $m = \dfrac{1}{4}(m + n)$

    $4m = m + n$

    $3m = n$

    $m = \dfrac{1}{3}n$

11. **(B)** This is a situation or word problem. Make a note of the final solution that will answer the question asked:

    $$\dfrac{\text{students}}{\text{non} - \text{students}}$$

    Then, use the data you're given to fill in the solution:

    $$\dfrac{\text{students}}{\text{non} - \text{students}} = \dfrac{45\% \text{ of Total}}{55\% \text{ of Total}} =$$

    $$\dfrac{0.45}{0.55} = \dfrac{9}{11}$$

12. **(E)** Here's another situation problem. Your final solution will be:

    $\$42 + (2 \times \$x) = 3 \times \$26$

So:

$$42 + 2x = 3(26)$$

$$2x = 78 - 42$$

$$2x = 36$$

$$x = 18$$

13. **(C)** This is a composite figure because the single triangle is divided into two smaller triangles. You can find the value of x as follows:

$$50 + 2x + 30 = 180$$

$$2x = 100$$

$$x = 50$$

And x is also the measure of the smaller triangle that includes the angle with measure of y:

$$50 + x + y = 180$$

$$50 + 50 + y = 180$$

$$y = 80$$

14. **(E)** This is also a composite figure problem. The figure consists of a triangle with vertices $(0,0)$, $(0,3)$, and $(4,0)$ and another triangle with vertices of $(0,0)$, $(0,2)$, and $(1,0)$. The shaded area of the figure is:

Triangle $(0,0),(0,3),(4,0)$ –
Triangle $(0,0),(0,2),(1,0)$ =

$$\frac{1}{2}(3)(4) - \frac{1}{2}(2)(1) = 5$$

15. **(A)** The problem just requires you to apply the Pythagorean Theorem:

$$PQ^2 = (60)^2 + (80)^2$$

$$PQ = \frac{\sqrt{3600 + 6400} =}{\sqrt{10,000} = 100}$$

So the difference is:

$$[60 + 80] - 100 = 40$$

Master Advanced Strategies for Difficult Items

19

Your knowledge of math is the foundation for your performance on Problem Solving, but there are two very powerful advanced strategies that can help you go beyond the limits of your knowedge.

ACTION PLAN **Advanced Strategies**

1. Test Answer Choices

2. Substitute Numbers

The multiple-choice format of the GRE is what gives it the ease of administrative convenience and makes it possible for over a million people to take the test each year. But the multple-choice format is also a signifiant weakness in the test structure—a weakness that you can exploit if you know how.

Test Answer Choices

One of the most important features of the multiple-choice format is that the answer choice is right there in front of you on the monitor screen. You just have to find it. And one way of doing that is by eliminating all of the wrong ones. When applied to Problem Solving items, this important principle says that you can test answer choices, eliminating wrong ones, until you find the right one. Here's how it works:

QUESTION   Which of the following is a solution to $5x + x^2 = -6$?

    (A) 6

    (B) 5

    (C) 2

    (D) 0

    (E) −2

ANALYSIS   The correct answer is **(E)**. You could dispose of this item by finding the roots of the equation. You'd first need to put the equation into standard form:

$$x^2 + 5x + 6 = 0$$

Then factor:

$$(x + 3)(x + 2) = 0$$

Therefore:

$$(x + 3) = 0 \text{ and } x = -3$$

or

$$(x + 2) = 0 \text{ and } x = -2$$

But the structure of the problem also tells you that one of the answer choices is a possible solution to the equation. All you have to do is test each choice until you find the one that works:

$5x + x^2 = -6$?

    (A) $5(6) + (6)^2 = -6$

         $30 + 36 = -6$ (Wrong.)

    (B) $5(5) + (5)^2 = -6$

         $25 + 25 = -6$ (Wrong.)

(C) $5(2) + (2)^2 = -6$

$10 + 4 = -6$ (Wrong.)

(D) $5(0) + (0)^2 = -6$

$0 + 0 = -6$ (Wrong.)

(E) $5(-2) + (-2)^2 = -6$

$-6 = -6$ (Correct.)

Here's another example:

QUESTION If x is a positive integer such that when x is divided by 6 the remainder is 1, and when x is divided by 9 the remainder is 4, which of the following could be the value of x?

(A) 43

(B) 61

(C) 76

(D) 85

(E) 104

ANALYSIS The correct answer is **(D)**. You don't need any fancy math to solve this problem. Just test answer choices until you find the one that satisfies the conditions set forth in the stem:

(A) 43

$43 \div 6 = 7$ plus remainder 1

$43 \div 9 = 4$ plus remainder 7 (Wrong.)

(B) 61

$61 \div 6 = 10$ plus remainder 1

$61 \div 9 = 6$ plus remainder 7 (Wrong.)

(C) 76

$76 \div 6 = 12$ plus remainder 4 (Wrong.)

(D) 85

$85 \div 6 = 14$ plus remainder 1

$85 \div 9 = 9$ plus remainder 4

(Correct.)

In this next example, which uses the ages of two people as variables, notice that the way that the ratio between the ages changes as time passes. This additional feature sets up a refinement on the advanced strategy that we've been studying.

19

QUESTION Today is Marie's 15th birthday and Karen's 40th birthday. How many years from today will Karen be twice as old as Marie at that time?

(A) 10

(B) 15

(C) 25

(D) 30

(E) 50

ANALYSIS The correct answer is **(A)**. The test-writers expect you to show your mastery of math by setting up an equation:

$$2(15 + x) = 40 + x$$
$$30 + 2x = 40 + x$$
$$x = 10$$

But you don't have to solve the problem that way. Instead, you could just test answer choices until you find the one that works. Start with (A), and assume that 10 years have passed. At that time, Marie will be 25 and Karen will be 50, and 50 is twice 25, so (A) is the correct answer.

You might think that this question makes things too easy simply because choice (A), the first one in the list, happens to be correct. But let's assume that the choices are reversed:

QUESTION Today is Marie's 15th birthday and Karen's 40th birthday. How many years from today will Karen be twice as old as Marie at that time?

(A) 50

(B) 30

(C) 25

(D) 15

(E) 10

ANALYSIS Now, you might think, it would be necessary to work your way through the entire list before you finally get to (E). But there is a short-cut: start with (C), the middle value.

Assume that 25 years have passed. On that assumption, Marie is 40 years old and Karen is 65 years old, but 65 is not twice 40; 65 is less than twice 40. That means that sometime before 25 years passed, Karen passed the mark at which she was twice as old as Marie. So the time that passes must be less, and you would test the next smaller answer choice, 15. On that assumption, Karen would be 55 and Marie 30—again, a wrong answer.

But the fact that 15 is also a wrong answer already tells you what the right answer is: **(E)**. It's the only one left that can possibly be correct.

In other words, by picking the middle value, you have to do only two calculations to get the right answer.

Here is another example:

QUESTION The Apex Cell Phone Company charges $20.00 per month for a connection fee and $0.10 per minute for calls. The SaveMore Cell Phone Company charges $10.00 per month for a connection fee and $0.15 per minute for calls. For a given month, at how many minutes of calls would the charges of the two companies be equal?

    (A) 50

    (B) 75

    (C) 100

    (D) 200

    (E) 250

ANALYSIS The correct answer is **(D)**. The test-writers think that you should set up an equation and solve for x:

$$20 + 0.1x = 10 + 0.15x$$
$$0.05x = 10$$
$$x = 200$$

But you can reach the same conclusion just by testing choices, starting with (C). Assume that a customer uses 100 minutes. The charge for Acme will be $20 + (100 \times \$0.10) = \$30$, and the charge for SaveMore will be $10 + (100 \times \$0.15) = \$25.00$. The lower initial connect charge of SaveMore makes it cheaper, so the break-even point must occur with more minutes. Test (D). If a customer uses 200 minutes, Acme will charge $20 + (200 \times \$0.10) = \$40$; and SaveMore will charge $10 + (200 \times \$0.15) = \$40$. That's the point at which the two charges are equal, so (D) is the correct answer.

The two problems that we just worked could be solved using what might be called the "pick (C)" method. In each of the situations, the final answer choice depended upon the magnitude of some variable or variables, e.g., the more minutes used the greater the cost. So given that choices are arranged in order, it made good sense to start the testing process with (C).

Answer choices are arranged in an order. So when magnitude matters, test choices beginning with (C). At worst you'll have to do two calculations. And if the correct choice happens to be (C), you get the right answer with only one calculation.

Substitute Numbers

Variables or unknowns are one of the most important advantages of algebra, but they are also a royal inconvenience for those of us who aren't always sure what to do with them. You can avoid this inconvenience on the test by working with real numbers instead of unknowns. Here's how:

QUESTION If $x \neq 0$, then $\dfrac{x\left(x^3\right)\left(x^2\right)}{x^2} =$

(A) x

(B) x^2

(C) x^3

(D) x^4

(E) x^5

ANALYSIS The correct answer is **(D)**. You can solve this item using the procedures for working with exponents:

$$\frac{x\left(x^3\right)\left(x^2\right)}{x^2} =$$

$$\frac{x\left(x^{3+2}\right)}{x^2} =$$

$$\frac{x\left(x^5\right)}{x^2} =$$

$$\frac{x^{1+5}}{x^2} =$$

$$x^{6-2} = x^4$$

But x is a variable, and a variable is a place holder for values. So you can assign a value to x, say $x = 2$:

$$\frac{x\left(x^3\right)\left(x^2\right)}{x^2} =$$

$$\frac{2\left(2^3\right)\left(2^2\right)}{2^2} =$$

$$\frac{2(8)(4)}{4} = 16$$

Now substitute 2 for x into each of the choices. The correct choice will return the value 162:

    (A) $x = 2$ (Wrong.)

    (B) $x^2 = 2^2 = 4$ (Wrong.)

    (C) $x^3 = 2^3 = 8$ (Wrong.)

    (D) $x^4 = 2^4 = 16$ (Right.)

 TIP

> To avoid working with variables, just assume real numbers for the unknowns.

Here's another example:

QUESTION   If $y = 3x$ and $z = 5y$, then in terms of y, $x + y + z =$

    (A) $\dfrac{3x}{5}$

    (B) $3x$

    (C) $5x$

    (D) $15x$

    (E) $19x$

19

ANALYSIS   The correct answer is **(E)**. You can solve the problem by reasoning as follows:

$$x + y + z = x + (3x) + 5(3x) = 19x$$

But you could also just assign a value to x, say $x = 1$. On that assumption, $y = 3$ and $z = 15$, and $x + y + z = 19$. Substitute 1 into the choices:

    (A) $\dfrac{3x}{5} = \dfrac{3(1)}{5} = \dfrac{3}{5}$ (Wrong.)

    (B) $3x = 3(1) = 3$ (Wrong.)

(C) $5x = 5(1) = 5$ (Wrong.)

(D) $15x = 15(1) = 15$ (Wrong.)

(E) $19x = 19(1) = 19$ (Correct.)

Here is another example:

QUESTION $\dfrac{x+y}{3+5} =$

(A) $\dfrac{x+y}{3} + \dfrac{x+y}{5}$

(B) $\dfrac{x+y}{8} + \dfrac{x+y}{8}$

(C) $\dfrac{x}{3} + \dfrac{y}{5}$

(D) $\dfrac{x}{5} + \dfrac{y}{3}$

(E) $\dfrac{x}{8} + \dfrac{y}{8}$

ANALYSIS   The correct answer is **(E)**. You could solve the problem by following procedures for manipulating algebraic terms:

$$\frac{x+y}{3+5} = \frac{x+y}{8} = \frac{x}{8} + \frac{y}{8}$$

But if you've forgotten exactly how to do the manipulation (and that can happen under the pressure of the test), you can assign a value to x. Again, try 1, since that is a convenient number to work with. On the assumption that $x = 1$:

$$\frac{x+y}{3+5} = \frac{1+1}{3+5} = \frac{2}{8}$$

And each of the answer choices becomes:

(A) $\dfrac{x+y}{3} + \dfrac{x+y}{5} = \dfrac{1+1}{3} + \dfrac{1+1}{5} = \dfrac{2}{3} + \dfrac{2}{5}$ (Wrong.)

(B) $\dfrac{x+y}{8} + \dfrac{x+y}{8} = \dfrac{1+1}{8} + \dfrac{1+1}{8} = \dfrac{2}{8} + \dfrac{2}{8}$ (Wrong.)

(C) $\dfrac{x}{3} + \dfrac{y}{5} = \dfrac{1}{3} + \dfrac{1}{5}$ (Wrong.)

(D) $\dfrac{x}{5}+\dfrac{y}{3}=\dfrac{1}{5}+\dfrac{1}{3}$ (Wrong.)

(E) $\dfrac{x}{8}+\dfrac{y}{8}=\dfrac{1}{8}+\dfrac{1}{8}=\dfrac{2}{8}$ (Right.)

And here is an example—with a twist:

QUESTION If $xy \neq 0$, $\dfrac{x+1}{xy}=$

(A) $\dfrac{1}{y}\left(1+\dfrac{1}{x}\right)$

(B) $\dfrac{1}{x}\left(1+\dfrac{1}{y}\right)$

(C) $1+\dfrac{x}{xy}$

(D) $1+\dfrac{y}{xy}$

(E) $xy+1$

ANALYSIS Pick a value for x and y, say $x = 1$ and $y = 1$. (Nothing says that x and y are different numbers.) Then substitute those values for x and y:

$$\dfrac{x+1}{xy}=\dfrac{1+1}{(1)(1)}=2$$

19

So when you substitute 1 for x and 1 for y, the correct answer choice must generate the value 2:

(A) $\dfrac{1}{y}\left(1+\dfrac{1}{x}\right)=\dfrac{1}{1}\left(1+\dfrac{1}{1}\right)=2$ (Correct?)

(B) $\dfrac{1}{x}\left(1+\dfrac{1}{y}\right)=\dfrac{1}{1}\left(1+\dfrac{1}{1}\right)=2$ (Correct?)

(C) $1+\dfrac{x}{xy}=1+\dfrac{1}{(1)(1)}=2$ (Correct?)

(D) $1+\dfrac{y}{xy}=1+\dfrac{1}{(1)(1)}=2$ (Correct?)

(E) $xy+1=(1)(1)+1=2$ (Correct?)

The strategy seems to have failed. Why? Because 1×1 is equal to $1 \div 1$. So the strategy really didn't fail; we just used values that coincidentally gave us the same result for all answers. So we need to try a different set of numbers, say $x = 2$ and $y = 3$:

$$\frac{x+1}{xy} = \frac{2+1}{(2)(3)} = \frac{1}{2}$$

(A) $\dfrac{1}{y}\left(1+\dfrac{1}{x}\right) = \dfrac{1}{3}\left(1+\dfrac{1}{2}\right) = \dfrac{1}{2}$ (Right.)

(B) $\dfrac{1}{x}\left(1+\dfrac{1}{y}\right) = \dfrac{1}{2}\left(1+\dfrac{1}{3}\right) = \dfrac{2}{3}$ (Wrong.)

(C) $1+\dfrac{x}{xy} = 1+\dfrac{2}{(2)(3)} = \dfrac{4}{3}$ (Wrong.)

(D) $1+\dfrac{y}{xy} = 1+\dfrac{3}{(2)(3)} = \dfrac{3}{2}$ (Wrong.)

(E) $xy + 1 = (2)(3) + 1 = 7$ (Wrong.)

A different set of values produces only one correct choice, so (A) is the correct answer.

CAUTION

> When you substitute numbers for unknowns, the value 1 may generate more than one right answer. Just test another number, and you'll have the correct response.

The technique is also useful for situation problems. Here's an example of how to use it in that context:

 For next year, a university has allotted 40 percent of its budget for faculty expenses, and the budget will be 20 percent higher than this year's budget of x dollars. In terms of x, how many dollars has the university allotted for faculty expenses for next year?

(A) $(0.4)(0.8x)$

(B) $(0.4)(1.2x)$

(C) $0.2(0.4)(x)$

(D) $\dfrac{1.2x}{0.4}$

(E) $(1.2x)(0.4) + (0.2)$

ANALYSIS If you find it inconvenient to work with the x in this problem, then just assign a dollar value to the university's budget for this year, say $100. True, that's not a realistic number, but it's a lot easier to work with than a realistic number like $83,147,246.13, and it will accomplish the same result. On the assumption that $x = \$100$, next year's budget will be $120 and faculty expenses will be 40% of $120 or $48. Now we substitute 100 for x in each of the answer choices until we find the one that generates the value $48:

(A) $(0.4)(0.8x) = (0.4)(0.8 \times 100) = \$32$ (Wrong.)

(B) $(0.4)(1.2x) = (0.4)(1.2 \times 100) = \$48$ (Correct.)

TIP

> If the answers to a word problem are algebraic formulas, try assuming a value for the unknown in the problem and then test answer choices.

This advanced strategy of substituting numbers even applies to some geometry problems. Here's an example:

QUESTION If the radius of a circle is decreased by 40 percent, by what percent will the area of the circular region be decreased?

(A) 20%

(B) 36%

(C) 40%

(D) 60%

(E) 64%

ANALYSIS This problem doesn't use a variable; but if it did, it would probably say "radius of length r." So you can just assume a value for the length of the radius, say 1. On that assumption, the original circle has an area of $\pi(1)^2$ or π. The new radius is 0.6, and the new area is $\pi(0.6)^2$ or 0.36π. So the percent decrease is:

$$\frac{\pi - 0.36\pi}{\pi} = \frac{0.64\pi}{\pi} = 0.64 = 64\%$$

So the correct answer is (**E**).

TIP

> Geometry problems that use unquantitied lengths or areas can often be solved by assuming a value even when the problem doesn't use a variable.

19

As you can see, testing choices and assuming values for variables are two very powerful strategies for raising your GRE quantitative score beyond the limit of your math knowledge. The next Workshop will allow you to practice these strategies.

Workshop B: Practice Advanced Strategies

The problems in this Workshop can all be solved using one of the two Advanced Strategies. There is no time limit. Work each problem and darken the appropriate oval. When you are finished, check your work against the explanations given in the Review portion of the workshop, below.

Drill

1. If n is an integer divisible by 6 but not by 9, then which of the following CANNOT be n?

   (A) 24
   (B) 42
   (C) 78
   (D) 96
   (E) 108

2. For which of the following sets of numbers is the product of the three numbers less than each member of the set?

   I. 3, −5, 7

   II. $-\dfrac{1}{4}$, −4, 8

   III. $\dfrac{1}{2}, \dfrac{1}{3}, \dfrac{1}{4}$

   (A) I only
   (B) III only
   (C) I and III only
   (D) II and III only
   (E) I, II, and III

3. If $n = 15 \times 16 \times 21$, which of the following is NOT an integer?

   (A) $\dfrac{n}{15}$

   (B) $\dfrac{n}{35}$

   (C) $\dfrac{n}{39}$

   (D) $\dfrac{n}{40}$

   (E) $\dfrac{n}{56}$

4. A coin bank contains exactly $11.90, all in dimes and quarters. If the number of dimes is equal to the number of quarters, what is the total number of coins in the bank?

   (A) 34
   (B) 50
   (C) 62
   (D) 68
   (E) 80

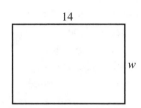

14

w

5. If the perimeter of the rectangle above is 48, then $w =$

   (A) 18
   (B) 14
   (C) 12
   (D) 10
   (E) 7

6. If integer n is divided by 13, the quotient is 7 with a remainder of 2, then $n =$

   (A) 91
   (B) 93
   (C) 98
   (D) 100
   (E) 103

7. If $x > 0$, then $\sqrt{0.36x^4} =$

   (A) $0.06x^2$
   (B) $0.06x^3$
   (C) $0.06x^5$
   (D) $0.6x^2$
   (E) $0.6x^3$

8. Dr. Gowda has exactly 5 years more experience with a certain procedure than Dr. Aman but exactly 3 years less experience with the procedure than Dr. Demeter. If Dr. Gowda has x years of experience with the procedure, then how many years of experience do Drs. Aman and Demter have with procedure *combined*?

   (A) $2x - 8$
   (B) $2x - 3$

   (C) $2x - 2$
   (D) $2x + 5$
   (E) $2x + 8$

9. If x is an even negative integer and y is an odd positive integers, then xy must be

   (A) even and negative
   (B) even and positive
   (C) odd and negative
   (D) odd and positive
   (E) zero

x y 0

10. If x and y are numbers on the number line shown above, which of the following statements must be true?

   I. $xy < 0$

   II. $x + y > 0$

   III. $x - y < 0$

   (A) I only
   (B) II only
   (C) III only
   (D) II and III only
   (E) I, II, and III

11. If $y = 3x + 1$, what is the value of x in terms of y?

   (A) $\dfrac{y+3}{1}$

   (B) $\dfrac{y}{3} + \dfrac{1}{3}$

   (C) $\dfrac{y}{3} - \dfrac{1}{3}$

   (D) $\dfrac{y}{3} - 1$

   (E) $\dfrac{y}{3} + 1$

19

12. $(N-1)(1-N) =$

   (A) 0
   (B) 1
   (C) $(N-1)^2$
   (D) $-(N-1)^2$
   (E) $-(N+1)^2$

13. If m and n are integers such that $m < n < 0$, how many integers are there between m and n, not including m and n?

   (A) none
   (B) one
   (C) $m - n$
   (D) $m - n - 1$
   (E) $n - m - 1$

14. Which of the following points on the number line shown above has a coordinate most nearly equal to xy?

   (A) P
   (B) Q
   (C) R
   (D) S
   (E) T

15. If the cost of renting a car is d dollars for the first day and $\frac{2}{3}d$ dollars for each additional day, what is the cost, in dollars, for renting the car for 7 days?

   (A) $\frac{12}{5}d$
   (B) $2d$
   (C) $3d$
   (D) $\frac{14}{3}d$
   (E) $5d$

16. Two college classes, P1 and P2, are fully subscribed, and there are 60 more students enrolled in P1 than in P2. If 10 students from each class drop out, there will be three times as many students enrolled in P1 as in P2. How many students are enrolled in P1 and P2 combined?

   (A) 140
   (B) 120
   (C) 100
   (D) 90
   (E) 80

17. If the width of a rectangle is decreased by 10% and the length is increased by 20%, what is the percent change in the area of the rectangle?

   (A) A decrease of 30%
   (B) A decrease of 10%
   (C) A decrease of 8%
   (D) An increase of 8%
   (E) An increase of 10%

18. What was the original price of a kitchen appliance if a 20% discount reduced the price of the appliance to $100?

   (A) $80
   (B) $100
   (C) $120
   (D) $125
   (E) $150

19. If 45 percent of the customers who bought tickets to a certain performance of a drama were students, what was the ratio of the number of students who purchased tickets to the number of non-students who purchased tickets?

(A) $\dfrac{5}{9}$

(B) $\dfrac{9}{11}$

(C) $\dfrac{9}{10}$

(D) $\dfrac{11}{9}$

(E) $\dfrac{9}{5}$

20. The rate for a limousine service ride from a hotel to the airport in a car that can accommodate 4 passengers is $42 for one passenger plus x dollars for each additional passenger. If 3 people take the limousine service to the airport and each pays $26, what is the value of x?

(A) 3

(B) 4

(C) 9

(D) 12

(E) 18

Review

1. **(E)** Just test each answer choice until you find the one that is divisible by 6 and by 9.

2. **(C)** Test each of the Roman numeraled statements. The product of the numbers in statement I is –56 which is less than each of the three numbers in the set. The product of the numbers in statement II is 16 which is larger than $-\dfrac{1}{4}$ and larger than –4. The product of the numbers in statement III is $\dfrac{1}{24}$ which is smaller than each of the three numbers in the statement.

3. **(C)** You can just do the arithmetic here and test choices:

   $15 \times 16 \times 21 = 5040$

   And $5040 \div 15$ is 336, $5040 \div 35$ is 144, but $4725 \div 39$ is 129 with a remainder.

4. **(D)** Just test each choice, starting with (C). If there is a total of 62 coins, that would be 31 dimes and 31 quarters for $3.10 in dime and $7.75 in quarters and a total of $10.85. But that's less than the $11.90 specified in the stem. So you should try the next larger number to get more money. If there are 68 coints, that would be 34 dimes and 34 quarters for $3.40 in dimes and $8.50 in quarters, for a total of $11.90.

5. **(D)** You can probably solve this item using w for a variable, but "just in case," here's how to get the answer by testing choices. Start with (C). If $w = 12$, then the perimeter is $12 + 12 + 14 + 14 = 52$, which is more than 48. So w is less than 12. Try 10: $10 + 10 + 14 + 14 = 48$, so (D) is the correct answer.

19

6. **(B)** You could solve this item by reasoning than $13(7) + 2 = 93$ is the integer asked about. But you can reach the same result by testing choices, this time starting with (A) since the result will not depend upon the magnitude of n. $91 \div 13 = 7$ with no remainder. So (A) is incorrect, and you would next test (B). $93 \div 13$ is 7 with a remainder of 2, so (B) is correct.

7. **(D)** This is a fairly difficult Problem Solving item because it uses the square root of a decimal number less than one, a potentially confusing concept. So why not assume that $x = 1$. On that assumption, the expression in the stem has the value $\sqrt{0.36(1)^4}$ or 0.6. And now test choices. (A), (B), and (C) all produce the value 0.06 and are wrong. (D) and (E) produce the expected value. At this point you could simply guess and move along (depending on how you're doing with time) or try another number, say $x = 2$. On this second assumption, the expression in the question stem has the value 2.4. (D) produces the right value but (E) does not.

8. **(C)** Assume a value for x, say Dr. Gowda has 10 years of experience. Then Dr. Aman has 5 and Dr. Demeter 13; together, Drs. Aman and Demeter have 18 years of experience. When you substitute 10 for x into the choices, only (C) produces the expected result.

9. **(A)** Instead of trying to reason about the properties of numbers, you can just assign values to x and y, say -2 for x and 1 for y. Then xy is -2, and only (A) correctly describes the value -2.

10. **(C)** Again, you can assign some values to x and y, say -2 for x and -1 for y. This shows that statements I and II are not always true. But statement III tests out as true.

11. **(C)** Just give x a value, say $x = 1$. On that assumption, y has the value 4. Next, substitute 4 for y into each choice to find the choice that returns the value 1.

12. **(D)** Assume a value for N, but watch out. If you choose 1, you'll wind up with 0 as the value of the expression in the stem and more than one seemingly correct choices. So you'd do better with a number like 5. On the assumption that $N = 5$, the expression in the stem has the value -16. Then substitute 5 for N into each of the choices until you get the expected value.

13. **(E)** Just pick a couple of values for m and n, say $m = -5$ and $n = -1$. On that assumption, there are 3 integers between m and n: -4, -3, and -2. Next, substitute -5 for m and -1 for n in the choices until you find the one that generates the value 3.

14. **(A)** Instead of reasoning about the properties of x and y, just assign them values, say $x = -1$ and $y = 3$. Then $xy = -3$, and that would be point P.

15. **(E)** Assign a value to d, but make it one that's easy to take $\frac{2}{3}$ of, say $d = 60$. On that assumption, the first day of the rental costs $60, and each additional day costs $40. So the total cost of the rental is $60 + (6 \times \$40) = \$300$. And when you substitute 60 for d into the answer choices, only (E) produces the value 300.

16. **(C)** Test choices starting with (C). If $P1$ has 100 students, then $P2$ has 40 students; and after the drops, $P1$ has 90 students and $P2$ has 30 students. Since 90 is 3 times 30, (C) is the correct answer.

17. **(D)** Just assume a value for the dimensions of the rectangle, something easy such as width of 10 and length of 10. On that assumption, the original area is 100. The new width is 9 and the new length is 12 for a new area of 108. And that is a percent increase of 8%.

18. **(D)** Test the choices, starting with (C). If the original price was $120, then a 20% discount would have a dollar value of $24, and the new selling price would be $96. That's wrong, and it means that our original assumption was too small. So test the next larger number. If the original price was $125, then a 20% discount would have a dollar value of $25, and the new, discounted price would be $100, as the stem specifies.

19. **(B)** This problem may look familiar to you: it appeared in Workshop A above. There you saw how to handle it as a common type. Now dispose of it by assuming a number for the purchasers, say 100. On that assumption, 45 students bought tickets and 55 non-students bought tickets. The ratio is $\frac{45}{55}$ or $\frac{9}{11}$.

20. **(E)** This problem too appears in Workshop A. Now test choices, starting with (C). If $x = 9$, then the cost of the ride should be $42 + 2(\$9) = \$60$; but we know the actual cost was $26 \times 3 = \$78$. So we should test the next larger number. If $x = 12$, then the cost of the ride would be $42 + 2(\$12) = \$66$. Again, too small. So we know the correct answer must be (E). Not sure? Test (E): $42 + 2(\$18) = \$78$.

19

Develop a Fail-Safe Plan for Emergencies

The Basic Technique for Problem Solving covers the majority of the items that the GRE has in its data base, and the Advanced Strategies can help you answer even when you're stumped by the math. Even so, you'll probably find that your going to have guess on some items. When you have to guess, you can maximize your chances of getting the right answer by following some guessing guidelines.

ACTION PLAN   **Fail-Safe Plan for Emergencies**

     1. Eliminate impossible choices and guess.

     2. Use estimates for the values of π and radicals.

     3. Rely on the figure as it is drawn.

First, when you have to guess, step back from the problem to get some perspective. Ask yourself what conclusions you can reach just using a little common sense. Then use those conclusions to eliminate choices. Here's an example:

QUESTION   Two teenagers were hired to shovel snow from a driveway for a total $27. In order to complete the job, one of them worked for 1 hour and 40 minutes and the other worked for 50 minutes. If they apportion the $27 according to the time each spent working on the job, how much should the person who worked for 1 hour and 40 minutes receive?

     (A) $13.00

     (B) $15.00

     (C) $18.00

     (D) $19.50

     (E) $21.00

ANALYSIS   The correct answer is (**C**). The two worked a total of 150 minutes, of which the one worker accounted for $\frac{100}{150} = \frac{2}{3}$ of the effort. And $\frac{2}{3}$ of $27 is $18. But let's assume that you weren't able to reach that conclusion. Just looking at the situation, you can see that one person worked considerably longer than the other, so they shouldn't split the money equally. That eliminates (A). And even (B) seems overly generous to the one who did less. This leaves you only (C), (D), and (E), and gives you a 1 out of 3 chance of answering correctly.

A second guessing strategy is to use approximate values in lieu of numbers like $\sqrt{2}$ and π. Here is an example:

QUESTION $\left(\sqrt{3}\right)-\left(\sqrt{2}\right)^{2} =$

(A) $1-3\sqrt{6}$

(B) $1-2\sqrt{6}$

(C) $5-2\sqrt{3}$

(D) $5-2\sqrt{6}$

(E) $5+2\sqrt{6}$

ANALYSIS The correct answer is (**D**):

$$\left(\sqrt{3}-\sqrt{2}\right)^{2} =$$

$$\left(\sqrt{3}-\sqrt{2}\right)\left(\sqrt{3}-\sqrt{2}\right) =$$

$$3-2\sqrt{6}+2 = 5-2\sqrt{6}$$

But let's assume that you couldn't remember the procedure for manipulating the radicals. You could approximate. $\sqrt{2}$ is about 1.4, and $\sqrt{3}$ is about 1.7. That makes the expression in the stem about $(1.7 - 1.4)^2 = (.3)^2 = 0.09$. Now look at the answer choices. (A) and (B) are both negative numbers, so they have to be wrong. (E) is greater than 5, so it too is wrong. This leaves (C) and (D). Can you advance the issue even further with this technique? Yes. (C) is about $5 - 2(1.7) = 1.6$, not very close to 0.09. (D) is 5 minus a larger number, so (D) is even closer to 0.09 and must be correct.

Finally, if you have a geometry problem with a figure and simply must guess, then go ahead and make your best estimate of the magnitude of the angle, line, or area asked about. Here is an example:

QUESTION In the figure above, the ratio of x to y is 4 to 5. What is the value of x?

(A) 4

(B) 5

(C) 20

(D) 80

(E) 100

ANALYSIS The correct answer is **(D)**. In order to find the magnitude of x, you need to divide 180 by 9, the number of ratio parts. Then $x = 4(20) = 80$ and $y = 5(20) = 100$. But let's assume that you just couldn't see your way to this solution and have to guess. Look at the figure. x seems to be a little less than a right angle, so (C) is the closest answer.

Guessing strategies are just that. Don't expect that they can substitute for a solid working knowledge of math. But, in a pinch, they're better than nothing.

Workshop C: Practice the Fail-Safe Plan

Use the 5 Problem Solving items below to practice the Fail-Safe methods outlined above. Don't use math to answer the questions, but do try to eliminate choices using the guidelines given above. Darken the appropriate oval. Then check your work against the explanations given in the Review portion of the workshop, below.

Drill

1. What is the distance between two points on a number line with coordinates $3 + \sqrt{3}$ and $2 - \sqrt{3}$?

    (A) 5
    (B) 1
    (C) $5 + \sqrt{3}$
    (D) $1 + 2\sqrt{3}$
    (E) $1 - 2\sqrt{3}$

2. Which of the following equals the ratio of $3\frac{1}{2}$ to $2\frac{1}{2}$?

    (A) 4 to 35
    (B) 5 to 7
    (C) 2 to 3
    (D) 7 to 5
    (E) 3 to 2

3. If 20 identical machines can produce x units in 6 minutes, how many fewer minutes would be required to produce the same number of units if 10 additional machines operating at the same speed are used?

    (A) 2
    (B) $2\frac{1}{3}$
    (C) $2\frac{1}{2}$
    (D) 3
    (E) $3\frac{1}{2}$

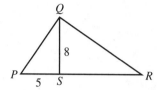

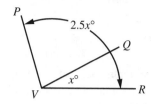

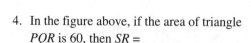

4. In the figure above, if the area of triangle
   PQR is 60, then *SR* =

   (A) 5
   (B) 8
   (C) 10
   (D) 12
   (E) 15

5. If $x = 30$, then angle *PVR* =

   (A) 75
   (B) 90
   (C) 100
   (D) 120
   (E) 150

Review

1. **(D)** You can find the distance between the two points by subtracting the coordinate of one point from that of the other. Let's assume that you couldn't remember how to work with radicals. You still know that $\sqrt{3}$ is about 1.7. So one point has a coordinate of about $3 + 1.7 = 4.7$, and the other a coordiante of about $2 - 1.7 = 0.3$. So the distance between the two points is about $4.7 - 0.3 = 4.4$. (A) is too large, and (B) is too small. (C) is way too large because it's more than 5, and (E) is way too small because its actually a negative number. So by the process of elimination, the correct choice must be (D); and, in fact, $1 + 2(1.7)$ is as close to 4.4 as you'd ever hope to get.

2. **(D)** Just by looking at the ratio, you know that the first element has to be larger than the second, so you can eliminate (A), (B), and (C). Then, you know that the ratio of $3\frac{1}{2}$ to $2\frac{1}{2}$ cannot be *exactly* 3 to 2, so (E) has to be wrong. That leaves only (D).

3. **(A)** Six machines in addition to the original 20 would reduce the time required substantially but not by as much as half, so (D) and (E) have to be wrong. (C) also looks a bit optimistic, so your best guess would be either (A) or (B).

4. **(C)** The figure shows that *PS* is 5 units long. So take a good look at *SR* and compare it to *PS*. It seems to be about twice as long, so the answer is probably (C). If you need to, take a piece of scratch

19

paper and measure *PS* and then
compare it to *SR*.

5. **(C)** Just estimate the size of angle
PVR. It looks larger than 90°, so
(A) and (B) must be wrong. And it
doesn't look as large as 120°, so
(D) and (E) must be wrong.

Get Answers to Frequently Asked Questions

Q: How long should I spend on an individual Problem Solving item?

A: About a minute and fifteen seconds—less on some, but more on others. By follow-ing this guideline, you'll spend about 15 minutes or so working on Problem Solving items in the math part. But you have to remember, they are not all presented sequentially (they're mixed in with QCs and graphs), so you won't have any way of keeping a running total of the time for an individual question type.

Q: Why do Problem Solving items seem difficult when I work them but easier when I read the explanations?

A: Problem Solving is not just a test of math but a test of math reasoning ability. So you may understand the math needed to answer a question but have trouble because you can't quite see how to apply what you know. That's one reason that you need the Advanced Strategies and the Fail-Safe Plan to make sure that you get your maximum score.

Q: Are there any Problem Solving kinds that I should hope that I don't get?

A: No. The test-writers have several different ways of adjusting the level of difficulty of items, so you can't conclude that one kind of problem is necessarily harder than another. In any case, as perverse as it sounds, you should really hope to see hard problems. That would mean that you're doing well. But don't place too much emphasis on your subjective impression about difficulty. The algorithm should be choosing items for you that are at the upper limit of your math ability—challenging but not outrageously difficult.

Q: Are Problem Solving geometry figures *always* inaccurate?

A: No. Many of them are accurately drawn. The problem is determining which are and which are not. Those that have the note "Drawn to Scale" are accurate, but those that don't have the note may or may not be accurate. The safest strategy is to answer geometry questions based on your knowledge of the principles of geometry, but you can use the figure to estimate if you have to guess.

Today's Review

1. Problem Solving items are as close to "pure math" as the GRE gets. If you have a good command of the basics, then you should be able to dispose of many items using the math techniques that you learned in school.

2. Many GRE Problem Solving items fall into one of six categories. When you recognize one, use the appropriate math technique to get your answer.

3. Your knowledge of math, as applied to the common types of Problem Solving items, is the basis on which you build your GRE math score for this part. The advanced strategies of testing choices and substituting numbers will boost your score beyond that limit.

4. Intelligent guessing is the icing on the cake. By eliminating choices that are not possible or that are less likely, you maxmize your chances of guessing the right response. And one or two extra points can help give you that top score you want.

19

Apply Your Action Plan to Problem Solving

Day

20

Today, you'll be using the Action Plan that you developed in Day 19. After a quick review of some important points, you'll revisit the Problem Solving items in the Math PreTest to see how the Action Plan would have helped you perform better. Then you'll have the opportunity to do timed exercises for further practice and to see the Action Plan applied to those items.

Review Your Action Plan

In Day 19, you learned that Problem Solving can be complicated by three added-difficulty factors: multiple math concepts, additional baggage, and unexpected question stems. Then you developed an Action Plan for Problem Solving items. The overall plan looks like this:

> **ACTION PLAN** **Step 1. The Basic Technique. Use familiar math techniques to solve the most common types of problems:**
>
> 1. **Problems about Operations**
> 2. **Problems about Approximations**
> 3. **Problems about Properties**
> 4. **Problems about Unknowns**
> 5. **Problems about Situations**
> 6. **Problems about Figures**

What You'll Do Today

- Review Your Action Plan
- Apply Your Action Plan to the PreTest
- Workshop A
- Workshop B
- Get Answers to Frequently Asked Questions

Step 2. Advanced Strategies

1. **Test Answer Choices**

2. **Substitute Numbers**

Step 3. Fail-Safe Plan for Emergencies

1. **Eliminate impossible choices and guess.**

2. **Use estimates for the values of π and radicals.**

3. **Rely on the figure as it is drawn.**

Now let's apply the integrated plan to the Problem Solving items from the PreTest.

Apply Your Action Plan to the PreTest

QUESTION $\dfrac{(13)(23) - (23)(7)}{13 - 7} =$

(A) 0

(B) 7

(C) 13

(D) 20

(E) 23

ANALYSIS The correct answer is (**E**). This is an operations problem. You can handle it with nothing more than multiplication, subtraction, and division; and while doing the actual manipulations is not the most elegant solution, it is effective:

$$\frac{(13)(23) - (23)(7)}{13 - 7} =$$

$$\frac{299 - 161}{6} = \frac{138}{6} = 23$$

But you could also save yourself some trouble by first simplifying the calculation:

$$\frac{(13)(23) - (23)(7)}{13 - 7} =$$

$$\frac{23(13 - 7)}{13 - 7} = 23$$

QUESTION A certain book sells for $15.00 in the bookstore, but the book can be purchased on-line for $12.00. An on-line purchaser saves what percent of the bookstore price of the book?

(A) 0.20%

(B) 0.25%

(C) 3%

(D) 20%

(E) 25%

ANALYSIS The correct answer is **(D)**. This is a problem about a situation, and the item can be done just with arithmetic; but you want to make sure that you answer the question that is asked:

Savings is what percent of price?

$$\frac{\$15.00 - \$12.00}{\$15.00} = \frac{15 - 12}{15} = \frac{3}{15} = \frac{1}{5} = 20\%.$$

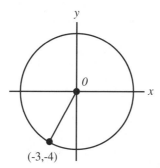

(-3,-4)

QUESTION If O is the center of the circle above, what is the circumference of the circle?

20

(A) 5π

(B) 7π

(C) 10π

(D) 25π

(E) 49π

ANALYSIS   **(C)** This is a problem about a figure, and it requires the use of two math concepts. First, you should use the Pythagrean Theorem to find the length of the
radius of the circle:

$$r^2 = (-3)^2 + (-4)^2$$
$$r^2 = 25$$
$$r = 5$$

And then you find the circumference of the circle:

$$C = 2\pi r$$
$$C = 2\pi(5)$$
$$C = 10\pi$$

If you found it necessary, you could have used the third fail-safe strategy and measure the
radius. You'd find it to be 5 units, or thereabouts. Then you would find the circumference
of the circle using 5 as the radius.

QUESTION   If 12 identical stamping machines require 20 hours to fill an order, how much
less time, in hours, will be required to fill the order if 4 additional stamping
machines are used?

(A) 5

(B) $9\dfrac{4}{5}$

(C) 10

(D) 15

(E) 18

ANALYSIS   **(A)** This is a problem about a situation, and it does contain some additional
baggage, but you can simplify things for yourself by assuming a number to make
the situation more concrete. Assume that the order is 240 units. That's a convenient
number because $12 — 20 = 240$. On that assumption, each machine produces one unit per
hour. When the four machines are added, the new production capacity will be $12 + 4 = 16$
units per hour, and the time required to process the order will be $240 \div 16 = 15$ hours. So
the time savings will be 20 hours – 15 hours = 5 hours. If you were absolutely stymied by
the item, you could use the fail-safe strategy of eliminating impossible choices. You would
reason that four machines in addition to the original 12 would not cut the time in half and
eliminate (C), (D), and (E). Furthermore, (B) seems to close to 10, which is half the
original time, so you'd want to eliminate it as well—leaving you only (A).

QUESTION The length of a rectangular room R is 1 meter longer than the side of square room S, and the width of room R is 1 meter shorter than the side of room S. If x^2 is the floor area of room S, what is the floor area, in square meters, of room R?

    (A) $x^2 - 2$

    (B) $x^2 - 1$

    (C) x^2

    (D) $x^2 + 1$

    (E) $x^2 + 2$

ANALYSIS **(B)** This is a problem about a situation, that is, a word problem. And you can solve it using algebra. But why bother? Instead, you can just cut to the chase and assign a value to the variable. Make it easy on yourself and use 100 for x^2. On that assumption, each side of the square is 10; the length of the rectangle is 11; and the width of the rectangle is 9. The area of the rectangle is $11 \times 9 = 99$. Substitute 100 for x^2 in the choices:

    (A) $x^2 - 2 = 100 - 2 = 98$ (Wrong.)

    (B) $x^2 - 1 = 100 - 1 = 99$ (Right.)

    (C) $x^2 = 100$ (Wrong.)

    (D) $x^2 + 1 = 100 + 1 = 101$ (Wrong.)

    (E) $x^2 + 2 = 100 + 2 = 102$ (Wrong.)

QUESTION At a certain company, 60 percent of the employees are women. If 20 percent of the women and 15 percent of the men hold MBAs, what percent of the total number of employees hold MBAs?

    (A) 6

    (B) 9

    (C) 12

    (D) 15

    (E) 18

20

ANALYSIS **(E)** This is a situation problem, and you could solve it by using algebra. But again, you could also just cut to the chase: pick a number for the total employed by the company. Again, 100 seems like a possibility. The problem says that 60% of the 100 employees or 60 people are women and that 20 percent of those or 12 people hold an MBA. Then, there are 40 men, of whom 15 percent or 6 hold an MBA. So the total number of MBAs is 18, and $\frac{18}{100} = 18\%$. N.B.: If you use a number like 10 for this problem, you wind up with fraction of people like 1.2 women with an MBA. That's somewhat counterintuitive, but it won't make any difference in the outcome.

QUESTION If a triangle in the coordinate plan has vertices of (–2,2), (4,4), and (0,0), what is the perimeter of the triangle?

(A) $2 + 6\sqrt{2}$

(B) $2 + 6\sqrt{10}$

(C) $4 + 2\sqrt{10}$

(D) $4\sqrt{2} + 6\sqrt{10}$

(E) $6\sqrt{2} + 2\sqrt{10}$

ANALYSIS **(E)** This is a problem about a figure—even though the figure itself doesn't appear. You can get the right answer by using the Distance Formula or the Pythagorean Theorem. You could also draw the figure on a piece of scratch paper. And if you draw it, then you know it's to scale. Now, use one of the fail-safe strategies: measure. The shortest side seems to be about 1.5; the next longer side about 8.5; and the longest side about 6⁺. So the perimeter looks to be about 15⁺. Now use another fail-safe strategy and estimate the choices:

(A) $2 + 6\sqrt{2}$ or about 2 + 6(1.4) or 10.4

(B) $2 + 6\sqrt{10}$ or about 2 + 18⁺ or 20

(C) $4 + 2\sqrt{10}$ or about 4 + 6⁺ or 10⁺

(D) $4\sqrt{2} + 6\sqrt{10}$ or about 5.6 + 9⁺ is 15 or so

(E) $6\sqrt{2} + 2\sqrt{10}$ or about 8.4 + 6+ is 15 or so

So the correct answer seems to be either (D) or (E), and you can make your guess. (You can't expect greater precision from a guessing strategy.)

QUESTION If a solid right circular cylinder of diameter 4 and height of 5 inches is placed into a rectangular box that is 3 inches by 3 inches by 5 inches, the volume of the box that is not occupied by the cylinder is how many cubic inches?

(A) 45 – 20pi

(B) 45 – 16pi

(C) 15 – 5 pi

(D) 20pi – 30

(E) 16pi – 45

ANALYSIS **(A)** This is a geometry problem involving a composite figure—with a twist. In this case, the composite figure is three-dimensional. The volume of the box not occupied by the cylinder is:

Volume of Cylinder – Volume of Box

$45 - 20\pi$

QUESTION If x and y are different positive integers, then the ratio of $\frac{x}{y}$ to its reciprocal is

(A) $\dfrac{y^2}{x^2}$

(B) $\dfrac{x^2}{y^2}$

(C) $\dfrac{x}{y}$

(D) $\dfrac{y}{x}$

(E) 1

ANALYSIS **(B)** This problem belongs to the common type of algebra-based items, but you can solve it using an advanced strategy: assume some numbers. Let $x = 3$ and $y = 2$. On that assumption, $\frac{x}{y}$ has the value $\frac{3}{2}$; its reciprocal is $\frac{2}{3}$; and the ratio $\frac{x}{y}$ to $\frac{y}{x}$ is $\frac{\frac{3}{2}}{\frac{2}{3}} = \frac{9}{4}$. Now plug numbers into the choices:

(A) $\dfrac{y^2}{x^2} = \dfrac{4}{9}$ (Wrong.)

(B) $\dfrac{x^2}{y^2} = \dfrac{9}{4}$ (Right.)

(C) $\dfrac{x}{y} = \dfrac{3}{2}$ (Wrong.)

(D) $\dfrac{y}{x} = \dfrac{2}{3}$ (Wrong.)

(E) 1 (Wrong.)

20

QUESTION Which of the following is the graph of all x values such that $x \geq 1$ and $-x \leq -2$?

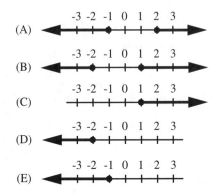

ANALYSIS **(C)** This item doesn't seem to fit neatly into any of the common type categories, but you can solve it using an advanced strategy: test the answer choices. Choices (A), (B), (D), and (E) all indicate that x can be 5, but 5 does not fit either condition of the stem. So the correct answer must be (C).

Workshop A

This workshop consists of drill and review. The drill has a time limit, but you should spend as much time as you need on the evaluation and review portions of the workshop.

Drill

This drill consists of 10 Problem Solving items. The time limit is 15 minutes. This reflects the general strategy of spending *on average* no more than a minute and 15 seconds per item.

10 Questions • Time—15 Minutes

1. If $3x - 6 = 30$, then $x =$
   (A) 12
   (B) 8
   (C) 6
   (D) 5
   (E) 4

2. The price of a certain stock increased by $12 per share, then decreased by $4 per share, and then increased by $3 per share. If the price of the stock before the changes was x dollars, which of the following was the price, in dollars, after the changes?
   (A) $x + 11$
   (B) $x + 9$
   (C) $x + 8$
   (D) $x + 5$
   (E) $x - 7$

3. A consumer purchases a computer for a price that is 20% off the list price of $930. If the consumer also received a $50 rebate from the manufacturer of the computer, what is the final cost of the computer after the discount and the rebate?
   (A) $744
   (B) $704
   (C) $694
   (D) $654
   (E) $632

4. If $3x + 2 = 11$, and $y = x^3$, then $y =$
   (A) 1
   (B) 3
   (C) 6
   (D) 9
   (E) 27

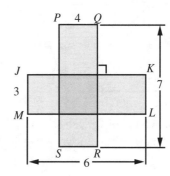

5. In the figure above, rectangle PQRS overlaps rectangle JKLM. What is the area of the shaded region?
   (A) 10
   (B) 12
   (C) 28
   (D) 34
   (E) 46

6. The cost to send an international letter is 75 cents for the first ounce and 50 cents for each additional ounce. If z is an integer greater than 1, what is the cost in *dollars* for a letter weighing z ounces?
   (A) $\dfrac{5z}{4}$
   (B) $\dfrac{2z + 1}{4}$
   (C) $z + 2$
   (D) $\dfrac{z - 1}{4}$
   (E) $\dfrac{2z - 1}{4}$

20

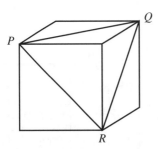

7. The volume of the cube shown above is 27. What is the perimeter of triangle PQR?

(A) $3\sqrt{3}$

(B) 9

(C) $9\sqrt{3}$

(D) 27

(E) $27\sqrt{3}$

8. What is the least prime number greater than 73?

(A) 74

(B) 77

(C) 79

(D) 83

(E) 87

9. The roots of the equation $x^2 - 5x + 6 = 0$ are

(A) 2 and 3

(B) −2 and 3

(C) 2 and −3

(D) −2 and −3

(E) none of the above

10. If $y \neq 0$ and $c = \frac{xy}{3} + z$, then what is x in terms of c, y, and z?

(A) $\dfrac{3c + z}{y}$

(B) $\dfrac{3(c + z)}{y}$

(C) $\dfrac{3c - z}{y}$

(D) $\dfrac{3(c - z)}{y}$

(E) $\dfrac{3(c - 2z)}{y}$

Review

Use the following answer key, and compare your performance to the graph below. Then review your performance by studying the explanations that follow.

1. (A)

2. (A)

3. (C)

4. (E)

5. (D)

6. (B)

7. (C)

8. (D)

9. (A)

10. (D)

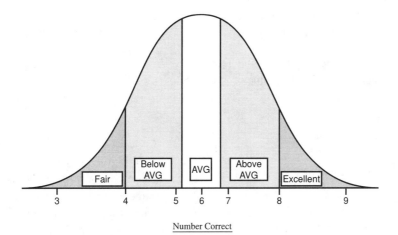

Number Correct

1. **(A)** This is a common question type: one equation with one unknown. So just solve for x:

$$3x - 6 = 30$$
$$3x = 36$$
$$x = 12$$

You could also test answer choices by substituting the value given in each choice for x in the equation in the stem. For example, you would use 12 to test choice (A):

$$3(12) - 6 = 30$$
$$36 - 6 = 30$$
$$30 = 30$$

So (A) is correct. You should remember, however, that the advanced strategies are for use on more difficult problems. The best approach to a simple problem like this is the conventional one you learned in school.

2. **(A)** Here you have another simple problem involving algebra, so you should set up the manipulation indicated in the question stem:

$$x + 12 - 4 + 3 = x + 11$$

Again, you could, if you choose to do so, use an advanced strategy. Assume that $x = 0$, an arbitrary and unrealistic assumption but perfectly okay for doing math. On that assumption, the price goes from 0 to \$12 per share, then down to \$8 per share, then back up to \$11 per share. And when you substitute 0 for x, only (A) gives you the value 11. But again, the advanced strategies usually take longer than the conventional math, so you should save them for those items when you really do need them.

3. **(C)** The is a common manipulation problem, and there is no better approach than just doing the arithmetic indicated. A 20% discount from the price of \$930 leaves the

20

price at 80% of $930 or $744. Then a $50 rebate reduces the price to $694.

4. **(E)** Here you have another simple algebra problem. First, find the value of x:

$$3x + 2 = 11$$

$$3x = 9$$

$$x = 3$$

Then find the value of y:

$$y = (3)^3 = 27$$

5. **(D)** This item belongs to the basic category of problems about figures, and it uses a composite figure built from two rectangles. The shaded area of the entire figure is the sum of the areas of the two rectangles less the overlap:

Area of *PQRS* + Area of *JKLM* – Overlap =

$$(4 \times 7) + (3 \times 6) - (3 \times 4) = 34$$

6. **(B)** This item belongs to the basic category of problems using algebra. And you can create the formula needed to answer the question as follows:

$\frac{3}{4}$ dollar for first ounce plus $\frac{1}{2}$ dollar for each additional ounce

And since z designates the number of ounces the package weighs:

$$\tfrac{3}{4} + \tfrac{1}{2}(z \, 1)$$

(Remember, the first ounce is already included in the 75 cents, so your second term is for *additional* ounces.)

$$\frac{3}{4} + \frac{z-1}{2} = \frac{3}{4} + \frac{z}{2} - \frac{1}{2} = \frac{1}{4}$$

$$+ \frac{z}{2} = \frac{1}{4} + \frac{2z}{4} = \frac{1+2z}{4} =$$

$$\frac{2z+1}{4}$$

Creating a formula like this can be tricky, even if you know what you're doing because you have to get the formula in the same form as the correct answer. The advanced strategy of assuming a value for a variable is a good back-up plan for problems like this. Let $z = 2$. On that assumption, the cost to send the package would be 75 cents plus 50 cents or 1.25 dollars. Now substitute 2 for z into the choices:

(A) $\dfrac{5z}{4} = \dfrac{10}{4} = 2.5$ (Wrong.)

(B) $\dfrac{2z+1}{4} = \dfrac{2(2)+1}{4} = 1.25$
(Correct.)

(C) $z + 2 = (2 + 2) = 4$ (Wrong.)

(D) $\dfrac{z-1}{4} = \dfrac{2-1}{4} = 1.75$
(Wrong.)

(E) $\dfrac{2z-1}{4} = \dfrac{2(2)-1}{4} = 1$
(Wrong.)

7. **(C)** This is a three-dimensional variation on the composite figure theme. Each side of triangle *PQR* is also a diagonal of the face of the cube. So we first find the length of the edge of the cube:

$$edge^3 = 27$$

$$edge = 3$$

Next, we use the Pythagorean Theorem to find the length of the diagonal of the face:

$$d^2 = (3)^2 + (3)^2$$

$$d = \sqrt{18} = 3\sqrt{2}$$

So the perimeter of triangle PQR is $3 \times 3\sqrt{2} = 9\sqrt{2}$

Is there any other way to go? Although this is a three-dimensional figure, the front face of the cube is drawn to scale, so you can compare the diagonal to the known length of the edge of the cube which is 3. The diagonal appears to be about 5 and change, so the perimeter of the triangle is 15 or maybe 16. That pretty much eliminates every choice but (C).

8. **(D)** This is a problem about the properties of numbers. Just examine each choice until you find the first prime, and that is 83.

9. **(A)** You can solve this algebra problem by factoring:

$$x^2 - 5x + 6 =$$

$$(x - 3)(x - 2)$$

$$x = 3 \text{ or } x = 2$$

If you "blank" when it comes to factoring, this would be a good time to use the advanced strategy of testing choices, starting with (A). Plug 2 and 3 into the equation for x, and you'll find that both work. So those are the two possible solutions for this equation.

10. **(D)** This is a fairly difficulty algebra problem:

$$c = \frac{xy}{3} + z$$

$$c - z = \frac{xy}{3}$$

$$3(c - z) = xy$$

$$x = \frac{3(c - z)}{y}$$

This would also be an appropriate time to use the advanced strategy of choosing a value for unknowns, say $x = 1$, $y = 1$, and $z = 1$. On that assumption:

$$c = \frac{(1)(1)}{3} + 1 = \frac{4}{3}$$

So you would use 1 for both y and z and $\frac{4}{3}$ for c in the answer choices, and the correct answer will return the value 1 for x:

(A) $\quad \dfrac{3c + z}{y} = \dfrac{3\left(\dfrac{4}{3}\right) + 1}{1} = 5$

(Wrong.)

(B) $\quad \dfrac{3(c + z)}{y} = \dfrac{3\left(\dfrac{4}{3}\right) + 1}{1} = 7$

(Wrong.)

(C) $\quad \dfrac{3(c - z)}{y} = \dfrac{3\left(\dfrac{4}{3}\right) - 1}{1} = 3$

(Wrong.)

20

(D) $\dfrac{3(c-z)}{y} = \dfrac{3\left(\frac{4}{3}\right) - 1}{1} = 1$

(Correct.)

(E) $\dfrac{3(c-2z)}{y} = \dfrac{3\left(\frac{4}{3}\right) - 2(1)}{1}$

$= 2$ (Wrong.)

Workshop B

This workshop consists of drill and review. The drill has a time limit, but you should spend as much time as you need on the evaluation and review portions of the workshop.

Drill

This drill consists of 10 Problem Solving items. The time limit is 15 minutes. This reflects the general strategy of spending *on average* no more than a minute and 15 seconds per item. Indicate your response by darkening the appropriate oval.

10 Questions • Time—15 Minutes

1. $\dfrac{6.082}{0.76}$ is most nearly equal to

   (A) 0.08

   (B) 0.8

   (C) 8

   (D) 80

   (E) 800

2. If $3 \times 8 = n \times 12 \times 2$, then $n =$

   (A) 12

   (B) 8

   (C) 6

   (D) 4

   (E) 1

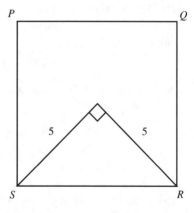

3. What is the figure area of square region *PQRS* in the figure above?

   (A) $25\sqrt{2}$

   (B) $20\sqrt{2}$

   (C) 50

   (D) 80

   (E) 100

4. $\left| -3 \right| + \left| 5 \right| + \left| -5 + 3 \right| =$

   (A) 0
   (B) 3
   (C) 5
   (D) 8
   (E) 10

5. Which of the following is greater than 1?

   (A) $\dfrac{0.00025}{0.000025}$

   (B) $\dfrac{0.006}{0.03}$

   (C) $\dfrac{0.0001}{0.00001}$

   (D) $\dfrac{0.0075}{0.00025}$

   (E) $\dfrac{0.05}{0.5}$

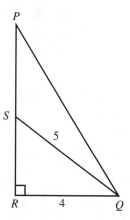

6. In the figure above, the area of triangular region PQR is 12. What is the area of triangular region PQS?

   (A) 3
   (B) 6
   (C) 9
   (D) 12
   (E) 15

7. The ratio of $\left(\dfrac{1}{2} \right)^4$ to $\left(\dfrac{1}{2} \right)^3$ is

   (A) $\dfrac{2}{1}$

   (B) $\dfrac{3}{2}$

   (C) $\dfrac{3}{4}$

   (D) $\dfrac{1}{2}$

   (E) $\dfrac{1}{4}$

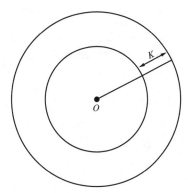

8. The circles above both have center O. If the area of the smaller circle is 36π and the area of the larger circle is 81π, then $k =$

   (A) 3
   (B) 4
   (C) 6
   (D) 12
   (E) 45

20

9. $\left(\dfrac{x}{x-1}+1\right)-\dfrac{x+1}{x-1}=$

(A) 2

(B) 0

(C) $x-2$

(D) $\dfrac{x+2}{x+1}$

(E) $\dfrac{x-2}{x-1}$

10. A government grant was distributed in such a way that Foundation J received $\frac{1}{3}$ of the money and Foundations K, L, and M each shared equally the balance. If Foundation J and Foundation K received a total of $100,000, what was the total amount of the grant?

(A) $180,000
(B) $165,000
(C) $153,000
(D) $137,000
(E) $125,000

Review

Use the following answer key, and compare your performance to the graph below. Then review your performance by studying the explanations that follow.

1. (C)   5. (D)   8. (A)
2. (E)   6. (B)   9. (E)
3. (C)   7. (D)   10. (A)
4. (E)

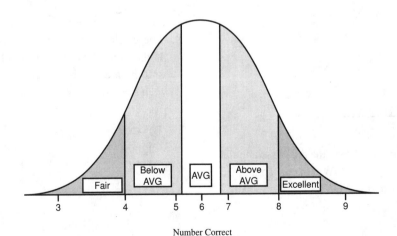

Number Correct

1. **(C)** This item falls into the basic category of approximation. The answer choices tell you that you really only need to keep track of the decimal point, and 0.7 goes into 6 about 8 times.

2. **(E)** This is a simple algebra-based problem, so just solve for n:
$$3 \times 8 = n \times 12 \times 2$$
$$24 = n \times 24$$
$$n = 1$$

3. **(C)** Here you have a problem that falls into that last category of basic problems that you studied, and it involves a composite figure: the hypotenuse of the right triangle is also the side of the square. So find the length of the hypotenuse:
$$h^2 = (5)^2 + (5)^2$$
$$h = \sqrt{50} = 5\sqrt{2}$$

And now find the area of the square:
$$5\sqrt{2} \times 5\sqrt{2} = 25 \times 2 = 50$$

4. **(E)** This is a simple manipulation problem:
$$|-3| + |5| + |-5 + 3| =$$
$$3 + 5 + |-2| = 3 + 5 + 2 = 10$$

5. **(D)** Here is an approximation problem. The stem tells you what to look for: only one of the choices is greater than 1. And that choice must be the one in which the numerator is greater than the denominator.

6. **(B)** This is a composite figure problem. First, you can find the length of PR, which happens to be the altitude of triangle PQR:

$$\frac{1}{2} \times PR \times 4 = 12$$
$$PR = 6$$

And you can find the length of SR using the Pythagorean Theorem. You can set up an equation, or, better, just notice that RSQ is a 3–4–5 triangle. So $SR = 3$. That means that $SP = 3$. Now you can use SP as a base and RQ as an altitude for triangle PQS:

$$Area = \frac{1}{2} \times 3 \times 4 = 6$$

(You might need to imagine the figure rotated 90° in a counter-clockwise direction in order to see that SP is a base and RQ an altitude of PQS.

7. **(D)** The arithmetic required here is manageable, so the best approach is probably just to do it:

$$\frac{\left(\frac{1}{2}\right)^4}{\left(\frac{1}{2}\right)^3} = \frac{\left(\frac{1}{16}\right)}{\left(\frac{1}{8}\right)} = \frac{8}{16} = \frac{1}{2}$$

And if you get lost in all of that? Use the fail-safe plan. Since these are fractions, the first element of the ratio is smaller than the second, and that means that when put into fraction form, the numerator of the fraction will be smaller than the denominator. That allows you to eliminate (A), (B), and (C) without doing any arithmetic.

20

8. **(A)** This is a geometry-based problem. The larger circle must have a radius of 9 and the smaller circle a radius of 6. So $k = 3$.

9. **(E)** This is one of those algebra problems that can cause trouble because you have to make sure that your manipulation produces the same form of the data as the answer choice:

$$\left(\frac{x}{x-1} + 1\right) - \frac{x+1}{x-1} =$$

$$1 + \frac{x}{x-1} - \frac{x+1}{x-1} =$$

$$1 + \frac{x - x - 1}{x - 1} =$$

$$1 + \frac{-1}{x-1} =$$

$$\frac{x - 1 - 1}{x - 1} = \frac{x - 2}{x - 1}$$

That's a lot of work. You might prefer the advanced strategy of assuming a value for x, say $x = 3$:

$$\left(\frac{x}{x-1} + 1\right) - \frac{x+1}{x-1} =$$

$$\left(\frac{3}{3-1} + 1\right) - \frac{3+1}{3-1} = \frac{1}{2}$$

(A)   2 (Wrong.)

(B)   0 (Wrong.)

(C) $x - 2 = 3 - 2 = 1$ (Wrong.)

(D) $\frac{x+2}{x+1} = \frac{3+2}{3+1} = \frac{5}{4}$
(Wrong.)

(E) $\frac{x-2}{x-1} = \frac{3-2}{3-1} = \frac{1}{2}$
(Correct.)

10. **(A)** Here you have a situation problem with a good bit of additional baggage. You can solve the problem this way:

$$J + K = \frac{1}{3}T + \left(\frac{1}{3} \times \frac{2}{3}T\right) = 100{,}000$$

$$\frac{1}{3}T + \frac{2}{9}T = 100{,}000$$

$$\frac{5}{9}T = 100{,}000$$

$$T = 180{,}000$$

Or you could use the advanced strategy of testing answer choices, starting with (C). If the grant total was $153,000 that would mean that J got $51,000 and K got $\frac{1}{3}$ of the remaining $102,000 or $34,000. So together J and K would have received $85,000. But that's less than the $100,000 stipulated by the stem. So (C) is wrong, and you need a larger answer choice.

Now look at (A) and (B). Which had you rather work with? Given that you know its one or the other of those two, it doesn't matter which you test, and (A) just looks a little easier to work with. If the grant was $180,000, then J got $60,000 and K got $\frac{1}{3}$ of $120,000 or $40,000 and that does make $100,000. So (A) is correct.

Get Answers to Frequently Asked Questions

Q: **I sometimes find I need more time on a Problem Solving item than a minute and fifteen seconds. What should I do?**

A: It won't hurt if you run over every now and again, so long as you can make up the lost time on another problem. Just remember, however, that you need to finish all the problems in the section (even if you have to guess). Also, if you are good at the mechanics of the computer testing (mousing the answer, confirming, etc.), then you can make up some time there.

Q: **If I know how to do the basic math, should I try one of the advanced strategies anyway?**

A: Not unless you're pretty sure the basic math is going to take too long. The way the Action Plan is structured, the basic technique is supposed to dispose of most of the items because this is largely a test of math. The advanced strategies are really alternative approaches to be used when you can't do the regular math.

Q: **Are the guessing guideliness really that big a deal?**

A: Yes and no. No, they're not a first-line strategy, and you can't expect for them to substitute for a good working knowledge of math. On the other hand, when you have to guess, the fail-safe plan is all that you've got to help you, so it becomes *all* important—by default. Use it.

Q: **The distinction between when to use the figure and when not to use the figure is a little confusing. What's a simple rule to remember?**

A: Don't trust the figures—unless you absolutely have no other choice. When you reach the point at which you have no other choice, you are guessing, so you can't hurt yourself by guessing using the figure.

20

Teach Yourself Graph Problems

Today, you'll teach yourself how to solve GRE graph problems. Graph problems are multiple-choice math questions that are based upon data presented in graphic form.

Get All the Inside Info on GRE Graphs

Graph problems are math questions that require you to use arithmetic and sometimes algebra to answer questions using data presented in graphic form. In fact, the only significant difference between graph problems and word problems is the use of the graphs to present the data that you need to answer the questions.

Psychologically, the most important thing that you have to learn about GRE graphs is to ignore the illusion of difficulty. In this respect, graphs are a lot like the Reading Comprehension in the verbal part: smoke and mirrors. Once you've learned how the illusion is created, you'll be less likely to be dazzled by its effect and better able just to answer the question asked.

GRE graphics are intentionally created to be imposing. If the GRE used graphs taken from a weekly news magazine or a daily paper, then the fear factor associated with GRE graphs would largely disappear. What helps to make GRE graphs so intimidating is the very fact that they lack those user-friendly features of the front-page feature of *USA Today*. GRE graphs aren't in full color; they don't have those nifty 3-D and other enhancements; they aren't supported by a text article; and they carry a lot of excess baggage in the form of data irrelevant to the two or three questions that you'll be asked.

Here's how things work. This is a simple graph dedicated to one notion:

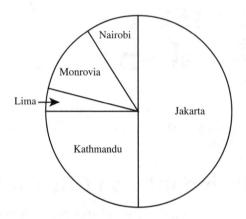

Destination of Shipment of
Widget Production of Factory F
(Projected 2025)

Questions based on this one graph would have to be simple and to the point. For example:

QUESTION What proportion of the widgets are projected to be shipped to Jakarta in 2025?

(A) 6.25%

(B) 12.5%

(C) 25%

(D) 37.5%

(E) 50%

ANALYSIS And the correct answer is **(E)** because that slice is about $\frac{1}{2}$ of the whole pie. In order to give you a more difficult question, the GRE would have to give you more data:

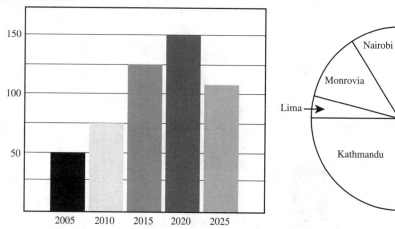

Widget Production of Factory F
(Projected 2005 - 2025)

Now it's possible to ask:

QUESTION For the year 2025, it is projected that how many more widgets will be shipped to Jakarta than to Kathmandu?

(A) 250,000

(B) 125,000

(C) 75,000

(D) 25,000

(E) 5,000

ANALYSIS The correct answer is **(D)**, but you have to look at two slices of the pie (Jakarta and Kathmandu) plus the projected total for 2025.

And if the test-writer wanted to give you a really difficult question, even more data would have to be incorporated into the graphic presentation:

21

Widget Production of Factory F
(Projected 2005 - 2025)

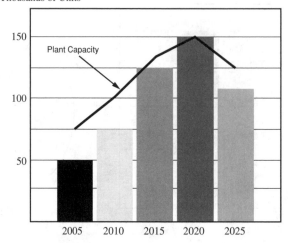

Thousands of Units

Now it's possible to answer some really complicated questions such as:

QUESTION If the projected distribution pattern of widgets for 2015 is the same as that for 2025, and the actual total of widgets produced in that year is equal to 125% of the projected factory capacity, how many more widgets will be shipped to o Nairobi than to Lima in 2015?

But we don't have to go there. The question is too complicated even for the GRE. It does, however, illustrate a very important point: the most complicated, difficult GRE graph question is really just a concatenation of much simpler questions.

Put another way, there are no hard graph questions on the GRE. The hardest question is just several easy questions rolled up into one large mess of a question that takes time to sort out. The most important thing that you can teach yourself about GRE graphs questions is how to wade through the data as quickly as possible, and that is what this lesson is about.

There are no hard graph questions. The most complex graph question is really just several simple questions strung together. Answer all the simple questions, and you have the answer to the complex one.

Here is your Action Plan for graphs:

 Step 1: Read the Graph

Step 2: Analyze the Question.

Step 3: Look for Short-Cuts.

We'll go over each of the three steps in detail.

Learn to Read the Most Commonly Used GRE Graphs

The first step of your Action Plan is to read the graph. And there is no getting around this requirement. You'll have to invest some time reading the graph before you can even begin to answer a question, and then you may only have two questions on that graph. So the minimum investment of time required to get one question right of this sort may be as much as three minutes.

The return on your investment of time is so meager that you can't afford to spend any more time than absolutely necessary before you cash in with an answer choice. So the main objective of this step is to learn about the common patterns so that you'll be able to process information as quickly as possible.

The GRE uses five common types of graphs. They are:

1. Table
2. Bar Graph
3. Cumulative Bar Graph
4. Line Graph
5. Pie Chart

Each type has special characteristics, and we'll discuss each in turn.

 NOTE

> Tables and pie charts are not, technically speaking, graphs, but we'll talk about them as though they were. That way we can say "graphs" instead of "tables, graphs, and charts"

21

1. Table

As the name implies, a table presents data in the form of rows and columns. Here is an example:

Purchase of Residential
Fire Protection Equipment

(value in millions of dollars)

Region	1991	1992	1993	1994	1995
United States	1,926	2,013	2,334	2,765	3,109
Western Europe	1,507	1,822	2,002	2,209	2,813
Pacific Rim	1,022	1,233	1,448	1,548	1,999
Latin America	936	1,051	1,109	1,278	1,560
Other Regions	722	801	855	942	1,088
Total	6,113	6,920	7,748	8,742	10,569

And here is how to "read" the table. The data needed to answer questions are located by referencing column and row, and there is no great mystery to that. You've been reading tables since you first looked up the start time for your favorite television show in the newspaper when you were 4 or 5 years old.

The descriptive information is always very important. In this case, the title tells you what the various values represent, and there is an important note: millions of dollars. So the value of residential fire protection equipment purchased in the United States in 1991 was not $1,926 but $1,926 million or $1,926,000,000, which is $1.926 billion.

NOTE

GRE graphs typically use at least five categories for its key measures, e.g., five or more consecutive years, five or more countries of origin or destination, five or more ingredients. Why? For the simple reason that the questions must have five answer choices. So the graph is built to support the GRE question format.

2. Bar Graph

A bar graph is easy to identify because it uses unbroken bars. The most important feature of a bar graph is that distance (from the base line to the top of the bar) represents magnitude. Here is an example:

DAIRY FARMING IN COUNTY K

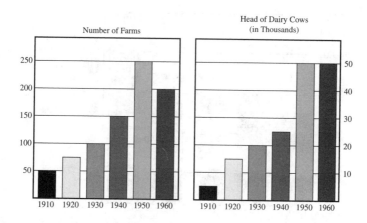

Here you have two related bar graphs. In each, the magnitude of a reading is represented by the length of the bar. For example, the number of dairy farms in County K in 1910 was 50, and you can read the value "50" from the scale immediately to the left of the bar. But what gives the bar the value 50 is the length of the bar: it runs from the base line (or zero) to the value of 50 on the scale. Similarly, the number of farms in 1950 was 250, and the bar for 1950 is 250 units long, running from the base line (zero) to 250 on the scale.

The graph on the right is also a bar graph and is read in the same way, but notice the additional information provided by the title of that graph: in thousands. So the total head count in 1960 was not 50 but 50,000,

NOTE

> The bars in a graph do not necessarily have to be oriented vertically. They can be oriented horizontally with the base line on the left or the right. The base line could even run vertically down the center of the page with bars extended to both the left and right to show something like "profit" and "loss."

21

3. Cumulative Bar Graph

The cumulative bar graph may be trickiest of the five common types. Here is an example:

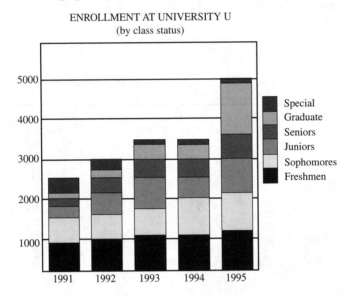

ENROLLMENT AT UNIVERSITY U
(by class status)

The key feature of the cumulative bar graph is that only the bottom component and the total are read from the base line. All other components are read from the top of the component immediately below to the bottom of the component immediately above (or the top of the bar in the case of the topmost component). So in this graph, the number of freshman can be read directly from the scale: 900 or so in 1991, 1,000 in 1992, and so on. And the total enrollment at University U can be read from the scale: 2,500 or so in 1991 and 3,000 in 1992. But you *cannot* read the value of the other components directly from the scale. The number of sophomores in 1991 was about 600 (1,500 – 900) *not* 1,500; and the number of special status students in 1995 was about 100, *not* 5,000.

 CAUTION

> Wrong answer choices often correspond to mistakes commonly made in reading a graph. With a cumulative bar graph, wrong answers can make the mistake of attempting a reading directly from the scale rather than correctly finding the length of that component of the bar.

4. Line Graph

A line graph is similar to a bar graph in that value is determined by the distance from the base line to the intersection of the line and the scale reading. Here is an example:

Marriage and Dissolution
(1998)

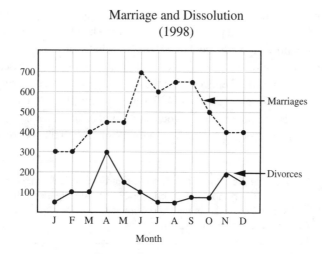

There are two measurements displayed on this graph, marriages and divorces; but each
line is independent of the other. For example, the number of marriages in June was 700
and in December 400. The number of divorces in February was 100 and in November 200.

CAUTION

Occasionally, a line graph will show a "break" in the scale. This is done to
conserve space and only when no values fall into the deleted part.

5. Pie Chart

A pie chart is easy to recognize and so named because the division of the circle into
sectors resembles a pie cut into pieces. Here is an example:

Composition of Timber Tract

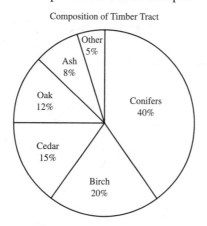

T = 4.2 million board feet

21

In a pie chart, the size of the sector represents value, and usually a value is attached to each sector. Additionally, a pie chart, without supplemental information, does not give a real value, as opposed to a percent or a share. For that, you need to know the total value represented by the pie, and this is often given in a note. So in this case, the percentages are given and you could, if asked, compare those directly, e.g, there is twice as much timber (measured in board-feet) in conifers (40%) as in birch (20%). And because you have the "T" or total given for the entire pie, you can calculate values for each sector, e.g, the number of board-feet of cedar is 15% of 4.2 million or 630,000 board-feet.

 CAUTION

> A single pie chart can only show one time period, e.g, year, or one source, e.g., country. So when a graph includes multiple elements such as a bar graph and a pie chart, the pie chart applies to only one of the bars in the graph—not to all of them.

You've reviewed the five most common graphs used by the GRE, now it's time to practice what you've learned.

Workshop A: Most Commonly Used GRE Graphs

This workshop consists of five graphs, each represents one of the common types. Following each graph is a series of questions. The questions are not multiple-choice; those come later in this lesson. There is no time limit for this exercise.

Drill

Below are five graphs followed by a series of questions. The questions are not multiple-choice. Instead, enter your answers in the spaces provided. Then compare your thinking to the explanations given in the Review portion of this drill.

Population of Five Communities
By Age (in years)

	0 -5	6 - 12	13 - 18	19 - 25	25+
Allenburg	2,476	2,104	2,003	1,987	8,976
Briarcliff	8,442	10,993	9,476	9,882	42,172
Cliffwood	5,002	4,998	5,127	6,101	31,272
Dreamville	3,427	3,427	3,109	5,885	23,976
Eagleston	1,004	998	972	1,804	6,432

1. What kind of a graph is this?

2. What is the total population of Allenburg?

3. What is the total population of Eagleston?

4. What is the total population 5 or under in the five communities combined?

Gross Revenues: Select Retailers

Hundreds of
Thousands of Dollars

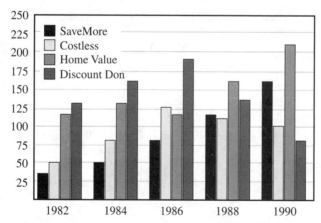

5. What kind of a graph is this?

6. What were gross revenues of Discount Don in 1984?

7. What were total gross revenues for all four retailers in 1990?

8. What were total gross revenues for Home Value for the five years shown?

21

Employment by Category Region R
(by sector)

Thousands of Workers

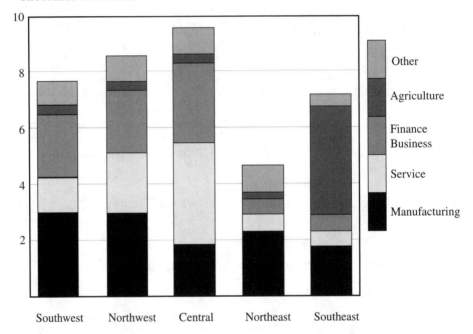

9. What kind of a graph is this?

10. How many people are employed in the Southwest sector of R in Manufacturing?

11. How many people total are employed in Central R?

12. How many people in the Northwest sector of R are employed in Service?

Vehicle Registrations in County X

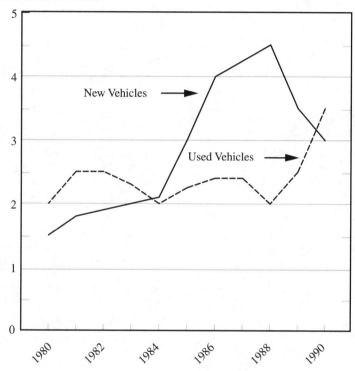

Thousands of Vehicles

13. What kind of a graph is this?

14. How many new vehicles were registered
    in County X in 1986?

15. How many used vehicles were registered
    in County X in 1980?

16. How many vehicles total were registered
    in County X in 1990?

21

Budget for School District #10
T = $8 Million

Sources   Outlays

17. What kind of a graph is this?

18. What fraction of the budget for School District #10 came from local school taxes?

19. How much money in the budget for School District #10 came from state aid?

20. How much money did School District #10 allocated for faculty salaries?

Review

1. Table

2. 17,546

3. 11,210

4. 20,351

5. Bar

6. $5 million

7. $55 million

8. $46.5 million

9. Cumulative Bar

10. About 3,000

11. About 34,000

12. About 2,500

13. Line

14. About 4,000

15. About 2,000

16. About 6,500

17. Pie

18. 45% or $\dfrac{5}{11}$

19. $2 million

20. $4.8 million

Review the Most Common GRE Graph Questions

The next step in your Action Plan is to analyze the question from the standpoint of what you need to answer and then to gather the data from the graph. Most of the questions asked fall into one of three major categories:

1. Reading values

2. Manipulating values

3. Drawing an inference

We'll look at examples of each category, but we'll need a graph for the examples:

Gross Revenues Publisher P

1. Reading values

Questions that ask about values ask for one of two things: a specific value or a comparison of values. Spend a minute or so getting familiar with the graph, and then we'll look at some questions.

QUESTION   What was the dollar value of revenues derived from book sales in 1987?

    (A) $400,000

    (B) $600,000

    (C) $750,000

    (D) $1,000,000

    (E) $1,200,000

21

ANALYSIS The correct answer **(E)**. Just read the value of "Book Sales" at the year 1987.

Here is an example of a question that asks for a comparison of values:

QUESTION In which year did revenues from software first exceed $600,000?

  (A) 1981

  (B) 1982

  (C) 1983

  (D) 1984

  (E) 1985

ANALYSIS The correct answer is **(E)**. Locate the line for software sales and find the first year (among those listed) in which the line broke across the 0.6 mark: 1985.

Here's another "compare" values question:

QUESTION For how many years shown, were revenues from Subrights Licenses less than revenues from Software Sales?

  (A) One

  (B) Two

  (C) Three

  (D) Four

  (E) Five

ANALYSIS The correct answer is **(B)**. Those years were 1985 and 1986.

It's possible for reading values questions to be more complicated, but only because the question stem asks you to retrieve more data from the graph. Here's an example of a question stem that goes way beyond what the GRE would ask, but it makes the point:

QUESTION In how many years in which revenues from Book Sales were greater than revenues from Subrights Licenses were revenues from Software Sales greater than revenues from Consulting Fees?

ANALYSIS This question would likely require a few minutes to work out because you'd first have to identify all of those years in which Book Sales generated more revenue than Subrights Licenses and then those in which Software Sales generated more revenue than Consulting Fees, and then compare the two, and count up the number of years that satisfy all of the conditions in the stem. But, and this is the important point, while that is time-consuming, it's not theoretically difficult.

In other words, it's just donkey math, and graduate programs don't expect their students to do donkey math. So reading values and comparing values are usually fairly simple procedures.

> **NOTE** Reading value questions ask you to read a value or to compare values, but no calculations are usually required.

2. Manipulating Values

The second group of questions require a calculation of some sort. One group asks for addition or subtraction, the other for an expression in fractional terms. Here is an example of the first type:

QUESTION Book Sales generated how much in revenues in years 1981, 1982, and 1983, combined?

    (A) $2,300,000

    (B) $2,100,000

    (C) $1,800,000

    (D) $1,250,000

    (E) $900,000

ANALYSIS The correct answer is (A). You locate the data for Book Sales and add the three numbers:

$$0.8 + 0.8 + 0.7 = 2.3$$

And that's 2.3 million or $2,300,000.

Other questions like this might ask you to add all four categories together for a certain year:

QUESTION What were gross revenues for Publisher P in 1986?

Or you might be required to subtract:

QUESTION Book Sales in 1988 accounted for how much more in revenues than Consulting Fees in the that year?

Or:

QUESTION In 1983, Subrights Licenses and Book Sales combined accounted for how much more revenue than Software Sales and Consulting Fees combined?

21

Again, there is no reason to pause now to work out answers to such questions because they're not really different from one another.

The other group of manipulation questions asks not for addition and subtraction alone but for you to express some value in fraction, percentage, or ratio terms. Here is an example:

QUESTION Consulting Fees accounted for what approximate percent of Publisher P's total revenues in 1987?

   (A) 4%

   (B) 13%

   (C) 18%

   (D) 23%

   (E) 39%

ANALYSIS The correct answer is (**B**). Total revenues for 1987 were:

$$1.2 + 0.9 + 0.6 + 0.4 = 3.1$$

And:

$$\frac{0.4}{3.1} \approx 0.13 = 13\%$$

And here's another example:

QUESTION In 1982, the ratio of revenues derived from Subrights Licenses to revenues derived from Consulting Fees was

   (A) 3:1

   (B) 2:1

   (C) 1:1

   (D) 1:3

   (E) 1:5

ANALYSIS The correct answer is (**A**):

$$\frac{0.9}{0.3} = 3 \text{ to } 1$$

Again, it is theoretically possible to create questions that are several degrees more complicated, but the added difficulty would just be donkey work.

> For questions that require manipulations, analyze the question stem to
> determine what data you need and make a note on your scratch paper. Then
> find the data on the graph and enter it on your note. And then do the
> manipulation.

3. Drawing Inferences

The final kind of question asks you to draw an inference from the data. In other words, the
first question type (read a value) just asks you to demonstrate that you know how to read
the graph. The second question type (manipulate the values) requires you to manipulate
the data in order to arrive at a solution. For this third type (draw an inference), you have to
draw a further conclusion from the data explicitly given. Here is an example:

QUESTION   How much money was spent by Publisher P on manufacturing costs in 1990?

    (A) $1,200,000

    (B) $1,600,000

    (C) $560,000

    (D) $400,000

    (E) $250,000

ANALYSIS   The correct answer is **(B)**. To get the answer, you have to see that the pie chart
provides the breakout for 1990. So you need first to find total revenues for 1990:

    $1.4 + 1.3 + 1.1 + .2 = 4.0$

And then take 40% of that sum:

    40% of $4.0 = 1.6$

So the amount of money for manufacturing costs in that year was 1.6 million dollars or
$1,600,000.

Workshop B: Most Common GRE Graph Questions

21

In this Workshop, you'll get to practice answering the common kinds of questions asked
by the GRE in this part. You'll notice that the graphs are the same ones used in Workshop
A—ones you already know how to read. So you can concentrate just on the forms of the
questions. You can check your work against the Answer Key in the Review part below.

Drill

Answer the following questions based on the graphs. There is no time limit for this exercise.

Population of Five Communities
bt Age (in years)

	0 -5	6 - 12	13 - 18	19 - 25	25+
Allenburg	2,476	2,104	2,003	1,987	8,976
Briarcliff	8,442	10,993	9,476	9,882	42,172
Cliffwood	5,002	4,998	5,127	6,101	31,272
Dreamville	3,427	3,427	3,109	5,885	23,976
Eagleston	1,004	998	972	1,804	6,432

1. Which community has the largest population in the age group 6 to 12?

   (A) Allenburg
   (B) Briarcliff
   (C) Cliffwood
   (D) Dreamville
   (E) Eagleston

2. The total population in the five communities age 25 years or more is approximately

   (A) 81,000
   (B) 92,000
   (C) 103,000
   (D) 112,000
   (E) 123,000

3. For which of the five communities is the ratio of the number of people age 6 to 12 years to the number of people 0 to 5 years the greatest?

   (A) Allenburg
   (B) Briarcliff
   (C) Cliffwood
   (D) Dreamville
   (E) Eagleston

Gross Revenues: Select Retailers

Hundreds of
Thousands of Dollars

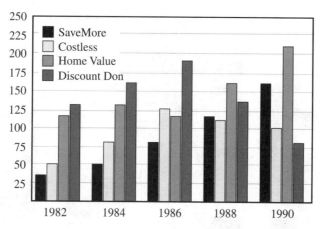

4. Gross revenues of Home Value in 1986 were

(A) $12.5 million
(B) $10 million
(C) $8 million
(D) $6 million
(E) $3 million

5. The four retailers had combined gross revenues in 1990 of

(A) $55,000,000
(B) $42,500,000
(C) $36,300,00
(D) $32,000,000
(E) $27,600,000

6. The ratio of gross revenues of Home Value in 1982 to gross revenues in 1990 was

(A) 1:4
(B) 1:3
(C) 1:2
(D) 1:1
(E) 6:5

21

Employment by Category Region R
(by sector)

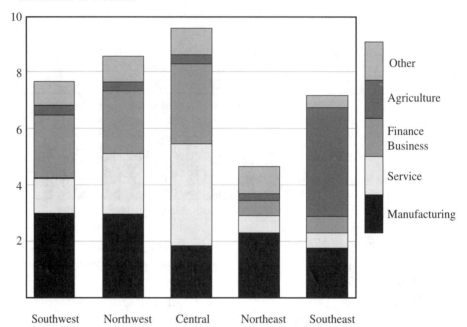

Thousands of Workers

7. In which sector of Region R is employ-
   ment in Agriculture the greatest?

   (A) Southwest
   (B) Northwest
   (C) Central
   (D) Northeast
   (E) Southeast

8. Approximately what fraction of the workers in the Northwest sector of Region R
   are employed in Manufacturing?

   (A) $\frac{1}{5}$

   (B) $\frac{1}{4}$

   (C) $\frac{1}{3}$

   (D) $\frac{1}{2}$

   (E) $\frac{2}{3}$

9. In the Northeast sector, how many workers are employed in Service?

   (A) 700
   (B) 1,500
   (C) 2,200
   (D) 2,900
   (E) 3,500

Vehicle Registrations in County X

Thousands of Vehicles

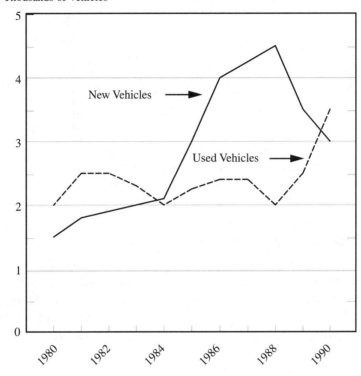

10. For how many years shown did registrations of Used Vehicles exceed registrations of New Vehicles?

    (A) 1
    (B) 2
    (C) 3
    (D) 4
    (E) 5

11. The total number of registrations of new and used vehicles combined in 1988 was

    (A) 2,000
    (B) 2,500
    (C) 4,500
    (D) 6,500
    (E) 7,500

12. What was the ratio of used vehicle registrations to new vehicle registrations in 1989?

    (A) 1:2
    (B) 5:7
    (C) 9:10
    (D) 7:5
    (E) 14:5

21

Budget for School District #10
T=$8 Million

Sources   Outlays

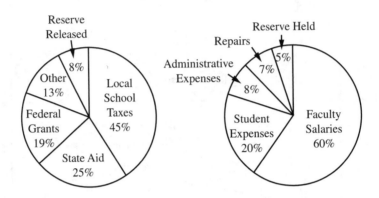

13. The amount of money allocated to student expenses was most nearly equal to money from what source?

(A) Local School Taxes
(B) State Aid
(C) Reserve Released
(D) Federal Grants
(E) Other

14. Funding for School District #10 from sources other than local school taxes amounted to

(A) $4.4 million
(B) $4.8 million
(C) $5.2 million
(D) $6.0 million
(E) $6.4 million

15. The net change in the Reserve was

(A) an increase of $3 million
(B) an increase of $130,000
(C) an increase of $240,000
(D) a decrease of $240,000
(E) a decrease of $3 million

Review

1. (B)

2. (D)

3. (B)

4. (A)

5. (A)

6. (C)

7. (E)

8. (C)

9. (A)

10. (E)

11. (D)

12. (B)

13. (D)

14. (A)

15. (D)

Master Advanced Strategies for Graphs

As you learned earlier in this lesson, nowhere else on the GRE is time more important than graphs. Fortunately, there are shortcuts:

1. Approximation
2. Simplification
3. Meastimation

Some graphs questions, as you have already seen, explicitly invite you to approximate. Question stems are particularly likely to include words such as "approximately" or "about" or "most nearly" when the graph uses large values and an exact value cannot reliably be read from the graph. Thus, a graph entitled "Budget of Town X" with values in the millions of dollars is not going to permit a reading of $1,197,268.17. You can round off, usually to the nearest integer or sometimes the nearest tenth: $1.1 million.

A second way to avoid doing arithmetic is to set up your solution and then simplify the numbers before doing the calculation. Suppose, for example, that you are asked to find the difference between two budget categories, one that is 25% of the budget and the other 40%, when the budget totals $9.9 million. You'd first round-off the $9.9 million to $10.0 million and set up your solution:

(40% of 10) – (25% of 10) =

Instead of doing two multiplications and then a subtraction, you can subtract first (40% – 25% = 15%) and then do one multiplication: 15% of 10 is 1.5.

A third shortcut is to use the picture itself to "meastimate" quantities. "Meastimate" is a made-up word that just indicates a combination of measuring and estimating. Here's an example:

21

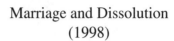

Marriage and Dissolution
(1998)

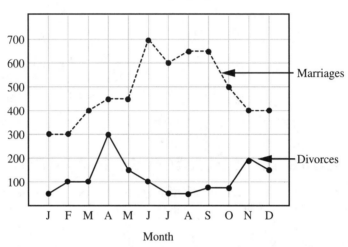

Month

QUESTION In which of the following months was the difference between the number of marriages and the number of divorces the greatest?

(A) January

(B) March

(C) July

(D) October

(E) December

ANALYSIS The correct answer is **(C)**. You can meastimate the answer just by looking at the difference between the two lines: of the five months given, the difference between the two lines is greatest in July.

Here's another example:

QUESTION What was the difference between the number of marriages in May and the number of divorces in November?

(A) 150

(B) 200

(C) 250

(D) 300

(E) 350

ANALYSIS The correct answer is **(C)**. You can get the answer by subtracting or you can use your pencil or the edge of a sheet of scrap paper to measure the difference between the two values and then compare that difference to the scale for the graph. That way, you can use the principle that "distance equals value" to meastimate the answer.

CAUTION Lengthy calculations are score-burners. If you're doing anything more time-consuming than calculating with a couple of two-digit numbers, then you're losing time. Try a short-cut instead.

Workshop C: Advanced Strategies for Graphs

Use the following items to practice your short-cut techniques. There is no time limit for the Drill, but check your work against the explanations in the Review part.

Drill

Gross Revenues: Select Retailers

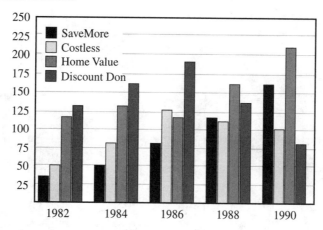

21

1. In which year was the difference between the gross revenues of Home Value and Cost Less the greatest?

   (A) 1982
   (B) 1984
   (C) 1986
   (D) 1988
   (E) 1990

2. In which year was the difference between the gross revenues of Discount Don and Home Value the least?

   (A) 1982
   (B) 1984
   (C) 1986
   (D) 1988
   (E) 1990

3. Which of the following increases showed the greatest percentage change in gross revenues?

   (A) Discount Don 1982 to 1984
   (B) Discount Don 1984 to 1986
   (C) Discount Don 1986 to 1988
   (D) Cost Less 1986 to 1988
   (E) Cost Less 1988 to 1990

Employment by Category Region R
(by sector)

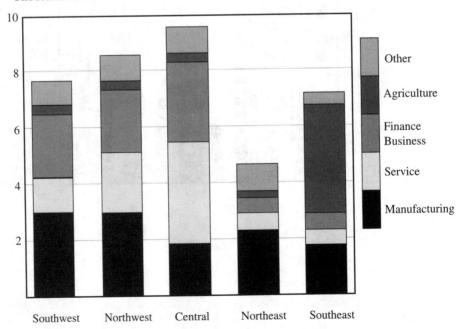

4. Which sector has the most workers employed in Service?

   (A) Southwest
   (B) Northwest
   (C) Central
   (D) Northeast
   (E) Southeast

5. For which sector is the ratio of the number of workers employed in Service to the number of workers employed in Manufacturing the greatest?

   (A) Southwest
   (B) Northwest
   (C) Central
   (D) Northeast
   (E) Southeast

6. For the Southeast sector, the ratio of the number of workers employed in Agriculture to the number of workers employed in Manufacturing is approximately

   (A) 3:1
   (B) 2:1
   (C) 3:2
   (D) 6:5
   (E) 5:6

7. Approximately how many more workers are employed in Finance and Business in the Central sector than in the Northeast sector?

   (A) 4,900
   (B) 4,200
   (C) 3,500
   (D) 2,700
   (E) 2,000

21

Vehicle Registrations in County X

Thousands of Vehicles

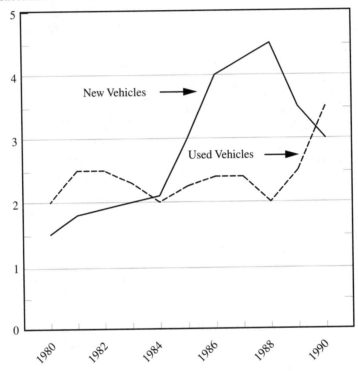

8. In which year was there the greatest difference between the number of new vehicles registered and the number of used vehicles registered?

(A) 1985
(B) 1986
(C) 1987
(D) 1988
(E) 1989

9. The greatest percent increase in the number of new vehicles registered occurred from

(A) 1980 to 1981
(B) 1983 to 1984
(C) 1984 to 1985
(D) 1985 to 1986
(E) 1986 to 1987

10. In which of the following years, was the number of used vehicles registered most nearly equal to the number of new vehicles registered?

(A) 1980
(B) 1983
(C) 1984
(D) 1988
(E) 1990

Review

1. **(E)** Just meastimate the difference in length between the two bars: the greatest difference occurs in 1990.

2. **(D)** Just look for the year in which those two bars were most nearly equal.

3. **(C)** Percentage change is a function not only of the absolute change in value (the increase or decrease) but the base or starting point as well. There are two choices that show large absolute increases than (B). (D) is an increase of 45 and (E) an increase of 50, but those are fractional increases of $\frac{45}{80}$ and $\frac{50}{160}$. (B) is a fractional increase of $\frac{30}{50}$ which is 60%.

4. **(C)** Just look for the sector where that component is the longest.

5. **(C)** Just meastimate and compare the lengths of those two bars for each sector. The greatest ratio is in the Central sector where the bar for Service appears to be about twice as long as the bar for Manufacturing.

6. **(A)** The bar for Agriculture appears to be about three times as long as the bar for Manufacturing.

7. **(E)** Measure the length of one bar using the edge of a sheet of scratch paper. Then, measure the other along the same edge. The difference in length is the difference in value: compare it to the scale.

8. **(D)** Just look for the year in which the two lines are separated by the greatest distance.

9. **(C)** Approximate, but be sure to remember that percent increase is also a function of the base or starting value: $\frac{3.0-2.1}{2.1}$ $\approx \frac{1}{2}$. (D) shows a greater absolute increase, 1, but a smaller percent increase: $\frac{4-3}{3} = \frac{1}{3}$.

10. **(C)** Look for the year listed in which the vertical distance separating the two lines is the least.

21

Get Answers to Frequently Asked Questions

Q: How much time should I spend on graph questions?

A: On average, somewhat less than $1\frac{1}{2}$ minutes each. That will give you three minutes for a pair of questions: a minute to become familiar with the graph and 45 seconds or so per question to answer.

Q: Are the graphs necessarily drawn to scale?

A: Yes, all graphs (except tables which aren't really pictures) are drawn to scale. Unless they were, there would be absolutely no point in using a graph. So you don't even have to look for the "*Note:* Drawn to Scale" that accompanies the graph.

Q: Is there any possibility at all that I could conceivably get a graph that doesn't fall into one of the common categories?

A: Yes, and there is also a quantifiable risk that a giant asteroid will strike your testing center at the exact moment you begin your GRE. But the odds are so small, they're not worth worrying about. Besides, even if you get a graph that is out of the ordinary, it will still use the common types of questions that you studied in this lesson.

Today's Review

1. From the standpoint of the number of questions, graphs are the least important part of GRE math. *But* because they pose the greatest hazard as time-burners, they are very important as potential disasters. Now you know how to work through them quickly.

2. You'll save time because you're familiar with the five common types of graphs—table, bar, cumulative bar, line and pie—knowing how to read them and what features they typically have.

3. The common question types—reading values, manipulating values, drawing inferences—pretty much exhaust the possibilities. Solutions are not mathematically difficult, though there is always a temptation to waste time.

4. Approximating, simplifying, and mestimating will save you even more time. You can't answer a graph question with greater precision than the graph itself, so questions often invite you to approximate. And even when the question doesn't specifically call for an approximation, you'll save time if you use one of the shortcuts.

Apply Your Action Plan to Graphs

Today, you'll be using the Action Plan that you developed in Day 21. After a quick review of some important points, you'll revisit the graph that appeared on the Math PreTest to see how the Action Plan would have helped you perform better. Then you'll have the opportunity to do timed exercises for further practice and to see the Action Plan applied to those items.

Review Your Action Plan

In Day 21, you learned that the critical point for graphs is timing because you have to invest the extra effort of reading the graph before you can even start on the first question. The Action Plan for Graphs was designed to familiarize you with the common types of graphs, the common types of questions, and valuable shortcuts. The overall plan looks like this:

ACTION PLAN

Step 1: Read the Graph

Table, Bar, Cumulative Bar, Line, or Pie.

Step 2: Analyze the Question.

Read a value or values, manipulate a value or values (by adding or subtracting or expressing as a fraction or percent), or draw an inference.

Step 3: Look for Short-Cuts.

Approximate, simplify, or meastimate.

Now let's apply the integrated plan to the items from the PreTest.

What You'll Do
- **Review Your Action Plan**
- **Apply Your Action Plan to the PreTest**
- **Workshop A**
- **Workshop B**
- **Get Answers to Frequently Asked Questions**

Apply Your Action Plan to the PreTest

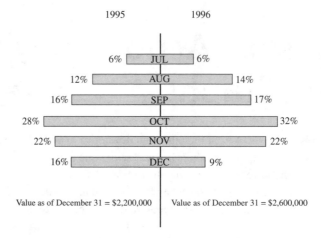

Warehouse Inventory for Company X
By Month of Acquisition

This is a bar graph. As with all bar graphs, distance from the base line to the end of the bar represents value—even though the bars extend left and right from a center line. The values in this case are percents of the total inventory held as of a certain date.

QUESTION   21. For 1995, what percent of the dollar value of inventory held on December 31 was acquired in September?

    (A) 1%

    (B) 15%

    (C) 16%

    (D) 28%

    (E) 34%

ANALYSIS   (C) This is a good example of a reading values question: just take the value directly from the graph.

QUESTION 22. During which of the following months was the dollar value of inventory acquired the greatest?

22

(A) August, 1996

(B) September, 1995

(C) September, 1996

(D) November, 1995

(E) December, 1996

ANALYSIS (D) Remember that distance on a bar graph represents value. So the longer the bar, the greater the value. In this case, the bars represent percents, so you can only compare directly bars with the same total, e.g., 1995 or 1996. That permits you to compare (A),(C) and (E) directly, and (C) is the largest value in that group because the bar for September is the longest of that group. Similarly, November 1995 is the larger of (B) and (D). Now you have to compare the two: 17% of $2.6 = 0.442 and 22% of $2.2 = 0.484.

QUESTION 23. If Company X acquired $500,000 of inventory in September, 1996, what was the dollar value of the inventory acquired that month that was no longer in the warehouse on December 31, 1996?

(A) $58,000

(B) $110,000

(C) $165,00

(D) $390,000

(E) It cannot be determined from the information given.

ANALYSIS (A) The dollar value of the September inventory still in the warehouse at the end of the year was 17% of $2.6 million or $442,000. That means that 500 – 442 or 58,000 was no longer in the warehouse.

QUESTION 24. What was the dollar value of the inventory held by Company X on August 31, 1996?

(A) $520,000

(B) $450,000

(C) $360,000

(D) $275,000

(E) It cannot be determined from the information given.

ANALYSIS (E) You must remember to read the accompanying information carefully. This graph provides information about inventory still in the warehouse on December 31. It does not provide information about the value of the inventory acquired in individual months. (This is the reason for the stipulation in the preceding question.)

QUESTION 25. Which of the following statements can be inferred from the graph?

    I. Company X had fewer units in the warehouse on December 31, 1995 than on December 31, 1996.

    II. The total cost of inventory acquired by Company X for the period August, 1996 through November, 1996 was $2,210,000.

    III. Company X acquired $880,000 more in inventory during November, 1996 than November, 1995.

    (A) none

    (B) I only

    (C) III only

    (D) II and III only

    (E) I, II, and III

ANALYSIS **(A)** Statement I cannot be inferred because the title of the graph talks about dollar value, not about units. Based on this conclusion, you would have eliminated choices (B) and (E). II and III cannot be inferred because the graph gives information about the dollar value of inventory on hand on December 31, not about the value of inventory acquired in the various months.

Workshop A

This Workshop consists of drill and review. The Drill portion contains 15 questions. The time limit is 20 minutes. Do the drill under timed conditions, then evaluate your work using the tools in the Review part of the Workshop.

Drill

15 Questions • Time—20 Minutes

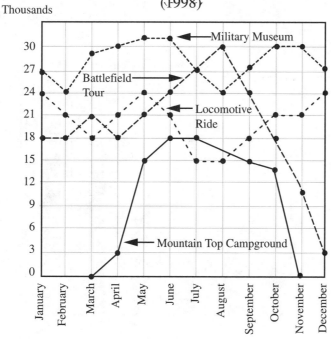

Number of Visitors to
Tourist Sites in Historic Park
(1998)

1. For the year shown, the greatest number
   of people visited the Locomotive Ride in

   (A) March
   (B) May
   (C) June
   (D) August
   (E) October

2. The total number of visitor to Historic Park
   for the month of April was most nearly

   (A) 72,000
   (B) 69,000
   (C) 58,000
   (D) 48,000
   (E) 42,000

3. For how many months was the number of
   visitors to the Locomotive Ride greater
   than the number of visitors to the Battlefield Tour?

   (A) Three
   (B) Five
   (C) Seven
   (D) Nine
   (E) Ten

4. The difference between the number of visitors to the Military Museum and the number of visitors to the Battlefield Tour was greatest in the month of

   (A) March
   (B) April
   (C) June
   (D) July
   (E) October

5. The greatest month-to-month percentage increase in the number of visitors to the Locomotive Ride occurred

   (A) from April to May
   (B) from May to June
   (C) from June to July
   (D) from July to August
   (E) from August to September

Donations to Two Charities

Millions of Dollars

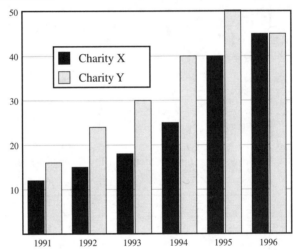

6. The ratio of contributions to Charity Y to contributions to Charity X was greatest in which of the following years

   (A) 1991
   (B) 1993
   (C) 1994
   (D) 1995
   (E) 1996

7. Total contributions to Charity X for the years 1991, 1992, and 1993 were approximately

   (A) $30 million
   (B) $36 million
   (C) $45 million
   (D) $52 million
   (E) $60 million

8. The yearly average (arithmetic mean) of contributions to Charity Y for the period shown was most nearly

   (A) $24 million
   (B) $32 million
   (C) $34 million
   (D) $39 million
   (E) $42 million

9. For how many years shown did contributions to Charity Y exceed contributions to Charity X by more than $10 million dollars?

    (A) zero
    (B) one
    (C) two
    (D) three
    (E) four

10. Which of the following statements can be inferred from the graph?

    I. In 1996, contributions to Charity X accounted for 100% of contributions to the two charities combined.

    II. In 1995, contributions to Charity X were less than 75% of the contributions to Charity Y.

    III. In 1992, contributions to Charity Y were 160% of contributions to Charity X.

    (A) I only
    (B) III only
    (C) I and III only
    (D) II and III only
    (E) I, II, and III

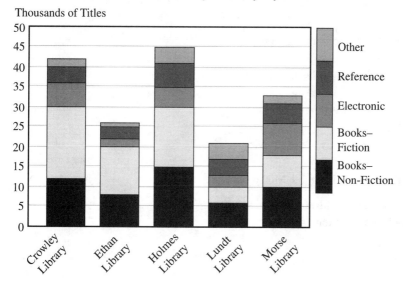

Holdings of the Five Member Libraries
of the North County Library System

Thousands of Titles

Other

Reference

Electronic

Books–
Fiction

Books–
Non-Fiction

11. The holdings of Morse Library include approximately how many Electronic titles?

    (A) 8,000
    (B) 12,000
    (C) 15,000
    (D) 18,000
    (E) 26,000

12. The total number of titles in the Holmes Library that are not Books/NonFiction titles is

    (A) 15,000
    (B) 24,000
    (C) 30,000
    (D) 36,000
    (E) 41,000

13. The number of Books/NonFiction in the Ethan Library is most nearly equal to the number of

    (A) Book/NonFiction titles in the Holmes Library
    (B) Books/Fiction titles in the Lundt Library
    (C) Electronic titles in the Morse Library
    (D) Reference titles in the Crowley Library
    (E) Reference titles in the Morse library

14. The total number of Reference titles in the entire Library System is most nearly

    (A) 18,000
    (B) 22,000
    (C) 27,000
    (D) 31,000
    (E) 35,000

15. Which of the following statements can be inferred from the graph?

    I. The total number of Books/Fiction titles in the Library system is greater than the total number of Electronic titles.

    II. The number of titles classified as 'Other' in the Lundt Library is less than the number of titles classified as 'Other' in the Morse Library.

    III. The largest number of Books/Fiction titles is held by the Crowley Library.

    (A) I only
    (B) III only
    (C) I and II only
    (D) I and III only
    (E) I, II and III

Review

Check your answers against the key and assess your performance to the graph below. Then compare you thinking with the explanations given.

1. (D)	6. (B)	11. (A)
2. (A)	7. (C)	12. (C)
3. (B)	8. (C)	13. (C)
4. (D)	9. (C)	14. (B)
5. (A)	10. (B)	15. (A)

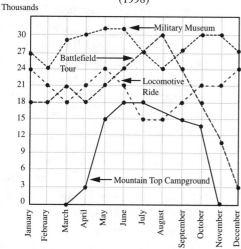

Number of Visitors to
Tourist Sites in Historic Park
(1998)

The first graph is a line graph. Notice that the units are in thousands of visitors.

1. **(D)** Just compare values by looking for the 'highpoint' of the line for the Locomotive Ride.

2. **(A)** This question requires you to manipulate some values, so quickly add the numbers for April. (The numbers are easy to work with.)

3. **(B)** This is a comparison question. Just count the number of months in which the line for the Locomotive Ride was above that for the Battlefield Tour.

4. **(D)** Save some valuable time: Look for the month in which the two lines are the farthest apart.

5. **(A)** Remember that a percentage increase depends upon the starting point or base value. April-May began a sequence of four periods in which the absolute increase was 3,000 visitors. But the greatest percent increase for those periods occurred when the base was the smallest. ((E) describes a drop, so it's not even in the running.)

The second graph is a bar graph, and the units are *millions* of dollars.

6. **(B)** Meastimate, and find the year in which the bar for Charity Y was the greatest in comparison to the bar for Charity X. You can do this using the edge of a sheet of scratch paper. Measure the length of the left-hand bar and divide that into the length of the right-hand bar. How many times does the shorter distance go into the longer distance?

(A) about $1\frac{1}{3}$

(B) about $1\frac{2}{3}$

(C) about $1\frac{2}{3}$

(D) about $1\frac{1}{4}$

(E) about 1

This eliminates (A), (D), and (E). Tidy up the loose ends: (B) = $\frac{30}{18}$ = $\frac{5}{3}$ = 1.66; (C) = $\frac{24}{15}$ = $\frac{8}{5}$ = 1.6. So (B) is greater.

7. **(C)** You can quickly manipulate the values by adding: $12 + 15 + 18 = 45$. Or you could even measure the lengths of each of the bars in questions, adding the length of the next to the length of the preceeding and then measure the result against the scale on the left.

8. **(C)** You can manipulate the values directly: $16 + 24 + 30 + 40 + 50 + 45 = 205$ and $205 \div 6 = 34+$. You can also meastimate the answer. Mentally draw a horizontal line through the approximate middle of the bars for Charity Y—so that

about as much distance for bars is above the line as below. That will be the average. And it seems to be about 35.

9. **(C)** You can quickly manipulate numbers. The two years are 1993 and 1994. Or you can meastimate an answer. Mark off a distance equal to the value of $10 million on the edge of a sheet of paper or your pencil. Then compare that distance with *difference* between the lengths of the two bars for each of the six years. (Compare your measurement for 10 with the part of the dark bar that extends above the end of the light bar.)

10. **(B)** This is an inference question. Statement I cannot be inferred; in that year, the two bars are equal. Eliminate choices (A), (C), and (E). Statement II cannot be inferred because the length of the lighter bar for 1995 is *more* than $\frac{3}{4}$ the length of the darker bar. So the correct answer is (B). And a quick meastimation confirms that III is inferrable.

This is a cumulative bar graph, and the units are *thousands* of titles. Remember that with a cumulative bar graph, only the bottom component and the total are read from the base line. The other components of the bar must be read from the bottom to the top *of that component.*

11. **(A)** You can manipulate the values: $26 - 18 = 8$. Or you can meastimate by measuring the length of the 'Electronic' component with the edge of a sheet of paper or a pencil and comparing that distance against the scale to determine value.

12. **(C)** Again, you can manipulate the values directly: 45 – 15 = 30, which is 30,000. Or you can meastimate by taking a measurement for the length of the Holmes bar for everything except the category Books/Non-Fiction.

13. **(C)** Again, you have your choice of methods. The number of Books/Non-Fiction in the Ethan Library is 8. (That's the bottom component of the bar, and you can read the value directly from the scale.) Next, look at the values for each choice until you find one that is approximately 8. Or, you could meastimate: measure the length of the bar for Books/Non-Fiction in the Ethan Library, but don't even bother to convert that to a number. Just compare that distance (value) to the distance (value) of each. The one that matches up best in terms of distance is correct.

14. **(B)** Here is a question where meastimating is the preferred method. Yes, you could solve the question by first calculating the value of the components for Reference titles for each library and then adding: 4 + 3 + 6 + 4 + 5 = 22. More efficient is to measure each of those little components, adding each to the cumulative measure of the others, until you have a distance marked on your yardstick (a sheet of paper or a pencil) that represents the value of all those components combined. Then read the value of that distance directly from the scale.

15. **(A)** This is an inference question. Statement I can be inferred using meastimation: for each library, the Books/Fiction component of the bar is longer than that for Electronic titles. So the total of the one is greater than the total of the other. Statement II is not inferrable. And statement III is not inferrable because the bar for that component is longer at the Holmes Library.

22

Workshop B

This Workshop consists of drill and review. The Drill portion contains 15 questions. The time limit is 20 minutes. Do the drill under timed conditions, then evaluate your work using the tools in the Review part of the Workshop.

Drill

15 Questions • Time—15 Minutes

Number of Registered Voters
By Party Affiliation

	Ward				
	First	Second	Third	Fourth	Fifth
Democratic	436	182	946	314	607
Republican	515	344	822	407	356
Liberal	102	76	149	103	119
Conservative	127	152	126	166	84
None	49	33	89	47	112

1. The total number of registered voters in the five wards who indicated no party affiliation is

   (A) 330
   (B) 278
   (C) 244
   (D) 198
   (E) 125

2. The number of registered voters who indicated Liberal as their party affiliation is most nearly equal in

   (A) the First and Second Wards
   (B) the First and Fourth Wards
   (C) the Second and Third Wards
   (D) the Second and Fourth Wards
   (E) the Fourth and Fifth Wards

3. In the Third Ward, the number of registered voters who indicated Democratic as their party affiliation is approximately what percent of all registered voters in that ward?

   (A) 18%
   (B) 37%
   (C) 44%
   (D) 51%
   (E) 58%

22

4. The number of registered voters in the Fourth Ward who indicated no affiliation is approximately what fraction of all registered voters in that ward?

(A) 0.45%
(B) 0.80%
(C) 4.5%
(D) 8%
(E) 12%

5. The ward in which registered voters who indicated a Democratic affiliation constitutes the greatest fraction of all registered voters in the ward is the

(A) First
(B) Second
(C) Third
(D) Fourth
(E) Fifth

Median Annual Income
High School Graduates versus Nongraduates

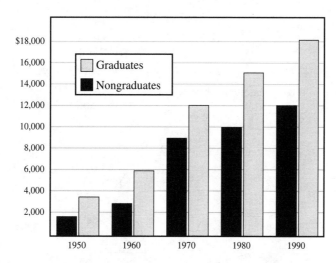

6. The median annual income for Nongraduates in 1980 was approximately

(A) $3,000
(B) $8,000
(C) $10,000
(D) $12,000
(E) $15,000

7. The difference between the median annual incomes of Graduates and Nongraduates was greatest in

(A) 1950
(B) 1960
(C) 1970
(D) 1980
(E) 1990

8. The average of the median annual incomes for Graduates and Nongraduates in 1990 was approximately

   (A) $6,000
   (B) $12,000
   (C) $15,000
   (D) $18,000
   (E) $30,000

9. The ratio of the median annual income of Graduates to Nongraduates was greatest in

   (A) 1950
   (B) 1960
   (C) 1970
   (D) 1980
   (E) 1990

10. Which of the following statements can be inferred from the graph?

I. The smallest ten-year increase in the median annual income of Nongraduates for the period shown on the graph was from 1970 to 1980.

II. The greatest percentage increase in the median annual income of Graduates for the period shown on the graph was from 1960 to 1970.

III. The median annual income of Nongraduates in 1980 was greater than the median annual income of Graduates in 1970.

   (A) I only
   (B) II only
   (C) I and II only
   (D) I and III only
   (E) II and III only\

Enrollment by School

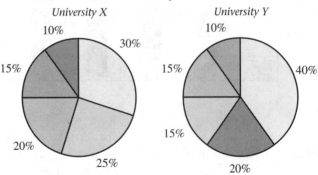

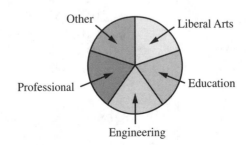

22

11. The number of students enrolled in Professional schools at University Y was approximately

    (A) 2,000
    (B) 3,000
    (C) 5,000
    (D) 9,000
    (E) 20,000

12. The number of students at University X enrolled in a school other than Engineering was most nearly

    (A) 1,500
    (B) 2,000
    (C) 5,000
    (D) 7,500
    (E) 15,000

13. The number of students enrolled in Liberal Arts at Univeristy X was most nearly equal to the number of students enrolled in

    (A) Liberal Arts at University Y
    (B) Education and Engineering at University Y
    (C) Professional school at University Y
    (D) Professional school at University X
    (E) Engineering school at University X

14. The ratio of the number of students enrolled in Liberal Arts at University X to the number of students enrolled in Education at University X is most nearly

    (A) $\dfrac{3}{2}$
    (B) $\dfrac{7}{5}$
    (C) 1
    (D) $\dfrac{5}{7}$
    (E) $\dfrac{2}{3}$

15. Approximately, how many more students were enrolled in Engineering school at University Y than in Professional schools at University X?

    (A) 250
    (B) 500
    (C) 650
    (D) 900
    (E) 1150

Review

Check your answers against the key and assess your performance to the graph below. Then compare you thinking with the explanations given.

1. (A)	6. (C)	11. (B)
2. (B)	7. (E)	12. (E)
3. (C)	8. (C)	13. (A)
4. (A)	9. (A)	14. (A)
5. (E)	10. (C)	15. (A)

Number of Registered Voters
By Party Affiliation

	Ward				
	First	Second	Third	Fourth	Fifth
Democratic	436	182	946	314	607
Republican	515	344	822	407	356
Liberal	102	76	149	103	119
Conservative	127	152	126	166	84
None	49	33	89	47	112

This is a table, and there are no tricks here.

1. **(A)** Just quickly add the values.

2. **(B)** Notice that the question specifically invites you to approximate, so don't start off by subtracting numbers. Think: well, 102 and 76 are not very close, so I'll check (A) later; 102 and 103 are very close, so it's probably (B); but I'll look at the other choices quickly. And the correct choice is (B).

3. **(C)** Manipulate the values, but remember to approximate. Think: $950 + 825 + 150 + 125 + 100 = 2150$ and $\frac{950}{2150} = \frac{95}{210}$ which is slightly less that $\frac{1}{2}$. So (C) is the closest answer.

4. **(A)** Meastimate. The toal number of voters in the Fourth Ward is about $300 + 400 + 100 + 160 + 50$ or 1050, of which 50 or so are 'none.' And that's about 5% or a little less.

5. **(E)** Instead of doing several calculations (a time-burner), try to meastimate an answer. In each ward, Democratic and Republican are the two biggest numbers, so the best starting point is to find the ward

or wards where Democrats outnumber Republicans. This is true of the Third and Fifth, but in the Fifth, Democrats outnumber the Republicans by almost 2 to 1. So that's your answer.

This is a bar graph. And there are no tricks in the units.

6. **(C)** Just read the value right off the graph.

7. **(E)** It would be a waste of time to do calculations here. Instead, the difference in the lengths of the two bars is the difference between the median incomes. For which pair of bars is the difference between the right and the left bar the greatest? 1990.

8. **(C)** You could run the numbers for this question: $18 + 12 = 30$, and $\frac{30}{2} = 15$. But easier would be to use the graph itself to find the midpoint between the tops of the two bars: about 15.

9. **(A)** Don't start calculating before you've tried meastimation on this item. The ratio between the two bars in each pair is expressed by the relative lengths of the bars. For 1950, the right bar is about twice as long as the left bar, and that's the biggest ratio.

10. **(C)** Statement I is inferrable. Use a yardstick to meastimate, and you'll see that the smallest difference between bars for two consecutive years was that for 1970 to 1980. Statement II is also inferrable. The 1970 bar for graduates is twice as long as the 1960. Statement III, however, is contradicted by the graph—as you can see from the lengths of the bars.

Here you have two pies. The totals are given as 20,000 for the pie on the left and 15,000 for the pie on the right.

11. **(B)** 20% of 15,000 is 3,000.

12. **(E)** Engineering at University X accounts for 25% of students, so non-Engineering is 75% of 20,000 or 15,000.

13. **(A)** The number of students enrolled in Liberal Arts at University X is 30% of 20,000 or 6,000. And at University Y, 30% of the 20,000 students or 6,000 are enrolled in Liberal Arts.

14. **(A)** You don't need to calculate a number. Just compare slices of the pie: $\frac{30\%}{20\%} = \frac{3}{2}$.

15. **(A)** Engineering at University Y has 15% of 15,000 students or 2,250 students; Professional schools at University X have 10% of 20,000 students or 2,000 students. And the difference is 250.

22

Get Answers to Frequently Asked Questions

Q: When I estimate and use similar techniques, don't I risk getting a wrong answer? Shouldn't I use exact numbers and be sure?

A: Yes there is a risk; no you shouldn't try to be more precise. First of all, meastimation is a reliable technique *because* the answer choices permit it. Trying to be more precise than the choices themselves is a time-burner. Second, since time is of the essence on this part, you just can't afford the luxury of double-checking each step.

Q: What if I'm running out of time and the last two or three questions are graphs?

A: Guess immediately. If you only have a minute or two left, you probably don't have time to read the graph and try to answer even the first question. And you are penalized if you don't finish the section. Plus, if you're lucky, those questions will be embedded experimentals.

Take the Math Final

Today, you'll take the Math Final.

The Math Final has a format similar to what you will encounter on your computer-based GRE. (A small adjustment has been made to the number of questions—30 rather than 28.) The Final uses the three math types presented in an order similar to that of the actual exam. Do the Final under strict timing conditions. After the Final proper, evaluate your performance and review your work.

What You'll Do
- Take the Math Final
- Evaluate Your Performance
- Review Your Work
- Get Answers to Frequently Asked Questions

Take the Math Final

This is the Math Final. It consists of 30 questions with a time limit of 45 minutes. Mark your answers by filling in the oval next to the answer choice that you select.

1 Ⓐ Ⓑ Ⓒ Ⓓ Ⓔ	9 Ⓐ Ⓑ Ⓒ Ⓓ Ⓔ	17 Ⓐ Ⓑ Ⓒ Ⓓ Ⓔ	25 Ⓐ Ⓑ Ⓒ Ⓓ Ⓔ	
2 Ⓐ Ⓑ Ⓒ Ⓓ Ⓔ	10 Ⓐ Ⓑ Ⓒ Ⓓ Ⓔ	18 Ⓐ Ⓑ Ⓒ Ⓓ Ⓔ	26 Ⓐ Ⓑ Ⓒ Ⓓ Ⓔ	
3 Ⓐ Ⓑ Ⓒ Ⓓ Ⓔ	11 Ⓐ Ⓑ Ⓒ Ⓓ Ⓔ	19 Ⓐ Ⓑ Ⓒ Ⓓ Ⓔ	27 Ⓐ Ⓑ Ⓒ Ⓓ Ⓔ	
4 Ⓐ Ⓑ Ⓒ Ⓓ Ⓔ	12 Ⓐ Ⓑ Ⓒ Ⓓ Ⓔ	20 Ⓐ Ⓑ Ⓒ Ⓓ Ⓔ	28 Ⓐ Ⓑ Ⓒ Ⓓ Ⓔ	
5 Ⓐ Ⓑ Ⓒ Ⓓ Ⓔ	13 Ⓐ Ⓑ Ⓒ Ⓓ Ⓔ	21 Ⓐ Ⓑ Ⓒ Ⓓ Ⓔ	29 Ⓐ Ⓑ Ⓒ Ⓓ Ⓔ	
6 Ⓐ Ⓑ Ⓒ Ⓓ Ⓔ	14 Ⓐ Ⓑ Ⓒ Ⓓ Ⓔ	22 Ⓐ Ⓑ Ⓒ Ⓓ Ⓔ	30 Ⓐ Ⓑ Ⓒ Ⓓ Ⓔ	
7 Ⓐ Ⓑ Ⓒ Ⓓ Ⓔ	15 Ⓐ Ⓑ Ⓒ Ⓓ Ⓔ	23 Ⓐ Ⓑ Ⓒ Ⓓ Ⓔ		
8 Ⓐ Ⓑ Ⓒ Ⓓ Ⓔ	16 Ⓐ Ⓑ Ⓒ Ⓓ Ⓔ	24 Ⓐ Ⓑ Ⓒ Ⓓ Ⓔ		

GRE Math Final

30 Questions • Time—45 Minutes

DIRECTIONS: Each of the following items consists of two quantities, one in Column A and one in Column B. Compare the quantities and choose:

(A) if the quantity in Column A is greater;
(B) if the quantity in Column B is greater;
(C) if the two quantities are equal;
(D) if the relationship cannot be determined from the information given.

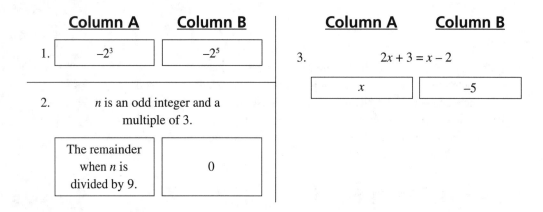

	Column A	Column B
1.	-2^3	-2^5

2. n is an odd integer and a multiple of 3.

Column A	Column B
The remainder when n is divided by 9.	0

	Column A	Column B
3.	$2x + 3 = x - 2$	
	x	-5

DIRECTIONS: Each of the following questions has five answer choices. For each question, choose the best answer given.

4. $(48 - 47 - 46 - 45) - (47 - 46 - 45 - 44) =$

(A) −52
(B) −48
(C) −2
(D) 45
(E) 92

5. Of the following, which is closest to $\sqrt[3]{65}$?

(A) 2
(B) 3
(C) 4
(D) 8
(E) 22

DIRECTIONS: Each of the following items consists of two quantities, one in Column A and one in Column B. Compare the quantities and choose:

(A) if the quantity in Column A is greater;
(B) if the quantity in Column B is greater;
(C) if the two quantities are equal;
(D) if the relationship cannot be determined from the information given.

23

Column A	Column B

6. m is a positive integer.

$$\frac{3}{8} = \frac{m}{n}$$

$n - m$	5

Column A	Column B

7.   The area of Circle O is 24π.

The radius of Circle O	4

8. | $(0.51)^2(0.51)^3$ | $(0.51)^6$ |

DIRECTIONS: Each of the following questions is based on the graph. For each question, choose the best answer given.

Income and Expenditures for Foundation F

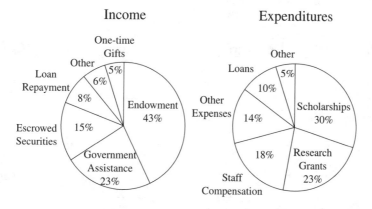

Income

One-time Gifts 5%
Other 6%
Loan Repayment 8%
Escrowed Securities 15%
Endowment 43%
Government Assistance 23%

T = $30 Million

Expenditures

Other 5%
Loans 10%
Other Expenses 14%
Scholarships 30%
Staff Compensation 18%
Research Grants 23%

T = $30 Million

9. How much of the Foundation's income came from government assistance?

   (A) $5.2 million
   (B) $6.3 million
   (C) $6.9 million
   (D) $7.4 million
   (E) $8.1 million

10. Expenditures for which of the following categories was most nearly equal to $4.5 million?

    (A) Staff Compensation
    (B) Office Expenses
    (C) Research Grants
    (D) Scholarships
    (E) Loans

11. How much more money was paid out in loans than was received as income in loan repayments?

    (A) $600,000
    (B) $2,400,000
    (C) $3,000,000
    (D) $3,600,000
    (E) $5,400,000

DIRECTIONS: Each of the following items consists of two quantities, one in Column A and one in Column B. Compare the quantities and choose:

   (A) if the quantity in Column A is greater;
   (B) if the quantity in Column B is greater;
   (C) if the two quantities are equal;
   (D) if the relationship cannot be determined from the information given.

Column A	**Column B**		**Column A**	**Column B**

12.
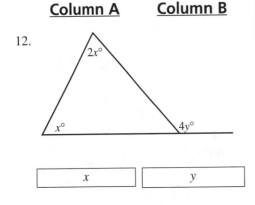

13. $0 > x > y$

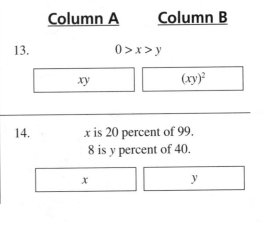

14. x is 20 percent of 99.
     8 is y percent of 40.

23

DIRECTIONS: Each of the following questions has five answer choices. For each question, choose the best answer given.

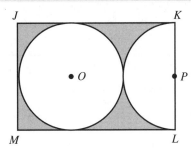

15. In the figure above above, *JKLM* is a rectangle, and *O* and *P* are the centers of circle *O* and semi-circle *P*, respectively. What portion of the figure is shaded?

(A) $\dfrac{1}{4}\pi$

(B) $1 - \dfrac{1}{4}\pi$

(C) $6 - \dfrac{1}{4}\pi$

(D) $4\pi - 1$

(E) $\dfrac{1}{4}\pi - 6$

16. By weight, ingredient *I* is 8.0 percent of dry mixture *M* and 15.0 percent of dry mixture *N*. If 2 kilograms of dry mixture *M* is combined with 3 kilograms of mixture *N*, then ingredient *I* accounts for what percent of the resulting dry mixture?

(A) 7.0%
(B) 11.5%
(C) 12.2%
(D) 23.0%
(E) 50.0%

DIRECTIONS: Each of the following items consists of two quantities, one in Column A and one in Column B. Compare the quantities and choose:

(A) if the quantity in Column A is greater;
(B) if the quantity in Column B is greater;
(C) if the two quantities are equal;
(D) if the relationship cannot be determined from the information given.

Column A	Column B		Column A	Column B

17. $x^2 = y^2 - 1$

$$x^4$$ $$y^4 + 1$$

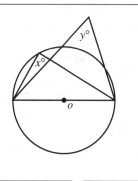

18. x y

19.   A tertiary number is a two-digit number such that the units' digit of the number is equal to $\frac{1}{2}$ the tens' digit.

| The number of tertiary numbers between 10 and 99 | 4 |

DIRECTIONS: Each of the following questions has five answer choices. For each question, choose the best answer given.

---

20. For the one hour period from 10:00 am to 11:00 am, x persons entered a certain store every 2 minutes and $x - 1$ persons left the store every 5 minutes. In terms of x, how many more people were in the store at 11:00 am than at 10:00 am?

(A) $24x - 8$
(B) $30x - 12$
(C) $36x - 24$
(D) $18x + 12$
(E) $36x + 30$

21. If x, y, and z are positive numbers,
$$x + \frac{1}{y} = \frac{1}{z} =$$

(A) $\dfrac{x + y}{z}$

(B) $\dfrac{xz + yz + 1}{z}$

(C) $\dfrac{xyz + y + z}{z}$

(D) $\dfrac{x + y + z}{xyz + 1}$

(E) $\dfrac{xyz + x + z}{yz + 1}$

DIRECTIONS: Each of the following questions is based on the graph. For each question, choose the best answer given.

Pilot Data for Airline A

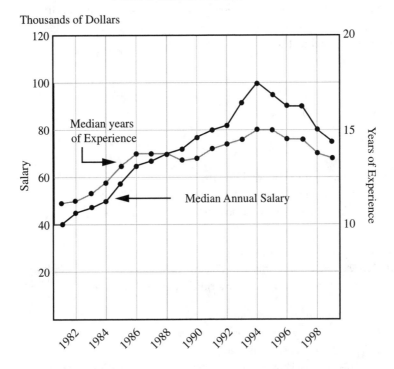

22. The Median Annual Salary rose by approximately what percent from 1981 to 1994?

    (A) 60%
    (B) 150%
    (C) 175%
    (D) 250%
    (E) 600%

23. Which of the following statements can be inferred from the graph?

    I. Median Annual Salary declined by approximately 25% from 1994 to 1999.

    II. The Median Years of Experience rose by approximately 20 years from 1982 to 1988.

    III. In 1988, pilots with the Median Years of Experience earned the Median Annual Salary.

    (A) I only
    (B) II only
    (C) I and II only
    (D) I and III only
    (E) I, II, and III

24. A survey questionnaire requires a respondant to choose 2 out of 5 options in Part I and 3 out 4 options in Part II. How many diferent combinations of options are possible on a completed questionnaire?

    (A) 4
    (B) 6
    (C) 14
    (C) 24
    (E) 40

25. A group of n students is divided into two team such that the number of students on one team is three more than twice the number on the other team. Which of the following represents the number of students on the team with more students?

    (A) $\dfrac{n+3}{2}$

    (B) $\dfrac{2n+3}{2}$

    (C) $\dfrac{n-3}{2}$

    (D) $\dfrac{2n+1}{3}$

    (E) $\dfrac{2n+3}{3}$

Column A	Column B
26. $(0.12345)^2$	$\sqrt{0.12345}$

Column A	Column B
27. Maxine and Robert were hired at a wage of x dollars per hour. Since then, Maxine has been awarded two separate raises of 10 percent each and Robert has been awarded one raise of 20 percent.	
Maxine's present hourly wage	Robert's present hourly wage

Column A	Column B

28.   Point *P* on the coordinate
        plan has coordinates of (3,4)

The distance from *P* to the origin	The distance from P to (*a*,0) where $0 < a < 6$

23

DIRECTIONS: Each of the following questions has five answer choices. For each question, choose the best answer given.

29. The average (arithmetic mean) of five numbers is 30. If one number is removed, the average (arithmetic mean) of the remaining numbers is 28. What number has been removed?

(A) 2
(B) 8
(C) 10
(D) 14
(E) 38

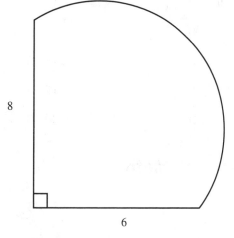

8

6

30. The figure above is bounded by two straight lines and the arc of a circle. What is the area of the figure?

(A) $24 + \dfrac{25\pi}{2}$

(B) $24 + 25\pi$

(C) $48 + \dfrac{25\pi}{2}$

(D) $48 + 25\pi$

(E) cannot be determined

Evaluate Your Performance

Use the following answer key to find out how many questions you answered correctly, then compare your performance on the Math Final with the graph below.

1. (A)	11. (A)	21. (E)
2. (D)	12. (A)	22. (B)
3. (C)	13. (D)	23. (A)
4. (C)	14. (B)	24. (E)
5. (C)	15. (B)	25. (E)
6. (D)	16. (C)	26. (B)
7. (A)	17. (D)	27. (A)
8. (A)	18. (A)	28. (A)
9. (C)	19. (C)	29. (E)
10. (B)	20. (D)	30. (A)

Overall Math

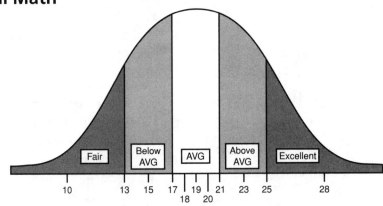

Number Correct

Review Your Work

1. **(A)** It would not be wrong just to do the arithmetic indicated. Column A is –8, and Column B is –32. But you could also reason that both columns will be negative, that Column B will have the greater absolute value, and that Column A is greater.

2. **(D)** This is a good time to test some numbers. n might be 9 or 15. When 9 is divided by 9, there is no remainder (remainder = 0), and when 15 is divided by 9, the remainder is 6. So the relationship is indeterminate.

3. **(C)** Here you see an equation with one unknown centered above the two columns, so you should immediately think "Solve for x:"

   $2x + 3 = x - 2$

   $x = -5$

4. **(C)** The math here, as written, would just take too long to do. So you should look for a way to simplify things. You should notice that there is a pattern: –46 and –45. So the problem can be simplified to:

   $(48 - 47) - (47 - 44) =$

   $1 - 3 = -2$

5. **(C)** This item specifically calls for an approximation. $\sqrt[3]{64} = 4$, so the correct answer must be slightly more than 4.

6. **(D)** Since m is a positive integer, the minimum values for m and n are 3 and 8,

respectively, because $\frac{3}{8}$ is the fraction in lowest terms. And if $m = 3$ and $n = 8$, then $n - m = 5$ and the two columns are equal. But m and n could also be numbers like 30 and 80, in which case $n - m$ would be 50 or some other number.

7. **(A)** This is a geometry manipulation problem, so just find the value of the radius of the circle:

   $Area = \pi r^2$

   $24\pi = \pi r^2$

   $r^2 = 24$

   $r = 2\sqrt{6}$

   Now, if it's still hard to see that Column A is larger, you could divide the columns by 2. You'd have $\sqrt{6}$ in Column A and 2 in Column B. But $\sqrt{6}$ must be greater than $\sqrt{4}$, which is 2, so Column A is greater.

8. **(A)** Trying to do the math indicated here would take too long. You can simplify matters by using the rules for manipulating exponents. Column A becomes $(0.51)^5$, and since (0.51) is a positive fraction, Column A is larger. (Remember that positive fractions get smaller as you raise them to higher powers.) You could also have used a proxy problem here. You could substitute (0.5) for (0.51) and probably do the arithmetic. Better yet, you could change the problem to read:

   $(0.5)(0.5)^2$ compared with $(0.5)^4$

   And you can do that arithmetic fairly easily.

23

9. **(C)** This is a set of pie charts. For this problem, just retrieve the values and do the multiplication: 23% of $30 million is $6.9 million.

10. **(B)** $4.5 million dollars worth of expenditures would be 15% of the expenditures pie. And the slice of the pie closest to 15% is Office Expenses.

11. **(A)** Ten percent of the expenditures went toward loans while 8% of the income was loan repayment, for a difference of 2%: 2% of $30 million = $600,000.

12. **(A)** The measure of the exterior angle of the triangle is equal to the sum of the measures of the two, alternative interior angles:

    $x + 2x = 4y$

    $3x = 4y$

    $\dfrac{x}{y} = \dfrac{4}{3}$

    And since degree measures on the test are positive, x must be greater than y.

13. **(D)** x and y are negative, so you don't want to use the technique of dividing across the comparison. You can, however, use the technique of substituting numbers. Say that $x = -1$ and $y = -2$. Column A would be 2, and Column B would be 4. And you would eliminate choices (A) and (C). Next, let $x = -\dfrac{1}{2}$ and $y = -1$. On that assumption, Column A is $\dfrac{1}{2}$ and Column B is $\dfrac{1}{4}$. That eliminates choice (B) as well. So the correct answer is (D).

14. **(B)** The arithmetic here is so simple enough, that you can go ahead and do it. But you might also notice that y is 20 and that x must be slightly less than 20.

15. **(B)** This is a composite figure problem. The shaded area is the difference between the area of the rectangle and the sum of the areas of the circle and the semicircle. Let r be the radius of the circles. The sum of the circular areas is $\pi r^2 + \dfrac{\pi r^2}{2}$ or $\dfrac{3\pi r^2}{2}$. The area of the rectangle is $3r \times 2r = 6r^2$. And the shaded area is $6r^2 - \dfrac{3\pi r^2}{2}$. And we're looking to find what fraction of the whole figure the shaded area is:

    $$\dfrac{6r^2 - \dfrac{3\pi r^2}{2}}{6r^2} = 1 - \dfrac{1}{4}\text{pi}$$

    This is also a good question for picking some numbers. Assume that the radius of the circle is 1. The circular regions would have an area $\dfrac{3\pi}{2}$, and the rectangle would have an area of 6. And you can finish the problem in the same way. Plus you can also eliminate some choices using common sense. The shaded area looks to be about $\dfrac{1}{4}$ or $\dfrac{1}{3}$ of the entire figure, and that eliminates (A) (which is about $\dfrac{3}{4}$), (C) and (D) (which are larger than 1), and (E) which is a negative number.

16. **(C)** You can solve this item using algebra, but a couple of the advanced strategies that you learned are more effective. You can, for example, just work with numbers. In 2 kilos of M, there are 0.16 kilos of I; and in 3 kilos of N, there are 0.45 kilos. When

you mix the two quantities together, you get 0.61 kilos of I out of a total weight of 5 kilos: $\frac{0.61}{5} = 0.122 = 12.2\%$. You can also use the fail-safe plan to eliminate several choices. Since the two concentrations are 8% and 15%, the resulting mixture must have a concentration in between those two numbers: eliminate (A), (D), and (E).

17. **(D)** You need to get x^4 into the problem, so square both sides of the centered equation. You get:

$x^4 = y^4 - 2y^2 + 1$

And once you've substituted for x^4 in Column A, you can subtract y^4 and 1 from both columns, leaving you with 0 in Column A and $-2y^2$. But you don't have any information about y.

18. **(A)** Since the vertex of angle x is on the circumference of the circle, x is called an inscribed angle. And an inscribed angle intercepts twice its measure of arc. Since the line that passes through O is a diameter, the arc measures 180°, and x is equal to 90°. Now what judgment can you make about y? Since angle y is located outside of the circular region, angle y is smaller than angle x.

19. **(C)** Don't let the fancy terminology throw you. The numbers in question are 21, 42, 63, and 84.

20. **(D)** You can treat this as an algebra problem. The number of persons inside the store grows at the rate of

$\frac{x}{2} - \frac{x-1}{5} = \frac{5x-2x+2}{10}$. And that goes on for 60 minutes: $\frac{5x-2x+2}{10} \times 60 = 18x + 12$. But you can also use the advanced strategy of assuming a number. Let x be 5. At the end of an hour, at the rate of 5 people every 2 minutes, 150 people would have gone in, and at the rate of 4 people every 5 minutes, 48 would have left, for a net gain of 102. Then substitute 5 for x into the choices until you find the one that works.

21. **(E)** You can do the lengthy algebra required here, or you can opt for an advanced strategy: assume some numbers. For example, let x, y, and z all be 1. On that assumption, the expression in the stem has the value $\frac{3}{2}$. Substitute 1 for all variables in the answer choices, and only (D) and (E) return the value $\frac{3}{2}$. Try another number, and you'll eliminate (D).

22. **(B)** The median annual salary rose from $40,000 in 1981 to $100,000 in 1994, an increase of $\frac{100-40}{40} = 1.5 = 150\%$.

23. **(A)** Statement I is inferrable because the median annual salary dropped from $100,000 in 1994 to $75,000 in 1999, a drop of $\frac{100-75}{100} = \frac{25}{100} = 25\%$. Statement II is not inferrable. II mistakenly reads the scale intended for salary. The median years of experience increased from about 10 to about 12.5. III makes the same kind of error.

24. **(E)** This problem is not one commonly used, but a little common sense can get you the answer. Just count on your fingers. For Part I, there are ten pairs of

responses, and for Part II there are four. And $10 \times 4 = 40$.

25. **(E)** You can do this problem using algebra, but one of the advanced strategies is going to be quicker: make up some numbers. Pick a number for the team with fewer students, say 10. On that assumption, the other team has 23 students. That's a total of 33 students, so $n = 33$. Next, just substitute 33 for n in the choices until you find the one that generates the value 23.

26. **(B)** Don't even think about doing this arithmetic. A positive fraction (between 0 and 1) when squared is smaller than the fraction itself, and its square root is larger.

27. **(A)** Just assign a value to x. Say $100 per hour. Maxine got a $6 per hour raise to $106 and another 6% raise on top of that to $106 + 0.06($106) = $112.36 per hour. Robert got just one raise: $100 + 0.12($100) = $112.00 per hour.

28. **(A)** You might want to sketch a figure on a piece of scratch paper, but it's not absolutely necessary. The distance from P to the origin is 5—as in a 3, 4, 5 right triangle. Then, since a is a point on the x-axis between 0 and 6, the distance from P to $(a,0)$ ranges from just less than 5 to 4.

29. **(E)** The total of the five numbers is 150. The total of the remaining four numbrs is 112. So the missing number is 38.

30. **(A)** Sketch in the hypotenuse of the right triangle. It will have a length of 5. Now, the triangle has an area of 24, and the semi-circle an area of $\frac{25\pi}{2}$.

Get Answers to Frequently Asked Questions

Q: Do I need to do more work on the math part?

A: Probably not. You have learned all about the three types of math questions and have mastered strategies for each one. Plus, you have done the equivalent of *six full-length practice exams* for this area.

Q: Should I be worried if I still miss some questions?

A: No. You have to remember that the GRE is a challenging exam. It's not like the tests you're used to taking. Only a handful of people every year answer all of the questions correctly. Even the people who are scoring in the 700s on the math are missing questions.

Q: What if I want to practice my math on the computer?

A: That would be a good idea. You've mastered the content of the math part, but you could still probably benefit from some hands-on experience with a computer-based delivery system—get a feel for the figures on the screen and using scratch paper and so on. Plus, even if you are computer literate, you still need to get used to the idiosyncracies of the GRE program.

Part IV

Analytical Skills

Test Your Analytical Skills

Today, you'll take the Analytical PreTest and use specially designed evaluation tools to make some judgments about where you stand. You'll also review explanations of the correct answers to the items used in the PreTest as a first step in your in-depth study of GRE analytical questions.

Preview the Analytical PreTest

You'll be taking the GRE on computer. This diagnostic exercise, which is presented in pencil-and-paper format, has been carefully designed to yield results that are comparable to a computer-based version of the test. You'll get the most out of this PreTest if you keep the following important points in mind.

The GRE CAT uses the two different kinds of Analytical Questions you learned about in Day 1. You'll find both of in today's Analytical PreTest.

Analytical Reasoning

Analytical Reasoning is the "logical puzzles" question type. Each group of items is related to a set of initial conditions that describe a common situation such as people standing in a line, different colored boxes with different contents, a group of people who must be divided into smaller groups. The initial conditions remain in effect for all the items in that group. Any additional assumptions that you are asked to make by a question apply to that question alone. You may find it useful to draw a diagram for some questions; for others, a diagram may not be useful. Here is an example to refresh your memory about puzzles:

What You'll Do Today

- Preview the Analytical PreTest
- Take the Analytical PreTest
- Evaluate Your Performance
- Review the Correct Answers

QUESTION Five people—Jamal, Katie, Lorna, Mary, and Nat—are to be awarded prizes—first (highest) through fifth (lowest)—based on their participation in a competition. Each person will receive exactly one prize, and no prize is shared.

Jamal will receive a higher prize than Katie.

Lorna will receive a higher prize than Mary.

Nat will receive a higher prize than both Jamal and Lorna.

Which of the following must be true?

    (A) Jamal receives first prize.

    (B) Nat receives first prize.

    (C) Lorna receives second prize.

    (D) Mary receives fourth prize.

    (E) Katie receives fourth prize.

ANALYSIS The correct answer is (**B**). Nat receives a higher prize than either Jamal or Lorna who, in turn, receive higher prizes than Katie and Mary.

QUESTION If Mary receives third prize, then which of the following must be true?

    (A) Katie receives second prize.

    (B) Jamal receives second prize.

    (C) Jamal receives fourth prize.

    (D) Lorna receives fourth prize.

    (E) Lorna receives fifth prize.

ANALYSIS The correct answer is (**C**). A rough diagram might be useful. Nat receives the first prize, and this question asks you to assume that Mary receives the third prize:

```
1  2  3  4  5
N     M
```

But Lorna receives a higher prize than Mary:

```
1  2  3  4  5
N  L  M
```

And Jamal receives a higher prize than Katie:

```
1  2   3   4   5
N  L  M   J   K
```

Logical Reasoning

Logical Reasoning is the "arguments" question type. Each item consists of an initial statement or paragraph, a question stem, and five choices. The initial statement or paragraph states a position or develops an argument. The question stem tells you what to do with it, e.g., describe it, find an assumption, attack it. Here is an example:

QUESTION The East Coast Eagles, a professional football team, unveiled an innovative five back offense in their game last week against the Southwest Wolves and won by the impressive score of 18 to 0. The five back offense is obviously highly effective and will soon be adopted by all other teams in the league.

The argument above can be criticized because it

    (A) relies on the opinion of an expert who may be biased

    (B) reaches a broad conclusion based on limited evidence

    (C) draws an analogy between two situations that are not similar

    (D) assumes uncritically the conclusion that the argument is supposed to prove

    (E) shifts the burden of proof to anyone who wishes to disprove the conclusion

ANALYSIS The correct answer is **(B)**. The speaker reaches a very large conclusion (all other teams will adopt the new offense) based upon very slim evidence: one team won one game with it.

NOTE Analytical reasoning is also called "logical puzzles" or sometimes just "puzzles." Logical reasoning is sometimes called "arguments."

The PreTest has been carefully crafted to give results that are comparable to those generated by a computer-based test. The mix of questions, the range of difficulty, and the 30-minute time limit are features that help to make this a true diagnostic exercise.

Since the computer-based GRE CAT does not give you the option of omitting a question, you should answer *all* items. You don't lose points for wrong answers.

Take the Analytical PreTest

Analytical PreTest

25 Questions • Time—30 Minutes

> **DIRECTIONS:** Each question or group of questions is based on a passage or a set of conditions. You may find it useful to draw a rough diagram for some questions. For each question, select the best answer choice given.

Questions 1–5

Seven people—Jane, Karl, Len, Mai, Nina, Olga, and Pietri—were candidates for a certain office. After the voting, they were ranked according to the number of votes they had received. The candidate receiving the most votes was ranked first, and every candidate received a different number of votes. The voting results include:

Jane received more votes than Olga.

Olga received more votes than Karl.

Karl received more votes than Mai.

Nina did not receive the fewest votes.

Pietri received more votes and Nina and more votes than Olga but fewer than Len.

1. Which of the following statements must be true?

   (A) Jane received more votes than Nina.
   (B) Karl received more votes than Nina.
   (C) Len received more votes than Jane.

   (D) Nina received more votes than Olga.
   (E) Pietri received more votes than Karl.

2. Which of the following could be an accurate list of the seven candidates ranked in order of the number of votes they received?

   (A) Jane, Len, Karl, Olga, Mai, Nina, Pietri
   (B) Jane, Len, Pietri, Olga, Karl, Mai, Nina
   (C) Len, Pietri, Jane, Nina, Olga, Karl, Mai
   (D) Len, Pietri, Nina, Olga, Karl, Jane, Mai
   (E) Pietri, Len, Jane, Olga, Nina, Mai, Karl

3. How many candidates could possibly have enough votes to finish first?

   (A) two
   (B) three
   (C) four
   (D) five
   (E) six

4. If Pietri, Olga, and Karl are ranked consecutively in that order, which of the following statements CANNOT be true?

(A) Jane received more votes than Len.
(B) Jane received more votes than Pietri.
(C) Nina received more votes than Mai.
(D) Nina received more votes than Olga.
(E) Olga received more votes than Nina.

5. If Pietri received more votes than Jane, then ranks of how many candidates can be determined?

(A) two
(B) three
(C) four
(D) five
(E) six

6. When asked whether or not electronic books might someday replace printed and bound volumes, Professor de la Paz smiled and responded, "No, once you have held a first folio of Shakespeare's work in your hands, you know electronic documents are just a curiosity that will never seriously threaten to replace the written word."

Which of the following, if true, most seriously weakens the Professor's conclusion?

(A) Shakespeare was only one great English writer among many.
(B) A substantial number of authors still use typewriters rather than word processors.
(C) Museums contains many artifacts that were replaced by new inventions.

(D) A first folio of Shakespeare has a special connection to a famous author.
(E) Many students graduate from college without having studied Shakespeare.

7. Complaints that public eduation has been hijacked by professional educators and that this is the cause of a general sickness in the education of our children are gross exaggerations. Virtually every school district in the country is under the direction of a school board that consists of members elected by the taxpayers who reside in that district.

Which of the following, if true, would most weaken the claim that professionals do not control the education of children?

(A) Across the nation, parent organizations share information about goals and policies at conferences and on the world wide web.
(B) Most decisions affecting educational policy are made by principals who are insulated by contract from the oversight of school boards.
(C) Most of the members elected to the local school board are parents who have children who are enrolled in the districts supervised by the boards.
(D) Recently, state-wide funding restrictions have been loosened to permit local school districts greater flexibility in desiging and implementing curriculum.
(E) Most states encourage but do not require local school districts to hire only teachers who have been certified by a state testing process.

24

8. Between major cities, Universal Parcel guarantees overnight delivery of a package weighing less than one pound for $15. Rapid Courier offers a second-day guaranteed services for packages of less than one pound for $8. If the guarantee of next day delivery is more important than the cost of shipping, a business will choose Universal Parcel over Rapid Courier.

Which of the following is an assumption made by the analysis above?

(A) The next day guarantee is worth at least $15.

(B) Price and delivery date are the only relevant considerations.

(C) Universal has a better reputation for on-time delivery than does Rapid.

(D) The $8 fee charged by Rapid is not justified by the service that it provides.

(E) Businesses will not choose Universal over Rapid for packages that weigh more than one pound.

Questions 9–13

A cosmetic company prepares complementary packages of its products for promotional purposes. The items included are samples from the following product lines: shampoos, conditioners, soaps, lotions, creams, and colognes. The packages must be prepared according to the following restrictions:

Each package must include at least three samples and represent at least three of the different products lines.

At most two samples can be shampoos.

At most two samples can be conditioners.

A package cannot contain more than one sample each from the soap, lotion, cream, or cologne lines.

If a package contains a sample of soap, then it must contain a sample of cologne.

If a package contains a sample of lotion, then it cannot contain a sample of cream.

9. The maximum number of samples that can be in a package is

(A) three

(B) four

(C) five

(D) six

(E) seven

10. Which of the following is an acceptable mix of samples for a finished package?

(A) Two shampoos and two conditioners.

(B) Two lotions and two colognes.

(C) One shampoo, one conditioner, one cologne, and one lotion.

(D) Two shampoos, one conditioner, one cream, and and soap.

(E) Two shampoos, three conditioners, one lotion, and two colognes.

11. If exactly one sample of shampoo and one sample of conditioner are included in a package, then which of the following must be true?

    (A) The package does not include a sample of cologne.
    (B) The package does not include a sample of soap.
    (C) The package includes a sample of lotion.
    (D) The package includes exactly six samples.
    (E) The package contains five or fewer samples.

12. If a package includes a sample of conditioner and a sample of cologne, any of the following additional samples could complete the package EXCEPT:

    (A) a sample of shampoo and a sample of conditioner
    (B) a sample of cologne and a sample of conditioner
    (C) a sample of cream and a sample of shampoo
    (D) a sample of soap and a sample of cream
    (E) a sample of lotion and a sample of shampoo

13. If a finished package includes exactly two shampoos and three other samples, each of a different product line, which of the following could NOT be included?

    (A) cologne
    (B) soap
    (C) lotion
    (D) cream
    (E) conditioner

Questions 14–18

Six people—Freda, Glen, Hilda, Justin, Kirsten, and Lorna—are going to attend a training session. The session will be held twice during the day, in the morning and again in the afternoon. Each person will attend one or the other session but not both.

> Three people will attend the morning session; three people will attend the afternoon session.
>
> Kirsten and Lorna cannot attend the same session.
>
> Either Freda or Glen must attend the same session as Hilda.

14. Which of the following groups could attend the morning session?

    (A) Freda, Glen, Kirsten
    (B) Freda, Glen, Lorna
    (C) Freda, Hilda, Glen
    (D) Glen, Kirsten, Lorna
    (E) Hilda, Glen, Lorna

15. If Hilda and Lorna attend the afternoon session, then which of the following pairs must attend the morning session?

    (A) Freda and Glen
    (B) Freda and Justin
    (C) Freda and Kirsten
    (D) Glen and Kirsten
    (E) Justin and Kirsten

24

16. If Justin and Lorna attend the morning session, then which of the following pairs must attend the afternoon session?

    (A) Freda and Hilda
    (B) Freda and Kirsten
    (C) Glen and Hilda
    (D) Glen and Kirsten
    (E) Hilda and Kirsten

17. Which of the following pairs CANNOT attend the same session?

    (A) Freda and Glen
    (B) Freda and Justin
    (C) Hilda and Lorna
    (D) Justin and Kirsten
    (E) Justin and Lorna

18. If Freda attends the morning session and Justin attends the afternoon session, then which of the following must be true?

    I. Glen and Justin attend the same session.

    II. Hilda and Kirsten attend the same session.

    III. Freda and Kirsten attend the same session.

    (A) I only
    (B) II only
    (C) I and II only
    (D) II and III only
    (E) I, II, and III

Questions 19–22

In a city, the public transportation system consists of a subway line, a bus route, and a commuter rail line.

Subway trains go from station J to K to L to M to N to O, stopping at each station, and make the return trip in reverse order.

Buses go from station K to S to R to M to T to O, stopping at each station, and make the return trip in reverse order.

Commuter trains go from station K to R to T to O, stopping at each station, and make the return trip in reverse order.

Transfers are possible at all stations served by more than one mode of transportation.

19. Which of the stations is not served by train?

    (A) K
    (B) L
    (C) N
    (D) S
    (E) R

20. In order to make the trip from J to M, a passenger must stop at which of the following?

    (A) K only
    (B) K and L only
    (C) K and R only
    (D) K and S only
    (E) K, S, and R only

21. Using the bus only, a passenger cannot go from

    (A) K to M
    (B) K to T
    (C) M to O
    (D) O to N
    (E) O to M

22. If N is closed, in order for a passenger to get from O to L, it is necessary to pass through

    (A) K
    (B) M
    (C) S
    (D) R
    (E) T

23. U-Park, which operates the below ground parking facility in the High Tower Apartment building, recently announced that it was increasing the rental on spaces leased to residents of the building by 25 percent. Many residents have said they will not renew their leases, preferring instead to take their chances of finding on-street parking. U-Park's greed is short-sighted because the company stands to lose a lot of revenue.

    Which of the following, if true, would most weaken the conclusion of the speaker?

    (A) Residents of High Tower Apartments already pay fees substantially above the city average for leases on their parking spaces.
    (B) On-street parking in the vicinity of the High Tower Apartment building is relatively easy to find on most days.

    (C) U-Park will be able to fill spaces with short-term transient vehicles that pay rates considerably in excess of those paid by long-term lessors.
    (D) The building management of High Tower Apartments leases the parking facility to U-Park for a percentage of the gross annual revenues generated.
    (E) Long-term parking leases are not subject to a 10 percent surcharge that is levied on parking rentals of less that 24-hour's duration.

24. So-called professional wrestling is contributing to a culture of violence among children. A recent survey of 50 episodes of professional wrestling broadcast on cable television found nearly a thousand instances in which particpants were struck by sticks, chairs, or other objects, almost 250 incidents of simulated sexual activity, and over 2,000 uses of profanity.

    The argument above depends upon which of the following assumptions?

    (A) Professional wrestling is also broadcast over network television.
    (B) Children watch professional wrestling on cable television.
    (C) Children who hear profanity on television do not hear profanity elsewhere.
    (D) The incidents of violence mentioned were actual and not merely simulated.
    (E) The majority of professional wrestling fans are children.

24

25. It was surprising to hear a medical doctor state that no child or adult has ever been harmed by eating any amount of fruits and vegetables produced using approved and regulated pesticides. Unlike food poisonings, infections, and allergic reactions, the causes of which can be traced, it is difficult to determine whether exposure to a substance—natural or nonnatural—10 or 20 years ago is responsible for a disease like cancer, multiple sclerosis, or muscular dystrophy, the causes of which are not well understood.

The speaker implies that

(A) some diseases may be caused by eating fruits and vegetables treated with approved pesticides

(B) approved pesticides are the likely cause for diseases such as cancer, multiple sclerosis, and muscular dystrophy

(C) medical doctors are not competent to determine whether pesticides cause disease in a particular patient

(D) any harmful effects of pesticides will be manifested relatively soon afeter the pesticides have been ingested

(E) the use of pesticides on fruits and vegetables for human consumption should be discontinued

STOP:
IF YOU FINISH BEFORE TIME EXPIRES, USE THE ADDITIONAL TIME TO CHECK YOUR WORK.

Evaluate Your Performance

Use the following answer key to score your Analtyical Diagnostic Test. (Put a "✓" beside those items you answered correctly.)

Analtyical Reasoning

1. (D)		13. (B)
2. (C)		14. (E)
3. (A)		15. (E)
4. (D)		16. (E)
5. (B)		17. (A)
6. (D)		18. (A)
7. (B)		19. (D)
8. (B)		20. (A)
9. (E)		21. (D)
10. (D)		22. (E)
11. (E)		
12. (B)		

Number of Analytical Reasoning
Correct: _____

Logical Reasoning

23. (C)
24. (B)
25. (A)

Number of Logical Reasoning
Correct: _____

TOTAL CORRECT: _____

24

When you ask "How did I do?", you probably have in mind a couple of different questions. You want to know how you did overall and whether you did significantly worse (or better) on one part of the test or another. The following "bell curves" will help you answer those questions.

Analytical Reasoning

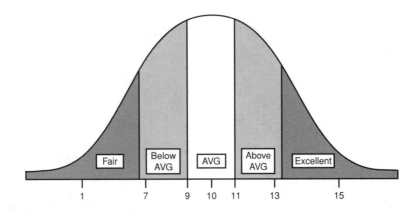

Number Correct

Logical Reasoning

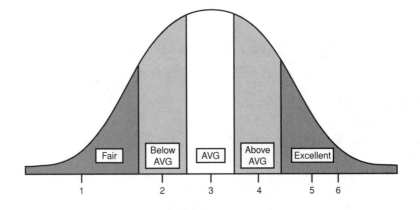

Number Correct

Overall Analytical

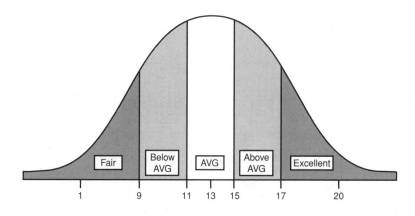

Number Correct

Review the Correct Answers

Now, you should review the explanations for the correct answers to the Analytical PreTest.

1. **(D)** Mai received fewer votes than Jane, Olga, and Karl; Nina received fewer than Len and Pietri; but since Nina did not receive the fewest votes, Mai must have received the fewest votes.

2. **(C)** Only choice (C) is consistent with all of the inital conditions.

3. **(A)** Only Jane or Len could have polled the greatest number of votes.

4. **(D)** Since Pietri received more votes than Nina, Nina could not have received more votes than Olga (because Olga is ranked directly behind Pietri, according to the question stem).

5. **(B)** If Pietri got more votes than Jane, then Len got the most votes, and Pietri ranked second. We know that Mai finished last. So the ranks of three different candidates can be determined. The ranks of the others depend on how Nina finished.

6. **(D)** The Professor reaches a very broad conclusion (electronic documents don't threaten the written word) based upon a single piece of evidence (the first folio). This is especially weak since the piece of evidence is very special, suggesting that it will not support the general conclusion.

7. **(B)** The speaker claims that elected school boards control educational policy. (B) directly contradicts this claim: principals, who are professional educators and free of oversight, really make the decisions.

8. **(B)** The information given talks only about price and delivery schedule. So the speaker assumes that those are the only two relevant factors. (There could be others, e.g., treatment accorded a package.)

9. **(E)** The maximum number is seven: two shampoos, two conditioners, soap and cologne, and either lotion or cream.

10. **(D)** Only (D) is consistent with all of the initial conditions.

11. **(E)** In addition to the one shampoo and one conditioner, the package could include soap and cologne and either lotion or cream. That's a maximum of five items, but it could contain fewer.

12. **(B)** The initial conditions say only one cologne can be included.

13. **(B)** The inclusion of soap would require cologne as well.

14. **(E)** The first condition eliminates both (C) and (D), while the second condition eliminates (A) and (B).

15. **(E)** If Hilda and Lorna attend the same session, then the third person in that session must be either Freda or Glen. Thus, Justin and Kirsten must attend the other session.

16. **(E)** If Justin and Lorna attend the morning session, then Kirsten must attend the afternoon session along with Hilda and either Freda or Glen.

17. **(A)** If Freda and Glen attend the same session, then Hilda would also attend that session; but that would leave both Kirsten and Lorna attending the same session.

18. **(A)** If Freda and Justin do not attend the same session, then (given that Kirsten and Lorna do not attend the same session) Hilda and Glen attend different sessions. But Hilda will attend the same session as Freda and Glen the same session as Justin.

19. **(D)** S is served only by bus.

20. **(A)** The only connection to J is K. From there, it is possible to via subway (to L and to M), by bus (to S to R and to M), and by commuter rail and subway (to R to M).

21. **(D)** The bus does not stop at N.

22. **(E)** With N closed, it is necessary to pass through T.

23. **(C)** The conclusion is that U-Park will lose money, and the evidence for that conclusion is the loss of a certain sort of revenue—the long-term lease. (C) weakens this conclusion by saying, in effect: there is other revenue to be had.

24. **(B)** The argument asserts that the broadcasts help to create a culture of violence for children, but that assumes that children see the programming.

25. **(A)** The speaker makes only the minimal claim that it is not possible to exclude pesticides as causes for diseases the causes of which are not certain.

24

Day

25

Teach Yourself Analytical Ability Questions

Get the Inside Info on Analytical Ability

The Analytical Ability part of your GRE will use two different question types: analytical reasoning, which is also called puzzles, and logical reasoning, which is also called arguments. Here are the directions for the Analytical Ability part of the GRE:

> **DIRECTIONS:** Each question or group of questions is based on a passage or a set of conditions. You may find it useful to draw a rough diagram for some questions. For each question, select the best answer choice given.

These directions cover both puzzles and arguments, but there is a big difference between the two question types. Let's look at each in greater detail.

The Inside Info on Puzzles

There are three important facts to keep in mind about puzzles. First, puzzles are almost entirely a matter of pure logic. You have to use techniques of reasoning such as "It's either P or Q; but it's not P; therefore, it's Q" and "If P, then Q; if Q, then R; P; therefore, R." In this respect, puzzles seem to be like math questions: they're open and shut; the answer is right or wrong.

What You'll Do Today

- Get All the Inside Info on Analytical Ability
- Learn How to Answer "Puzzle" Questions
- Workshop A: Puzzles
- Learn How to Answer "Argument" Questions
- Workshop B: Arguments
- Get Answers to Frequently Asked Questions

> **NOTE** Because they use logical connections, puzzles have the "flavor" of math questions. But unlike math, puzzles don't require that you memorize formulas.

Second, all puzzles are controlled by a group of set-up conditions. These set-up conditions describe a situation such as:

QUESTION Six people are going to address a meeting. Each one will speak exactly once, and some restrictions apply such as a certain person can't go first and two other people won't speak one directly after the other.

You have to answer questions about the order in which the people can speak.

Or:

QUESTION Eight chemicals on a shelf are going to be used in an experiment. A couple of the chemicals must be used; this chemical can only be used if that chemical is also used; and some chemicals cannot be used with others.

You have to answer questions about the possible combinations of chemicals that are permitted.

Or:

QUESTION A campground has several campsites joined by paths. It's possible to go directly from some campsites to others, but other campsites require you to take circuitous routes through intermediate locations.

You have to answer questions about possible routes to and from various places in the campground.

In each case, the questions in the group ask you about possibilities that are left open by the set-up conditions. This is an important design element of this question type: the set-up conditions leave open the possibilities that the questions then ask about.

> **CAUTION** Don't waste a lot of time trying to figure out all possibilities, because there are too many.

The third important characteristic of puzzles is that individual questions can provide more information. This is done by asking you to make assumptions such as "If Jones is the third speaker," "If chemical K and chemical P are combined," and "If the path from P to Q is closed." In this way, the questions work with the original set-up to create the series of questions.

> Additional information introduced by an "if" clause is good for one question only.

The Inside Info on Arguments

Arguments are made up of an initial paragraph, a question stem, and answer choices. Let's look at each element more closely.

> Arguments in the Analytical Ability part are a lot like reading comprehension questions in the Verbal part—only shorter. So you can apply what you learned about Reading Comprehension to arguments.

The initial paragraph is fairly short, sometimes only one sentence long and at most a few sentences long. The most important thing to notice about an initial paragraph is that it states a position. For example:

The shelf space given by retail stores to a book is a function of the sales retailers expect to realize from the title. The greater projected sales, the larger the display. Therefore, a consumer who sees multiple copies of a title on display should not assume that this means the book has literary merit.

In this case, the position, which is also called the conclusion of the line of reasoning, is signaled by the "therefore:" shelf space does not equal literary value. Everything else in the initial paragraph is the evidence or support for that position.

The second important element of an argument question is the stem. The stem is the instruction that follows the initial paragraph. It tells you what you're supposed to do: draw a conclusion, weaken the argument, comment on the argument, find a similar argument, and so on.

> Argument question stems often use the phrase "if true." This means that you are supposed to accept the information as factual and to assess its impact as though it were true—even if it seems to you problematic or untrue.

25

The third element of argument questions is the answer choices. The answer choices to arguments are a lot like the answer choices to reading comprehension questions: every word counts. You have to be sure that you read what is actually written and not just what you think you'd like to find.

TIP — Forget about the formal directions for Analytical Ability. You'll be able to recognize puzzles and arguments just by looking at them, and you'll already know what to do with them. So when you see the directions, point and click on the "DISMISS DIRECTIONS" icon on the screen and start answering questions.

Learn How to Answer "Puzzle" Questions

Because puzzles are almost pure logic, answering questions is almost entirely a matter of processing information. In fact, puzzles require very little intelligence. Given enough time, you could work out all of the possibilities permitted by the set-up conditions, and that list of possibilities would include every correct answer choice. The problem is that you don't have unlimited time, so puzzles become a race against the clock. You have to process information as efficiently as possible, and that is where your Action Plan is focused:

 Step 1: Process the information given in the set-up.

A. Identify the type.

First, determine what kind of puzzle set you have based on the initial description and the kinds of connections it uses. Most fall into one of three common categories.

B. Summarize the information.

Second, set up an initial diagram or summarize the information. Your choice will depend on the type of problem set-up you've got.

C. Draw further conclusions.

Third, look for further conclusions that might be drawn from the initial description.

Step 2: Answer the questions.

A. If the question provides no additional information, answer using only the set-up conditions.

Questions that provide no additional information can be answered using what you already know. This may require a further inference drawn during Step 1, or it may be just a matter of comparing answer choices against the conditions given in the initial set-up.

B. Process any additional information provided by the stem.

If a question provides additional information, process that information for additional conclusions before selecting your answer choice.

One of the most important components of the first step of the Action Plan is identifying the type of problem set-up you have. The set-ups used by the GRE usually fall clearly into one of three categories—though some overlap is possible. Here are the three types you'll most likely have to deal with.

Ordering Problems

The most common type of puzzle is the ordering problem, so we'll start with that category. Ordering problems, as the name implies, involve putting individuals into a sequence. Here are some examples of ordering set-ups:

Seven people—John, Kim, Leslie, Moses, Nolan, Oliver, Pam—are standing in a single-file line waiting to buy tickets for a movie.

John is closer to the ticket window than both Kim and Leslie.

Nolan is standing directly behind Moses and directly in front of Oliver.

Pam is not the last person in line.

A professor must schedule conferences with seven students—J, K, L, M, N, O, P— during a certain day. Each conference will start on the hour and last 60 minutes. The first conference is scheduled for 9:00, the last for 3:00. The professor will see each student exactly once during the day.

The professor must see J sometime before she sees either K or L.

The professor must see N immediately after she sees M and immediately before she sees O.

The professor cannot see P last.

A bio-chemist has discovered that seven different molecules—J, K, L, M, N, O, P—are found in sequences that determine important genetic characteristics.

25

Each molecule appears exactly once in a sequence, and the positions in the sequence are numbered from 1 through 7.

J always appears earlier in a sequence than both K and L.

N always appears directly behind M and directly after O in a sequence.

P is not the last molecule in a sequence.

You'll notice that while these three problem set-ups differ in descriptive terminology, the underlying logic is the same:

Sequences of J, K, L, M, N, O, P.

J earlier than K in the order

J earlier than L in the order

M then N then O

P is not last in the order

CAUTION

> Be careful to distinguish between set-up conditions that specify "directly" or "immediately" and ones that require only "somewhere." For example:
>
> *John is directly in front of Kim versus John is somewhere in front of Kim.*
>
> *Leslie is immediately to the left of Moses versus Leslie is somewhere to the left of Moses.*

TIP

> Some ordering problems use names, others use letters in place of names. There is no difference in the underlying logic, but you can save yourself time if you reduce any names to first initials, e.g, *John = **J*** and *Karl = **K***.

Now let's apply the Action Plan to an ordering problem set:

The awards committee of a civic club will recognize seven members—J, K, L, M, N, O, P—for their contributions to the community at the club's annual awards dinner. Each member will be recognized exactly once according to the following conditions:

J will be recognized last.

K will be recognized before both L and M are recognized.

O must be recognized immediately after P and immediately before N or immediately after N and immediately before P.

This set has the distinguishing feature of an ordering set: individuals who must be ordered into acceptable sequences. Notice also that the set-up conditions don't determine the order in which the individuals will appear in the sequence. (Except for J, who must appear last.)

The first thing that you should do is summarize the information you've been given on the scratch paper you have available. Use whatever shorthand you normally use, but your summary should look something like this:

J = 7th

K before L & M

N-O-P or P-O-N

It doesn't appear possible to determine even a partial order, so you would proceed to Step Two.

Here is the first question:

QUESTION Which of the following is a complete and accurate listing of the individuals who could be recognized first?

(A) K

(B) K and N

(C) K, N, and P

(D) K, N, O, and P

(E) K, L, N, O, and P.

ANALYSIS The correct answer is (**C**). The set-up conditions say that N, O, and P come in that or the reverse order, so of that group, only N and P could be recognized first. Then, K must be recognized before L and M. So the possibilities for first position are K, N, and P.

Here is the second question:

QUESTION K could be recognized in all the following positions EXCEPT:

(A) first

(B) second

(C) third

(D) fourth

(E) fifth

ANALYSIS The correct answer is **(E)**. K must come before L and M. Since J is already designated as seventh, K cannot come later in the sequence than fourth.

And here's the third question:

QUESTION If M is recognized third, then which of the following must be true?

(A) L is recognized second.

(B) N is recognized fourth.

(C) P is recognized fourth.

(D) N is recognized sixth.

(E) P is recognized sixth.

ANALYSIS The correct answer is **(A)**. For this question, you'll probably want to use a diagram:

```
1 2 3 4 5 6 7
    M       J
```

Then N-O-P will have to be in positions 4, 5, and 6, though not necessarily in that order:

```
1  2   3  4   5  6   7
      M N/P O P/N  J
```

And that means that K and L will be first and second:

```
1  2  3  4   5  6   7
K  L  M N/P O P/N  J
```

And here is the fourth question:

QUESTION If N is recognized immediately before K, then all of the following must be true EXCEPT:

(A) P is recognized first.

(B) O is recognized second.

(C) N is recognized third.

(D) K is recognized fourth.

(E) L is recognized fifth.

ANALYSIS The correct answer is **(E)**. Again, you'll need to see what the new information tells you. Since K can be recognized no later than fourth:

1	2	3	4	5	6	7
P	O	N	K	L/M	M/L	J

Selection Problems

The second common type of puzzle is selection problems. In this type of problem, you are given a group of individuals and must choose several according to the initial conditions. Here are some examples:

The chair of an academic department must appoint six professors to serve on a committee. The list of possible appoints includes Martin, Neckar, Ovitz, Pharr, Quinn, Rahm, Seton, Taub, and Urbano.

Martin will not serve on the committee with either Pharr or Rahm.

If Neckar is appointed to the committee, either Quinn or Seton must be appointed but not both.

Either Taub or Urbano must be appointed to the committee.

A coach has ten players—J, K, L, M, N, O, P, Q, R, S—who must be assigned either to the first team or the second team.

Each team will consist of five players.

If J is assigned to the first team, then R must also be assigned to the first team.

Both S and N cannot be assigned to the same team.

If L is assigned to the second team, then O must be assigned the first team.

K can be assigned to the first team only if Q is also assigned to the first team.

A dispatcher has five pilots—F, G, H, J, K—four copilots—M, N, O, P—and three navigators—X, Y, Z—who must be assigned to three flights with different destinations—Great Gorge, Pine Terrace, and River Bend. Each crew will consist of one pilot, one copilot and one navigator.

F will not fly with either N or Z.

If G is assigned to the River Bend flight, then O and P are assigned to the Pine Terrace flight.

If J is assigned to the Great Gorge flight, then Y must also be assigned to the Great Gorge flight.

25

CAUTION Pay careful attention to asymmetrical requirements, e.g., *If F is chosen, then G is chosen.* (G can be chosen without F but not vice versa.)

Now let's apply the Action Plan to a selection set:

> A florist is creating a display. The display will include three flowers in bloom selected from J, K, L, M, and N and two types of greenery selected from P, Q, R, and S. The display must be created according to the following constraints:
>
> J cannot be used unless S is also used.
>
> If L is used, then both K and P must be used.
>
> If either R or S is used, then Q cannot be used.

You should begin by summarizing the conditions on your scratch paper for ready reference:

> J ——> S (J cannot be used unless S is also used.)
>
> L ——> (K & P)(If L is used, then both K and P must be used.)
>
> (R or S) ——> not-Q (If either R or S is used, then Q cannot be used.)

Here is the first question:

QUESTION Which of the following is an acceptable display?

    (A) J, L, M, K, R

    (B) J, L, K, P, S

    (C) K, L, M, R, S

    (D) K, M, N, Q, S

    (E) K, N, P, R, S

ANALYSIS The correct answer is **(B)**. Since this question provides no additional information, you can answer based just on the set-up conditions. (A) is not acceptable because it includes J without S in violation of the first set-up conditions. (C) is not acceptable because it includes L without including both K and P, in violation of the second set-up condition. (D) is not acceptable because it includes both S and Q, in violation of the third set-up condition. And (E) is not acceptable because it uses only K and N from the flowers-in-bloom group, but the set-up requires three from that group.

Here is the second question in the series:

QUESTION   If R and S are both used in the display, then which of the following CANNOT be used?

(A) J

(B) K

(C) L

(D) M

(E) N

ANALYSIS   The correct answer is **(C)**. This question provides additional information, so add it to the set-up conditions and process it for further conclusions. R and S are the two from the greenery group, so you need three from the flower-in-bloom group. L cannot be used, since P is not used.

Here is the third question in the series:

QUESTION   If P is not used, then which of the following must be used?

(A) J

(B) L

(C) M

(D) N

(E) S

ANALYSIS   The correct answer is **(E)**. If P is not used, then both R and S have to be used. (Q could not be used with either R or S.) The three flowers-in-bloom must be chosen from the group J, K, L, and M, but no one of them is required.

And here is the final question:

QUESTION   If the florist has already used J and R, how many acceptable group of elements can complete the display?

(A) 1

(B) 2

(C) 3

(D) 4

(E) 5

ANALYSIS   The correct answer is **(C)**. With J selected, S must be used, so the two greenery components are R and S. Then since P is not used, L is not used, which leaves K, M, and N for the flowers-in-bloom. You'll need two of the three: K and M, K and N, or M and N.

25

Map Problems

The third type of puzzle commonly used by the GRE involves a map of some sort. Here is an example:

A system of canals connects the following villages:

J and K   M and O

J and L   O and P

L and M   P and Q

M and N

The canals pass through the center of the villages, and none of the canals intersects another canal.

Boat traffic moves in both directions on all canals.

There is a feeder canal that connects Q to K, but the flow of water in the feeder canal does not permit boats to travel from K to Q.

With this type of problem, a diagram is virtually a necessity:

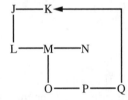

And here's the first question:

QUESTION In order to go by boat from N to K, it is necessary to go through

(A) J

(B) K

(C) L

(D) M

(E) O

ANALYSIS The correct answer is (D). The diagram shows that the only way out of town N is through town M. From there it is possible to go to L or to O and on to K via other towns.

And now the second question in the series:

QUESTION In order to go from K to P, what is the minimum number of other towns through which a boat must pass?

(A) 1

(B) 2

(C) 3

(D) 4

(E) 5

ANALYSIS The correct answer is (**D**). Since it is not possible to go from K to Q directly (only from Q to K), it is necessary to pass through J, L, M, and O en route.

Here is the third question in the series:

QUESTION If the canal through town L is closed, then it is not possible to go by boat from

(A) J to K

(B) J to O

(C) M to P

(D) P to J

(E) Q to K

ANALYSIS The correct answer is (**B**). If L is blocked, then it is not possible to go from J to O. The other trips are possible, however. J and K remain connected; and M, P, and Q are connected to J and K via the one way feeder canal.

And here is the final question in this series:

QUESTION If a new lock is constructed on the feeder canal that makes it possible to travel by boat from K to Q, then the minimum number of towns that a boat must pass through in order to go from J to P is *reduced* by how many

(A) 0

(B) 1

(C) 2

(D) 3

(E) 4

ANALYSIS The correct answer is (**B**). Prior to the construction of the canal, it was necessary to go through L, M, and O. With the new canal, it is necessary only to pass through K and Q. So the number has been reduced by 1.

25

NOTE   With a map problem set, your diagram will usually tell the whole story. All of the possible connections will be summarized in it.

Workshop: Puzzles

In this workshop you will find an example of each of the three major types of puzzles. Follow the Action Plan developed above. Indicate your answer choices in your book, then review your work. The time for the Drill is 20 minutes.

Drill

15 Questions • Time—20 minutes

DIRECTIONS: Each question or group of questions is based on a passage or a set of conditions. You may find it useful to draw a rough diagram for some questions. For each question, select the best answer choice given.

Questions 1–5

During the running of a race, seven monitors—J, K, L, M, N, O, P—are each stationed at a different checkpoint. The checkpoints, evenly spaced, are numbered 1 through 7 from the start of the race to the finish and are staffed according to the following conditions:

The distance separating J's checkpoint from K's is the same as the distance separating L's checkpoint from M's.

N is stationed at a checkpoint immediately before or immediately after the checkpoint at which O is stationed.

P is not stationed at the finish line.

1. Which of the following is an acceptable assignment of monitors to the checkpoints, 1 through 7 respectively?

   (A) J, K, M, L, P, O, N
   (B) J, M, K, P, L, O, N
   (C) K, J, M, L, N, O, P
   (D) M, L, P, O, J, K, N
   (E) M, L, O, J, N, K, P

2. If O is stationed at checkpoint 6, which of the following must be true?

   (A) J is stationed at checkpoint 1.
   (B) L is stationed at checkpoint 2.
   (C) M is stationed at checkpoint 4.
   (D) P is stationed at checkpoint 5.
   (E) N is stationed at checkpoint 7.

3. If J and K are assigned to checkpoints 2 and 6, respectively, then which of the following must be true?

   (A) K is assigned to checkpoint 2.
   (B) L is assigned to checkpoint 7.
   (C) N is assigned to checkpoint 4.
   (D) O is assigned to checkpoint 5.
   (E) P is assigned to checkpoint 1.

4. If N and O are assigned to checkpoints 3 and 4, respectively, then which of the following must be true?

   (A) J is assigned to checkpoint 1.
   (B) K is assigned to checkpoint 5.
   (C) L is assigned to checkpoint 2.
   (D) M is assigned to checkpoint 7.
   (E) P is assigned to checkpoint 5.

5. If J and L are assigned to checkpoints 5 and 6, respectively, then which of the following must be true?

   (A) K is assigned to checkpoint 1.
   (B) N is assigned to checkpoint 2.
   (C) O is assigned to checkpoint 3.
   (D) M is assigned to checkpoint 4.
   (E) K is assigned to checkpoint 4.

Questions 6–10

A caterer is planning a buffet. The buffet must offer at least three but no more than five of the following dishes.

> The hot main dishes are roast beef and broiled fish; the cold main dish is quiche.

> The hot side dishes are scalloped potatoes, green beans, and asparagus; the cold side dish is tossed salad.

> The buffet must include either one or two main dishes.

> The buffet cannot include four side dishes.

> The buffet must include at least one cold dish.

> If the tossed salad is included, at least one hot side dish must be included.

6. Which of the following could be the menu for the buffet?

   (A) Scalloped potatoes, green beans, asparagus
   (B) Roast beef, broiled fish, asparagus, green beans
   (C) Roast beef, broiled fish, tossed salad
   (D) Roast beef, broiled fish, scalloped potatoes, asparagus
   (E) Broiled fish, asparagus, green beans, tossed salad

7. If the only cold dish included is tossed salad, the buffet must also include

   (A) exactly two other dishes
   (B) exactly three other dishes
   (C) exactly three hot side dishes
   (D) two hot main dishes plus one hot side dish
   (E) at least one hot main dish plus either one or two hot side dishes

25

8. If five items are offered on the buffet, which of the following must be true?

   (A) Exactly two main dishes are included.
   (B) Exactly three hot side dishes are included.
   (C) Exactly four side dishes are included.
   (D) Both cold dishes are included.
   (E) Only one hot main dish is included.

9. If three hot side dishes are offered, which of the following must also be offered?

   (A) Tossed salad
   (B) Quiche
   (C) Roast Beef but not steamed fish
   (D) Roast beef and quiche but not steamed fish
   (E) Steamed fish and tossed salad

10. If both cold dishes are offered, an acceptable buffet can be made by the addition of each of the following EXCEPT:

    (A) one hot side dish
    (B) two hot side dishes
    (C) three hot side dishes
    (D) roast beef and asparagus
    (E) steamed fish and two hot side dishes

Questions 11–15

An intelligence network consists of six spies—F, G, H, J, K and L. For security reasons, messages can only be sent from:

F to G

G to H and K

H to F, K, and L

K to H and J

J to F and L

L to J

A spy who receives a message can in turn relay that message.

11. Which of the following spies CANNOT receive messages directly from two other spies?

    (A) F
    (B) G
    (C) H
    (D) J
    (E) K

12. Which of the following is a complete and accurate list of spies who can send a message, either directly or indirectly, to G?

    (A) F
    (B) F, H, J
    (C) F, H, K
    (D) F, H, J, K
    (E) F, H, J, K, L

13. Which of the following messages requires the greatest number of intermediate relays?

    (A) K to J
    (B) J to G
    (C) H to G
    (D) K to H
    (E) L to H

14. All of the following links can be broken without disrupting the flow of messages EXCEPT:

    (A) F to G
    (B) G to K
    (C) H to F
    (D) H to L
    (E) K to J

15. If J is eliminated from the network, which of the following spies can no longer send message to any other spy?

    (A) F
    (B) G
    (C) H
    (D) K
    (E) L

Review

1. (A)   6. (D)   11. (B)
2. (E)   7. (E)   12. (E)
3. (E)   8. (A)   13. (E)
4. (E)   9. (B)   14. (A)
5. (D)   10. (C)   15. (E)

25

Now find out how you did by comparing your results to the graph below.

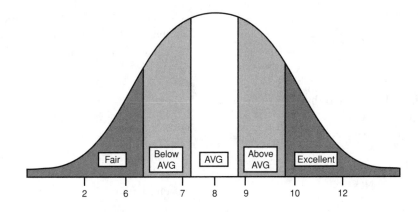

Fair   Below AVG   AVG   Above AVG   Excellent

2   6   7   8   9   10   12

Number Correct

Questions 1–5

This is an ordering set, and you'll want to begin by making a couple of notes:

J – K = L – M

N-O or O-N

P ≠ finish

1. **(A)** This question doesn't supply any additional information, so you can answer it based upon the set-up conditions. Just use the set-up conditions to eliminate choices until only one remains. The first condition eliminates answer (B) and (E). The second condition eliminates (D). And the third condition eliminates (C). Only (A) is consistent with all of the set-up conditions.

2. **(E)** The additional information stations O at 6:

    1 2 3 4 5 6 7
               O

    The only next step that's possible is to think about where N should go. N can go either at checkpoint 5 or at checkpoint:

    1 2 3 4 5 6 7
    NO ON

    As for the first possibility, since P cannot be assigned to 7, P will be assigned to 1, 2, 3, or 4. But that means that J, K, L, or M will be assigned to 7, and it won't be possible to observe the first set-up

condition. So N must be assigned to 7. The other choices are possible but not required.

3. **(E)** You'll want to enter the new information on a diagram:

    1 2 3 4 5 6 7
      J   K

    Since J and K are separated by 3 positions, L and M must be separated by 3 positions as well. This means that L and M must be assigned to checkpoints 1 and 5 or 3 and 7, though not necessarily respectively:

1	2	3	4	5	6	7
L/M		J			L/M	K
		J	L/M		K	L/M

    And then N and O must be assigned to the two checkpoints that are in sequence, again not necessarily in that order:

1	2	3	4	5	6	7
L/M		J	N/O	N/O	L/M	K
		J	L/M	N/O	N/O	K	L/M

    But since P cannot be assigned to checkpoint 7, P must be assigned to the first check point:

1	2	3	4	5	6	7
~~L/M~~		~~J~~	~~N/O~~	~~N/O~~	~~L/M~~	~~K~~
P	J	L/M	N/O	N/O	K	L/M

4. **(E)** Put the new information on a diagram:

1 2 3 4 5 6 7
 N O

Where should J and K be assigned? They can't be assigned to 1 and 5 because that would require that L and M be assigned to 2 and 6—with P at the finish. So J and K must be assigned to checkpoints 1 and 2, though not necessarily respectively:

1   2   3   4   5   6   7
J/K J/K N   O

And L and M to checkpoints 6 and 7, not necessarily respectively, with P at 5:

1   2   3   4   5   6   7
J/K J/K N   P
L/M L/M   O

5. **(D)** You'll need to process the new information:

1 2 3 4 5 6 7
      J L

You next move should be to think about what the first set-up condition requires for K and M:

1   2   3   4   5   6   7
K   M   J   L
    K   M   J   L
        K   M   J   L
        K   J   L   M

There seem to be four possibilities, but you also have to worry about the other three individuals:

1   2   3   4   5   6   7
K̶   M̶   J̶   L̶
    K̶   M̶   J̶   L̶
        K̶   M̶ J̶ L̶
        K   J   L   M

So only the fourth line is possible. Now, it doesn't appear possible to draw any further conclusions, but the diagram already has the answer: K is assigned to 4.

Question 6–10

Begin by processing the set-up information. This is a selection set, and you can use the following table to help keep track of the information:

	Hot	Cold
Main	beef, fish	quiche
Side	pot., beans, asp.	salad

3–5 dishes total

1–2 main dishes

1–3 side dishes

1 or more cold dishes

ts ——> pot. or beans or asp.

6. **(E)** The question doesn't provide any additional information, so use the set-up conditions to eliminate choices until you are left with only one. (A) doesn't include

a main dish; (B) has no cold dish;(C) has tossed salad but no hot side dish; (D) doesn't include a cold dish.

7. **(E)** If the only cold dish is the tossed salad, then the menu will include two or three hot side dishes with one of the two other main dishes.

8. **(A)** If five dishes are offered, the menu must include two main dishes and three side dishes.

9. **(B)** If the three hot side dishes are included, then tossed salad is not; and that means that quiche must be the cold dish.

10. **(C)** Three hot side dishes in addition to the cold side dish would violate the requirement that no more than three of the side dishes be offered.

Questions 11–15

This is a map problem, so you will need a diagram:

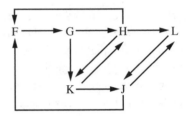

11. **(B)** G can only receive messages directly from F.

12. **(E)** Every spy can get a message to G.

13. **(E)** L's message must go through J, F, and G.

14. **(A)** Breaking the F to G link breaks the loop.

15. **(E)** J is L's only link for sending messages.

Learn How to Answer "Argument" Questions

Arguments are the other question type used in the Analytical part of the GRE, the ones that look like small reading comprehension questions. Here is your Action Plan for arguments:

 Step 1: Read and analyze the initial paragraph.

Step 2: Read the question stem and select the choice that best responds to the stem.

Each element of the Action Plan is designed to focus your attention on one of the important components of the argument question. Whether it's the initial paragraph, the stem, or the answer choices, you need to read that part specifically looking for what the GRE wants you to find there. Let's look at each step.

Step 1: Read and analyze the initial paragraph.

As you read the paragraph, analyze the logical structure of the speaker's reasoning. Logical structure is the defining characteristic of the initial paragraphs used in this part of the GRE. They are not merely reports of events of the sort that you read in the newspaper; they are reasoned presentations that have a main point. The main point is also called the conclusion.

The conclusion of a line of reasoning is most easily seen in those arguments that we associate with a college course in logic. For example:

> All swans are birds.
>
> All birds have feathers.
>
> Therefore, all swans have feathers.

The conclusion of this argument is the last sentence, and it is signaled by "therefore." But most of the initial paragraphs used by the GRE don't have a neat structure like this one, so you'll have to work a little to find the conclusion.

As you read the initial paragraph, look for a conclusion signal such as "therefore." Here's an example more like one you'd find on the GRE:

> Most sport utility vehicles are built on a truck chassis, which means that they are not designed to absorb a fair share of the impact of a crash. Plus, they ride so high that they override the bumpers and door sills of ordinary cars. Therefore, the government should get them off of our roads.

Again, the conclusion is signaled by "therefore." So even though the argument doesn't have the crisp, clear structure of the "swans" argument above, it's still pretty easy to find the conclusion.

> **TIP**
>
> The following words and phrases often signal the conclusion of the argument:
>
> *therefore, consequently, so, hence, thus, as a result, it follows that, this proves that, this demonstrates that, it is likely that.*

25

Some GRE arguments, however, don't use a signal for the conclusion. In that case, you have to read the argument consciously asking yourself "What is the main point the speaker wants to prove?" Here's an example:

> The objective of the census is to count people as accurately as possible. It's difficult, however, to be sure that everyone is counted because not everyone wants to participate. If people could be encouraged to participate voluntarily, then the census would be more accurate. To increase the accuracy of the census, the government should have random drawings and give lotto prizes to people who fill out the questionnaires.

This paragraph doesn't include a "therefore" or similar signal, so you'll have to find the conclusion by looking for the main point. Fortunately, except for those questions that ask you to draw the conclusion yourself, the conclusion is one of the sentences in the paragraph. So ask yourself, "Is this the main point?"

Is this the main point?

> The objective of the census is to count people as accurately as possible.

No, this is a starting point of the argument.

Is this the main point?

> It's difficult, however, to be sure that everyone is counted because not everyone wants to participate.

Again, the answer is "no" because this too is something the speaker takes for granted, not the point the speaker wants to prove.

Is this the main point?

> If people could be encouraged to participate voluntarily, then the census would be more accurate.

No, again this is an idea assumed by the speaker to be true. It's not the point the speaker hopes to make.

Is this the main point?

> To increase the accuracy of the census, the government should have random drawings and give lotto prizes to people who fill out the questionnaires.

Yes, the speaker wants to prove that the government should adopt a system of lotto prizes for the census.

> If the conclusion of the argument is not signaled by a key word or phrase, ask yourself what is the point that the speaker wants to prove.

Step 2: Read the question stem and select the answer that best responds to the question asked.

The second step is to read the question stem to learn what you're supposed to do with the argument. Most of the question stems used for arguments fall into one of the following categories.

The argument above is based on which of the following assumptions?

When the GRE uses the word "assumption," it means "premise." And when a question asks you to identify an assumption or premise of an argument, it's *not* asking about one that is explicitly stated in the argument. Instead, it's asking about one that is only implicit in the argument. The following example illustrates the distinction:

QUESTION Sometimes the artistic value of an object is not apparent because of the context in which we encounter it. A quilt that appears to be quite ordinary when lying on a bed becomes a work of abstract art when mounted on a wall. A ceramic pitcher on the kitchen counter is a container for holding liquids; but when it's placed in a glass box with suitable lighting, it becomes a sculpture. Thus, the people who created these objects were frustrated artists whose aesthetic vision went unrealized.

The argument assumes that

(A) many folk artists who created quilts also worked in other areas such as ceramics

(B) the makers of quilts and ceramics realized their work had an artistic dimension

(C) all ordinary household objects can be elevated to the status of art in the right context

(D) critics who see quilts and ceramics as art do not use such objects for their intended purposes

(E) all true works of art have practical applications that could be realized in a suitable context

25

The correct answer is (**B**). The speaker argues that seemingly ordinary objects may be works of art, though their real status may be obscured by the context in which we find them. From this, the speaker concludes that the people who made them were frustrated artists. But that assumes that the people who made them understood that they were creating art—and not just ordinary household objects. This is the hidden assumption that (B) brings to light.

CAUTION

> When you're looking for a hidden assumption, don't pick an idea explicitly stated by the speaker. An explicit statement is not a suppressed or hidden idea.

Which of the following, if true, would most weaken the conclusion above?

This type of question focuses on a hidden or suppressed premise of the argument and involves refuting it in order to weaken the argument. Here' an example:

QUESTION Motorcycle organizations argue that the decision not to wear helmets is like the decision to invest in the stock market. They ask what business is it of anyone else if an individual chooses to assume a risk. They conclude, therefore, that laws requiring motorcyclists to wear helmets are an unwarranted infringement upon personal liberty.

Which of the following, if true, most seriously weakens the conclusion drawn above?

(A) Most new motorcycles are equipped with warning lights, scientifically designed breaking systems, and other features to make motorcycling safer.

(B) Insurance rates for motor vehicles are higher for all owners because of the need to cover the cost of increased injuries or deaths of motorcyclists who fail to wear helmets.

(C) Government regulations require employers in many industries to ensure that employees in certain jobs wear hard hats to protect their heads.

(D) In a motorcycle accident, a cyclist or a passenger who is not wearing a helmet is more likely to incur serious injury than one who is.

(E) The overall rate for motorcyclists involved in accidents is higher in jurisdictions that require helmets than in those that do not.

ANALYSIS The correct answer is (**B**). The argument assumes—without saying so—that only the injured motorcyclist suffers harm, as when the investor loses money in the stock market. (B) contradicts this hidden assumption by suggesting that people other than the motorcyclist are injured. Notice that this type of question goes one step further than the first type. Not only do you need to find the hidden assumption, you also need an answer choice that negates it in order to weaken the argument.

You should also note that only one of the answer choices really attacks the argument. So when even though the stem uses the phrase "most weakens," you are not being asked to rank different choices according to how well they attack the argument. Only one of the five choices will be an attack, and that's the right choice.

 NOTE

> A "most weakens" question does not ask you to compare the strengths of different attacks. Instead, only one of the choices will be an attack, so, by definition, it is the one that most weakens the argument.

Which of the following, if true, would most strengthen the conclusion above?

25

This is the mirror-image of the second question type. Just as the wrong answers to a weakening question are not less powerful attacks on the conclusion, so too the correct answer to a strengthening question is not the most powerful of several ideas that strengthen the conclusion. Instead, the correct answer to a strengthening question is the only one that strengthens the argument at all, and it usually does this by eliminating a possible weakness in the argument. In other words, the correct answer to a strengthening question is usually the mirror-image of the correct answer to the same item if it asked about an attack on the argument. Here's how this looks:

QUESTION Over the past 30 years, we've seen a general decline in the quality of teaching in our public school systems. An explanation is not difficult to find. Thirty years ago, women were not encouraged to enter law, medicine, or business—professions traditionally reserved for men. So, the brightest and most capable women chose teaching as an alternative. As other professions gradually opened up to them, fewer and fewer women turned to teaching. Consequently, the pool of teachers is today less talented than it was thirty years ago.

Which of the following, if true, would most strengthen the claim above?

(A) Men who 30 years ago have might have chosen law, medicine, or business but today are competitively excluded have not chosen teaching as an alternative.

(B) The salary and benefits levels for teachers in public schools relative to law, medicine, and business are today about 50 percent higher than they were 30 years ago.

(C) The percentage of teachers in the public schools who today hold advanced degrees is considerably lower than the percentage of such teachers 30 years ago.

(D) More jurisdictions today require teachers to pass standardized certification examinations and have continuing education requirements than did 30 years ago.

(E) Public schools today are mandated by law to provide to students who need them special educational resources that did not exist 30 years ago.

ANALYSIS The correct answer is **(A)**. The speaker reasons that the pool of teachers today is less qualified than that of 30 years ago because highly qualified women no longer go into the pool. A possible objection is that the men who have been displaced from the law, medicine, and business pool would choose teaching. If that were so, then one would expect the quality of the pool as a whole to remain constant. (A) eliminates this idea by saying that men do not go into teaching. In other words, by eliminating a possible objection to the argument, (A) strengthens the argument.

CAUTION   In a weakening or a strengthening situation, watch out for choices that do the opposite of what you're really looking for. For example, if a question asks you to weaken an argument, an idea that strengthens the argument can be deceptively attractive just because it is so clearly relevant to the issue.

What conclusion can be most reliably drawn from the statements above?

This type of question is an exception to the general rule about finding the conclusion in the speaker's argument. As the wording of the stem suggests, the conclusion is *not* stated in the paragraph; instead it's your job to draw the conclusion. Here's an example:

QUESTION The city has proposed auctioning off over 100 city-owned lots now being used by local residents as community gardens. City officials maintain that the sale of these lots would result in new housing, thereby benefitting all members of the community. This move is opposed by hundreds of community leaders and concerned citizens. And, in fact, most of these lots, because of their size and location, are not likely to be developed for housing. Ninety percent of similar properties auctioned by the city ten years ago remain vacant.

The speaker is mostly likely leading up to which of the following conclusions?

(A) City officials are not interested in creating new housing.

(B) Community gardens do not serve any useful function.

(C) The city should not auction off the lots used as gardens.

(D) The city should change the regulations on developing residential property.

(E) The city should reacquire the properties that it sold ten years ago.

ANALYSIS The correct answer is **(C)**. The author points out a weakness in the city's justification for selling the properties: it won't result in more housing. So the speaker believes that it is a mistake to proceed with the auction. Notice that the other answer choices go far beyond the scope of the statements in the paragraph. As for (A), what evidence is there for such a large claim about the *intentions* of city officials? As for (B), the speaker's position seems to be that the properties are currently serving a useful function. And (D) and (E) go way beyond what has been said.

TIP When you're asked to draw a conclusion, choose the most limited answer available that is supported by the statements in the initial paragraph. The more limited the claim, the more likely it can be supported by those statements.

25

Which of the following best describes the argument?

Some argument questions just ask that you describe the structure of the reasoning in the initial paragraph. Here is an example:

QUESTION Most of what passes for learning in our institutions of higher learning is really just attempted fraud. One professor of literature, analyzing Nathaniel Hawthorne's *The Scarlet Letter*: "insights into the contingent possibility of a genderized structure unaugurate a disinterested conception of hegemony." What gibberish!

The argument above could be criticized because it

(A) assumes the conclusion that it hopes to prove

(B) attacks the credibility of an opponent

(C) generalizes on the basis of on example

(D) confuses a cause with its effect

(E) fails to consider a third possibility

ANALYSIS The correct answer is **(C)**. The conclusion of the argument is a general indictment of "learning," but the author provides only a single example.

NOTE

The following phrases are often used to describe the kinds of arguments used on the GRE:

generalizes, attacks the source, begs the question, uses an ambiguous term, mistakes a cause for an effect, overlooks another possible explanation

---

The argument above is most like which of the following?

This question stem asks you to choose an argument that has the same logical structure as the speaker's argument. Here is an example:

QUESTION Only applications received before midnight will be reviewed. Ellen's application was received at 11:59. Therefore, Ellen's application will be reviewed.

Which of the following is most similar in its logical structure to the reasoning above?

(A) Everyone who submits a term paper will receive a grade. Ralph submitted a term paper. Therefore, Ralph will receive a grade.

(B) Only fences built prior to 1960 are legal structures. The fence around Harvey's house was built in 1961. Therefore, Harvey's fence is not a legal structure.

(C) No letter will be delivered that lacks sufficient postage. Hank put the correct postage on his letter to Jeremy. Therefore, Hank's letter will be delivered.

(D) Not all requests for parking submitted on time will be honored. George's request for parking was submitted on time. Therefore, George's request for parking will not be honored.

(E) Any one who fails to register his car with campus security is subject to being towed. Bob did not register his car with campus security. Therefore, Bob's car will be towed.

ANALYSIS The correct answer is **(C)**. The mistake in the reasoning of the initial paragraph is confusion over what are often called necessary and sufficient conditions. A necessary condition is a circumstance that is needed before some outcome ensues, but it is no guarantee of that outcome. A sufficient condition, as the name implies, is sufficient to guarantee the outcome. In this case, submitting the application on time is a necessary condition for review, but it is no guarantee of a review. Similarly, the right postage is a necessary condition for delivery—but not, in and of itself, a sufficient condition.

A logical similarity question asks you to *replicate* the reasoning of the speaker. Don't try to correct the mistake.

Workshop: Arguments

This workshop will give you the opportunity to practice the Action Plan for augments. Indicate your answer choice in your book, then review your work. The time for the Drill is 10 minutes.

Drill

7 Questions • Time—10 Minutes

DIRECTIONS: For each question, select the best answer choice given.

25

1. Equating business size with success is a holdover from a market place driven by the economies of scale created by mass manufacturing and mass marketing. When it comes to return on investment, bigger isn't necessarily better as small-time entrepreneurs with homegrown web sites demonstrate.

   Which of the following conclusions can be most reliably drawn form the information above?

   (A) Small entrepreneurs are more aggressive than large, established businesses.

   (B) Small businesses do not rely on the economies of scale of mass manufacturing and marketing.

   (C) The web is not particularly well-suited to conducting business on a large scale.

   (D) Large businesses are no longer able to compete effectively against small businesses.

   (E) Mass manufacturing and marketing are business techniques that have outlived their usefulness.

2. It is true that aggressive enforcement of tough laws against crack cocaine have succeeded in keeping levels of usage of that drug below those of powdered cocaine but only at the cost of fairness. Persons arrested for possession, use, or sale of powdered cocaine are less likely to be charged, less likely to be charged with the most serious offense possible, and less likely, if convicted, to be sentenced to the maximum term because authorities see powdered cocaine as less serious than the crack variety. Fairness requires, however, that crack cocaine be treated more leniently in order to eliminate the disparity of treatment.

Which of the following, if true, most weakens the argument above?

(A) The disparity could be eliminated by treating offenses involving powdered cocaine more seriously.
(B) Crack cocaine and powdered cocaine are different forms of the same drug.
(C) Authorities have discretion to prosecute some crimes more vigorously than others.
(D) As the dangers of taking a certain drug become known, fewer people take it.
(E) More aggressive enforcement of laws against powdered cocaine would result in decreased usage.

3. The solution to the problem of unleashed dogs in city parks is obvious. The crackdown on drunken drivers which involves seizing the cars of anyone suspected of driving while intoxicated has been very effective. The city should immediately impound any dog that is not on a leash.

The speaker reasons primarily by

(A) drawing an analogy
(B) generalizing on an example
(C) pointing out an inconsistency
(D) citing statistics
(E) introducing a distinction

4. Representatives of the union have objected to the appointment of Johnson as mediator in this dispute, claiming that Johnson is pro-management. But the record shows that he has decided in favor of labor in just about half the cases he has heard. Johnson's record proves that he is a fair and impartial arbiter.

The argument above is flawed because it ignores the possibility that

(A) the evidence shows that Johnson should have decided far more cases in favor of labor than he did
(B) decisions reached in favor of labor could have been appealed by management to a court of law
(C) many of the cases decided in favor of management did not involve large sums of money
(D) some of the cases decided in favor of management could have been initiated by labor
(E) some of the cases could have been decided on technicalities rather than on merit

5. Last year, over 125 foreign nationals dropped out of State University citing lack of financial resources to continue their studies. This was an increase of nearly 100 percent from the previous year. The result is quite surprising since tuition remained virtually unchanged and the price of room and board rose only slightly.

Which of the following, if true, best explains the result mentioned above?

(A) The students who dropped out last year had higher academic standing than those who dropped out the previous year.

(B) Global economic events caused an unfavorable shift in the exchange rate for the national currencies of those students who dropped out.

(C) The total number of all State University students who dropped out citing inability to continue their studies declined over the past year.

(D) The university has announced that it will make increased financial aid to foreign students in the upcoming year.

(E) The university liberalized work-study rules allowing foreign students to work an additional five hours per week.

6. A famous entertainment personality recently won a large judgment against an advertiser who featured a look-alike to promote its product, even though the advertisement clearly warned "This is not a famous person." Advertisers use look-alikes because they don't have to pay them as much as the real personalities, but now they will be reluctant to continue to use look-alikes. Consequently, the cost of producing such advertisement will increase.

The conclusion above depends upon which of the following assumptions?

(A) The viewing public cannot distinguish between the look-alike and the real personality.

(B) Advertisers will use real personalities to promote their products.

(C) Advertisements using look-alikes are no less effective than those using real personalities.

(D) Some personalities refuse to do commercial advertisements.

(E) Advertisers will create promotional pieces that don't rely on personalities.

25

7. One of the problems faced by today's military is the retention of experienced officers. Many leave after only 7 or 8 years for civilian positions. The problem is evidently the level of retirement benefits. A substantial increase in the retirement benefits would help to keep experienced officers in the service.

Which of the following, if true, would most weaken the conclusion above?

(A) Most officers who leave the military in the middle of their careers do not cite inadequate pay as a reason for retiring early.

(B) The time of service required to vest retirement benefits in the military is comparable to the time required for other government jobs including civil service.

(C) Ratings systems used by the military to determine promotions are designed so that no more than half of the officers will be promoted and qualify for retirement benefits.

(D) Increased pay for the lowest ranks and enlistment incentives have significantly reduced the shortfall of recruits.

(E) Over the past years, the risk of being sent to a high risk duty area has been significantly lower than in previous times.

Review

1. (B)
2. (A)
3. (A)

4. (A)
5. (B)

6. (B)
7. (C)

Now evaluate your performance using the graph:

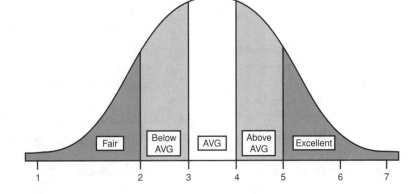

Number Correct

1. **(B)** This problem asks you to draw a further conclusion, and it is important to "stay as close to home as possible." (B) does this. The speaker concludes that bigger isn't necessarily bigger because certain business strategies are no longer essential, namely those that require large scale manufacturing and marketing. Consequently, you can infer that small businesses today don't rely on those strategies.

2. **(A)** With this type of question (weaken) you should be looking for a possible hidden assumption. The speaker here argues that X is more severe than Y, so to bring them into alignment, it is necessary to mitigate the severity of X. But that overlooks the possibility of increasing the severity of Y to attain the balance. Now, it might

be objected this change would have some unwanted consequences, but remember that the question has asked you to weaken the argument presented—not analyze the larger question of the wisdom of anti-drug laws.

3. **(A)** This is a straight-forward "describe the argument" questions. The speaker creates an analogy between dogs off their leashes and drunk driving and concludes: if seizure is good in one case, then it should be good in the other.

4. **(A)** This question asks you to find a weakness in the argument, so you should be looking for an unstated assumption to attack. In this case, the speaker reasons: Johnson decided for labor in half the cases, so Johnson is fair. But that assumes that the cases were

25

correctly decided. As (A) points out, it may be that Johnson should have decided even more cases in favor of labor.

5. **(B)** This is one of those questions that asks you to explain a seemingly surprising result: the students dropped out even though costs did not increase. (B) suggests a possible explanation: the cost to the students rose because the purchasing power of their currency declined.

6. **(B)** This question asks for a hidden assumption. The speaker reasons that the cost of producing the advertising will rise because the cheap alternative is no longer available. But that presupposes that advertisers will use the more expensive real personality.

7. **(C)** For this weakening question, you should be looking for a hidden assumption to attack. The speaker argues that an increase in retirement benefits would keep officers in the service, so you need a choice that highlights an oversight on the speaker's part: officers can't get to retirement because of promotions policies.

Get Answers to Frequently Asked Questions

Q: **The 60-minutes time limit make this part seem like the most important section of the GRE. Is it really more important than the other parts?**

A: No. First of all, the time limit is not a function of the importance of the questions. It's a function of how many items the CAT algorithm needs to finish off a score for you and how long it takes you to answer them. Second, remember that you get three GRE scores: verbal, math, *and* analytical. So the questions in this part don't affect your other scores.

Q: **Would a college course in logic be useful for this part?**

A: One *could be* useful because it probably would include topics such as analysis of arguments, examples of faulty reasoning, and maybe even some diagraming techniques. But the overlap is not really that great. The GRE is what it is. So if you haven't taken such a course, you're not really at a disadvantage.

Today's Review

1. There are two types of analytical ability questions: puzzles and arguments.

2. The most common types of puzzles are ordering, selection, and map set-ups.

3. Argument questions test your ability to analyze the logical structure of arguments. The most common types of arguments are: hidden assumption, weaken, strengthen, draw a conclusion, describe, and parallel.

25

The Analytical Final

Day 26

In Day 25, you developed Action Plans for the Analytical Reasoning ("puzzles") and Logical Reasoning ("arguments") that appear in the Analytical Reasoning part of the GRE. Today you'll get a chance to apply those strategies as you take the Analytical Ability Final.

What You'll Do Today

- Take the Analytical Final
- Evaluate Your Performance
- Review the Correct Answers

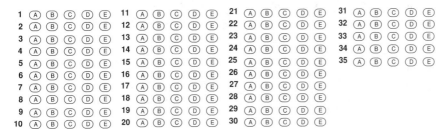

1 Ⓐ Ⓑ Ⓒ Ⓓ Ⓔ 11 Ⓐ Ⓑ Ⓒ Ⓓ Ⓔ 21 Ⓐ Ⓑ Ⓒ Ⓓ Ⓔ 31 Ⓐ Ⓑ Ⓒ Ⓓ Ⓔ
2 Ⓐ Ⓑ Ⓒ Ⓓ Ⓔ 12 Ⓐ Ⓑ Ⓒ Ⓓ Ⓔ 22 Ⓐ Ⓑ Ⓒ Ⓓ Ⓔ 32 Ⓐ Ⓑ Ⓒ Ⓓ Ⓔ
3 Ⓐ Ⓑ Ⓒ Ⓓ Ⓔ 13 Ⓐ Ⓑ Ⓒ Ⓓ Ⓔ 23 Ⓐ Ⓑ Ⓒ Ⓓ Ⓔ 33 Ⓐ Ⓑ Ⓒ Ⓓ Ⓔ
4 Ⓐ Ⓑ Ⓒ Ⓓ Ⓔ 14 Ⓐ Ⓑ Ⓒ Ⓓ Ⓔ 24 Ⓐ Ⓑ Ⓒ Ⓓ Ⓔ 34 Ⓐ Ⓑ Ⓒ Ⓓ Ⓔ
5 Ⓐ Ⓑ Ⓒ Ⓓ Ⓔ 15 Ⓐ Ⓑ Ⓒ Ⓓ Ⓔ 25 Ⓐ Ⓑ Ⓒ Ⓓ Ⓔ 35 Ⓐ Ⓑ Ⓒ Ⓓ Ⓔ
6 Ⓐ Ⓑ Ⓒ Ⓓ Ⓔ 16 Ⓐ Ⓑ Ⓒ Ⓓ Ⓔ 26 Ⓐ Ⓑ Ⓒ Ⓓ Ⓔ
7 Ⓐ Ⓑ Ⓒ Ⓓ Ⓔ 17 Ⓐ Ⓑ Ⓒ Ⓓ Ⓔ 27 Ⓐ Ⓑ Ⓒ Ⓓ Ⓔ
8 Ⓐ Ⓑ Ⓒ Ⓓ Ⓔ 18 Ⓐ Ⓑ Ⓒ Ⓓ Ⓔ 28 Ⓐ Ⓑ Ⓒ Ⓓ Ⓔ
9 Ⓐ Ⓑ Ⓒ Ⓓ Ⓔ 19 Ⓐ Ⓑ Ⓒ Ⓓ Ⓔ 29 Ⓐ Ⓑ Ⓒ Ⓓ Ⓔ
10 Ⓐ Ⓑ Ⓒ Ⓓ Ⓔ 20 Ⓐ Ⓑ Ⓒ Ⓓ Ⓔ 30 Ⓐ Ⓑ Ⓒ Ⓓ Ⓔ

Take the Analytical Ability Final

Analytical Ability Final

35 Questions • Time—60 Minutes

DIRECTIONS: Each question or group of questions is based on a passage or a set of conditions. You may find it useful to draw a rough diagram for some questions. For each question, select the best answer choice given.

Questions 1–5

The desk clerk of a hotel must assign eight guests—J, K, L, M, N, O, P, and Q—to eight empty rooms, one guest per room. The only empty rooms are located on floors one (the lowest) through five (the highest) of the hotel.

Exactly two of the floors have more than one vacant room.

O is the only guest who will be assigned to the third floor.

M and N are assigned rooms on the third floor above the room to which Q is assigned.

P is assigned a room on a floor higher than the room K is assigned.

1. Which of the following CANNOT be true?

   (A) O's room is on a floor higher than K's room.

   (B) L's room is on a floor higher than J's room.

   (C) K's room is on a floor higher than N's room.

   (D) L's room is on the same floor as N's room.

   (E) J's room is on the same floor as K's room.

2. Which of the following must be true?

   (A) There are three vacant rooms on the floor to which M and N will be assigned.

   (B) There are exactly three vacant rooms to be filled on one of the floors.

   (C) Exactly one guest will be assigned to the first floor.

   (D) Exactly two guests will be assigned to the fifth floor.

   (E) Q will be the only guest assigned to the second floor.

3. If Q and J are the only guests assigned to the second floor, which of the following must be true?

   (A) K is assigned to a floor with one vacant room.

   (B) L is assigned to a floor with one vacant room.

   (C) P is assigned to a floor with one vacant room.

   (D) P's room is higher than N's room.

   (E) L's room is on a floor lowers than O's room.

4. If M, N, and K are assigned to the same floor, which of the following must be true?

   (A) J is assigned to the first floor.

   (B) Q is assigned to the first floor.

   (C) L is assigned to the second floor.

   (D) J and L are assigned to the same floor.

   (E) J and Q are assigned to the same floor.

5. If L is given a room on a floor higher than P's room, which of the following CANNOT be true?

   (A) L and Q are assigned to the same floor.

   (B) L and J are assigned to the same floor.

   (C) M and P are assigned to the same floor.

   (D) P is the only guest assigned to the first floor.

   (E) K is the only guest assigned to the first floor.

6. Rail is the safest way to ship hazardous waste materials. In recent years, there have been more than 10 times as many spills associated with highway transportation of hazardous waste materials as with rail, in spite of the fact that both modes of transportation moved about the same volume of material.

Which of the following, if true, most weakens the argument?

   (A) Because rail transportation involves large containers linked together, a single spill of hazardous waste is likely to be more than 10 times as serious than a highway accident.

   (B) Federal regulations require all shippers of hazardous waste to comply with a variety of regulations designed to minimize the risk of a mishap and to contain damage in the event of one.

   (C) During the past five years, there have been virtually no truck-train accidents involving trucks and trains that were transporting hazardous material.

   (D) Because sites that accept hazardous waste materials being closed, the volume of hazard waste materials transported to those that remain open is expected to double in five years.

   (E) Because the infrastructure was built to handle heavy traffic, rail cars can incorporate protective plating and other features that add weight that trucks cannot handle.

26

7. Over the past ten years, membership in pipe band associations is up over 40% and the number of solo bagpipers has increased by 600. The number of animal skin bags sold for instruments has remained relatively constant, while the number of synthetic bags made from material like that used for ski parkas and windbreakers has increased dramatically. This is somewhat surprising since the bag is the least expensive part of the instrument.

Which of the following, if true, best helps to explain the surprising trend described above?

(A) New students of the bag pipe tend to buy inexpensive instruments so the cost of the bag is a greater part of the total investment than for the high-priced instruments used by more experienced players.

(B) Synthetic bags wear out more quickly than animal skin bags, and once they begin to leak cannot be repaired as an animal skin bag can.

(C) When the instrument is played in public, the bag is concealed in a tartan cover so that it's not possible to determine from appearance what material was used for the bag part of the instrument.

(D) Both animal skin and synthetic bags must be carefully maintained to prevent excessive moisture buildup from the blowing of the player that can cause reeds to become soggy and fail.

(E) Traditionalists prefer animal skin bags and tend to look down on players who use synthetic bags.

Questions 8–12

Seven countries—P, Q, R, S, T, U, V—have entered into a cooperative trade agreement. Q is permitted to import goods from any other country in the cooperative; all other exports and imports are subject to the following restrictions:

P can export goods to R.

R can export goods to S and U.

S can export goods to P, T, U, and V.

U can export goods to V and R.

Goods imported by one country from another can be exported to other countries in the cooperative subject to the other rules.

8. V can import goods directly from how many countries?
    (A) 0
    (B) 1
    (C) 2
    (D) 3
    (E) 4

9. How many of the countries in the cooperative can export goods to a country from which they can also directly import goods?
    (A) 1
    (B) 2
    (C) 3
    (D) 4
    (E) 5

10. If a country imports goods directly only from T and V, then that country is

   (A) P
   (B) Q
   (C) R
   (D) S
   (E) U

11. Goods originating in P would have to pass through a minimum of how many other countries before being received by V?

   (A) 1
   (B) 2
   (C) 3
   (D) 4
   (E) 5

12. Goods originating in S that pass through *exactly* one other country could arrive in how many different countries?

   (A) 1
   (B) 2
   (C) 3
   (D) 4
   (E) 5

13. Some people argue that gun makers intentionally manufacture and sell more guns that can be distributed through legitimate channels. These guns, according to the theory, are diverted into illegal channels and wind up in the hands of criminals who use them to commit crimes. On this theory, gun manufacturers are partly responsible for crime. But the "supersaturation" theory proves too much. If the oversupply of guns is significant, then the guns cannot be going to criminals, who constitute such a small portion of the population.

Which of the following, if true, most strengthens the analysis above?

   (A) Starting in 1985, there was a tripling of the murder rate among inner-city teenage males that was associated with the widespread use of crack cocaine.
   (B) A disproportionate number of the crimes committed with illegal handguns use powerful, automatic models that are costly to manufacture and expensive to buy.
   (C) The vast majority of illegal gun owners are not violent criminals but otherwise law-abiding citizens who purchase guns for self-defense.
   (D) Several states have recently passed concealed-carry laws that make it possible for owners to obtain permits to carry handguns for self-defense.
   (E) European nations have a lower rate of gun ownership and also have a lower crime rate for violations associated with gun use.

14. Scientists looking for intelligent life would do well to concentrate on planets outside of our solar system. The Milky way includes billions of other stars similar to our sun, many millions of which could be planetary systems that include a planet with conditions similar enough to those on Earth to make the emergence of life possible.

The argument above makes which of the following assumptions?

26

(A) It is probable that intelligent life would arise elsewhere out of circumstances that are similar to those on Earth.

(B) Millions of stars in the Milky way are associated with planets on which conditions are similar to those of Earth.

(C) If the appropriate physical requirements are satisfied, intelligent life will eventually evolve on a planet.

(D) Life does not exist in our solar system on any planet other than Earth.

(E) Living creatures on planets with conditions similar to those on Earth would have a similar physical appearance to those on Earth.

15. The price of honey jumped from $3 for an 8-ounce jar two years ago to $5 for an 8-ounce jar this season. It seems that the new Association of Honey Growers has been successful in encouraging its members to actinically inflate prices. The government should step in and end this collusive behavior and roll prices back to a level determined by the market.

Which of the following, if true, most weakens the demand made above?

(A) Honey producers are not subject to any government health regulations or inspections.

(B) An infestation of aphids killed off a substantial portion of the honey bee population curtailing honey production in the region.

(C) Honey is usually produced in rural areas by farmers who use the revenue from the sale of honey to supplement their incomes.

(D) Honey production doesn't rely on technological innovation and is carried on today in much the same way that it was 50 years ago.

(E) Honey prices have gradually risen over the past 25 years at a rate approximately the same as that of prices in general.

Questions 16–22

A spy is putting a message into code. The message will consist of exactly six words: M, N, O, P, Q, and R. Each word will appear in the message exactly once according to the following conditions:

Both M and R must appear after Q.

M must be appear before P.

N is the third word.

16. Which of the following could be the order in which the words appear in the message?

(A) N, O, Q, R, P, M
(B) N, Q, R, M, P, O
(C) P, M, N, R, O, Q
(D) Q, O, N, M, R, P
(E) Q, R, M, P, N, O

17. Which of the following must be true of the order in which the words appear in the message?

   (A) N appears before O.
   (B) Q appears before P.
   (C) N appears before Q.
   (D) P appears before R.
   (E) M appears before R.

18. Which of the following could be true?

   (A) The first word is N.
   (B) The second word is P.
   (C) The third word is Q.
   (D) The sixth word is M.
   (E) The sixth word is R.

19. If O is the first word in the message, then the second word must be

   (A) M
   (B) N
   (C) P
   (D) Q
   (E) R

20. If P appears immediately before R and immediately after O, then M must appear

   (A) first
   (B) second
   (C) fourth
   (D) fifth
   (E) sixth

21. If O is the sixth word in the message, which of the following could be the first and second words, respectively??

   I. Q and M

   II. Q and R

   III. M and R

   (A) I only
   (B) II only
   (C) I and II only
   (D) II and III only
   (E) I, II, and III

22. All of the following could appear immediately after N EXCEPT

   (A) J
   (B) O
   (C) P
   (D) Q
   (E) R

Questions 23–28

Nine people—F, G, H, I, J, K, L, M, N—are to be seated at three tables with different colored tablecloths—red, blue, and white. Three people will be seated at each table according to the following restrictions:

   H and M must be seated at the same table.

   J and K must be seated at the same table.

   N and I cannot be seated at the same table.

   L is seated at the table with the blue tablecloth.

   Either I or L or both must be seated at the table with G.

26

23. Which of the following groups could be seated at the same table?

    (A) F, K, N
    (B) F, I, L
    (C) J, H, L
    (D) M, H, I
    (E) N, H, I

24. Which of the following groups CANNOT be seated at the table with the white table-cloth?

    (A) J, K, N
    (B) J, K, I
    (C) F, G, I,
    (D) F, H, M
    (E) F, I, H

25. Which of the following CANNOT be seated at the same table as J?

    (A) F
    (B) H
    (C) I
    (D) L
    (E) N

26. Which of the following CANNOT be true?

    (A) H is seated at the table with the blue tablecloth.
    (B) G is seated at the table with the white tablecloth.
    (C) N is seated at the table with the white tablecloth.
    (D) I is seated at the table with the red tablecloth, and G is seated at the table with the white tablecloth.
    (E) F is seated at the table with the red tablecloth, and J is seated at the table with the white tablecloth.

27. If L and M are seated at the same table, and if G is seated at the table with the red tablecloth, which of the following people must be seated at the table with the white tablecloth?

    (A) H, I
    (B) H, N
    (C) I, K
    (D) K, F, J
    (E) K, J, N

28. If I and J are seated at the table with the white tablecloth, then which of the following people must be seated at the table with the blue tablecloth?

    (A) F
    (B) G
    (C) H
    (D) K
    (E) N

29. It is sometimes said that Samuel Beckett, through his lawyers, sued to stop the American Repertory Theater from staging "Endgame." In fact, Beckett's view was that because of substantial changes in stage directions the play was unacceptable to him and argued only that the playbill and publicity should not describe him as author. The company staged the production as it wished but conformed the billing and publicity to Beckett's wishes.

    The speaker is primarily concerned to

    (A) clarify an ambiguous term
    (B) correct a misunderstanding
    (C) defend a moral concept
    (D) explain an ethical dilemma
    (E) illustrate a thesis

30. Translating poetry, which has always been a difficult task, has become even more problematic but not because, as Robert Frost said, "poetry is what gets lost in translation." Rather the act of turning writing of another language into our own language is disparaged as an imperialistic project, an attempt to superimpose our own linguistic conceptual framework onto the writing of another whose independence is thereby negated. But, ironically, this attitude actually reinforces the linguistico-centric viewpoint it attempts to subvert by announcing in advance that any attempt to transcend the national and cultural boundaries of English is in principle doomed.

The speaker's point is that

(A) the refusal to translate poetry into English is ultimately self-defeating

(B) it is impossible to translate poetry into English without losing its essence

(C) only great poets can be effectively translated without sacrificing their insights

(D) poetry written in English cannot be translated into other languages effectively

(E) the English language enjoys a privileged position in the writing of literature

31. The Bridge and Tunnel Authority promised that technical glitches in its Auto-Pass system would be worked out within a few months. The system, which allows motorists to prepay tolls, was designed to speed the flow of traffic through toll booths. But after nearly a year, traffic is moving more slowly through the toll booths than it was before the inauguration of the Auto-Pass system.

Which of the following, if true, helps to explain the result?

(A) It took six months for the Bridge and Tunnel Authority to get the new system working properly.

(B) Motorists using the Auto-Pass system pay the same amount in tolls as other motorists.

(C) The Auto-Pass system is available for commercial vehicles but only at specially designated lanes.

(D) The Auto-Pass system worked so well that new motorists attracted to the roadway clogged the system.

(E) Other jurisdictions have experienced a similar problem after installing the Auto-Pass system.

Questions 32–35

The manager of a college bookstore is scheduling part-time student help. The available workers are J, K, L, M, and N. Exactly one worker will be scheduled to work in the morning and one in the afternoon each day during the upcoming week, Monday through Friday, according to the following conditions:

J and L can only work in the afternoons.

M and N can only work in the mornings.

No student can work both in the morning and in the afternoon of the same day.

26

No student can work on two consecutive days.

K will work Wednesday afternoon.

N will work Thursday morning.

32. Which of the following must be true?

    (A) J works Tuesday afternoon.
    (B) J works Friday morning.
    (C) K works Friday morning.
    (D) L works Thursday afternoon.
    (E) N works Tuesday morning.

33. If K works on Monday afternoon, which of the following must be true?

    (A) K does not work on Friday morning.
    (B) M works on Monday morning.
    (C) J works on Tuesday afternoon.
    (D) L works on Tuesday afternoon.
    (E) Neither J nor L works Tuesday afternoon.

34. If K works only one afternoon during the week, which of the following must be true?

    (A) J works exactly two days during the week.
    (B) K works exactly three days during the week.
    (C) L works only one day during the week.
    (D) N works on Monday morning and Friday morning.
    (E) K works more times during the week than M.

35. If J is not scheduled to work at all during the week, all of the following must be true EXCEPT

    (A) K works on Friday afternoon.
    (B) M works on Friday morning.
    (C) L works on Tuesday afternoon.
    (D) N works on Monday morning.
    (E) K works on Monday afternoon.

STOP:
WHEN YOU HAVE ANSWERED THE LAST QUESTION, THE FINAL IS OVER. YOU ARE NOT PERMITTED TO CONTINUE TO WORK ON THE SECTION

Evaluate Your Performance

Use the following answer key to score your Analytical Diagnostic Test. (Put a "✓" beside those items you answered correctly.)

Analytical Reasoning

1. (C)	12. (C)	24. (E)
2. (B)	16. (D)	25. (B)
3. (A)	17. (B)	26. (D)
4. (B)	18. (E)	27. (E)
5. (A)	19. (D)	28. (B)
8. (C)	20. (B)	32. (E)
9. (B)	21. (C)	33. (B)
10. (E)	22. (D)	34. (A)
11. (B)	23. (D)	35. (D)

Number of Analytical Reasoning Correct: _____

Logical Reasoning

6. (A)	14. (A)	30. (A)
7. (A)	15. (B)	31. (D)
13. (C)	29. (B)	

26

Number of Logical Reasoning Correct: _____

TOTAL CORRECT: _____

When you ask "How did I do?", you probably have in mind a couple of different questions. You want to know how you did overall and whether you did significantly worse (or better) on one part of the test or another. The following "bell curves" will help you answer those questions.

Analytical Reasoning

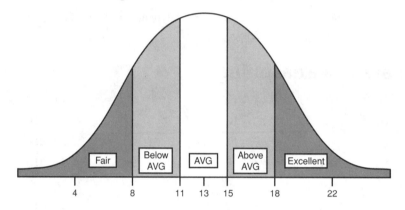

Number Correct

Logical Reasoning

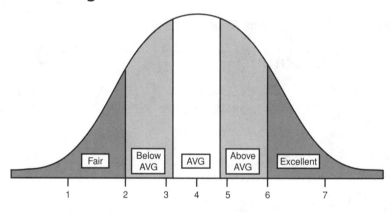

Number Correct

Overall Analytical

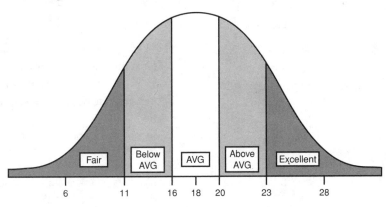

Number Correct

Review the Correct Answers

Questions 1–5

This is an ordering set. You should begin by processing the set-up conditions.

O = 3rd (and only O)

(M & N) = Q + 3 (M and N are 3 floors above Q)

P > K (P on a higher floor than K)

1. **(C)** This problem does not give you any additional information, so you can find the correct choice using only the set-up conditions. The incorrect answers can all be shown to be possible by constructing examples:

1st	2nd	3rd	4th	5th
Q	K	O	M	P
	J		N	
			L	

This is not the only possible assignment of rooms, but the diagram shows that (A), (B), (D), and (E) are possible. (C), however, is not possible. K has to have a room no higher than the fourth floor since P has a room higher than K's. M and N can't be on a floor lower than four since they have rooms three floors above Q's room. So it is impossible for K to have a room higher than N's.

2. **(B)** Again, you have a question that doesn't supply more information. (B) is necessarily true because the distribution of vacant rooms is 1, 1, 1, 2, and 3 rooms per floor (though not necessarily in that order). As for the incorrect answers, the following diagram shows that they are not necessarily true:

26

1st	2nd	3rd	4th	5th
Q	K	O	M	P
J				N
L				

3. **(A)** Here you have additional information:

1st	2nd	3rd	4th	5th
	Q			M
	J			N
				?

M and N must be assigned to the fifth floor, and a third person must be assigned to the fifth floor in order to meet the 1–1–1–2–3 distributional requirement. (A) is the correct answer since P must have a room on a floor above K's. This means that K is not on the fifth floor, and K cannot be on the second floor. This means that K must be either on floor one or four, floors with only one vacant room. (B), (C), (D), and (E) are all possible, but not necessarily true.

4. **(B)** Since P's room must be higher than K's, and since M's room and N's room can only be on the fourth or the fifth floor, the stipulation that K's room is on the same floor as M's and N's means that M and N are on floor four. This requires Q

to be on the first floor. The remaining statements are all possible but not necessarily true.

5. **(A)** If L's room is on a higher floor than P's room, then the fourth floor is the lowest possible floor for L (P's room must be higher than K's). However, the highest floor to which Q can be assigned is the second. So L and Q cannot be assigned to the same floor.

6. **(A)** This is a weakening question. Begin by finding the conclusion of the argument: rail is safest. And the evidence for this conclusion is the fact that there are fewer spills. But what if those are really big spills? This is the attack suggested by (A). The difficult with the argument is that it assumes, tacitly, that all spills are equal. Like most weakening questions, (A) attacks the hidden assumption. (E) is your attractive distractor. It's high relevant to the argument—but it actually strengthens rather than weakens the argument.

7. **(A)** This is one of those questions that ask you to explain a seemingly contradictory or paradoxical result: the bag is the least expensive component, but people save money on that component. (A) explains why: comparatively speaking, the bag is a fairly substantial part of the cost of an inexpensive instrument.

Questions 8–12

This is a map set, so you'll need a diagram:

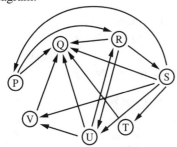

8. **(C)** V can import goods directly from S and U.

9. **(B)** Both R and U can export directly to and import directly from each other.

10. **(E)** As the diagram shows, only Q can import directly from T and V.

11. **(B)** The most direct route would be P to R to U to V.

12. **(C)** Goods leaving S could go:

    To T and then to Q.

    To U and then to R.

    To U and then to V.

    To U and then to Q. (But Q is already included.)

13. **(C)** This question is a "strengthening" question. And with a question like this, the correct answer is often an idea that preempts a possible attack on the argument. In this case, the argument would be vulnerable to the objection that the guns are indeed going to criminals, even though criminals are a small part of the population, because criminals simply own more than they can use at any given time. (C) preempts this by saying that the guns are actually going to otherwise law-abiding citizens who want them for self-defense.

14. **(A)** This is an assumption question, and you know from your Action Plan that you should be looking for an unstated premise. (A) is the correct choice. The speaker says that the Milkyway is a good place to look for other life because there are many planets out there that might have conditions similar to those on earth. That assumes, however, that these are the conditions that would give rise to life.

15. **(B)** This is a "weakening" question. (B) takes on the argument directly by denying the speculative link between the Association and the price rise. According to (B), there is an alternative explanation for the price increase that has nothing to do with collusive behavior.

Questions 16–22

16. **(D)** The first condition eliminates (C); the second condition eliminates (A); and the third condition eliminates both (B) and (E).

17. **(B)** Since Q comes before M and M before P, Q must come before P.

18. **(E)** The third condition eliminates (A) and (C). Then, (B) is not possible because both Q and M must come before P. Finally, (D) is not possible because M must come before P.

26

19. **(D)** Q must come before M, P, and R. So if O is the first word (and N the third), Q must be the second word.

20. **(B)** If O-P-R are played consecutively in that order, then they must be the fourth, fifth, and sixth words of the phrase. Then since Q must be played before M, Q must be the first word and M the second.

21. **(C)** If O is the sixth word, then there are exactly three possible messages:

1	2	3	4	5	6
Q	M	N	P	R	O
Q	M	N	R	P	O
Q	R	N	M	P	O

22. **(D)** Q cannot appear as the fourth word, because Q must appear before M, R, and P.

Question 23–28

This is a selection set. You should begin by summarizing the information:

H = M
J = K
N ≠ I
L = blue
I or L or both = G

23. **(D)** This question provides no additional information, so use the set-up conditions to eliminate the wrong choices. You can eliminate (C) and (E) because H is at a table without M. You can eliminate (A)

because K is at the table without J. And you can eliminate (B) because either I or L must sit with G.

24. **(E)** Again, use the set-up conditions—this time to find the one grouping that is not possible. (E) is not acceptable because H and M must sit together.

25. **(B)** J and H cannot sit together because J must sit with K and H must sit with M.

26. **(D)** Seating I at the red table and G at the white, would leave G without either I or L because L is seated at the blue table.

27. **(E)** Now you'll probably need a diagram to keep track of things:

Red	Blue	White
G	L,M	

I must be seated with G, since L is not:

Red	Blue	White
G,I	L,M	

And that means that J and K are at the white table:

Red	Blue	White
G,I	L,M	J,K

With H at the blue table and N at the white:

Red	Blue	White
G,I,F	L,M,H	J,K,N

28. **(B)** Again, a diagram is probably a good idea:

Red	Blue	White
	L	I,J

And that puts K at the white table:

Red	Blue	White
	L	I,J,K

And G must sit with L:

Red	Blue	White
	L,G	I,J,K

29. **(B)** This question just asks for you to describe the development of the argument. The speaker says that there is a common conception that Beckett tried to stop the ART production of "Endgame." But this is incorrect, according to the speaker. And the speaker then explains what actually transpired.

30. **(A)** This question asks you to draw a further conclusion. The speaker explains that there is a tendency now to deny that it is possible to translate other languages into English because the other languages have their own validity. But, the speaker argues, this misguided attempt to acknowledge the validity of other languages actually says, in effect, that English is too powerful to permit other works to be translated into English.

31. **(D)** This type of question asks you to explain a seemingly paradoxical result. In this case, (D) suggests that the system worked too well: it sped up the flow of traffic which in turn attracted more people to the faster route which in turn slowed things down again.

Questions 32–35

This is an ordering problem, so begin by processing the set-up conditions:

	M	Tu	Wed	Th	F
a.m.				N	
p.m.			K		

Since K works Wednesday afternoon, K cannot work Tuesday or Thursday. Further, with N working on Thursday, N is not available for Wednesday morning. This means M works Wednesday morning and N works Tuesday morning:

	M	Tu	Wed	Th	F
a.m.		N	M	N	
p.m.			K		

32. **(E)** Our further conclusions show that M works Wednesday morning and N works Tuesday morning. (A), (B), (C), and (D) are all possibly true; only (E) is necessarily true.

33. **(B)** Begin by processing the additional information. Since K works Monday afternoon, K cannot work Monday morning or on Tuesday. So either J or L will work on Tuesday afternoon, and M will work Monday morning:

26

	M	Tu	Wed	Th	F
a.m.	M	N	M	N	
p.m.	K	J/L	K		

The diagram shows that (A), (C), and (D) are possibly true and that (E) is necessarily false. Only (B) is necessarily true.

34. **(A)** The additional information says that K works only one afternoon. We can't draw any specific conclusion about a particular day, so we should look at the answer choices. (A) is correct. J and L must work Monday, Tuesday, Thursday, and Friday afternoons. And since a student cannot work on consecutive days, J must do either Monday or Tuesday and either Thursday or Friday. (B) is incorrect since M could do both Monday and Friday mornings, and then K would only work once. (C) is incorrect because L must work two days; (D) is incorrect because

N cannot work on Monday or Thursday; and (E) is possibly, though not necessarily, true. We don't know whether Monday and Friday mornings will go to K or to M.

35. **(D)** Begin by processing the additional information:

	M	Tu	Wed	Th	F
a.m.	M	N	M	N	M
p.m.	K	L	K	L	K

If J does not work at all during the week, then L must work on Tuesday and Thursday. This means that K must work on Monday afternoon and Friday afternoon. Further, we must assign M to Monday and Friday mornings. The diagram shows that (A), (B), (C), and (E) are all necessarily true and that (D) is necessarily false.

Part V

Writing Skills

Day
27

Test Your GRE Writing Assessment Skills

Preview the GRE Writing Assessment

The GRE Writing Assessment consists of two essays: a 45-minute "issue" essay and a 30-minute "argument" essay. The "issue" topic states an opinion about a topic of general interest; you have to take a position on the topic and write an essay defending your position. The "argument" topic requires you to critique an argument.

On the actual Writing Assessment, you'll have the option of using the computer to write your essay or writing it out in long hand. So too, here you have your choice. If you have access to a computer with word processing capability, then you can use that. Or, you can write your responses in hand in the space provided.

The "Issue" Essay PreTest

In this part, you will respond to an "issue" topic. The time limit is 45 minutes, so set aside some time when you won't be disturbed and use a watch or a clock to time yourself. Use a computer for word processing, or write your response by hand using a separate piece of paper. Then evaluate your essay by comparing it with the samples given in the Review part of this section.

"Issue" PreTest

Issue Task

Present Your Perspective on an Issue

Time—45 minutes

You have 45 minutes to plan and write an essay on the topic below. *An essay on any other topic is not acceptable.*

The topic is a brief statement about an issue of general interest. You may accept, reject, or qualify the statement. Support your views with reasons and examples drawn from your reading, experience, observations, or study.

Your essay will be graded according to how well you:

—Appreciate the complexities and implications of the issue

—Organize, develop, and support your ideas with reasons and/or examples

—Express your ideas and control the elements of standard written English

Spend a few minutes organizing your thoughts before you begin writing, and leave yourself some time at the end to edit your response.

Issue Topic

The sole function of public schools should be to teach academic and practical skills and not to inculcate ethical values.

Review

Here are two sample responses to the topic above. Compare your essay to them. In making your comparison, think about the following questions:

1. In terms of overall effectiveness, where does my answer rank?

2. How are the different essays organized? Which organization is easier to follow?

3. What kinds of reasons are given? Are examples used? How do the reasons/examples add to the effectiveness of the essay?

4. Are the ideas clearly expressed? Which essay is more interesting to read?

(You'll notice that the samples contain some errors. This is to be expected since they are "draft" quality and not final versions.)

Strong "Issue" Essay

Providing a public school education to children is one of the most important functions of government because most children (except those in private schools) have to attend public school until they are at least 16 years old. Children are in school several hour every day, so the content of the curriculum influences them in some important ways. But what should be the limits of a public school curriculum in a democracy where freedom of conscience is so important?

On the one hand, it might be thought that the sole function of public schools should be to teach academic and practical skills and to avoid ethical issues altogether. Certainly, government through public education should avoid dictating religious views. It is no business of the schools to tell children that they should be Protestant, Catholic, Jewish, Muslim, or any other religion. And related issues such as abortion and sexual activity should be left to parents.

On the other hand, it seems impossible to avoid such issues altogether. While it might be possible to teach pure math without ethical overtones, history and even literature are about human activities. It's impossible to teach about the Holocaust without saying that it was morally wrong. Teaching the history of western expansion would be one-sided if it didn't raise questions about the actions of the white settlers. Hamlet wouldn't be Hamlet without the dilemma of "to be or not to be." And even in the so-called "hard" sciences, questions about the environment and the appropriate use of and conservation of resources raise ethical issues that just cannot be avoided. Biology and human reproduction are legitimate academic subjects that also start to raise ethical questions including evoltion.

It's easy in theory to say that government shouldn't be in the business of teaching ethics in the public schools. But in practice, the ethical issues are impossible to avoid. Instead of pretending that schools can avoid morality altogether, we should insist that when such issue come up, they are present from a variety of perspectives so that children are exposed to different viewpoints but not told what to believe.

27

Weak "Issue" Essay

Public schools are important in America and teach academic and practical subjects, but they should not teach ethics. One of the important reasons for the founding of this country was freedom of religion. People came here to get away from the prosecutions they had experienced in their homeland. So it would be wrong to set up a new system that tries to tell them what they ought to think.

The fact that our past leaders thought that religious freedom was important is expressed in the Constitution. The Bill of Rights says that the government cannot set up a state religion. That should also be read to mean that the government cannot set up a quasi-state religion through the schools. If government attempts to tell children what to think about important ethical issues, then that is the moral equivalent to a state religion.

America was built upon experience with other forms of government. One of the primary experiences was religious prosecution. Steering clear of that sort of thing in the future will continue to ensure that we remain freedom.

The "Argument" Essay PreTest

In this part, you will respond to an "argument" topic. The time limit is 30 minutes, so set aside some time when you won't be disturbed and use a watch or a clock to time yourself. Use a computer for word processing, or write your response by hand using a separate piece of paper. Then evaluate your essay by comparing it with the samples given in the Review part of this section.

"Argument" PreTest

Argument Task

Analysis of an Argument

Time—30 minutes

You have 30 minutes to plan and write a critique of an argument. *An analysis of any other argument is not acceptable.*

The topic is a brief argument. You are not asked to agree or disagree with the conclusion of the argument but to analyze the argument. Consider what assumptions underlie the thinking and how the evidence is related to the conclusion. You can also discuss what other evidence, if available, might strengthen or weaken the argument.

Your essay will be graded according to how well you:

—Identify and analyze important elements of the argument

—Organize, develop, and support your ideas with reasons and/or examples

—Express your ideas and control the elements of standard written English

Spend a few minutes organizing your thoughts before you begin writing, and leave yourself some time at the end to edit your response.

Argument Topic

Two years ago, the Fort Ann School purchased twelve new computers and implemented a requirement that all students take at least two hours of computer instruction each week. The Hudson Falls School, which is near Fort Ann School and has about the same number of students, doesn't have such a requirement. Over the past two years, the number of Fort Ann School seniors going on to college has increased by 20 percent while the number of Hudson Falls seniors going on to college has remained constant. Therefore, if Hudson Falls wants to give its students the opportunities they deserve, it should buy new computers and teach students how to use them.

27

Review

Here are two sample responses to the topic above. Compare your essay to them. In making your comparison, think about the following questions:

1. In terms of overall effectiveness, where does my answer rank?

2. How do the essays differ in their analysis of the argument? How are the different essays organized? Which organization is easier to follow?

3. What kinds of reasons are given? Are examples used? How do the reasons/examples add to the effectiveness of the essay?

4. Are the ideas clearly expressed? Which essay is more interesting to read?

(You'll notice that the samples contain some errors. This is to be expected since they are "draft" quality and not final versions.)

Strong "Argument" Essay

The argument is interesting but not entirely persuasive. It will obviously appeal to many people who uncritically accept the idea that "computers" are a silver bullet for all of our educational woes. A closer look, however, shows that much more would be needed to support the conclusion.

First, it is necessary to determine in what respects, if any, the education at Hudson Falls School is deficient. The argument doesn't says that Hudson Falls students are prevented from going to college because they don't learn about computers. For all we know, Hudson Falls already has all of the computer equipment that it needs and gives its students instruction in computers. Additionally, the number of students who go to college is not the only measure of a school's effectiveness. Not every student wants to go to college. It would also be important to learn whether Hudson Falls effectively serves the needs of students who want vocational training using computers.

Second, it would be important to ask whether or not the computers used at Fort Ann School made the difference in the number of college-bound students. Perhaps Fort Ann already had enough computers to begin with, and the twelve new computers were really just extra resources that didn't have a real impact. And what was taught during the two hours of "computer instruction?" Word processing, graphics, bookkeeping, internet research? Some computer skills are more relevant to college preparation than others. Nothing in the argument draws a causal connection between the computer instruction and the number of students going to college.

Third, it is necessary to consider what would be the overall effect of investing in new computer equipment and requiring computer study. We don't know anything about the size of the student body at Hudson Falls School, but new computer equipment may mean a substantial investment compared to the overall budget. That could mean money not available for texts, library books, newspaper subscriptions, field trips, and even sports. Additionally, time spent in a computer lab is time not spent learning a second language or working in the chemistry lab. These other activities may be even more important for college preparation than learning a little about computers.

In conclusion, the argument fails to prove the conclusion. It doesn't establish that there is a problem at Hudson Falls; it doesn't identify the real cause of the supposed problem; and it doesn't consider the overall effect of spending more money on computers. The word "computers" has a nice ring to it; but a lot more research would have to be done before it could be concluded that new computers and required courses are needed at Hudson Falls School.

27

Weak "Argument" Essay

The argument is well-presented and argued, but it is not completely persuasive. It gives statistics to support the conclusion that computers help to prepare students for college. (A 20% increase at Fort Ann school.) The argument also points out that students have to know how to use computers. (Required two hours each week.) A computer sitting on a desk is not helping anyone.

Unfortunatley, the argument fails to note many other things. For example, some students may not even want to go to college or even to learn about computers. Other students may want to go to college and may already have computers in their homes. Also, computers are good for many different things such as word processing and bookkeeping. Some of these are college skills and some are not.

In conclusion, the argument presents some reasons why Hudson Falls should buy computers and require students to use them. The reasons may be somewhat good. But more information should be learned before the school makes the investment.

Day
28

Teach Yourself the Writing Assessment

Today, you'll teach yourself how to write the essays for the Writing Assessment. The Writing Assessment includes two essay tasks that are in some ways different but in other ways alike. It will be necessary to use slightly different approaches for the content of the two essays, but both are graded on organization, clarity of expression, and mechanics (grammar, etc.), so there is some overlap. Here are your goals for today:

Get the Inside Info on the Writing Assessment

The GRE Writing Assessment consists of two essays: a 45-minute "issue" essay and a 30-minute "argument" essay. The "issue" topic states an opinion about a topic of general interest; you have to take a position on the topic and write an essay defending your position. The "argument" topic requires you to critique an argument. According to the GRE, the two writing tasks are complementary: one asks you to create your own argument for a position; the other asks you to attack someone else's argument. (This is an important difference that will help define your approach to the two exercises.)

The Writing Assessment directions and topics are presented on the computer, and you can use the keyboard to input your essay. The word processing program used for the Analytical Writing is fairly simple. You can type, delete, cut, and paste, but you won't have any of the advanced functions you may be used to. Additionally, you have the option of handwriting your essay.

What You'll Do Today

- **Get All the Inside Info on the Writing Assessment**
- **The "Issue" Essay**
- **The "Argument" Essay**
- **Writing Correctly**
- **Get Answers to Frequently Asked Questions**

> **TIP** If you are used to doing word processing on a computer, then use the computer. If you are not comfortable with composing at the computer, then choose the hand writing alternative.

You may be given a choice of topics for each exercise, but don't count on it. You may be assigned your topics; and even if you're given a choice, you'll only have a couple of options, so it's no big deal. Here are some sample "issue" topics:

The architecture of public buildings reflects the values and aspirations of the society that built them.

Urbanization and advances in communication have brought us closer together. But even as we meet more and more people, we find that we are lonelier.

Ultimately, the environmental problems that we face will not be solved by governments or business. They can only be solved by individuals.

You'll notice that these topics don't require any special knowledge. They're general enough so that if you were assigned one, you should be able to find something to say. Argument topics tend to be more concrete, and that's because they present a real-life situation for you to analyze. Here are some examples:

For many years, *The Standard* was the only newspaper in the city of Evertville. Two years ago, however, a new paper, *The Chronicle*, was started; and since then, circulation of *The Standard* has declined by 10 percent. *The Chronicle* includes more coverage of neighborhood events and local stories like crime than *The Standard*. So if *The Standard* wants to regain the readers that it lost, it should devote more space to events that will be of interest to readers in the Evertville area.

Two years ago, the Fort Ann School purchased twelve new computers and implemented a requirement that all students take at least two hours of computer instruction each week. The Hudson Falls School, which is near Fort Ann School and has about the same number of students, doesn't have such a requirement. Over the past two years, the number of Fort Ann School seniors going on to college has increase by 20 percent while the number of Hudson Falls seniors going on to college has remained constant. Therefore, if Hudson Falls wants to give its students the opportunities they deserve, it should buy new computers and teach students how to use them.

A recent review of the records of the Putnam volunteer rescue squad shows that its average response time is greater than that of the Empire Ambulance Service, a for-profit company. Putnam should disband the rescue squad, sell the equipment, and contract ambulance services out to Empire. We'd get much better emergency care for our citizens.

Even though these topics are purely hypothetical, they resemble real-life situations in that they reach specific conclusions based upon the kind evidence you would ordinarily use in such situations.

MAKE CONNECTIONS

The Writing Assessment topics are selected from a list of topics that you can study in advance. You'll find them in a variety of GRE publications, and you can download the list from: *www.gre.org/*

Your essays will be scored on a 6-point holistic scale according to criteria developed by the GRE. Each of your essays will be assigned at random to two readers who have been trained to apply the criteria, and there are special procedures for resolving differences of opinion about the score that an essay should be given. Your scores will be available a couple of weeks after you've taken your test.

What counts as a good essay and what makes an essay bad? For an answer to that question we need to look at the criteria used to grade the essay and to what graders themselves say about how they apply those criteria. Although the essay topics are different for the two exercises, there is considerable overlap in the grading criteria.

First, here are the most important elements of the grading system:

28

Strong Essay	Weak Essay
Develops a position using reasons and examples	Limited development of a position on the issue
Focused and well organized	Poorly focused and poorly organized
Ideas expressed using varied sentence structures; demonstrates command of standard written English	Problems expressing ideas clearly and lacks sentence variety; numerous errors in grammar, usage, and mechanics

And what do graders say about how they apply these criteria? As for the first, a strong essay is one that "examines the multi-faceted implications of the issues," while a weak essay "lacks development," "repeats ideas" stated earlier, or "consists of unsubstantiated generalizations." As for the second criteria, the strong essay allows "reader to move effortlessly from point to point," and ideas are connected "through the use of appropriate transitions" such as "but," "usually," and "for instance." As for the third, the strong essay displays a "mastery of the elements of effective writing," while the weak essay lacks "control over syntax, usage, and word choice."

A good way of understanding all of this is to think about the graders as judges in a gymnastics or similar competition. Your essay-routine has to have a certain number of moves, and you get added points for degree of difficulty and style. On the other hand, you lose points for breaks. You can use the first two criteria outlined above to add points to your essay, and you use the third criteria to avoid having points subtracted.

TIP   Make liberal use of examples. First, they'll help you to have something rather than nothing to say; second, they'll help you be specific rather than vague; third, the graders themselves say they love examples.

Our analysis so far tells you exactly what you need to do to get a good score on the essay. They key factors are:

1. Articulate a position and have ideas to support it.
2. Write an organized, coherent essay using those ideas.
3. Use sentences that are clear, and don't make unnecessary mistakes.

Although there are some minor differences, this analysis applies to both of the essay tasks. We talk about the differences as we discuss each in turn.

> Think of Writing Ability as a competition against yourself. The graders are the judges. Your essay is your routine. Your routine has to have certain required moves; it must flow; and you can earn points for added difficulty. You gain with style points. Points are deducted for breaks and sloppiness.

The "Issue" Essay

The "issue" topic requires you to develop your own position on the assigned topic. Here's your Action Plan for the "issue" essay:

Step 1: Plan your essay.

Read the topic, articulate to yourself the position that you want to defend, then outline your essay on the scratch paper you've been given.

Step 2: Write your essay.

Your essay can have a brief introduction. Then follow your outline and write one paragraph for each of the major points. You may also include a conclusion if you wish.

Step 3: Proofread your essay.

For proofreading, you'll need a checklist of the most common errors that students make on the essay part. (We'll take care of that at the end of today's lesson.)

Now let's discuss each step of the Action Plan.

Before you try to write anything, you need to plan your essay. Planning means first articulating the position that you plan to defend. This is essential. The directions and the commentary about the essays are very clear that points are awarded for responding to the essay prompt; points are deducted for failing to address the topic specifically.

What position should you take? It really doesn't matter. There is no right or wrong answer; there is no preferred and no disfavored position. If you have some reflective thoughts about the topic, then you can let them guide you. But the topics are written to avoid giving anyone an advantage of specialized knowledge, so don't expect to find a topic that you know a lot about.

Additionally, the topics tend to be very broad. So broad, in fact, that you probably would need to narrow one down before you could write an ordinary college essay on the topic. And another feature of this broadness is that the topics are sufficiently vague as to allow different interpretations. Or, you saw above, the graders say that the issue is "complex."

28

Instead of trying to nail the topic down, exploit the ambiguity (complexity). Make it the centerpiece of your essay. Here's how to do it.

We'll use the following topic for the discussion:

> In this age of computers, some people complain that our lives are being controlled by machines. But, in reality, computers actually improve the quality of our lives.

Does "controlled" literally mean that every aspect of our lives is dictated by some machine? If it does, then the topic is really pretty silly, because there are obviously a lot of things that we do that aren't controlled by machines. But maybe "controlled" is only used to dramatize the point and means that machines have a big impact on our lives. In that case, the statement doesn't seem to be so exaggerated. So what is it exactly that the statement means? It's impossible to say. We'd call that ambiguity, but the graders call it complexity. So let the complexity work for you, and (to quote one of the graders) "explore the intricacies" of the issue.

The easiest way to "explore the complexities" of an issue like this is to focus on a key word in the topic. Define that key word one way, and then define it another way. That's what we did in the sketch above with the word "control."

Once you've decided what you want to say, then you need to outline your essay. (You can use the scratch paper that your given.) This step is also essential. One of the important criteria on which you'll be graded is how well organized and developed your essay is, so you need to know where you're going before you start. The approach that we're taking naturally lends itself to a three paragraph development:

I. Computers are so important that it may seem like they control us.

    A. They handle a lot of important tasks like helping pilots fly planes and doing scientific research.

    B. They handle a lot of less important but useful tasks like opening doors and controlling microwaves.

    C. Sometimes they even intrude when we don't want them, e.g., automatic dialers for telemarketers.

II. Computers don't really control us.

    A. We control them by programming.

    B. There are places where there are no computers.

    C. We can always turn them off.

III. On balance: computers affect our lives but don't control us.

You may think that this approach "waffles" on the issue, but the grader is going to think that it "explores the complexities" of the issue. (One person's "waffling" is the GRE's "complexity.")

> **TIP**
>
> For the "issue" essay, focus on a key word or phrase in order to say that the topic presents "complex issues." Then give the reader the old one-two punch ("on the one hand; but on the other").

The second step in your Action Plan should follow directly from the first if you've made a proper outline. Write your essay according to the outline. Think about each sentence before you begin to write, and express yourself in a clear, direct, and concise manner. Here's is what an essay using the outline above might look like:

Computers are so ubiquitous that it sometimes seems as though they control every aspect of our lives. Certainly, they handle a lot of very important tasks that are literally matters of life and death. For example, large government and private computers keep track of air traffic, tracking individual airplanes, plotting safe routes, and monitoring the skies for emergencies. Or, to take another example, computers are also essential for doing advanced medical research. Whether or not we get a new drug or treatment seems to depend on whether a university computer "concluded in a study" that the therapy improved the chances for treatment of a certain disease. Computers also are responsible for a lot of small but useful tasks: they open and close doors automatically, regulate the temperature of buildings, and operate various appliances like VCRs and microwaves. And they seem to do this all behind our backs and without our asking for it or consent. Sometimes, computers are really intrusive. Who hasn't been interrupted during dinner by the computerized dialer of some telemarketer? Also, most of us worry that computers have so much information about us that we can't control.

On the other hand, in spite of all of this, computers don't really control us. We control them. In the first place, computers depend on us for their very existence. We manufacture them, and then we program them. Moreover, we can always escape from them. We can go camping in the wilderness or even just take a walk in the country without the help of a computer. In the final analysis, we can always "pull the plug" if we want to. You don't have to program your VCR if you don't want.

On balance, while it may seem that computers "control" us, a closer look at things shows that we really control them. If there are ways that computers adversely

continues

28

affect us when we don't want them to, it's not really the computer's doing. It's the person behind the computer. The telemarketing computer did not tell itself to call me during dinner; the salesperson did. So if there's any blame to be assigned, it belongs to people, not inanimate machines.

 CAUTION Don't overburden a sentence. Trying to string together too many thoughts into a single sentence results in unclear writing. And even if your sentence is clear, you reader may get lost and blame you.

Workshop A

This workshop includes three "issue" topics for practice. There is no time limit for the exercises and no right or wrong answer.

Drill

For each of the following topics, outline an essay. The template following each topic gives you some suggestions. Then check your work against the explanations given in the Review part of this Workshop.

Topic 1

When asked about the key to success, most successful people say "Hard work." Yet, hard work alone is not sufficient to guarantee that one will be successful.

Focus on the term "hard work" and complete the following outline.

I. _____

    A. _____

    B. _____

    C. _____

II. _____

    A. _____

    B. _____

    C. _____

III. _____

Topic 2

Power over other people is only the illusion of power. Real power comes from having control over one's own destiny.

Focus on the term "power" and complete the following outline.

     I. _____

          A. _____

          B. _____

          C. _____

    II. _____

          A. _____

          B. _____

          C. _____

   III. _____

Topic 3

The news and entertainment media are driven by the profit motive, and that is the cause of the poor quality of news and entertainment that we receive.

Focus on the term "driven by the profit motive" and complete the following outline.

     I. _____

          A. _____

          B. _____

          C. _____

    II. _____

          A. _____

          B. _____

          C. _____

   III. _____

28

Review

Outline for Topic 1

    I. Successful people all seem to share one characteristic: they work hard.

        A. Political leaders work hard. The President is never officially "off duty."

        B. Athletes work long, hard hours. The games are short but training and conditioning require time.

        C. Artists work hard. Dancers have to practice and rehearse; painters make sketches and studies; actors have to study and learn their lines.

    II. But what do such people mean by "hard work?

        A. Many successful people seem to enjoy what they do. It can't just be the money, e.g., politicians, not-so-famous athletes, starving artists.

        B. Work is hard for people who do not enjoy what they do, e.g., farming or working on an assembly line.

        C. Perhaps even successful people who don't enjoy what they do think it's hard work.

    III. On balance, it's easy to say that hard work is the key. But the term means different things to different people.

Topic 2

    I. Having authority over other people may seem to make you powerful.

        A. The general of an army has life and death control over the soldiers.

        B. The head of a corporation can hire and fire people.

        C. Parents can tell their children what to do.

    II. But power is an illusion.

        A. You can't be sure other people will do what you tell them. Soldiers may disobey. You can fire someone, but that doesn't make them do what you want. Children can be obstinate.

        B. Even the most powerful people are not invulnerable. A general can be killed, a corporate head can be replaced by stockholders, parents can be hurt by their children.

    III. The person who seems to be in control is also controlled because the person is dependent on the others.

Topic 3

I. It may seem as though the "profit motive" results in poor quality news and entertainment.

    A. Newspapers. Tabloids look for sensational stories. Even established papers give coverage to titillating stories like the private lives of famous and powerful people.

    B. Television programs like Rivera and Springer exploit people in order to attract viewers. And advertisers pay to be featured during those times.

    C. Movies and the music industry seem to worry only about the bottom line, looking for a box office blockbuster or a new genre like gangsta rap.

II. Clearly people want these products.

    A. People buy tabloids. And established papers have determined that circulation improves with the addition of titillating stories.

    B. Rivera and Springer have ratings that justify what their producers charge advertisers.

    C. By definition, a box office blockbuster is a movie that people go to see.

III. If bad media sells, it can only be because someone is buying the product. So blame for poor quality should be placed on the consumer as well as on the provider.

> **NOTE** If you can find time in your study schedule for the GRE, you'd benefit from actually writing essay responses using the outlines above.

The "Argument" Essay

The "argument" topic requires you to critique someone else's argument. Here's your Action Plan for the "argument" essay:

Step 1: Plan your essay.

Read the topic, identify at least three major weaknesses in the argument, then outline your essay on the scratch paper you've been given.

Step 2: Write your essay.

Your essay should have a brief introduction. Then follow your outline and write one paragraph for each of the major points. You may include a conclusion if you wish.

28

Step 3: Proofread your essay.

For proofreading, you'll need a checklist of the most common errors that students make on the essay part. (We'll take care of that at the end of today's lesson.)

You notice that the Action Plan for the "argument" essay differs from that of the "issue" essay primarily in the first step.

> The argument topic doesn't ask you to agree or disagree with the ultimate conclusion of the argument. Instead, you are asked to evaluate how well the reasoning provided supports the conclusion.

Now let's discuss each step of the Action Plan. We'll use this topic for the discussion:

> A recent review of the records of the Putnam Township volunteer rescue squad shows that its average response time is 6 minutes greater than that of the Empire Ambulance Service, a for-profit company operating in the Putnam area. Putnam should disband the rescue squad, sell the equipment, and contract ambulance services out to Empire. We'd get much better emergency care for our citizens.

First, read the topic and identify at least three major weaknesses in the argument. As you look for weaknesses, ask the following questions:

1. Does the evidence show that a problem exists? If so, how significant is the problem?
2. Can the problem be corrected in a way other than that suggested by the topic?
3. Would adopting the plan of the topic result in any unintended and disadvantageous side-effects?

> When analyzing an argument topic, ask:

1. Does a serious problem exist?
2. Can it be corrected otherwise?
3. Would the plan of the argument result in side-effects?

Here are some possible answers to those questions.

First, does a problem exist? The only evidence for the existence of a problem is the 6 minute difference in response time of the volunteer squad and the professional service.

Does the 6 minutes make a significant difference? Perhaps it does make a difference, but certainly the argument doesn't prove that it does. It's easy to imagine serious cases in which immediate treatment means the difference between life and death, but the evidence doesn't show that the professional service provides immediate treatment. For example, it's possible that the average response times are 21 minutes and 27 minutes and that the 6 minutes just doesn't make a difference.

Or, you might ask whether the average response times is a fair comparison. For example, do the rescue squad and the ambulance company service *exactly* the same area? Perhaps the rescue squad responds to emergencies in remote areas where the ambulance can't go and that accounts for the response-time difference. Or, were the records reviewed representative of the quality of service provided by the two organizations? How many cases were reviewed? Was there anything unusual about those cases?

CAUTION | Don't accept the evidence for the conclusion at face value. In fact, the evidence given in the argument topic doesn't *prove* the conclusion of the topic. Otherwise, the directions wouldn't ask you to question it.

Second, even granting that a problem exists, perhaps the problem could be solved by some "minor adjustments" to the existing system. Perhaps, the rescue squad needs new radio equipment or a new vehicle to speed up response time. Maybe members of the rescue squad are in need of further training that would make them more effective and thereby reduce response time. Perhaps the rescue squad should work more closely with the professional service, allowing the professional service to respond to those calls where it would be more effective but holding open the option of using the volunteers where they would be equally as and perhaps more effective.

Third, would adopting the course of action called for result in any unwanted side-effects? Usually, there is a monetary cost associated with any such plan. In this case, it would be appropriate to ask how much it would cost Putnam Township and its citizens to make the change to the professional service. And it is also possible that they would end up with even worse service. After all, they would be dependent upon a vendor. If Empire doesn't perform adequately, the town may have some legal recourse, but a lawsuit doesn't make ambulance calls. Suppose, further, that the squad is disbanded and the equipment sold and things don't work out. Will it be possible to reorganize the squad? Would people again volunteer to serve? How much would replacement equipment cost?

28

This is not to suggest that any of these issues can be resolved just by the wording of the topic. That is not the point. The directions specifically tell you to look for:

- questionable assumptions
- whether the evidence supports the conclusion
- additional evidence that would be useful
- changes in the argument that would improve it

In other words, you don't have to answer the questions; you just have to ask them.

Let's assume that you considered all these points and decided to use the following ones in your essay:

I. The six-minute time difference doesn't prove that Empire is more effective than the volunteer squad. More information would be needed about:

 A. The number of cases studied and the time period covered.

 B. The methods of response and location of the cases.

 C. The effect of the time difference on effectiveness.

II. If a problem is determined to exist, Putnam should first consider improving the rescue squad.

 A. It should review the training procedures.

 B. It should look at the equipment being used.

 C. It should consider working more closely with Empire.

III. Before adopting the radical proposal suggested, Putnam should consider the following:

 A. It should review the training procedures.

 A. Contracting out such a service may be expensive and may take money away from other pressing problems.

 B. A private contractor may not be completely responsive to the town's wishes.

 C. If the new plan doesn't work, it may be difficult and expensive to return to the old system.

The second step of the Action Plan calls for you to write your essay. And, as you can see, it is practically written for you in the outline. You may want to add a brief introduction and perhaps a conclusion. Then, write three paragraphs, one for each of the main points. Here's what your essay might look like:

The argument to abolish the volunteer rescue squad in favor of a professional ambulance service is not persuasive for three reasons. First, the evidence cited doesn't prove the existence of a serious problem. Second, any problem that does exist can perhaps be solved with less drastic measures. Third, the radical plan called for might have serious side-effects.

First, the six-minute difference in response time doesn't, in and of itself, prove the existence of a serious problem. The evidence refers simply to "a review of records" but says nothing more about how that review was conducted. It would be important to determine that a representative time-slice was taken and that representative cases were reviewed. A single difficult case, for example during a snow storm, could skew the statistics. Additionally, the information given in the argument doesn't prove that the six-minute difference is an important difference. It is entirely possible that the volunteer squad responds to calls according to their survey. For example, a minor traffic accident doesn't calls for break-neck speed.

Second, if a problem does exist, Putnam should consider ways of improving the performance of the rescue squad. At minimum, it should look at the equipment now being used. Is the squad properly equipped? Is its dispatch and radio equipment reliable? Are its vehicles in good working order. Beyond that, it should look at training procedures, perhaps compare them with those of similar rescue squads elsewhere. If improvement is needed, more training would be in order. Finally, it could even consider working more closely with Empire, calling on Empire to answer those calls when it is unable to respond.

Third, Putnam should also consider the possibility that eliminating its rescue squad may cause new problems. Of course, it has to determine what the cost of such a move would be. Additionally, it has to realize that a private company might not be as cooperative as volunteers from the community. Further, if the new plan should be a complete failure, it might be difficult to reinstate the old system. People might be reluctant to volunteer again; leadership might be lacking; equipment might not be available or available only at a prohibitive cost.

In conclusion, there are at least three good reasons why Putnam should proceed cautiously and get more information before it makes a decision.

28

TIP

Make liberal use of transitions such as ordinal numbers (*first, second,* etc.) to signal new points, thought-sustainers (*additionally, further, furthermore, moreover, also*) to let the reader know you're still developing the same idea, and thought-reversers (*however, yet, though, although, but*) to announce a change in direction.

The final step of the Action Plan is to proofread what you have written. But again, we'll defer that discussion until later in this Day.

Workshop B

This workshop includes three "argument" topics for practice. There is no time limit for the exercises.

Drill

For each of the following topics, outline an essay. The prompts following each topic gives you some suggestions. Then check your work against the explanations given in the Review part of this Workshop.

Topic 1

People are becoming more interested in food and drink as entertainment. Last year, of the 35 new titles published by MidDay Books, 20 were on cooking and wine. Evening Books produced only one new title in that area out of a total of 30 new titles. Revenues at MidDay increased by 10 percent to $23 million while revenues at Evening Books remained a constant $25 million. If Evening Books wants to increase revenues, it should concentrate on bringing out more books on food and drink.

Does the evidence prove that there is a problem with sales at Evening Books?

If Evening Books does have a problem, can it be solved without concentrating on books about food and drink?

If Evening Books does concentrate on books about food and drink, what is it risking?

Topic 2

The patented Steering Wheel Lock is your best protection against having your car stolen. The Lock is so effective that we make the following guarantee: if you send in proof of purchase within 10 days of buying your Lock, then later if your car is stolen while protected by the properly installed Lock, we will pay the cost of any deductible on your car insurance in excess of $500. In the past two years, over 250,000 Locks have been sold, and our company has paid out just 995 claims. Made from a patented steel alloy, the Lock is stronger than other competing models. So if you want your car to be safe no matter where you park it, buy and use the Lock.

Does the viewer have a need for the Lock?

What is the reason for the small number of "paid" claims?

What evidence is there that the Lock prevents auto theft?

Are there any possible "negatives" to owning and using a Lock?

Topic 3

Artkraft, which produces high quality, custom-made graphics, has been using Rapid Messenger, a motorized delivery service, for all of its local deliveries. In a typical week, Rapid picks up from Artkraft and delivers (usually within four hours) about 120 packages for a cost of about $1,500 per week. A new firm, Cycles'r'Us, uses bicycle messengers and guarantees to deliver packages to the same area with four hours at only 80 percent of the cost. In order to save money and get the guarantee of a four-hour delivery, Artkraft should use Cycles'r'Us as its messenger service.

Is there any problem with Artkraft's present delivery service?

If there is a problem, can it be solved by working with Rapid rather than abruptly changing services?

Is there a downside to going with a new and untested firm that uses bicycles rather than motorized vehicles?

28

Review

Here are suggested outlines for the topics above. Don't be concerned if the particular points raised in these outlines are not the same that you would raise. Instead, try to compare your work with the suggested outlines in terms of the organization each exhibits and the development each would permit. If your outlines would score high on those two scales, then you've made good ones.

Topic 1

I. The evidence doesn't prove that Evening Books needs to change its publication policies.

    A. Another company's success doesn't prove that Evening Books is falling behind. It would be important to analyze last year's sales for trends such as a large client that was late paying or one particular title that "flopped."

    B. The numbers don't prove that the growth in sales at MidDay was attributable to the new titles in the area of "food and drink."

II. Even granting that "food and drink" is a new market, it should be possible to tap that market without "concentrating" on it.

    A. Evening Books can contract for a few titles in this area to test the waters.

    B. Evening Books should also review its existing publishing policies to determine whether it needs to make reforms in areas where it is already established.

III. A shift in editorial policy is not without risk.

    A. Last year's fad may not be the best basis for planning a strategy for next year—food and drink may no longer be hot topics.

    B. Shifting focus would require reallocation of administrative resources, e.g., perhaps the company's editors will not be as effective at editing "food and drink" books as other titles. Shifting the company focus could undermine sales if the sales force has to be retrained and redirected.

    C. Finally, such books may be more expensive to produce because consumers expect "name" authors and elaborate photographic spreads.

Topic 2

I. The argument doesn't prove that any particular driver needs a Lock.

    A. First, it would be important to learn the odds of a particular vehicle's being stolen. A car that is not likely to be stolen in the first place doesn't need one.

    B. Also, a vehicle that is otherwise protected, e.g., an alarm system or a locked garage, may not need a Lock.

II. The argument doesn't prove that the Lock is effective.

    A. The argument does not provide the most important comparison: number of cars of certain kinds in certain circumstances that were stolen versus the same with the Lock that were not stolen.

    B. The low number of claims paid may be due to the restrictive nature of the guarantee: proof of purchase within 10 days, Lock properly installed, and then the high threshold of the $500 deductible.

    C. How easy is it for a professional thief to circumvent the Lock?

III. The Lock may actually cause problems.

    A. The clever wording of the guarantee suggests that the company may not be very cooperative in addressing problems.

    B. Unwarranted faith in the Lock could lead drivers to fail to exercise normal prudence, e.g., they might park in unlighted areas, thinking "The Lock will keep the car safe."

Topic 3

I. The argument doesn't prove that Rapid is in any way deficient as a messenger service.

    A. The argument says that most deliveries now are made within four hours. Is a guarantee really important?

    B. Equally important to delivery time is the response time to a request for pick-up.

II. Artkraft could negotiate with Rapid for more favorable terms now that there is a new competitor.

    A. Artkraft could ask for some kind of a guarantee.

    B. Artkraft could ask for a reduction in price.

III. Changing to Cycles'r'Us to save a little money entails a risk.

    A. The firm is new. It will surely have growing pains, and it may not survive. Can it handle the volume Artkraft has? Or what happens when the cyclists begin to organize a union and demand higher wages?

    B. The use of bicycles may be a good idea in some circumstance but not in others. What happens if it rains?

    C. Artkraft produces graphics that presumably require careful handling. A bicyclist pedaling through traffic may not be able to provide the needed care. A single

28

important client may be worth more than Artkraft would ever save in delivery charges.

Writing Correctly

Although it may seem somewhat surprising, grammar and mechanics are probably the least important aspects of preparing for the GRE Writing Assessment. We tend to think of them as very important, but only because we associate grammar and mechanics with the courses we took in the English department in college. So quite naturally, we think of the GRE Writing Assessment in familiar terms: it's an English test, so I'd better get out the grammar book. The GRE Writing Assessment, however, is a different kind of exercise. Content, organization, and development are more important than mechanics.

This doesn't mean, however, that grammar and mechanics are completely irrelevant; but you need to remember that graders will forgive a few "literary indiscretions" if your essay is otherwise good. Grammar and mechanics come into play primarily as penalty points and only if you are obviously inattentive to such matters.

In this section, you'll do a review of the mistakes that people are most likely to make writing essays of the sort required by the GRE Writing Assessment. And after you reviewed the discussion to make sure you understand the distinction between correct and incorrect usages, you'll have a checklist of common errors to use when you proofread your Writing Assessment essay.

1. Subject and Verb

- Every sentence has to have a main (conjugated) verb.

A sentence without a main (conjugated) verb is called a sentence fragment, and fragments are not acceptable in standard written English. Here is an example of a fragment:

Granting that books on food and drink were important last years, projected sales in upcoming years of other kinds of books.

The fragment lacks a main verb, so you need to insert one:

Granting that books on food and drink were important last years, projected sales in upcoming years may come from other kinds of books.

 CAUTION Non-conjugated verbs forms such as -ing forms can sometimes look like main verbs even though they are not.

- The verb has to agree with its subject.

A subject is either singular or plural; so too, the verb must agree by being singular or plural. The following sentence is incorrect because the verb doesn't agree with the subject:

Sales of books about an important area such as entertainment is likely to increase as the standard-of-living increases.

The verb "is" is singular, but the subject "sales" is plural. The sentence should read:

Sales of books about an important area such as entertainment are likely to increase as the standard-of-living increases.

> **TIP** Point your finger at the subject and at the verb, so that you'll know you're looking at the right element (like "sales") and not some other element in the sentence (like "entertainment") that may cause you to become confused.

- Verb tenses must be consistent.

Verb tenses are used to show how various actions and events relate to one another in time. The following sentence fails to respect this requirement:

The 10 percent increase in sales that occurs last year at MidDay is a powerful reason for Evening Books to investigate the new market area.

The use of the present tense "occurs" suggests an event that occurs in the present and in the same time frame as the other verb in the sentence, "is." But the sentence means to refer to an increase that took place in the past. The sentence can be correct in this way:

The 10 percent increase in sales that occurred last year at MidDay is a powerful reason for Evening Books to investigate the new market area.

> **TIP** Pay careful attention to verb tenses as you proofread your essays. Make sure that past events are described with a past tense, present events with a present tense, and future events with a future tense.

28

2. Pronoun Usage

- A pronoun must have a referent.

A pronoun is a word that takes the place of another word, usually a noun but sometimes another pronoun. The word that it replaces is called the referent (because it is the word referred to) or sometimes the antecedent (because it comes before the pronoun). The technical terminology is not important. What is important is that you know that every pronoun has to have a referent. The following sentence doesn't follow this rule:

> Eating out is always popular with young professionals who have money to spend, so they will probably sell better than other books Evening Books might produce.

The problem here is that the pronoun "they" does not have a referent. It seems to refer to something like "books about food and drink," but you don't find that or a similar phrase. You can correct the sentence by using a noun instead of a pronoun:

> Eating out is always popular with young professionals who have money to spend, so books about food and drink will probably sell better than other books Evening Books might produce.

- A pronoun must agree with its referent.

Most pronouns have identifiable singular and plural forms, so you have to use the correct form as determined by the number of the pronoun's referent. The following sentence illustrates the "failure of agreement" error:

> A beautifully designed book on food an drink with full color photos is a gift many people would be proud to give, so they would probably sell well during the holiday season at the end of the year.

The pronoun "they" is plural, but its referent is the singular noun "book." You have your choice in how to correct the error. You can use a plural noun, or you can change the pronoun as shown here:

> A beautifully designed book on food an drink with full color photos is a gift many people would be proud to give, so it would probably sell well during the holiday season at the end of the year.

TIP

For each pronoun, put your finger on its referent. If it doesn't have one, rewrite the sentence; if they don't agree, change the pronoun.

3. Style

- Parallel elements must have parallel forms.

If you are trying make your sentence structures interesting, you are likely find that they contain series of examples or other elements, e.g., "menus of good restaurants, recipes for outstanding dishes, and lists of fine wines." You want to make sure that the elements of the series all have the same form. The following sentence demonstrates this kind of error:

NOTE

> In a properly written sentence, elements in a series should all have the same grammatical form, e.g., "writing, editing, and publishing such books" *not* "writing, editing, and publication of such books."

- Modifying phrases must clearly modify.

You've probably heard a lot about the notorious dangling modifier, but it's really just one of a group of errors about which we can speak generally: modifying phrases must clearly identify what they modify. And that usually means placing the modifier as close as possible to what it modifies. Here's what happens when you don't:

Illustrated by beautiful drawings and photographs, the consumers will think that the new books are well worth the price.

That's fine if you really think that consumers can be "illustrated by beautiful drawings and photographs." Of course, the sentence means to say that it is the new books that are illustrated. So you need to rewrite the sentence and reposition the modifier:

Illustrated by beautiful drawings and photographs, the new books will impress consumers who will think that they're well worth the price.

TIP

> Put your modifying phrases as close as possible to the words they are supposed to modify.

4. Clarity and Conciseness

- Avoid the passive voice.

The passive voice is the verb structure that uses a form of "to be" to invert the relationship between the subject and the verb. The following pair of sentences illustrates the distinction:

Books on food and drink would be bought by young professionals, who have a lot of disposable income.

Young professionals, who have a lot of disposable income, buy books on food and drink.

28

The first sentence uses the passive voice, the second the active voice. Prefer the second form. It's not the case that the passive voice is necessarily incorrect; rather, the passive voice tends to sound contrived and stilted. You can't go wrong with the active voice.

- Avoid unnecessary wordiness.

Given the nature of the Writing Assessment, there is a temptation to use too many words to express an idea (either to sound "important" or to try to fill up space). Graders, however, will count off for this sin. Here's an example of a sentence that is needlessly wordy:

Given the current conditions of the market place as they now exist, Evening Books could expect to achieve and obtain higher sales and larger revenues by diversifying into other areas of publishing and book distributing.

Just cut to the chase:

Given the current conditions of the market, Evening Books could expect to achieve higher sales by diversifying into other areas of publishing.

Don't sacrifice accuracy or clarity for the sake of shorter sentences, but do make sure that your sentences are not needlessly wordy.

5. Punctuation

Punctuation is one of those "bugaboos" of English teachers. In fact, punctuation is a lot simpler than we were told in school. And punctuating your Writing Assessment essays is even easier.

- Use commas for clarity.

Wherever you would pause briefly in reading a sentence aloud, you probably need a comma. Read the following sentence aloud:

Full color photographs of beautiful presentations reproductions of menus of famous restaurants and wine lists with impressive prices all work to create a certain snob appeal.

If you read the sentence so that it made sense, your pauses probably indicated that commas are needed in the following places:

Full color photographs of beautiful presentations, reproductions of menus of famous restaurants, and wine lists with impressive prices all work to create a certain snob appeal.

Apply the same technique to the following sentences:

Although restaurants in the highest price ranges may be outside the budgets of some readers pictures will permit them to enjoy a meal there in vicarious fashion.

The book should include a variety of visual elements that will make it appeal to an up-scale consumer and the price should be high enough to say to a potential buyer that the book gives its owner status.

You probably paused in the following places:

Although restaurants in the highest price ranges may be outside the budgets of some readers, pictures will permit them to enjoy a meal there vicariously.

The book should include a variety of visual elements that will make it appeal to an up-scale consumer, and the price should be high enough to say to a potential buyer that the book gives its owner status.

About the only uses you'll have for commas is separating elements of series, separating a subordinate clause from a main clause, and separating two main clauses joined by a conjunction such as "and" or "but."

TIP | When in doubt, leave it out. If you are not sure whether you are writing something correctly, use a different form that you know to be correct.

NOTE | You don't have to worry about arcane points of grammar such as *who* versus *whom* or shifting usages such as the split infinitive. Even the venerable OED now allows that these conventions have outlived their usefulness.

Get Answers to Frequently Asked Questions

Q: How important is the Writing Assessment in the admissions process?

A: The weight given to the Writing Assessment varies from program to program. For some graduate schools, it may not be relevant at all; for others it may be very important; for others, it may act as a tie-breaker. One thing is certain, however. A good essay score cannot hurt your application; a bad one might. So you want to do your best on the Writing Assessment.

Q: Do I need to do a big grammar review and study topics like punctuation?

A: No. The quality expected of the essay is "first draft." So the readers realize there will be some errors in your essay, even if you've proofed it at the end. And keep in mind that the two most important elements are content and organization. Grammatical

28

correctness is fairly low on the list. So long as your sentences are clear, straight-forward and easy to understand, you'll get a good score.

Q: Since topics are published, can't I prewrite my answers to all of them?

A: Theoretically, you could—if you have the time to write answers to a couple of hundred topics and then memorize what you've written. But even then, there's no guarantee that one of those topics would be used. The GRE can always add new topics to the pool. So a better use of time would probably be to use the pool of topics for practice. Just pick a topic at random, and write an essay under timed conditions. Then go over it in light of what you learned this day.

Today's Review

1. The Writing Assessment consists of two essay tasks: an "issue" essay and an "argument" essay.

2. You are graded on analysis, organization and development, and execution (mechanics, etc.) And the order of the list reflects the emphasis given by the graders.

3. The "issue" essay uses a topic about an issue of general concern. A good approach is to focus on a key term in the statement of the issue and then explore its "complexities" by pointing out the ways in which it is an oversimplification.

4. The "argument" essay is more concrete and reaches a conclusion based on evidence. Your task is to explain that the conclusion is not justified. Try to find at least three major weaknesses in the argument and turn those into the three major points (paragraphs) of your essay: there is no problem, the problem could be solved in other ways, and the conclusion of the argument, if acted on, is likely to cause other problems.

5. Finally, you have created for yourself a checklist of errors that people commonly make. You can memorize this checklist and use it to proofread your essays on the test.

Day

29

The Writing Assessment Final

The "Issue" Essay Final

In this part, you will respond to an "issue" topic. The time limit is 45 minutes, so set aside some time when you won't be disturbed and use a watch or a clock to time yourself. Use a computer for word processing, or write your response in hand using the space provided below. Then evaluate your essay by comparing it with the samples given in the Review part of this section.

What You'll Do Today

- "Issue" Essay Final
- "Argument" Essay Final
- Review the Finals

Issue Task

Present Your Perspective on an Issue

Time—45 minutes

You have 45 minutes to plan and write an essay on the topic below. *An essay on any other topic is not acceptable.*

The topic is a brief statement about an issue of general interest. You may accept, reject, or qualify the statement. Support your views with reasons and examples drawn from your reading, experience, observations, or study.

Your essay will be graded according to how well you:

—Appreciate the complexities and implications of the issue

—Organize, develop, and support your ideas with reasons and/or examples

—Express your ideas and control the elements of standard written English

Spend a few minutes organizing your thoughts before you begin writing, and leave yourself some time at the end to edit your response.

Issue Topic

Great people should be remembered for their accomplishments in their fields—politics, science, art, or business—and not for their shortcomings as human beings.

The "Argument" Essay Final

In this part, you will respond to an "argument" topic. The time limit is 30 minutes, so set aside some time when you won't be disturbed and use a watch or a clock to time yourself. Use a computer for word processing, or write your response by hand on a separate piece of paper. Then evaluate your essay by comparing it with the samples given in the Review part of this section.

Argument Task

Analysis of an Argument

Time—30 minutes

You have 30 minutes to plan and write a critique of an argument. *An analysis of any other argument is not acceptable.*

The topic is a brief argument. You are not asked to agree or disagree with the conclusion of the argument but to analyze the argument. Consider what assumptions underlie the thinking and how the evidence is related to the conclusion. You can also discuss what other evidence, if available, might strengthen or weaken the argument.

Your essay will be graded according to how well you:

—Identify and analyze important elements of the argument

—Organize, develop, and support your ideas with reasons and/or examples

—Express your ideas and control the elements of standard written English

Spend a few minutes organizing your thoughts before you begin writing, and leave yourself some time at the end to edit your response.

Argument Topic

The City Parks Department has authority over all of the City's recreational facilities. The City opens the swimming pools on the Memorial Day Weekend and closes them on Labor Day. During the summer, however, all of the City's indoor facilities are closed. In response to a survey question that asked "Do you want children to have the opportunity to play sports such as basketball and handball during the summer?", 98 percent of City residents answered "yes." It is clear, then, that City residents want all of the City's recreational facilities open during the summer. So the City should adopt a new policy that keeps the indoor facilities open during the same months the swimming pools are open.

29

Evaluate Your Essays

Here are sample responses to the topics above. Compare your essays to them. In making your comparison, think about the following questions:

1. In terms of overall effectiveness, where does my answer rank?

2. How do the essays differ in their analysis of the argument? How are the different essays organized? Which organization is easier to follow?

3. What kinds of reasons are given? Are examples used? How do the reasons/examples add to the effectiveness of the essay?

4. Are the ideas clearly expressed? Which essay is more interesting to read?

(You'll notice that the samples contain some errors. This is to be expected since they are "draft" quality and not final versions.)

Strong "Issue" Essay

"Great" people are always remembered for their accomplishments. Thomas Jefferson is remembered as a patriot and a profound political thinker who wrote the Declaration of Independence. Albert Einstein is remembered as the brilliant physicist who developed the Theory of Relativity. Were it not for these accomplishment, these great people would not be considered great and likely would not be remembered at all.

It is currently fashionable, however, to try to bring great people down a notch or two by parading out their shortcomings to show that they really weren't so "great" afterall. Evidence has recently become available to prove that Thomas Jefferson carried on an affair with a woman who was his slave and that he fathered a child or children by her. A popular way of scoring points in trivia is to point out that Einstein was notoriously poor at math and got Cs in algebra in high school. But do these shortcomings make them any less great? Only if one has an unrealistic definition of greatness. Would Jefferson have been as deep a thinker had he been less complex? Would Einstein have grasped the fundamental intution of relativity had he been enslaved to mathematics?

It seems likely, then, that great people will always be remembered for their shortcomings as well as their accomplishments. It's a way of making them seem human and not so distant from the rest of us. And, in a real sense, balancing a person's shortcomings with their accomplishments is appropriate. That is because a "great person" is also, by definition, a person, and as Hegel said of Napoleon, who he idolized but realized had faults, "No man is a hero to his valet."

Strong "Argument" Essay

29

The evidence provided does not support the recommendation regarding indoor facilities for three reasons. First, it is not clear that residents support the plan. Second, there is no proof that children are lacking any recreational oppotunities. Third, implementing the ambitious plan could actually undermine the recreational programs.

First, it is not clear that residents think that children need other opportunities. The wording of the question includes the phrase "such as." Many of those who responded "yes" might have interpeted the question to include "swimming."

Second, there is no evidence that children are denied the opportunity to play basketball or racketball. Presumably, the City also has outdoor recreational facilities with "hoops" and "walls." Those can certainly be used during the summer months. Plus, many other activities such as softball and soccer are avalailable during the summer months.

Third, the attempt to keep the indoor facilities open year-round might actually undermine the quality of the City recreational programs. Obviously, there will be an attendant cost for hiring additional workers to staff the additional facilities. Money spent on indoor facilities during the summer might draw needed money away from outdoor facilities that are traditionally used only during those months. Additionally, it is logical to schedule maintenance tasks on the indoor facilities during the summer months when the weather won't interfere with work. Trying to keep the facilities open year-round could make it more difficult to keep them in top condition. Finally, some indoor facilities may not even be usable during the hot summer months due to lack of suitable ventilation.

While everyone would agree that, in prinicple, children should be given the widest range of recreational opportunities possible, sometimes hard decisions have to be made about what is realistic. Without further evidence that there is a real need for the indoor recreational facilities to remain open, the City should continue its policies.

Part VI
Putting It All Together

Getting Ready for the Big Day

Think About the Test Day

There's no doubt about it. The GRE is a big day. So you want to be ready to peak. In order to do that, your long-term preparation and your short-term preparation have to come together at that moment.

You've invested a lot in your long-term preparation. Your short-term preparation is also important: how you feel physically and mentally on that day can have an effect on your score. So here is an Action Plan to implement beginning a couple of days beforehand and taking you right through the test.

ACTION PLAN

Step 1: Two or three days before the test, start to relax.

Step 2: The day before the test, double check that you've attended to all of the administrative details.

Step 3: The night before the test, relax and get some sleep.

Step 4: The day of the test, arrive early and settle in.

Step 5: During the test, concentrate on what your doing and maintain a positive attitude.

Let's talk about each one of the steps.

What You'll Do Today

- **Think About the Test Day**
- **Review Everything You've Learned**

Step 1: Two or three days before the test, start to relax.

Two or three days before the test, stop studying for the GRE altogether[md]except for leisurely reviewing the imortant points listed below. Your mind needs a break and some time to absorb everything, and learning one more thing about the GRE at the last minute isn't going to help you.

Ideally, you also want to some time off from your other studies,but that may not be feasible. Still, if you can, plan to take care of other responsibilities like an important paper well in advance of your GRE. That way, it won't be hanging over your head.

So the last couple of days before the test, there's nothing else terribly important that you absolutely have to do.

 CAUTION

Don't keep studying right up until the time of the test. The GRE tests knowledge acquired over time. What you've done in this book is reviewed what you already knew and focused it directly on the GRE. "Cramming" one more factoid into your brain isn't going to help.

Step 2: The day before the test, double check that you've attended to all of the administrative details.

For most people, the GRE is an "away game." You'll have to travel to another location and sit in an environment you're not familiar with. This adds an additional pscyhological burden. You can minimize the burden by planning in advance and having everything ready to go:

- **Know where you're going and how to get there.** If you're not familiar with the testing center, plan your route in advance. And make sure you know precisely where the testing center is if it is in a complex of buildings, e.g., where on campus.

- **Pack your bag.** Put together everything you're going to need including the necessary i.d., your admission ticket. Include whatever personal items you think you might need such as tissues, medicine, extra clothing, and a snack. (You won't be allowed to eat in the testing room, but you may need to eat before or immediately after the test; and you'll find that whatever vending machines are around run out of things quickly.)

Step 3: The night before the test, relax and get some sleep.

This should go without saying, but it can't hurt to say it anyway. You won't be doing yourself a favor if you stay out late the night before partying. Go to bed at a reasonable hour and get up a little early to give yourself some extra time to get to the testing center.

Step 4: The day of the test, arrive early, and settle in.

30

Plan to get to the testing center early. This will give you a time cushion against unforseen events like a construction detour, a late-running train, a traffic accident, and so on. (Even if you've planned your route carefully and think you know what entrances and parking areas are available, you can just about bet that someone will have decided that would be a good day to close off half the campus for a major road repair.) Once there, you can stand around, sit around, read the paper, eat your donut, or do something until the administrators start processing you. From that point on, everything is pretty much out of your control, e.g., what room you go in, where you sit, what you can and cannot have on your desk.

Step 5: Concentrate on what you're doing and maintain a positive attitude.

Once testing has begun, you have to maintain your concentration. You'll find that now and again your mind begins to wander off the task. That's normal. Just take a few seconds to compose yourself and put yourself back on track.

> **TIP**
> When your mind begins to wander (and it will), take a few seconds to compose yourself and get back to work.

Finally, maintain a positive attitude. You've done a lot of work to get ready for this test. (Even if you've cut a few corners, you're still way out ahead of the curve.) You're ready for your best performance.

Review of Everything You've Learned

We assembled a list of the important points and Actions Plan for you to review on this last day. Remember this is just a review. You've learned and practiced these points already; but if one or more are not clear, refer to the appropriate chapter for clarification.

Verbal Skills

Sentence Completions (Day 3)

 Action Plan for Sentence Completions

The Basic Technique

Step 1: Read through the sentence for meaning.

Step 2: Formulate a possible completion and choose an answer.

Advanced Strategies

Step 1: Dispose of any excess baggage.

Step 2: Use the verbal signals.

Fail-Safe Plan

Step 1: Test answer choices.

Step 2: Choose the most obscure word.

Analogies (Day 5)

 Action Plan for Analogies

The Basic Technique

Step 1: Summarize the relationship in a sentence.

Step 2: Adjust the sentence if necessary.

Advanced Strategy

Use a prepared template.

- place for
- device for
- kind of
- part of
- sequence
- degree
- key element
- absence of

Fail-Safe Plan

Step 1: Eliminate non-starters.

Step 2: Use templates 7 and 8.

Antonyms (Day 7)

 Action Plan for Antonyms

The Basic Technique

Step 1: Read the capitalized word and try to formulate possible opposites.

Step 2: Match your formulated responses to an answer choice.

Advanced Strategies

Step 1: Correct for part of speech.

Step 2: Work backwards from the answer choices.

Fail-Safe Plan

Step 1: Associate the capitalized word with a context.

Step 2: Guess.

Reading Comprehension (Day 9)

 Action Plan for Reading Comprehension

Read for Comprehension

Step 1: Read the first and last sentences.

Step 2: Track the development.

Step 3: Read "through" details.

Step 4: Summarize the development.

Step 5: Identify Question Stems and Choose the Right Answer

Thesis Questions

Right Answer: Describes the main theme of the selection

Wrong Answers: Describes only a subpart of the selection or refers to material beyond the passage altogether

30

Fact Questions

Right Answer: Specifically mentioned in the text (though perhaps not in the same words)

Wrong Answers: Nowhere mentioned in the text, a distorted rendering of a fact mentioned in the text, or a fact mentioned that is not responsive to the question asked

Development Questions

Right Answer: Explains *why* the author introduces a specific point or *how* the entire selection is organized

Wrong Answers: Fail to explain *why* the author makes a certain point or fail to explain *how* the selection is organized

Implication Questions

Right Answer: A statement logically inferrable from the text of the selection

Wrong Answers: Statements that do not follow from the text either because they are not supported or because they go too far

Application Questions

Right Answer: A statement that is *plausibly* a conclusion the author would accept

Wrong Answers: Statements that it is *unlikely* the author would accept

Judgment Questions

Right Answer: A description that reflects the author's attitude or tone

Wrong Answers: Descriptions that are too positive, too negative, or simply not descriptive of the author's tone or attitude

Math Skills

Quantitative Comparisons (Day 17)

 Action Plan for Quantitative Comparisons

Step 1: The Basic Technique: For simple QCs, do the arithmetic, the algebra, or the geometry.

Step 2: Advanced Strategy: For difficult QCs, simplify the math by simplifying expressions, eliminating redundant elements, or redefining a figure.

Step 3: Fail-Safe Plan: For very difficult QCs, use one of the guessing guidelines. Use a proxy problem, test numbers, or distort a figure.

Problem Solving (Day 19)

 Action Plan for Problem Solving

Step 1. The Basic Technique. Use familiar math techniques to solve the most common types of problems:

- •Problems about Operations
- •Problems about Approximations
- •Problems about Properties
- •Problems about Unknowns
- •Problems about Situations
- •Problems about Figures

Step 2. Advanced Strategies

A. Test Answer Choices

B. Substitute Numbers

Step 3. Fail-Safe Plan for Emergencies

A. Eliminate impossible choices and guess.

B. Use estimates for the values of π and radicals.

C. Rely on the figure as it is drawn.

Graphs (Day 21)

 Action Plan for Graphs

Step 1: Read the Graph. The most common types are table, bar, cumulative bar, line, or pie.

Step 2: Analyze the Question. The most common questions ask you to read a value or values, manipulate a value or values (by adding or subtracting or expressing as a fraction or percent), or draw an inference.

Step 3: Look for Short-Cuts. Approximate, simplify, or meastimate.

30

Analytical Skills

Puzzles

Step 1: Process the information given in the set-up.

A. *Identify the type.* Most fall into one of three common categories: ordering, selection, map.

B. *Summarize the information.* Set up an initial diagram or summarize the information.

C. *Draw further conclusions.* Look for further conclusions that might be drawn from the initial description.

Step 2: Answer the questions.

A. *If the question provides no additional information, answer using only the set-up conditions.*

B. *Process any additional information provided by the stem.* If a question provides additional information, process that information for additional conclusions before selecting your answer choice.

Arguments

Step 1: Read and analyze the initial paragraph. Look for the conclusion of the argument.

Step 2: Read the question stem and select the choice that best responds to the stem. The most common types of questions are: hidden assumption, weaken, strengthen, draw a conclusion, describe, and parallel.

Writing Assessment (Day 28)

The "Issue" Essay

Step 1: Plan your essay.

Read the topic, articulate to yourself the position that you want to defend, then outline your essay on the scratch paper you've been given.

Step 2: Write your essay.

Your essay can have a brief introduction. Then follow your outline and write one paragraph for each of the major points. You may also include a conclusion if you wish.

Step 3: Proofread your essay.

Use the checklist below.

30

The "Argument" Essay

Step 1: Plan your essay.

Read the topic, identify at least three major weaknesses in the argument, then outline your essay on the scratch paper you've been given.

Step 2: Write your essay.

Your essay should have a brief introduction. Then follow your outline and write one paragraph for each of the major points. You may include a conclusion if you wish.

Step 3: Proofread your essay.

Use the checklist below.

Proofreading Checklist

1. Subject and verb.

   • Every sentence has to have a main (conjugated) verb.
   • The verb has to agree with its subject.
   • Verb tenses must be consistent.

2. Pronoun Usage.

   • A pronoun must have a referent.
   • A pronoun must agree with its referent.

3. Style

   • Parallel elements must have parallel forms.
   • Modifying phrases must clearly modify.

4. Clarity and Conciseness

- Avoid the passive voice.

- Avoid unnecessary wordiness.

5. Punctuation.

- Use commas for clarity.

A Final Word

As you reviewed the list above, one thing should have been obvious: you've learned a lot about the GRE. You know what kinds of questions to expect, how to tackle them, how to separate correct answers from wrong ones, time-saving techniques, short-cuts, guessing strategies, and many other things that will help you get that top score. So there's only one thing left to be said:

Good Luck!